Building Web Sites All-in-One Desk Reference For Dummies®

Cheat Sheet

Top Ten Design Tips

1. Create reusable graphics.
2. Use templates whenever possible.
3. Use CSS (cascading style sheets) in place of the <font> tag.
4. Resize and optimize graphics before adding them to a web page.
5. Do not resize graphics using the <img> tag.
6. Do not use Flash introductions; they're no longer in style.
7. Avoid long paragraphs.
8. Use Heading styles to break up a page.
9. Break up large amounts of text with graphic images.
10. Keep the home page short and simple.

Sample Site Map

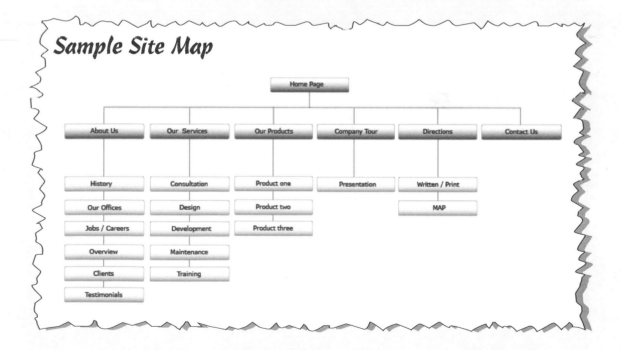

Building Web Sites
All-in-One Desk Reference
For Dummies®

Cheat Sheet

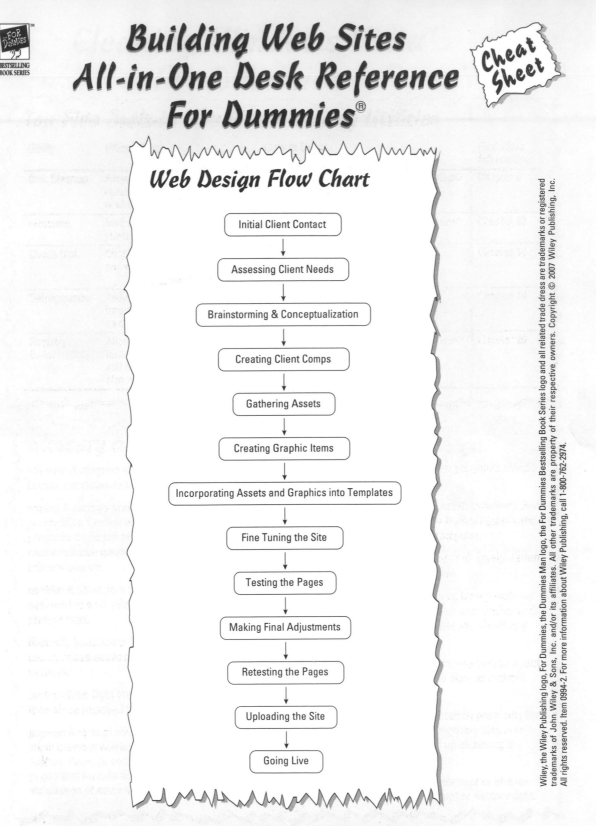

Web Design Flow Chart

Initial Client Contact

Assessing Client Needs

Brainstorming & Conceptualization

Creating Client Comps

Gathering Assets

Creating Graphic Items

Incorporating Assets and Graphics into Templates

Fine Tuning the Site

Testing the Pages

Making Final Adjustments

Retesting the Pages

Uploading the Site

Going Live

For Dummies: Bestselling Book Series for Beginners

Building Web Sites
ALL-IN-ONE DESK REFERENCE
FOR
DUMMIES®

by Doug Sahlin and Claudia Snell

Wiley Publishing, Inc.

Building Web Sites All-in-One Desk Reference For Dummies®

Published by
Wiley Publishing, Inc.
111 River Street
Hoboken, NJ 07030-5774
www.wiley.com

Copyright © 2007 by Wiley Publishing, Inc., Indianapolis, Indiana

Published by Wiley Publishing, Inc., Indianapolis, Indiana

Published simultaneously in Canada

For general information on our other products and services, please contact our Customer Care Department within the U.S. at 800-762-2974, outside the U.S. at 317-572-3993, or fax 317-572-4002.

For technical support, please visit www.wiley.com/techsupport.

Wiley also publishes its books in a variety of electronic formats. Some content that appears in print may not be available in electronic books.

Library of Congress Control Number: 2006936836

ISBN-13: 978-0-470-00994-9
ISBN-10: 0-470-00994-2

Manufactured in the United States of America

10 9 8 7 6 5 4 3 2 1

1B/SY/RS/QW/IN

WILEY

About the Authors

Doug Sahlin is an author, photographer, and Web designer living in central Florida. His clients include attorneys, authors, artists, doctors, and musicians. He has written and coauthored over 16 books on office applications, Web design applications, and digital photography. His books have been translated into five foreign languages. When he's not busy writing, photographing clients, or designing Web sites, he enjoys playing the guitar and dabbling in watercolor painting.

Claudia Snell is a new media designer based in Worcester, MA. She currently works as an online producer at the Worcester Telegram & Gazette, where she works with Web and multimedia design and video for Web. Previously, she has worked in an agency, as a freelance new media designer, and as a contract Web/multimedia designer in large corporate environments. She has been a guest speaker at the Boston Macromedia User Group, Society of Professional Communicators, Worcester Computer Society, and on the WPI Venture Forum radio show. She founded and managed the Worcester Macromedia User Group and was a frequent presenter. She has written for Macromedia *The Edge* and for FlashGoddess.com.

Dedication

From Doug: Dedicated to the memory of Barry Murphy: songwriter, musician, friend, and world-class human being.

From Claudia: This book is dedicated to my family: my husband, Jason Snell, and my kids, Sarah and Damon Bousquet.

Authors' Acknowledgments

From Doug: Thanks to Steve Hayes for making this project possible. Kudos to project editor Nicole Sholly for her sense of humor and dedication to the task at hand. Thanks to the fastidious Heidi Unger — who must be related to Felix — for rendering squeaky clean text and providing insightful questions. Special thanks to fellow authors Bonnie Blake, Joyce Evans, and Ken Milburn for their friendship and inspiration. Thanks to literary agent extraordinaire, Margot Maley Hutchison, who shall go forward in time with the nickname Ollie. As always, thanks to my friends, mentors, and relatives, especially you Karen and Ted.

From Claudia: I would like to acknowledge the great support I have gotten from the faculty at Assumption College and most especially: Dr. Robert Fry, Scott Glushien, Brian Bercier, and Dr. Rockie Blunt. Their support and guidance has made it possible for me to pursue my career.

I would also like to acknowledge the Macromedia User Group program, the team at Macromedia, Ed Sullivan, and Amy Brooks, and all the managers. Participating in the User Group program gave me tremendous opportunities to learn. The user group managers are a fantastic resource. I always appreciated their thoughts and advice on Web design and development.

I'd also like to acknowledge the people at Wiley publishing, including Steve Hayes and Nicole Sholly who patiently guided me through this project. Thanks also to the team of editors, reviewers, and production staff who have worked hard to make this book better. And finally, a special thanks to my coauthor, Doug Sahlin.

Publisher's Acknowledgments

We're proud of this book; please send us your comments through our online registration form located at www.dummies.com/register/.

Some of the people who helped bring this book to market include the following:

Acquisitions, Editorial, and Media Development

Project Editor: Nicole Sholly

Senior Acquisitions Editor: Steve Hayes

Copy Editor: Heidi Unger

Technical Editor: Danilo Celic

Editorial Manager: Kevin Kirschner

Media Development Manager:
Laura VanWinkle

Editorial Assistant: Amanda Foxworth

Sr. Editorial Assistant: Cherie Case

Cartoons: Rich Tennant
(www.the5thwave.com)

Composition Services

Project Coordinator: Jennifer Theriot

Layout and Graphics: Claudia Bell,
Lavonne Cook, Denny Hager,
Stephanie D. Jumper, Heather Ryan,
Ronald Terry

Proofreaders: Laura Albert,
Christine Pingleton, Techbooks

Indexer: Techbooks

Anniversary Logo Design: Richard Pacifico

Publishing and Editorial for Technology Dummies

Richard Swadley, Vice President and Executive Group Publisher

Andy Cummings, Vice President and Publisher

Mary Bednarek, Executive Acquisitions Director

Mary C. Corder, Editorial Director

Publishing for Consumer Dummies

Diane Graves Steele, Vice President and Publisher

Joyce Pepple, Acquisitions Director

Composition Services

Gerry Fahey, Vice President of Production Services

Debbie Stailey, Director of Composition Services

Contents at a Glance

Table of Contents

Introduction

Web sites can be very complex or very simple. When you're building a site, you have many decisions to make, all dependent on the needs of a particular project. This can be overwhelming, but don't fret — you have *Building Web Sites All-in-One Desk Reference For Dummies* to help you. It's so comprehensive and so flexible that it will help you in all aspects of Web design, from the initial planning phases to testing and publishing your masterpiece.

This book can help you take on the role of project manager, graphic designer, developer, or multimedia designer, and it has information about interacting with different specialists on larger or more complex projects. So whether you're undertaking your first Web design project or are a veteran taking on a Web design team, this book is for you.

About This Book

Here are some of the things you can do with this book:

+ Plan your Web site project.

+ Assemble and manage a Web team.

+ Create layouts, graphics, navigation menus, and Web pages from scratch.

+ Optimize graphic elements for your Web pages.

+ Work with HTML and CSS to create and maintain your pages.

+ Create HTML forms.

+ Add multimedia content such as Flash movies and video clips.

+ Integrate e-commerce into your Web site project.

+ Maintain and promote a Web site.

+ Explore server-side and client-side code.

Foolish Assumptions

We have, perhaps foolishly, made a few assumptions about our readers. We expect that you have basic computer skills (either Windows or Mac) and a basic understanding of how to use a browser and the Internet. The authors and publisher of this book assume you're a bright, intelligent person who wants to learn but doesn't have the time to read a book from cover to cover. We assume you'll find the information you need by perusing the index and then cut to the chase and read that section.

If you don't have any prior knowledge of HTML, CSS, or graphics software, that's okay; we give you the basics here. We do assume that you have more than a passing interest in Web design. In fact, this book is geared for Web designers, or anyone with aspirations of becoming a Web designer. If you don't have any prior experience with Web design or managing Web site projects, that's okay, too. This book starts at the beginning before moving into more advanced topics.

Conventions Used in This Book

By *conventions,* we simply mean a set of rules we've employed in this book to present information to you consistently. When you see a term *italicized,* look for its definition, which we've included so that you know what things mean in the context of Web site construction. Sometimes, we give you information to enter on-screen; in this case, we've **bolded** what you need to type. We've placed Web site addresses and e-mail addresses in `monofont` so that they stand out from regular text. Code appears in its own font, set off from the rest of the text, like this:

```
Never mind the furthermore, the plea is self-defense.
```

When we present complex information with copious amounts of code, we present examples and then dissect the code. Blocks of code are neatly bundled into a listing, which looks like this:

Listing Intro-1: Everything you wanted to know about code, but were afraid to ask.

Throughout the book, you'll find icons such as Tips, Warnings, and Remember. These little tidbits are cold, hard facts we found out the hard way. We sprinkle this information liberally so you won't fall into the same chuckholes we did, or worse, end up with egg on your face.

What You Don't Have to Read

We've structured this book *modularly* — that is, it's designed so that you can easily find just the information you need — so you don't have to read whatever doesn't pertain to your task at hand. We include sidebars here and there throughout the book that contain interesting information that isn't necessarily integral to the discussion at hand; feel free to skip over these. You also don't have to read the paragraphs next to the Technical Stuff icons, which parse out uber-techie tidbits (which might or might not be your cup of tea).

How This Book Is Organized

Building Web Sites All-in-One Desk Reference For Dummies is split into nine minibooks. You don't have to read it sequentially, you don't have to look at every minibook, you don't have to review each chapter, and you don't even have to read all the sections in any particular chapter. (Of course, you can if you want to; it's a good read.) The Table of Contents and the Index can help you quickly find whatever information you need. In this section, we briefly describe what each minibook contains.

Book 1: Preparations

This minibook covers all the things you need to do before you start actually creating a Web site. The topics of planning, managing your project, flying solo on a project, and assembling and managing a Web design team are all covered here. We've also included information about creating a site that portrays the client and her organization in a flattering light while providing visitors with content that keeps them coming back for more.

Book 11: Site Design

Site design is about the nuts and bolts of how a site works and about making the visual aspects work within the technical needs — this minibook helps you make these two worlds come together. In short, if you're looking for information about creating layouts and planning site structure, implementing appropriate design, and collecting and using feedback, you'll want to read this minibook.

Book 111: Site Construction

Book III takes you into the hands-on creation of your site. The minibook begins with an overview of the tools and materials necessary for Web design; other chapters introduce you to graphics and Web design software before delving into the details of preparing a site to go live. Book II is about being an architect and designer; Book III is about being the crew that gets the job done.

Book IV: Web Graphics

A Web site without graphics is text, which won't keep a visitor interested for very long. Book IV begins with a section on finding inspiration. After you're inspired, it's off to the races with information on how to create graphics in Photoshop and Fireworks.

Book V: Multimedia

Book V shows you how to add multimedia content to your designs. We start out by showing you how to incorporate Flash elements into your designs. If your client wants music or other joyful noise on her Web site, read Chapter 2 of this minibook. If it's full-motion video your client is after, we show you how to add it in Chapter 3 of this minibook. If your client has copious amounts of images to display in a short amount of space, check out Chapter 4, where we show you how to add a *tres-cool* slide show to a Web site.

Book VI: Audience Interaction

Web sites come in many flavors. If your client has the need to give and receive information via the World Wide Web, this minibook is your Rx for Web interactivity. If your client's site needs forms, see Chapter 1. In the latter chapters of this book we also show you how to incorporate additional inter-activity, such as databases and pages that change depending on the needs of the visitors. We end this book with an introduction to other forms of inter-activity, such as blogs, forums, and other such delights.

Book VII: E-Commerce

If your client wants to take his local, bricks-and-mortar business worldwide, we show you how to accomplish this feat in Book VII. E-commerce is indeed complex, but we do our best to simplify it for you. First, we explore basic concepts such as credit card packages, secure Web sites, and PayPal. Then, we move on to the technological and legal considerations of an e-commerce Web site. Last but not least, we show you what you need to consider when building and maintaining an e-commerce site.

Book VIII: Site Management

If you build it they will come. *Not.* The only way to get people to flock to a Web site in droves is to promote it. We begin this book by exploring methods you can use to promote a site and get it recognized by the search engines. Of course, after the site has a steady stream of visitors, you or your client will need to maintain the site. And if the site really catches on, your client will probably need you to revise or redesign the site. We show you how to maintain and expand a Web site in Chapters 2 and 3 of this minibook.

Book IX: Case Studies

The final minibook of this lofty tome is four chapters of case studies. We learn a lot by surfing the Net and dissecting what's good, bad, and downright ugly about what's out there. You can too. To give you an idea of what goes into planning and then creating a site, we explore the needs of four different clients and the resulting Web sites.

Icons Used in This Book

For Dummies books are known for those helpful icons that point you in the direction of really great information. In this section, we briefly describe each icon used in this book.

The Tip icon points out helpful information that is likely to make your job easier.

This icon marks an interesting and useful fact — something that you might want to remember for later use.

The Warning icon highlights lurking danger. With this icon, we're telling you to pay attention and proceed with caution.

When you see this icon, you know that there's techie stuff nearby. If you're not feeling very techie, you can skip this info.

Where to Go from Here

While the book is written so that more experienced Web designers can skip around to the parts they need, novice users probably need to start with Book I, which gives a good foundation of building Web sites, before proceeding to the other books. If you're one of those experienced designers, scour the index for the material you need and then read those sections.

Experience is the best teacher. After immersing yourself in those topics you want to know more about, launch your favorite HTML editor and begin noodling with designs you've previously created, and tweak them, using the information from this book. And if — like the plumber with leaky faucets — your personal Web site was designed around the turn of the century, by all means spiff it up using the techniques we show you.

Book I

Preparations

The 5th Wave   By Rich Tennant

HORNER BROS.
MAKERS OF PREMIUM
BELLS & WHISTLES

"As a web site designer I never thought I'd say this, but I don't think your site has enough bells and whistles."

Contents at a Glance

Chapter 1: Planning a Web Project

As with any project, planning and gaining support are crucial to your success. Web site projects are sometimes deceptive. They look as if you can just toss one together without too much fuss, but don't be fooled by that; you can't skimp on the planning process. You need assistance regardless of the size of the project, so make sure you've got everyone you need on board — including, for example, department managers or IT personnel. Although the players might be different when looking at fully inhouse productions as opposed to a collaboration between inhouse and hired teams (the topic of Chapter 2 of this minibook), the need to research and plan still exists. It's easy to get excited when you start a Web project, but don't let that get you into trouble later.

Something to keep in mind as you work is that Web projects are *iterative*. By that, we mean that a Web project requires many cycles of review and revision as you move along. You must develop a flow to move through the project, and you need a clear vision of the project, too — but don't get hung up on working out every single detail beforehand. Being flexible to adjustments while not deviating from the plan is a difficult but important balancing act. In this chapter, we lay out the information that will help you stay balanced.

Defining the Audience

You might not realize this, but your Web site has multiple audiences — internal stakeholders and external Web site visitors — and each set has its own needs. You must consider everyone when defining your audience and goals.

Internal stakeholders

Internal stakeholders are the people who work for the company that has hired you to create its Web site — managers, public relations people, IT and marketing professionals, customer service reps, sales people, and so on. All of these people have needs that you must consider when planning and creating the site.

The best way to gain support is to do a little upfront legwork. As much as possible, talk to key players; ask them what they want to get out of the Web site. Doing this helps you make sure that you address their actual needs and concerns as you prepare to make your formal presentation. It also ensures that when you make the formal presentation of your project, you can speak to their needs and anticipate their questions. Web builders commonly make the mistakes of not letting other people have input and wasting the stakeholders' time by presenting information that doesn't help them decide how to support your project.

Some helpful questions to ask before you start your project are

> What are your expectations for this Web site?
>
> What do you want the results to be and what sort of functionality do you want?
>
> Do you have an established site or printed materials?
>
> Do you have a corporate brand, logos, and other look-and-feel materials that need to be incorporated?
>
> Are there people within your organization that will help support the site? If so, what are their roles?
>
> Do you have a project point person?

If your client does not know what she's looking for, ask her to go look at some Web sites. Tell her to look at competitors' sites and also at sites that have similar purposes (informational, e-commerce, or whatever). Ask the client to make a list of things she likes and doesn't like. Set a time for a follow-up meeting to discuss what she finds. As you review the sites, ask her to explain what she likes or dislikes and why. The process of analyzing these other sites will help you and your client develop a better vision of what the client needs.

External audience

Oddly, the users of a Web site are often the most overlooked part of the equation. Getting caught up in all the other details of planning and deciding how the site will support the goals of the organization can easily take you away from considering the *real needs* of your external audience. Often, the visitors are referred to as a *target audience* and are described in very broad terms. Unfortunately, the discussion of a target audience is generally a short one and not very detailed.

As a Web site project manager/designer, though, you must be careful to dig a little deeper into what kinds of people are in the target audience and what they want; otherwise, the site will try to be everything to everybody instead of being just what it needs to be for that audience. Luckily, certain techniques can help you avoid the common pitfalls of designing for your users — profiles. *Profiles* (also known as *personas*) are detailed descriptions of your users as individual people. While you're developing your content and design, you might forget that your users are individual people. Generalizing your audience makes it much harder to deliver truly helpful and engaging content. Profiles help you think about your users' needs.

Here are some easy steps to help you create a profile:

1. **Start with a general target audience description and then imagine one of those people standing out in the crowd.**

   What does that person look like?

2. **Create a detailed description of that individual, even giving the person a name or using photos that fit the description to help you envision this person.**

3. **Choose several more individuals from that target audience crowd.**

   If your site is servicing multiple crowds, create several profiles for each crowd. For instance, if you're making a site that helps kids with homework, you need to think of a group of teachers, a group of parents, and a group of kids.

4. **Select just a couple individuals to be representatives for the whole group.**

   Starting with several individuals and then narrowing it down to only a few gives you more information at first, which you can focus on later. If you've really thought about your individuals, you should start to notice patterns that can help you focus on what their needs really are.

After you have the profiles in hand, develop a list of how to meet the needs of those individuals. Try to come up with specific ideas of how you will meet their needs. For example, if you're building an e-commerce site for people who are not so technologically savvy, you need a plan for how to help them use your site. You could plan to include an online tutorial and informational minisite that explains to them the process and addresses the concerns they may have. Consider a glossary or other materials that would help your users learn about e-commerce. Doing so can help customers feel more confident about doing business with the company.

Paying careful attention to your users helps you create a site that delivers what they need and expect. You should be able to develop a good idea of what works well for them. Doing this upfront work helps you decide everything from look and feel to voice and functionality. Making sure your site is what your visitors need and want helps your site be a success.

Setting Goals

Each Web site needs a purpose. Even if you're designing a small site about your hobby, you need to have a reason for building the site. You also need to decide what you will use to measure the success of the site. People often talk about a "successful" Web site, but what does that really mean? Is the goal to raise awareness or to increase sales? Is the purpose to cut down on customer service calls or to obtain a large volume of traffic? If a site doesn't have a goal or a definition of success, it becomes impossible to develop or maintain it. You determine these goals in part by talking with the internal stakeholders of the site (what are their expectations?) and also by determining what it is that the external audience needs. (We discuss these two groups in the preceding section.)

Usually, a site has more than one goal, so make a list and prioritize them. You have to decide what goals and features are must-haves and what are simply nice to have. Concentrate your efforts on the must-haves first and create a game plan for future development to add the nice-to-have stuff. The great thing about Web sites is that if you plan them well, adding things can be fairly simple.

Another important reason to have goals is that it helps you set project *milestones*. These milestones are short-range goals that help you measure the progress of your project and keep everyone on track. When working for a client, having milestones is important because it enables the client to sign off on the progress, showing approval of the work to that point. If the client does not approve of the work, you need to get specific feedback about what the concerns are, refer to the original plans for the site, and determine whether the requests fit within the scope of the project. If they do, make the changes and then request a review/sign-off of those changes. This process ensures that there is no confusion about whether a client approves of the work and that the client agrees that the product has been delivered as expected. For more about checking your progress at milestones, see the "Revising Your Original Plans — Using Feedback to Improve" section, later in this chapter.

Creating a Scope Document

Define your Web projects in terms of what features and content you intend to include. Having a general idea of what the site will include is not enough because everyone has their own vision of that. A well-run project needs good communication right from the start. The success of a project depends on everyone agreeing on what the project includes. This project definition — or *scope* — should be written out in a *scope document* and distributed to all members of the team. Any changes to the scope of the project need to be recorded as changes to the scope document and then redistributed to team members.

Creating the scope document involves defining what the project is, but don't forget to also define what a project is *not*. If the site will include Flash but not video, the scope document needs to say so. Define each element clearly. Simply including "Flash element," for example, in a list in the scope document is not enough. With each element, spell out what the project functionality *is* and *is not* in very definite terms. So, to properly reflect the "Flash element" in your document, you must be specific, like this: "Flash document to include animated bulleted list as provided by client and supporting graph from client's PowerPoint presentation. This Flash element will not include audio or video." By being specific, you protect yourself and your client from being unpleasantly surprised when you produce the Flash piece.

All projects suffer to some degree from something called *scope creep,* which happens when people start throwing in little extras that weren't part of the original scope. Keep these things to a minimum. If you need to revise a portion of a project in any substantial way, make sure you amend the original scope document, adjust the timelines as necessary, and then get all the key players to sign off. Failing to rein in scope creep can kill your project.

Preparing to Get Started

Your preparation doesn't have to be a giant project. Smaller or less-complicated sites require just a little time — you can accomplish a lot with a couple of hours, a cup of coffee, and a pad of paper. Just sit down and start focusing on the details of the project, such as defining your purpose, coming up with specific ideas, considering budget and timeline, and so on. Of course, you'll need more time and more people on the team if you're planning a large or complicated project — so make that a whole *pot* of coffee (and maybe some donuts, too).

Defining why you're doing the project

This might sound obvious, but you should define why you're going to build or redesign a site in the first place. Companies commonly start a Web project because their colleagues or competitors have Web sites. While "keeping up with the other guy" is a reason, it can't be the only reason. Without a strong message or clear direction, your site can end up being a bland imitation of other sites, and that is usually counter-productive. A Web site can be a great tool for an organization if you focus on why you're building it and what can make your site better than everyone else's.

Brainstorming and evaluating your ideas

As with any type of a project, the first thing you can do after you have some basic information about the needs of your internal stakeholders and external audience is have a brainstorming session. Do this alone or with the core team so that you can get the ideas flowing with minimal complications. You can (and in many cases, should) have additional brainstorming sessions with the team later. The important thing at this point is to write down everything that pops to mind.

After you have had your brainstorming session, it's time to consider the ideas from that session in a more practical way. Compare what you have with your defined goals and reasons and start discarding things that just don't fit. Again, this part of the Web project is similar to many other types of projects. Web project managers can easily fall into the trap of thinking that because it's a Web project, all the work will be done on a computer, and old-school techniques don't apply — resist the urge to fall into that trap. Getting away from the computer and technology can help you focus on the purpose of your project and the content you plan to deliver without the distraction of the computer and technology.

Looking at budget and timelines

Even an inhouse project has a budget and a timeline. These things can change during the course of a project: Sometimes, deadlines cannot be met or need to be pushed forward. But remember that time and money, as in any project, are tied together.

As you work on your first Web projects, you'll probably find that budgeting time and money is difficult. Projects usually are more complicated than they seem; even small projects need input from multiple individuals, and those individuals will need to agree and collaborate. While we can't give you a magic formula for calculating how these changes and collaborations will impact your project, keep in mind the following guidelines when you're planning the budget and deadlines:

✦ **Clearly establish deadlines up front, specifying what elements team members will deliver on those deadlines and what resources team members will need from stakeholders for the project to continue on track.** Include information about what will happen if stakeholders or clients delay the project. When a client is responsible for delivering materials, such as photos or text, and he doesn't get it to you on time, you cannot proceed. It's standard practice to add the number of days the materials were late to the timeline. If clients are two days late with text, the deadline pushes out two days.

✦ **Whether you are working as a freelance Web designer or as part of an internal team, put everything in writing.** This way, you avoid the he said/she said scenario that only causes frustration and is counterproductive.

✦ **Use a *rush fee*.** This is extra money that you charge if the client wants you to deliver the project faster than originally agreed. You can also use a rush fee when a client asks for a project on extremely short notice — for example, a client calls and asks you to create a minisite in only two days.

Considering collaborations

As you complete your own planning, consider the possible reactions to what you're planning to do. There might be some opposition from individuals who don't think a Web site is a good thing. On the other hand, some overly enthusiastic people might want to pitch in and help. Try to think about the people who will be impacted by the project and be prepared to address concerns, using all the information you've gathered to this point. Thinking of how (or if) you'll collaborate with those who want to help is a good idea, which can help you with the next steps — selling the idea and having a meeting to officially get things rolling.

Selling the Idea

Whether you work in a large, corporate environment or you're a freelancer/design firm, you need to sell your plan to the stakeholders. Remember, *selling* is not a dirty word. You're not trying to get people to agree to buy something they don't need. In fact, if you've done your preplanning, your project will actually help them solve problems.

Be prepared to address the stakeholders' concerns as you point out how your plans will solve problems for them, and don't forget to discuss the negative points or other impact your project might have. You can gain respect and important feedback if you show that you're open to discussion and knowledgeable enough to know that the project is not all about fun and glamour.

In short, present your idea, answer their questions — be prepared for their concerns.

Holding a Kick-Off Meeting

Another form of selling the idea, the kick-off, is a meeting to get all the hands-on people involved. The main purpose for this meeting is to explain the project and set expectations among the members of the team and give them copies of the scope document so they can review and understand fully what is expected. In addition to that, open up a discussion among team members, giving them an opportunity for sharing ideas and honing the plan.

When presenting your idea and defining the project, ask questions of your team regarding feasibility and capabilities. Also, be prepared for their questions — production people and IT folks need details in order to do their jobs correctly. Don't confuse their questioning for "being difficult." Also, try to understand any issues that are raised. Sometimes, features or functionality are possible but just not practical to create or support, so you might need to suggest a compromise. Work with your team to come up with the best solutions.

Make brainstorming ideas a part of the process. Allow everyone to give input about big-picture concepts on features and functionality. However, when the actual work begins, respect people's expertise. Writers should be the ones responsible for the written content; designers create the designs; and developers work with the code. It's great to share ideas, but when members of the team start doing each other's jobs, it becomes counterproductive. As a project manager, you should establish that collaboration is good, but second-guessing expertise creates friction and generally hurts the finished project. Make sure you hire the right people and then define the roles and build a good environment for teamwork.

The final task for a kick-off meeting is setting the next steps — make sure all team members understand what they need to do after the meeting. Be clear about what you expect from each team member and give deadlines. A good way to start the project off right is to follow up with an e-mail that includes a summary of the meeting, a list of tasks, and an outline of expectations.

Revising Your Original Plans — Using Feedback to Improve

As a Web project progresses, it moves through a cycle of review, feedback, and revision. Each iteration of the project (hopefully) helps the finished product be better. Establishing project milestones (which we discuss in the earlier section, "Setting Goals") is an important part of the initial planning phases. The milestones provide points along the way when all stakeholders can have a look at the site and give feedback about the progress.

Whether formal or informal, *usability testing* (a process where you let people play with the site to see what works and what doesn't) at key milestone points can provide useful feedback. To conduct a quick, informal usability test, select some people who are representative of your target audience — preferably people who are not involved in the project at all — and ask them to try to use your site; then have them provide feedback about their experiences. Book III, Chapters 9 and 10 contain more information about usability testing and getting feedback.

When you're asking others to preview the site — whether they're usability testers or internal stakeholders — make sure you label place holder text and graphics clearly and let people know that they are not going to be part of the finished project. *Place holder* items do just that in a layout — they hold the place while finished text and artwork are being created. A large, red, "For Placement Only" statement across a graphic often helps people stay on track while they review a project in progress.

Make sure you show your work to stakeholders whenever you've made significant progress or hit a project milestone. They need to know that you're staying on track. Also, keep in mind that some of your stakeholders might not be able to envision the finished product. When you notice that someone is getting bogged down on a temporary item — such as a place holder graphic — thank them for their feedback and then try to redirect their attention to items you do need feedback on.

Receiving feedback

If you're looking for a particular type of feedback, make sure you ask specific questions that prompt users to comment on the elements or issues you want to focus on. In general, it's not very productive to just send out a link with a note that says, "What do you think?" You'll get responses like, "Looks good" — which is great for a final okay before launching a project but is not so good when you're midproject and looking for something more solid. In some cases, you might even want to direct their attention to a particular piece of functionality, such as the subnavigation or a new Flash presentation, and ask them to comment specifically about just that piece. Here are some tips that can help you get the information you need:

✦ **Don't ask for general feedback unless that's what you really want.** The best way to get a group of random comments and personal opinions like, "I like it" is to just send a link without any explanation, or with a vague explanation like, "Check this out."

✦ **Make sure you ask for specific feedback from individuals based on their expertise.** Any Web project involves many details and many different disciplines working together. Make sure you have experts to help keep you on track. In other words, it's best to ask writers to help you proofread your content; designers can make sure your colors are working for you. Rely on experts you trust for detailed feedback on details specific to what they know.

✦ **Never assume that a person has nothing useful to contribute.** While the finer details should be picked over by an expert, a fresh set of eyes is very helpful when looking at the project as a whole. Remember, your actual visitors don't have inside knowledge or expertise and will also be looking at your site from a fresh perspective. For example, I've even gotten great feedback from an 8-year-old child about some icons that weren't working — you never know who will have a useful tip.

✦ **Include a list of what is new since the last time you sent out a link for review.** It's not polite or productive to expect people to play compare and contrast to figure out what you've been up to. Keep in mind that most of your usability testers and sources of feedback are trying to look at your project and comment on it between working on their own projects. They won't take the time to help you if you don't take the time to direct their attention to the important issues.

✦ **Make sure you don't ask for feedback if you're unable to use it.** If you know that you're locked into a particular piece of functionality or presentation, don't ask people to comment on whether it should be there. It wastes their time, and they might not want to help you the next time. Let people know up front about situations that are beyond your control. For instance, if you must display a particular logo in a specific place, include that information in your note requesting feedback.

✦ **Ask open-ended questions.** Try to come up with questions that will make people interact with your site and really think about what they are experiencing. You need to get honest input from people even if it's not a bunch of compliments. If you collect useful information and act on it, you will get plenty of compliments when you launch a great Web site.

✦ **Thank them for their input.** Make sure you thank them for their time — you'll need to call on them again as your project progresses. Keep them interested in helping you. It's easy to forget this little detail when you're wrapped up in your project, but people want to know that their time was well spent. Make sure you send out a follow-up after you've collected feedback, including a summary of the feedback and what you intend to do as a result of the comments given.

Giving feedback

Giving feedback can be trickier than getting it, so follow these pointers that can help you give feedback without stepping on any toes:

✦ **Take your time.** When you're evaluating a project to give feedback, take your time and look at the site. Your feedback isn't helpful if you immediately start reacting without taking a few moments to look at it and consider what you're going to say.

✦ **Stay polite, and don't get personal in a negative way.** It might sound strange, but being polite goes a long way when giving feedback. People often forget that someone has put a lot of time and effort into her work, and no one likes to be criticized. Make sure that when you give feedback, you take that into consideration. Blurting out comments shuts down communications pretty quickly. Ultimately, it's the project that suffers for it.

✦ **Balance positive and negative comments.** Launching into a laundry list of everything that is wrong with the site is a bad idea. Remember, a human being did the work — not a machine. The best way to have your suggestions ignored is to sound like you're launching a nitpicky attack. Try to balance your negative comments with positive ones. For instance, instead of saying, "I don't like where the logo is, It's crunched up in the corner," try, "I see that you've put a lot of work into this. It's looking good, but I think I'd like to see the logo with a little more space around it. It seems a bit crowded." The second approach takes a few seconds longer but helps build and maintain a good working relationship. Web projects take a long time and can be difficult and frustrating. To avoid creating problems, take a few moments to consider delivery of comments.

✦ **If something doesn't look right, ask questions.** Web sites go through a lot of changes throughout the process. If you think something looks wrong, ask what is going on. Sometimes, there is a good explanation for why something looks strange. For example, if the logo is missing, don't just say, "The logo is missing." Instead, try something like, "I noticed the logo is missing, why is that?" It could be an oversight; it could be that a new logo is being developed. Again, delivery of critical comments makes the difference between a healthy collaboration and a confrontation.

✦ **Keep your feedback mostly objective.** Remember that the project is not your personal, artistic statement. If you don't like the color but the colors have already been decided, accept the decision and move on to other issues. It's okay to have some personal reactions to the site and comment on them, but don't be offended if you're overruled. Everyone has something to contribute, but not every idea can be included — or the site will look like a crazy quilt!

✦ **When giving feedback on an interactive piece — be specific!** It's not helpful to look at the functionality of a piece and respond to the developers with, "It's broken." Designers and developers that are working on interactive pieces need specific information about what went wrong. They need to know what you did (for example, "I clicked the Shop Now button"), what you expected to have happen ("I thought it would take me to the shopping cart page"), and what actually happened ("I got a page that said, '404 error — Page Not Found'"). This tells the developer or designer exactly what to look at. "It's broken" doesn't tell them anything. If you encounter an error message or error code, tell the designer/developer what it is, *specifically,* and what action you took right before it occurred. The more information you give, the better. If you don't give specific information up front, you can count on playing a game of 50 questions later as designers and developers try to wrestle the details from you.

Preparing to Redesign an Existing Site

Most of the preparations that you need to do for a new site also apply to an existing site. Some differences that you should take into consideration as you prepare to redesign a site include these:

✦ **Evaluate your current Web site.** The first task is to look at the current site and evaluate how well it aligns with your needs. Look at the content, functionality, and look and feel as separate elements. Take each aspect of your site into consideration — technologies used, coding techniques, site structure, colors, style of writing, and so on. List them all and rate them based on whether they can be used on the new site.

✦ **Have experts look at what you have.** Large or complex sites need to be evaluated by selected experts or consultants. In particular, coding and technologies need to be evaluated to make sure that you don't reuse old, outdated technologies instead of using a redesign as an opportunity to make important upgrades.

Don't get caught up in the "newer is always better" line of thinking because it isn't. You know the old saying — "If it isn't broken, don't fix it." Sometimes that's the best course to take. Make sure you weigh the pros and cons of keeping or replacing code carefully before you dive into a big project.

✦ **Include all stakeholders in the initial evaluation process.** This can help you verify that the information on your site is current and accurate. A site redesign is a good opportunity to involve all interested parties in looking at and updating materials that have been posted for a while. It's common for certain types of information to be posted to a site and then forgotten. Be sure to look at contact information and directions pages — they often harbor out-of-date information.

✦ **Check the front-end code.** Look at the code that handles the display of your interface — HTML and Cascading Style Sheets (if your site has them). These technologies have undergone many rapid changes over the past few years, and many sites could benefit from recoding the pages. Book III, Chapters 2 and 3 have information about current HTML and CSS coding.

✦ **Gather the data and make decisions.** When the analysis and evaluation is done and you've collected all the feedback from interested parties and *content owners* (people responsible for the content of part or all of a site), it's time to start the planning process. Compare what you currently have with what you need your site to be and decide what parts of the current site can be used as is, repurposed and used, and what needs to be thrown out. As you're deciding what to do, keep in mind that it's often better to put a little more effort into recoding or reworking an existing item than it is to roll a cumbersome or badly developed piece of functionality into a new site. One of your project goals is to make the site more efficient than it currently is. With the analysis in hand, you're ready to start working on meeting with stakeholders and your team to plan your approach.

Chapter 2: Build a Web Team or Go It Alone

In This Chapter

✔ Evaluating what you need to do it yourself

✔ Knowing who can help

✔ Giving the reins to the client

*W*eb design projects require a blend of skills. The unique blend of creative and technological requirements means that an aspect of Web design and development draws on skills you've used in other positions — or on skills you don't necessarily consider your strengths. The most effective Web professionals are those who know how to leverage their own personal skills and talents and find others who can fill in any skill gaps. Specializing in what you're good at and aligning yourself with others who share your work philosophies enables you to build long-term relationships with those who can work with you to get the job done — whether you go it alone or are part of a team. This chapter covers both scenarios to help you decide which route is the best for you.

Flying Solo: Skills You Need to Go It Alone

You need many skills to single-handedly undertake a Web design project. Some of these skills are tangible — you must know some HTML and CSS and how to effectively use Photoshop and other graphics programs — while others are intangible — you must be able to provide good service while managing the project and your time and keeping the budget under control. This section lists and describes some of the necessary skills you need to fly solo on a Web-design project.

Managing the project

If you're doing most or all of the work yourself, you must be able to work on several aspects of the project simultaneously — which calls to task your project, time, and money-management skills — in addition to communicating all of that to your client. You can make these tasks easier by

✦ **Keeping notes.** Get a notebook and write down what you've done, why you have done it, and what you'll do next.

✦ **Making a special e-mail folder for project-related e-mails.** If you can, set up your e-mail to direct all mail pertaining to the project to that folder. (Many e-mail programs, including Microsoft Outlook, Entourage, and Lotus Notes, have this capability.)

✦ **Drawing up a budget.** Your budget should include your fees for doing the work (Hourly Rate x Time = Cost of Work), fees for any contractors you hire, and also fees for project management. You should also include fees for extra services — such as image scanning or writing content — if you want to make those available to the client. Another possible thing to add is special software or equipment. If your client *requires* that you buy something, build the cost of it into the budget.

✦ **Establishing a timeline.** Clients often don't understand the amount of work and time a Web project requires — they just know that you make it look simple and easy. The process of developing a quality site is not quick, but creating a to-do list for each week (or day) and also marking deadlines on a calendar helps you track what you need to do and when.

✦ **Devising a troubleshooting plan.** Technological issues are inevitable. For instance, multimedia elements sometimes don't download fast enough, certain functions don't work as expected, or layouts have CSS issues. These sorts of problems can take some time to troubleshoot and fix. Your plan for the troubleshooting process should include staying task oriented and *not* participating in finger-pointing. During trouble-shooting, work with the server administrators and others that are involved with the project to find a solution. Communicate with your client; explain the problem and what you're doing to fix it. Stay calm and confident so that your client feels reassured that you are in control and dealing fairly with them. If you need to bring in help, tell your client who you're bringing in and why.

The bottom line here is that if you don't figure out how much time you have to complete the project and how much money is in the budget *very early in the process* — and communicate that to your client — you could end up wasting a lot of time and energy planning a project only to find out that the client is unrealistic in her expectations.

Serving your customer

Part of a Web project manager's job is customer service. Providing good customer service can help ensure that your clients are happy, and that can help you build a solid reputation. The following list describes four important aspects of customer service:

✦ **Communicate often and minimize jargon.** You must communicate often about the status of the project so that your client knows what's going on. Communicating with clients, however, can be a little awkward — don't talk down to them, but also, don't use a lot of jargon (which can make a less-than-Web-savvy person feel stupid). Try to ease into the techno-talk gently unless you're sure they speak geek too.

✦ **Stay professional.** Web jobs can be a lot of fun for everyone if they're well run and everyone has a good attitude. Unfortunately, sometimes you won't mesh well with a client. If that happens, you must keep a professional attitude, do the work, treat the client with respect, and just suffer through it. That's business. However, in rare situations — for instance, if a client becomes abusive — you might find it impossible to continue working with that client. In that case, you must decide how to wrap things up with the client; you can either finish the job or hand it off to another designer. Either way, you must carefully explain to the client that they would be better off working with someone else. For those rare occasions when a working relationship goes sour, be sure that your contract allows you to get out of an abusive situation.

✦ **Know when to say no to a project.** Accepting every job that comes your way might seem like a good idea. It isn't. Some clients don't have the money or game plan in place to make it worth your time to work with them. If you are wasting time on someone who can't make a commitment, you could be missing out on a client that is ready and able to start a project. If a client isn't ready right now, stay in touch with him. He will appreciate your interest in his project and might just give you the job when it's time.

✦ **Take only projects that you can execute well.** Your portfolio and reputation are important. Delivering a good product is a great thing, and your client will recommend you to their colleagues — that's free advertising. Delivering a bad product can have the opposite effect — you might lose that client and anyone who asks them for advice on hiring a Web designer. This doesn't mean that you should never take a project unless you can do every part of it. If a project has some components you can't do on your own, call in a specialist — make sure you let the client know you're working with a team. The fewer surprises to your client, the better off you will be.

Dealing with HTML, CSS, and other scripting

Web pages are made of code, so — no matter how you look at it — you can't avoid code. Luckily, basic Web code — HTML and CSS — is fairly easy to learn. It might seem complicated at first, but with practice and patience, you'll be hand-coding pages pretty quickly. Many tools can help you generate code, but you still have to understand the code because sometimes you have to roll up your sleeves and get in there.

✦ Even the most sophisticated software package is still just software and can make mistakes.

✦ Many advanced techniques will require a deeper understanding of the underlying code and how it works.

✦ Taking on an existing site to redesign or maintain requires that you know how to analyze the code that's there — if you can't, you might find that you can't work with the site.

Book III covers coding by hand, using Dreamweaver, and techniques to help you take advantage of both. Figure 1-1 shows an example of HTML code. The first few times you look at the code, it might seem confusing, but it will quickly become familiar.

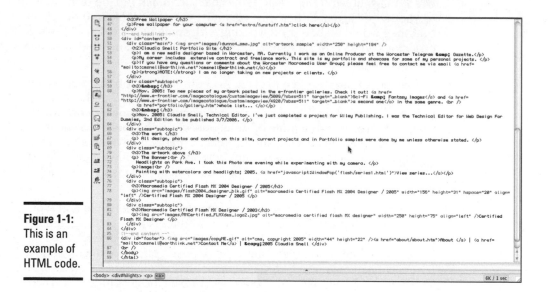

Figure 1-1: This is an example of HTML code.

Using Photoshop, Fireworks, and other graphics applications

If you're going to do design work, you need some design skills. In addition to understanding how to use color, fonts, and images to support your content and how to use layout effectively, you need to know some basics in a variety of graphics programs, including these three:

✦ **Adobe Photoshop CS2/Image Ready:** This is a great pair of tools for doing practically everything you need to do with Web graphics. Photoshop/Image Ready is the industry standard for working with graphics. With Photoshop/Image Ready, you can work with photos and create supporting graphics (such as banners and buttons) and any other graphics you need. Image Ready has tools that enhance Photoshop, such as a tool that helps you create buttons with rollover effects. If you want to pursue a professional career in design, you need Photoshop skills. See Book III, Chapter 4 for a brief introduction to the Photoshop CS2 interface and toolbox.

✦ **Fireworks:** This is a Web graphics creation tool, and you can also use it to manipulate photos and create other graphics. Fireworks' functionality fits in between Image Ready and Photoshop. In other words, it has similar functionality to Image Ready with some of Photoshop's included. Its strength is in being tightly integrated with Dreamweaver and Flash. (You can launch Fireworks easily from within either program via a handy icon.) Fireworks also has great optimization tools and a helpful and easy-to-use batch processing tool (which is good for resizing a large number of photos at once, among other things).

✦ **Adobe Illustrator/Freehand:** In these programs, you can create and edit vector graphics. A *vector graphic* is one that is made up of mathematical information defining points and lines that make up shapes. A discussion of bitmap versus vector graphics is in Book III, Chapter 4. Vectors are great for building graphics with hard lines — such as logos.

Note: You have to convert vectors into bitmaps to use them on a Web site. Photoshop and Fireworks are primarily bitmap editing programs; bitmaps are the choice for photographs. Figure 1-2 shows a vector graphic (on the left) and a bitmap graphic side by side. Notice the jagged edges created by pixilation in the bitmap.

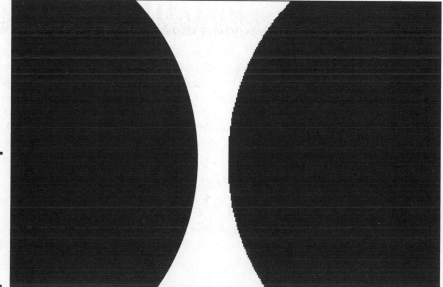

Figure 1-2:
Vector graphic on the left versus bitmap graphic on the right.

Information about how to create, use, and prepare graphics for use on a site is included in Book IV.

Developing content

Good Web writing skills are essential to a successful Web site because a site without good content isn't useful to anyone. Whoever creates the site's content — whether it is you or a partner — must understand how people use Web sites and why they go to the site in the first place.

Good writing skills also come in handy when you're preparing presentations and proposals. Almost all projects require some degree of writing skill for preparing contracts, proposals, scope documents, and other communications. Short paragraphs and bullet points help readers find what they need quickly.

Considering basic computer and Internet skills

Not that we want to state the obvious, but you need some computer skills if you are going to design Web sites.

✦ **Word processing:** Whether you're using Microsoft Office or AppleWorks, the ability to prepare documents efficiently ensures that you can prepare contracts and proposals and keep track of the business side of things.

✦ **E-mail/IM (instant messaging):** Communicating with clients is important for your success. With e-mail and instant messenger, staying in contact with clients has never been easier.

✦ **Browsers:** Having some familiarity with and testing your site on the popular Web browsers (Internet Explorer, Safari, and Firefox) ensures that the site will work no matter how visitors are viewing it.

✦ **Windows/Macintosh platforms:** Developing skills on both Macintosh and Windows computers broadens your range and eases testing of your Web pages on both platforms. Professional Web designers work to make their sites function under a wide range of conditions. Book III has more details about things you need to look for and how to deal with platform issues.

Incorporating multimedia in your project

If you're planning to work with Flash, audio, or video, you'll need some multimedia skills. You have a choice of many types of multimedia, and what you use depends on what you're trying to accomplish. Book V has information about technologies and techniques for using multimedia elements in your project.

Handling a solo project

If you decide to take on a project by yourself, here's a brief list that can help keep you on the right track:

✦ **Prioritize your tasks and develop a workflow.** Some parts of the project are more enjoyable than others, but you still have to complete all of them. After you've done a few projects, you start to develop a workflow that enables you to work effectively through all the parts of the project (even the ones that aren't as enjoyable). Prioritizing your tasks (based on what needs done when) and breaking up creative and analytical tasks (so you don't burn out on one aspect of the project) can help you meet your deadlines.

✦ **Establish a workflow with your client.** Do this *at the beginning* of the project. Working with one contact person can help reduce misunderstandings.

✦ **Notify your client of personnel changes.** If you find it necessary to bring in some help, make sure you let the client know.

✦ **Treat your home office like a "real" office.** If you're freelancing from your home, make sure you have a good workspace with all the equipment you need. Treat it like a regular job. Make regular hours for yourself. It's also a good idea to save some days strictly for production and others for meeting days.

✦ **Network and market yourself.** You'll need to build time into your schedule to look for your next project. When you're writing proposals and discussing projects with clients, don't forget to build "lost" days into the timeline. *Lost* days are those spent going to meetings or other events. If you know that you'll need 40 hours to complete a job, don't tell the client that you'll have it in five business days. You won't have it done. The 40 hours is the time that you'll spend on their project specifically — but you'll have other tasks that take up your time. The "40-hour-job" can be more like a month-long project.

Hiring Members of the Team

You might choose to hire some help with your projects for many different reasons. Some projects might have components that you don't have time to complete yourself. The client might need things that are beyond the scope of your capabilities. It's more common that you'll be good at some aspects of the work and not so good at others. For instance, you might find that you're excellent at developing code, but colors and design issues mystify you. Individuals who are great at everything aren't the norm. Even if you're one of those who can do it all, it's often more cost- and time-effective to work with a team.

An effective way of working is to establish relationships with individuals or companies that provide the services you need. After you find people you can work with, you can quickly build project teams that are tailored to the needs of your client. Your "regulars" can develop a smooth workflow. You will also expand the size and scope of projects you take on.

Note: Job titles in the Web-design industry vary greatly and even overlap. For instance, a Web/New Media designer and Project Manager might both be dubbed the Producer. When interviewing people, ask them what their actual experience is over what their job title is. You might also want to ask them whether they've worked on teams before and if they like the team environment. Assembling people who are team players helps ensure that the team will collaborate.

Project manager

A *project manager* for a Web project — like the project manager for any project — keeps everyone on the same path and makes sure issues are dealt with as quickly and smoothly as possible. The project manager should be organized and detail oriented enough to responsibly do the following: make sure members of the team are hitting deadlines, keep track of hours spent on the project, and inform team members of situations that might affect them.

A Web project manager needs to know about the workflow and time traps that can accompany the type of project you're planning. Experience working with creative individuals is also important because a project manager must understand each individual's needs concerning workflow and how materials are to be delivered (both to and from team members). The project manager also has to estimate the time needed to complete different types of projects. Familiarity with industry standards and terms can help the project manager when dealing with professional designers. In some environments, the Web project manager is sometimes referred to as a *producer*.

Web designer/new media designer

A true Web designer knows how to hand code HTML and CSS and might know some other scripting technologies, like JavaScript. Web designers are responsible for the visual design of the interface, creation of graphics, and *optimization* (resizing and compressing them for Web use) of photos. (Book III, Chapter 7 has more information about optimizing graphics.) Web designers are also responsible for coding the pages, HTML, and CSS development.

Watch out for Web designers that "don't do" code. Web designers that downplay the importance of strong HTML and CSS skills aren't really Web designers. They're graphic designers who make graphics that coders can use to create Web pages. It will save you time, money, and aggravation if you shop around for someone who can take care of the whole job, as opposed to someone who needs other members of the team to complete the tasks of creating the interfaces.

Web developer/programmer

Web developers and programmers design and create the back-end systems that make your site do more than just deliver static information. If you need or want your Web site to interact with your users, you need databases and the supporting programming to be in place.

As with Web designers, the importance of a good developer is often misunderstood. The availability of point-and-click development tools gives some people the impression that it's simple and easy to create databases and Web pages that will work with them. These easy-to-use tools are generally fairly limited in what they can do. If the site will have a lot of people interacting with it or if people will be performing complicated functions on the site, you should hire developers to build your system for you. If you want to add shopping functionality, you'll need developers that understand how to make a safe, secure, and easy-to-use site, or users won't buy the advertised products.

Content developer/writer

A good content developer or Web writer understands that writing for the Web is different than writing for other media because visitors interact with Web sites differently than they do with traditional, printed materials.

When looking for Web writers, you want to hire someone who can deliver the following:

✦ **Easy to understand information:** You should look for a writer who can deliver concise text that has a good tone for the Web. Most successful Web sites have a more conversational tone.

✦ **A good call to action:** A good Web writer can get a site's users to act. Every site has a goal, but without a good call to action, users might not perform the tasks you want them to while on the site. A good call to action is irresistible. A savvy Web writer knows how to craft the content so it drives people to the pages and actions that you want them to see and do.

✦ **Organization:** Content developers must understand how to create a flow of information and leverage the nature of the Web to provide users and site owners with the best results.

✦ **Search engine optimization (SEO):** Content developers must know how to create text and meta tags that enable users to find the site through search engines. More information about meta tags is in Book III, Chapter 2. Book VIII, Chapter 1 covers SEO.

Webmaster/host

Hosting is a service usually provided by a third party. Web hosts own and care for Web servers. A *Web server* is a computer that has server software installed and is connected to the Internet. For a fee, the owners of the server, or *host,* allow individuals to copy their Web site files to the Web server so that they're accessible to everyone with an Internet connection.

In addition to owning servers and renting space, Web hosts take care of the servers. They might also provide additional software that tracks the number of visitors your site has. Many Web hosts also offer *URL* (Web site address — for example, `www.yourname.com`) purchasing services. Most Web hosts will sell a complete package, including space for your site, e-mail, *traffic reports* (number of visitors to your site), and URL purchasing.

Other professional help

You should consult with other professionals as you start to work on Web site projects. Designing Web sites is just like any other business, and it's important to get some help so that everything runs smoothly. We suggest that you contact the following types of professionals:

✦ **Lawyer:** If you plan to work for clients, you'll need a lawyer. Make sure you hire someone who specializes in technology and creative industries. A knowledgeable lawyer can prepare contracts that spell out copyrights, address deliverables and timelines, and make sure everyone gets a fair deal. You will need someone who is an intellectual property specialist.

A good contract makes sure that everyone understands the scope of the project, the responsibilities of the parties, and when the project will be delivered. It also spells out how the fees for services work — whether it's an hourly rate or a flat fee, everyone needs to understand and be in agreement. Also make sure that if the client requests or requires you to purchase stock photography, extra software, or fonts, that they're responsible for the costs.

✦ **Accountant:** As with any business, you need an accountant. Seek the advice of an accountant before you start to take in fees or hire others to work for you. She can advise you how to set up your business so that everything runs smoothly.

Managing the team

After you've assessed the needs of a project and called in the necessary team members, it's a good time to have a kick-off meeting. Chapter 1 of this minibook covers kick-off meetings and how to run them successfully. In short, everyone needs to get together and discuss the project, timelines, expectations, and next steps. These two steps are particularly important in keeping the project moving smoothly:

✦ **Establish the workflow during the planning phase.** This is especially important if you're working with more than one service provider. Everyone needs to know how to communicate with one another. Will you be using instant messenger to stay in touch? Make sure everyone has contact information for each other. Find out what the daily schedules will be to facilitate communications.

✦ **Set up weekly production meetings.** To facilitate the meeting, the project manager should prepare a job grid (generally just in Excel) of all the tasks, who is responsible for what, expected delivery dates, status, priority, and any contingencies. All members of the team should update the team on their progress, any issues, and next steps. Make sure that you get good feedback from everyone — statements like, "I'm working on it," aren't really helpful. At the very least, find out when each individual expects to finish assigned tasks. After the meeting, send out a follow-up e-mail that outlines what was agreed on. Include a new job grid reflecting progress and next steps.

Giving feedback that helps

Web projects have a lot of details to be taken care of. Don't forget to establish a process of asking for and receiving feedback. The project manager should inform members of the team that he is going to send materials to the client for review and await confirmation that everyone is ready for the client to see the work. If some pieces won't be ready on time, don't hold up a scheduled review. Inform the client about the status as soon as you're aware of an issue. Proceed with the scheduled review and be prepared with adjusted timelines.

Establish a contact person within the client organization and communicate with that person only. It might sound unfriendly, but it isn't. Having only one contact person ensures that there won't be confusion as multiple people give feedback. The contact person should be responsible for asking people in their organization for feedback, getting *signoffs* (formal acceptance of the work as complete), obtaining materials that she's responsible for, and communicating with you or your project manager. The project manager is responsible for communicating with the team, presenting materials to the client for review, and making sure the project flows smoothly.

For more information about communicating feedback with the team and feedback (giving and receiving), see Chapter 1 of this minibook.

Keeping the team on track

One of the hardest things to control is something called *scope creep*. This is what happens when, during the course of a project, someone — a client or development team — decides to add "little extras" to make the project better. It is the job of the project manager to keep track of those little extras and make sure that they don't add up to a whole bunch of extra functionality that wasn't in the original agreement or budget.

If the client asks for things that are outside the scope of the project, you have two options for moving forward:

✦ **Incorporate the extra request into the current plan.** In this case, you have to tell the client that the extra request is beyond the scope of the agreed project and that amending the current scope document (and timeline and budget) is necessary.

✦ **Discuss the additional functionality as a future project.** If the client agrees to hold off on the new idea for later, you can proceed with the project as planned. The good news is that you now have a future job already lined up.

In either case, let the team know about the requests so they can adjust accordingly.

If your client decides to amend the scope of the current project, you must prepare a new scope document, timeline, and budget. You and the client will have to sign and agree to it.

Handing Off a Project to a Client

Whether you complete the whole project on your own or with a team, you might at some point need to hand off the project to someone else. When you're planning a project, you need to think about the ongoing maintenance of the Web site and either include a maintenance agreement in your proposal or outline how you'll hand off the project.

A *maintenance agreement* should outline how much it will cost to maintain the site and what services you'll provide. Clients must know that requesting large additions to the site will require a new proposal, scope document, and contract.

If you're planning to hand off the Web site to the client, you and the client must agree on the following:

✦ **What will you hand off?** If you're turning over development materials, how much and in what format?

The choice of what to do with production graphics is up to you. Some designers keep their original, editable versions of their graphics. Others hand over all the files. Whichever you decide, make sure that the client understands what they're going to get and how they'll get it.

Whatever you decide as far as the deliverable materials to the client, you need to make sure you keep copies for your own records. Burn the files to discs, collect the site notes, and gather the electronic documents that you've used (e-mails, word documents, contracts, invoices, and so on). Put all the materials together and keep them for your records. Sometimes clients that take on a project come back to you for follow-up work.

✦ **How much transitional support will you give at hand off?** You might want to offer some training if the client doesn't have inhouse staff with skills to maintain the site on her own. Make sure you figure any training or transitional support work into your budget.

✦ **How will you transport the material to the client?** It's standard to deliver the site itself to the client's Web server using a method called *FTP*, or File Transfer Protocol. This technique is covered in Books III and IV. Or you might deliver the site files — and other files, too — on a CD or DVD.

Whatever you decide, make sure you get it all in writing. Make sure that everyone understands what you're delivering and how. Consult your lawyer regarding your copyrights and how to protect against your materials being used in a way that you don't intend.

Chapter 3: Developing the Content

In This Chapter

- ✔ Researching site content
- ✔ Defining goals for the site
- ✔ Keeping the site relevant

So you've got a client who has signed on the dotted line and wants you to create a drop-dead gorgeous Web site with all the bells and whistles that the law allows. When you brainstorm with the client and ask him what he wants on the site, you get an answer like, "You know, the usual." Arggggggh. Wrong answer. The problem with many Web sites is that they don't have content that's relevant to what's out there. So instead of trying to read the client's mind and put together a site that will fail and inevitably taint your reputation as a Web designer, your best course of action is to do some research with the client to steer him in the right direction. Then, when he's developing the text content for the site, you can do what you do best: Design an aesthetically pleasing site that keeps visitors returning time and again. In this chapter, we show you how to guide your client in the right direction.

Knowing What to Put on Your Site

When you go to a bookstore and open a book on cooking, you find recipes and information on how to prepare them. When your client's customers visit her Web site, they expect to find content that relates to the title of the site. You know, truth in advertising and all that bunk? In most cases, the client is responsible for the text content. If your client has created content for the Web, or is experienced in marketing, you're home free. If not, you'll have to act as the voice of reason and steer your client in the right direction.

As the Web designer, you're responsible for the look and feel of the site. This includes elements such as navigation menus; the colors used for the background, buttons, and text; fonts used for the text; and so on. Your choices are driven by your personal taste, experience, and your client's vision. However, factor in two additional parameters: your client's intended audience and competing sites. After all, people don't expect to find a picture of a girl in a bikini on the cover of that Bam guy's cookbook, do they? In the upcoming sections, we show you how to guide yourself and your client in the right direction.

Finding out what your client's visitors need

During the initial stages of the client/designer relationship, you need to figure out what your client's grand vision for the site is. If your client doesn't have a grand vision but wants a Web site because everyone else has one, you might have a problem. If, however, your client does have a viable product, service, or cause, there are probably several hundred sites devoted to the same product, service, or cause. The following list shows some methods of ascertaining what visitors will require from your client's site:

✦ **Visit the Web sites of your client's fiercest competitors.** Imitation is the sincerest form of flattery. If your client's competitors have successful Web sites, explore the sites in depth. Make sure you do your exploration with the client so she knows what type of material you'll require from her to complete your design. Bookmark the sites and refer to them when creating your design. Of course, creating a blatant copy of the competitor's site is not good practice. Put your own spin on what you consider are the most successful elements of the sites you visit.

✦ **Find out which elements are considered standard for a Web site in your client's industry.** For example, all photographers have galleries of portfolios, and most e-commerce sites have some sort of catalog and online shopping cart. Savvy Web site visitors expect to see these elements when they visit sites. If your client's site doesn't have these elements, visitors might go elsewhere for their needs.

✦ **Poll existing customers.** If your client has an established bricks-and-mortar business, he has another excellent resource for determining content for the site. Ask existing customers which Web sites they frequent that offer services similar to your client's.

✦ **Decide whether the site should be interactive.** Many Web site owners have customers fill out questionnaires, while other Web sites entertain customers with interactive games or quizzes that relate to the product or service being offered. Find out if interactive elements are usually associated with Web sites that sell products or services similar to your client's.

✦ **Find out what technology your client's intended audience uses to access the Internet.** All Web site visitors want a fast-loading site, and this information can help you provide that. Your goal as a Web designer is to make an attractive, fast-loading site. The definition of *fast-loading* varies greatly depending on whether your client's intended audience uses dialup modems, DSL modems, or cable modems.

✦ **Find out whether visitors of Web sites of businesses similar to your client's expect bells and whistles such as Flash movies or PDF documents.** If they do, make sure that your content is backward compatible.

For example, if you create Flash content that works with only the latest version of Flash Player, you're potentially alienating a large part of your client's potential customers.

✦ **Find out whether visitors like to personalize their experience on Web sites similar to your client's.**

Dealing with copyright issues

Copyright laws protect creators of original content — such as writing, art, photographs, and so on — from people using unauthorized copies of their work. The copyright laws also apply to Web designers. When you create a Web site, you're using content supplied by your client. If your client indeed created the text and images you're using on the site, he owns the copyright to this material. If, however, you use material such as photographs and music that were not created by the client, you must license the right to use this material as part of your design. If you've purchased a collection of clip art or purchased stock images from one of the stock art houses *and your license allows you to use the image as part of a Web design,* you're covered under the copyright laws. Notice the caveat we include regarding your license? That's right. Just because you bought it, doesn't mean you can use it. Some licenses are very rigid and allow a limited number of uses for an item. Many licenses also prohibit significantly altering clip art.

The best defense here is to read the fine print before using any item that you've purchased, or are contemplating purchasing, for use in a Web design. If you purchase a collection of images or music for use in your designs, make sure they are royalty free. If not, you're responsible for paying royalties to the copyright owner of

the work. Copyright laws also protect logos. If your client sells a product line and requests that you use the product logo on the Web site, make sure this is permissible by the company who manufactures the product. In most instances, your client has to agree to certain terms in order to display the licensed version of the logo on the Web site. The written word is also copyrighted. If your client provides you with verbatim descriptions from a product catalog or another Web site, he might be in violation of the copyright law. Certain items can be copied and used under the Fair Use Doctrine. Even though you're using material that might be copyrighted by others, the manner in which the material on your site is presented is unique and should be copyrighted by the owner of the site you're designing.

Another copyright issue is the completed site. You can copyright the site by adding the following at the bottom of each page: `Copyright 2007 by your client. All rights reserved.` In the end, the best defense is a good offense, which, in this case, means that you and the client should create as much of the content as possible. If your client presents any material that might be questionable, strongly suggest that he contact legal counsel. Attorney's fees are a lot cheaper than paying for duking it out in court.

Finding out what your client needs from site visitors

Before you launch your favorite HTML editor, you've got to do your homework and find out as much as possible about your client and the type of Web site she envisions. If you've already designed sites for similar clients, your knowledge can help guide the client when she's at a loss for answers. Ask your client what her goals are for the site. Get your client to go into detail concerning site goals. Learn as much as you can about her business, and make sure to take copious notes. The following are a few questions you can ask your client to clarify her goals:

✦ **Does your client want to sell goods to visitors?** If so, will the client rely on the site as an online catalog and have personnel fill orders via phone, or will the site be a full-blown, e-commerce site on a secure server?

✦ **Does your client want to inform visitors?** If the client has an established bricks-and-mortar business that is profitable, she can use a Web site to cut down on overhead. For example, instead of giving out catalogs, the client can provide product specifications on the Web site — which eliminates mailing and printing costs. It can also cut down on the number of personnel needed to staff the phones.

✦ **Does your client want a service-oriented site?** Clients use service-oriented sites to answer frequently asked questions from customers, handle service issues, and so on.

✦ **Does your client want repeat visitors?** If so, you have to design a site that gives visitors a reason to return. You also have to tell your client that the site must be updated frequently in order for visitors to return.

✦ **Does your client want to collect contact information to keep visitors apprised of new information about his products or services?**

✦ **Does your client want to frequently update the site?** If so, negotiate a separate contract for ongoing updates. If the client wants to update the site, create the site using templates that have locked areas that the client can't edit. If your client updates the site, we strongly advise you to suggest that the client use Adobe Contribute to do that.

✦ **Does your client want to maintain ongoing communication with site visitors?**

Tell your client when his goals require technology or design elements that exceed his budget. If your client insists on using these elements, give him the price for the additional elements and be prepared to write an addendum to your contract.

Reconciling the content with the goals

After you know what visitors expect from sites similar to your client's and you know what your client's goals are, you're ready to create the site. Your client should provide you with a good deal of the content. In an ideal world, the client submits all images to you in electronic format, optimized and ready to pop into your design. However, it's been our experience that the client is most likely to send you images that you need to scan and optimize, or images in electronic format that you need to resize and optimize for the Web. Your client should also provide text for the site. In the Zen tradition of less is more, make sure that your client doesn't go over the top by providing too much information or by providing information that isn't relevant to site visitors. When reviewing text for the site, think like the site visitor and ask the question, What's in it for me? If some of the information doesn't address a customer question or need, suggest that your client delete it.

In addition to what your client supplies, you're creating content for the site. The content that you create should be based on customer needs and your client's goals. Based on this information, you might need to add or create the following to the site:

✦ A secure server and an online shopping cart are necessities if your client wants to sell merchandise from the site.

✦ Create an online catalog if your client wants to inform visitors about his goods and services.

✦ Include an e-mail newsletter if one of your client's goals is to keep customers informed.

✦ A *blog* (a Web log) is an easy way for your client to maintain ongoing communication with site visitors.

✦ The Web site needs forms and databases if the client wants to collect contact information from people visiting the site.

✦ Use cookies if customers want to personalize their experience while visiting the site. *Cookies* are software that is downloaded to the user's computer. When the visitor next visits the site, the information from the cookie is recognized by the HTML code.

✦ Use templates in your layout of sections of the site your client wants to frequently update. Templates save time and trouble. Creating templates enables you to delegate the work to a less-experienced designer. If the client wants his staff to update the site, templates are imperative. Templates prevent inexperienced editors from corrupting navigation menus and so on. When you create templates, lock out the areas you don't want the client or other designers to modify.

✦ If the client's staff is going to update the site, design your site so that it can be edited with Adobe Contribute and include the price of the application as part of your Web design fee. Also, make sure to include training sessions in your contract. Cover additional training and consultation in a separate contract or separate clause of your Web design contract.

Keeping It Fresh: An Ongoing Process

If you've done your best to create a compelling site for your client, and you've optimized the site 27 ways to Sunday, people will visit the site. But like anything else, the bloom is off the lily rather quickly. People might watch a good movie many times, but it's rare that people visit a Web site with the same content over and over again. To keep visitors returning, you or your client have to give visitors a reason to return. If interested visitors know that the content is updated on a regular basis, they will return.

Assigning content development tasks

If your client decides that he wants the site updated frequently, either you or your client's staff is responsible for updating the pages and uploading them to the server. If your client has contracted you to do the updates, you and your staff can schedule updates at a convenient time. If your client does the updates, he can coordinate the task with his staff. If your client's staff is doing the updates, make sure you design the site with templates, locking the areas with which you don't want the client to tamper. Make sure your client's staff has the knowledge and software to update the site without destroying your hard work. For personnel with little or no Web experience, Adobe Contribute is an ideal application to update a site.

Keeping the graphics fresh

When people visit your Web site for the first time, it's a shiny new face. But like the man in the mirror, the shiny, new face grows old after a while. In this regard, the graphics on the Web site should be updated on a regular basis. Anything with the client's logo, such as the site banner, should not be updated. After all, you do want some continuity in the site. The graphics you do want to update are any Flash movies and graphics used for news, information, and the like. If your client will update the site, get her to supply you with several images that will be rotated in certain parts of the site — for example, the home page and the What's New page, if the client has one. Size the graphics to fit the spots on the page where they will be displayed, optimize them for Web viewing, and then return the optimized images to your client. If your client uses Flash movies on the Web site, create a few alternatives that are the same size and show your client's staff how to swap out the movies when needed.

Chapter 4: Creating Relevant Site Content

In This Chapter

✔ Putting the company in a favorable light

✔ Offering information

✔ Developing content

A Web site is a very important thing. At least, it better be. When you're hired to create a Web site, you're creating a worldwide presence for your client. As a Web designer, you do your best to create a site that portrays your client's business or service at its best. But it's a two-way street. You can be the best designer in the world, but if your client doesn't know what he wants or needs for his Web site, your best design efforts are in vain. A Web site is all about marketing a company, product, or service. It's an extension of the client's bricks-and-mortar business, if he has one. If not, the Web site serves as the identity for your client's business. Your job as a designer is to work with the client in order to portray his company in the best possible light. This chapter gives you some information that you can use to guide your client in the right direction.

Portraying Your Client's Company

When you develop a Web site for a client, you're presenting your customer's professional image for the world to see. Your client might be selling goods or services or providing information for customers. A Web site works 24/7 and has the potential for drawing a worldwide audience. The organization portrayed on the Web site might or might not have a bricks-and-mortar location in which it does business. Even if it does have a bricks-and-mortar business, that won't matter to an audience whose opinion of the company is defined by its Web site. Therefore, it is paramount that you paint the best portrait possible when you create a Web site for a client.

Defining your client's voice

Your client's voice encompasses many things: the manner in which your client does business, your client's mission, the image your client portrays to his customers, and so on. When you define your client's voice through a Web site, you're answering the question: Do I want to do business with this company or individual? In order to gain the trust of Web site visitors, the site must leave a positive impression. But more than that, the site should be unique enough to stand out against the client's competition.

Most of your client's competitors probably have Web sites. And it's almost a given that Web sites within a certain industry will have a common look. Therefore, the only way you can make your client's site rise above the competition is to portray your client's unique assets — the client's voice, if you will. When defining the voice of a company, the message you portray on the Web should be consistent with the client's other communications, such as printed ads, television commercials, and audio advertisements. If your client has a startup company, the Web site helps define the client's essence. To define this intangible, you need to brainstorm with your client and consider the following:

✦ **Audience:** Who is the client's intended audience? What's unique about your client's intended audience? How do you portray your client as part of this clan? What type of message will set your client apart from his competition, in the eyes of his intended audience?

✦ **Mission:** What is your client's intended mission? How does your client plan to serve the intended audience? When defining the client's mission, steer clear of the usual clichés, such as highest quality, superior service, satisfied customers, and so on. You can reword clichés to make your client stand out from his competition. In addition to instilling confidence in your client's intended audience, his mission statement must portray his unique core values.

✦ **Style:** What is your client's style? Is she an entrepreneur? Where does the client fall in the broad spectrum of similar businesses? Is she smack-dab in the middle? Or is she conservative or bold and brash?

✦ **Customers:** How do your client's customers perceive her? The competitors? Do the answers to these questions match your client's perception of herself and her business?

✦ **Future goals:** Where does your client see herself in five or ten years? Will the message your client portrays now be viable in five or ten years?

Armed with this information, you and your client can begin making some decisions about how you'll portray the company on the Web. While you're at it, have the client distill the information into a few paragraphs that describe the company, its core values, and future vision. You can incorporate this information into an effective mission statement.

Developing your client's look

After you and the client define her voice, it's time to think of how you'll incorporate this with the Web site you create. In essence, you're defining your client's look on the Web. The amount of creativity you can employ in defining your client's look on the Web depends on whether the client has an established, bricks-and-mortar business.

If your client has an established bricks-and-mortar business, you'll have to create a Web site that has a similar look and feel. The site has to incorporate the client's logo and images that are used in corporate brochures and advertising. Your client's presence on the Web is defined on how well you assimilate your client's bricks-and-mortar look with your Web design. When you're designing a Web site for a client who has already established a look, ask yourself these questions:

✦ **Does the Web site have the look and feel of the client's bricks-and-mortar business?** When established customers visit the Web site, the site should seem like an extension of the client's bricks-and-mortar business. The design should feel right to the client as well as his customers.

✦ **Does the design effectively portray the client's voice?** The design you create needs to portray the client's manner of doing business, his mission statement, and his style of doing business. Your design must also be consistent with the expectations of the client's current audience and intended audience.

✦ **Can the design be modified to fit the client's future goals and needs?** If your client's long-term goals are substantially different than current goals, you'll probably end up doing a complete redesign at some point in the future. However, if your client's future goals are to grow and increase customer base with the same or similar product designs, your initial design has to be flexible enough to incorporate future expansion, such as the addition of new sections, changes in product lines, and so on.

If you're designing a site for a client that will do business only on the Web, you have considerably more leeway when developing a client's look. With the client's help, you can establish the client's Web presence. If the client already has a logo, you use this as a starting point. The colors in the client's logo help define the color palette you use to design the Web site. After deciding on the color palette, your next step is to assimilate graphics into the design. If the client is a *solopreneur* (runs a one-person business) or has a small business, you can make the business seem larger than life with the creative use of clip art. If your client is an aggressive businessperson, you can depict your client's style of doing business with the creative use of color and fonts. The finished site must effectively communicate your client's style of doing business, mission, and goals to potential customers in the most positive manner. (See Figure 4-1.) This design incorporates the colors from the client's logo.

Figure 4-1:
Creating a
site that
portrays
the client's
voice.

Selling Goods or Services

If you're creating a site that sells goods or services, your goal is to create a compelling site that piques customer curiosity and instills customer confidence. There are a lot of snake oil salesmen on the Web, and buyers definitely err on the side of caution. Therefore, it is your job as a designer to instill trust in your client's potential customer while also bringing the product or service to the forefront of the visitor's mind, hopefully resulting in a click of one or more Buy Now buttons. It's a shame that Buy Now buttons don't make a noise your client can hear, as this would be music to his ears.

Emphasizing key points

When you sell a product or service online, you design your pages in such a manner as to instill customer confidence while emphasizing the key points of your client's product or service. The old, Zen-like maxim of "Less is more" definitely applies here. Instead of barraging the Web site visitor with each and every subtle nuance about the product, you point out major features of a product without engaging the visitor in several paragraphs of text. You can easily sum up a product line by showing the key points about a product in a succinct paragraph or two. Better yet, use bullet lists to emphasize the key points of a product line. Your goal is to pique the buyer's curiosity and get her to take action.

You can also emphasize key points by using different colors for text, bold-facing text, and so on. If you're using bullet points, consider boldfacing the word(s) that define the bullet point and perhaps using a different color text. If you use a different color text to emphasize a key point, choose a color that is harmonious with the design. (See Figure 4-2.)

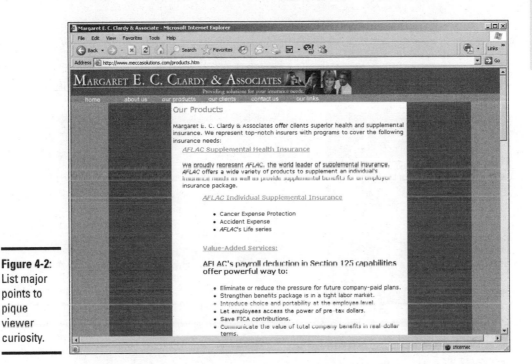

Figure 4-2: List major points to pique viewer curiosity.

The same rules apply when you're presenting information about a service. Emphasize the service with bold text and an introductory sentence followed by bullet points. To emphasize the key points of the service, use a different color for the text of the key points. This directs the viewer's eye to the most important information.

Highlighting the product

When the goal of a Web site is to sell products, or present information about a product, your design should make that readily apparent to the viewer. When you're working with products, you need to get high-quality images from your client. Armed with good pictures, you can then employ other methods to highlight the product.

If you're dealing with a complex product line, it's best to devote a single page to each product. Including too many products on a single page dilutes the effectiveness of the message. Figure 4-3 shows a product page. The product image is the highlight of the page, followed by two paragraphs of concise text that tells visitors key information about the product.

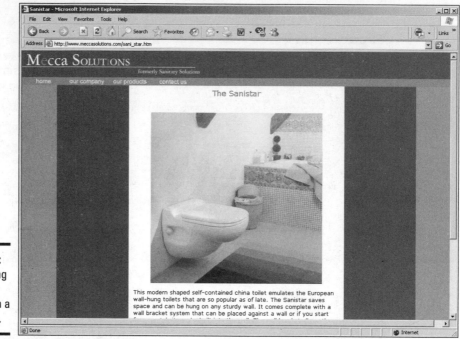

Figure 4-3: Highlighting a single product on a Web page.

Providing Information

If your client's goal is to provide information about his services, you'll create a site that provides information about the client's products or services, but has no option to purchase the product or service online. When you create an information-driven Web site, you use text or brochures supplied by the client to create the content for the site. You might also assimilate information created by others, such as articles or multimedia content. The client is responsible for the accuracy of the material. You, however, are responsible for providing the information via your Web design in a manner that is easy to digest and understand.

Handling large amounts of content

If your client has copious amounts of information to dispense through his Web site, you've got a challenge on your hands. The attention span of most

Web site visitors is minute, which means they're not going to read pages with voluminous amounts of text. It's your job as a designer to break the information down into bite-size pieces. Here are a few techniques you can use for achieving that goal:

✦ **Break large amounts of text into several pages.**

✦ **Intersperse images with the text to break up the content.**

✦ **Break up large amounts of text with headlines that visitors can use to ascertain whether they want to read the content.** Savvy visitors also use headlines to get the gist of what information is presented on a page.

✦ **Create a newspaper-style page where the information is presented in columns.** Each article has a headline. Instead of including all of the information on a page, include the first paragraph or two and then include a More link at the end of the last sentence. When clicked, the More link opens the full article in another window.

✦ **Create a home page that contains links to the information you need to present.** (See Figure 4-4.)

✦ **Create a site map.** The site map has a text description of every page on the site. Each text description doubles as a hyperlink, which, when clicked, reveals the applicable page.

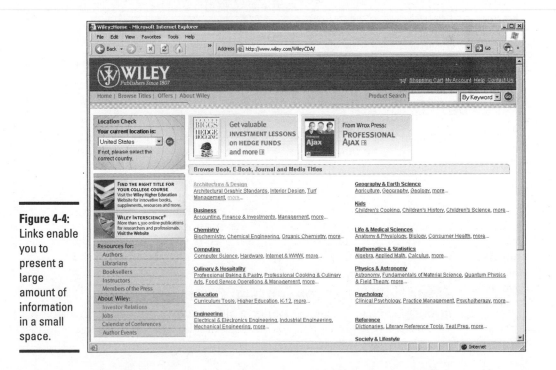

Figure 4-4:
Links enable you to present a large amount of information in a small space.

Presenting information

Presenting information on a Web page is an art unto itself. The information you present depends on the type of site you design and what the client gives you to work with. The typical Web site is a mixture of images and text, with, perhaps, some multimedia content added for grins and giggles.

✦ **Break major ideas into bullet points.** Bullet points make a page look less cluttered. See Figure 4-5.

✦ **Arrange the page so that the information has a logical flow.** You can break up big blocks of information using header styles. Readers should be able to sum up the information presented on a page by glancing at the headlines and then deciding what information they want to read.

✦ **Break up text with pictures.** If applicable, add a caption to each picture on a page. Busy site visitors can use captions to sum up the information presented on a Web page at a glance.

✦ **Don't use color combinations that are hard to read.** For example, pink text on a dark-colored background is difficult to read. The old tried and true black text on a white background is always legible.

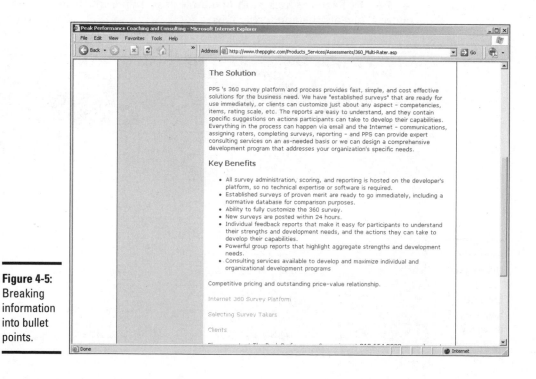

Figure 4-5:
Breaking information into bullet points.

✦ **Don't use small fonts.** A text size smaller than 10 points is almost impossible for visitors to read, unless they have extremely acute vision. If your intended audience is getting on in years, the text shouldn't be smaller than 12 points.

✦ **When you're designing your site, make sure you view it using the smallest desktop size of your intended audience.** As of this writing, 52 percent of Web site visitors are surfing the Net with a desktop size of 1024 x 768. Make sure your design flows logically and is easy to read.

✦ **If you're using a newsletter style with multiple columns for your Web page, make the columns different widths.** Also, don't exceed two columns, especially if your audience uses a small desktop size. (See Figure 4-6.) If you're using a horizontal menu, you can increase to three columns.

✦ **Don't use nonstandard font faces when designing your pages.** Your intended audience might not have the font installed on their machines, which causes the browser to use the default system font. This might cause usability issues and make the page difficult to read. When in doubt, stick to the fab four: Arial, Georgia, Times New Roman, or Verdana.

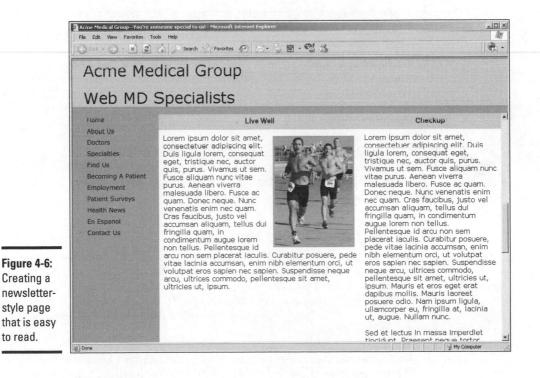

Figure 4-6:
Creating a newsletter-style page that is easy to read.

✦ **Don't use a busy background for your pages.** The busyness makes text hard to read. If your client insists on a tiling background (when a small image is repeated on the page, which when the page loads looks like a single image), choose a simple design and lower the opacity in an image-editing application such as Fireworks or Photoshop.

✦ **Use hyperlinked text to draw a viewer's attention to pertinent content.** If you use this technique, make sure you don't disable hyperlink decoration with a cascading style sheet. Your goal is to make the hyperlink easy to see when the page loads. If you don't like underlined hyperlinks, use the style sheet to modify the color of the hyperlink text.

✦ **Use bold-faced text to direct the viewer's eye to important information.**

✦ **If several authors write the Web site content, make sure the style and voice is similar.** A Web site should read like a book. Consistency is important.

✦ **Make sure the terminology and spelling is consistent sitewide.** For example, don't use *Website* (one word) in one section, and *Web site* (two words) in another. At the risk of being redundant, consistency is important.

✦ **Make sure the structure and the layout of the pages is consistent.** Pages might have to vary, depending on the content, but the look and style needs to be consistent.

✦ **If you're using multimedia content such as movies and sound files, make sure they're all the same file format.** For example, don't use the Windows Media Format for some of your movies and Apple's QuickTime for the rest. Choose a file format that the majority of your client's intended audience can view and stick with that standard.

Read the information provided by the client before adding it to the page. If, in your opinion, the client is presenting too much information (also known as stuffing 50 pounds of text into a 30-pound bag), ask the client to edit the text and be more concise.

Including e-learning materials

If your client is creating a Web site that instructs end users on how to use a particular application or accomplish a specific task, include material that can accomplish this task. There are many methods of accomplishing this. In fact, specific software packages are available to create content for e-learning Web sites. The following is a list of some of the items currently used on e-learning Web sites:

✦ **Instructional video:** Nothing gets the point across like video. If the site is showing users how to master a software application, a video capture of the application in action is the ideal teaching tool. In conjunction with the teacher's audio instructions, video is a powerful e-learning tool. You can capture a video of an application using Camtasia or HyperCam software. The video you post online can vary depending on the type of Internet connection used by your client's intended audience. You can post streaming video using the Windows Media Format, Apple's Quick-Time format, or Flash video.

✦ **Flash interactive content:** Flash is a wonderful tool for creating animations. You can also use Flash to create content such as quizzes, interactive learning exercises, and so on. If you're adept at ActionScript, you can get Flash to do some wonderful things, such as tally the score of a quiz, or direct a user to a different part of the Flash movie based on the response to a question.

✦ **PDF documents:** Adobe Acrobat is another wonderful tool that you can use to create tutorials. Many people think that PDF documents can be used to show only text and images. This is not true. In the hands of an experienced Acrobat user, a PDF document can include multimedia content such as audio and video. Acrobat PDF documents can also be interactive. Acrobat has built-in actions that you can use to link to open other documents, play video or audio, and so on. An Acrobat document can also use JavaScript to perform tasks.

You include links to your e-learning materials in your HTML documents. You can set the learning material to open in the same browser window or a new window. You can embed e-learning material such as video in the document, complete with a player. This is the preferred method, as some people rely on the Back button to recall previously viewed content. When a document is opened in a new window, this luxury is not available.

Using Personas to Develop Content

When you create a Web site for a client, part of your job is to find out who the client's intended audience is. After you find out who the client's intended audience is, you need to find out as much about the audience as possible. Your client should be able to provide you with the majority of the information. You might be able to find other information, such as demographics, online. Armed with this information, you can tailor the content to the intended audience. In other words, the site you design connects with viewers on a personal level, a task that is easier said than done.

If your client's goal is to connect with viewers on a personal level, you can create one or more personas to define your client's archetypical visitors. A *persona* is a hypothetical person whose characteristics and demographics fit your client's intended audience to a tee and therefore has all of the information you need to define the audience. When considering what content to use on the site, you use the persona to guide you. In other words, you tailor your content to the persona, and your client's intended audience will think the content was written personally for them. Depending on the scope of your client's intended audience, you might have to create multiple personas. For example, if the intended audience is young males between the ages of 24 and 35 with a college degree who live in the U.S. and make between $45,000 and $75,000 per year, you can get by with one persona. However, if your intended audience is male and female with varying degrees of education and varied socioeconomic groups, you'll have to create multiple personas.

Defining your client's customers

When creating personas, you have to rely on your client to provide the information. After all, you are a Web designer, not a marketing guru. If your client is not familiar with creating personas, here are a few guidelines:

+ Create a one- or two-page description of each persona. Include information such as gender, age, ethnicity, education, profession, income, and so on.

+ Include information about the habits and daily routine of each persona.

+ What are the hobbies and pastimes of each persona?

+ What are the habits of each persona?

+ What computer skills does the persona have?

Your client will probably end up with between three and six personas. If the number gets larger than that, you'll have a hard time tailoring content for that diverse a group. The whole idea behind personas is focusing on the type of individuals who will use your client's product or service, not the general public.

Delivering what they want

With multiple personas defined, your client can begin creating content for the site. Of course, the content your client provides will be text. The authors will create text that is appropriate for the age, gender, and education level of the personas. You'll create a navigation menu and design that is concurrent with the likes and computer skills of the personas defined by your client. If you're using multimedia elements, such as background music, the personas defined by your client will guide you to the proper choice.

The content created for the Web site is also governed by the area in which the personas live. If the personas reside locally, you'll want to include information about your client's local events. If the personas live in all areas of the country or world, you can include information about worldwide events pertaining to the client's business or service.

Book II

Site Design

The 5th Wave   By Rich Tennant

SITE MAP STRATEGY BY JERRY

"Okay, well, I think we all get the gist of where Jerry was going with the site map."

Contents at a Glance

Chapter 1:
Conceptualizing Your Site

In This Chapter

✔ Deciding what types of pages you need

✔ Choosing the right delivery methods

✔ Creating printer-friendly materials

*B*ook II, Chapter 3 covers developing content. This chapter discusses how to present content to your visitors. You must keep some content in a database; you store other content as plain HTML pages. And you can consider several multimedia methods of delivery. Not every method is good for every type of information. You must determine what types of pages you need, how to deliver those pages to your viewers, and whether to include printable pages.

Deciding What Types of Pages You Need

The types of pages are *static* Web pages (plain HTML pages) and *dynamic* Web pages (pages that can react to site visitors; more on that in a bit). Different situations require these different types of pages. Either type of page can include multimedia elements. When determining what types of pages you need, consider the following:

✦ **The amount of information you have and how you want to organize it:** Some sites have only a few pages with some pictures and a little text. Other sites have massive amounts of information that needs a database (or more than one database) to manage it all. Most sites fall somewhere in between.

✦ **How you want visitors to use your information:** Do you want them to passively read, or would you like them to interact with the content? Do you want them to be able to download anything?

✦ **Users' expectations:** To get an idea of what users want from your site, look at similar sites to get an idea of what sorts of features and functionality they have in common. Visitors to your site will most likely have an idea of what is typical and expect that your site have similar features. For instance, if you build a site that sells children's stories, the target audience will probably expect some downloadable coloring pages and other free fun things for kids. If your site doesn't have those types of features, your audience might abandon your site for one that does.

✦ **Layout considerations:** Some sites have a unique home page layout and then two or three subordinate page designs. Other sites have a consistent layout for every page. Which method you choose depends on the needs of your site. Having a unique home page layout helps unify a site that has several sections that have different needs. For instance, for sections of your site that primarily display text, you need a layout that works for that type of information. The same site can include a catalog section for products. The layout for that section is different because you must display the products. The home page for a site like that works as a jumping off point that unifies the two areas of the site. The home page also is a good place to highlight information or drive traffic to a specific feature of your site. A unique home page layout can effectively support that functionality.

Other page layout considerations are whether the site will have charts and graphs or tables, which need to be delivered as graphics or multimedia elements. In some situations, the best way to handle this type of information is to embed the chart/graph directly into the HTML document. This works best if you can display it effectively along with any supporting text on the monitor without having to scroll — even on monitors with lower resolutions (800×600, for instance). If you need the chart or graph to be larger, you can have it launch in a second browser window. That way, it can use more space while keeping the supporting text information easily available.

✦ **Multimedia considerations:** How do you want multimedia elements to display? The considerations are the same for charts and graphs. Look at the content and decide whether it will work best embedded in the page or displayed in a second browser window. The second window can be smaller, which allows visitors to see and use the original page. Figure 1-1 shows a Flash element launched in a smaller browser window.

Considering static Web pages

Static Web pages are plain HTML pages. They can include some JavaScript and should include some CSS for formatting. This type of page is called static because the elements in it don't change unless the Webmaster makes changes to it. Each time the page loads, it is pretty much the same. The content remains the same regardless of who views it.

Figure 1-1:
Using a
smaller,
second
browser
window can
help visitors
access your
information.

When a visitor tries to view a static Web page, a request to view the page is sent to the server that holds the HTML document. The document and any supporting files are delivered to the visitor's browser. The HTML document that is stored on the server is a whole document with all of its elements included in it. The only external pieces are CSS, images, and some JavaScript. The same HTML document is delivered every time, regardless of who is trying to view it or what they have done previously.

Static Web pages can include some JavaScript that can give the illusion of dynamic content. An example of this is script that displays different images in a specific place each time the page loads. If you've browsed a few sites, you've probably seen this effect. You can use it to switch out CSS files, also. Figure 1-2 shows an example of a Web page that has a bit of JavaScript randomizing an image. This might appear to be changing content, but it really isn't. The JavaScript has a list of image files to choose from, and it randomly chooses from that list each time the page loads.

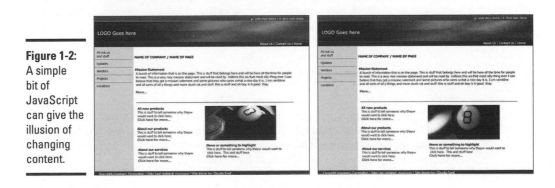

Figure 1-2:
A simple
bit of
JavaScript
can give the
illusion of
changing
content.

Freshening the content with dynamic Web pages

Dynamic Web pages are built when a visitor comes to your site. That might sound a little strange, but it's true. When a visitor tries to view a page that is dynamic, requests for information are sent to the server. The server reacts to the request and assembles the pieces of the page as requested and delivers them to the visitor's browser as an HTML document.

The big difference between dynamic pages and static ones is that dynamic ones can react to your visitors. You can include scripts in parts of your code that help your site remember visitors when they return. The scripts assemble customized pages based on those visitors. A good example of this is the Amazon.com Web site. Each visitor's experience is customized to that person based on previous visits. This is accomplished by using a series of communications between the server and the user's browser.

Dynamic pages allow users to send you information via forms that can be stored in a database. And you can allow your visitors to request information and perform searches on your site content.

Dynamic pages are made up of pieces of information and pieces of pages. Where the code for a static page is included in only one document, dynamic pages are made up of headers, footers, and include files. Each of these is a mini-HTML document that isn't complete on its own. But when assembled by the server and delivered to a browser, they become complete. The content in these pages is typically pulled from a database. It's easy to spot pages that are dynamic while you're browsing. A page with an `.asp`, `.jsp`, or `.cfm` file extension — rather than `.htm` or `.html` — is a dynamic page.

You can create dynamic pages using any of several technologies. You're likely to hear about ASP, JSP (JavaServer Pages), and ColdFusion when you start looking into dynamic Web sites. (You can find more information about using ASP to create dynamic Web pages in Book VI, Chapter 2.) If you want a page to really interact and react to your visitors, you need dynamic functionality. The pages can be the same for each visitor, and you don't need to pull out the big guns.

When talking about dynamic Web sites, you'll hear certain terms, including these:

✦ **Front end:** This is code that deals with how the information is displayed — the CSS and HTML that is wrapped around the information that is being delivered from the database.

✦ **Back end:** This refers to the database and supporting structures.

✦ **Middleware:** This is the collection of code that communicates with the server, the database, and the front-end code. It's just what it sounds like — it's the middleman between the front and back.

Each area — front, back, and middle — requires different skill sets to create. If you'll be collecting personal information or allowing purchases on your site, you need to take special care in building the middle- and back-end pieces to avoid any problems.

Evaluating multimedia element choices

Multimedia is a broad term that includes video, sound, animations, and other presentations. Multimedia is not a series of HTML pages that are navigated in a linear fashion. Although the effect is similar to a presentation, it's not considered multimedia unless it's actually a self-contained piece embedded in a Web page.

Multimedia elements can be dynamic, depending on what type of multimedia you use. For instance, Flash can communicate with databases and serve dynamic content — so it's *dynamic multimedia*. Flash can also collect information from your visitors by using forms, and can then deliver the information to your server. When you use Flash in this way, the Flash element is said to be the *front end*. You can use Flash to create a form (shown in Figure 1-3) that passes information to a database.

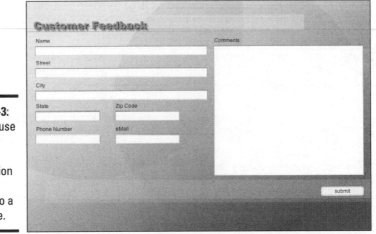

Figure 1-3:
You can use Flash to collect information to be passed to a database.

You can deliver multimedia content in many different ways, and which way you choose to use depends on many factors. The most important things to consider are what the multimedia content is and what you're trying to accomplish. Are you trying to let your visitors hear some music? You'll need to look into formats that let you get the music to your visitors easily and well. Figure 1-4 shows a Flash-based jukebox used to deliver MP3 files to users.

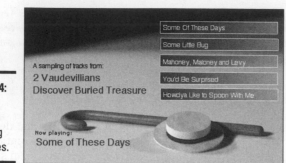

Figure 1-4:
A Flash
jukebox
delivering
music files.

A sampling of tracks from:
**2 Vaudevillians
Discover Buried Treasure**

Some Of These Days
Some Little Bug
Mahoney, Maloney and Levy
You'd Be Surprised
Howdya Like to Spoon With Me

Now playing:
Some of These Days

Making a decision about what types of multimedia to use (if any) is an involved process. You must think about the pros and cons: Essentially, you're weighing functionality against the technological constraints of your audience and your own ability to build and maintain the piece. You have to consider your individual situation on each project. To help you decide, consider the following:

+ **Your current resources:** Do you have software to create multimedia elements? Can you purchase the software? After you purchase software, do you, or anyone on your team, know how to use the software well enough to create your project? Is it feasible to call in a specialist if you don't have the software and skill set available to you?

+ **Target audience:** You must know whether the site's visitors appreciate multimedia elements or find them annoying. Are you targeting individuals that have newer machines and good connections to the Web, or are you trying to target a more general audience? Broader audiences generally mean that you should stay more conservative in your multimedia methods and deliveries and pay special attention to file sizes and download speeds.

+ **User preferences:** Everyone benefits from different types of experiences — differently. Some people get a lot out of charts. Others prefer text. Some users appreciate graphics or video to help them understand the content. Not all users are the same. Sometimes your best bet is to make your information available through a variety of methods. For example, post a video for those who appreciate visual and audio information, but also include a text version for those who prefer written text or aren't able to use the video content.

In general, users appreciate your site more if you create navigation that allows them to move freely through the content as much as possible. The Web offers users the unique opportunity to experience your content their own way. No two users will take the same path, and any user can choose different paths on return visits.

The speed of multimedia evolution: Make sure that if you're trying to target an audience that generally has older machines, you create multimedia that uses older versions of browser plug-ins. This also helps you make sure that the piece won't require too much processor power. If you use the latest and greatest in multimedia on your site, older machines will have a difficult time with or won't be able to display your multimedia at all, resulting in a bad experience for visitors.

Number of versions of the project you can create: You must decide whether the benefits of offering pieces with different specifications are worth the extra time and effort required to build and maintain sites that have more than one version of multimedia elements. You go through the initial process of creating the project only once, but then you have to *export* (publish) different versions of the project. The process of creating the different versions can be time consuming because creating each version is a process of trial and error, to a degree. You can develop some good starting points (as far as settings to make), but each project is a little different and the results are a little different. You have to work at it until you get the right balance between quality and performance.

To provide different versions, export versions with different plug-in and compression settings. The basics of compression are *the more you compress a file, the smaller it gets, the faster it downloads*. The down side of that is that you also lose quality in the file. Compression is always a game of balancing quality and performance.

✦ **Server space:** Multimedia files are typically larger than other files. Make sure that the server you're storing them on has enough room. If you're hosting your site remotely, make sure you have enough monthly bandwidth to support the amount of traffic you expect. Each time users view your files, they use up some of your bandwidth. Hosting plans typically allow a certain amount of bandwidth per month. If you exceed the amount of bandwidth, you can incur extra charges. Make sure you have enough bandwidth to handle the amount of traffic you expect, and find out how much it will cost if you go over.

If you opt for multiple versions of multimedia files, you have to upload those different versions to the server. That uses up more server space. You'll also have to provide ways to navigate to the alternate versions of the multimedia elements. Each version needs an HTML document so that it can play in visitors' browsers. You want to make the user experience as seamless as possible. Plan navigation elements in advance, not as an afterthought.

TIP

Making multimedia elements available to all users

A target audience using older machines or slower connections doesn't mean that you can't use multimedia elements. It does mean that you have to consider how you can make your content work for them. If you need to make your multimedia more efficient, consider these options:

- **Use a photograph instead of video.** You can slowly move the photograph to give the impression of a video element (this is called the Ken Burns effect).

- **Use vector graphics in your animations.** If you use Flash to create animated elements, make sure you take advantage of vector elements and their ability to reuse elements. See Book V, Chapters 1, 2, and 3 for more information about using Flash.

- **Download only parts of your multimedia as they're needed.** You can use Flash to download only the pieces of your multimedia that

are needed. You can also plan your files so that they play parts of the presentation while more is still downloading (which is called *progressively downloading*).

- **Publish your files to an older version of the player.** For example, instead of using the latest features of QuickTime, opt for fewer bells and whistles and publish the file so that older versions of the player can use it. This also works in Flash; publish to Flash Player version 6 or 7 to accommodate users that might not have updated machines.

If you know that a larger number of your audience has updated machines and better connections, feel free to create content that plays best using the latest technologies. Another option is to make multiple versions available. As always, weigh the benefits against how much work it will take to create and maintain multiple versions.

Choosing the Right Delivery Method

You can create Web sites made up of all static pages, a few templates created to work with dynamic information, or a combination of the two. You can use multimedia elements throughout the site on either static or dynamic pages. Figure 1-5 shows a page that has multimedia elements on a static page.

Knowing when static pages suit your purpose

Static HTML works well for information such as directions to your facility and general contact information. If you intend to post a large number of contact people, consider a dynamic solution.

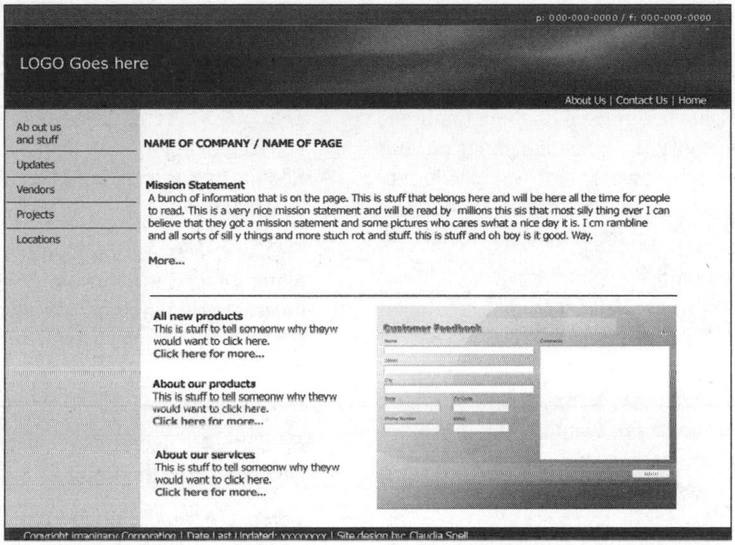

Figure 1-5:
Static HTML and multimedia work together to create a total experience for your users.

Pages with content that doesn't need to change very often are also good candidates for static HTML. Make sure that the content appears in only a couple of places. Because the content is embedded directly in the HTML, you have to update each file separately to make sure they're consistent. If you use a *WYSIWYG* (what you see is what you get) editor to create pages, you can use a Find and Replace feature.

Using dynamic pages to manage complex information

Manage large amounts of information that the Web team or visitors will need to search using databases and dynamic pages. Sites with content that changes often also are good candidates for dynamic pages.

Using a database and dynamic pages to deliver your content also makes content easier to repurpose. With static pages, the content is embedded directly in the code. Dynamic sites hold all their content in databases; therefore, more than one location can use the same content at the same time. You can have more than one site using the database, or you can enable more than one section of your site to display the same information. Because the information is all coming from one source, it's consistent. Static pages run the risk of becoming out of synch with each other if information is updated on one page but not another.

Using Find and Replace in Dreamweaver

The Dreamweaver Find and Replace feature is a very useful tool when updating pages on your site. This tool allows you to simply locate instances of a specific piece of text or code and replace it with something else. (Book III, Chapters 5 and 6 contain information about using Dreamweaver.) To use the Find and Replace feature in Dreamweaver, follow these steps:

1. **In the Code view window, select the piece of text or code you want to find in another place in the document.**

2. **Choose Edit⇨Find and Replace.**

   The Find and Replace dialog box opens. It has your selected text and/or code in the Find field.

   You can decide to search just the selected text, the current document, the whole site, all open documents, selected files, or a selected folder of the site. You have the choice of doing a *Find* (Dreamweaver searches for the term) or a *Find and Replace* (Dreamweaver replaces the found term with the term you enter in the Replace field).

3. **For a Find and Replace, enter the text and/or code that you'd like to replace the current selection with in the Replace field.**

4. **Click the button to the right that represents the function you'd like to perform.**

   Your choices are

   Find Next: Moves the cursor to the next instance of the term you're looking for.

Find All: Finds all instances of the term you're looking for and displays a list in the Results box, which launches automatically when needed.

Replace: Moves the cursor to the next instance of the term you're looking for, deletes it, and replaces it with the term you typed in the Replace field. Then it hops to the next instance and awaits your next instruction.

Replace All: Replaces all instances of the Find term with the Replace term.

Close: Closes the dialog box when you're done.

Warning: Before you do a Find and Replace All, you should be very sure that you really want to make the change. This is especially true if you choose to do a Find and Replace that involves files that aren't open. You can't Undo the changes you make to those files.

Remember that global Find and Replace operations can sometimes create undesirable results. In cases where the selected text to be replaced occurs in locations that you hadn't thought of, you can damage your content or your code.

If you're unsure about the impact of a Find and Replace action, use Find All first, and then individually select the instances from the list that you want to change.

There are several choices for delivering multimedia elements on your site. The most common ones are Flash, QuickTime, Windows Media Player, and Shockwave. The right choice depends on the content you're delivering and the target audience. Each option can deliver video, audio, and animations to your users. We discuss things to consider when choosing what type of multimedia to use in the next section.

Considering multimedia

Multimedia can be a good way to make very boring information more interesting. You can use animations to establish information or clarify your point; they can enforce your message and clarify your information. When deciding whether to use multimedia on your site, however, you must consider the time, your resources, and whether there will be a good return on the investment. Also, make sure that the content itself is better presented as multimedia. Some content is not well suited for multimedia treatment. Think about how using multimedia enhances your information; see the "Evaluating multimedia element choices" section earlier in this chapter.

**Book II
Chapter 1**

Conceptualizing
Your Site

Handling Printable Materials

Sometimes you want to allow your visitors to print or download materials from your site. You have different ways to handle this task.

For smaller sites, it's fine to create PDFs from your printable documents, post those PDFs to your server, and provide links to them. This method is effective if you have only a few printables that don't change very often. We don't recommend posting Word documents. They're too easy to download and change. PDFs allow you to control the content of the documents.

You can write CSS that instructs the browser how to display the page on-screen and also instructs the browser/printer how to print the document. CSS — which stands for Cascading Style Sheets — is generally thought of as a tool to control your layout on the screen, but that is just one thing that CSS can do. You can specify different media types for CSS to control. One of the options is Print, which controls the way the page prints. For more about working with CSS, see Book III, Chapter 3.

To create a style sheet for print, follow these steps:

1. **Create a screen CSS file.**

   A *screen CSS* is the same thing as CSS without a media type specified.

2. **Create a print CSS file.**

Make sure that the names of your selectors are the same in both files. There will be different values for some of the selectors depending on the intended use of the CSS, but they both need to have the same names to apply styles to. Otherwise, your code can become very messy with code that is intended for use by different style sheets.

3. **Link to the CSS files and give them the correct media types, as follows:**

```
<LINK href="myPrint.css" rel="stylesheet" type=text/css
 media="print">
<LINK href="myScreen.css" rel="stylesheet" type=text/css
 media="screen">
```

Using the media type tells the browser which style sheet to use for printing and which one to use for displaying the page in a browser. There are many different values that are recognized for media type. For your purposes, you need to know only about `print` and `screen`.

In addition to common browsers and printers, some other types of media that CSS can work with are

- *Screen readers:* This is software used by visually impaired users; it reads the pages.

- *Braille devices:* These are devices that translate the pages into Braille.

- *TTY & Handheld:* This is for devices with limited display capabilities, such as terminals or Web-enabled handheld devices.

- *TV and projectors:* Makes pages usable for television monitors or on-screen projectors where scrolling and resolution may be issues.

Information and a more complete listing of media types are at the World Wide Web Consortium (W3C) Web site. The W3C is an organization that develops recommended standards for Web coding technologies.

```
http://www.w3.org/TR/CSS21/media.html
```

4. **In the HTML, create the layers and name them.**

More information about how to create HTML documents and apply styles to elements is in Book III, Chapters 2 and 3.

To use the print and screen style sheets together in a document, follow these steps:

1. **Type the following three lines of code for the CSS for screen display:**

```
body{color: #fff; background-color:#000;}
```

This creates a black page with white text

```
h1 {color: #ccc; background-color:#999; }
```

Creating printable style sheets

Printable style sheets are CSS that are created for the purpose of controlling the layout of Web pages when users print them from their browsers. If the owners of the site have not included instructions for printers, the user will get everything that's on the page delivered the way the printer decides to interpret it. A *printable style sheet* allows you to instruct the printer to print your page the way you want it to be printed. You can even instruct the printer to ignore or replace areas of your page with more printer friendly versions, such as the banner graphics. You can create a special header that is invisible in the browser but replaces the banner when the visitor prints the page.

Printable style sheets are relatively easy to develop and implement. From a user perspective, printable style sheets make it easier to print a page. Visitors can choose File⇨Print in their browser and skip clicking a special button and awaiting a new version of the page. There are two good reasons to create printable style sheets:

✔ **Printable style sheets make things much easier on your visitors.** And they show consideration for their ink cartridges. Those are things that add to the overall good (or bad, if you don't do them) impression that visitors have of a site. Not all sites need printable CSS because not all of them have content that people will want to print.

✔ **Creating printable style sheets means you won't have to create or maintain separate documents for your visitors to download and print.** Webmasters use various methods for producing printable versions of their pages. Some use coding or scripts to strip out the elements that aren't printer friendly (such as navigation). That process requires a visitor to click a Print This Page button that sends a request to the server to create and deliver a page that has the important content but strips things such as navigation, advertisements, or graphics the user won't want to print.

This makes the h1 headings display as gray on gray.

```
#banner{background-color: #009; color: #ccc;}
```

This code instructs the browser to display the area of the page marked as a banner with a dark blue background with gray text.

2. **In the HTML, include the following code:**

```
<div id="banner">This is my banner area</div>
```

3. **In the CSS document, include this code:**

```
body{color: #000; background-color:#fff;}
```

This creates a white page with black text

```
h1 {color: #000; background-color:#cccc; }
```

This makes the `h1` headings display as black text over a light gray background.

```
#banner{display: none;}
```

This last bit makes the banner area in the HTML document disappear. This also works for elements that you want to display in the printed document but not on the Web page. Just use the technique in reverse.

This method lets you make sure that the content on your site prints nicely for your visitors. It also ensures that the content in the HTML document matches what your visitor downloads. With PDFs, there is the possibility that the content on your site won't match what's in your PDF. Depending on what your content is, that might be all right — or it might not be.

Chapter 2: Creating Effective Layouts

In This Chapter

✓ Identifying and organizing page contents

✓ Including essential Web page elements

✓ Emphasizing important information

✓ Making pages usable and accessible

✓ Creating wire frames

This chapter helps you begin the process of designing the pages for your Web site. Before you proceed with the page-level design process, you must have a clear idea of what your pages need to include. (If you want help defining your project, check out the information about this important step in Book I, Chapter 3.) You also need a site map that shows how the pages you're designing relate to one another within the site.

Creating wire frames for page-level layouts is an important and helpful step in the process of building a Web site. *Wire frames* are working sketches of the page-level layouts for your site. The process of creating these sketches gives you an opportunity to think about how the elements of your site (the pages) work together regardless of details like specific colors and photos.

In addition to showing you how to create wire frames, this chapter gives you basic design rules, tells you what essential elements to include, and advises you how to fashion an accessible design.

Wire frames should not include finished art. The point of creating wire frames is to make sure that the elements you want to include lay out on your pages in a useful and aesthetically pleasing way. Figure 2-1 shows a sample wire frame; notice that the sample represents page elements but not completed artwork.

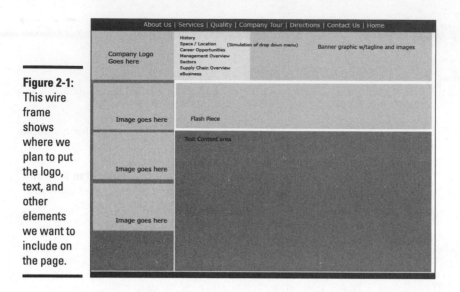

Figure 2-1: This wire frame shows where we plan to put the logo, text, and other elements we want to include on the page.

Content Is Key: Making Sure It's All Included

In Book I, we discuss a few important steps that make your project go more smoothly: listing goals, evaluating potential users, and so on. Here, we help you decide what content you need to include. Planning a Web page layout requires that you consider all the types of information the pages need to accommodate. You might want to include tables, lists, headers, paragraphs, images, and multimedia elements — just make a list of them all. Look at all the content you've collected and determine the best way to present each piece. Also, you can make a list of content that you want to add in the future and include these elements in your list. The reason for this is that figuring out now how you'll handle everything saves time later.

Consider what would happen if you were building a house. If halfway through the project you figure out that not all of the rooms are big enough, you're stuck with a lot more work when you try to rework what has already been done to accommodate the new requirements. The same thing applies to a Web site. If you know that in the future you would like to add some graphs, for instance, figure out during this phase how you would like to display them and where they will fit into the site. That way, when the time comes, you can quickly add the new content instead of having to shoehorn it in somewhere.

Creating Order from Chaos: Consistency Is Your Friend

Always remember that consistency is your friend. Being creative doesn't mean that each page of a site becomes a freestanding document with its own design. Apply creativity on a global scale with the entire site being treated as a whole and consider both sides of your site in this. You must include both the *front end* (the stuff your user sees) and the *back end* (all the files that make it work) during this phase and the site-map-building phase. (See Figure 2-2 for a sample site map.)

✦ **On the front end, consistency involves a cohesive and uniform layout for all pages.** Banner, global navigation, and main content areas need to be located in the same places on every page. (See the later section, "Including Things That Every Page Needs," for more about the banner and other necessary elements.) Using the Web site should not feel like a task in itself; the site should be a transparent delivery system for your information. If a layout is not working for all of your content, rethink your layout.

As with anything, there are a couple of exceptions to the "always be consistent" rule:

• *Creating a home page that has a different layout:* If you choose to do this, all the elements should have a common look and feel to the rest of the site. Navigation elements should have the same style throughout the site so that users understand that they are used for navigation. The names on buttons, colors used, and style in general must be consistent throughout the site.

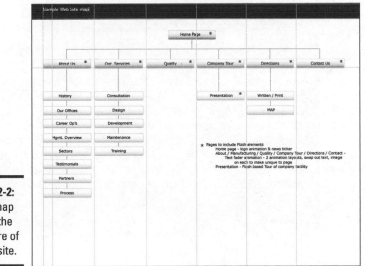

Figure 2-2:
A site map
shows the
structure of
a Web site.

- *Launching multimedia elements into a separate, smaller window:* If you do this, make sure the content has a consistent look and feel with the rest of the site. Figure 2-3 shows an example of launching a multi-media element in a new window. Note how the elements in both windows share a common look and feel. This signals to users that, while different, these pieces are part of a whole.

✦ **On the back end, consistency involves employing file organization.** The back end of your Web site is the collection of documents, images, media, and other elements that make it all work. Any project, no matter what the size, should have a planned file structure. Put images in a folder together; group content documents in a logical way. Develop a standard way of naming files, explain the naming convention to other team members, and stick to it. This task might take you more time in the beginning, but as the site grows, you'll benefit from huge time savings in maintenance. Sharing the work with others, if you need to, is also easier if file organization is implemented and adhered to.

Whatever naming conventions you create, make sure that you and your team members stick to them and especially make sure that your system is logical, easy to follow, expandable, and *Web legal* (that is, use file names that work on the Web). Avoid names like `IMG001.jpg` and `pagetwo.html`. These types of names end up causing confusion because they are not descriptive. Maintenance can become difficult when file names give no clue about what they are.

Figure 2-3:
Sample of a Flash piece launched into a secondary browser window showing a different layout, but consistent style to the rest of the site.

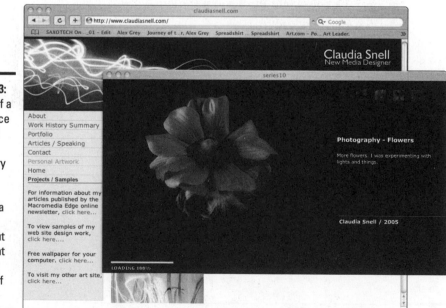

Staying Web legal

The term *Web legal* has nothing to do with the law. It simply refers to file names that work on the Web. Page names with spaces and characters in them might cause problems or not work at all. Names that are too long also can cause trouble. In other words, avoid calling a file `"company "picnic" with lots of great food & drinks.jpg"`.

One common way of labeling folders for Web documents is to match them to the major navigation areas. For example, if your global navigation includes About Us, Our Products, and Services links, your file structure can include folders named About, Products, and Services. All Web documents pertaining to those areas are then organized by how they logically appear. In a similar fashion, include information on the type of graphic (such as a button, icon, thumbnail, and so on) and sometimes the size dimensions (for instance, 50 x 10) in a graphic file name. For example, you can name the file for your About Us button `about_but_50x20.gif`.

**Book II
Chapter 2**

Creating Effective
Layouts

Including Things That Every Page Needs

You want to include some elements on every page of your Web site. These things should be located in the same place on each page (except in the cases we mention earlier: alternate home page or multimedia layouts), and should have the same look and feel on every page. It isn't helpful to users of your site, or to your organization, to express your creativity by changing things on each page. First-time Web designers often make this mistake.

The short list of must-haves we include in this section might seem to you like common sense. Surprisingly, though, many sites fail to include the most basic page elements on every page. Don't let it happen to you. In Figure 2-4, all the important page elements are represented. Note how the site's name and organization are clearly displayed. Navigation is obvious, as are highlighted features. Including these items helps your users to understand your Web site.

Banner

Adding a *banner* (a headline graphic that identifies a site and establishes a look and feel) to each page lets users know that they are on the same site, even though they've navigated to different pages within it. For example, in Figure 2-4, the graphics, logo, and links at the top of the page appear on every page of the site that you navigate to. The banner conveys information such as branding and the name of the organization and/or site name. It gives a page a finished look and grounds the design. It's also a good place to put some contact information, a link to a site map, or a search function.

Figure 2-4: This Web page has all the necessary stuff, including user-friendly navigation, a banner, and a page headline.

Page headline

The page headline sets user expectations of what they'll find on the page. It also helps users orient themselves on your site. If they're looking for information about your products, for example, a page headline with the name or type of product lets them know that they're in the right place. In Figure 2-4, the headline "About Marc & Susan Smith" lets users know that they can find biographical information on that page.

Global navigation

Every site has a collection of major sections. Whether those sections are made up of one page each or many, the *global navigation* is the way that users access those areas. In the preceding Figure 2-4, notice that clicking one of the links on the left side of the page takes you to one of the primary areas of the site. This same global navigation feature appears in the same place on every page of the site.

Larger sites certainly need *supplementary navigation,* and so a larger site structure can have multiple levels. For example, the user starts on the home page, and clicks About Us from the global navigation, which takes them to the main page of that section. On that page, the user finds some basic information and a second navigational area that allows her to dig deeper for more specific information: *secondary navigation.* You may even have to provide subnavigation within those pages: *tertiary navigation.* If you're designing a site that requires supplementary navigation, make sure you place that secondary (and tertiary if you need it) navigation in consistent place(s) on each page. The secondary and tertiary navigation should also share a common look and feel throughout the site.

Page title

The page title is not the same thing as the headline. The *page title* is information that needs to be included in the head section of the HTML. You can find information about how to create and implement these in Book III, Chapter 2. This text shows up in the browser window and also serves as the link text in a search engine, among other things. Make sure you include a page title on each page of your site. In Figure 2-4, you see that the page title "The Kreisau Project" appears at the top edge of the browser above the Web address field.

Page description and keywords

Other information that you should add to each page include page descriptions and keywords. Descriptions and keywords are important to your site, although it's easy to overlook them because they aren't visible on the actual page.

The *page description* is just what it sounds like: a description of the page's content; it's what shows up in search engine listings. Page descriptions give the users a quick summary of what your site is about. Keep the description short but informative. Short is important because of space constraints in search engine listings; only the first sentence or two will be visible. You can't see the page description in Figure 2-4, but here's what it looks like in the HTML:

```
<meta name="Description" content="The Kreisau Project:
    Production to result
     in a book and a TV series telling the remarkable history
    of Germany&#8217;s
     von Moltke family and its family estate at Kreisau." />
```

Be considerate of your users' needs. If your description isn't accurate, users will leave your site to find one that delivers what they need. Also, avoid marketing rhetoric.

Keywords are the terms that you expect your users to search for your site with. They are the words that your users think of to describe your product, service, or organization. If your users would call your organization a *daycare* or *preschool*, put that in the code even if the correct industry term is *child care center*. Keywords are most effective if they reflect accurately the content of the page. If, for example, your keywords include *puppies*, but the page is actually about *tractors*, the keywords are not effective because the Web surfer is directed to a page they're not looking for. Search engines use a combination of keywords, meta tags, content, and other factors to determine the relevance and placement of a page in the listings and to generate useful links to the information people need.

Here is an example of keywords:

```
<meta name="Keywords" content="kreisau, krzyzowa, vonmoltke,
    von moltke, freya, germany, anti-nazi resistance, marc
    smith, blue pumpkin productions " />
```

Here is some code you can use to implement some sample page information:

+ **Page Title:** Claudia Snell:: New Media Designer

    ```
    <title>Claudia Snell:: New Media Designer</title>
    ```

+ **Keywords:** Web design, flash designers, Website, new media, video, streaming, presentations, online demonstrations, video, worcester, massachusetts

    ```
    <meta name="Keywords" content="Claudia Snell, Web
        Design, Web Development, Flash, Flash Developers,
        Website, new media, video, streaming, e-learning,
        presentations, online demonstrations, video,
        worcester, massachusetts, claudia, bousquet, jason,
        snell" />
    ```

+ **Description:** Claudia Snell is a new media designer based in Worcester, MA.

    ```
    <meta name="Description" content="Claudia Snell is a
        new media designer based in Worcester, MA." />
    ```

Put the code for your page information in the head section of the HTML code. See Book III, Chapter 2 for more information about the parts of an HTML document. Figure 2-5 shows how the content is included in the code. Notice that the description is in the form of a sentence, the keywords are single words or phrases separated by commas, and the title is the name of the site or page. In Figures 2-6 and 2-7, note how some of this information is used by the browser and search engines.

```
Source of http://www.jcnewmedia.com/
<?xml version="1.0" encoding="iso-8859-1"?>
<!DOCTYPE html PUBLIC "-//W3C//DTD XHTML 1.0 Transitional//EN" "http://www.w3.org/TR/xhtml1/DTD/xhtml1-transitional.dtd">
<html xmlns="http://www.w3.org/1999/xhtml">
<head>
<title>jason and claudia snell :: new media designers</title>
<meta http-equiv="Content-Type" content="text/html; charset=iso-8859-1" />
<link rel="shortcut icon" href="../Icon4.ico" />
<meta name="Keywords" content="Web Design,Web Development,Flash,Flash Developers,Website,new media,video,streaming,e-commerce, e-learning,
presentations,online demonstrations, video,production,post production, animation,worcester, massachuestts,claudia, bousquet,jason, snell" />
<meta name="Description" content="Portfolio site of Jason Snell, motion graphics/video production and Claudia Snell, new media designer." />
<meta name="revisit-after" content="14 days" />
<meta name="ROBOTS" content="index,follow" />
<meta name="copyright" content="2000-2004, jason and claudia snell" />
<meta name="publisher" content="jason and claudia snell" />
<meta name="author" content="claudia snell" />
<script language="JavaScript" type="text/javascript" src="../functions.js"></script>
<link href="siteStyle.css" rel="stylesheet" type="text/css" />
</head>
<body>
<table border="0" align="center" cellpadding="0" cellspacing="0">
```

Figure 2-5: This is how meta tag information looks in a block of code.

Figure 2-6: The browser uses meta tag information to display content on-screen.

Figure 2-7: The page title and description from the meta tags of the page show up in the search engine listings.

jason and claudia snell :: new media designers
jason and claudia snell is a full service web, multimedia and video production studio based in Central Massachusetts.
www.jcnewmedia.com/ - 8k - Cached - Similar pages

Claudia Snell
For **Jason's** bio: http://www.jcnewmedia.com. Meetings are free, all are welcome. Hope to see you there! posted by **claudia snell** at 11:19 AM 0 comments ...
claudiasnell.blogspot.com/ - 20k - Cached - Similar pages

Book II Chapter 2

Creating Effective Layouts

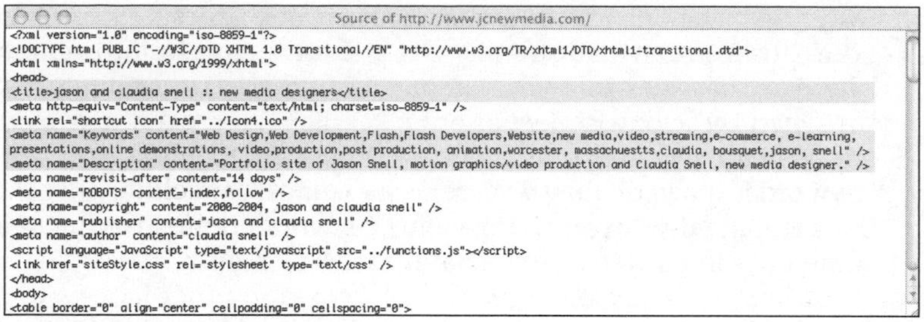

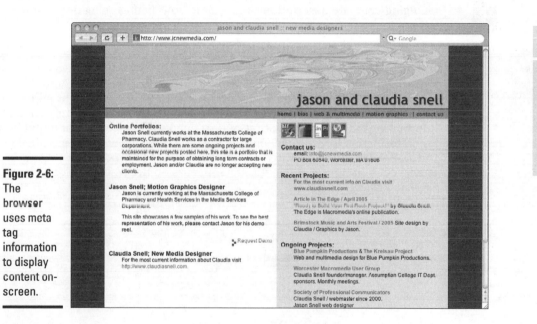

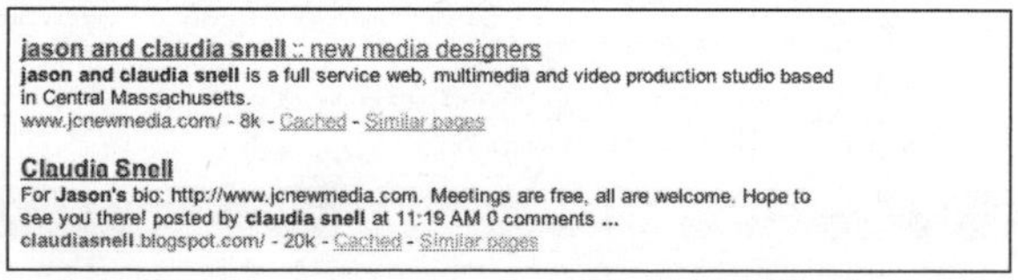

Note: Descriptions and keywords are just one way that search engines find your site. You can also submit your site for inclusion into search engines. There are services that you can pay for and also free submission tools like the Open Directory Project at `http://dmoz.org`. When you submit your site, you are given an opportunity to include information, descriptions, and keywords. When dealing with search engines, remember that they do not update instantly. If you change your keywords or descriptions, expect for some time to pass before the databases catch up.

The combined effect of submitting your site with alternate descriptions or changing your site description can result in your listing being different from your actual descriptions as they are shown on your site.

Page footer

You should put a footer at the bottom of every page, where the footer belongs. Important elements to include in the footer are copyright information, links to any legal or privacy policies you include on your site, contact information for your organization, and so on. It's also a good spot to put contact information for your Webmaster, the date the page was last modified, the global navigation mirrored as text links, and Web production credits. In Figure 2-8, you can see the footer that appears on the Web page for The Kreisau Project.

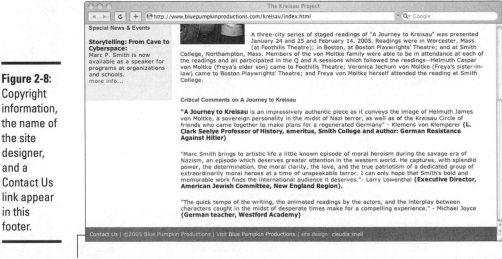

Figure 2-8:
Copyright information, the name of the site designer, and a Contact Us link appear in this footer.

Footer

Planning How to Emphasize Important Information

A well-designed Web page draws the user's attention to one key piece of information without that element looking so far out of place that it looks wrong. Planning for where and how you'll emphasize an element on your site saves you time later. You'll already know how to handle that special announcement before you have to add it. A little planning now also prevents strange or awkward-looking retrofitted elements, so keep these points in mind:

+ **Emphasis is good, but your page can have too much of a good thing.**
  Good Web designers tend to break a page into three levels of emphasis. There should be one major piece of information on the page, and the second and third are lesser pieces of information. Convey the emphasis to the visitor by using text size (larger equals more important) and text position (higher and in the middle equals more important). You can also use color to help convey emphasis.

  When using color to show emphasis, be careful! Too many colors can make a page look garish. Another consideration is that many people might not be able to see the colors as you see them. For instance, a user might be color blind or visually impaired, so make sure to incorporate more than one cue to bring the visitor's attention to your major point of focus. We discuss usability and accessibility further in the next section.

+ **Be sparing in your use of special font treatments to create emphasis.**
  Keep the number of treatments to a minimum to avoid visual confusion and amateurish-looking pages. Keep it simple. Plan areas for headings and for content text for any special promotional items you need to include on your site. Make sure that these elements match the look and feel of your site. Don't create elements that clash with the rest of the site; it creates a bad impression for your site and organization and also confuses visitors. Remember, no one will be standing there to explain your design choices to your users. The site must convey its message all by itself.

+ **Remember that nothing is emphasized if everything is emphasized.**
  If too many things are fighting for attention, the site is difficult to use, and visitors are confused by too many messages that demand equal amounts of attention. This sort of thing can make users feel bombarded, and they'll miss out on the information you're working hard to make available to them — or worse, they'll leave your site and go to one that doesn't confuse or assault them.

TIP

About fonts

When choosing fonts, each color and size of text used counts as a separate font. For instance, if you have Arial text but it's in three different colors and five different sizes, count that as eight different font treatments. In a case like that, rethink your design and eliminate some of the treatments. A good rule to live by is to limit the number of fonts on a page to three. Notice how the fonts in the top image shown here compete for attention; this site uses too many fonts, which creates a confusing layout. The bottom image shows the actual page, which uses only a limited number of fonts; using fewer fonts helps bring emphasis without confusing the visitors. For more information about working with fonts, see Book II, Chapter 4.

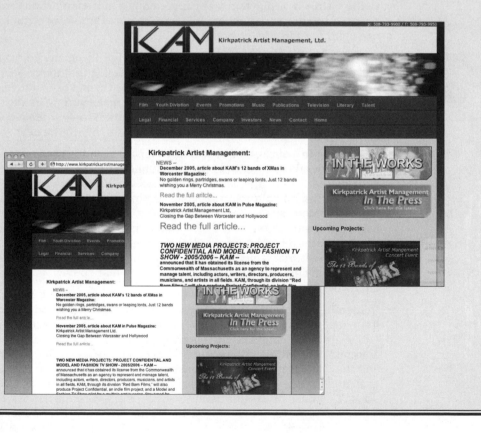

Understanding the Basics of Usable and Accessible Design

If you spend any time around Web site design projects, usability and accessibility are words that you hear a lot. *Usability* refers to how easily your visitors can use your site, and *accessibility* refers to how well your site performs on technologies other than browsers and/or for visitors with disabilities. As often happens, these are two more buzzwords thrown into a presentation to sound impressive. Unfortunately, in practice, these concepts are generally misunderstood or overlooked.

Everyone involved in a Web project knows that people view Web pages using a computer and browser. Often overlooked are the increasing numbers of other devices, such as handhelds and cellphones, that are Web enabled. And don't forget about screen readers and screen magnifiers, which enable users who are blind or have limited vision to use the Web.

From screen readers for blind users to handheld devices, people are visiting sites in many different ways other than traditional browsers. You want your site to be easy for them to use.

Common usability testing traps

Often, Web designers fall into a common trap. They think, "I find my site easy to use, and I'm a *normal* person, so the site is very usable." Or worse, they ask their friends or others that are closely involved in the project to check the site. Generally, these so-called testers don't give accurate feedback. No one wants to hurt their friends' feelings, so they simply say that they like the site. Also, people who are involved with the project are too close to it to see its flaws; they have a lot of inside information that helps them understand the site. In most cases, your target audience isn't as intimately involved with your content as you are, so your site might not make as much sense to them as it does to the team that created it.

Testing the usability of your site is an ongoing process. You should look for feedback throughout the process of planning and building your site. Correcting usability issues along the way is easier than having to rework things later.

Give testers a list of tasks like, "Find information about *Product X*" or "Locate our company profile." Observe while the tester tries to accomplish these tasks. After the user completes the tasks, ask her for feedback about whether she found the tasks easy or hard. Also, ask her why a task was hard and solicit comments that can help you solve the issues. The point is to see your site from other people's points of view and make it as easy for them to use the site as you can. See Book III, Chapter 9 for more about usability testing.

Usability and accessibility are vital to the success of a site. If visitors can't understand or use your site, they'll leave and not return. To prevent that scenario — and to ensure usability — consider these points when planning your site:

✦ **All clickable or otherwise interactive elements need to work, and they all need to work as expected.** This means that if a button reads Click Here to Search the Site, clicking that button activates a search function — or at least brings the user to a site search function. It should not, for example, launch a photo gallery — or worse, do nothing at all.

✦ **A site should download quickly, and the content should be easy to get to.** In general, navigation of a site should be easy to figure out and easy to remember. Visitors don't like frustrating navigation or confusing content structures. Try to keep everything within just one or two clicks away.

✦ **Make sure you plan ways for your site to react to human errors.** Your visitors sometimes make mistakes, especially if you have forms or other types of interactivity. Try to make correcting an error easy for your visitors. If making a mistake throws a visitor completely out of a transaction, he won't appreciate having to start all over again; he might, instead, abandon the task and not come back.

✦ **Your image counts.** People do assess an organization by what its site looks like. Try to remember that visitors might have only one impression of an organization — its Web site. If it looks amateurish or inappropriate, they're less likely to trust the site. You could lose valuable visitors/customers to a competitor that has a better-looking site.

Accessibility shares many of the same considerations as usability but also brings a few more items to keep in mind:

✦ **Make sure that images, especially navigational ones, are properly tagged for screen readers.** This is a sample of an *HTML image tag*. For example, a screen reader that detects the code that follows reads "artwork sample" to the user. Using descriptive tags like this is vital for visually impaired users. Without them, a page can become confusing or tedious to visit, depending on how their reader deals with untagged images.

```
<img src="images/graphic.jpg" alt="artwork sample"
    width="250" height="184" />
```

✦ **In addition to color coding, use a secondary method of emphasizing information.** Color coding is good for some people but not so good for color blind and visually impaired people. Make sure you group content by using positioning, headings, and other visual cues (icons), to separate content.

✦ **Make sure that the colors you choose have enough contrast so that people can read the text.** We're surprised by how many sites sport gray backgrounds with gray text — it might look cool, but for anyone over 35, it might be hard to read.

✦ **Make sure your site includes site maps, breadcrumbs, and other orientation tools.** *Breadcrumbs* refer to a list of links, generally displayed at the top of a page, that shows the path to where the user is — think Hansel and Gretel. Figure 2-9 shows an example of breadcrumbs.

Breadcrumb trail

Figure 2-9:
This breadcrumb trail shows that the user went from the Home page to the About page.

We cover these important topics in more depth in Chapters 1 and 3 of this minibook and also Book III, Chapter 9.

Creating a Layout Wire Frame

A *wire frame* is a page-level layout sketch — like a blueprint of the main areas where you intend to put images, text, headings, links, and so on, on a page; see Figure 2-10. You can create wire frames with traditional drawing tools (pen, pencil, paper, or crayons, if that's what you like) or with a graphics program such as Photoshop, Illustrator, or Fireworks. Claudia generally starts to work out her ideas on paper and then re-creates the wire frames in Illustrator.

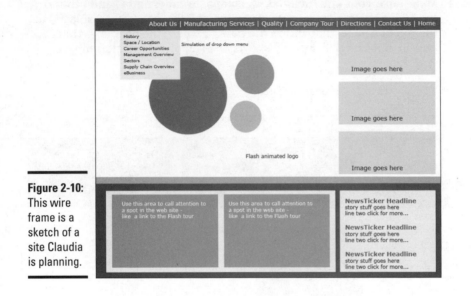

Figure 2-10: This wire frame is a sketch of a site Claudia is planning.

The number of wire frames you need to create depends on the individual needs of the site you're creating. Some sites work well with one layout for all the pages, and other sites need multiple layouts. Remember, these are just layouts at this point, not finished designs.

To create a layout wire frame using Photoshop CS2, just follow these steps:

1. **Open Photoshop and choose File⇨New to create a new document.**

The New dialog box opens. (See Figure 2-11.)

2. **Fill in the following information and click OK.**

- **Name:** Set the name of the file to myInterfaceLayout (or something else you like better). Because this becomes the name of the file, create a name you'll remember.

- **Width:** Set at 800 pixels.

- **Height:** Set at 600 pixels.

The current standard Web screen resolution is 800 x 600. You can set this number to any size you like, but by starting with 800 x 600 pixels, you can see how your layout works at the standard Web size.

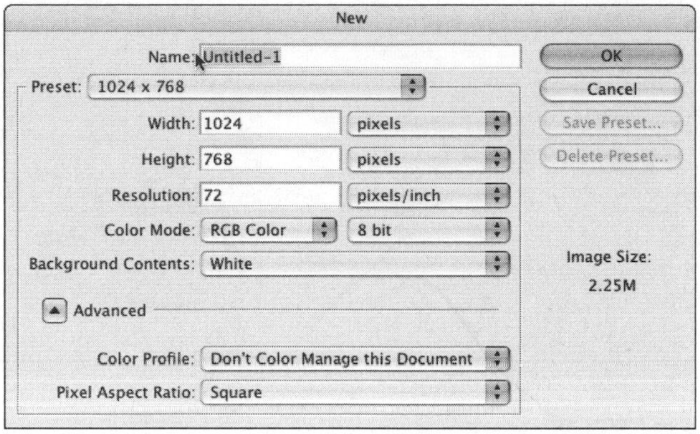

Figure 2-11:
The New
dialog box.

- **Background contents:** Set to white or any other background color.
  (You can change this later if you change your mind.) This just starts
  your work area off with a background color.

After you click OK, the dialog box disappears, and the new document
appears in its place.

3. **In the new document (see Figure 2-12), create the main element areas
(banner, content, navigation, and so on):**

   a. Click the Rectangle tool on the tool palette.

     It is the third tool from the bottom in the second column. Your
cursor now looks like a plus sign.

   *b. Click and drag to create rectangles to represent all the areas of your
page — banner, navigation, content, and so on.*

     Each time you click and drag, a new layer is created.

   *c. On the Layers palette, double-click the name of the new layer and give
it a descriptive name.*

     If you don't, you'll end up with a bunch of layers with the names
Layer 1, Layer 2 (or Shape 1 if you've used the shape tool), and so
on. Unless you can remember what each layer number represents,
it's hard to change your layout later.

   *d. Position the elements by selecting the layer you wish to move, clicking
the Move tool, and dragging each element.*

   *e. Resize an element by selecting the layer, choosing Edit➪Transform➪
Scale, and then clicking and dragging in the main window.*

Move tool   Rectangle tool

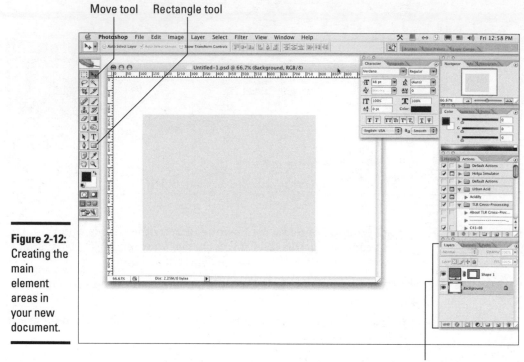

Figure 2-12:
Creating the
main
element
areas in
your new
document.

Layers palette

    *f. Change the color of elements by double-clicking the layer thumbnail on
the Layers palette.*

    g. In the Color Picker dialog box that launches, choose a color and click OK.

4. In the main window, create place holder text. (See Figure 2-13.)

    a. Select the Text tool.

    b. Click a location in the main window and type some text.

    *c. Format the text by double-clicking the large T on the Layers palette and
making changes on the Options palette or on the Character palette.*

    You can move text the same way you moved the layout elements: by
dragging with the Move tool.

When you're finished, your wire frame should be a layout grid that will
drive the graphic design and page development process.

Text tool

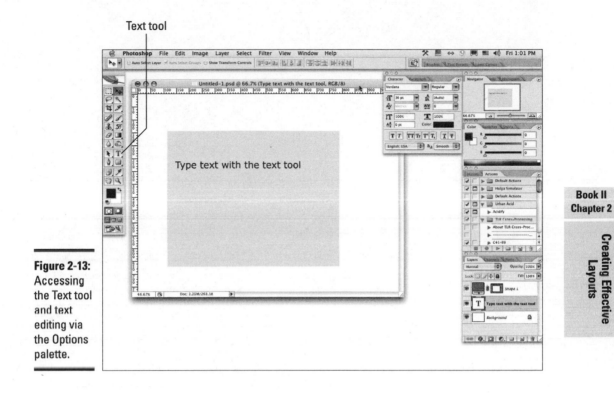

Figure 2-13:
Accessing
the Text tool
and text
editing via
the Options
palette.

Chapter 3: Organizing Your Content

In This Chapter

✔ **Establishing and sharing file management conventions**

✔ **Developing Web site content**

✔ **Keeping best practices in mind**

*B*ook II, Chapter 2 helps you figure out what content to include on your site. Although, by now, you might have collected much of it, your content will evolve as you develop it. Web site content actually continues to develop throughout the life of the site. For this reason, planning and building a good organizational structure is very important, and that's why we devote this chapter to that topic. As you collect information, it's tempting to just dive right in to the artwork part of designing your site. Resist the temptation. The following pointers can help you organize the content (and save yourself some headaches in the process):

✦ **Keep all site files in one set of folders.** Typically, you have pictures, text documents, and other things, such as PowerPoint files and Excel spreadsheets. Some of these files will end up directly on your site and others just provide information. In either case, keep the original files together in a set of folders. Keep this set of folders in the local copy of your site. A *local copy* refers to the version of the site that's on your computer hard drive. You work on these files and then publish them to a Web server.

✦ **Do first things first.** It's actually important to start with designing the structure and maintenance of your site first. If you start with creating artwork first, you're likely to design something that looks great but doesn't work for the purpose of the site.

✦ **Keep site maintenance manageable.** A good way to make sure the maintenance doesn't get done is to make it difficult for people to work on the site. For instance, if you create content that needs to be updated often, you'll need to assign the editing to people who probably already have other jobs. Or the task might fall to someone who doesn't know how to do it, which means that you need to train that person. So if you don't think through all aspects of the site upfront, you risk ending up with a hard-to-manage site and overworked people.

One small update shouldn't be a big deal, but if you have several, they can accumulate into a large project. It might be a good idea to look for ways to automate part of the maintenance or create content that doesn't need to be updated as often. The decision of what is best depends on your needs and what your resources are.

✦ **Remember that design includes the whole project, not just the pretty graphics and layout.** The *whole project* includes functionality, maintenance, usability, graphics, layout, and expandability. You need to consider all users of the site, from content owners to the people who maintain the site to potential visitors. A beautiful-looking site that doesn't work for the intended purpose is a failed design. The life of such a design is not as long as one that you've thought through and designed well.

The rest of this chapter elaborates on these ideas and also explores the issues of file management, content placement, and best practices in terms of what's best for the site user.

Considering File Management

You might think of file management as boring and tedious, but it's necessary. Whether you're building a site that multiple people will maintain or you're working alone, make sure you have a plan for managing files. As you work on a Web project, you accumulate a lot of files — Word documents, Excel spreadsheets, images, audio, HTML, sketches or notes on paper, and so on — and developing a logical method of organizing these documents is essential to the project. Part of the file management process includes keeping copies of original files, for these (and other) reasons:

✦ **Future reference:** Suppose you need to reconstruct a page or section of a Web site. If you back up your entire site periodically (which is a good practice in case of a major problem with your Web servers), you can easily backtrack and redo that part.

✦ **Repurposing content:** In many cases, you can repurpose existing print content, such as logos, fliers, product catalogs, and so on, to the Web site. Naturally, you want to keep copies of all of those resources. With these resources at hand, you can

  • Pull up the original quickly and make changes.

  • Keep track of the original content.

  • Build a source of information for other parts of your project.

While, for the most part, the information stays the same from print to Web, the layout changes. You might find that you need only parts of the material on a particular page. For instance, if you have a presentation that has five slides with bullet points, you might want to condense the information to three bullet points for the Web. Two months after you launch your site, if you decide to freshen the content and give your visitors even more information, you can refer back to the original document and add those other bullet points.

✦ **Revision of graphics:** With most images, whether they're photos or art, you edit them, apply effects, or add them to other elements and use the finished version of the images on the Web. If you crop and prepare your photos and other graphics for use on your Web site without saving the originals, you can't revise the images as easily. Keeping a copy of the originals ensures that you can reuse the graphics with the most flexibility. To keep a copy, just choose File⇨Save As and name the file something descriptive.

Book II
Chapter 3

Organizing Your
Content

When revising a file, do a File⇨Save As and change the name *immediately* after opening the file so you don't accidentally ruin your original. This technique works no matter what software package you're using — Fireworks, Photoshop, Illustrator. Saving the original with a name that's different from the names of the files in-progress and the finished file ensures that you can go back to your starting point if you need to.

With graphics files, you typically have a working file and a final version. The *working file* is the version that has all the editable pieces still intact. The important thing to know here is that as you work in graphics software, you generate a series of layers with pieces of your graphic on each layer. One image, actually, is made up of multiple layers that you can edit. When you generate the final copy of the graphic you'll use on your site, the resulting file is *flattened* — in other words, the layers no longer exist in that file. Because the layers don't exist anymore, you can't easily make changes to the file, and some changes become impossible. In most cases, you have to open the working copy and edit the layers.

Keeping copies of these working files — along with the other support and content files — in the Production Files folder means that you don't have to reconstruct the project every time you want to make a change to the graphics. (Book IV has more information about how to use graphics software.) And keeping the Production Files folder within your local site means that you can easily find the files you want to edit.

The *final version* of a graphics or multimedia file is the JPEG, GIF, or SWF file (to name a few) that you use on your actual Web page. Put these files in your Images folder with the other site graphics. Here's an example of how you take a working file to its final version: When you work with Flash, it generates an editable `.fla` file — your working file. When you're ready to publish the Flash project to your live site, you save it as a `.swf` file — the file that a browser with the Flash player plug-in can run. You store the .fla file in your Production Files folder so that you can edit it in the future if you need to, and you save the .swf file in your Images folder to publish on the Web site. Figure 3-1 shows the Save for Web dialog box in Photoshop; in this example, a photograph is being optimized for use on a page. By choosing File⇨Save for Web, you can prepare a graphic to use on your site by choosing a format, optimizing the graphic for the Web, and even resizing it if you need to.

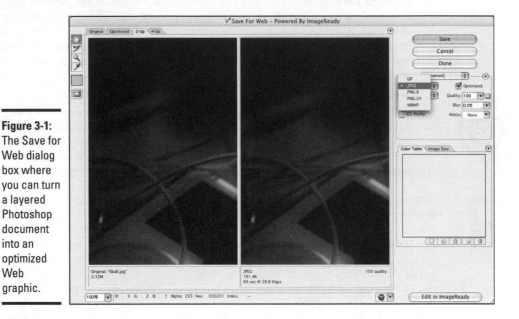

Figure 3-1: The Save for Web dialog box where you can turn a layered Photoshop document into an optimized Web graphic.

Keeping It Tidy

You need to keep your production files somewhere, and if you're working alone, it's all right to keep them within your local copy of the site. If you're working on a team, you might want to find a place that all team members can use, such as a shared network drive. That way, they can do what they need to do and keep the site consistent. It also ensures that the live server doesn't become cluttered in the process. Regardless, whether you're using your local copy of the site or a shared drive, the following points can help you continue good file management after initially implementing it:

✦ **Create a system for naming your files before you start building the site.** This applies whether you're working alone or with a team. If you're working as a team, make sure everyone on the team understands the naming conventions and uses them correctly. Create a document explaining the site structure and naming conventions and make sure that everyone has access to it. This document of standards helps everyone understand how to work on the site without creating a mess.

✦ **Write down maintenance procedures as you create them.** Attempting to figure out how you need to update something is frustrating, even for seasoned Web professionals. The task of producing consistent results becomes much more difficult when you make your teammates guess how they should do things. The techniques of keeping documents and notes aren't only for large, complex sites with lots of people working on them. It can save you, the one-man band, when you need to get some work done on a site that you haven't worked on in a while.

✦ **Don't waste precious hosting space on production files.** Production files tend to be very large, so they take up a lot of space. Also, Web staff can access anything on your Web server. Files can become inadvertently available to people you don't want having your files, and that can result in unwanted changes (or worse). The best rule is to not post files unless they need to be there.

✦ **Archive obsolete files.** If you're no longer using a graphic on the *live site* (the published version of the site), remove it from the Web server. It's all right to create an archive on your local or shared network drive, but remove it from the live server. This is especially important for large, complex sites and sites that have multiple people working on them. Make sure that each member of the team knows that she is responsible for archiving the files that she makes obsolete. This is also true for whole sections of the site. If you intend to remove a file (or more) from the site, remove it fully from the server. Make a backup of it so you can recover it if you need to.

✦ **Create a flexible file structure that can handle your site now and into the future.** Most likely, you'll want to add to your site at some point. Make sure you structure your site in a way that makes that easy. Consider how much of a particular type of content you intend to have. If you think you'll have a lot of multimedia elements, put them in a folder together. Start off with subcategories within that folder. It might look and sound strange when you initially launch your site to have a folder with other folders in it for only a few multimedia files, but when you start adding files, you'll see a great benefit in having planned ahead.

Implementing Information Architecture

Information architecture involves building the structure of your site from a content standpoint — that is, deciding what information to put in each section. Part of organizing and designing your site entails deciding how to present the content. Upfront, you must determine how to treat images and graphics (whether or not to use captions, for instance), how to handle text and other content (presented in tables or bulleted lists?), and of course, how to handle overall site organization (placing information where it's easy to find but not confusing or crowded).

Information architecture sounds complicated, and it can be for larger sites. Generally, though, it's just deciding what works best as a group. Organize content in groups, which become the sections of your site. For example, in the site map in Figure 3-2, you can see that this site has sections named About Us, Our Services, Our Products, Company Tour, Directions, and Contact Us.

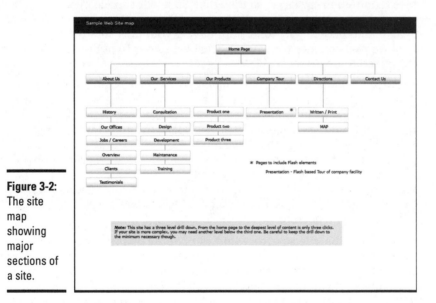

Figure 3-2:
The site map showing major sections of a site.

Those groups are then broken into smaller groups to become the page-level content. In Figure 3-2, for example, you can see that the About Us section includes a History page, an Our Offices page, and a Jobs/Careers page, among others. Organize this information in a logical way, somewhat like you would do if you were creating an outline.

If your information architecture plan for your site is successful, site visitors (as well as your Web staff) can find what they're looking for easily. If you've done a poor job of planning the structure of your site, visitors can get lost and frustrated. For instance, it's not a good idea to hide your contact information in a section filled with games, where your users can't find it. And remember that someone has to maintain the site once it goes live. Structuring the site in a way that makes sense also makes it easier to maintain. If things are in odd places, you'll have a harder time finding what you need.

On the back end, make your folder structure consistent with your site map. Keep the content for each section in its own folder, with subfolders (if needed) that contain the page-level content. That way, everything is easy to find when you need to make updates. The folder structure should match the site navigation. This is not to say, though, that you must create a navigation button for each folder in your structure. Some folders contain elements such as documents, multimedia, style sheets, and graphics.

Developing section-level information architecture

As with your page-level information architecture, you'll find that within your sections there are main pages and subordinate pages. As you consider how to structure your information, keep in mind that users don't like having to click through too many links. About three levels of information is a good amount. This means that from the home page of a site, a user should have to click through only two pages *maximum* to reach the deepest level of your content.

From the home page, you drive your traffic into your section content areas. Make sure your section page and secondary pages reward your users with useful information. Make sure it's high-level, summary-type information so that you can quickly fill the needs of visitors. The summary approach also benefits visitors by letting them know that they're headed down the right path. For instance, on the home page, you can feature a teaser with some marketing-type language about caring for house plants. Include a picture of a beautiful plant with an enticing blurb about what the visitor can find in the House Plants section of your Web site. End the blurb with a `Click here to get more information about caring for house plants` (or similar) link.

The included link, naturally, takes the visitor to the House Plants section and the promised information about caring for house plants. Also, from these secondary pages, you can include links to deeper information about the topic. With the house plant example, you'd link to main pages about specific types of plants or groups of plants (such as cacti or ivy).

So, still using the example of the House Plants section with a page about cacti, you can include general information about cacti and other succulents and add links to a specialized page with specific information — such as a customized aloe vera plant page. If you have a large amount of deeper information, you can offer a bit more content on this page than the upper-level pages. You might also choose to deliver the more detailed information as downloadable documents so that users can download, print, and read at their leisure.

This method of structuring content produces what is called a *drill-down*. Users drill down from the summary on the main page through successively deeper information until they get to the level they need. This makes your site useful to a wider variety of users and uses.

Arranging page-level information

The page layout phase of site design is easiest if you've organized your content first. You'll know how much information you need to accommodate on each page. When deciding how much information to include on a page, remember that visitors get frustrated with pages that scroll excessively. If a page becomes very long, take a second look at your content to see if you can reorganize it. Or use the technique of breaking long lists into multiple lists. Alphabetical order works well for many of them.

When planning how you'll arrange content on a page, make sure that you design your pages so that the main point of the page is obvious. Lack of focus can create a confusing situation for your users. Lead them to what you want them to see by placing the main idea toward the top of the page so it appears within the browser window. In Figure 3-3, for instance, the main content goes in the large space below the names Jason & Claudia Snell. Tertiary information is best placed on the page below everything else. That way, if users don't scroll to the bottom of the page, they're not missing the important stuff.

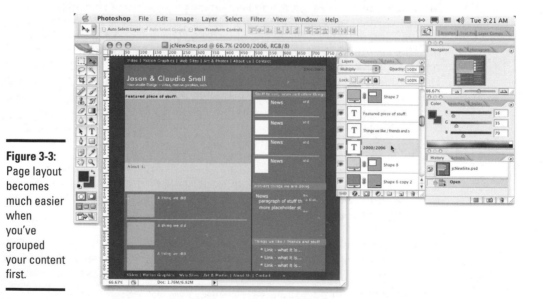

Figure 3-3: Page layout becomes much easier when you've grouped your content first.

Avoiding Content Problems

Other important things to remember about site structure and information architecture follow:

✦ **Make each page deliver real content.** Web site visitors should find that even pages that are at the higher levels — and therefore, made up of more shallow, summary information — provide useful content. *Shallow* and *summary* shouldn't mean *useless.* Sometimes, useful information is concise — such as, `Click here to learn about cacti!` Simplicity is appropriate if you know your users will understand what they'll get when they click a link.

If you think your higher-level information needs a little explanation, include a short paragraph to get users interested. There are no truly hard rules with this other than you should think about what your users will need in order to decide what they're going to do after they find your site.

✦ **Avoid compiling lists of links.** Sometimes, you can group a few links effectively, but we can't think of very many good reasons (other than search results or possibly task lists for groups or students) that a visitor to your site should click a link only to be confronted by another list of links — or worse: a list of links that don't include any explanations.

The worst site design mistake is a happy invitation to `Click here for information` that sends users to a page that invites them to `Click here for more information`, and so on, until users get tired of clicking and not finding what they want. Users will find a different site to visit if they find that your site doesn't have any actual information, just a series of links to nothing.

In other words, make sure you allow your users to drill down to the level of information they want. Keep the vague `Click here` links to a minimum, and ideally, don't use them. Try to use link text that tells the user what they will get when they click it, include the link directly in your content by making the relevant phrase into a link. This will invite your users to follow the trail of information deeper into your topic.

✦ **Don't include unfinished work on your site.** Most people agree that clicking a link and finding an `Under Construction` or `Coming Soon` page is a waste of time. It's all right to allude to features that you intend to add to your site, if you like. This gets people excited about making repeat visits to your site. However, we advise against including links on your page to `Under Construction` pages or sections. If the content isn't ready to roll out, don't include it in any navigational element.

✦ **Announce an upcoming new feature shortly before its launch.** Frequent users notice when an announcement is up for a prolonged period. They also notice when you announce a new feature that doesn't

Book II Chapter 3

Organizing Your Content

materialize. Sometimes, planned features just don't work out — or they aren't ready as soon as you intend them to be. Don't make promises that you might not fulfill.

✦ **Give your visitors the ability to customize their experience as much as possible.** Simply making sure they can flow through your information in different ways makes your site more useful and interesting. Be creative about how you help visitors flow through your site. Give them options that allow them to choose their own path while also rewarding them with useful content along the way.

✦ **Avoid hiding your content under a pile of lists.** Presenting users with large lists of links with little or no explanation about what they get when they click will not produce a good user experience. You'll want to guide people through your information, gently, by including links to broader content areas within your site's navigational areas. Use links within your text to guide people into deeper information.

✦ **Use images and multimedia elements thoughtfully.** Don't include an element just because you like it. Make sure it fits your content. If your site is about cacti, find pictures of cacti. Include a chart of care statistics or create a short, multimedia presentation about how to care for cacti. Leave the pictures of kittens off the page about cacti. They might be cute, but an image that is there for no other reason than that it's cute makes your page look amateurish.

Especially, use Flash and other multimedia with care. Plan and develop each piece of multimedia, whether it's a Flash presentation or a video, making sure it conveys information in addition to being nice to look at. If you expect your users to wait for media to download, make it worth their time. (You can find more about developing and using multimedia elements in Book V.)

Call to action

You might hear the term *call to action* when you start working with Web sites. This term refers to the practice of including an overt direction to your visitors: `Click here` or `Order now`.

A call to action is generally used along with some explanation to visitors about why they would want to follow your directions. You can drive traffic very effectively using a call to action. `Click here for sale prices` is sure to catch attention and get your users to follow the link.

When you don't use a call to action, you're leaving your visitors to decide what they'd like to do next on their own. If your content is confusing enough or your navigational elements don't look like navigation (links that are hidden), your users have no idea what they're expected to do. They might leave the site in favor of a site that helps them find what they need.

Chapter 4: Ensuring Visual Appeal

In This Chapter

✔ Understanding colors on Web sites

✔ Getting to know JPEGs and GIFs

✔ Choosing font families

✔ Buying stock images

✔ Refreshing an existing site

As you start to work on the visual aspects of your site — also known as the *look and feel* — you have to make a few decisions. You have to choose colors and imagery that support your message and convey a sense of what your organization is about. In some cases, you might have to buy images to use. You might also have to work with existing printed materials. You have many details to tend to, but don't let that overwhelm you. Within a short period of time and with the help of this chapter, getting the artwork under control will become second nature to you.

Colors on the Web

One of the first things you might encounter is a situation where an organization already has printed materials and is looking to enhance its presence with a Web site. The printed materials might have a look and feel already established and most certainly have a logo and color scheme in place.

Color on the Web is different than color on paper. This might sound like an obvious statement, but it actually isn't. Color in printed materials is represented by a system called CMYK (cyan, magenta, yellow, and black). In short, it refers to the colors of ink that are used when printing. Web pages and Web graphics don't use CMYK; they use a system called RGB (red, green, blue), which is represented in HTML, CSS, and other Web scripts with hexadecimal code. More on that later in this chapter. In order to understand *why* it is important that the color systems are different, you need a bit of information about *how* the color systems are different.

CMYK color

CMYK is the color system used to produce printed materials. It refers to the colors of ink that are used to print things. CMYK is what is called a *subtractive color system*. With a subtractive color system everything starts off white. White is the color you get when all the colors are being reflected back to your eye from a surface. Subtractive colors absorb, or subtract, some of the color in the light, which creates the effect of colors. CMYK colors are represented by percentages of how much of each ink color are to be used. The Photoshop Color Picker window shown in Figure 4-1 features the CMYK settings.

Figure 4-1: Color Picker window showing the CMYK settings.

RGB color

Red, green, and blue are the primary colors of light. Because computer monitors use light to display colors on-screen, the RGB system is what computers use. RGB is an *additive color system,* which means that you add different amounts of red, green, and blue to create colors. Black is the absence of light and so is the absence of color in the RGB system. As you add different values of the three primaries, you get different colors. RGB colors are represented as numbers between 0 and 255 — one number for each R, G, and B. Zero means that none of that color exists and 255 means that the maximum amount of the color exists. So for example, 0, 0, 245 represents a very blue color (0 for the value of red, 0 for the value of green, and 245 for the value of blue).

Hexadecimal colors

Hexadecimal colors are the way browsers like to see color. When you're using HTML or CSS code to produce colors, you will, most likely, use hexadecimal colors to do it. You can use other methods of displaying colors (such as using color names), but hexadecimal is the preferred standard. Hexadecimal (or hex) uses six digits or letters to display colors. These digits are actually seen as three pairs of numbers; the first pair represents the amount of red in the color, the second pair represents the amount of green in the color, and the third pair (you guessed it right) represents the amount of blue. You use hexadecimal colors for background colors, font (typeface) colors, and link colors.

Computer monitors use light to display images, so RGB is what they're using. Hexadecimal is just a way to communicate with the browser about what color you want a Web element to be.

To find out more about using hexadecimal in code, refer to Book III, Chapters 2 and 3, which are the chapters that cover HTML and CSS.

Making nice with established color schemes

If you're going to design graphics for an organization that has a color scheme already in place, you must have them supply the correct RGB or hexadecimal values that correspond to the CMYK colors they're already using; otherwise, you might not get the colors right. We don't recommend "just using the eyedropper," as some print designers might tell you to do. The colors often shift or aren't accurate when you use that method. A best practice is to get the colors straight from the client so that you're sure they're what the client wants. In Figure 4-2, you can see the different color systems available for you to work with in Photoshop.

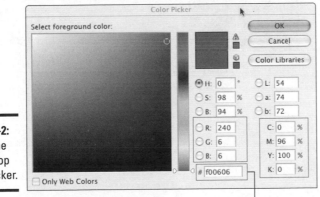

Figure 4-2:
This is the
Photoshop
Color picker.

Hexadecimal

Despite your best efforts, though, a subtle shift in colors is likely to occur. You can't perfectly match the colors of a brochure to the colors on the computer screen. The reason for this is that the appearance of the colors on the brochure change depending on the lighting conditions in the room, and every computer monitor is a little different. If you hold the brochure up next to the monitor and work at it, you might get them to match visually, but as soon as you go to a different monitor or change the lighting in the room, they won't match any more. In other words, if you're trying to match perfectly, don't. You can get them close enough so they'll be consistent, and that should be the goal. The way to do that is to make sure you get the right colors from the client. Figure 4-3 shows the Eyedropper tool in Photoshop.

Eyedropper tool

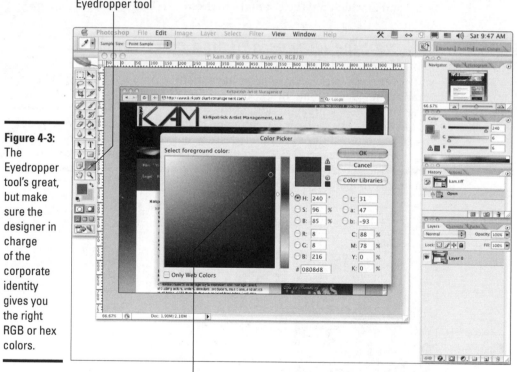

Figure 4-3:
The Eyedropper tool's great, but make sure the designer in charge of the corporate identity gives you the right RGB or hex colors.

Use the eyedropper to match colors.

Web-safe colors

In addition to RGB and hexadecimal colors, you hear about *Web safe* or the *Web 216* palette. *Web safe* and *Web 216* refer to the set of 216 colors that display reliably across the different platforms. The use of Web-safe colors was more important years ago when people didn't have computers and monitors that could handle millions of colors. A system was developed to make sure that colors could be displayed correctly on both Mac and Windows computers. Now that computers and monitors are much improved, it's becoming increasingly mainstream to disregard strict adherence to the Web-safe, 216-color palette. Figures 4-4 and 4-5 illustrate the difference between a Web-safe, 216-color palette (Figure 4-4) and a nonWeb-safe palette (Figure 4-5).

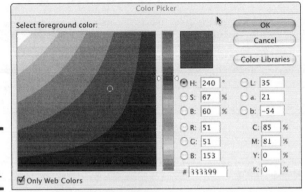

Figure 4-4: The Web-safe palette.

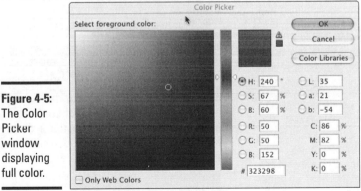

Figure 4-5: The Color Picker window displaying full color.

While in many cases, you can pick colors without worrying too much about strict adherence to the Web 216 (Web-safe, 216-color) palette, sometimes you need to. One of those times is when you're making a graphic that needs to sit next to an expanse of code-generated color — for instance, in a banner. If you want to match the background color of the banner and the color in a graphic sitting over the background color, you should use a Web-safe color. That way, you can be sure there isn't a slight color shift between the graphic and the background. *Color shift* is what happens when two colors that should be the same are very slightly off. A color shift between a graphic and the background can be slight to severe but is always distracting. See the example in Figure 4-6 to see how this can produce undesirable results.

Figure 4-6:
A color shift between a graphic and the background can be slight to severe but is always distracting.

This is the color shift between graphic and background.

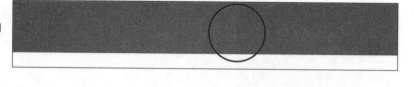

Bandwidth

As you start to become familiar with graphics for the Web and Web site design, you need to learn about bandwidth. *Bandwidth* is the amount of information that has to be sent to the user's machine in order for her to see your Web pages.

Each Web page is made up of several files working together, including an HTML file, graphics files, CSS files, and possibly some script files or other data that is being transferred from a database. Each element that has to be sent to the user's machine takes up bandwidth. Keep that in mind as you're designing pages. Slow Web pages are a very serious problem for a Web site.

As you work on your site, you might find that you need to increase the download speed of your pages. If you find yourself in that situation, you should look at the following:

✔ **Graphics:** Have they been compressed well, or could they be worked with?

✔ **HTML:** Is the code clean and well written, or does it have a lot of issues like nested tables and unnecessary globs of old HTML?

✔ **Back-end systems:** Have your databases and other support systems all been optimized the best way, or has there been sloppy design and coding in the building and maintenance of your back end?

✔ **Multimedia:** Have the multimedia elements been designed and developed so that they download gracefully? Have the elements been properly optimized?

Information about how to work with these elements to deliver the best quality while not ruining the download speed appears in Books IV through VI.

Another fix for the color shift (or *dithering*) is to create transparent images that float over the background color. Book IV has instructions and examples of how to create transparent images and other graphics tricks.

Getting Familiar with Graphics File Formats

There are two *main* graphics file formats in use on the Web. It's true that there are many other formats in use on the Web, but they're not as popular as the big two: JPG (or JPEG) and GIF. A third, much-less popular format that you might encounter is PNG.

JPEG and GIF files are popular because they work well for most graphics that a Web site needs, and they're viewable by any browser that has graphics-display capabilities. Users don't need to make any special modifications or change any settings.

The JPEG and GIF formats *compress* images, meaning they make image file sizes smaller than they originally were. *File size* refers to the amount of space an image takes up on the computer, not how large it is on your screen. Changing the display size doesn't necessarily change the file size unless you're actually resizing the image in a graphics program.

File compression is important for Web graphics because the larger the file sizes are, the longer it takes for them to download. So compressing files helps them to download more quickly. On the Web, speed is everything.

While JPEG and GIF both compress graphics, they work in different ways. Each has its purpose:

Book II
Chapter 4

Ensuring Visual
Appeal

+ **JPEG Joint Photographic Experts Group:** This format is named for the organization that created it. JPEG is good at compressing pictures — images with a lot of tonal changes in them, such as photographs, or graphics with a lot of gradients in them. JPEGs aren't good at compressing graphics that have large areas of solid color. Graphics with large areas of solid colors in JPEG format tend to get strange smudges (called *artifacts*) on the image and can also make text hard to read. Figure 4-7 illustrates JPEG artifacts. The only way to eliminate JPEG artifacts is to start over and recompress the original image with higher-quality settings. The trade off is that the file size will be larger. The whole trick to graphics compression is to balance quality with size; you want the perfect balance of the two. It's different for each graphic, but you will quickly learn how to compress graphics well.

Figure 4-7:
JPEG
artifacts
make words
hard to
read.

JPEG artifacts make text look messy.

Text in my banner

You can adjust the JPEG's quality and download properties to get the best quality with the smallest file size. You can set JPEGs to *progressively download,* which means that the image begins to display as it's downloading. If you've seen an image that appears to be materializing in waves, it's probably a progressively downloading JPEG. Using this method, you can make larger images start to appear quickly, which helps your visitor know that something is coming. Otherwise, they might be looking at a blank space for a few seconds.

✦ **GIF (Graphics Interchange Format):** GIFs are great for buttons and other graphics with large areas of solid color and sharp lines — such as graphics with text. Where JPEGs get artifacts and leave text looking pretty bad at times, GIFs can deliver clean graphics at much smaller file sizes. GIFs don't get artifacts, so the text stays clean, even at small file sizes. You might be wondering why everyone doesn't use GIFs for all their graphics. The reason is that GIFs also have limitations. They don't compress photos or other tonal images well. A photograph that has been compressed as a GIF often gets what is called *dithering.* This is when the image has too many colors for the GIF format to deal with, so it starts shifting some of the colors to colors that are close but not the same. Figure 4-8 shows an example of an image that doesn't work well as a GIF (the image on the right). Dithering can be mild, or it can be severe to the point that gradients end up looking like bands of spray paint. Figure 4-9 is an example of an image that works well as a GIF.

Figure 4-8:
The image
on the
left was
prepared
for the Web
using JPEG,
on the right
as a GIF.

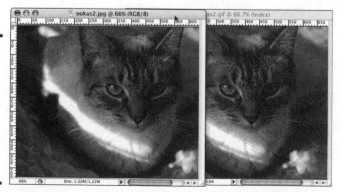

Figure 4-9:
GIF images
do great
with solid
colors and
sharp lines.

Look to Book IV, Chapter 1 for more information about these file formats.

Using Fonts Effectively on Web Sites

Web sites are different from other media in that you have to rely on the users' fonts to display the site content. Web sites draw from the fonts available on the Web site visitor's machine. When you choose fonts for your Web pages, you need to make sure you choose common ones that most users have on their computers. Otherwise, the computer has to make a substitution, and the results of that can be very unexpected and not at all pleasant. But you must plan for this scenario.

The *font-family method* of choosing fonts for your pages is a tried-and-true practice. With this method, you instruct the browser to use one of a few different fonts. For example, if you specify that the font should be `Verdana, Arial, Helvetica, sans-serif`, the visitor's machine tries to use Verdana first. If that is not available, it looks for Arial, and so on. If none of the three named fonts are available, the visitor's computer uses its own, default, sans serif font. *Serif fonts* have little feet or tails attached to the character; *sans serif fonts* don't. See Figure 4-10. (Book IV, Chapter 1 has more information.) The result of using this font-family method is that you don't have exact control over the font for every single user, but you can establish a look and feel with fonts that are similar. That way, your users can have roughly the same experience. It's a safe bet that no one will be able to tell that your site has Verdana on one machine and Arial on another — unless the person looking is a typography fan.

Figure 4-10:
Serif fonts
versus sans
serif fonts.

Some elements, such as banners and logos, require that you absolutely use a special font. In those cases, you must make a graphic that has the text in it and place that on your page. Display text within graphics only sparingly for these reasons:

✦ **Text in graphics adds a lot to the information to download.** Make sure you deliver text as graphics only when it's absolutely necessary — like when it is part of your logo or corporate look and feel. Do not deliver body copy as a graphic for the purpose of maintaining a particular layout or font choice. Revise your layout so it works on the Web instead. It will make the site work better for your client and the site's visitors.

✦ **Text within graphics requires a very large `alt` attribute for the image (also called *alt tags* or *alt text*) for screen readers and other devices.** If people are trying to access your site via screen readers, they won't be able to read your content unless you include the large <alt> tag. (See Book III, Chapter 2 for more information about alt tags.) Problems can arise if the graphic is inline with other content. The screen reader will read things in the order that they appear in the code. The content can end up being read in a different sequential order than you would expect, which is confusing for the visitor.

In general, though, the aesthetics of using a special font are overshadowed by the poor user experience that is created by placing all your text in a graphic.

As with many other aspects of Web design, always design for the medium you're using. Web sites aren't the same as printed materials. Printed materials allow for a lot more control over body copy than Web pages do. Make sure you don't make the mistake of choosing the pretty font over your visitor's ability to use the site.

To get the best results from the fonts you choose, just remember a few rules:

✦ **Web is not print.** Web pages are not printed brochures minus the trip to the printer. Choose fonts that are available on the visitor's machine. Don't try to use a special font that you bought. Users won't have it, and their systems will substitute the font they don't have with one they do.

✦ **Be a designer but not a control freak.** You have a lot of control over the way your pages look, but ultimately, the user can make many adjustments and settings that can change the way his computer displays your design. Fonts can be substituted, sizes can be changed, and CSS can be overridden to help the visitor. It's a fact of the Web. Embrace it; don't try to force it to act like print.

+ **Make your site user friendly.** Don't embed your text in graphics unless it is a logo, a masthead, or a special promotional graphic that really needs a special font. When you do embed text, make sure you include an alt text that has the same text in it — otherwise, some of your visitors won't know what the text in your graphic says.

+ **Use modern standards to build your site.** Use CSS to make modifying and updating your site easier and the user experience better for your visitors. Make sure your code is compliant, well written, and clean. Not everyone using the Web is using a traditional browser.

Implementing Stock Images and Other Elements

Sometimes, you need to use photos, audio files, or other materials that were produced by someone else. When you do so, make sure that you respect the copyrights of others. Stealing images or other materials from a Web site is never okay and can cause large problems if the rightful owner finds out you have been stealing. Everything is subject to copyright laws: multimedia, audio and music, graphics, photos, text, fonts — everything. It's never okay to use things you have found on the Web without permission of the rightful owner.

There are many places that sell stock photography, video footage, and music or audio files. Make sure you understand what you're purchasing before you buy.

Different types of licenses are applied to materials available on the Web. Keep these points in mind as you shop around:

+ **Buy only from the person that actually has the right to sell the material.** When you're using materials produced by someone else, you must buy them from the person that actually has the right to sell them. We recommend buying from reputable companies, which might cost you more, but the quality of the materials and the knowledge that you're getting legal materials is well worth it.

+ **Make sure that the license for the materials you buy specifically states that you can use them for the purpose you're buying them for.** Sounds strange, but sometimes, for example, a license clears you to use an image in printed materials but not on the Web — or the other way around. Read the license carefully, and if you have questions, consult your lawyer. Make sure that if a time frame is involved (you can use the song on your site for one year, for instance), you adhere to the restriction.

✦ **If you intend to modify the materials, make sure the license allows modification.** Some licenses state that you can't create derivative works — and so making a different item out of it would not be okay.

✦ **When buying on behalf of a client, make sure that it's okay for you to do so.** If it isn't, your client will have to purchase the images. Some clients prefer to do it that way anyway.

While shopping for stock imagery, you're likely to run into stock photo jargon. The following list highlights just some of the terms you might see. Make sure you always read the licensing terms before using any stock materials.

✦ **Royalty free:** These materials will have specific rules that you will have to abide by while using them. When you buy access to royalty-free materials, you're buying the right to use the materials for the specific purpose stated in the license. You don't own the copyright to the materials. The copyright remains with the copyright holder (the originator or, in some cases, a company that has purchased the rights).

✦ **Terms of use:** These are the rules that come along with royalty-free materials. You must read the terms of use carefully and make sure that the materials you're buying access to can be used for your intended purpose. Remember, you don't actually own the materials, just the right to use them as specified in the terms of use.

✦ **Educational use:** Some materials might be marked as "for educational use" or something similar. Again, read the documentation that accompanies the materials because the copyright holders have the right to create their own terms. In general, the term *educational use* — as applied to any materials, including software — means just that: The materials are to be used by educational institutions, students, and teachers for projects relating to the institution or to educational pursuits. Copyright owners restrict what types of projects are allowed. In general, educational use licenses are less expensive than commercial licensing. Because of this, commercial use is probably prohibited.

✦ **Rights managed or managed rights:** These types of materials are licensed on a use-by-use basis. The fees for these images vary based on what the image will be used for, how long the image will be used (is it for a short promotion or a longer one?), where it will be used (just in one state or all over the world?), what medium it will be used in (print, Web, video — all three?), and other factors.

✦ **Comp or preview images:** These are versions of the materials that you can use temporarily in a project while you are in the design/approval phase of the project. They are usually provided at a lower quality and with a *watermark* (overlaid text or logo that makes them unusable). They serve the important function of making sure everyone approves of the materials before any money is spent obtaining licensing to use them. It's not all right to use preview or comp images in final projects. Figure 4-11 shows a sample of what a watermark looks like. If a client provides you with images that have similar marks, ask them where the licensed copies are. Licensed copies don't have a watermark.

Figure 4-11:
Sample of a water marked image.

TIP

Consult your lawyer

Before you start creating Web sites professionally, we recommend consulting with a lawyer concerning copyright and intellectual property laws. A lawyer can help you to protect your rights and help you understand how not to infringe on someone else's rights.

One common misconception with Web graphics is that they are all free for the taking. While it might be very easy to copy graphics from a Web site, you can't legally use them in your work without permission from the person who holds the copyright. This and many other confusing and seemingly contradictory rules can get you in a lot of trouble. If you choose a lawyer that specializes in copyright and intellectual property, ask her to help you understand how to stay on the right side of the law.

Another thing a lawyer can help you with is to protect you in the event that a client supplies you with graphics that are questionable in their origins. Make sure you have a clause that allows you the right to refuse graphics that can get you in trouble so that you will be protected if you need to be.

Facelifting an Existing Site

Knowing a little bit about fonts, colors, and images — all of which are discussed in the previous sections of this chapter — can help you effectively apply these elements to a project. A graphical makeover on a small- to medium-sized site can be a quick and easy project if your site is constructed well. If you haven't already done some planning for your project, refer to Book I, Chapter 1, which contains information that can help you get organized before you roll up your sleeves and get into the work of making changes to a site.

Sometimes a site has good content but just needs a quick freshening up. If you design your sites using HTML and CSS, you can easily modify the look and feel. A *facelift* differs from a *redesign* in that a facelift requires only that you change colors and graphics. Layouts, site structure, and content all stay the same. When you need to redesign a site, you must examine the content, code, layout, structure, and all components to determine what to change or re-integrate into the new site. A redesign is a major project. A facelift — which we discuss throughout the rest of this chapter — is just a little sprucing up.

Choosing a new color scheme

Make sure you choose colors that work with any established printed materials your client is using and that convey the right message. For example, if your site is for a toy store, choose bright, happy colors. If your site is about a more serious subject, choose a conservative palette. As you are choosing your colors, remember you will need a main color, a second complementary color, and a third accent color. You can even choose two complementary colors, but don't try to use too many or your design will become confusing to users. Choose your accent color carefully and use it sparingly, as shown in Figure 4-12. You should use the accent color in small amounts to bring attention to an area of the page. For example, you could use a bright accent color in a thin line at the bottom edge of a banner to bring attention to the main navigation area. Make sure you don't overdo it, though. A little is great; a lot will overpower the design.

Figuring out which graphics to replace

Make a list of all the graphics your site is currently using, taking note of the file names, functions, and pixel dimensions. Look for banners, promotional graphics, and navigational buttons. Make sure you haven't left anything out. Also, make a list of photos or other elements you will need to revamp. The other elements will range from customized bullet points to multimedia elements.

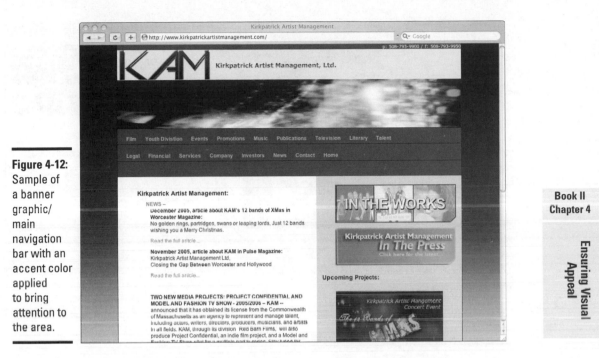

Figure 4-12:
Sample of
a banner
graphic/
main
navigation
bar with an
accent color
applied
to bring
attention to
the area.

Decide how you will handle multimedia elements. If their look and feel is very different from the Web site's new look, you might want to revamp them to match. During this process, take the time to clean up old or unused graphics. Figure 4-13 shows a Web site that is considered for redesign; notice the areas that need new or updated graphics. If you find files that aren't being used, don't add them to your list. That way, when it comes time to make the new graphics, you don't waste time making new versions of these obsolete graphics.

Creating a new prototype

Using Photoshop CS2 (or another graphics program of your choice), create a design prototype. Remember to keep the same basic layout as your current design. This is just a facelift, not a redesign. Everything will stay in the same place. Only the graphics and colors will change. Experiment with your new colors. The following steps get you started.

To create a template to work from:

1. **Open your current Web site in a browser.**

2. **Take a screen shot of it.**

Figure 4-13:
Note the
graphics on
the page
and decide
whether to
replace
them. Make
sure you
look at all
the pages
on the site.

On a Windows-based PC:

a. *Press the Print Screen key.*

b. *Open Photoshop and choose File⇨New Document⇨OK.*

Photoshop defaults to the same size as your screen capture.

c. *Place your cursor in the new document window and press Ctrl+V to paste the screen capture into the new document.*

On the Mac, use Grab:

a. *Choose Capture⇨Window.*

b. *From the dialog box, select Choose Window.*

c. *Click the browser window your current Web site is in.*

d. *Save the file.*

e. *Quit Grab.*

f. *In Photoshop, open the screen shot file.*

3. **Copy content areas of your page to use as place holders with the rectangular Marquee tool. (See Figure 4-14.) Draw a box around a block of text and then press Ctrl+J (Windows) or ⌘+J (Mac) to make a copy of the block on a new layer but in the same place as the original.**

Figure 4-14: Use the Rectangular Marquee tool to copy content areas of your page.

Repeat for all blocks of text.

4. **Create page layout elements with the Rectangle tool. (See Figure 4-15.) Draw Rectangles over the banner, navigation areas, and each content block area, making sure you match the size of the elements.**

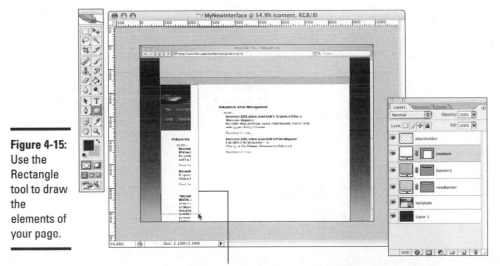

Figure 4-15: Use the Rectangle tool to draw the elements of your page.

Creating layout elements with the Rectangle tool.

5. **Apply the new color scheme to your page elements:**

    a. With the Move tool, select the layer that contains the rectangle you're changing.

    b. With the layer selected, double-click the layer — but not on the name or icons.

    The Layer Style palette opens; see Figure 4-16.

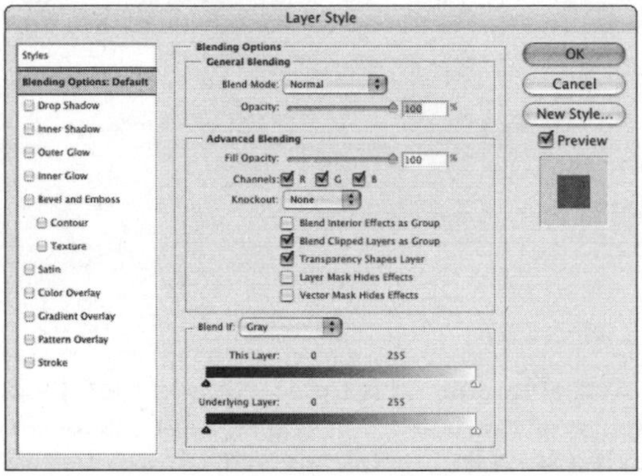

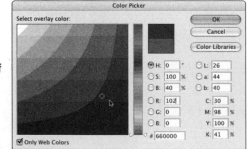

Figure 4-16: Select the layer and launch the layer style.

    c. Select the Color Overlay check box at the lower left of the palette.

    The Color Overlay dialog box appears.

    d. Click the colored rectangle next to the Blend Mode menu.

    The Color picker appears.

    e. Click in the window to select a color — drag the arrows next to the rainbow-colored window to select different colors; see Figure 4-17.

Figure 4-17: Select the Only Web Colors check box if you want only Web-safe colors to be displayed.

   f. *Click OK.*

   g. *Adjust the Opacity or Blend mode, if desired.*

     Opacity affects how transparent the color is. 100% is completely opaque; 0% is completely transparent. *Blend modes* affect how the element reacts to other layers and elements. Experiment with Blend modes to achieve different looks.

6. **Create a new banner, buttons, and other functional graphics.**

   a. *In your old Web site, rename your Images folder by adding* old *to the name. (For example, change the name of the Images folder to ImagesOld, or something similar.)*

     By doing this, you have copies of the old images to refer to or revert to if you need them.

   b. *Create a new Images folder with the same name as the original.*

     This is where your new graphics go. Book IV, Chapter 3 covers making the graphics you need in a project like this.

As you work, make sure you create graphics that are the same size as your existing ones. If you change sizes, you need to adjust your existing layout accordingly.

Name the new graphics the same names as the old graphics and place them in the new Images folder. If you don't, the graphics won't appear on your pages because the HTML code will be trying to place graphics with the old name and location information. It is important to replace those old name and location graphics with new ones that are named exactly the same thing and are in the same folder where the original graphics were. If you don't, you'll have to manually change the file names and locations in your HTML files.

Applying the new colors to your CSS file

In previous steps, you decide what color to use for the banner area, and what color to use for the elements on your pages, such as headlines, banner area, footer — any areas that can be colored through the use of code in the style sheet. You need to sort out what color goes where and apply those changes in the style sheet. To do so, follow these steps:

1. **Look in your HTML document and make note of class and ID selector names.**

Look for code that looks like this:

```
<div id="banner"><h1>My banner text </h1></div>
```

or

```
<p class="footer">my footer content here</p>
```

2. **Open the CSS file and apply the hexadecimal colors to the corresponding classes and IDs.**

   The corresponding CSS will look like this:

   ```
   #banner h1{color:#000000; font-weight: bold;}
   ```

   or

   ```
   .footer{font-size: small; color: #000000;}
   ```

   The #000000 is the hexadecimal color; this code would make the text black. Yours might be a different hexadecimal color.

3. **Change the hexadecimal color value in the #banner h1 set, and all instances of an h1 within a <div> tag with the ID selector of banner are updated.**

   You don't have to open, change, and save each HTML document.

4. **Follow the same procedure of changing values for all attributes you need to affect in order to create your new look and feel.**

   You can change colors, font sizes, weights — anything you like. If you change padding, margins, or positioning, your layouts will change. Make sure you test carefully when you make changes that affect the layout. Also, be aware that if you make drastic changes in font weights or sizes, your layout might be affected.

   For more information about CSS and HTML, please refer to Book III, Chapters 2 and 3.

   After you make all your changes and test all your pages in a browser to make sure everything looks the way you want it to, it's time to publish your new site.

5. **Publish (also referred to as *post*) the new graphics files and the CSS file to your Web server.**

   If you didn't add or change the HTML, you don't need to update those files. Please refer to Book III, Chapter 10 for more about File Transfer Protocol (FTP), the method by which Web pages and sites are published to a Web server.

Book III

Site Construction

The 5th Wave   By Rich Tennant

"Well, it's not quite done. I've animated the gurgling spit sink and the rotating Novocaine syringe, but I still have to add the high-speed whining drill audio track."

Contents at a Glance

Chapter 1: Pulling Together Tools and Materials

In This Chapter

✔ Understanding why you need all this stuff

✔ Choosing hardware

✔ Carving out a workspace

✔ Selecting graphics, multimedia, Web design, and browsing software

As part of the decision-making process, you need to consider the future along with the current needs. Your hardware and software needs to grow with the needs of the sites you're building and with your growing skill set. Buying hardware or software based on current needs and skills alone can result in your gear becoming obsolete more quickly. You can also accidentally limit your personal growth by opting for less-robust software or hardware. For some designers, the issue of outgrowing software and hardware can be a problem; for others, it might not be. If you're looking to build a simple, functional Web site and don't need to build it beyond the basics, you might not need to worry about becoming more ambitious with your Web site's features. As you work on more and more sites, though, your skills will grow along with your creativity. You will want to explore and learn more as you go. Nonprofessional-grade software and hardware — perhaps the perfect match for you when you're starting out — can become very limiting when you get a little experience under your belt. This chapter shows you the hardware, software, and accessories that will grow with you as your skills and demands change.

Matching the Tools to Your Needs

Before you get to the business of building Web sites, make sure you have the hardware and software and other tools that you need. Start out by assessing your needs so that you can make informed decisions about whether you need to buy additional equipment or software.

You have many choices when you're setting up your Web production environment. At the bare minimum, you need the following:

✦ **Computer, monitor, and other hardware:** If you're planning on having a hands-on part in designing and building the site, you'll need to make sure you have a computer to use. This can be your current computer, as long as the computer's specifications meet the needs of the software you decide to use.

✦ **Workspace:** At first, you might get by with a workstation set up in the guest bedroom (or your own). Eventually, though, as you take on more projects and get more clients and have more work to do (good for you), you will need more space (and plenty of it) dedicated to Web design.

✦ **Web design and other software:** You might need to buy additional software in order to build Web sites. As with the hardware, the decision of what to buy is based on your particular needs. If you're in an environment that requires you to use a specific piece of software, make sure you have that software. If you don't have any required programs, you'll need to decide what software you'll buy, based on what you're going to do yourself and what sorts of elements the sites you're building will have.

✦ **Equipment for the whole team:** Remember, it's common to have multiple people working on a site. If you have a team working on the site, make sure everyone has the hardware and software needed to do the work. Adding special features to your site, like multimedia or video, also means that you'll have to get equipment and software to support those features.

The rest of this chapter explores these tools in more detail. More importantly, it helps you decide which tools and equipment are right for your projects and situation.

No matter what sort of equipment you decide you need, don't forget that there is going to be a period of learning. Even the most basic software, and sometimes hardware, requires a little time to get used to. The more complicated the software and hardware, the more time you need to master it. Professional software has more flexibility, along with a steeper learning curve. The good news is that it's all "learnable" — just give yourself time, be patient, and keep working. You'll be surprised at how quickly you can learn how to build Web sites if you stick to it.

Hauling Out the Hardware

Obviously, you need a computer to build Web sites, and other hardware can make things much easier for you as you work. This section suggests a few things for you to consider — but is by no means a complete list.

A computer

You *do* need a computer. As soon as you start talking about building a Web site, you start to get advice from everyone about what type of a computer to buy. You'll hear arguments about PCs versus Macintosh computers. Some people believe that if you're going to do design work, you must have a Macintosh. Other people say that if you're going to do Web design, you have to use a PC because "everyone" uses PCs. These opinions are just that — opinions. The fact is that you can outfit either a PC or a Mac computer with professional-grade graphic and Web design software. Both types of computers are just fine to do Web design work. The choice for you comes down to what you want to use. If you have a computer that can handle your graphics software already, use that. In general, graphics and Web design software requires between 256MB of RAM and 320MB of RAM.

Many professional Web designers actually work on both Macintosh and PC computers. Working cross-platform helps the designer to ensure that the site and graphics look good on both types of machines. There *are* differences between the two in how their browsers render Web pages. And PCs tend to display colors a little darker than Macs. As a Web designer, you don't have any control over what machines and browsers your visitors use and what their personal settings are. That's why it's so important that you test your site on a variety of machines before going live to make sure everything works and looks right. If you don't have both types of machine, find a way to check Web pages on both platforms to ensure things are working right and looking good.

When you look into buying a machine or deciding to use a current machine for production, assess the software you intend to use. Check the specifications that the software needs (RAM, operating system, available hard drive space, processor type, graphics card requirements, and so on). All legitimate software comes with a list of specifications for you to look at. You need to make sure your machine at least meets those requirements. When making the decision, make a list of all the software you intend to use, figure out what each package needs, and then consider your working style. If you like to have many things going on all at once — such as e-mail, graphics, and Web design software — consider that and buy a machine that can handle the workload. If you're more focused on completing one thing at a time, you might not have to consider buying a more powerful machine. In general, a slightly better-than-average machine is probably all right.

Computer monitor

As with all equipment, a better-quality monitor can help you when you work. First rule: *You must have a monitor that displays colors properly.* While users with a huge variety of computer and monitor configurations can and will visit your site, you should make sure you're working with a monitor that is accurate. If you have an older or less-reliable monitor, consider getting a newer or better one. It is also a good idea to make sure you calibrate (adjust) your monitor regularly.

Your monitor and/or system will likely include tools to help you, or you can buy calibration tools to get a more accurate adjustment. One tool you might find useful is one of the Spyder series calibrators from ColorVision, (`www.colorvision.com`). These calibrators analyze your monitor's colors and adjust its accuracy. Many professional designers and photographers use Spyder calibration devices to ensure accurate color.

Another thing you might want to consider is setting up two monitors on your computer. (Check first to make sure your computer supports a dual monitor setup or that you can upgrade it to allow for a dual monitor in the future.) A two-monitor setup gives you twice the screen space. Graphic and Web design software tend to have a lot of palettes and work areas. Dual monitors allow you to spread things out a bit.

The two monitors work as one large one unless you set them up to *mirror* — meaning that the displays are identical. Figure 1-1 shows an example of a dual monitor workspace setup. This example shows Flash being used with two monitors. Monitor one (on the left) accommodates the stage, timeline, and palettes, while monitor two displays the ActionScript window, Flash help, and other code-helpers. This setup greatly increases productivity. Note how palettes can be moved out of the way while you work. This setup is not necessary, but it does improve efficiency.

Figure 1-1:
A dual monitor setup can allow you to work more comfortably.

Backups and storage

As you start to work with graphics, you quickly find that you need a way to store all the large files that you generate. This is particularly important if you're going to work on a large site or on multiple sites. The hard drive of your computer starts to clutter up with pictures, Photoshop documents, and old versions of pages. The answer to the clutter is to have a plan for handling the files in the short term and a plan for storing the files on a more long-term basis.

If you need extra space for handling files, consider an external hard drive. Shop around; you can get hundreds of spare gigabytes for a good price. If you're planning to do work for clients, consider buying different types of readers, such as a Zip drive and/or a floppy disk drive. While these formats aren't as popular as they used to be, plenty of people still use them. It can be a great convenience to your customers if you're equipped to handle a wider variety of media. If you're working with video, your storage needs are much more robust.

In the long run, a good way to store Web graphics files is on either CD (capable of storing 650MB) or DVD (capable of storing as much as 10GB). Make sure your computer can create CDs or DVDs and you have any necessary software. Find a good solution before you accumulate a lot of files. And back up files so that you can have enough room on your machine to work on newer projects. Plus, backing up older files enables you to recover them if you need to.

Make a schedule or routine for yourself for making backups. When it's time, make your discs and then label them well. Be clear about what's on the disc and when you made it. That way, when you need to find something, you won't have to dig through lots of discs trying to find a digital needle in a haystack. A good technique is to burn the digital files to discs and put the discs in a folder along with any hard copies of documents pertaining to the project (signed contracts, brochures, and other materials). That way, you can locate all the materials related to one project very quickly if you need to revisit older projects.

Printers and scanners

It might seem odd to need a printer if you're doing Web design work, but you'll find that it's very handy. Part of the process of designing sites involves making presentations and outlining the plans, and can also include creating and signing contracts. If you're creating a Web design studio, make sure you can copy and print documents.

The other important thing you'll need is a scanner. It's common for photos or other documents to be available only in a physical form. If you don't have a way to scan those items, you'll have a difficult time using them on your site. If you expect to scan a relatively small number of images for use on Web pages only, you can use a common flatbed scanner. If you intend to scan large numbers of images and want to use them for print projects, you'll need a more professional scanner. Make sure you consider what type of work you will do and match the equipment to the task. ***Note:*** If you do choose to scan client materials, make sure you build the time it takes to scan those images into your proposal with an option for them to opt out and scan and deliver them to you in a suitable format. (Specify the format.)

Cameras and camcorders

Whether you're shopping for a still camera or a video camera, make sure you get quality gear that can produce professional results and allows for future needs. The benefit is that you get equipment that's versatile and expandable while remaining affordable.

When you start looking for equipment, talk to professionals that are already working. They can give you advice on what they're using and what they like or dislike about what they use. Also, check out message boards and consumer feedback sites. When you're reading message boards, look for comments that include information about what the poster is doing with the equipment and what his experience level is. Look for people who are experienced and doing similar work to what you're looking to do. Also, make sure you read from several sources; that way, you can get a broad overview of what people are saying. The only thing to keep in mind is that you ultimately don't know any of the people posting. Reading many comments from different sources can help you get a more-accurate picture.

Marketing materials generally promise professional results, but not all equipment actually produces truly professional quality. Many times, the automatic features actually produce undesirable results. The more the camera controls itself, the less you can use your judgment. In situations the camera isn't programmed to handle, the automatic modes can become confused and produce poor-quality video. Make sure that whatever you buy for a camera or a camcorder, it allows you to take complete, manual control if you need to. The reason that this is important is that you need to compress pictures and videos before using them on a Web site. You need to start with the highest-quality source material you can get. That way, you'll have high-quality Web productions. If your fully automatic camera makes some bad decisions for you, you might be left with video or images that aren't good enough to use.

Digital still cameras

If you need to take photos for your clients, make sure you have a good-quality camera. Buy a camera that allows you to take professional-quality images. The better the images are to start, the more flexible they are as you work. It's also common for clients to want to multipurpose photos. Your camera needs to be able to take good enough pictures that you can use them in other projects, such as printed materials. Research well before buying and try to stick with prosumer or professional gear. *Prosumer* (PROfessional + conSUMER = prosumer), in this context, refers to equipment that is considered to be of a higher quality than consumer-grade, lower-end equipment — these products straddle the fence between hobbyist and professional. In general, you want to look for a digital SLR camera that can take pictures that are at least 5 or 6 megapixels.

Video cameras

Although consumer-grade video cameras have improved, they really aren't made for professional production. The better the quality of your equipment, the better the quality of your video — and it really shows in the final product. A higher-quality camera has features that will help you produce better-quality video under a wider variety of situations. Make sure you get information from actual users and not from marketing materials.

If you're looking at doing video, consider how you're going to get the video into your computer for editing and preparing it for the Web. You can connect the camera itself to the computer, but it's not necessarily the best way. Each time you use the camera for taping or for getting the video into the computer, you're producing wear and tear on the camera. If you plan to do a lot of video, you might want to consider buying a VTR (also called a *deck*) to do the job of getting the footage onto your computer. A *VTR* is a device that can play back the tapes from your camera — a *VCR* is a VHS deck. There are many available; look for one that can handle your needs. Check the format(s) your camera uses to make sure the deck works with it.

Accessories

Consider the accessories when you're deciding your budget for purchasing camera equipment. The extras can add up quickly. In addition to actual cameras and camcorders, you might want to consider these add-ons:

✦ A **camera bag** for storing and transporting the equipment.

✦ **Cleaning equipment and supplies** to keep everything in good, working order.

✦ **Tapes** for video cameras.

✦ **Audio equipment** for capturing better sound. Your video camera will come with some type of microphone but not of great quality. It is generally a good idea to buy extra microphone(s) to improve the quality of your productions.

✦ **Lights** for improving shooting conditions when available light is not good. There are a wide range of lights available for still and video cameras ranging from on-camera lights and flashes to whole lighting kits. What you need depends on what type of work you are doing.

✦ A **tripod** that fits your camera (or camcorder). Make sure you have one that fits your intended use and supports the weight of your equipment.

✦ **Storage cards and a card reader.** *Card readers* are devices that attach directly to your computer and allow you to download your pictures easily by removing the card from your camera and inserting it into the reader. From there, you can download your pictures as you would if you had your camera connected to the computer. This can protect your camera from being damaged while waiting to download pictures. Generally speaking, you want at least two or three 512MB storage cards so you don't run out of space. Larger cards are available, but keep in mind that if you have a 1GB card and you fill it, you will have to unload all those pictures. It can be more efficient to have two smaller cards so you can be unloading pictures from one and shooting on the other at the same time.

Graphics tablet

Some designers find a graphics tablet useful. A *graphics tablet* is a flat device ranging in size from that of an average mouse pad to about 12 inches by 19 inches. Designers use a penlike device, called a *stylus,* to draw, paint, or write on the tablet. The tablet/stylus is pressure sensitive and generally includes a couple of buttons to substitute for the mouse buttons. The pressure sensitivity works with graphics software to produce more real-looking graphic effects. Whereas a mouse has a more-uniform response to your hand, a stylus or tablet senses how hard you press and produces stronger or thicker lines the harder you press. You can also set the tablet to affect opacity. The settings are up to the user and you can change them to suit your needs.

Actually, a tablet and stylus can completely replace your mouse if you prefer it, but not all designers use tablets. Whether to use one depends on your personal tastes and what you're trying to do.

Setting Up Your Web Design Studio

If you're working on a corporate Web site for your employer, you already have a workspace. If you plan to create Web sites for clients, you need to create your workspace. Some resources to have in your Web design workspace include these:

✦ **A comfortable desk and chair:** Building Web sites takes a lot of time. Make sure your chair is comfortable for you to sit in for a long time. It's true that you can work with a hard folding chair and a little table, but you'll be more productive if you make a space that is comfortable and has enough room for you to sit and work for prolonged periods.

✦ **Bookshelves:** Web and multimedia production involves a lot of details. As you progress, you'll accumulate reference books, inspirational art books, trade magazines, and other books and materials. If you've got a bookcase near your desk, it's easier for you to get to those materials while you work.

✦ **Enough desk area to accommodate all of your equipment:** It's a good idea to have a little extra room for future growth. At least have some idea of how you can rearrange your workspace to accommodate more equipment if need be. If you choose to set your computer up with two monitors, you'll need enough space to have the monitors side by side so you can use them both comfortably.

✦ **Space to do paperwork:** Building Web sites also requires some paperwork. You'll find it's a good idea to have enough space to work on proposals, design prototypes, and other paper documents that help you stay on track.

✦ **Peace and quiet:** Your workspace needs to be quiet. You'll need a place that lets you focus your attention on all the details involved. If you set up in a major traffic area in your house, you might find it hard to be productive, especially when you have to work through a problem. Professional Web design does require an inquisitive nature and a place that supports reading and problem solving.

Desperately Seeking Software

Throughout this book, we cover many different types of software, but this section gives you a quick-and-dirty list of what you should consider. Software is referred to as *industry standard* when it's the preferred package for a particular function amongst professionals. If you're concerned about building a resume, use industry-standard software whenever possible. It can give you a skill set that is valuable to the widest number of employers. If you don't intend to pursue a career or to work with other professionals, industry standard software is less of an issue for you.

When you're looking for Web and graphic design software, check out bundled packages. Adobe has packages that include everything you need — graphics, Web, and multimedia software. Buying a bundle can save you a bundle of money because the price of the bundle ends up being less than the prices of buying each piece of software individually. On the other hand, if you choose to use software from different companies, the bundled software might not work for you.

Note: The software discussed in this section is available for both PC and Macintosh computers, unless otherwise specified.

Researching software before you buy

Much of the professional-grade software we overview in this section doesn't come cheap. Before you plunk down your hard-earned cash for a piece of software, do a little research on it. You have several avenues to find out about software, including

✦ **Trial versions:** Trial versions of software allow you to test-drive a package before you buy it. Often, some features are disabled because the purpose of the software is to let you try it, not to give you free access to it. Trial software generally has a time limit (two weeks or a month), after which the software ceases to function. If you're unsure about whether a piece of software will do what you want it to, look for a trial version.

✦ **People you know:** Ask around to see if anyone you know is using the software. That way, you can get some firsthand advice about what the software can do for you.

✦ **User groups:** Research on the Internet to see if any Web design or software-specific user groups are in your area. A couple of hours at a meeting can get you a lot more information than you could find on your own in several hours of surfing the Web.

✦ **Developers' sites:** When you read about software, make sure you read Developer or Community sections of the Web sites in addition to the marketing sections of the sites. It seems that all software boasts of being full featured, professional grade, and easy to learn/use — make sure that their idea of what those things mean match with the reality of your needs before you make the leap. Communities and developer sites can give you a much clearer picture of what it's like to work with the software on a daily basis.

Something that's easy to use for a seasoned professional can be a bit more daunting for individuals just starting out. Don't let that stop you; just be aware that the easier the software, the fewer the features, the quicker you outgrow it.

Graphics software

This category includes software for manipulating photos, drawing illustrations, and creating layouts. You can't build Web sites without them.

Note: Adobe and Macromedia are now the same company. Adobe purchased Macromedia in 2006.

Adobe Photoshop

Photoshop is the industry standard for creating graphics and manipulating photos. It's an extremely powerful program with a wide range of uses. Designers who work with Web, video, multimedia, and print all use Photoshop, as do photographers. Figure 1-2 shows the Photoshop interface in its default layout. Chapters 4 and 7 of this minibook cover using Photoshop in Web site design.

A "lite" version of Photoshop is available, called Elements. Elements consists of the most popular and most used features of Photoshop but leaves out many of the professional tools. If your needs are for just basic photograph manipulation and simple graphics creation, Elements might work for you. If you plan to work as a professional designer, you'll want to learn and use the full version of Photoshop.

Photoshop comes with ImageReady integrated. As with many of the graphics packages, with the combination of tools in Photoshop and ImageReady, you can create buttons, banners, and GIF animations.

You can purchase Photoshop alone or as part of one of the Adobe software bundles. The choice of how to purchase depends on your needs.

Figure 1-2:
Adobe
Photoshop
interface.

Macromedia Fireworks

Fireworks (shown in Figure 1-3) is another program that is widely used in professional environments to create graphics and manipulate photos. It also has some useful features, such as batch processing of images and good Web compression tools.

As with Photoshop, you can create layouts and slice them for use as Web graphics — see Chapter 7 of this minibook for details about how to use Photoshop to make a Web page layout and prepare it to be a Web page. Fireworks also has good tools for making *rollovers* (graphics that change when users place their cursors over them — such as with buttons that appear to light up), and other effects.

Fireworks was created specifically for use as a Web graphics software package, so its tools are specialized for Web designers' use. The focus is on creating great-looking, well-optimized graphics. Fireworks comes alone or bundled in the Studio 8 package from Adobe/Macromedia and integrates well with Dreamweaver and Flash.

Figure 1-3:
Macro-
media
Fireworks.

Adobe Illustrator

Illustrator is the industry standard for creating vector images. Vector images tend to look more like line drawings. Illustrator is particularly useful for creating logos. To design a proper logo, you need to create artwork that can scale to any size. Vector artwork does scale without losing quality, so you'll want to create all logos as vector artwork. Figure 1-4 shows an example of the type of art you can create in Illustrator.

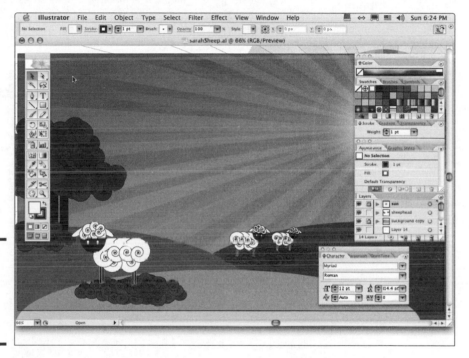

Figure 1-4:
A vector image created in Adobe Illustrator.

Macromedia FreeHand

Macromedia FreeHand is a popular, vector art package. Many professional designers use FreeHand to create logos and other artwork — like layout prototypes. As with Photoshop and Fireworks, you can use both FreeHand and Illustrator to create artwork that you can use in Flash or other programs. Figure 1-5 shows the workspace in FreeHand.

Combining the best tools from multiple graphics programs

It's common to use more than one piece of software to create graphics and multimedia elements. It's not necessary, but you might find that each piece of software is particularly good at some things but not everything. For instance, Adobe/Macromedia Flash is excellent for creating multimedia. It has a fine toolset for creating graphics, too, but FreeHand and Illustrator are much more powerful in that respect. You might find that it works better for you to create the graphics in FreeHand or Illustrator and then import them into Flash. If you're using bitmapped images, you need to use something like Photoshop or Fireworks to do the job — then import the resulting graphics into Flash. See Chapter 4 of this minibook for an explanation of vector and bitmapped art.

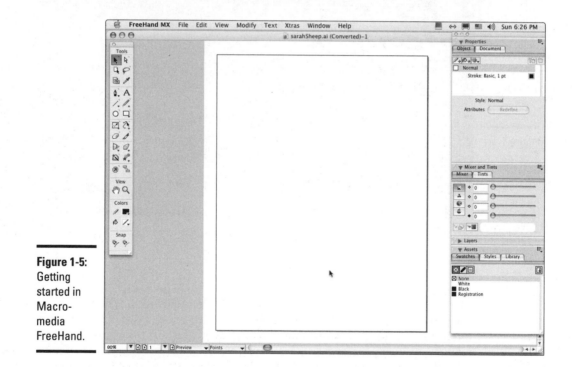

Figure 1-5: Getting started in Macromedia FreeHand.

Multimedia software

You use multimedia software to create animations, presentations, and other multimedia elements on your site. If you plan to work with video, you need video editing software. What follows isn't a complete list of all the software available, but it can give you some ideas of where to start.

Macromedia Flash

Flash (shown in Figure 1-6) is the industry standard for creating multimedia interfaces, animations, games, and other multimedia elements for Web pages and CDs. Flash features a design environment where you can create graphics, a timeline for making animations, and a scripting language (called *ActionScript*) that allows developers to create applications or interfaces for applications. For information about incorporating Flash elements into Web pages, see Book V.

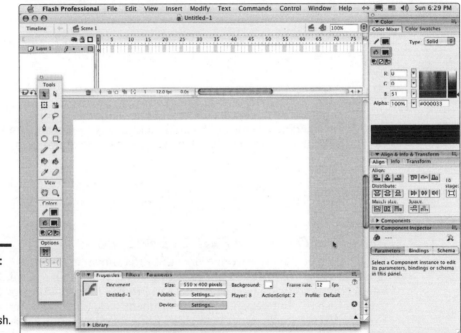

Figure 1-6: Getting started in Macromedia Flash.

When you use Flash elements on your site, visitors need the Flash Player installed on their machine in order to see Flash content — but most users do have Flash Player. When you create Flash content, it's a good idea to include either a link to the Adobe site where visitors can get the player (www.adobe.com/downloads). Another option for handling visitors that don't have the player is to include alternate content in the HTML document that instructs people what to do. Flash also has settings within the publishing settings that can put code into your project that checks the visitor's machine and gives instructions to the visitor if the player isn't the right version. After you get more comfortable with code, you can also create your own detection script.

For information about or trial versions of Adobe or Macromedia software, you can visit the Adobe Web site at www.adobe.com.

Toon Boom Studio and Toon Boom Studio Express

Toon Boom Studio is the professional version and Toon Boom Studio Express is the "lite" version of the software. You can use both to create animations for use in Flash. If you plan on doing a lot of animations — especially if you expect to have a lot of character animation in your work — you might want to check out one of these packages. They specialize in animation and have tools that are intended for that purpose. Trial versions are available on the Web site, so you can try it out before you buy it.

For information about Toon Boom Studio or Toon Boom Studio Express software, you can visit the Web site at www.toonboom.com.

Electric Rain Swift 3D

Swift 3D specializes in creating 3D art and animations for Flash. Electric Rain offers two different versions of Swift 3D, a full-blown program and a plug-in for Flash. Which one works best depends on the type of projects you intend to create.

You can find additional information about Electric Rain products at www.erain.com.

Apple Final Cut Pro and Final Cut Express HD

For Macintosh computers only. Final Cut Pro (shown in Figure 1-7), sold alone or as part of the Final Cut Pro Studio, is a professional, nonlinear, video editing software package. Final Cut Pro has more features than Final Cut Express HD, but depending on your needs, you might find that Final Cut Express HD is enough. Most Web video projects don't require the more robust features that are available in the Pro version. Before you decide which works best for you, you'll have to determine what your plans are.

If you do decide to start with Final Cut Express HD and then later move up to Final Cut Pro, you'll find that it's an easy transition because the interfaces of the two are so similar. You'll just have to learn the additional features. Whichever one you choose, you'll also have to figure out if you want to put motion graphics *(animations)* in your videos. If you do, you need to make sure you have additional software to create the animations — such as Adobe After Effects, Apple Motion, or LiveType.

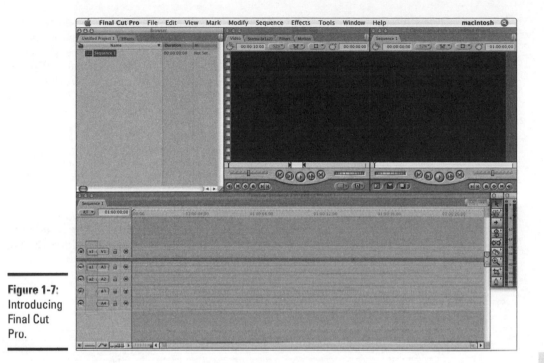

Figure 1-7:
Introducing
Final Cut
Pro.

For more information about the Final Cut products and other software by Apple that can help you with your video projects, go to www.apple.com.

Adobe Premiere Pro

Available for Windows only. Adobe software's professional, nonlinear, video editing software provides the tools that you need to edit and prepare video. Like the Final Cut products, you need additional software if you want to do fancy, motion graphics in your videos. Premiere is available bundled with other software. Visit www.adobe.com/products for more information about Premiere Pro.

There are many other video editing software options but many of them are more robust than you need to create Web video — and have price tags to match. If you find that Final Cut Pro, Final Cut Express HD, or Premiere Pro doesn't have the features you need, you might want to look at Avid (www.avid.com) software.

Web design software

Your Web design studio needs some type of Web design software. You can create pages in a plain, text editor or you can buy what is called a *WYSIWYG* (what you see is what you get) Web page editor. WYSIWYG page editors include both the coding environment and a designer mode that shows you what your page will look like. Your other option is to use software that isn't quite full WYSIWYG but is more robust than a text editor (such as BBEdit). Here are some tips on what type of Web design software might work for you:

✦ **WYSIWYG software:**

 • *Macromedia Dreamweaver:* Dreamweaver, considered to be the industry standard for Web design, works with Contribute and other Macromedia products — Flash, Fireworks, and Adobe Photoshop (via the Edit With command). It comes alone or as part of a package. The Dreamweaver 8 user interface is shown in Figure 1-8. We cover Dreamweaver in Chapters 5 and 6 of this minibook.

 • *Adobe GoLive:* This Web editing software has many of the same features as Dreamweaver, and many professionals use it. Adobe GoLive is available alone or as part of the Creative Suite Premium bundle.

 You can find more information about Dreamweaver and GoLive at www.adobe.com.

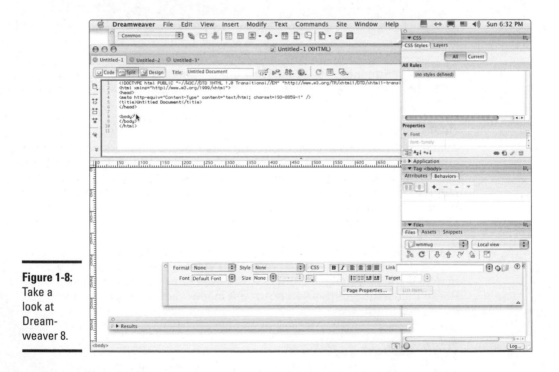

Figure 1-8:
Take a look at Dream-weaver 8.

- *Microsoft FrontPage:* Microsoft's professional Web design and maintenance software features a full set of tools for creating and maintaining sites for individual users and for larger Web teams.

All three WYSIWYG software packages have features that help keep teams on track. Dreamweaver is the most widely used and integrates with Contribute (which is Macromedia's software for nontechnical Web editors). GoLive's interface looks familiar to those Web team members who already use other Adobe products. Choose Microsoft FrontPage if you and your team are more familiar with Office products — and already have the software. Microsoft FrontPage is no longer being made but is still being used by some design/development teams.

✦ **Bare Bones Software BBEdit:** BBEdit is a widely used HTML and text editor (which means that it's good for all sorts of tasks — CSS and JavaScript included). It's available for Macintosh computers only. BBEdit is good for individuals who are more comfortable with a code-only environment. Some of its features and functions are similar to those of the more robust WYSIWYG editors, but as the name implies, it really is a pretty bare-bones package. Some developers prefer the stripped-back interface and the reduced toolset for its less-cluttered environment.

Ideally, you'll learn HTML and CSS well enough to be able to create pages in any environment.

✦ **HomeSite:** This is Macromedia software's HTML/text editor for PC computers only. Like BBEdit, the tool is geared toward people who are more comfortable with code than a visual approach to Web site design. HomeSite is a very good package for creating Web page code — HTML, CSS, JavaScript, and others.

The choice of what software you use is really up to you. If you're going to make a career out of creating Web pages, learn HTML and CSS along the way. That will ensure that you're able to handle real-world Web page creation and maintenance. Remember, the more the software does for you, the more you have to trust a machine to figure things out for you. Software is good, but it's still no match for human judgment.

Browser software

You need to have copies of the most popular browsers available on your machine. Ideally, you have copies available on both platforms. At least make sure that you have access to a way to view your pages on both Mac and PC. Some of the most popular Web browsers that you need to make sure you have are Firefox, Safari, Internet Explorer, and Netscape. You might also need to look at your site in AOL.

Book III
Chapter 1

Pulling Together
Tools and Materials

Look at your pages in all the most popular browsers because they don't interpret code in exactly the same way. Additionally, pages can look different in PC and Mac versions of a browser. Each browser and platform has quirks that you have to work with. The process of building pages does require a cycle of build, test, adjust, test, and so on until you get acceptable results in the targeted browsers.

The list of browsers and versions that are in common use changes often. Some browsers are no longer in common use or are no longer being supported — such as Internet Explorer for the Mac. You probably don't need to worry about checking your pages in old or outdated browsers. The exception to this is cases where the client or audience will be using older technologies. Make sure you talk with your client about the technological needs of the site before you start building. If you don't, it isn't possible for you to know what to build.

Chapter 2: Making a Web Page with HTML

In This Chapter

✔ Getting started on coding your Web page

✔ Adding body content

✔ Creating bullet lists, numbered lists, and tables

✔ Introducing style

✔ Developing good coding practices

This chapter helps you understand the basics of HyperText Markup Language (HTML). HTML is the underlying code that makes all Web pages work in a browser. In this chapter, we deconstruct an HTML document and show some basics of how to create a Web page.

This chapter focuses on the most basic Web page layout, but there are many technologies that can be added to a site — and the code — to create much more complicated pages. HTML isn't able to use information from a database or to create any multimedia effects on its own. For that, you need other scripting and programming languages (covered in Book VI) and plug-ins, such as Flash or QuickTime (covered in Book V).

Getting Acquainted with the Basic Parts of an HTML Document

The essential parts of an HTML document are pretty simple. Each HTML page consists of a head and a body that are contained in *tags*. In fact, all elements on an HTML page must be contained in tags. The absolute minimum tags needed are the HTML <head> and <body> tags, as shown here:

```
<html>
<head>Your header information goes here.</head>
<body>The content of your page goes here.</body>
</html>
```

Note that most tags travel in pairs. Each element has an *opening tag* (<html>, <head>, <body>) and a *closing tag* (</body>, </head>, </body>). The opening and closing of tags lets the browser know where each part of your document begins and ends. All tags in HTML should be closed; in the current version of HTML, or XHTML, they *must* be closed. Some tags are *container tags* — that is, one opening tag is followed by some content, which is then followed by the closing tag, as in the preceding example. Other tags, such as a break (`<br />`), are *single tags*. Notice how the single tag also has a / to close itself.

If you'd like to have a look at the HTML of any page, you can view the source code in your browser. It's a good way to see how others are creating their pages. Be aware though, that browsers are very forgiving of bad coding practices. Many older sites and sites created by less-skilled developers might not have standard code. Make sure you verify that a technique is a good one before you put it to use on your own site. To view the source code of a page in Internet Explorer, for example, you can either right-click in your browser window and select View Source, or choose View➪Source on your browser menu bar. (You can also view source code with other browsers. The location of View Source might be different but will be found under a similar view-type menu.) Figure 2-1 shows an example of the HTML code and the page it produces.

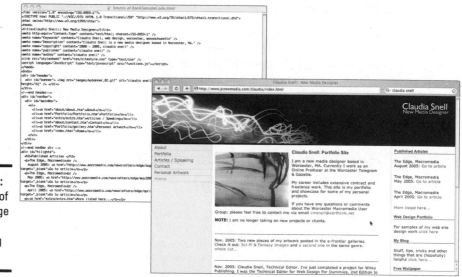

Figure 2-1: A sample of a Web page and its underlying code.

Starting Your HTML Document Right

Throughout this chapter, we work through an HTML document from top to bottom and explain the parts. This will help you develop good, solid code

Picking up pointers from reliable sources

Elsewhere in the chapter, we recommend that you look at what others are doing when you're beginning to write code. We also recommend that you supplement what you're learning with information from the World Wide Web Consortium (W3C). The W3C is the organization that creates the recommendations and standards for properly coded Web sites. Consulting the W3C site (`www.w3.org`) can help you ensure that you are picking up the best habits while avoiding bad ones.

As you develop as a Web designer, make regular visits to the W3C site to make sure you stay up to date with the current standards. A very important part of being a competent Web designer is keeping your skills current.

---

when you start to work on your site. By *good, solid code,* we mean code that is consistent with Web standards, is free of typos and other errors, and also is well commented. This section explains the document type definition (DTD) and the head and body tags. Each site you create will always have at least these three elements.

As you start to build your HTML document, you might notice when you preview it that it is pretty ugly. The default look of headings and paragraphs can be very unattractive. Don't try to make it look good at this point. The CSS (Cascading Style Sheets) file you create will take care of all the visual aspects of your page. *Cascading Style Sheets* are a type of coding that controls layout. CSS are the instructions for the browser about how to display different elements of your HTML document. CSS can control how much space is between the elements on the page, what colors things are, and how large the text appears. Some very old methods of making HTML look good (such as using the `<font>` tags) should not be used anymore. They create code that is difficult to edit and maintain. The old methods are also not as compliant with modern browsers and devices. Remember, a well-coded HTML document is a pretty bland and ugly thing.

The document type definition

The first thing your page needs is the opening document type definition (DTD) and HTML tags. These tags tell the browser what type of HTML document you are sending it. There have been several versions of HTML, and telling the browser which version you're using helps the browser display it correctly. This example is from a page that is using XHTML 1.0 Transitional, a modified version of HTML 4.01:

```
<!DOCTYPE html PUBLIC "-//W3C//DTD XHTML 1.0 Transitional//EN" "http://www.w3.
    org/TR/xhtml1/DTD/xhtml1-transitional.dtd">
```

HTML versus XHTML

While you're learning about HTML, you're probably going to hear about XHTML (eXtensible HyperText Markup Language), too. XHTML is, in the simplest terms, the next generation of HTML. It's very similar to HTML with some very subtle but important differences. These differences are currently in place and will be enhanced in future versions of XHTML to help documents work with XML (eXtensible Markup Language) better. The technical aspects of the differences are beyond the scope of this book, although the World Wide Web Consortium (www.w3.org) has information for the curious.

Older versions of HTML allowed tags to be left unclosed. The current standard is to close all tags and to use XHTML. One of the differences is that XHTML needs all tags to be closed. This is because HTML "sees" the tags as markup; XHTML "sees" them as containers holding distinct types of content within your document. XHTML needs to know where each piece starts and ends. This all becomes important when you want to develop content that works well within many different systems and on different devices. XHTML is designed to be more compatible with XML (which is a widely used standard for storing and delivering content across different systems and devices). Older versions of HTML were not designed to work the same way and so are more forgiving of less consistent coding practices.

In HTML you would code a paragraph this way:

```
<p>This is a very short
   paragraph
<p>Here is another very short
   paragraph
```

Closing the tags would be optional.

In XHMTL, it would be like this:

```
<p>This is a very short
   paragraph</p>
<p>Here is another very short
   paragraph</p>
```

In XHTML, all tags need to be closed; in HTML, it is a nice thing to do but not required.

This code also tells the browser that this page is in English (note the EN) and more information about how to display your page.

The head tag and what goes in it

The head of the HTML document is where information called *meta data* (information about the document) is contained. Tags associated with meta data are *meta tags*. The purpose of meta tags and the information they contain is to

✦ Inform the browser about what type of document it is receiving.

```
<meta http-equiv="Content-Type" content="text/html; charset=ISO-8859-1" />
```

✦ Give information to the search engines.

```
<meta name="Keywords" content="Claudia Snell, Web Designer, massachusetts "
   />
<meta name="Description" content="Claudia Snell is a new media designer
   based in Worcester, MA." />
```

✦ Provide a title for the page. This page title is displayed in the title area of the browser and also in most search engine results lists.

```
<title>Claudia Snell:: New Media Designer</title>
```

✦ Link associated files like CSS and JavaScript files.

```
<link rel="stylesheet" href="css/sitestyle.css" type="text/css" />
<script language="JavaScript" type="text/javascript" src="functions.js">
    </script>
```

✦ Provide information about when the page was published and by whom.

```
<meta name="copyright" content="2000 - 2005, claudia snell" />
<meta name="publisher" content="claudia snell" />
<meta name="author" content="claudia snell" />
```

Note that all the samples of code in the preceding list are closed either with a closing tag or with a / at the end of the code. A good way to tell if a tag is a container tag is to determine whether it "contains" anything. The <head> tags encapsulate all the header information, so they are container tags. The meta tags merely convey a piece of information and so are not containers.

There are several more meta tags available, and header information can also contain other types of information, like CSS styles and JavaScript. To see examples of these in CSS, check out Book III, Chapter 3; Book VI, Chapter 1 covers JavaScript.

So, to have a look at how the code examined so far works together to create the beginning of your HTML document, examine this code:

```
<!DOCTYPE html PUBLIC "-//W3C//DTD XHTML 1.0
    Transitional//EN" "http://www.w3.org/TR/xhtml1/DTD/xhtml1-
    transitional.dtd">

<head>
<title>Claudia Snell:: New Media Designer</title>
<meta http-equiv="Content-Type" content="text/html; charset=
    ISO-8859-1" />
<meta name="Keywords" content="Claudia Snell, web design,
    worcester, massachusetts" />
<meta name="Description" content="Claudia Snell is a new media
    designer based in Worcester, MA." />
<meta name="copyright" content="2000 - 2005, claudia snell" />
<meta name="publisher" content="claudia snell" />
<meta name="author" content="claudia snell" />
<link rel="stylesheet" href="css/sitestyle.css"
    type="text/css" />
<script language="JavaScript" type="text/javascript" src=
    "functions.js"></script>
</head>
```

This code communicates important information like the name of the site, the author and publisher of the content, a description of the site content, and what version of HTML/XHTML the page is using. This information is used by the browser, search engines, and the site's visitors. The code will also make sure that all the correct CSS and JavaScript needed to make the page work is loaded. Figures 2-2 and 2-3 show how the search engine and browser use the head tag information to help your visitors find and use your Web site.

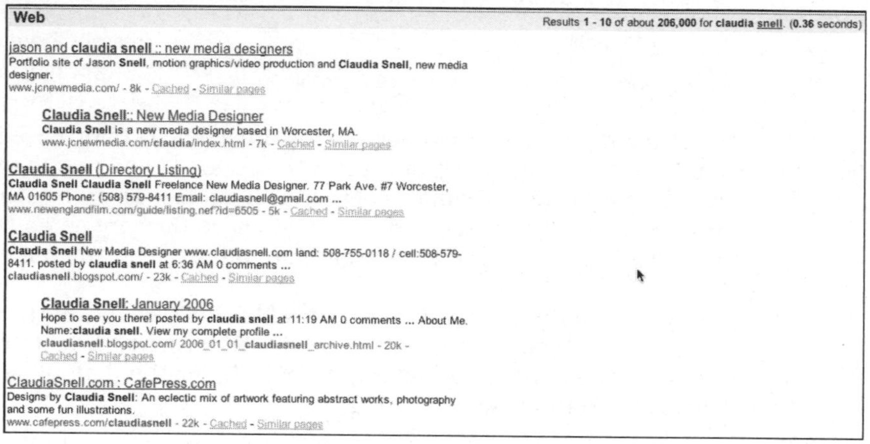

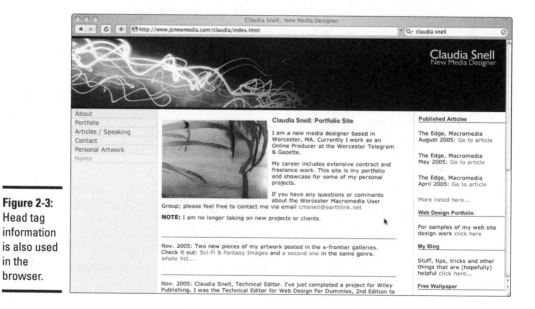

Figure 2-2:
Head tag information is used in search engine results.

Figure 2-3:
Head tag information is also used in the browser.

Now for some body!

The main part of a page is the body. This is where all the visible content of a page goes. All the graphics, images, banners, headings, and paragraphs of text must be contained between the <body> and </body> tags.

Before you start coding, organize the content as an outline with a main topic heading and then supporting subheadings under each. While there are several layers of headings available, we recommend that you stick with three levels or less. If a subheading has enough supporting information to require <h4> and above, it might be a good candidate for being its own page. Remember, people like short, easy-to-access information on a Web page. The cleaner your outline, the cleaner your page, and the better the experience for site visitors.

Adding headings

Headings on your page belong between heading tags. These are container tags that should be used in order of your content structure — <h1>, <h2>, <h3>, and so on. The <h1> tag is for the main heading of your page, <h2> is for subheadings, and <h3> is for subheadings under the <h2> subheadings.

```
<!DOCTYPE html PUBLIC "-//W3C//DTD XHTML 1.0 Transitional//
    EN" "http://www.w3.org/TR/xhtml1/DTD/xhtml1-transitional.
    dtd">
<head>
<title>Claudia Snell:: New Media Designer</title>
<meta http-equiv="Content-Type" content="text/html; charset=
    ISO-8859-1" />
<meta name="Keywords" content="Claudia Snell, web design,
    worcester, massachusetts" />
<meta name="Description" content="Claudia Snell is a new media
    designer based in Worcester, MA." />
<meta name="copyright" content="2000 - 2005, claudia snell" />
<meta name="publisher" content="claudia snell" />
<meta name="author" content="claudia snell" />
<link rel="stylesheet" href="css/sitestyle.css" type="text/
    css" />
<script language="JavaScript" type="text/javascript" src=
    "functions.js"></script>
</head>
<body>
<h1>Main Heading Of the Page</h1>
<p>An opening paragraph is sometimes nice</p>
<h2>A subheading</h2>
<h3>A subheading of the above h2</h3>
<p>This is a good place for a paragraph</p>
</body>
</html>
```

If you'd like to see what this code looks like as an actual Web page, you can copy it directly into a plain text document. Save the document with an `.html` file extension instead of `.txt`. Open the document in a browser. It won't be very nice looking, but you will be able to see what parts of this code are visible on the page, which parts are in the title bar, and which parts are invisible. You will also be able to see what the different heading types look like by default (before styling). You'll most likely want to apply CSS to make them look better.

Also, notice the closing tags on these container tags. If you don't close the heading or paragraph tags, the browser doesn't know that section has ended. It will treat the rest of the document as if it is part of that section. Imagine an entire page displayed as a main heading!

Coding paragraphs

As you might have noticed in the preceding code example, the container tags for paragraphs are `<p>` and `</p>`, and you use them to separate text into paragraphs. Each paragraph must have its own set of paragraph tags. As you look at HTML of other sites, you might notice that they do not use the `<p>` tags, they use `<br>` tags instead — sometimes several of them — to create the visual effect of having paragraphs. This is an incorrect use of the break tag and should never be done. The break tag should be used only when you need a hard break, like in a very long bullet. The reason using multiple `<br>` tags is incorrect is that when you apply style sheets, you can get inconsistencies in your design because the style sheet will apply attributes to things like paragraphs. The `<br>` tags will not get the same attributes unless you clutter up your CSS with code to make them the same. Also, coding your site properly will make your content more compatible with other technologies, such as screen readers and handheld devices.

The anatomy of a whole page

Headings and paragraphs aren't always enough. Sometimes you need lists and tabular data on your pages, too. When deciding how to present your data, consider your other options. If the text fits into short bullets, present it that way. Bulleted lists work very well on the Web where your audience will be looking for quick, easy-to-access information. Tables should be used whenever your information needs that type of structure, like contact lists or price lists. These are scenarios when columns and rows really are best.

Using bulleted and numbered lists

Bulleted lists and numbered lists help your visitors get the point quickly. The code for lists — bulleted or numbered — is fairly simple. You can put the heading for a list in either a paragraph tag or in a heading tag, whichever suits the situation best. Take a look at the following HTML, which creates a simple bullet list:

```
<p>My list of fruit</p>
<ul>
    <li>apples</li>
    <li>bananas</li>
    <li>oranges</li>
</ul>
```

Note that the paragraph tag is closed before the list tags begin. The `<ul>` tag in the set means *unordered list* and the `<li>` is for *list item*. To turn this list into a numbered list, use `<ol>` (for *ordered list*) in place of the `<ul>` tag — and don't forget to close it with the `</ol>` tag.

Sometimes a list has nested sub-items in it. The code to make that happen looks like this:

```
<p>My list of fruit</p>
<ul>
    <li>apples
    <ul><li>red</li>
        <li>green</li>
        <li>yellow</li>
    </ul>
    </li>
    <li>bananas</li>
    <li>oranges</li>
</ul>
```

In this example, the sub-items in the `apple` item are part of a second unordered list. Notice how the sub-items list begins and is closed between the `<li>` and `</li>` of the `apple` item. The browser displays them as indented items under `apple` in the main list.

Building tables for your site

Another situation you will likely encounter is a need for tabular data. Tables usually turn up in the form of contact lists on sites but are very common with many types of data, such as price lists or comparison charts. In the old days of Web design, tables were used to control layout of the page, and many sites are still built this way. There are some instances where it is necessary to use some form of layout tables.

If you're using layout tables, avoid nesting tables excessively. *Nesting* refers to the practice of creating a table within a table, within a table, and so on. Building a page with nested tables creates these problems:

✦ **The pages load slowly.** If the tables have significant nesting, the browser has a lot more information to interpret and display, and the page loads can be slowed considerably.

✦ **The information is less accessible.** Nested tables can make a Web page difficult to view by people who are using devices without traditional browsers — such as PDAs or Web-enabled phones — to visit your site. And they can make your Web page nearly impossible to use by people using screen readers.

✦ **Pages are difficult to maintain and update.** Excessively nested tables create a confusing pile of code that is easy to break, hard to repair, and even more difficult to edit, expand, and modify. Edits that should take seconds can end up taking hours.

✦ **Pages are difficult to reuse when it's time to redesign.** With rigid table structures in place, it becomes impossible to implement new layouts. Your "new" design will amount to just changing out a few graphics — as long as the new graphics are the same size and shape as the originals.

When you're creating HTML documents, think about how the structure of the code will affect the site's visitors and maintenance of the site. Spending a little time considering the code saves a lot of time when you or your team needs to update or add to your site. Figure 2-4 shows an example of code that has been built with nested tables. Figure 2-5 is an example of the same information built with CSS. The use of CSS allows the designer to create the layout with much less code. The content of the page is easier to identify, and edits are easier because you need to apply only a few HTML tags as opposed to trying to figure out a complex table and inserting or deleting content from it.

Tables can also be difficult for smaller devices to handle. They don't have as much screen space, so it can be difficult to display content that is in nested tables — especially those that have specific widths included in the code. Try to picture an 800-pixel-wide table trying to be displayed on a handheld device. When you examine the code, it becomes easy to see which page would be easier to maintain or expand.

A table (properly coded, of course) is sometimes appropriate and necessary. Make sure you keep your table structure as simple as possible. Don't put tables inside the cells of another table unless you must.

The code to create a basic table with three rows and two columns is

```
<table>
   <tr>
      <th colspan="2" scope="col">Table Heading</th>
   </tr>
   <tr>
      <td>Content goes here</td><td>And here</td>
   </tr>
   <tr>
      <td>Content goes here</td><td>And here</td>
   </tr>
</table>
```

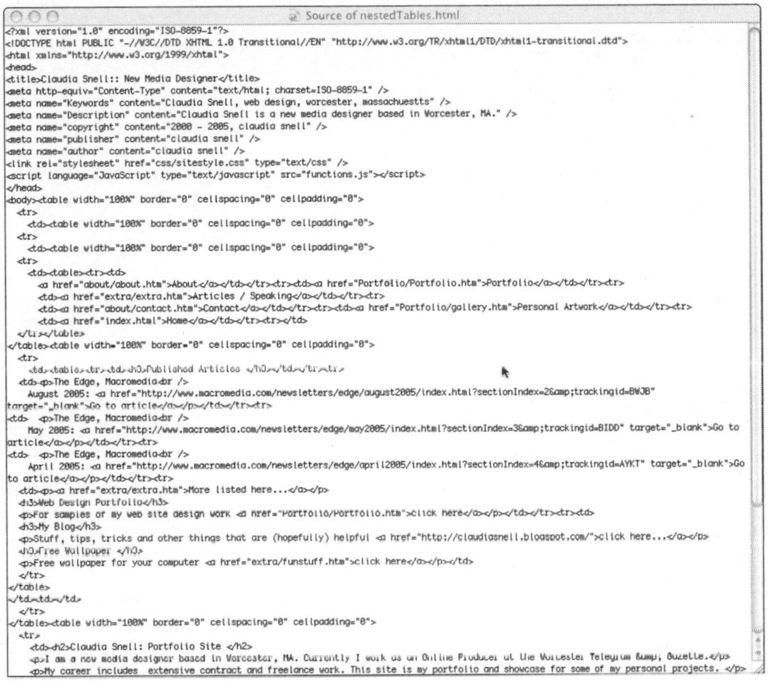

```
Source of nestedTables.html
<?xml version="1.0" encoding="ISO-8859-1"?>
<!DOCTYPE html PUBLIC "-//W3C//DTD XHTML 1.0 Transitional//EN" "http://www.w3.org/TR/xhtml1/DTD/xhtml1-transitional.dtd">
<html xmlns="http://www.w3.org/1999/xhtml">
<head>
<title>Claudia Snell:: New Media Designer</title>
<meta http-equiv="Content-Type" content="text/html; charset=ISO-8859-1" />
<meta name="Keywords" content="Claudia Snell, web design, worcester, massachuestts" />
<meta name="Description" content="Claudia Snell is a new media designer based in Worcester, MA." />
<meta name="copyright" content="2000 - 2005, claudia snell" />
<meta name="publisher" content="claudia snell" />
<meta name="author" content="claudia snell" />
<link rel="stylesheet" href="css/sitestyle.css" type="text/css" />
<script language="JavaScript" type="text/javascript" src="functions.js"></script>
</head>
<body><table width="100%" border="0" cellspacing="0" cellpadding="0">
  <tr>
    <td><table width="100%" border="0" cellspacing="0" cellpadding="0">
  <tr>
    <td><table width="100%" border="0" cellspacing="0" cellpadding="0">
  <tr>
    <td><table><tr><td>
      <a href="about/about.htm">About</a></td></tr><tr><td><a href="Portfolio/Portfolio.htm">Portfolio</a></td></tr><tr>
      <td><a href="extra/extra.htm">Articles / Speaking</a></td></tr><tr>
      <td><a href="about/contact.htm">Contact</a></td></tr><tr><td><a href="Portfolio/gallery.htm">Personal Artwork</a></td></tr><tr>
      <td><a href="index.html">Home</a></td></tr><tr></td>
  </tr></table>
</table><table width="100%" border="0" cellspacing="0" cellpadding="0">
  <tr>
    <td><table><tr><td><h3>Published Articles </h3></td></tr><tr>
  <td><p>The Edge, Macromedia<br />
    August 2005: <a href="http://www.macromedia.com/newsletters/edge/august2005/index.html?sectionIndex=2&amp;trackingid=BWJB"
target="_blank">Go to article</a></p></td></tr><tr>
<td>  <p>The Edge, Macromedia<br />
    May 2005: <a href="http://www.macromedia.com/newsletters/edge/may2005/index.html?sectionIndex=3&amp;trackingid=BIDD" target="_blank">Go to
article</a></p></td></tr><tr>
<td>  <p>The Edge, Macromedia<br />
    April 2005: <a href="http://www.macromedia.com/newsletters/edge/april2005/index.html?sectionIndex=4&amp;trackingid=AYKT" target="_blank">Go
to article</a></p></td></tr><tr>
  <td><p><a href="extra/extra.htm">More listed here...</a></p>
  <h3>Web Design Portfolio</h3>
  <p>For samples of my web site design work <a href="Portfolio/Portfolio.htm">click here</a></p></td></tr><tr><td>
  <h3>My Blog</h3>
  <p>Stuff, tips, tricks and other things that are (hopefully) helpful <a href="http://claudiasnell.blogspot.com/">click here...</a></p>
  <h3>Free Wallpaper </h3>
  <p>Free wallpaper for your computer <a href="extra/funstuff.htm">click here</a></p></td>
  </tr>
</table>
</td><td></td>
  </tr>
</table><table width="100%" border="0" cellspacing="0" cellpadding="0">
  <tr>
    <td><h2>Claudia Snell: Portfolio Site </h2>
    <p>I am a new media designer based in Worcester, MA. Currently I work as an Online Producer at the Worcester Telegram &amp; Gazette.</p>
    <p>My career includes  extensive contract and freelance work. This site is my portfolio and showcase for some of my personal projects. </p>
```

Figure 2-4: Example of nested table code within a page. Note how the sea of <td>s and <tr>s makes the code difficult to decipher.

Notice in this code that the first row of cells has a `<th>` tag. This represents *table heading*. The other tags in this table are `<tr>` for *table row* and `<td>` for *table data*. You might also notice that the `<th>` row has `colspan` and `scope`. Those two pieces of information, respectively, tell the browser that the first row is two columns wide (as in "column span") and that the table heading is for the columns instead of the rows. If the headings were in the first column, the `scope` would be `"row"`.

Coding a whole Web page

The following block of code — which is the code for a whole HTML document that is ready to work with the CSS document in Book III, Chapter 3 — shows just the basic structure of an HTML document; the content has been minimized to make it easier to see the code we want to focus on. If you type this code directly into your HTML editor, you will see a very plain document. By adding CSS, the page will become a well-designed and well-coded page. Add this code to the code in the "The head tag and what goes in it" section for the head elements, and you've got a whole page.

Note: The `begin header area` in this code refers to the top/banner portion of the visible page — not the head information discussed earlier in this chapter.

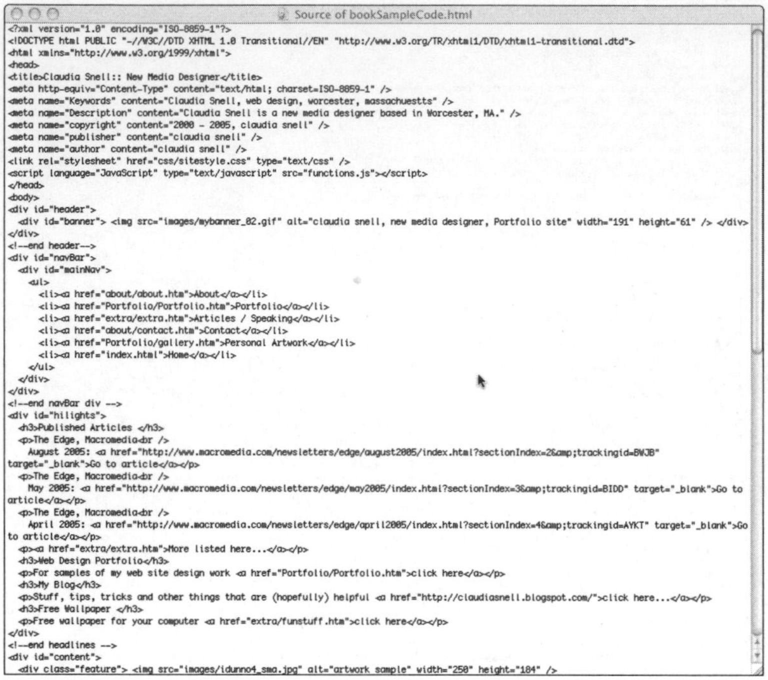

```
Source of bookSampleCode.html
<?xml version="1.0" encoding="ISO-8859-1"?>
<!DOCTYPE html PUBLIC "-//W3C//DTD XHTML 1.0 Transitional//EN" "http://www.w3.org/TR/xhtml1/DTD/xhtml1-transitional.dtd">
<html xmlns="http://www.w3.org/1999/xhtml">
<head>
<title>Claudia Snell:: New Media Designer</title>
<meta http-equiv="Content-Type" content="text/html; charset=ISO-8859-1" />
<meta name="Keywords" content="Claudia Snell, web design, worcester, massachuestts" />
<meta name="Description" content="Claudia Snell is a new media designer based in Worcester, MA." />
<meta name="copyright" content="2000 - 2005, claudia snell" />
<meta name="publisher" content="claudia snell" />
<meta name="author" content="claudia snell" />
<link rel="stylesheet" href="css/sitestyle.css" type="text/css" />
<script language="JavaScript" type="text/javascript" src="functions.js"></script>
</head>
<body>
<div id="header">
  <div id="banner"> <img src="images/mybanner_02.gif" alt="claudia snell, new media designer, Portfolio site" width="191" height="61" /> </div>
</div>
<!--end header-->
<div id="navBar">
  <div id="mainNav">
    <ul>
      <li><a href="about/about.htm">About</a></li>
      <li><a href="Portfolio/Portfolio.htm">Portfolio</a></li>
      <li><a href="extra/extra.htm">Articles / Speaking</a></li>
      <li><a href="about/contact.htm">Contact</a></li>
      <li><a href="Portfolio/gallery.htm">Personal Artwork</a></li>
      <li><a href="index.html">Home</a></li>
    </ul>
  </div>
</div>
<!--end navBar div -->
<div id="hilights">
  <h3>Published Articles </h3>
  <p>The Edge, Macromedia<br />
    August 2005: <a href="http://www.macromedia.com/newsletters/edge/august2005/index.html?sectionIndex=2&amp;trackingid=BWJB"
target="_blank">Go to article</a></p>
  <p>The Edge, Macromedia<br />
    May 2005: <a href="http://www.macromedia.com/newsletters/edge/may2005/index.html?sectionIndex=3&amp;trackingid=BIDD" target="_blank">Go to
article</a></p>
  <p>The Edge, Macromedia<br />
    April 2005: <a href="http://www.macromedia.com/newsletters/edge/april2005/index.html?sectionIndex=4&amp;trackingid=AYKT" target="_blank">Go
to article</a></p>
  <p><a href="extra/extra.htm">More listed here...</a></p>
  <h3>Web Design Portfolio</h3>
  <p>For samples of my web site design work <a href="Portfolio/Portfolio.htm">click here</a></p>
  <h3>My Blog</h3>
  <p>Stuff, tips, tricks and other things that are (hopefully) helpful <a href="http://claudiasnell.blogspot.com/">click here...</a></p>
  <h3>Free Wallpaper </h3>
  <p>Free wallpaper for your computer <a href="extra/funstuff.htm">click here</a></p>
</div>
<!--end headlines -->
<div id="content">
  <div class="feature"> <img src="images/idunno4_sma.jpg" alt="artwork sample" width="250" height="184" />
```

Figure 2-5: Example of the same page but coded with HTML and CSS. Cleaner, easier, friendlier to all.

```
<!DOCTYPE html PUBLIC "-//W3C//DTD XHTML 1.0
   Transitional//EN" "http://www.w3.org/TR/xhtml1/DTD/xhtml1-
   transitional.dtd">
<head>
<title>Claudia Snell:: New Media Designer</title>
<meta http-equiv="Content-Type" content="text/html; charset=
   ISO-8859-1" />
<meta name="Keywords" content="Claudia Snell, web design,
   worcester, massachusetts" />
<meta name="Description" content="Claudia Snell is a new
   media designer based in Worcester, MA." />
<meta name="copyright" content="2000 - 2005, claudia snell"
   />
<meta name="publisher" content="claudia snell" />
<meta name="author" content="claudia snell" />
<link rel="stylesheet" href="css/sitestyle.css" type=
   "text/css" />
<script language="JavaScript" type="text/javascript" src=
   "functions.js"></script>
</head>
<body>
<!-- begin header area -->
<div id="header">
   <div id="banner">
      <h1>Welcome to the site</h1>
```

```
        </div>
    </div>
    <!--end header / begin left nav bar-->
    <div id="navBar">
        <div id="mainNav">
            <ul>
                <li> <a href="#">About</a> </li>
                <li> <a href="#">Products</a> </li>
                <li> <a href="#">Contact</a> </li>
                <li> <a href="#">Home</a> </li>
            </ul>
        </div>
    </div>
    <!--add hilights here if you have them -->
    <div id="hilights">
        <h3>Come to our open house</h3>
        <p>Come visit us on April 1 for our first <a href="#">open
        house</a></p>
        <h3>Come to our other event</h3>
        <p>Come visit us on April 2 for our <a href="#">other
        event</a></p>
        <h3>Check out our latest project</h3>
        <p>Click here to see our <a href="#">latest project</a></p>
    </div>
    <!--end left nav bar / begin main content area -->
    <div id="content">
        <div class="main">
            <h2>Claudia Snell: Portfolio Site </h2>
            <p>This is my web site. This is a good place for some
        opening text</p>
        </div>
        <div class="subtopic">
            <h2>Another topic</h2>
            <p>Here is a sub topic on my page</p>
        </div>
    </div>
    <div class="subtopic">
        <h2>Another topic</h2>
        <p>Here is a sub topic on my page</p>
    </div>
    </div>
    <!--end main content area / begin footer -->
    <div id="footer">&copy; 2006 Claudia Snell | contact me |
        other important footer information here </div>
    <br />
    </body>
    </html>
```

The page that is generated by the preceding code is not very pretty to
look at. (See Figure 2-6.) Still, it is all ready to work with a CSS file to be

a well-designed Web page. Note in the head tag portion there is a line of code that links this HTML document to the CSS file:

```
<link rel="stylesheet" href="css/sitestyle.css" type="text/css" />
```

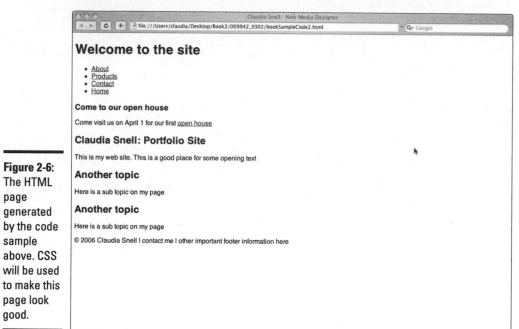

Figure 2-6:
The HTML page generated by the code sample above. CSS will be used to make this page look good.

Controlling layouts with CSS

The old style of building Web sites used a series of tables and nested tables to create rigid grids that held all the pieces of a page together. Remember, the original purpose of the Web was not to support great design, it was to convey information quickly.

The method of using tables to control layout was a misuse of the code to produce a visual effect. It used to be the best solution, but that was before CSS (Cascading Style Sheets) were developed. Another issue that slowed progress in the implementation of better techniques was browser support. In the early days of CSS-driven designs, the browsers didn't support them properly. Pages would sometimes have serious issues. Those times are gone now. CSS has been developed beyond a few font-formatting tricks and the major browsers now have good support for CSS 1 and 2.

The World Wide Web Consortium Web site (www.w3.org/) is a good place to go for information about CSS. CSS guru, Eric Meyer, has a Web site (http://meyerweb.com/eric/css/) that is also a good reference. If you're curious to see what others are doing with CSS, check out the CSS Zen Garden at www.csszengarden.com. All the designs are created using identical HTML with only the CSS and graphics files changing. The variety of layouts and design possibilities are amazing.

Book III, Chapter 3 shows you how to create a CSS document and make it work with your HTML document.

Helpful Development Practices

Here are some techniques that can help you as you work on your Web site projects:

✦ **Use comments in your code.** *Comments* are notes to yourself and other people who might have to work with your files. Whether you're working alone or in a group, commenting your code is an important habit to develop. Common things to include in comments are when the code was added to the document, what the piece of code does, who added it, and so on. Make sure your comments are clear and concise to avoid confusion and frustration. Remember, though, that some comments will be visible via View Source, so don't type things you don't want the general public to read.

You can comment your code whether you're writing HTML, CSS, Action-Script, JavaScript, or any other code. Scripting, markup, and programming languages have their own format for how to create comments. HTML comments are contained between <!-- and -->. Everything between the comment tags will be visible only to people who are editing the HTML document and to those who view source on your pages. CSS comments look like this: /* comment goes here */.

✦ **Use version control.** Make sure you have something in place to prevent members of the team from overwriting each other's work. Even if you're working solo, it is easy to accidentally overwrite a file. Make sure you have backups so you can recover the work if something does happen. Explore your software for version control options. For instance, Dreamweaver has some tools to help. Power users like tools like Visual Studio Visual SourceSafe 6.0.

In general, version control tools warn or prevent other members of your team from opening and working on files that are already open and being edited. They all work a little differently and some are more effective than others — that is, they prevent more than one person from opening and

Book III
Chapter 2

Making a Web Page
with HTML

working on a file instead of just issuing a warning that someone else is working on the file but letting a second person work on it anyway.

Other version and source control features include warning a user when she is trying to post an older version of a file to the server when the file that is currently on the server is newer and presumably has been posted by someone else very recently. Another way to make sure files don't get overwritten is to limit the number of people who have the power to publish files to the site. The designated person acts as a gatekeeper, making sure that members of the team are not overwriting each other's work.

Remember to also keep track of original versions of the photos associated with your site in case you need them later.

✦ **Keep communication open.** There cannot be enough communication between members of a Web team. The nature of the work makes it easy for members to run to their respective corners and hibernate until they're done with their piece. Typically, details of what each person is working on morphs, as planned techniques do not always work when they're put into practice. Communication is especially important when this happens.

For example, if your team decides to use HTML to deliver a company tour and then later discovers that Flash would be a better method, tell all team members about the change of plans. If someone else is developing the content for an HTML page and doesn't realize that you've changed direction, the time spent on content development has been wasted. In fact, the team needs extra time to develop the new content.

✦ **Organize your supporting files.** As you work on a site, you'll accumulate several files that aren't actual parts of the site. You will almost immediately start generating Word documents, Photoshop or Fireworks files, Illustrator files, Flash files, and a host of other files. Make a folder called something like Production Files to keep track of all these files. You should keep this folder with the site folder, but don't post it to your live site. You need to use these files when and if you need to revise your graphics or multimedia elements or if you need to refer back to original content documents. When you launch your site, burn a backup CD or DVD with the site and production files on it. Periodically make new backups.

✦ **Make all source documents available to everyone who will need to edit site elements.** Ensure that everyone on the team can edit or create new graphics as needed without having to try to completely re-create the original source files.

Chapter 3: Creating a Web Page Layout with HTML and CSS

In This Chapter

✔ Considering the benefits of using CSS

✔ Learning some simple CSS

✔ Using cool style tricks

I n Book III, Chapter 2 you explore a basic HTML document and find some basics about creating an HTML page. This chapter shows you how to create the accompanying Cascading Style Sheet (CSS) file. CSS is a simple language that is a flexible and powerful way to control the layouts of your Web pages. As your site grows, you will see huge benefits in ease of maintenance and the ability to repurpose or redesign sections of your site very quickly.

Introducing CSS

Before we jump into the mechanics of creating a Web page layout with HTML and CSS — what this chapter is all about — we first want to show you some reasons why using CSS is a good thing. Next, we tell you how you can use the View Source feature of a Web browser to examine other developers' code — it's a valuable way to see how things are done right (or wrong, as the case may be). We also quickly cover in this section how easy it is to use CSS with other tools, such as Dreamweaver.

Understanding why CSS can help your site — and you

We include many code examples in this chapter and the preceding one that show the old-fashioned HTML way of doing things — as compared to the new-fashioned CSS way. In some cases, such as with the borders and padding, the benefits of CSS are very clear. For example, you can apply borders to many different types of elements, such as paragraphs and bullets. You can also control the color, width, and style of borders with CSS. You can even specify that the borders appear only on some sides, such as the bottom and left, but not on others. HTML only allows for borders on tables, and those borders are either all the way around or none at all. In other cases, it might not be as clear to you until after you start to work with your site. But know that when you design your site with CSS, you're making things much easier for yourself. When using CSS, you can

✦ **Easily make changes to the presentation of your content.** Imagine having to find all the font tags and change them all in an extensive Web site. Simple Find and Replace often doesn't work because of the inconsistent way the tags are coded. It's possible to have hundreds of variations of the font tags that all look the same on the Web page but are coded differently, which makes Find and Replace utilities useless.

✦ **Easily discern the original meaning of your content.** When working with older, "anything that makes it look good" type techniques, you often cannot tell what the different parts of the page content are visually looking at it. Old-style HTML allows for using tags improperly, like applying properties to a font tag that makes a paragraph tag display as though it is a heading. Not easy to fix. If you manage to strip out the old font tags, you also strip out the visual cues that can help you to recode the page properly.

For example, if you set up your page as a block of content with `<br>` tags to separate it visually into paragraphs and `<font>` tags to make headings look different, it would be difficult to figure out what was what if the tags were disrupted or deleted. Also, users can create their own style sheets. The ability to create these style sheets is particularly important for people who are visually impaired, who develop their custom style sheets with the assumption that your paragraphs will be marked up as paragraphs and headings will be headings. If your site is not coded properly, it can make your site much more difficult for these individuals to use because their style sheets won't work as they expect them to.

✦ **Make your site friendly to all who visit — no matter where they are or what their situation.** Another reason to use CSS and HTML properly is that an increasing number of people are using the Web, and many of those people aren't using a computer to do it — they're using handhelds, phones, and other devices. In addition, some of your visitors don't have perfect vision and hearing, and many don't have a fancy computer with great speakers. The point is that the Web is more accessible than ever, and you have to be mindful of the wide variety of situations and visitors — and code your pages so that your visitors can easily use your site.

Again, some users will have customized style sheets so they can use the Internet. One reason a person would have a customized style sheet is to make font sizes larger or to specify how a screen reader will aurally signal different parts of a document to compensate for visual impairments. Information about aural style sheets can be found on the World Wide Web Consortium site at `www.w3.org/TR/REC-CSS2/aural.html`.

We spend time in this chapter showing how true the preceding bullets are, but first, we want to give you some quick notes about the View Source technique and integrating CSS with other tools.

Checking the source

To get a look at the CSS of a page, use the View Source technique. To view the source code of a page in Internet Explorer, for example, you can either right-click in your browser window and select View Source, or choose View⇨ Source on your browser menu bar. (You can also view source with other browsers. The location of view source might be different but is found under a similar view-type menu.) Look for a line of code in the <head> section of the page that refers to the CSS file *or* the actual CSS in the head of the file. If you find a reference to the CSS file, you can use your browser to view the file (more about that in a minute). CSS can also be applied within the document itself, but that method defeats one of the main strengths of CSS — the reusability of code that is kept in only one place.

You'll find it helpful to save the HTML code so you can play with it on your own. When you view the source, look for signs of CSS. Inline and embedded styles are easy to see. You can also get a look at external style sheets by looking for the path to the file in the head tag. Assuming the URL of the Web site is `http://www.examplesite.com`, the URL of the CSS would be `http://www.examplesite.com/css/sitestyles.css`. By typing the URL of the CSS into your browser window, you can view the CSS:

```
<link rel="stylesheet" href="css/sitestyle.css" type="text/css" />
```

Save a copy of the CSS and HTML files so you can play with them and see how they interact. To see a lot of examples of the power of using CSS to control your visual display of a page, visit The CSS Zen Garden at `www.csszengarden.com`. The CSS Zen Garden is a project created by Dave Shea for the purpose of encouraging and supporting the use of CSS design. There are a series of page designs that are all very different in appearance, but they all share the same HTML code; only the CSS changes from design to design.

As we mention in Book III, Chapter 2, you can learn by example. Look at what others are doing and use View Source to see how they are doing it. To check the CSS of a site, look for the link to the CSS file that you can use to download the site's CSS file.

For example, Claudia's site's URL is

`www.jcnewmedia.com`

If you go to that site and choose View⇨Source from Internet Explorer's menu, a file with the HTML for her site appears. About 16 lines from the top, you see the path to her CSS file:

```
<link rel="stylesheet" href="sitestyle.css" type="text/css" />
```

To access the CSS file, type this into your browser's address bar:

www.jcnewmedia.com/sitestyle.css

The CSS file opens, and you can view it or save a copy for reference.

Using CSS with other tools

As you begin to work with HTML and CSS, you will notice that there are many tools available to help you. Dreamweaver has excellent HTML and CSS support and many tools to help you along the way. Figure 3-1 shows an example of a handy Dreamweaver tool — a Color picker that pops up automatically when you need it. If you type **color:** into a CSS document in Dreamweaver, the Color picker pops up to help you. That way, you don't have to memorize all the hexadecimal color values possible — you can simply click the color that you like.

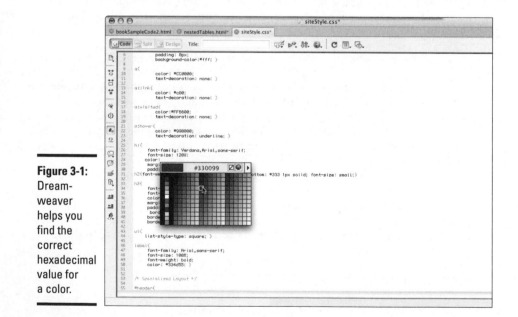

Figure 3-1: Dreamweaver helps you find the correct hexadecimal value for a color.

Hexadecimal colors

HTML and CSS "see" colors in special code called *hexadecimal code*. It's a series of six numbers and/or letters that represent the amounts of red, green, and blue that are present in a color. Red, green, and blue (or RGB) are the primary colors for light — and because colors are displayed by using light, RGB are the primary colors of computers, too.

As you look at a Web page's code, you might see code that looks like this: #000000 or #993366 — these are hexadecimal values for colors. When the browser reads the code #000000, it reads 00 for the value of red, 00 for the value of green, and 00 for the value of blue, and thus generates the color black. Or when the browser reads the code #993366, it reads 99 for the value of red, 33 for the value of green, and 66 for the value of blue, and generates a reddish purple color.

You might be wondering, how can I keep track of which numbers stand for which colors? Don't worry; many charts are available (one site that has a chart is W3Schools at www.w3schools.com/html/html_colors.asp), and virtually all Web design or graphics software has a color-picker tool that gives you hexadecimal values. (See the "Using CSS with

other tools" section in this chapter for an example.)

In CSS, you can use shorthand to represent Web-safe hexadecimal colors. To do so, you take the first number of each pair and use the three-digit shorthand equivalent of the whole six-digit hexadecimal color. So the shorthand for #993366, for example, is #936. The browser assumes that the other three numbers are 9, 3, and 6 (no commas or spaces in the code itself, just #936). But the shorthand works only on hexadecimal colors that have pairs for the values of red, blue, and green. NonWeb-safe colors often do not. For instance, the code #efefef represents a nonWeb-safe gray. That particular code doesn't have a valid shorthand because by typing #eee you would be telling the browser that the color is #eeeeee, which is not the same at all.

Hexadecimal values work in both HTML and CSS. They also work on all elements that can take a color value.

If you want to know more, check out *HTML 4 for Dummies,* 5th edition, by Ed Tittel and Mary Burmeister (Wiley Publishing, ISBN 0-7645-8917-2); it includes a super-size Cheat Sheet with a handy hexadecimal color chart.

Ways of Working with CSS

There are three ways that CSS can be implemented on your pages:

✦ **Inline:** *Inline CSS* refers to styles that are directly in the content. This method is the least desirable type because it affects only the content the styles are directly associated with.

✦ **Embedded in the head of the HTML document:** These styles offer more flexibility because they can be applied to many elements in the document, such as all the paragraphs. These styles will not, however, affect parts of other documents.

✦ **External:** To have styles that affect all the pages of a site, you need to create an external CSS file and create a link to that file in the head section of your HTML documents. This third way enables you to take advantage of the quick site-wide layout control discussed earlier in this chapter.

Note: These methods can be used alone or in combination with each other. If you do use more than one method, you must know about the Cascade. *The Cascade* refers to the fact that the style that is closest to an element is the one that takes precedence. For example, say you have styles set up for paragraphs in your external CSS file, and you decide that you need a special treatment for paragraphs on one page of your site. You can set up those styles in the header. The CSS in the header will take precedence over the CSS in the external CSS file because it is closer to the paragraphs of that page. If you then decide that one paragraph in that same document needs a third treatment, you apply inline CSS to just that paragraph. That paragraph — and only that one — will be styled by the inline style.

Inline styles

Inline styles are coded directly into the body of your document. For example, take a look at the following HTML for a paragraph:

```
<p style="color:#000000;">This would be black text</p>
```

While these are pretty quick to add on the fly, we don't recommend this technique. In essence, you're trading an old style of coding that created hard-to-maintain sites for a new flavor of the same thing. For example, in the code that follows, you can see that this style is applied directly within the <p> tag and will affect only this one instance of a paragraph. No other paragraphs will take on the attributes unless you apply the same style attributes to them.

```
<p><font color="#000000">This would be black text</font></p>
```

The problem with coding this way is that if you decide you want to change the color of your text on your site — or anything else coded with inline styles — you have to find *all* the places that you used these inline styling techniques and change them. It also makes for a lot of clutter that isn't necessary.

Styles embedded in the head of the document

When you *embed styles,* you create your CSS styles in the head portion of your HTML document and refer to them in the HTML, like this:

```
<head>
<title>Claudia Snell:: New Media Designer</title>
<style type="text/css">
<!--
p {color: #990099}
-->
</style>
</head><body><p>This text would be purple</p></body>
</html>
```

The advantage to using this technique is that you can have some specialized styles embedded in just one HTML document. This can come in handy if you want a special page for an event or some other reason.

Use this technique to implement styles for that HTML document only. The other pages of your site aren't affected by styles that are embedded this way or created inline. If you're creating styles that you intend to use throughout your site (which is most often the case), don't use this technique to do it. You'll end up with a site that is a pain in the neck to update because you'll have to open each document and edit each embedded style individually — unless you feel brave and want to use the Find and Replace feature of your software.

External style sheets

Using an external style sheet is generally the preferred method — especially if you want to implement your styles across the whole site. All the CSS are created in an external file, or files if you have a more complex site. The files are linked to the HTML document in the head portion of the HTML, like this:

```
<head>
<link rel="stylesheet" href="css/sitestyle.css" type="text/
    css" />
</head>
```

This code links the CSS file to the HTML document. Notice that the external style sheet's file extension is .css. When a visitor goes to your site, the CSS is loaded along with the HTML, and the page looks great. The major advantage to this technique is that if you decide you want to change anything about your design or layout, you can make a site-wide change simply by changing the styles in the CSS file. There is no need to open the HTML files to edit them. Of course, you'll want to preview your pages before publishing them, but that's the rule for all Web pages.

It is also possible to create more than one style sheet and link them to the same HTML document like this:

```
<head>
<link rel="stylesheet" href="css/sitestyle.css" type="text/
    css" />
<link rel="stylesheet" href="css/photogallery.css" type=
    "text/css" />

</head>
```

The benefit of doing this is that your site can have a unified look and feel, but you can also implement some specialized styles throughout just one section — for instance, you can implement a color-coding scheme by using this technique.

The Cascade (which is the name for how the priority of styles work together) is a strange but useful friend. The most basic explanation of how it works is that whichever style declaration is closest to an element is the one that will take effect. Sort of . . . in some cases, styles interact in unexpected ways. Be on the lookout for multiple styles applied to the same type of element or styles that will affect positioning of elements in relation to each other, such as margins and paddings. If you place a margin on a paragraph and a padding on a table, the two will interact when you put a paragraph in a table. You may need to adjust your styles when things don't look the way you expect. Don't get discouraged; the best way to master CSS is to get in there and work with it.

Commenting your code

Each type of coding has its own language style or *syntax* (it's like grammar for computers). You must use proper syntax when creating any code. If you don't, the code won't work — or it might do unexpected things. Even comments have proper markup and/or syntax. If you don't create code comments correctly, the browser may see it as content or code and treat it as such instead of keeping it hidden the way it should. (See Book III, Chapter 2 for information about using comments in general.) In CSS, comments look like this:

```
/*Banner and header styles - creates background color and
    places images*/
#banner{width: 100%; background-color: #000;}
#banner p{color: #fff;}
#header{border-bottom: 1px #333 solid;}
/*End banner and header styles*/
```

Note how the comments are between a /* and */, which signals to the browser that the information contained is a comment and is to be ignored.

Keep your style sheet clean and easy to understand by

✦ **Grouping styles that work together.** In the previous example, the `#banner` style establishes the width and background color of the banner area, and the `#banner p` style specifies that paragraphs within the banner area will be white. Grouping styles that work together this way in your CSS file is a good thing; that way, seeing all the pieces is easier.

✦ **Placing a comment at the beginning of a group of styles stating what the styles are affecting and what they're doing.** Keep it short, but make sure it's informative enough so that others (or yourself in six months) will understand it.

✦ **Including a comment at the end of the group.** By doing this, you keep the styles organized and reduce confusion about where one set begins and one ends.

Creating a CSS Document

It's time to start creating your first CSS document. A *CSS document* is the file where the styles you create are kept. The term CSS can refer to this file or to the actual styles. It can be confusing, but as you get more comfortable with the way everything works, you'll also get used to the lingo of Web design. For the sake of simplicity, we work with the HTML that we create in Book III, Chapter 2 to create a simple design that helps you get your footing as you set off into the Web design wilderness. While the actual styles work as inline, embedded, or external style sheets (which we explain in the preceding section), the examples given here refer to styles that are external.

CSS styles are made up of three parts:

✦ **Selector:** Specifies what the style will affect.

✦ **Property:** Indicates what exactly will be affected (font, color, background, and so on).

✦ **Value of the property:** Indicates how the property will be affected (fonts will be black and bold for instance).

The other thing to notice is that there are different types of selectors or ways of attaching styles to parts of your HTML content. Some affect HTML tags directly (`<p>`, `<table>`, `<body>`). Other styles create classes or IDs. Classes and ID's are a bit more complicated and are explained later in the chapter.

**Book III
Chapter 3**

**Creating a Web
Page Layout with
HTML and CSS**

Setting default selectors

As you get started, there are going to be some common elements that you want to create styles for to ensure a unified site style. Default paragraph, link, and heading styles are examples of these. These are all styles that will affect HTML tags directly; they are your most general default values for things like colors and fonts. Those types of styles are important, and we explore those in the next section.

You can start your CSS document by listing the default selectors you want to create. This helps you get started and ensures that you won't forget something very basic as you get into developing your CSS file:

```
body{}
p{}
h1{}
h2{}
h3{}
ul{}
li{}
```

These are some, but not all of the basic elements you will want to make sure you create styles for.

At this point, it's easy to begin to write your *base styles,* the styles for things like paragraphs, links, tables, headings, and other common elements that will appear on your site. These will serve as the basic default values for each element but can be changed by creating custom styles. We cover this in more depth later in this chapter. For right now, we focus on the basic parts of a CSS style. The *syntax* (or grammar) for writing CSS is

```
selector {property: value;
    property: value;
    property: value;}
```

A style can have several `property:value` pairs, or just one. A style can also have several selectors. For example, the style that follows has four selectors, all of which happen to be headers:

```
h1, h2, h3, h4 {font-weight: bold; color: #990000;}
```

So, here's an example of a style with one selector and five `property:value` pairs:

```
body{
      font-family: Verdana,Arial,sans-serif;
      color: #000000;
      margin: 0px;
      padding: 0px;
      background-color:#ffffff; }
```

The preceding example does the following:

+ Uses the default font of Verdana with Arial or sans serif as alternatives in case Verdana is not available on the user's machine.

+ Specifies that the default color of text is black (#000000).

+ Specifies that the HTML document should entirely fill the browser window with no margin (0px) or *padding* (0px) — spacing — between the edge of the browser window and the content of the page.

+ Creates a default background color of white for the whole site (#ffffff).

Setting class and ID selectors

The other types of styles are class and ID selectors. Class selectors can be applied to any element in your HTML document. ID selectors can be applied to only one element on a page. There are also differences in how these types of styles are applied.

Class selectors

Class selectors are enhancements to your default styles. You create them if you want to have more than one style of paragraph. For instance, suppose you set your default paragraph to be a straight, black, Verdana type with a margin of 5 pixels, but you also want to have a special paragraph type to emphasize a point. You would create the following styles:

```
p {color:#000000; font-family: Verdana, Arial, sans-serif;}
.special {color: #ffffff; background-color: #333333}
```

The first line, as you might already realize, establishes your defaults for paragraphs on your Web page. In the second line, .special is a class selector. This line tells the Web browser that when you assign the special class to a paragraph, the font of that paragraph should be white (#ffffff), and the background for that paragraph should be dark gray (#333333). As you look at it, notice that the selector starts with a period this time. This is important. This is the proper grammar for *this is a class selector.* You'll see that ID selectors have their own syntax (or grammar). You must use this syntax correctly and apply the styles according to that syntax, or they will not work properly.

In your HTML, you would use the following code to create a paragraph with the default styles:

```
<p>A regular paragraph would look like this</p>
```

And you would use this code to create a paragraph with the class styles you set up in your CSS:

```
<p class="special">A special paragraph would look like this</p>
```

In this example, the `.special` class can be applied to any element, such as a bullet in a list, a table cell, a paragraph, or any other element. You can also create the `special` class for use just with paragraphs like this:

```
p.special{color: #ffffff; background-color: #333333}
```

You might notice that the preceding example has no font-family property. You don't need to specify a new property unless you want to use a value that is different from the default. A good practice is to declare your font values in either the body selector or the p selector of your CSS. Then the fonts will be the same throughout your document, unless you indicate otherwise. If you decide you'd like to use a different font on a particular element, create a class and declare a new value for the property. When you apply the class to an element in your HTML document, it ignores the default setting you have made in the body selector in favor of the class values.

The general rule is that the `property:value` pair closest to the element wins, sort of. The more specific styles take precedence over less specific ones. So, a general paragraph selector will lose out to a more specific Class selector, which in turn will lose out to an ID selector.

In cases where nothing has been declared, the next value is used. So, using our example, the `special` paragraph would change its font color to white, its background color to dark gray, but would keep the font-family as specified in the `<p>` tag because no new font-family was declared. There are also other things that can affect how styles interact, but discussing those are beyond the scope of this chapter. You can find more information at the World Wide Web Consortium Web site at `www.w3.org/Style/CSS`.

Notice that, in these example styles, the class selector looks a little different than the tag selector — in this case, we're using the HTML tag itself to select content for styling. So, if you use a tag selector of p, then all paragraphs will pick up the style. You don't need to apply any extra code (other than the proper paragraph tags) in the HTML document, unlike the class and ID selectors, which require that you add some extra code so the browser knows where to apply the style.

So, to refresh where we are, with tag selectors, you just start with the tag. Class selectors start with a . (period) — this is an important thing to remember. The syntax rules of CSS must be followed carefully or the CSS won't take affect for the particular selector or property that is incorrect.

ID selectors

An *ID selector* is the third way that styles can be applied to content on your site. In general, you use these as a group of styles that affect several pieces of your content that work together — such as navigation or sidebar content. There can only be one instance of an ID tag per HTML document. ID tags are good for creating content groups with accompanying CSS that all work as a unit. An example of this in action is a CSS menu. By using HTML bulleted lists and a group of ID selectors, a designer can create a CSS menu that is easy to update, works well for all users, and is easy on the download times.

When you look at the code of an HTML document that works with CSS, you might see code that looks like this:

```
<div id="navBar">
    <div id="mainNav">
        <ul>
            <li> <a href="#">About</a> </li>
            <li> <a href="#">Products</a> </li>
            <li> <a href="#">Contact</a> </li>
            <li> <a href="#">Home</a> </li>
        </ul>
    </div>
</div>
```

The "mainNav" and "navBar" sections of this HTML example use an ID selector for its style information — it's marked in HTML with the `<div>` tag, which encapsulates the content to be included in the style in the code. In this sample, two sets of ID selectors are used together to create the effect of *rollover buttons* (buttons on a Web site that change appearance when you place your cursor over them), but without using JavaScript or graphics (the usual way of creating this effect). The ID selector information for this particular example looks like this:

```
#navBar ul a:link, #navBar ul a:visited {display: block;}
#navBar ul {list-style: none; margin: 0; padding: 0;}
#navBar{
        float: left;
        width: 20%;
        height:450px;
        margin: 0px;
        padding: 0px;
        background-color: #eeeeee;
        border-right: 1px solid #cccccc;
        border-bottom: 1px solid #cccccc; }

#mainNav{
        position: relative;
        margin: 0px;
```

```
            padding: 0px;
            border-bottom: 1px solid #cccccc;
            font-size: 90%;
            color:#000000; }

#mainNav h3{
            padding: 10px 0px 2px 10px; }

#mainNav a {
            display: block;
            border-top: 1px solid #cccccc;
            padding: 2px 0px 2px 10px; }

#mainNav a:hover{
            background-color: #dddddd; }
```

The preceding code, when applied to a bulleted list, will create a menu bar that interacts with users when they roll their cursor over the "button" areas. The visual cue of this effect helps users understand that they have their cursor over a link. These styles

Set the display of the list items to "block."

Remove the bullets and set the margins and paddings of the list items to 0.

Specify the position, color, borders, and size of the navigation bar itself.

Set the borders and display attributes of the links themselves.

The last style sets the color of the background of the links when the user's cursor is over it.

Note the new syntax introduced here. ID selectors are indicated by starting with a #. Also notice that ID selectors are implemented in the HTML with `<div id="`*selectorname*`">` *content* `</div>`. There is no need to apply styles to each element between the `<div>` tags. Everything contained between the `<div>` tags is seen as part of the whole. The browser understands that an `<h3>` heading occurring within the `<div id="`*selectorname*`">` `</div>` tags is to be styled according to the #mainNav h3 properties and values set in the style sheet. Again, if no style is set for an element, the default values are used.

In Figures 3-2 and 3-3, you can see that the difference between a basic HTML bulleted list and one with CSS can be very dramatic.

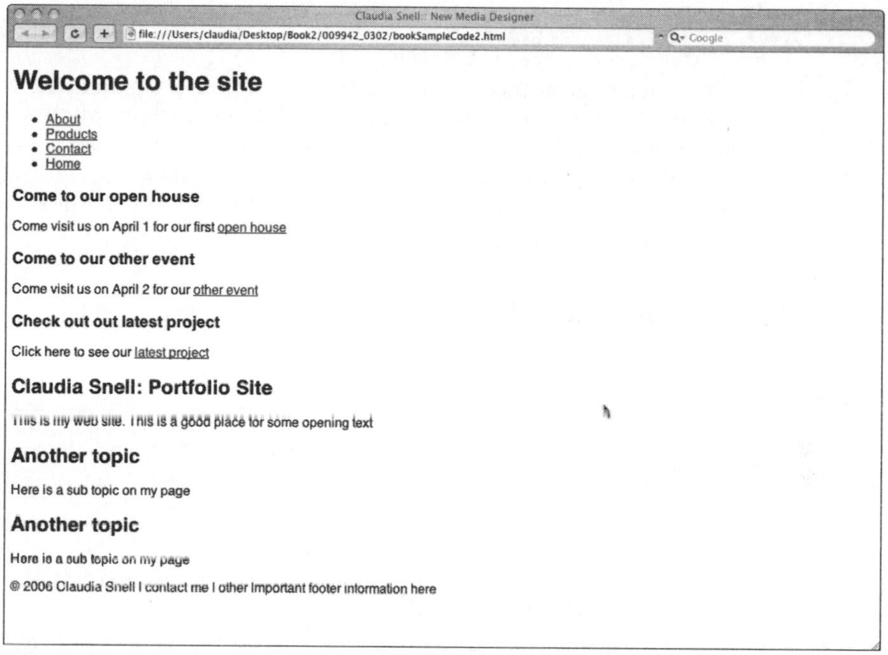

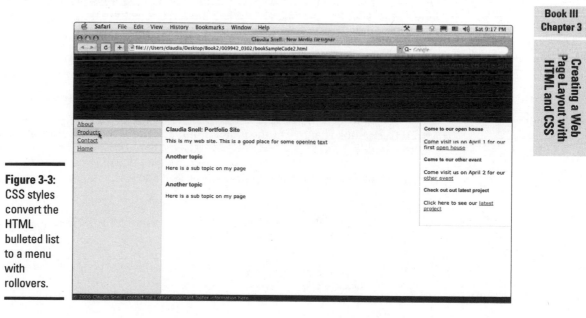

Figure 3-2:
An HTML bulleted list without CSS.

Figure 3-3:
CSS styles convert the HTML bulleted list to a menu with rollovers.

Special Effects with CSS

There are a few tricks that you can do with CSS that you can't do with HTML. You can create custom rollover effects like the ones we show you in the ID selector example (see the preceding section), and you can set custom looks for links on your page. Everyone has seen the default, brightly colored, underlined links of HTML. CSS allows you to style those links in a more aesthetically pleasing way.

Styling your links

You can set a specific color for everything that has an <a> tag (links are created in HTML by using <a href="http://www.linkgoeshere.html">), like so:

```
a{
      color: #CC0000;
      text-decoration: none; }
```

This style automatically works on all link tags in your HTML document because it uses a tag selector.

Or . . . you can spice up the way your links look by creating styles for the different states, which are link, visited link, hover, and active. We go into more detail about these next:

✦ **Visited:** A link is considered visited when the user has clicked it. The CSS selector for this is a:link.

✦ **Hover:** A link is in the hover state when the user's cursor moves over it. The CSS selector for this is a:hover.

✦ **Active:** A link is active at the moment it is clicked. The CSS selector for this is a:active.

Here is what the CSS code for these settings looks like:

```
a:link{
      color: #c00;
      text-decoration: none; }

a:visited{
      color:#FF6600;
      text-decoration: none; }

a:hover{
      color: #990000;
      text-decoration: underline; }
```

```
a:active{
      color: #990000;
      text-decoration: underline; }
```

As with other selectors, you can also nest these together:

```
a:hover, a:active{color:#990000; text-decoration: underline;}
```

Note also that you can have more than one set of these selectors. You can create a default set and then create others for use in different areas of your page, such as the footer:

```
#footer{
      clear: both;
      border: 1px solid #cccccc;
      font-size: 75%;
      color: #ffcc66;
      background-color:#000000; }
```

```
#footer a:link{color:#ffcc66; }
#footer a:visited{color:#ff0000; }
#footer a:hover{color:#ffffcc; }
#footer a:active{color:#FF6666; }
```

Cool headlines

Another interesting thing you can do with CSS is add some style to your heading tags.

```
h2{font-weight: bold;
color:#333333;
border-bottom: #333 1px solid;
font-size: small;}
```

Figure 3-4 shows how this code affects the <h2> tags in the HTML document. Note how the underline extends beyond the end of the text, making the heading a nice, page-separating device. Traditional HTML underlining is constrained to the length of the text, but CSS styles stretch across, making them more attractive and useful as page dividers.

Custom padding and margins

In CSS, you can set custom padding and margins. With plain HTML, you can set a padding value, but it's the same on all four sides. Same goes for margins. With CSS, you can set top, right, bottom, and left independently — you can have four completely different values! The flexibility this allows is a tremendous help to designers and makes *spacer graphics* a thing of the past. The old, spacer graphic technique was to use transparent .gif files or nested tables with tiny spacer cells in them to try to get nice layouts. These techniques create very messy, hard-to-maintain code. And it's a nightmare for anyone trying to visit your Web site with devices other than browsers. (Screen readers for blind users become confused in the sea of weird table structures and unnecessary .gif files.)

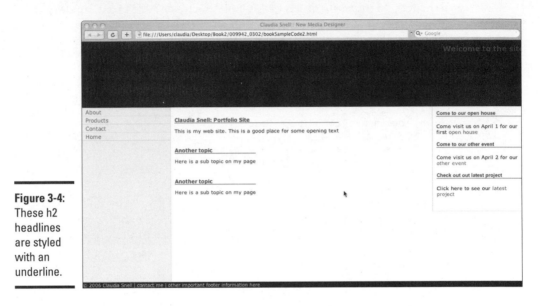

Figure 3-4: These h2 headlines are styled with an underline.

Figure 3-5 shows the CSS box model, which is the way that browsers and other devices actually see your content. Padding settings affect the space between the content and the "box" that contains it. Margin settings affect the actual space around the content. For more on padding and margins and how to use them effectively, visit the W3Schools CSS tutorials and reference at www.w3schools.com/css.

Custom borders

Just like padding and margins, in HTML you either have a border all the way around something or you don't. Also, you're limited to what you can apply a border to.

CSS allows you to put a border in just the place you want it. If you want just a top border, set border-top values, and you'll have only a top border. You can also apply borders to many more types of elements, such as heading tags and paragraphs. CSS borders also have more values to choose from. Designers can choose colors, positioning, thickness . . . and some browsers support type (solid lines, dotted lines, double lines, and so on).

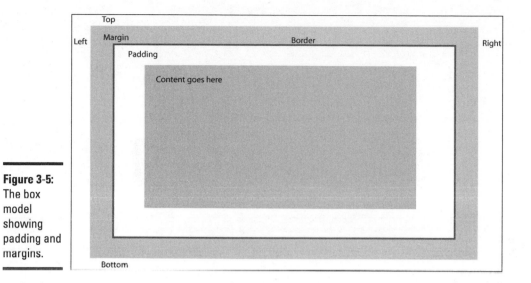

Figure 3-5:
The box model showing padding and margins.

REMEMBER

Figure 3-5 shows where the borders will be placed in relation to the margins and padding. Keep this in mind because it can affect your layout by placing borders in ways that you didn't intend — too close to the content for instance.

Book III Chapter 3

Creating a Web Page Layout with HTML and CSS

Chapter 4: Introducing Web and Graphics Software

In This Chapter

✔ Getting your graphics software

✔ Looking at Web-design software

✔ Taking a tour of Photoshop

✔ Getting to know the tools of the trade

Many tools are available to help you with the hands-on tasks of Web site design and maintenance. Eventually, choosing the right tools can be a matter of personal preference, but we do know of a few must-have tools for every Web designer. This chapter gives you a brief overview of these must-have tools plus a quick-and-dirty tour of Photoshop CS2.

Choosing Graphics Software

So many graphics software packages are available and so many manufacturers tout that their product can do everything and anything that you might be confused when choosing graphics programs. First, figure out what kind of work you want to do and then buy industry-standard software for that work. If you plan on creating lots of vector graphics, for instance, look for software that specializes in that; if you plan to work with photos, look for software that has tools for that. By sticking to industry-standard software, you can ensure better compatibility with other designers, better resources, better employability as a designer, better toolsets, and with practice, better overall quality of work.

Adobe Photoshop

The industry-standard software for working with bitmapped graphics is Adobe Photoshop. Photoshop offers a powerful set of tools that allows you to create and work with any graphics you need for your site, from concept to completion.

Bitmap versus vector images, part 1

The trick to successful graphics creation is understanding the strengths and weaknesses of the different formats and types of graphics. *Bitmapped images* are made up of pixels (tiny dots of color) laid out on a grid (or mapped). Think of a bitmap as a screen equivalent of a printed image — lots of dots that, together, make a picture.

Computer monitors display images at 72 or 96 dots per inch (dpi). Sometimes, this is referred to as ppi (for *pixels per inch*). When you prepare graphics for a Web page, make sure you save them with 72 dpi. By doing so, you make the file sizes smaller without making the image on-screen look worse.

Printers work with 150–300 dpi. This is why 72-dpi images don't look great when you print them. While it might be tempting to use higher resolutions to make your images look better, it

doesn't work that way. Always remember that larger files download slower, which is bad for your users.

Bitmapped images resize smaller fairly well. So an image that is 400px by 600px ("pixels" is abbreviated as px) downsizes to 200px by 300px fairly well. But scaling images up is another story. When making an image larger, the dimensions are made larger, but the amount of information stays the same. The computer has to make its best guess as to what color the additional dots that are needed to enlarge the picture should be. This is called *interpolation* and creates very jagged-looking images. If you've tried to scale up an image and noticed little stairs appearing along the edges of elements in the image, you have seen the effect of trying to scale up. This figure shows a bitmap image that has been scaled up.

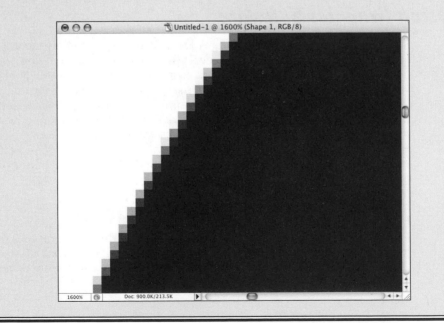

People in many different aspects of working with photos and graphics all use Photoshop. Photographers, designers, editors, and video professionals all use it because of its superior tools and vast number of uses. With Photoshop, you can create all original graphics, draw artwork, adjust or manipulate photos, apply effects, resize, optimize — virtually anything you might want to do with images is possible with Photoshop. Figure 4-1 gives you a peek at the Photoshop interface. The "Touring Photoshop CS2" section, later in this chapter, introduces you to the Photoshop interface and some of the program's features.

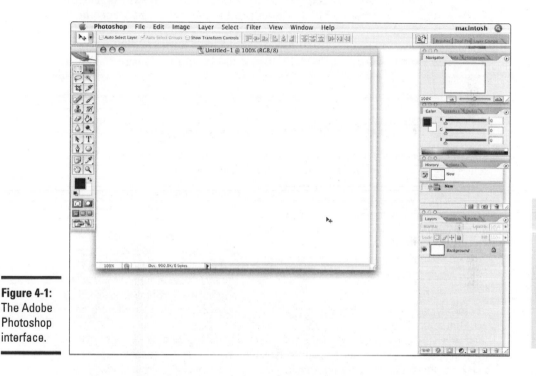

Figure 4-1:
The Adobe
Photoshop
interface.

Book III
Chapter 4

Introducing Web
and Graphics
Software

Adobe Illustrator

The industry standard for creating vector graphics is Adobe Illustrator. Like Photoshop, this tool has a very powerful set of tools but specializes in creating vector images. If you plan on creating logos or line art, this is an important piece of software to have. It's also useful to own if you want to do Flash design. Flash works well with vectors — all the drawing tools in Flash are vector based. By adding Illustrator to your set of tools, you can create Flash-friendly illustrations and other artwork. Figure 4-2 gives you a look at the

Adobe Illustrator interface. Notice how it is very similar to the Photoshop interface. Another benefit of sticking with industry standards and especially products from Adobe is that their interfaces share similar features. They also work together to help users get the job done more efficiently. More about integrated workflows is discussed throughout this book.

Other professional-grade graphics software

Other graphics software that you might encounter includes: Adobe Fireworks, Adobe FreeHand, and Adobe Flash. (Fireworks, FreeHand, and Flash are formerly Macromedia products. Adobe and Macromedia have merged.) The Adobe products have similar features, enabling designers to move easily from one product to another. There are also a few professionals who use Corel products: Painter, Paint Shop Pro, and CorelDRAW.

Bitmap versus vector images, part 2

Vector images are made up of mathematical statements that define individual objects that are made up of points, lines, and fills. Think geometry class. Because they're created by math, they scale up and down very well. They're also relatively easy to edit because the elements are separate objects as opposed to a series of self-contained dots. Designers can select an element, move points, and change properties of the lines and fills very easily.

Vector art works well for logos and other line art. Due to the nature of how they're created, they have very clean lines. The downside is that they don't do well with pictures and other types of images that require lots of tonal changes and soft transitions between those tones.

You will need to convert (or *rasterize*) vector graphics into bitmaps before using them on a Web page — with the exception of vector art created in Flash. The Flash player supports vector graphics where browsers don't. Some plug-ins that are available can support vectors, but not many people download and install them. The main strength of vector art is that you can

have very clean logos and line art that can be scaled to any size you need.

If someone sends you a graphic file, you can tell if it's a vector or bitmap by examining the pieces in your graphics software. Depending on the software you use and the software the graphic was created in, you may get a warning that shapes will be rasterized. This message is telling you that there are vector-based shapes in the graphic that the software is having trouble dealing with and so the software will convert the shape into a bitmap. Another way you can tell the difference between vector and bitmap is by selecting the objects within the graphic. If a series of lines, curves, and dots appears all around the edge of the object, you've got a vector. If however, you get a box that contains the object or no lines at all, you've got a bitmap.

Note: Simply opening a graphic in a vector graphics program, like Adobe Illustrator, and then saving it as an Illustrator file does not make the graphic a vector. Remember, a vector is a math-based graphic — think geometry class, lines, curves, and points.

Figure 4-2:
The Adobe Illustrator interface.

Considering Web-Design Software

While you can code Web pages entirely in Notepad (and some folks do it), we advise you to look at the Web-design software packages that are available. Some Web developers will tell you that these packages are bloated, and they write bad code. While there might be some truth to this, it's mostly just coder snobbery. You should choose tools that work best for you. The bloat they're referring to is actually a set of helpers and features that, if used properly, can help you be a better Web designer.

You shouldn't, however, substitute software helpers for learning HTML (HyperText Markup Language), CSS (Cascading Style Sheets), and the other technologies you intend to use. If you don't learn how it all really works under the hood, you can't fix problems beyond the software's capabilities. You also won't be able to clean up the mistakes that WYSIWYG (what you see is what you get, or *WHIZ-ee-wig*) editors often make — such as leaving tags behind after you've deleted the content.

In actuality, most people can't tell the difference between pages hand coded in Notepad and those hand coded with Dreamweaver. In fact, Dreamweaver has many tools that can help you write better code than someone with a stripped-back text editor. For instance, you can set up Dreamweaver to high-light coding errors in bright yellow. Someone using a text editor isn't alerted to simple typos in the code, a problem that can result in a really messed-up-looking page. Dreamweaver shows you exactly where your mistake is, and tells you what the mistake is — with a plain text editor you're left to find and figure it out for yourself. See Chapters 5, 6, and 7 of this minibook for more about using Dreamweaver for your Web-design projects.

While Adobe Dreamweaver is the industry standard and is most commonly used by professionals, a couple of other, common, professional-grade, Web-design software packages are available, including Adobe GoLive and Microsoft FrontPage. If Dreamweaver doesn't suit your personal tastes, one of the other two major packages might. The choice does become a matter of personal needs and tastes. If your whole team is using FrontPage, you should try to use FrontPage also so that you have more compatibility with your team. If you're working alone and feel more comfortable in GoLive, don't force yourself to use something else just to prove a point.

Some Web-design software packages are in-between the range of Notepad and Dreamweaver. You might encounter BBEdit for the Mac or HomeSite for Windows. These resemble stripped-back versions of the more full-featured packages. And some programmers prefer hardcore development environments, such as Visual Studio. Some designers prefer these; some don't. Again, the most important point is to learn HTML, CSS, and the other coding/scripting technologies you intend to use on a regular basis and pick your tool based on what you need and want it to do. You can develop quality Web pages in any of the packages mentioned.

Deciding on Multimedia Software

If you plan to include video, audio, presentations, and slide shows on your site, you need to consider what multimedia software you want to use. What you choose depends on what you want to do and who your target audience is. For instance, if you want to do a lot of animations, Toon Boom Studio (www.toonboom.com) specializes in animation and is probably a good choice for your work. To decide what works best for your situation, take a look at this list that briefly describes the most common multimedia programs available (visit the listed URLs for more information) and then pick the solution that best fits your needs:

✦ **Apple QuickTime and QuickTimePro:** QuickTime is available for both the Mac and PC. The player is free but the Pro version of the software that allows you to create multimedia is, at the time of this writing, $29.99. QuickTime Pro allows you to import and edit video, *capture* (record) audio, create slide shows, and do other similar types of projects. This tool is relatively easy to use but also doesn't have the more robust features of the more expensive and more sophisticated software. To find out more, visit `www.apple.com/quicktime/download`.

✦ **Microsoft Windows Media:** Microsoft has a player — Windows Media Player — and a version for creating projects — Windows Media Encoder. Windows Media Encoder can be used to capture audio or video. Windows Media Encoder is available for the PC; go to `www.microsoft.com/windows/windowsmedia/default.mspx` for more information.

✦ **Adobe Flash:** Flash also has a "player version" and a "developer software" version. Adobe Flash is used to create animations and Web interfaces (Web sites). Flash can compress and play back video. You cannot capture or edit audio or video with Flash. You also cannot edit video with Flash. Flash is available for both the Mac and PC. Check out Book V for more about Flash.

A lot of software programs have the capability to create multimedia files. Some software manufacturers claim that their products can create Flash; the reality is that these products can create .swf files (the files that play in the Flash plug-in in the browser), but there's only one, true Flash program. If you want all the functionality of Flash, you need to get the Adobe Flash software and create your .swf files with that.

Just because a piece of software can do something doesn't mean that it does it well. PowerPoint and Word can create Web pages and Web presentations, but they don't do it overly well. Using PowerPoint and Word to create a presentation is a good idea; when you want to put your presentation online, however, you'll need to convert it to a more Web-friendly format using specialized software.

**Book III
Chapter 4**

Introducing Web
and Graphics
Software

Touring Photoshop CS2

Before you dive right into Photoshop, it might be helpful to get familiar with the basic features. This quick tour can help you get acquainted quickly.

The Welcome Screen

The Welcome Screen is the first window that opens when you launch Photoshop (unless you disable the Show this Dialog at Startup check box). The Welcome Screen has links to helpful tutorials, tips and tricks from Photoshop experts, and other things that can help you get started. After you're comfortable with Photoshop, you might want to disable the Show this Dialog at Startup check box so that the Welcome Screen goes away. You can always get it back by choosing Help➪Welcome Screen. Figure 4-3 shows the Welcome Screen.

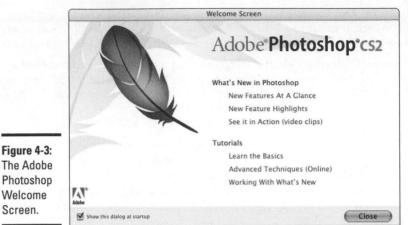

Figure 4-3:
The Adobe
Photoshop
Welcome
Screen.

The default workspace

When you click the Close button on the Welcome Screen (or first thing, if you've disabled the Show this Dialog at Startup check box), the default workspace appears. (Refer to Figure 4-1.) The most commonly used palettes are laid out on the screen, including the toolbox, Navigator, color sliders, swatches, styles, history, actions, and layers.

You can customize the workspace to your needs. So if you find that you like a particular layout of palettes or you find that you use some more than others, you can set up your own screen layout and save it. This feature can be very handy because it saves you time rearranging the screen if you have different preferences for different tasks.

To create a new workspace:

1. **Arrange the screen the way you like it and then choose Window⇨Workspace⇨Save Workspace.**

2. **In the Save Workspace dialog box that appears, give your workspace a name and choose any of the three options that you would like to save (palette locations, keyboard shortcuts, menus, and so on).**

   You can have custom settings for each of these or only some of them if you like.

3. **Click Save.**

To use the workspace you've saved, choose Window⇨Workspace⇨*the name you gave it.*

You can also delete a saved workspace. Just choose Window⇨Workspace⇨ Delete Workspace, select the name of the workspace you want to delete from the menu, and click Delete. Confirm the deletion by clicking Yes in the pop-up window.

Some specialized workspaces are available as presets. They are all available under the Window⇨Workspace menu. Explore them to see if they work for you and the tasks you're working on. Use the reset options if you'd like to put everything back where it started.

The work area

The work area is the window where your graphics will be. It's the canvas for your work. Figure 4-4 shows the New dialog box where you set up a new work area.

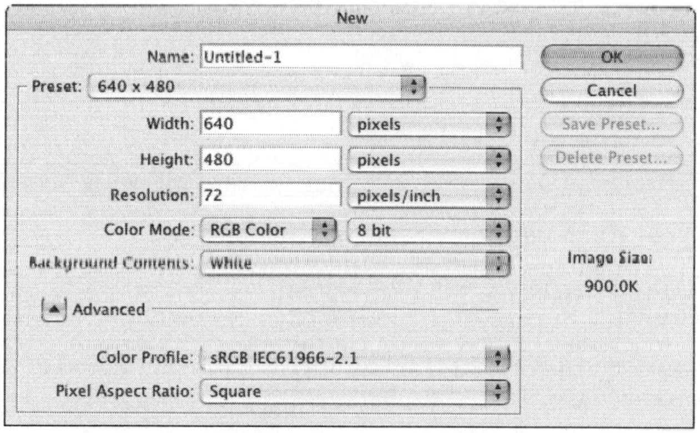

Figure 4-4:
The New dialog box.

To create a new work area:

1. **Choose File⇨New.**

2. **At the top of the New dialog box that appears, give your new graphics file a name by typing it into the Name text box.**

3. **Set the dimensions in the Width and Height fields.**

Choose pixels as the unit of measure because you're designing for the Web — the Web doesn't have inches.

4. **Set the resolution to 72 pixels/inch.**

The higher numbers are for print design. (See the explanations of graphics types in the sidebars, earlier in this chapter, that compare bitmaps and vector graphics.)

The Advanced button

If you're the curious type, you might notice that there is an Advanced button near the bottom of the New dialog box. If you click the Advanced button, you find settings for Color Profile and Pixel Aspect Ratio. These are important to you if you're working in print or video design. The Color Profile helps you set up your document so that it can communicate colors more accurately. (Go ahead — click it to check out the options.) Pixel Aspect Ratio is for setting up graphics for use in video. If you click that drop-down menu, you see many options as well. Video likes pixels that are rectangular — different projects have different needs, so you have several options. For Web design, you want square pixels.

---

5. **Select the RGB Color Mode.**

   Book II, Chapter 4 explains color space.

6. **Set the Background Contents of your file to be transparent or have a color.**

7. **Click OK to create the file.**

   Photoshop creates the new graphics file and places it on-screen.

8. **Save your document by choosing File⇨Save As.**

9. **In the Save As dialog box that appears, choose a location, name the file, and click Save.**

   Make sure you save it to your production files folder so you can find it easily later.

Another way to start a new workspace is to open a graphics file by choosing File⇨Open; browse to the image that you want and select it. Click Open. You might notice that when the file opens, the image is in a layer called Background. We discuss layers next.

Layers and the Layer palette

One of the most important palettes is the Layers palette. The elements that make up your graphics are held in *layers* — think of them as sheets of paper stacked one on top of another. But the big difference between layers and actual sheets of paper is that the layers can interact with each other. Some layers can be transparent so that layers underneath show through, or you can use *blend modes* (layer attributes that specify how a layer interacts with other layers below it) and *opacity* (the degree to which an object is not transparent) to blend the elements of your graphics together. Figure 4-5 shows the areas of the layers palette, and this list gives you a crash course in working with layers:

Photoshop files and keeping editable copies

When you create a new document in Photo-shop, the file saved by Photoshop is a .psd document by default. The .psd document contains all of your layers and editable text (as long as you don't convert or rasterize the text). See the "Bitmaps versus vector images, part 2" sidebar in this chapter for information about rasterizing. Make sure you keep a copy of your original .psd files so that you can quickly make changes or build new graphics based on the originals. After you've saved a graphic as a Web graphic file, you can't edit certain elements, such as text, in the file. Without the editable file, you might not be able to make changes to your graphics at all. At the very least, a simple task will be much more difficult and time consuming. On the other hand, on some occasions, you must rasterize text. If, for instance, you create a graphic with a special font and you intend to pass the Photoshop file to someone who doesn't have that font on their machine, you will need to rasterize the text (make it into a graphic layer). Otherwise, the other machine substitutes a different font for the one you used. Make sure you keep a copy of the original PSD file for editing, though.

✦ To create a new layer, just click the Create New Layer icon.

✦ Duplicate layers by using any of these methods:

- Select the layer you want to duplicate and press Ctrl+J (Windows) or ⌘+J (Mac).

- Right-click the layer you want to duplicate and choose Duplicate.

- Click the layer you want to duplicate and drag down to the New layer icon.

✦ Re-order layers by dragging them higher and lower in the window: Click a layer that you would like to move in the stacking order and drag it up or down the stack.

✦ Create new layers by using the Text or Shape tool, as follows:

1. **Click the Text tool (the large T in the toolbox).**

2. **Begin typing in the workspace.**

   The text appears on its own layer.

✦ Delete a layer by selecting the layer to be deleted and then clicking the Delete Layer icon (which looks like a trash can).

✦ Make a layer invisible by clicking the corresponding eye icon for the layer you would like to make invisible. To make it visible again, click the empty box where the eye icon used to be. (The eye disappears when the layer is invisible.)

Figure 4-5:
The Layers
palette and
its many
features.

Figure 4-5:
The Layers
palette and
its many
features.

Click to create
a new layer.

Tools and the toolbox

In this section we look at the most commonly used tools. As with other features we introduce to you, we recommend that you experiment with these tools to get an idea of how they work.

Playing with layers

If you haven't worked with layers much, follow these steps to get started playing with blend modes and opacity and see what the different settings do:

1. **Open a photo image.**

2. **Duplicate the layer. (See instructions in the "Layers and the Layer palette" section of this chapter.)**

3. **Select the top layer and then select a blend mode from the drop-down menu at the top of the Layers palette.**

   By default it will have Normal selected; when you click the menu, you will see the other options, like Multiply, Lighten, Darken, and Soft Light (to name a few).

4. **Experiment with the different blend modes to see what they do.**

You can also make multiple duplicate copies, use different blend modes on each, and then change the layer order or opacity on the different layers.

You can undo the changes you've made with the History palette, which shows a list of the actions you've done to the file. Open this by choosing Window⇨History. To step backwards, select the step in your process you'd like to go back to.

Remember: As long as you keep at least one layer that holds the original image, you can always delete layers that don't look so good.

Selection tools: Marquee, Lasso, and Magic Wand

The Marquee, Lasso, and Magic Wand tools select areas of a layer to be affected by filters or effects. They also help you work on a specific area of a layer without affecting areas you don't want to touch.

✦ The **Marquee tool** gives you a rectangular or elliptical marquee. With the marquee tools you select an area of your graphic. Depending on which version of the tool you select, the selection will be rectangular or rounded.

✦ The **Magic Wand tool** selects everything in your graphic that matches the color you click with it.

✦ The **Lasso tools** allow you to make customized selections. You can click around an area and create a selection of any shape with the Lasso tools.

Click the small black triangle in the lower-right corner of any tool icon to see the variations of the tool, like Rectangular Marquee or Elliptical Marquee. Many tools have different versions. You can tell which ones do by looking for the little black triangle. When you click it, the other versions will pop out as a mini menu with icons. You can then select which version of the tool works best for the task at hand.

To use a selection tool, select the layer you want to work on and then select the tool that will work best for what you're doing. (See the previous list.) Then take the appropriate action based on the tool you chose.

✦ **Marquee tools:** Click and drag over the area you want to select.

✦ **Magic Wand tool:** Click on an area that is the color you want to select, and your selection will appear as a dotted line around the selection — the dots move along the line, often described as marching ants (see Figure 4-6 for an example) — the marching ants appear around all selections regardless of what tool made them.

✦ **Lasso tools:** Click along the edge of the object you would like to select. Make sure you go all the way around and end by clicking on the start point — that way you have "drawn" a complete container around the object you'd like to select.

The Move tool

Use the Move tool to (what else?) move elements of your artwork around the work area. You just select the layer that holds the artwork you would like to move and then click and drag inside the work area window until the element is where you'd like it to be.

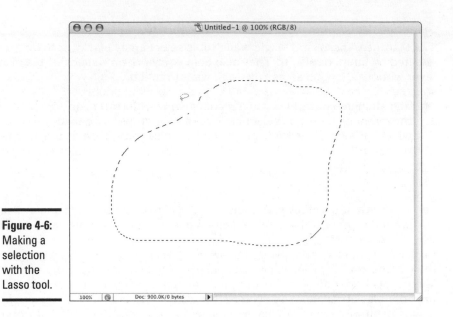

Figure 4-6:
Making a selection with the Lasso tool.

Interested in more precise movement? To move objects one pixel at a time, select the layer that contains the object you'd like to move, select the Move tool, and click anywhere in the work area, and then use the arrow keys on your keyboard. To move an object 10 pixels at a time, hold down the Shift key while pressing an arrow key.

By using the Move tool in conjunction with the Align icons, you can align multiple objects at once; just follow these steps:

1. **Select the layers you want to align by pressing and holding the Ctrl key (Windows) or Command key (Mac) and clicking each layer.**

2. **Click the Move tool.**

3. **Click the appropriate Align icon (located at the top of the screen; see Figure 4-7).**

Figure 4-7:
The Align tool helps you line up elements in your design.

The Crop tool

Use the Crop tool to cut down your file and remove any extra space that is floating around the main subject area. You can use the tool freehand-style by selecting it and clicking and dragging a box around the area you would like to keep. You can adjust the box if you need to and then press Enter. The entire document is cut down to the size of the selected area. Any elements that remain outside the box are deleted — completely. Make sure you don't cut off anything unless you mean to. Duplicating the image you're cropping and then working on the copy is a good idea; that way, you'll always have the original to go back to.

A more precise way to use the crop tool is to set dimensions that you want your cropped document to be.

1. **Open the photo you're cropping and click the Crop tool.**

   Notice how the options available in the palette at the top of the screen change as you choose different tools — this is a *context sensitive* palette. It allows the interface to make a lot more tools available to you without cluttering up the screen.

2. **At the top of the screen, type a number in the Width text box and another in the Height text box; also, enter a number in the Resolution text box.**

   If, for example, you want to make a 75-pixel x 75-pixel icon out of a 600-pixel x 400-pixel photo, type **75 px** in the Width text box and **75 px** in the Height text box. 72 dpi works for the resolution because computer monitors do not require a higher resolution; see the sidebar information earlier in this chapter about bitmaps and resolutions.

3. **Click and drag the Crop tool over the area you want your image cropped to.**

   Everything outside that area will be chopped off.

   When you click and drag your crop area, the result is a perfect 100-px by 100-px square at 72 dpi. Make sure you have placed your box over the area you want to keep; everything else will be lost when the crop is finalized. You finalize the crop by pressing Enter, or by clicking the check mark at the top right of the palette at the top of the screen.

   You can move around the crop area until you have the perfect image framed in the crop area, and then either press Enter or click the check mark in the context sensitive menu at the top of the screen. To remove the settings, just click the Crop tool and click Clear in the menu. See Figure 4-8 for an example of this technique.

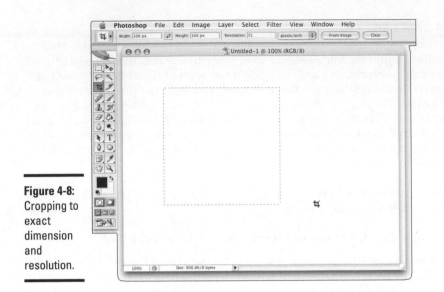

Figure 4-8:
Cropping to
exact
dimension
and
resolution.

The Slice tools

With the Slice tools (the tool in the toolbox that looks like a small knife), you can take a large graphic and cut it into smaller graphics to be exported out of Photoshop/Image Ready as graphics and an HTML document. This is useful when you have designed an entire interface and you need to break it up into the separate graphics that will make up the working HTML interface. Figure 4-9 shows a Photoshop file that has been sliced. See Chapter 7 of this minibook for more information about using this tool.

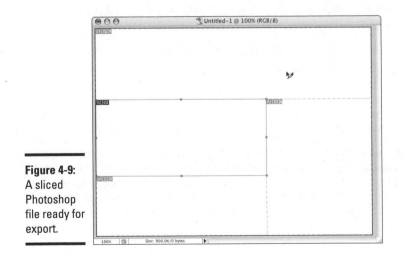

Figure 4-9:
A sliced
Photoshop
file ready for
export.

The Brush and Pencil tools

You use the Brush and Pencil tools to draw or paint in your document. Select one of the tools — for example, the Brush tool — and a menu appears at the top of the screen. (See Figure 4-10.) You can choose what color to paint with, the style and size of brush, and many other options.

Figure 4-10:
The Brush tool has many options to help you work with your graphics.

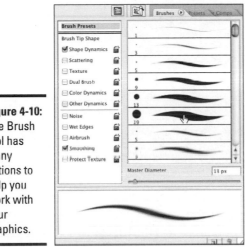

The Eraser tool

The Eraser tool does exactly that — it erases parts of a layer. To use it, select the layer you want to erase things from, click the Eraser tool, customize its size and other properties in the menu at the top of the screen, and start erasing. Things that are erased are gone forever (see Figure 4-11), so we recommend that you duplicate the layer and make the extra layer invisible (refer to the "Layers and the Layer palette" section for instructions on making a layer invisible) before you start erasing; that way you have a backup.

An alternative to using the Eraser tool (which is a destructive tool because what it erases is really gone) is to use *layer masks*. When you use a layer mask, part of the layer becomes invisible — it's still there; it's just hidden from view. When you use a layer mask, what you "erase" doesn't go away forever. This option offers a nondestructive way to alter your images.

This area has been erased.

Figure 4-11:
If you erase part of a layer, it is gone.

The Paint Bucket and Gradient tools

The Paint Bucket and Gradient tools color an entire layer or an entire selected area with the color of your choice. The Paint Bucket will just dump the color into the layer or selected area, filling it entirely. The paint brushes allow you to, well, actually *paint* the color in where you like. The Gradient tool fills the area with a gradient; you can select one from the context-sensitive menu or customize the gradient in the dialog box that opens when you double-click a preset.

Putting the Paint Bucket tool through its paces

To use the Paint Bucket tool:

1. **Select or create a layer or select an area of a layer.**

2. **Double-click the foreground color tile, select a color from the Color Picker (shown in Figure 4-12), and click OK.**

The foreground/background color tiles are at the bottom of the toolbox; they are two overlapping colored squares — the top one is foreground, and the other is background.

When you select a color from the Color Picker, your cursor will look like an eyedropper.

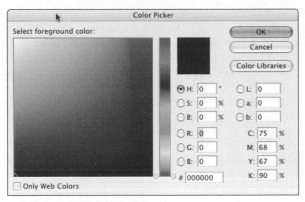

Figure 4-12:
Choosing a color to fill a layer with.

The new color will be shown in the top half of a rectangle at the top/center of the dialog box. The original color will be shown in the bottom half for comparison.

3. **Click the Paint Bucket tool and click inside the work area or selected area.**

The chosen area is filled with the color you picked in Step 2.

Experimenting with the Gradient tool

Gradients have different types, meaning they have different ways of displaying. Although you have several to choose from, two common ones are

✦ **Linear:** The linear gradient will display from left to right, top to bottom or diagonally — in a linear way, from one color to the other.

✦ **Radial:** The radial gradient will display in a circular fashion from one color to the other. One color will be a round circle and the gradient will radiate outward around it.

Experiment with the different types to see what they look like, there are icons in the gradient tool context-sensitive menu at the top of the screen.

The context-sensitive menu also contains a drop-down menu at the upper left that features a gradient sample as the menu choice instead of words. This is the menu that you use to select the colors of your gradient. If you click the menu button, you see all the available preset gradients. But the more exciting way to work with gradients is to click the color swatch in the menu itself, which launches the Gradient Editor (shown in Figure 4-16). In the Gradient Editor, you can change the colors of the gradient, add colors to the gradient, change the position of the colors within the gradient, and save gradients that you create (you save them a preset).

To change colors, select one of the presets that are available to start, and then either double-click one of the color chips that are displayed under the sample of that gradient or click the Color drop-down menu. Either one will launch the color-picker tool. You can move the position of the colors within the gradient by clicking and dragging the color chips or by clicking a color chip and then changing the number in the Location box. The "right" way depends on your personal tastes. Experiment with it and have fun.

To use the Gradient tool:

1. **Select a layer or create a layer or select an area of a layer.**

2. **Click the Gradient tool.**

3. **Click the Click to Edit menu at the top of the screen to open the Gradient Editor. (See Figure 4-13.)**

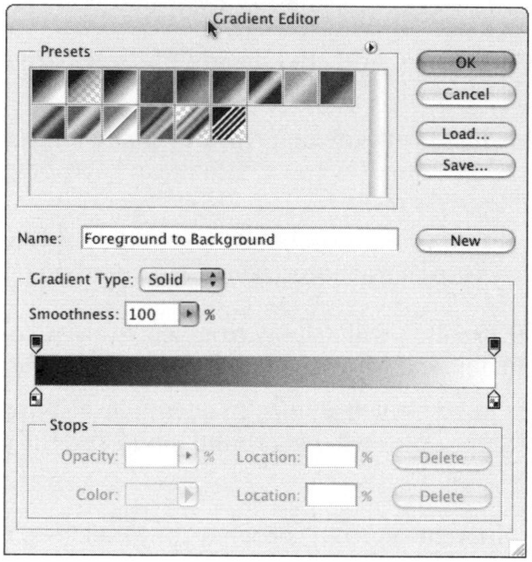

Figure 4-13: Calling up the Gradient Editor tool.

4. **Select a Preset or adjust the settings to create your own gradient and then click OK.**

5. **Click and drag across the layer you want to fill with the gradient.**

The layer is filled with the gradient you created in Step 4.

If you don't like the result, you can try again. Adjust the gradient or keep the one you already have and just drag again. Repeat until you get what you want.

The Text tool and palette

You can add text to your graphics with the Text tool. To use this tool, click it, click in the work area where you want your text to appear, and type. A new layer is automatically created with your new text. The Text tool has its own menu bar and a palette that contains more options for formatting, including options for handling paragraphs. Figure 4-14 shows the Text menu bar and palette.

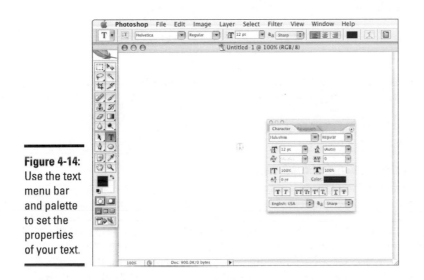

Figure 4-14: Use the text menu bar and palette to set the properties of your text.

Vector tools: Shape, Pen, and Path Selection tools

Photoshop has a few vector graphics tools — and these can be tricky to use, so we recommend experimenting with them until you feel comfortable using them. Here are the highlights:

✦ **Shape tool:** Draw shapes such as rectangles and ellipses. To use it, just select the tool, and then click and drag in the work area. The Shape tool has an option that allows you to draw a variety of preset shapes, see Figure 4-15.

✦ **Pen tool:** Draw lines, curves, and shapes. With the Pen tool, you click in the work area to create points; after you've created all your points, Photoshop connects them to create a shape.

✦ **Path Selection tools:** Edit *paths* — the lines in a vector graphic — that you have created.

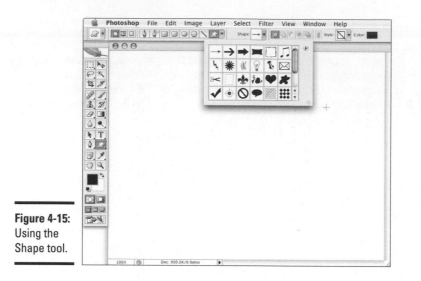

Figure 4-15:
Using the
Shape tool.

The Magnify and Hand tools and Navigator palette

The Magnify and Hand tools, along with the Navigator palette, help you move around your document and zoom in or out for a better look.

✦ **Magnify tool:** To zoom in on a portion of the work area, choose the Magnify tool and click on that area. Double-click the Magnify tool icon to go directly to 100%. Use the Navigator palette (by sliding the small red triangle under the preview window) or enter a percent value into the box at the lower left of the document window to zoom back out.

✦ **Hand tool:** This one moves your viewing area around the document; it doesn't move any of the artwork. Select the tool, click within the document work area, and then drag the work area around. The whole Photoshop file will appear to move around within the document window area. You are not actually moving the graphics — only the visible area. This is particularly helpful if you are zoomed in far enough that your whole document is not visible in your document window. You can drag the area that you are looking at without having to move the actual graphics around.

✦ **Navigator palette:** This palette performs the same functions as the pre-ceding two. The slider zooms in and out, and the red box indicates your viewing area. You can also use the Navigator to orient yourself in the document. Click the red box and drag it around the document thumbnail so that you can change the viewing area as you work. See Figure 4-16 for an example of how the Navigator works. If you cannot see the Navigator on your screen, open it by choosing Window➪Navigator.

Drag the red box to change the viewing area.

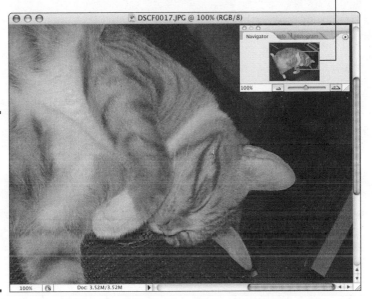

Figure 4-16:
Use the
Navigator
to zoom in
and out
and move
around your
work area
without
moving the
artwork.

Chapter 5: Getting Started with Dreamweaver

In This Chapter

✔ Touring the Dreamweaver interface

✔ Creating a Web site

✔ Creating pages and supporting files in Dreamweaver

✔ Testing your pages and validating the code

✔ Publishing your Web site

reamweaver 8, the industry standard software for Web design, has some great features and some very useful tools to help designers and developers to be more efficient. Some of the features include code formatting, comment features to help keep code understandable, and code collapsing to help you focus on an area of your code. The handy placement and functionality these features add are great assets as you start to work with your first Web pages and HTML code. This chapter gives you a quick-and-dirty tour of Dreamweaver before delving into using this very handy tool.

Before you start working in Dreamweaver, it is a good idea to make sure you have Web hosting and a URL purchased. You can actually work on your site before you do these things, but that's not a great idea because you must be sure you can find and afford hosting that will accommodate your site (not all hosts are the same). The URL is important, especially if the name of the site will be the URL. Designing a site only to discover later that someone else already owns the name is a real drag. This scenario has happened more often than you'd think — don't let it happen to you. Book I has information about choosing hosts and URLs.

Exploring the Dreamweaver Interface

Before you dive right into Dreamweaver and start making pages, you'll probably want to get acquainted with the interface. The following section gives you the quick rundown of the key features and a little about how they work. After you get familiar with Dreamweaver's default set of features, you can look for additional features to download at the Adobe Exchange Center at www.adobe.com/exchange.

REMEMBER

What's in a name? Local site, remote site, testing servers . . .

The following terms keep popping up throughout the site creation and management process:

✓ **Server:** This is just a computer that is hooked up to the Web that also has server software running on it. *Server software* receives requests for information from other computers and "serves" the requested information back to the requesting machine.

✓ **Local site:** This is a folder on your own computer that you keep all your working files for one Web site in. It is your unpublished Web site.

✓ **Remote site (or live site):** This is the site that's on the Web server. It's the collection of files that have been copied to the Web server and has your URL (Web address) pointed to it. This site is visible to anyone who has your URL or finds your site via a search engine or a link.

✓ **Testing server (optional):** A very good thing to have, the testing server is the place where you can publish the site so people within your team can see it, but it isn't visible to the whole world. It can be the same machine as your live server, but the files are put into a different folder than the live files — or you can put the files on a totally different machine. The testing server needs to be equipped with the same server software (or server software that supports the same features) as the live environment.

Note: If your testing server and live server are too different, you can end up with content that works on one server but not on the other. That's not a big deal if your Flash video doesn't work correctly on your test server but looks great on the live server — it's a very bad thing if it is the other way around. You could end up with content that took a lot of time and effort to produce, but you can't use it. That's no fun!

The first time you launch Dreamweaver, you see the Start page (more about that later). The other thing that happens the very first time you launch Dreamweaver is that you'll be asked to set up a Web site. A dialog box opens, giving you Manage Sites and Cancel options. What Dreamweaver is trying to do is to index and keep track of the files that will make up your Web site. This is important. Dreamweaver helps you with site maintenance (uploading, synchronizing versions, checking links, and so on) *if* you set it up properly. More on that later in this chapter. You can work in Dreamweaver without creating a site; just be aware that Dreamweaver will not be able to help you keep track of the files and their relation to each other. Either way, you'll need to deal with Dreamweaver's request to set up a site. To set up a Web site, click Manage Sites. To skip this step and begin working with Dreamweaver, click Cancel.

The benefit of setting up a site is that Dreamweaver keeps track of all the files associated with your Web site on your local machine, on your Web server, and on your (optional) test server.

Sometimes, you just want to work on one file that is not part of a whole Web site. Simply click Cancel in the dialog box and proceed. If you choose to work this way, Dreamweaver warns you that you aren't working with files that are part of a single site whenever you try to insert secondary files.

The Start Page

When you launch Dreamweaver, you're presented with the Start Page. (See Figure 5-1.) This page gives you the option to open a file you've recently worked on, create a new file, create a file from a sample, take a tour, or do a tutorial. It also provides information about updates or new products. Macromedia/Adobe sends these updates to your Start Page when you're connected to the Internet.

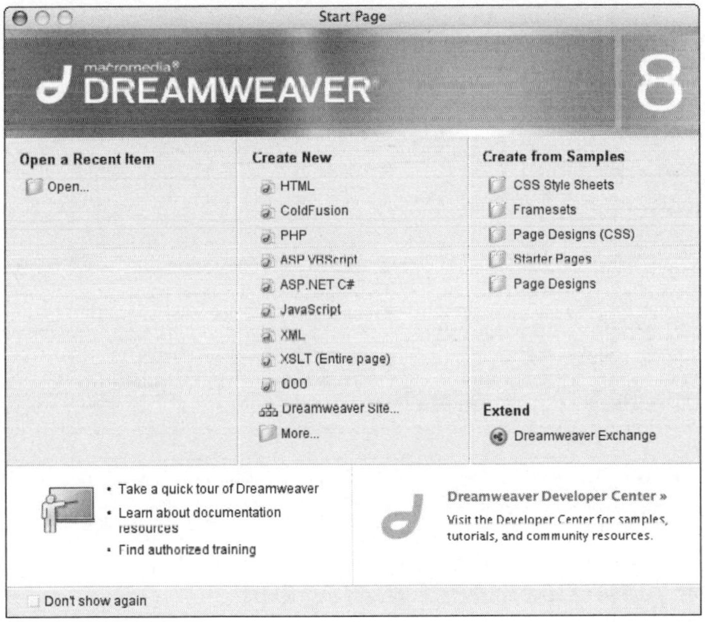

Figure 5-1: The Dreamweaver Start Page.

Book III
Chapter 5

Getting Started
with Dreamweaver

The Dreamweaver Start Page gives you tons of options for getting started, organized into three lists: Open a Recent Item, Create New, and Create from Samples. And in the same window you see some of the menus and panels that we discuss later in this chapter. If you haven't used Dreamweaver before, the Open a Recent Item list has only one item in it: the Open folder button. If you've worked in Dreamweaver and saved some files, you see a list of the ones you used most recently. To open a recent item, just click the file name. Or, you can click the Open folder button to see a list of the files in the last site worked on.

In the middle of the Start Page, the Create New list gives you the option to create an HTML, ColdFusion, PHP, or CSS document, among others. To immediately create a file, just click the type of file you need. To see more options, click More at the bottom of the list.

Dreamweaver comes with a large number of sample or starter files that can get you going quickly. To access them, you can click any option in the Create from Samples list (refer to Figure 5-1) to launch the New Document dialog box. (See Figure 5-2.) From that dialog box, you can select the type of file you would like to create, make some optional selections, or choose to start your document from a premade template. Read the next sections for more information about that.

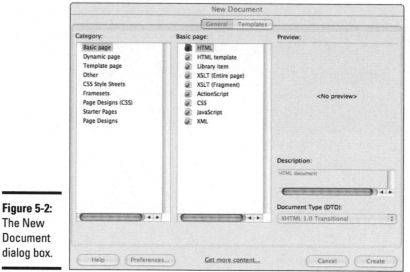

Figure 5-2:
The New Document dialog box.

The New Document dialog box

You can access the New Document dialog box by choosing File➪New from the menu. Click the appropriate tab (General or Templates), depending on whether you're creating a *new document* or a *new template*. A *new document* creates one document; a *new template* creates a file that you can use to make and maintain multiple files.

The Templates tab holds the custom templates you build, listed by the site they're associated with. For more on custom templates, see Book III, Chapter 6. The General tab has several categories, which we describe in the following sections.

The New Document dialog box is divided into three fields, starting with the Category field on the left. The Category field lists groups of files that you would typically want to build that you can use to start your HTML, CSS, or other site files. The middle field changes according to what Category you select, but it always gives you further options to select a different category. On the right side of the dialog box, you see the Preview pane. Once you've selected an item in each of the two fields to the left, the Preview pane gives you a rough sketch of what your selections translate to on the actual page.

Basic Page starter files

The Basic Page starter files create HTML, HTML templates, library items (see Book III, Chapter 6 for more), ActionScript (for use with Flash), CSS, and JavaScript files. These files are just starter files and include just the basics (tags for DTD, HTML, head, title, body) — for more about these initial tags, see Book III, Chapter 2.

In the case of HTML, Dreamweaver creates a document that has an HTML file extension and includes the document type, HTML tags, head tags, and body tags. It's all ready for you to begin creating your page.

Other options for the Basic Page files start off with just a comment at the top to identify what sort of page it is and the correct file extension to get you started. Although these files don't have any code in them, they do help you remember to save the file with the right extension. It's easy to make a mistake with all those files flying around. Whether to use them or not is really a personal preference. Claudia often starts a site with a CSS and an HTML document that she starts by using these starter files; she feels it's just a quick way to get going.

Dynamic Page starter files

The Dynamic Page starter files are for building ASP, JSP, ColdFusion, or other dynamic Web pages. If you're looking to build Web pages that communicate with a database or collect information at all, you might want to use one of these types of files. See Book VI for information about building dynamic pages.

CSS Style Sheets starter files

The CSS Style Sheets starter files aren't complete CSS, but they do include font treatments and basic color schemes to get your design started. See Figure 5-3 for a preview of a CSS Style Sheet starter file with the Basic: Arial option selected. Use these files to get the foundation styles set up, and then add your own custom styles to build your design.

**Book III
Chapter 5**

Getting Started
with Dreamweaver

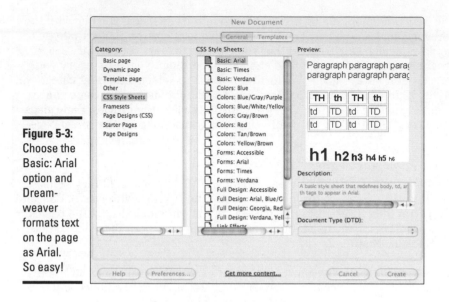

Figure 5-3:
Choose the
Basic: Arial
option and
Dream-
weaver
formats text
on the page
as Arial.
So easy!

Framesets starter files

Dreamweaver sets up the initial files you need to create a frame-based Web site when you select the Framesets category. (See Figure 5-4.) Framesets are a little different from regular Web pages. A regular HTML page has one Web page document. A *frameset* is one file that actually uses multiple HTML documents to create the whole page. The benefit of building a site this way is that you can have parts of your page stay the same while other pieces of the page change. For instance, you can put your navigation in the HTML document that loads into the left frame and launch different HTML documents in the right frame.

Using frames has a downside: Search engines sometimes find only part of the page and launch it without the rest of the page, so visitors can get the main content frame but no navigation or banner area. Another problem with frames is that it can reduce usability for some users because screen readers sometimes have trouble navigating frames. Framed layouts can also be a little more difficult to manage than straight HTML — for instance, linking to information within your site can present problems unless you take special care to direct the browser to load the new page into the right frames. Weigh the pros and cons before deciding to use frames in your design. Many designers do not use frames in their designs because of the associated cons.

Updates to Dreamweaver

If your categories in the New Document dialog box are different from those listed in the "Page Designs" section — for instance: Page Designs, Page Designs CSS, and Page Designs Accessible — you might need to download and install the Dreamweaver 8.02 updater. Checking for updates and making sure you've got the most recent updates of your software is always a good idea. Sometimes the updates are additional content and other times they are improvements to the functionality. Updating is easy, and you'll be getting better tools in the process.

You can check your version of Dreamweaver by doing the following:

On the Mac: Choose Dreamweaver⇨About Dreamweaver.

On the PC: Choose Help⇨About Dreamweaver.

On both: Click the Dreamweaver splash screen; the version number and other information is displayed in the lower-left corner of the splash screen. Click the splash screen again to make it disappear.

The Dreamweaver Start Page alerts you to updates if you're connected to the Internet. You can get more information about the update by clicking the provided link. Or, you can visit `www.adobe.com/support/dreamweaver/downloads_updaters.html` to see the updates that are available for Dreamweaver.

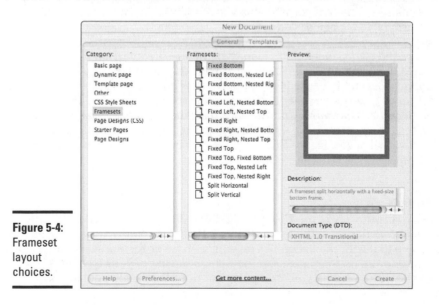

Figure 5-4:
Frameset
layout
choices.

Page Designs

Page Designs are sets of files that work together — HTML and CSS are created when you use these options. With page designs, you actually get an HTML and a CSS file that are already set up to work together and with layouts already started. Some are fairly complete while others are pretty simple. The other starter files (discussed in the preceding sections) don't include the layouts. The page designs are divided into three types: Page Designs (CSS), Starter Pages, and Page Designs. Find out how to build pages and sites using these prebuilt page designs in Book III, Chapter 6.

The Files panel

When you've made your selections in the New Document dialog box and clicked the Create button, the dialog box closes and you see

+ **The Document window:** This is the work area where you design and code Web pages.

+ **The panels on the right:** By default, these include the Files panel, the Tag Inspector panel, the Application panel, and the CSS panel. This can also include other panels that you choose to open — look under the Window menu for more panels and tools.

+ **The Properties inspector (at the bottom of the page):** This is a context-sensitive menu panel that helps you work with images, text, and other parts of your page or code.

You use the Files panel for site management and organization. The Files panel is the list of all the files in your Dreamweaver site. We specify a *Dreamweaver* site because files will only show up in this window if you have set it up as described earlier in this chapter. You can open site files from the Files panel. You can work with the Files panel in either the Expanded view for site management or file uploading or in Collapsed view while you work on individual pages. Figure 5-6 shows the Collapsed view of the Files panel. Note how the site structure is also displayed.

Expanded view

The Expanded view of the Files panel (shown in Figure 5-5) is divided into two main sections. On the left, you see (initially) an empty window. This will be populated with the list of files on your remote or testing server after you connect (more on that later). On the right is the list of your *local files* (the Web site files saved on your computer but not necessarily published to the Web).

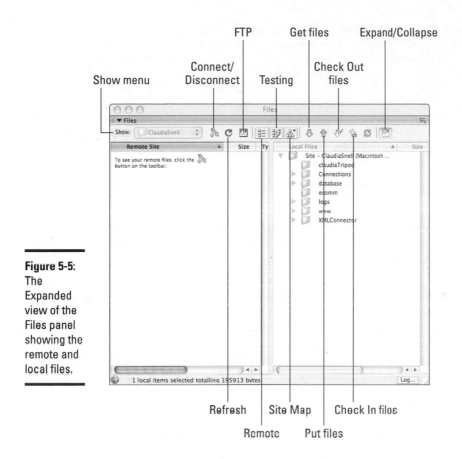

Figure 5-5:
The Expanded view of the Files panel showing the remote and local files.

Across the top of the Files panel (Expanded view), you see a menu and a series of buttons. From left to right, they are

✦ **Show:** This menu (click the arrow buttons to expand it) is a list of the different sites you have set up — you can set up multiple Web sites in Dreamweaver. Dreamweaver keeps track of each one separately. If you want to work on a different site, use the Show menu to select the site you want to work on. The files for that site will replace the current listing.

✦ **Connect/Disconnect:** Click this button to make a connection with your remote Web server. You have to do this before you can see a list of the files on that server and before you upload (or download) anything to it (or from it).

✦ **Refresh:** Clicking this button refreshes the file lists, both remote and local. This can take a few minutes if you have a very large site. Sometimes, you'll have better luck right-clicking just one folder within a site and clicking Refresh. It can be much faster.

✦ **FTP:** Clicking this button shows the details of your last FTP transaction with the server. FTP stands for *File Transfer Protocol* and refers to a protocol (or set of rules) by which computers and servers can communicate, as long as the server is set up to accept FTP and the person trying to send things to the server via FTP has a valid FTP address, username, and password (which are all provided to you by your host when you sign up for services). FTP transaction simply refers to sending or getting information via FTP. (*Note:* HTTP, which stands for Hypertext Transfer Protocol, is also a protocol and is the way that servers and browsers communicate.)

✦ **Remote view, Testing view, and Site Map view:** Use these three buttons to switch among the remote server, the testing server (if you're using one), and the Site Map views of your site. The Site Map view shows a flowchart of how your files are structured within your site. Also, note that if you don't have a testing server, nothing is displayed.

✦ **Get and Put:** These two buttons get (down arrow) files from the remote server or put (up arrow) files to the remote server. To *get* a file is to use FTP to retrieve a copy of a file from your Web server. To *put* a file is to publish (upload) it to the Web.

Put and get overwrite existing files on the destination computer, so if you Get the home page from the remote (or testing) server, you overwrite the copy on your local machine. When you put (or publish) a page from your local machine to the remote (or testing) server, you overwrite the copy that is there. If you're trying to overwrite a newer copy with an older copy, Dreamweaver warns you that you're about to do that and gives you the option to cancel. This is one of the benefits of allowing Dreamweaver to manage your site — it keeps track of and compares the dates and times on your files.

Both the Put and Get commands create the identical file structure, if it doesn't already exist. For instance, you add a new folder to your site on your local machine. When you publish the folder and new content, you don't need to create a place for it to go because Dreamweaver creates the new folder in exactly the right place on your remote server. The same thing goes when you download files from a site. The site structure is duplicated exactly. This ensures that your links work correctly and things are where you expect them to be. Pretty cool, huh?

✦ **Check Out and Check In:** These two buttons are for managing workflow for a team. Members of the team *check out* files when they're going to work on them. That way, anyone else on the team who tries to open and work on the file at the same time is alerted that someone is already working on it. This prevents members of a team from overwriting each other's work. When done working on the file, the team member simply has to *check in* the file so that others can work on it.

Using this built-in tool — or some other type of *source control* (also known as *version control*) — is very important so that multiple people simultaneously working on a site avoid overwriting each other's work.

✦ **Expand/Collapse:** Puts local and remote files side by side.

Collapsed view

The same functionality that is available in the Expanded view is also available in the Collapsed view. (See Figure 5-6.) This view can be helpful if you just need to make a quick change to one file and upload it. The drop-down menu on the left is the Site Management menu; use it to select the site you want to work on. The menu on the right is the Site View menu; use it to choose Local, Remote, Testing, or Site Map view. The same Connect/ Disconnect, Refresh, Get, Put, Check Out, Check In, and Expand/Collapse buttons (explained in the bulleted list in the preceding section) are available, too.

The buttons for Site Files, Testing Server, Site Map, and Synchronize are omitted from the collapsed view to conserve space. These functions and several others are available via a drop-down menu in the upper-right corner of the panel or via the pop-up menu available through the button at the extreme upper-right corner of the panel — look for an icon that looks like a tiny bulleted list. These show up in many panels, so be on the lookout.

Site Management   Site View

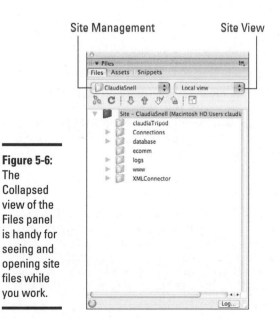

Figure 5-6: The Collapsed view of the Files panel is handy for seeing and opening site files while you work.

Book III
Chapter 5

Getting Started
with Dreamweaver

Other options that are available through the Files panel include file and site management tools. In the far, upper-right corner is a button that looks like a tiny bulleted list. If you click it, a pop-up menu opens with options to work with files and folders in your site, to group files for better organization, and to change the view you're using in the Files panel. One of the most important options is the Site menu, which enables you to do the following:

✦ **Create or edit site settings.** Find out more about this in the "Creating a Web Site with Dreamweaver" section, later in this chapter.

✦ **Set up a site to work with Adobe Contribute.** Contribute is content management/editing software.

✦ **Turn on or off cloaking.** *Cloaking* allows you to set some local files to not upload — a handy feature for working with files like raw Flash files and Photoshop documents.

✦ **Run site reports.** Running reports enables you to check links and do other tests to make sure your site is working well.

✦ **Synchronize files.** You can ask Dreamweaver to compare the files on your local machine to those on the remote server (or the other way around) and give you a list of files that have been updated more recently. You can then choose to upload all files, or you can individually select files to be skipped and upload just the ones you'd like to publish. This is helpful when you make several edits to a site, and you want to make sure you publish all the new files to the server. It can be easy to forget which files you need to upload; Dreamweaver can help you with that.

The Document window

The Document window is where the file you're working on is displayed. There are different ways you can work with this window. The "best" way depends on what you're doing and what you're most comfortable with. In this section, we show you the three views you can choose (Code, Design, and Split) and describe some of the Document window's features.

Code view

The Code view (shown in Figure 5-7) is just a window with the HTML in it. No graphics or colors are displayed, just the underlying code of your page. This view is good if you're comfortable with hand coding your pages or if you need to use as much space on your screen as possible to look at a larger block of code. The downside is that you can't see the end results of what you're coding without previewing in a browser or switching to a view that includes the Design view.

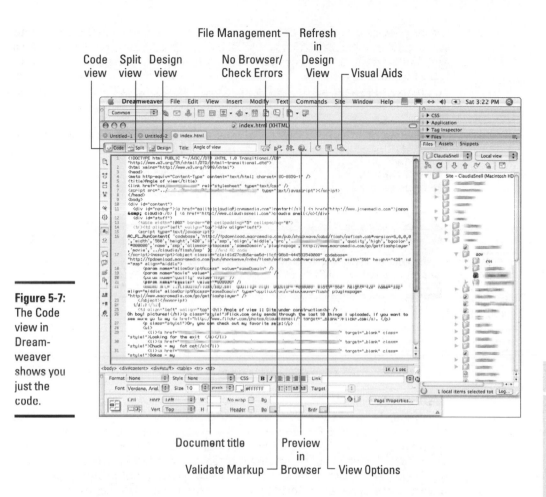

Figure 5-7:
The Code view in Dreamweaver shows you just the code.

Design view

The Design view is the opposite of the Code view. In Design view, you see only the visual aspects of your page (as shown in Figure 5-8). This can be helpful if you're not as comfortable with code or if you need to see more of your design for a moment. The downside to this mode is that you can't see what's happening with your code. Dreamweaver is a great tool but is no substitute for a person. Sometimes, edits that you make in the Design view can produce issues in the code, such as *empty tags* (tags that are left behind after the content in them has been removed). Check over your code with a validator (covered later in this chapter) before you go live with the page. A *code validator* is a test that you can run on a page's code to make sure it's written properly. The test results alert you to any issues so that you can fix them.

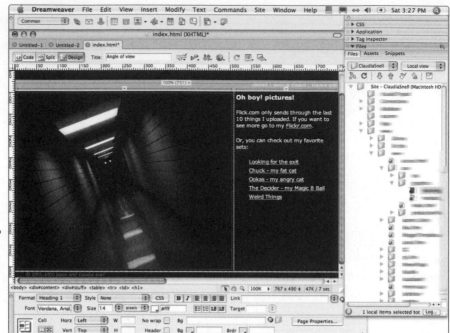

Figure 5-8:
The Design
view shows
the visual
appearance
of the page.

Split view

This mode is really the best of both worlds. You get the Code view at the top of the screen and the Design view at the bottom. In Split view (shown in Figure 5-9), you can hand code *or* make edits in the design window. It allows you to see the effects of your edits right away, whether you make them in the Code portion of the view or in the Design portion of the view. When it's necessary to update the Design portion of the view, a Refresh button appears in the Properties inspector. (We cover the Properties inspector later in this chapter.)

Document Title

At the top of the Document window is the Document Title box. It's important to give each document a proper title. Remember, the page title shows in browsers and in search engines, so make sure you give your page a title that makes sense. You can add a title by typing **<title>My Title Here</title>** in the head of the document. See Book III, Chapter 2 for more information about HTML. Dreamweaver automatically adds the title tags in the correct place if you create your HTML documents via the New Document dialog box. Simply replace the default `Untitled Document` with the title of your choice. (And now, you know why so many pages seem to be titled `Untitled Document` out there.)

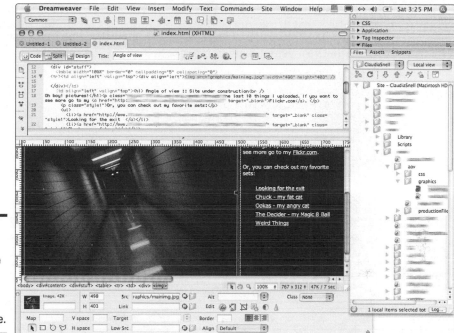

Figure 5-9:
Use Split view to see both the code and the visual appearance.

Check and validate code

The Document window toolbar (shown in Figure 5-10) offers code validating and checking functionality. Code *validators* and *checkers* are quick tests that you can run to make sure your page is going to work well for your visitors. The No Browser/Check Errors button (refer to Figure 5-7) enables you to deal with checking for browser errors and support; the Validate Markup button allows you to check the code for errors and see where the errors are.

Using checkers and validators is a good habit to develop. You can set up these tests to look for different things, such as problems with different types of browsers or different versions of HTML and CSS. Decide what versions of browsers or code you will support, based on your site's purpose and the target audience. Try to find out as much as possible about the types of technologies that work best for your audience, and then develop your site to work with those technologies.

File Management: Put and Get

The Put/Get buttons on the Document toolbar look the same as the ones in the Files panel. In the Document window, the Put button uploads the current document, and the Get button retrieves the live version of it for you. In all cases, Put/Get asks you if you'd like to upload (or download) the dependent files. This means, "Would you like all the graphics, CSS, JavaScript, and multimedia files that are linked to that, too?" It doesn't mean that Dreamweaver will download other HTML documents, though. Just the files that are needed to create the finished page you're posting or getting.

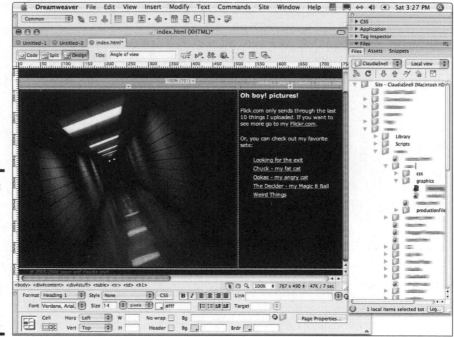

Figure 5-10:
The
Document
window
toolbar has
many
features to
help you be
more
productive.

Preview in Browser

Preview in Browser is really the only way to see what your page will look like. To see the preview, click the Preview in Browser button. (Refer to Figure 5-7.) While Design view shows a very close rendition, different browsers display things a little differently. You need to preview your pages in the actual browsers you're designing for. It's best to view your pages on both Mac and Windows computers and in all of the major browsers. Also, make sure you test all interactive and dynamic elements to make sure they work. Be especially careful with JavaScript and CSS because browsers can vary greatly in how they use them.

Refresh Design view

After you make changes in the Code view of the Document window, click the Refresh in Design View button (refer to Figure 5-7) to see the changes take effect.

View options

Some additional helpers are available to help you as you work. These include things like the following:

✦ **Word wrap:** Without this, the code and content can stretch out for miles. Word wrap keeps it all in the visible window without affecting the code.

✦ **Code line numbers:** Displays numbers in the right margin of the Code view window.

✦ **Highlight invalid code:** This one highlights errors in the code with bright yellow, which is very handy!

There are also code-formatting options and many other tools to make life easier. Explore them and find which ones work best for you.

The Preferences dialog box

You can customize the way Dreamweaver works for you. The Preferences dialog box (shown in Figure 5-11) is available by choosing Edit➪Preferences (on Windows) and Dreamweaver➪Preferences (on the Mac). You can enable or disable many settings in this dialog box; the best way to become familiar is to explore them. We highlight a few of its features in the text that follows.

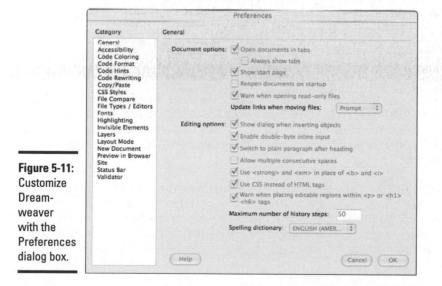

Figure 5-11: Customize Dream-weaver with the Preferences dialog box.

When you select the General category, you see (among other options) the check box that you use to turn the Start Page on and off. You also see options to adjust settings for how Dreamweaver handles spell checking and updating links. In this dialog box, you also have the option of setting Dreamweaver to warn you when you're opening *read-only files* (files that are locked and can't be edited, just viewed).

Other categories in the Preferences dialog box enable you to customize the handling of accessibility features, the colors used when displaying code (setting up different colors for different types of code helps you read your code), and the formatting of your code for easier reading.

Also, when you select the Code Hints category, you get the option of setting up Dreamweaver to give you hints when you begin typing tags. With this feature enabled, Dreamweaver attempts to finish tags as you type them to remind you of proper syntax or parameters available for that tag. Also, this feature shows a list of styles available if you have CSS set up for the page.

The Properties inspector (panel)

The Properties inspector is a *context-sensitive panel*, which means that its functionality changes depending on what you select in the Document window. If you select a table, the options for editing a table are displayed. When text is selected, the text formatting options are shown. You can edit elements using the Properties inspector or set alignments, change colors, join table cells, or apply CSS styles. Many other options are also available depending on what type of element you select.

Making links with the Properties inspector

One of the interesting tools in the Properties inspector is the Point to File tool (shown in Figure 5-12), which looks like a clock to the right of the Link text box. To use the tool, click and drag the clock to the file in the Files panel to make a link. A line drags out from the box to the file you point to. This is a quick and easy way to make a link. It saves time when linking to files within your site.

To link to files that aren't part of your site, type the full URL in the Link text box. You can also choose to target a window when you make a new link. The default is for pages to load into the same window as the page you are already viewing — replacing the current page with the new page to be viewed. For some links, you don't want the new page to replace the one the visitor is viewing — for example, when you link to another site, you probably want that to open in a new window so that the visitor can easily return to your site. In that case, you want to choose _blank from the Target drop-down list. This opens the new page in another window. When the user is done viewing the linked page, she closes that window and the original page is still there in its window. Use this technique sparingly because it can be annoying to visitors if your site launches a lot of windows.

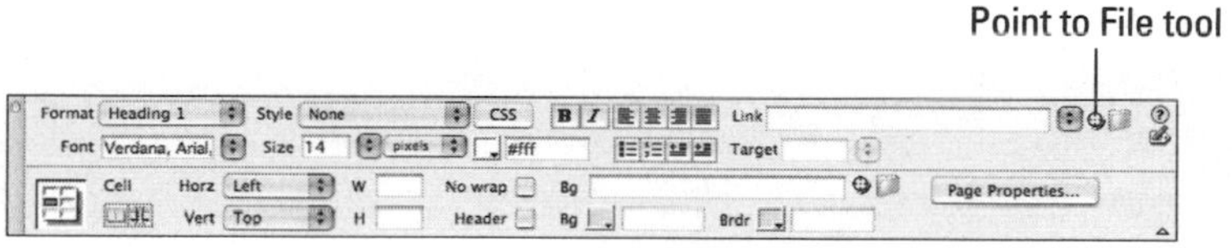

Figure 5-12:
The
Properties
inspector
shows you
the options
available for
the page
element
you are
working on.

Point to File tool

Setting page properties

Click the Page Properties button on the Properties inspector panel to adjust settings regarding default font and size, page color, and margin size. You can also customize the color of a link, including its *rollover color* (the color the link changes to when you hover your cursor over the link). Making settings on this panel automatically generates CSS in the head portion of your document. If you're building multiple pages that will share the same look and feel, you should cut the CSS out of the page head and paste it into an external CSS file. See Book III, Chapters 2 and 3 for more information about how to use CSS and HTML together.

The CSS Styles panel

The CSS Styles panel is where you can write and edit CSS styles. You can also write CSS directly into the HTML document or into the CSS document. Book III, Chapters 2 and 3 show you how to use CSS and HTML together. The CSS Styles panel (see Figure 5-13) gives a list of styles associated with the page.

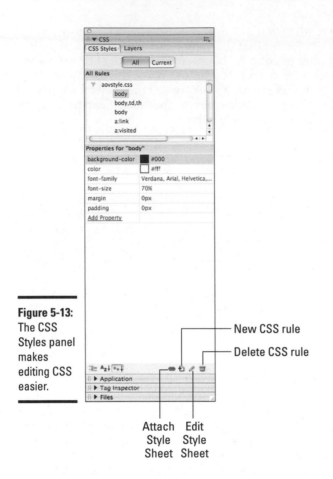

Figure 5-13:
The CSS Styles panel makes editing CSS easier.

New CSS rule

Delete CSS rule

Attach Style Sheet

Edit Style Sheet

Here are ways you can manipulate styles with this panel:

✦ Click the All tab to see all the styles, or click the Current tab to see the style associated with an element on your page.

✦ Double-click a style to edit it.

✦ Add new styles by clicking the New Style Sheet button.

✦ Attach a style by clicking the Attach Style Sheet button. A browse window opens so you can locate the CSS file you'd like to attach.

The CSS Properties, which appear in the middle section of the CSS Styles panel, allow you to edit the properties of a particular style. When you select a style in the CSS Styles panel, the panel is populated with the properties available (see the middle portion of Figure 5-13). Click in the area to the right of a property to see a menu of options for that property. You can also type a value into the field.

The Insert bar

The Insert bar (shown in Figure 5-14) is a narrow toolbar that appears near the top of the screen in the default workspace layout. This toolbar has several categories of tools for elements that you might want to quickly and easily add to a page. Some items in the default set include the following:

✦ **Common:** These elements are the basics: link, e-mail link, *anchor points* (those invisible links that make it so people can jump from place to place on your page), table, image, date (which has several options for formatting), and comment (for adding a code comment).

✦ **Forms:** Inserts the elements you need to build Web forms. (See Book VI for details about how to make a form.) The elements found under this toolbar are radio buttons, check boxes, and text boxes. Each of these has their own special attributes that you can set via the Properties inspector after you've added them to the page.

✦ **Text:** This is another place that has options for formatting text. Special types of formatting are available here, such as headings and definition lists.

✦ **Application:** Inserts elements you need while building dynamic pages. (See Book VI for more details.)

All the elements available on the Insert bar are available via the Insert menu. You can also add more categories by going to the Dreamweaver Developer Center at www.adobe.com/devnet/dreamweaver and finding extensions.

Book III
Chapter 5

Getting Started
with Dreamweaver

Figure 5-14:
The Insert bar has several categories of items you might want to insert on your pages.

Creating a Web Site with Dreamweaver

Now it's time to set up your first Web site. Although you can work with Dreamweaver without setting up a site, it's really a better idea to set one up. Dreamweaver creates a log of information about your site and the files included in it, called a *site cache*. This enables Dreamweaver to do many things. It can make sure that paths to linked files are correct, synchronize your content on your live server, and perform other, helpful, site management tasks. With that being said, it's time to set up your site.

Before you start working in Dreamweaver, it is a good idea to make sure you have Web hosting and a URL purchased. Book I has information about choosing hosts and URLs.

1. **Create a folder on your computer and name it after your project.**

This will be your local site; all site files will go in this folder. (Dreamweaver uses the term *local root folder* to refer to this.)

2. **Create a folder inside your project folder and call it Production.**

This folder is for all the working files you create while working on your site. Don't post this to the server when you publish. Use the cloaking feature to keep it local. (Refer to the "Collapsed view" section in this chapter for instructions on how to set this up in the Files panel.)

3. **Create a folder inside the Production folder and call it Images.**

This will be where all your site images go. (Dreamweaver refers to this as your *Default Images Folder.*)

4. **Create folders for the major areas of your Web site.**

For the About Us area of your Web site, create an About folder; for the Products area of your Web site, create a Products folder; and so on. Make sure you follow Web-legal naming conventions.

5. **Create a folder for your included files.**

This includes CSS, JavaScript, and any other special files that you want to keep organized.

6. **Launch Dreamweaver.**

7. **At the dialog box, select Manage Sites.**

8. **Choose New⇨Site.**

• **Select the Local Info Category.**

Name the site — this name appears in the site list, so make it something that you'll easily recognize.

Set the Local Root Folder by browsing to the folder you created in Step 1.

You can also set up the Default Images Folder by browsing to the folder you created in Step 3.

Select Enable Cache.

• **Select the Remote Info Category.**

Set access to FTP (or one of the others if your server requires it) We'll focus on the FTP settings because this is the most common.

The information you need to input into the fields at this point has to come to you from your Web host, usually via e-mail.

- **FTP Host** is the location of their server. It will look like a regular URL except that it will start with ftp instead of http. (FTP stands for File Transfer Protocol — the way that files are published to Web servers. Using the FTP tells the server what sort of communication is coming.)

- **Host Directory** (optional) Many hosts don't provide a directory name for you to input.

- **Login and Password** is the username and password as given to you by the Web host. You get all the necessary information to log in and FTP files when you sign up for Web hosting.

Make sure you choose a host that has FTP access. Otherwise, uploading and maintaining site files can be a time-consuming nightmare.

- The next three check boxes are optional. Your Web host tells you if you need to use them. If you're having trouble connecting and you're sure all the information you input is correct, ask your host if you should be using any of these options, too.

9. **Click Test to make sure you can connect.**

That's it. You're ready to build a site in the local folder and then publish it to the Internet.

There are other options also available through the Manage Sites dialog box. You can set up a test server and make settings on the types of files you wish to cloak, among other things.

Testing Your Pages and Validating the Code

When you validate your code and check it for browser compatibility or accessibility, you're making sure it's coded so that it complies with the version of HTML or XHTML you're using, making sure it works in the browsers you want to target, and making sure your site is accessible to as many users as possible. (See Book III, Chapter 9 for more about testing usability and accessibility.)

There are different versions of HTML, XHTML, and browsers. Make sure you decide what works best for your audience before you start coding. You can check the World Wide Web Consortium Web site for more information about the versions of HTML, XHTML, and other Web programming and scripting languages.

Use any of these methods to use Dreamweaver's built-in browser checkers and code validators:

✦ **The Site and Commands menu:** Click these menus and select the test you want to run.

✦ **The Results panel:** This panel (shown in Figure 5-15 with test results) automatically launches when you run tests using other methods, too. This is the place where the results of the tests and validators are displayed along with additional information where appropriate. Double-click a line item and Dreamweaver takes you to the error in the code; this helps you quickly locate and fix issues. Also, the Results panel gives the code line numbers for each error that it finds, if you want to use that method for finding issues reported. You need to turn on the code line numbers in the Code View Options; to do so, choose View⇨Code View Options⇨Line Numbers. The line numbers are displayed in the margin of the Code view.

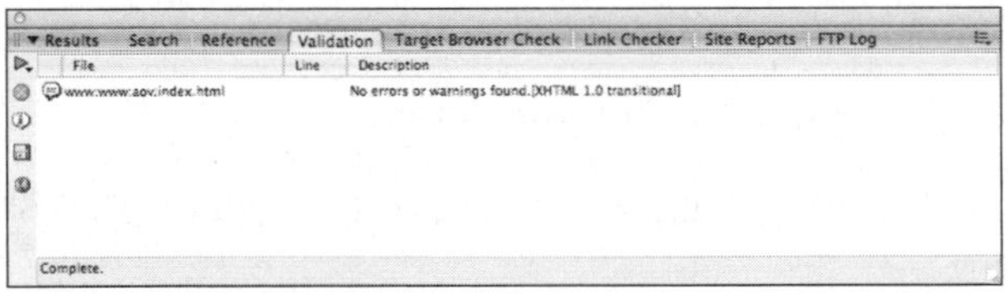

Figure 5-15:
The Results panel. The arrow activates the menus of options within each tab.

The Results panel has options to find and replace things within your code or text, which is handy if you find you've misspelled someone's name. You can also check the links on your page or within your site. Other site reports are also available; experiment with them to see which ones work best for you.

✦ **The Validate Markup button on the Document toolbar:** Refer to Figure 5-7.

To check your code's validity:

1. **Click the Validate Markup button on the Document toolbar.**

2. **From the pop-up menu, choose Current Document, Current Local Site (to do the whole site), or Selected Files in Site (to check a few files at once).**

The Results panel will display the results of the test along with information about what the error is, how severe it is, and where you can find it in your code. Double-click an item and Dreamweaver takes you directly to the error.

To check your page for browser compatibility:

1. **Click the Check Browser Support button on the Document toolbar.**

   This causes Dreamweaver to display your results in the Results panel.

2. **If you haven't set up Dreamweaver to check for the browsers and versions you want to test for, select Settings; if you already have, skip to Step 6.**

3. **Choose the browsers and versions you'd like to test for in the dialog box and click OK.**

4. **Click the Check Browser Support button.**

5. **Select Check Browser Support from the drop-down menu.**

6. **Review and handle any errors according to the information supplied by Dreamweaver.**

Additional tools to help you as you code are also available under the Commands menu. Code Formatting straightens out your code and makes it easier to read. It doesn't affect your site's performance or the validity of your code. Clean up Word HTML fixes errors in HTML code generated by Microsoft Word. These code clean-up tools look for common messy things that happen to code, such as empty tags. They clean up some of these things and alert you to possible issues it finds but can't clean up. It's a handy tool but shouldn't be used instead of validators and checkers.

Publishing Your Web Site with Dreamweaver

You're ready for this section when you have a completely designed site. You've bought your hosting and URL and made sure your URL is pointed to your space, and you've developed your content, designed your pages, run usability tests, and validated your code — and it's all ready to go.

In other parts of the book, we take you through all of the steps leading up to this point. When you're ready to FTP your files to the server, here's how you do it:

1. **Open the Files panel.**

Make sure that you have turned cloaking on for any files or folders you don't want to publish. (Working files, while important, just clutter your host space and take up room, and you pay for that space.) Take a look at the Collapsed view section of this chapter to find out how to turn cloaking on.

2. **Select the folder you would like to cloak.**

3. **Click the Options button in the upper-right corner of the Files panel; it looks like a tiny bulleted list.**

4. **Choose Site➪Cloaking➪Cloak to cloak the folder you selected. Or you can select from the same menu Settings to target specific file types.**

5. **Connect to your remote server by clicking the Connect button on the Files panel toolbar.**

6. **Click the Put button and click Yes when Dreamweaver asks whether you'd like to Put the entire site.**

If you've already posted your site, you can use the synchronize feature to post only new or updated content.

7. **Select the folder you want to synchronize (or select the main folder to synchronize the whole site).**

8. **Select the folder(s) or files that you'd like Dreamweaver to consider while checking files to synchronize. Click the option menu button in the upper-right corner of the Files panel and choose Site➪Synchronize.**

9. **Select a Direction — put new files to the remote server or get new files from the server.**

Synchronize works both ways. Make sure you choose the right direction or you could overwrite your newer files with older ones.

Your options are

- *Put Newer to Remote:* This uploads files from your computer to your remote Web server.

- *Get Newer from Remote:* This Gets files that are newer and copies them to your local site.

- *Put and Get:* This choice compares all the files and either Puts or Gets the newer files, depending on which copy is newest.

You can also elect to have any files that exist on the remote site but not on your local site deleted. If you're very careful to make sure this doesn't affect anything, it can be a great way to clean up site files on the remote server.

10. **Click the Preview button.**

Dreamweaver calls it Preview to let you know that it's not actually post-ing or getting anything yet. It is compiling a list for you to see.

Dreamweaver compares the local site with the remote site and presents you with a list of files that need to be updated. You can accept the list as is or you can select files in the list and remove them from the upload cue by clicking the Ignore File button (red circle with the line through it). Figure 5-16 shows the Synchronize dialog box with a list of files to be posted to the Web upon approval.

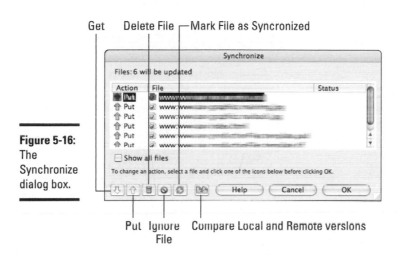

Get   Delete File ─ Mark File as Syncronized

Figure 5-16: The Synchronize dialog box.

Put Ignore   Compare Local and Remote versions
     File

Book III
Chapter 5

Getting Started
with Dreamweaver

11. **When you're ready to post, click OK.**

That's it. You should go to your URL and check to make sure all the files you wanted to post made it to your live site. If you don't see your changes, try refreshing your browser. If that doesn't work, you'll have to explore the pages for another issue, such as links going to older versions of pages.

Chapter 6: Using Dreamweaver: Advanced Techniques

In This Chapter

✔ **Using prebuilt page designs in Dreamweaver**

✔ **Creating your own templates in Dreamweaver**

✔ **Managing your assets and library items**

✔ **Implementing behaviors on your pages**

Dreamweaver 8 has several, built-in tools and features that make your job as a site builder easier. One especially useful feature is Dreamweaver's collection of prebuilt pages — pre-existing designs into which you place your content — that can help you get up and running very fast. You can also build special pages called *templates* — which are essentially the same as prebuilt pages, but you create these according to your specific needs — to make site building and maintenance easier for you and/or your team. The great thing about prebuilt pages and templates is that you can use the same ones over and over, instead of having to reinvent the wheel every time you start a new site project.

If you have content that will appear in multiple places on your site — such as footers, headers, and navigation aids — Dreamweaver also provides features that make handling this situation and updating a site easier. You can build little modules of code to include in your pages.

In this chapter, we look at a Dreamweaver-specific feature called *library items* (pieces of code that you can quickly add to a page and reuse countless times) and the Assets panel, where you can see all the elements of a site. We also cover *behaviors,* which are small bits of JavaScript code that you use to add functionality to your pages, such as opening a new browser window from a link or creating an image rollover effect. (An *image rollover* is when an image changes to a different image when a user moves his cursor over it.)

Creating a Site with Prebuilt Page Designs

Dreamweaver's prebuilt page designs can be good tools to get a project up and running very fast. Also, because you don't have to start entirely from scratch, using the prebuilt designs can be a great way to figure out how to create and code pages; you can change a few things in the HTML and CSS code and see what the effects are.

Some of the prebuilt designs are complete designs and others are just starters, like the CSS files that supply you with a basic HTML page and a CSS document that covers the basics of a color scheme and font choices but leaves the layout code to you. Each category has benefits; the decision of which to use depends on your needs and how comfortable you are with creating pages entirely on your own. The important thing to know is that Dreamweaver can help you if you need it in this area, or it can stay out of your way. The choice is completely yours.

To build a site using the Dreamweaver prebuilt page designs, just follow these steps:

1. **Create a folder on your hard drive and name it after your project. Put it somewhere you will be able to easily find it. This is a personal preference issue, so feel free to create a system that works for you.**

2. **Inside the first folder, create three more folders.**

   Name the folders Images, Includes, and ProductionFiles. (That's right, no spaces in folder names. Always use Web-legal naming conventions; see Book II, Chapter 2 for more information about Web-legal naming.)

   If your site has subsections that will have multiple pages in each, create a folder for each section. This helps you keep your site easy to maintain. Only very small sites (ten or fewer pages) are manageable with all the files in one folder together. It's best to start with a structure that will support expansion, so if you expect to have additional pages within your subsections later, start with folders for each subsection up front. Figure 6-1 shows the file structure for a basic site.

3. **Launch Dreamweaver.**

4. **Create a new site:**

   If Dreamweaver prompts you with a Site management dialog box with a Manage Sites choice, click the New button to do so. From the Manage Sites dialog box, select New.

   If Dreamweaver doesn't prompt you, open the Manage Sites dialog box by choosing Site⇨New Site.

   a. *In the New Site dialog box, set the local site folder to the folder you created in Step 1.*

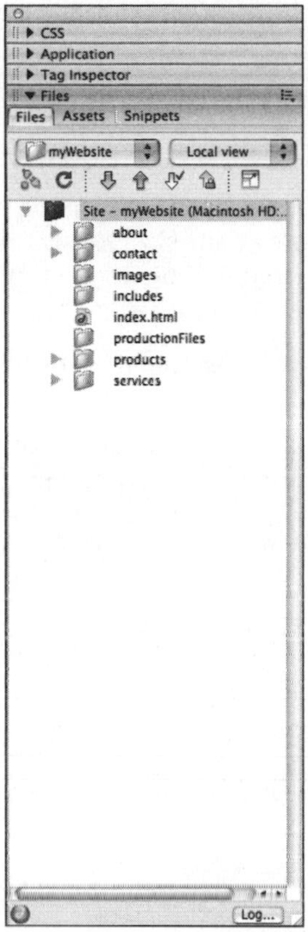

Figure 6-1:
The file
structure of
a basic Web
page.

    *b. Set the default images folder to the folder inside your local site folder
called Images, which you created in Step 2.*

    *c. If you have your Web site hosting set up, put the remote site information
in the appropriate fields. (See Book III, Chapter 5 for information about
setting up a site in Dreamweaver.)*

**5. Create your first page by choosing File⇨New, clicking the Starter
Pages Category, and then choosing a design in the field to the right of
the Category field. For purposes of exploring the interface, choose
Starter Pages⇨Entertainment-Home Page.**

The Preview pane displays a rough idea of what your design will look
like.

**6. In the lower-right section of the dialog box, select a document type
definition (DTD) for your pages. For now, choose XHTML 1.0 Transitional. See Book III, Chapter 2 for more information about DTDs.**

7. **Click Create to create the page.**

8. **When Dreamweaver prompts you to Save As, browse to the local site folder and save the file as `index.html`.**

   This is your site's home page.

   Dreamweaver then displays a Copy Dependent Files dialog box stating that additional files need to be copied to your site. *Dependent files* are the graphics, CSS, and any other files that will be needed for your page to display and work properly.

9. **Browse to the local site folder and click the Copy button in the Copy Dependent Files dialog box.**

   At this point, you have an HTML document open in the Document window, a CSS file that you can open and edit as you need to, and a few supporting sample graphics supplied by Dreamweaver. (Banner, place holders, and others — these vary depending on the design you have chosen.)

10. **Customize the HTML document with your content:**

    • *Replace the place holder text with your own.*

    • *Check image sizes so you can create your own graphics.*

11. **Open the CSS document and determine what (if anything) you'd like to change to create your own design.**

    Figure 6-2 shows how you can use a predesigned page as the base for your own design.

What is a DTD?

Although the code that makes up Web pages is generically referred to as HTML, there are actually several different versions of HTML — and also XHTML (the newer versions of HTML). As you're building pages and learning how to code, you should try to use the most current versions. Information about the versions of HTML can be found on the World Wide Web Consortium Web site at http://w3.org.

A DTD (document type definition) in an HTML or XHTML document should be the first line of code in your page. It tells the browser what version of HTML or XHTML your page is coded with. This helps the browsers know what your page is made of and assists with proper display of your pages. For more information about DTDs, you can visit the section of the World Wide Web Consortium Web site that deals specifically with Web document DTDs at www.w3.org/QA/2002/04/valid-dtd-list.html.

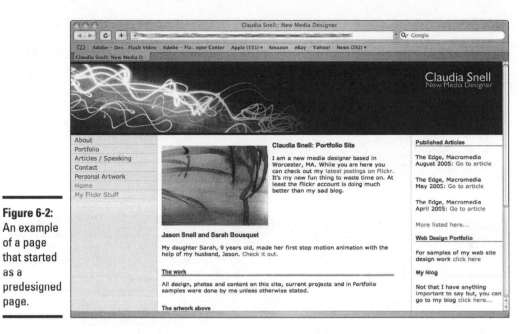

Figure 6-2:
An example
of a page
that started
as a
predesigned
page.

12. **Proceed with creating other pages on your site.**

You can select other layouts from the same set you have chosen for your home page or just use the Save As feature to rename the file you just created to make the other pages on your site.

Creating Templates to Ease Site Maintenance

In Dreamweaver, you can create your own templates. These templates can have sections of the pages locked, or uneditable, to protect content that is consistent on each page. You can set up templates that have several different layouts to accommodate different types of content.

The locked regions of these templates are editable only within the original template document itself. You create individual pages using the template to start and set the boundaries for the locked regions. These templates also work with Adobe Contribute, which is a Web page editing program that allows nontechnical content providers to update and maintain pages.

Making a template

If you don't already have a site set up, create the folders as described in the previous section. Also, adjust your site settings as described in Book III, Chapter 5. Then, follow these steps to create a template:

Why call your home page index instead of home?

You can actually call your home page file `index` or `default`, but not something else. The way that Web servers work is that they look in the folder for a file called `index.html` or `default.html` (or `index.asp`, `index.php`, `index.cfm`, or `index.jsp`, if you're building a dynamic Web site). These are the universal home page names. If you don't give your home page one of these names, people will have to type the whole path to your home page in order to see it. For example, if you call your home page `homepage.html`, a visitor has to type **http://www.*yoursite.com/*homepage.html** to see your site. If he doesn't, he gets an error message saying the site cannot be found or that a page cannot be displayed. If you name your home page properly, a visitor needs to type only **http://www.*your*** *site.com* to get to your site. The same rules apply to subfolders. If you have a section of your site inside a folder called Plants, name the main page `index.html` within that folder so that visitors only need to type **http://www.*your site.com*/plants** to see the page.

Another thing to know is that `.htm` and `.html` are not the same thing to all servers. Make sure you check with your host to see what their system is set up to recognize. If their server considers only `default.htm` to be the default page of a site (or home page) and you use `index.html`, the server won't recognize the home page. If you experience difficulty getting a site to show up after you upload it, this is one thing to check. Also, make sure you're using the right name and file extension for your host's setup.

1. **Create a new page:**

    a. Choose File⇨New from the Dreamweaver menu bar.

    b. On the General tab of the New Document dialog box that appears, click Basic Page in the Category field.

    c. In the field to the right of Category, click HTML.

        Take a look at the Preview pane to get a rough idea of what the design will look like.

    d. Click the arrows on the Document Type (DTD) drop-down menu and select the appropriate DTD.

        (For information on what a DTD is, see the nearby sidebar.)

    e. Click the Create button.

2. **Save the document to your site folder.**

    Design your page as you would for a normal page. See Chapters 1–5 of this minibook for information about creating pages. Or you can start your design with a prebuilt design, which we discuss in the preceding section.

3. **To make the page into a template, choose Insert⇨Template Objects⇨ Make Template from the Dreamweaver menu bar. A second way to do this is to choose File⇨Save as Template.**

   Like so many things in Dreamweaver, which one to use is a matter of personal preference. The good thing about having multiple ways to get a job done is that you can develop a working style that is comfortable for you. The way that is easiest for you to remember is the way you should do it.

   Make sure your template stays in the same folder with your site. If you move the template, your template won't work properly. Notice that Dreamweaver gives templates a special file extension (.dwt) and also creates a special folder (Templates) where it stores the template files for the site.

Including editable regions

Editable regions allow you to make changes to designated areas of a particular page. Changes to noneditable areas have to be made in the template itself and are reflected in *all* of the documents that have been created using the template. Follow these steps to include editable regions in your template:

1. **Highlight the area that you'd like to make editable — a table cell or a layer, for example — and choose Insert⇨Template Objects⇨Editable Region.**

2. **Name the editable region.**

Book III
Chapter 6

   These areas are the only areas that are directly editable within the pages created using the template. Figure 6-3 shows a page with editable pages included. These editable areas are where each page's unique content will go. Content that stays the same on each page should not be made editable. This helps you maintain consistency in areas where consistency is vital — such as navigation and site-branding areas.

Using Dream-
weaver: Advanced
Techniques

Creating a page using a template

After you create your own template for site building, creating a page with it is easy; just follow these steps:

1. **Choose File⇨New.**

2. **On the Templates tab of the New Document dialog box that opens, select the name of your site from the Templates For list.**

   Select the template you'd like to use. (You can create as many as you'd like.)

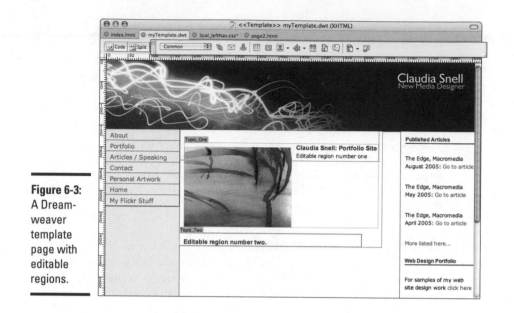

Figure 6-3:
A Dream-
weaver
template
page with
editable
regions.

3. **Enable the Update when Template Changes check box.**

   This allows you to make changes to just the template, and Dreamweaver changes all the pages that were created using the template. The benefit of this functionality is that you can build pages that allow other users to change the main content of a page but protect the banner and navigation areas from unauthorized edits. If edits need to be made, make them in the template, and the rest of the pages are updated, too.

4. **Click Create.**

Dreamweaver templates also work with Contribute, so you can build a site in Dreamweaver but supply Contribute to individuals who need to make regular changes to text or pictures. The combination of these two programs helps you protect your site from unauthorized changes or unintentional mistakes that break the pages while giving you the ability to hand off routine maintenance to nontechnical members of a team. Figure 6-4 shows what areas of a page would need to be editable on the average page. Notice how much of the page can have a consistent look protected by noneditable regions.

Updating a template

Updating a template is nearly as easy as creating and using one; just follow these steps:

1. **Open the template file you'd like to change. Opening a template is just like opening any other file in your site. Use File⇨Open or double-click it in the Files panel.**

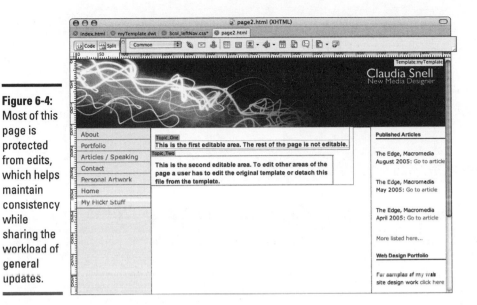

Figure 6-4:
Most of this
page is
protected
from edits,
which helps
maintain
consistency
while
sharing the
workload of
general
updates.

2. **Make the edits to the noneditable areas you need to update.**

3. **Save the document.**

   The Update Template Files dialog box (see Figure 6-5) opens, showing the files to be updated.

4. **Click Update to accept the list; click Don't Update to reject the updates.**

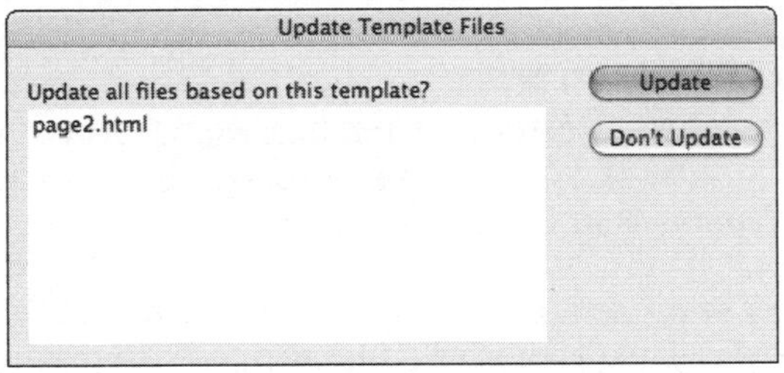

Update Template Files

Update all files based on this template?

page2.html

[Update]

[Don't Update]

Figure 6-5:
Choosing
files to
update.

The Update Pages dialog box appears, see Figure 6-6 for an example. This dialog box allows you to select the whole site that you want to update or just a folder on the site. It also gives you some other options and gives a report of the status of files to be updated.

5. **Click Update to update the files.**

Dreamweaver reports on the status of the changes.

6. Click Close when the updates are complete.

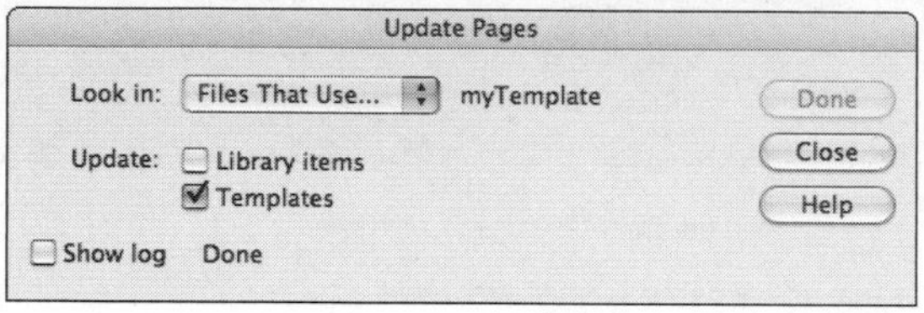

Figure 6-6:
The Update
Pages
dialog box.

Update Pages		
Look in: Files That Use... ⬍ myTemplate		Done
Update: ☐ Library items		Close
☑ Templates		Help
☐ Show log Done		

Exploring the Assets Panel and Library Items

Two other handy tools in Dreamweaver are the Assets panel and library items. They're grouped together and they both help you keep things organized, but they aren't exactly the same thing.

The Assets panel provides a quick-and-easy way to see all the things that are available within your site. It provides easy access to things like images, templates, multimedia elements, and color schemes. *Library items* are pieces of code that you make into modules that you can quickly add to a page. Unlike *Code Snippets,* which are also bits of code that you can use on your pages over and over, you build library items, and they're associated with a particular site. They work a bit like minitemplates. When you add them to a page, they aren't editable unless you detach them from the original library item. However, if you make changes to the library item itself, a similar Update Files dialog box appears.

Touring the Assets panel

If the Assets panel isn't open when you launch Dreamweaver, open it by choosing Window⇨Assets. The Assets panel groups on-screen with the Files panel when the Files panel is in Collapsed view.

The Assets panel has several categories, represented by buttons in the left margin. (See Figure 6-7.) The categories (from top to bottom) are

+ **Images:** Lists all the JPEGS, GIFs, and PNGs within the site.

+ **Colors:** Shows color chips and the hexadecimal code for the colors used on the site.

+ **URLs:** Lists the pages and URLs your site is linked to. You can quickly make links in your documents by highlighting the text or item you'd like to be the link, and dragging the desired link onto the highlighted element in your Document window.

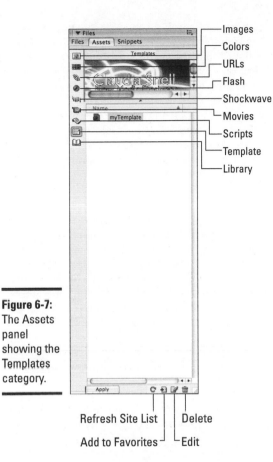

Figure 6-7:
The Assets panel showing the Templates category.

Refresh Site List

Add to Favorites ─ ─Edit

Delete

Book III
Chapter 6

Using Dream-
weaver: Advanced
Techniques

+ **Flash:** Lists all `.swf` files, which are different from the Shockwave files. If you want to use images or Flash pieces, click the Flash button on the vertical toolbar and drag the item from the list to the place in the Design view window you'd like to place it.

+ **Shockwave:** Lists multimedia created using Adobe Director. Flash files are sometimes referred to as *Shockwave,* but they aren't really Shockwave; they're Flash.

+ **Movies:** Lists all movie files that don't fit on the Flash or Shockwave tabs, such as QuickTime.

+ **Scripts:** Lists all the external scripts, such as JavaScript files, that are on your site.

+ **Template:** Lists the Dreamweaver templates you've built.

+ **Library:** Lists the library items you've created for the site.

You can access the assets of each type by clicking the appropriate button. This method of locating assets is helpful when you know you're looking for a particular item and you'd like a list of just that type of object. For instance, if you want to place a Flash element on a page, click the Flash button and you're presented with a list of the Flash elements available on that site.

At the bottom of the Assets panel, you'll notice a few more buttons (refer to Figure 6-7): Refresh Site List, Add to Favorites, Edit, and Delete (looks like a trashcan). At the top are a few more: Sort by Whole Site and Sort by Favorites. If you have marked elements as Favorites, you can use the second option to narrow your search for assets as you work.

Discovering library items

Webmasters have several methods at their disposal for implementing similar types of functionality on a Web site; using the library items feature is the Dreamweaver-specific method. The assets panel is usually open within the Files panel and can be accessed by clicking the Assets tab. If the assets panel is not open, you access library items through the Assets panel. (See Figure 6-8.) Choose Window➪Assets from the Dreamweaver menu bar to open the Assets panel. After you have created an HTML document, you can make parts of it into library items. With library items, you can reuse that content on other pages by dragging it from the Library into the spot on the document you'd like for it to be. By default, there aren't any library items, so you'll have to make them yourself.

+ **Create part of a page once and then quickly apply the code from it to other pages on your site.** You might find library items useful to implement and maintain consistency in footers, banners, and navigational elements.

+ **Update all instances of a library item at once.** Library items maintain an association to the library item file, so if you update the original, the other instances of it are updated, too.

Library items are sort of like minitemplate pieces with a few differences. As with templates, you can create as many library items as you like, but you should keep in mind that the more variations you have, the more difficult maintenance can become.

With Dreamweaver library items, the code of the item does appear in the individual HTML document but is linked in Dreamweaver to the originating file. Other HTML editors won't recognize the association, so if you implement this method, you need to maintain and edit the files within your Dreamweaver site.

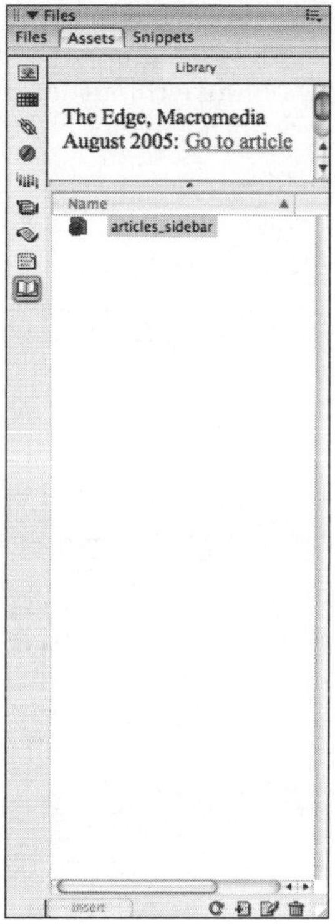

Figure 6-8:
Viewing library items in the Assets panel.

Creating a library item

To create a Dreamweaver library item, follow these steps:

1. **Create a Web page or open an existing one.**

2. **Create the element you'd like to make into a library item.**

   Create a navigation bar or site banner, for instance.

3. **Open the Assets panel by choosing Windows➪Assets from the Dreamweaver menu bar. Click the Library button on the Assets panel.**

4. **Highlight all the code that makes up the element.**

5. **Click the New Library Item button located in the lower-right corner of the Assets panel.**

   A dialog box warns you that style sheet information that applies to the code is not copied along with the code.

6. **Click OK.**

7. **Name the library item.**

Use a name that makes sense, such as `Navigation` for a navigation bar. Make sure you call it something Web legal. Making up strange naming schemes is not helpful and can actually confuse things later when you or other members of the team need to work with the files.

Dreamweaver automatically creates the library item folder called Library in your site. The new library item is in the folder with the name you gave it and the file extension of `.lbi`.

At this point, you might notice some new code in your document that looks like this:

```
<!-- #BeginLibraryItem "/Library/Navigation.lbi" -->
    <div id="links">
        <ul>
            <li><a href="about/about.htm">About</a></li>
            <li><a
href="portfolio/portfolio.htm">Portfolio</a></li>
            <li><a href="extra/extra.htm">Articles /
Speaking</a></li>
            <li><a href="about/contact.htm">Contact</a></li>
            <li><a href="Portfolio/gallery.htm">Personal
Artwork</a></li>
            <li><a href="index.html">Home</a></li>

        </ul>
    </div>
    <!-- #EndLibraryItem -->
```

The first line in this block of code alerts Dreamweaver that this is a piece of code that is linked to the library item called `Navigation`. The last line tells Dreamweaver that it has reached the end of the block. Do not remove this code, or Dreamweaver won't be able to update this properly.

The block of code is also highlighted in Code view. This is just a visual cue to help you see that you have a library item on your page. It won't affect the visual display of your page at all.

Using a library item

Inserting library items into a site is very easy and takes only a couple of steps:

1. **Create or open an HTML document that you'd like to use the library item in.**

2. **Drag the library item from the library panel into the Document window into the location you'd like to place the block of code.**

   Your page has a block of code that resembles the code generated when you created the library item.

Updating library items

To update the library item:

1. **Select the library item in the Assets panel list.**

2. **Click the Edit button. (It's in the lower-right corner of the Assets panel; refer to Figure 6-8.)**

3. **Dreamweaver opens the document in the Document window.**

4. **Make the desired edits.**

5. **Save the document.**

   The Update Library Items dialog box opens, displaying a list of documents that will be affected.

6. **Click Update.**

   The Update Pages dialog box appears, giving you additional options and a status on the update process.

7. **Make any additional optional choices and click Start in the Update Pages dialog box.**

8. **Click Done to close the dialog box.**

Detaching library items

In some cases, you might want to detach an instance of the library item from the main file. For instance, you could decide to expand an area of a site that has a library-item-generated navigation bar. You can detach that navigation bar from the library file, make changes, and then make a new, secondary navigation library item for use within that section.

To detach an instance of the library item from the parent file:

1. **Open the page that has the block of code.**

2. **Select the library item code. You'll be able to find it easily; library item code is highlighted by Dreamweaver.**

3. **In the Properties inspector, click Detach from Original.**

   An alert box opens, warning you that you will not be able to affect this section of code by editing the library item after detaching.

4. **Click OK to detach the item or click Cancel if you change your mind.**

   Note: You can also choose to edit a library item by selecting it and clicking Open in the Properties inspector. To select the Library item, just click anywhere in the library item code or click it in the Design view window.

An additional function you can perform by selecting an instance of a library item is Recreate. If you click the Recreate button in the Properties inspector, Dreamweaver creates a new copy of the library item. If the .lbi file (.lbi is the file extension for a Dreamweaver library item) already exists, a dialog box opens, warning you that you're about to overwrite the original.

Adding Functionality with Dreamweaver Behaviors

Dreamweaver *behaviors* are pieces of prebuilt, client-side JavaScript. *Client-side* refers to scripts that are executed by the browser on the user's machine as opposed to *server-side* scripts, which are executed by the server.

Behaviors allow Web designers to add functionality quickly and easily. Dreamweaver comes with several behaviors included. You can further customize Dreamweaver by downloading more and adding them.

Two popular behaviors are

+ **Open Browser Window:** A link opened via JavaScript allows for some customization and can also receive other commands via JavaScript. We give you instructions on how to use this behavior later in this section. When this code is added to a link, the linked file opens in a new browser window. (See Figure 6-9.) This is a little different than simply opening a link in a new window via HTML (`<a href="`*http://www.sample.com* `target="_blank">`*LINKED TEXT*`</a>`), which is shown in Figure 6-10.

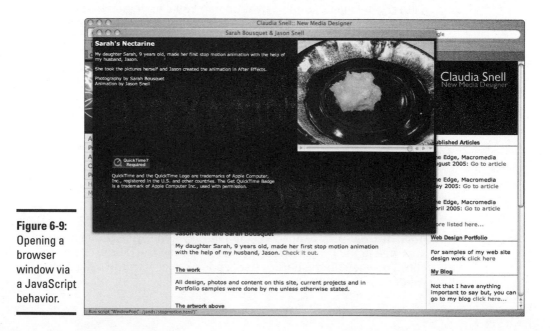

Figure 6-9: Opening a browser window via a JavaScript behavior.

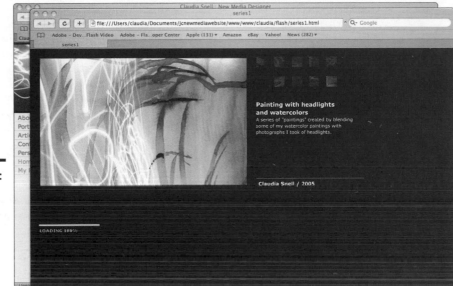

Figure 6-10:
Using
target="_
blank" to
open a
second
browser
window.

✦ **Pop-up message:** A *pop-up message* is a dialog box that pops up and
gives your users instructions or other information. (See Figure 6-11.)
Pop-up messages (or *alerts,* as some people call them) can be very helpful and useful, but be careful to use them only when they're the best
solution. Users tend to get annoyed by pop-ups and alerts, so you
should avoid them unless they're conveying important information.
Information about how to implement and work with pop-up messages
appears later in this section.

Figure 6-11:
An example
of a pop-up
window,
also called
an alert.

> JavaScript
>
> This is a popup message.
>
> OK

Other functionality available through the Behaviors panel includes functions
for DHTML (dynamic HTML) and rollover effects.

One thing to keep in mind as you use behaviors is that browsers support JavaScript in different ways. Some functionality that works fine in one browser doesn't work in other versions — or can work differently in other browsers. Before you start to use behaviors, decide what browsers and versions you want to support. You can then set up the Behaviors panel to show only the behaviors that work for your targeted browser(s). In the same menu that appears when you click the Add Behavior button (the plus sign at the top of the panel) is an option called Show Events For. If you choose that menu item, a list of available browsers is displayed. Scroll to the one you'd like to target and click it. Behaviors become available or unavailable depending on your selection immediately.

If you'd like to get more behaviors, you can click Get More Behaviors (which is also available through the Add Behavior menu). When you choose that menu item, Dreamweaver launches a browser and browses to the Dreamweaver Exchange Web site — as long as you're connected to the Internet, that is. If not, it asks you to connect. You can then select, download, and load new behaviors into Dreamweaver.

Including the Open Browser Window behavior

To include the Open Browser Window behavior in your code, follow these steps:

1. **Highlight the item you'd like to use as a trigger.**

   The trigger should be an image or bit of text; you need to have a link on the page so the user can make the window open.

2. **If the Behaviors panel isn't open, you can access it by choosing Window⇨Behaviors.**

3. **In the Behaviors panel, click the Add Behavior button (the plus sign at the top).**

4. **From the pop-up menu, choose Open Browser Window.**

5. **Make changes in the Open Browser Window dialog box that opens. (See Figure 6-12.)**

   a. *Type the URL you would like to open in the URL to Display text box, or click the Browse button and browse to the file within your site that you'd like to open.*

   b. *Set the window width and height to customize the size. Just enter the numbers; the unit of measure is pixels. So, if you'd like your window to be 500 pixels wide and 400 pixels high, enter **500** in the width box and **400** in the height box.*

   You can set the size to any size you'd like.

   c. *Enable the check boxes of the attributes you'd like to select.*

About extensions and the Extension Manager

Extensions are bits of code and other plug-ins created by Adobe/Macromedia or third parties and made available for download through the Adobe Exchange Web sites. You can download and install these extensions to add functionality to Dreamweaver, Flash, Fireworks, and/or other Adobe/Macromedia software. Some extensions are available for a fee, and others are free. Make sure you read the license agreements and user reviews before you download files. They can help you choose the most helpful tool for the task at hand.

To install behaviors or other items downloaded from the Adobe Exchange Web sites:

1. **Double-click the `.mxp` file.**

   (`.mxp` is the file type of Adobe/Macromedia extension files.)

Extension Manager launches and handles the installation. Extension Manager also has additional information about the file you've installed, sometimes including copyright information or tips for use. You can also *manage your extensions* — enable and disable them and keep track of which extensions you have installed — for your Adobe/Macromedia products. The image that follows shows the Extension Manager, which is actually a separate program that manages any extensions you collect for all of your Macromedia products.

2. **You must restart Dreamweaver for the new extension to be available.**

   (The same goes for all the Adobe/Macromedia products.)

Attributes further affect the features and appearance of the new browser window, such as whether scroll bars appear in the new window, whether the user can resize the window, and so on.

   d. *Type a name in the Window Name text box.*

Give the new window a name that can be referred to by other JavaScripts you might want to implement.

A benefit of using a window name is that you can prevent multiple new windows from opening by using the same name in other instances of the open browser window script within your site. If a visitor clicks an instance, a new window opens. When he clicks another instance that targets the same window, the new content replaces the old content.

Another benefit of using this method of opening another browser window — you can control that window via JavaScript that calls that new window by the name you give it. A downside is that a few users don't allow JavaScript to run in their browsers. It is possible that they could miss out on your content.

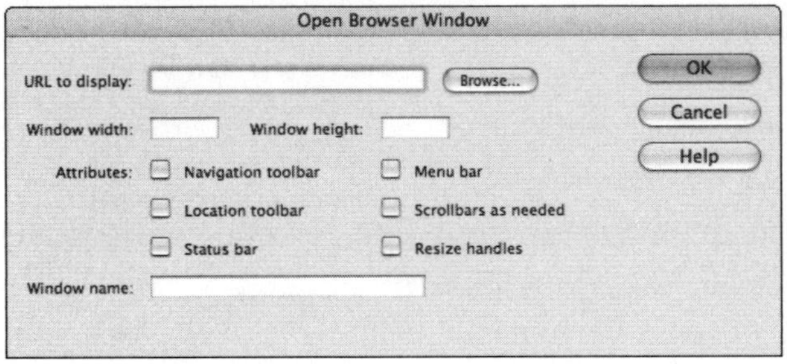

Figure 6-12:
The Open Browser Window dialog box.

Open Browser Window	
URL to display: [ ] Browse...	OK
Window width: [ ] Window height: [ ]	Cancel
Attributes: ☐ Navigation toolbar ☐ Menu bar	Help
☐ Location toolbar ☐ Scrollbars as needed	
☐ Status bar ☐ Resize handles	
Window name: [ ]	

6. Click OK.

Dreamweaver inserts code into the head section of your Web page that makes the behavior work. Dreamweaver also inserts some code at the location that you highlighted in Step 1. This code is there to trigger the behavior that is placed in the head.

If you want to reuse the code on multiple pages or if you'd like to keep your pages clean, you can cut and paste the JavaScript from the head of the document into an external JavaScript file by following these steps:

1. Choose File➪New from the Dreamweaver menu bar.

2. In the New Document dialog box, choose Category➪Basic➪JavaScript.

3. Click Create.

4. Save the new file to your local Web site folder.

If you don't have a folder called Scripts in the site folder, create one:

a. *Choose File➪Save As from the Dreamweaver menu bar.*

b. *Browse to the folder that holds your local Web site.*

    c. Click New Folder.

    d. Name the Folder Scripts.

    e. Save the new JavaScript file with a Web-legal name. (See Book II,
    Chapter 2 for information about Web-legal names.)

5. **Look for code that looks like the following in the head section of your HTML document:**

```
<script language="JavaScript" type="text/JavaScript">
<!--
function MM_openBrWindow(theURL,winName,features) {
   //v2.0
   window.open(theURL,winName,features);
}
//-->
</script>
```

6. **Cut all of the code that starts with** `function` **and ends with the second curly brace, like this:**

```
function MM_openBrWindow(theURL,winName,features) {
   //v2.0
   window.open(theURL,winName,features);
}
```

The curly brace is very important. If you don't have that curly brace, the code will be broken!

7. **Paste this code into the new JavaScript file.**

The remaining code looks like this:

```
<script language="JavaScript" type="text/JavaScript">
<!--
//-->
</script>
```

8. **Remove the comments and add a link to the JavaScript file:**

```
<script src="scripts/myscript.js" language="JavaScript"
   type="text/JavaScript"></script>
```

You can add this code to any of the pages of your site, and it will make the open browser window behavior available on that page, too.

The second piece of code that makes this work is in the body section of your HTML document:

```
<a href="onclick="MM_openBrWindow('http://www.YOURLINK.com',
   'windowName','menubar=yes,width=440,height=444')">Text
   that is linked</a>
```

Book III
Chapter 6

Using Dream-
weaver: Advanced
Techniques

This piece of code creates the link text that triggers the open browser window. It also sends instructions to the code called *parameters*. It tells the code how large the window should be, what URL should be displayed, and whether there should be scroll bars — all the things you set in the Open Browser Window dialog box. You can make changes to this code if you like by typing directly into this code. The JavaScript gets the new instructions and follows them. No need to open the JavaScript file at all. It's been built using variables that await the instructions that are passed by the preceding code.

Editing a behavior via the Behaviors panel

If you're not comfortable messing with the code (as we show you in the preceding section), you can use the Behaviors panel to alter behaviors. Just follow these steps:

1. **Select the trigger code in the body of the HTML document.**

2. **In the Behaviors panel, double-click the Edit Behavior button — it looks like a little yellow gear next to the name of the behavior.**

3. **In the Attributes dialog box that opens, make your edits.**

4. **Click OK to accept the changes.**

Another thing you can edit is the type of interaction that triggers your behavior.

You will notice that the behavior has some code that looks like onClick or onLoad. These are actions that trigger the code. In other words, onClick means that when someone clicks the spot you designated, the behavior executes. And onLoad means that the script will execute as soon as the page or other trigger element loads into the visitor's browser. You can change the trigger action by selecting a new one from the drop-down menu next to the edit gear in the Behaviors panel.

Creating a pop-up message

Another behavior that might come in handy is the pop-up message (also known as an *alert box*). If you've browsed the Web, you've seen alert boxes before. They're the little windows that pop up to give you some extra information. These windows require some acknowledgement from users that they have seen them — in other words, users have to click OK before the alert lets them proceed. Pop-ups are most often used to tell users that they need to include some extra information in a form and other things of that sort.

While many users don't like pop-ups, they can be a valuable tool when you need to convey information. But make sure you don't overuse them because they can lose their impact. Sometimes, users won't see the vital information, just another roadblock as they try to use your site. Also, make sure your message is easy to understand, concise, and doesn't include a lot of technical detail. Remember, it's just a quick alert, not a minisite. Be considerate of your users, and they will pay attention to your messages.

To include a pop-up message on your page:

1. **Open the document you're adding the message to and place the cursor in the body section of the document.**

Alternatively, you can highlight a section of the code.

2. **In the Behaviors panel, click the Add Behavior button (the plus sign).**

3. **In the Popup Message dialog box that appears (see Figure 6-13), type the message and click OK.**

Dreamweaver adds this code to the head of your document:

```
<script language="JavaScript" type="text/JavaScript">
<!--
function MM_popupMsg(msg) { //v1.0
  alert(msg);
}
//-->
</script>
```

Figure 6-13:
Type what
you want
users to see
in a pop-up
message.

Popup Message

Message: | This is a popup message.

OK
Cancel
Help

It also adds this code to the body of your document:

```
<body onLoad="MM_popupMsg('This is a popup message.')">
```

This particular example tells the browser to create an alert message box when the page loads and display the text: This is a popup message.

You can edit the message by changing the text in the code. You can also change the trigger and content of this behavior in the way we describe in the "Including the Open Browser Window behavior" section earlier in this chapter.

Chapter 7: Creating a Web Page from a Photoshop File

In This Chapter

✔ Finishing a wire frame design

✔ Dealing with graphics: Slicing and optimizing

✔ Creating a transparent image

*P*lanning and wire framing can save you a lot of headaches later because it's easier to fix mistakes before the whole site is built. In Book II, Chapter 1, we show you how to create a Photoshop wire frame that you can use for a page layout. In this chapter, we show you how to take that wire frame to the finished product. Creating a wire frame helps you decide what belongs on the screen, figure out the underlying structure of your site, and make adjustments as necessary before committing to a whole design. We also show you how to develop a layout, slice a document, and prepare graphics for use on your Web page.

Taking a Wire Frame to a Finished Design

With a complete wire frame, follow these steps to create your page layout:

1. **Launch Photoshop.**

2. **Open your wire frame file.**

3. **Choose your color scheme.**

When choosing colors for the Web site, check to see whether the organization has already chosen colors for its communications. If so, ask for the RGB or hexadecimal codes for the colors to ensure that you use the correct ones. Book IV, Chapter 1 has more details about the different types of colors and why you need RGB or hexadecimal colors instead of CMYK.

Some designers advise you to use the Photoshop Eyedropper tool to get the colors from a CMYK document, but this is not a good way of getting the colors. It can be unreliable, and the resulting colors can be incorrect.

If no set of graphics standards exists or if the site you're designing needs a unique look, you have to choose the colors yourself. If you need information about choosing a good color scheme, refer to Book II, Chapter 4. You can also make a custom palette (see Figure 7-1), a process that is explained further in the "Managing colors with customer palettes" sidebar.

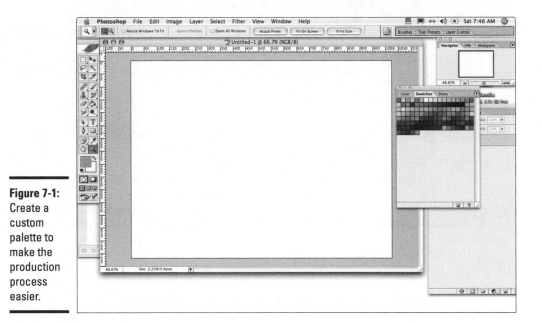

Figure 7-1:
Create a custom palette to make the production process easier.

4. Create place holder elements to fill in your layout.

To create the text elements, you use the Text tool.

a. *With the Text tool (the one that looks like a capital T in the tool bar) selected, click anywhere in the work area window.*

Notice that Photoshop automatically creates a text layer for your new text.

b. *Select a font and color by using the context-sensitive menu that appears at the top of the screen, under the default Photoshop menu bar.*

See Figure 7-2 for an example of the menu.

c. *Select a color from your custom palette by clicking the color chip in the Text menu and then clicking a swatch in your custom palette window.*

d. *Click the spot in the work area where you want your text. Type the text.*

Managing colors with custom palettes

A custom palette isn't necessary, but it can certainly make things easier. It allows you to keep colors consistent throughout the project. You can also e-mail the file to other members of the team so they can match the colors.

To make a custom palette, follow these steps:

1. **Create a layer.**

2. **Make boxes with the colors in your color scheme.**

3. **Choose File⇨Save for Web**

4. **In the color table palette, open the Color Palette menu (by clicking the *twirl-out menu* — the small black triangle icon at the upper-right of the palette).**

   Figure 7-1 shows you where to find the palette and menu selection.

5. **Select Save Color Table from the pop-up menu.**

   Photoshop saves it to the Adobe Presets folder called Optimized Colors, by default. You can save the file to your Production Files folder so that it stays with the project, even after you back up the files for storage.

6. **Name your file something that is easy to identify.**

   Using the project's name will help keep things tidy.

Load the custom palette by following these steps:

1. **In Photoshop, open the Swatches palette (Window⇨Swatches).**

2. **In the swatches pop-up menu, found when you click the small black triangle in the upper right of the swatches palette, choose Replace Swatches.**

3. **Select your palette and click Open.**

   Note: Replace Swatches removes the current palette and replaces it with your custom one. If you choose Append instead of Replace Swatches, your custom palette is appended to the end of the list of swatches already available in the swatch palette.

   You can bring the default palette back by selecting the twirl-out menu and choosing Reset Swatches — or you can replace it with another palette the same way you loaded your custom swatches.

You can edit, move, and change the text later, so don't worry if it's not perfect. If you know what some of your headings are, use that text. If not, use something like **Example Header** so everyone understands that the text is just for example, not the finished content.

Figure 7-3 shows the color swatches (from Step c), as well as typed text.

e. *Create headings of at least three sizes for primary, secondary, and tertiary headings. You will also want to apply colors, underlines, or any other special treatments you would like to apply to your headings.*

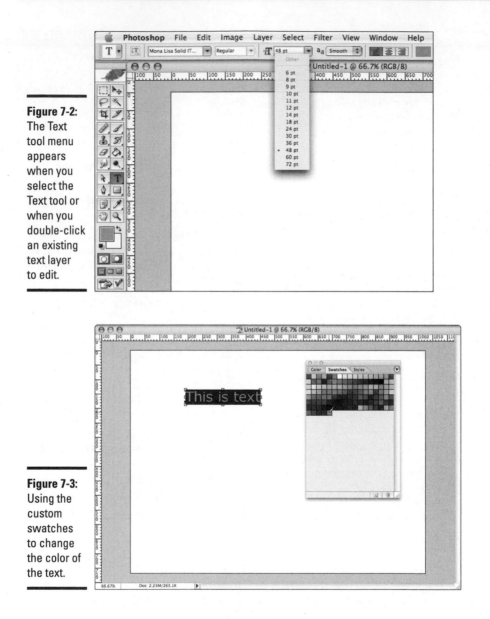

Figure 7-2:
The Text tool menu appears when you select the Text tool or when you double-click an existing text layer to edit.

Figure 7-3:
Using the custom swatches to change the color of the text.

Make sure that the priority of the headings is clear — Heading 1 should look more prominent than Heading 2, which is more prominent than Heading 3, and so on.

f. Create a fake paragraph with a font that is clear and easy to read.

Verdana is a good font to use for Web content. At this stage, just type some nonsense so that you can see what the paragraphs will look like within your final design. Place a few of them into your design. Make sure you also place headings into the layout, too (as discussed in Step e). Doing so gives you an idea of how everything will look together. The point is to make this version of your design look more like the finished product.

g. Create place holder buttons by using the rectangle tool to draw the shapes.

Click the small black triangle in the Rectangle tool's area to see other shape tools. Use the Line tool to create borders for your buttons. You can start applying the text to these if you know what that text will be. After you make the button shapes, double-click the layer that Photoshop made when you created the rectangle to launch the Layer Effects dialog box. Here you can apply drop shadows, gradients, patterns, and many other effects. Click the name of an effect to open the options for that effect.

It's easier to create a whole navigation bar with just one rectangle, and then break it up into buttons visually with the Line tool. This way, you have only one rectangle to contend with when it comes to lining things up, changing effects, or adjusting colors.

h. Create footer text.

With footer text, you'll want to make it small and discreet — the text will include things like copyright information and contact information. It's important information but shouldn't overpower the rest of the page.

i. Create banner text.

Banner text should make a big impression. This text is going to be the name of your site, and it's part of your brand. This text must be more eye-catching than other text on the page.

Figure 7-4 gives you an idea of what your design might look like at this point. Making these place holders helps as you make sure your content is readable and that emphasis is on the right elements without cluttering the design with finished artwork. Design is an iterative process: You will layer changes on changes until you have the completed product.

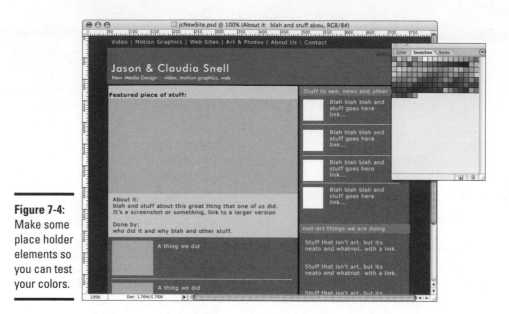

Figure 7-4:
Make some place holder elements so you can test your colors.

At this point you have a wire frame layout that is starting to have a little look and feel to it. It's by no means ready to go, but it is much more developed than a bunch of boxes. These next steps take you through the process of adding a little more personality to the layout by editing fonts and colors, adjusting text, and so forth. Just follow these steps:

1. **Edit fonts, content, colors, or any other properties of text after you've created it by double-clicking the text layer or single-clicking the layer, selecting the Text tool, and then directly selecting the text in the work area.**

2. **Apply the color scheme to the layout.**

3. **Double-click the color thumbnail to open the Color picker and change the color.**

    For the layout boxes, notice that the layers have two thumbnails. (See Figure 7-5.)

4. **Mouse over the custom swatches; the cursor changes to an eyedropper, and you can click one of your custom colors to apply it.**

    If you're not using Web-safe colors, you must uncheck the Web Only Colors box in the Color picker. See Book III, Chapter 4 for more details about how to use Photoshop's Color Picker palette.

5. **Adjust the colors of the text until it has enough contrast that you can easily read it.**

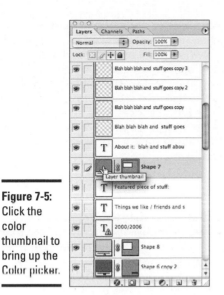

Figure 7-5:
Click the color thumbnail to bring up the Color picker.

6. **Adjust the headings, banner text, and other supporting text until they're readable and also have the amount of emphasis you want them to have.**

   This is a judgment you have to make, and it's different for each project's content and objectives.

7. **Apply color to the boxes — experiment until you produce the effect you want.**

As you're adjusting colors and making decisions, remember not to sacrifice readability for a cool design. The point of a site is to convey information. Low contrast (for example: light gray text over a medium gray background) might look very cool but is hard for many users to read. A design, even a nice-looking one, is a failure if visitors can't use the content. Visitors can and will look for a site that is easier to use. See Book II, Chapter 4 for more information and pointers about choosing colors and fonts for your site.

Finishing the Artwork

In Book II, Chapter 1, we show you how to create a wire frame. The first section of this chapter shows you how to apply a little look and feel to that wire frame by adding and adjusting color, text, headings, and so on. Here we continue to modify the wire frame by focusing on completing the banner. Note that the techniques can be applied to any of your site graphics.

Choose images or create artwork for your banner and your site pages. As with every other step in the process, choosing or creating artwork should be driven by reinforcing your message. Of course, you'll use your own taste when selecting images, but ultimately, the direction must be driven by communication, not artistic statements. Make sure you have licenses to use images and artwork that you didn't create. A license to use an image for print is not necessarily the same thing as a license to use it online. Read the agreement carefully before using images coming from another source. We will focus on the banner graphics for now, but keep in mind that your other images and graphics will need to match the look and feel.

Placing a photo in your banner

The *site banner* is that identifying strip that lies across the top of a page. Often, the banner contains a company logo or motto or other identifier that viewers can recognize and relate to. You can jazz up this element of your site by adding photos to it. To do so, just follow these steps:

1. **Open your layout in Photoshop and then open the images you're adding to the design.**

2. **Drag the image to the layout file.**

   Photoshop will automatically create a new layer for the image when it places it in the layout file.

3. **Select the image file and click the layer called Background.**

   The background layer is an initial layer that is created by Photoshop by default. In a new document, this layer is empty or contains only a solid color depending on the settings you make when creating the file. With a photo or other image, the background layer contains the image.

4. **Drag the layer into the layout document window.**

Creating a clipping mask

You create a *clipping mask* when you use a layer to constrain how much of another layer is visible. Here, we show you how to use a plain box (like the one you create in Step 4g in the "Taking a Wire Frame to a Finished Design" section) to constrain a photo to just the banner area — without having to distort or resize the photo. All you need is a rectangle that will represent the area you want to have as your banner. See Figure 7-6 for an example of a clipping mask used to constrain a graphic to the banner.

To constrain a graphic to the banner with a clipping mask, follow these steps:

1. **Move the new image layer you created in Step 2 of "Placing a photo in your banner" so that it is directly above the banner area box.**

Figure 7-6:
You can use this method any time you want to constrain the effects of a layer to only the layer used as the mask (second layer).

2. **If your image layer is not selected, click to select it.**

3. **Choose Layer⇨Create Clipping Mask.**

4. **Move, resize, and edit the image layer as you normally would. However, the only portion of the layer that will be visible is the area that is precisely above the box layer.**

Remember to keep the background directly behind text or other important elements relatively clear of patterns. In other words, keep it simple behind the text; it's harder to read text that is over a busy background.

Implementing filters, adjustment layers, and blend modes

As you're working with your banner, don't be afraid to try some filters to change the look of the graphic or apply a blend mode or adjustment layer to change the look of the image until it looks the way you want it to. Refer to Book III, Chapter 4 for information about using blend modes. Adjustment layers are covered later in this chapter.

To use a filter, follow these steps:

1. **Select the image layer.**

2. **Choose one of the selection tools. (Review Book III, Chapter 4 for a tour of the Photoshop tools.)**

3. Select the area you would like to affect — if you want to affect the whole image, select the whole layer — and then choose Filter⇨Filter Gallery.

This opens the entire gallery of filters (shown in Figure 7-7) and gives you thumbnail examples of what each does.

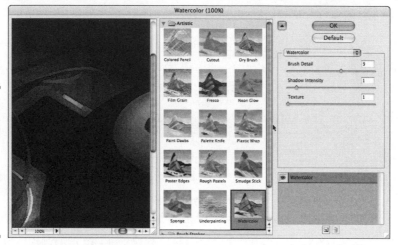

Figure 7-7: The filter gallery can help you decide which effect you'd like to apply to an image.

4. Select the filter you want directly from the Filter menu by clicking it.

The filter is applied and you see the effects. Some filters will present you with a dialog box with customization options. Most will allow you to preview the results before applying, so feel free to play with the options until it looks the way you want.

To use an adjustment layer, follow these steps:

1. In the Layers palette, click the Adjustment Layer button.

The Adjustment Layer button looks like a half black, half white circle at the bottom of the Layers palette.

2. Select the type of adjustment you'd like to apply.

Several options control things like brightness, color, and contrast. The best way to learn about them is to experiment. One that you will most likely find helpful is Hue/Saturation. You can change how the colors in your document look or you can click Colorize and tint everything to the color you select.

You can constrain an adjustment layer to only one layer, the same way you constrain an image to the banner area. For example, choose the Hue/Saturation adjustment layer. Make sure the Preview check box is selected. Click and drag the saturation slider. If you slide to the left, the colors in your image will *desaturate* (become less intense). Sliding to the right makes them more intense. Experiment with the other sliders to see how they affect the image. For a different effect, click the Colorize check box.

To use a blend mode, follow these steps:

1. **Select the layer you would like to affect.**

2. **From the drop-down menu at the top of the Layers palette, choose a blend mode.**

   This is another feature that is easiest to understand after you experiment a little. Basically, it affects how the chosen layer interacts with the layers below it. You can further augment the effect by changing the transparency of the layer (opacity)

3. **For an interesting experiment, apply different transfer modes to different layers, modify transparencies, and then reorder the layers.**

   The effects are different, depending on the images and transfer modes you select and any other adjustments you make. Have fun. If anything looks bad, you can step backwards in the History palette or just change the layer order for a different effect. Figure 7-8 shows the use of transfer modes to create effects.

Figure 7-8:
Use transfer modes to change the effects of layers on each other.

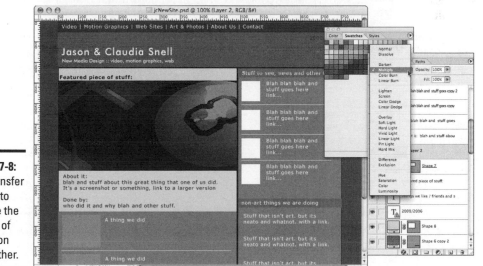

Slicing a Photoshop Document

After you create a Web page design in Photoshop, you're ready to turn it into an actual Web page. That involves creating graphics for the page and the HTML/CSS so that visitors can view your pages online. The process of creating graphics is called *slicing, optimizing, and exporting.* When you slice a Photoshop document, you're telling Photoshop where to create areas that will become a series of graphics and HTML files.

It is necessary to create slices only in areas that will need to be graphics on the finished page. Content areas that will be filled with text shouldn't be graphics, so you don't need to create slices for them. Large areas of continuous color also don't need to be sliced because you can tell the browser to display colors using code. It's best to use code as much as possible to generate your design because it's faster to download and also easier for more people to use.

Figure 7-9 shows you which areas of a document should be sliced and which will be generated with code.

Figure 7-9:
Slice only those areas that need to be graphics. Text and large areas of solid color are taken care of in the HTML.

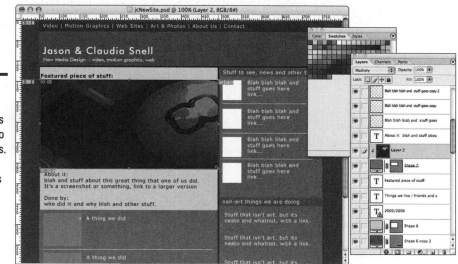

1. **Open the Photoshop document you created while designing your page.**

2. **Click the Slice tool — it's the one in the tool palette that looks like a little knife.**

Extra slice tool tricks

The Slice and Slice Select tools have additional tools to help you work with your graphics. As we recommend with all the tools in Photoshop, experiment with the options to see what works best for you. The basics (following) are simple, but you can explore many options after you get more comfortable:

✔ With the Slice Select tool active, double-click the small box next to the slice number (the one that looks like a rectangle with a jagged line in it). A dialog box opens that allows you to make some settings on the slice, such as a URL for a link, a target window, ALT text, and a message.

✔ In the context-sensitive menu bar, you'll also find a button that allows you to subdivide a slice. Click the button to see the dialog box with options for number of slices, orientation, and sizes.

✔ The Slice tool has options in its context-sensitive menu bar that allow you to specify a size or aspect ratio for your images.

Notice that there is a second option under the Slice tool called the Slice Select tool. That will be important after you've created a few slices. For now, select the Slice tool. (See Figure 7-10.)

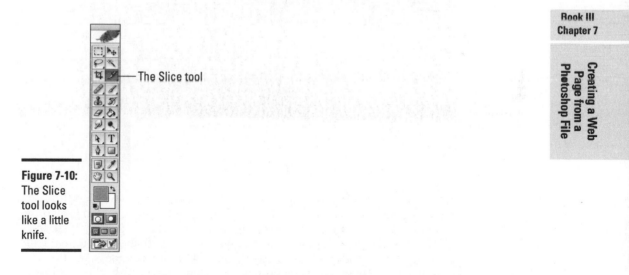

— The Slice tool

Figure 7-10: The Slice tool looks like a little knife.

3. **Create your slices by clicking and dragging with the Slice tool over an area that needs to be a graphic. Repeat the click and drag over each area.**

Be careful to get the slices as accurate as possible. If you're off, it can create undesirable results, like weird lines of color in your finished page that shouldn't be there. You can adjust your slices as necessary. If you are unsure about the accuracy, zoom in to get a better look.

4. **If necessary, click the Slice Select tool, click the slice, and then move or edit the slice.**

As you create your slices, you see numbered boxes appear over your document; these represent the borders of the graphics you're creating. Make sure the lines of those boxes are aligned with the edges of your graphics areas. Figure 7-11 shows you what a sliced document looks like.

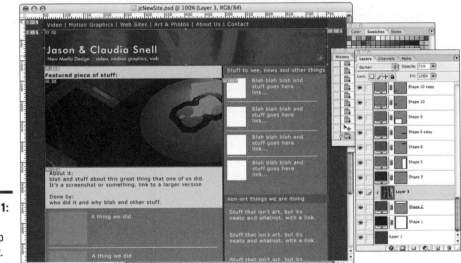

Figure 7-11:
A sliced
Photoshop
document.

Optimizing Graphics for the Web

After you have a Web page designed in Photoshop and have sliced the document, the next step is to prepare your graphics for export, which is also called *optimizing and exporting* your graphics. This is the process that actually creates the graphics for your Web page. The Photoshop document will stay intact and ready for you to use if you need to make changes to the graphics or design. Keep the Photoshop document with the rest of your production files in the Production Files folder of your Web site. See Chapter 3 of Book II about Web site structure and how to organize your files.

To optimize and export your graphics, follow these steps:

1. **Choose File⇨Save for Web.**

   Notice that your slices still have the lines and numbers but now look like semi-opaque white boxes over your document. Don't worry; the finished graphics don't have that appearance. Selected slices become transparent, so you can see what the graphics will really look like.

   The Save for Web dialog box launches. Tabs along the upper left allow you to choose among different ways of working in this window:

   - *Original:* Shows you the original document.

   - *Optimized:* Shows you the optimized version.

   - *2-Up:* Shows you the original in the left window and the optimized in the right.

   - *4-Up:* Shows you the original and three versions with different optimization settings, which is useful if you need to compare several possibilities.

2. **For these steps, select 2-Up (shown in Figure 7-12) because it lets you see what you're doing to your image as you compress it, but doesn't overwhelm you with too many things to look at.**

**Book III
Chapter 7**

Creating a Web
Page from a
Photoshop File

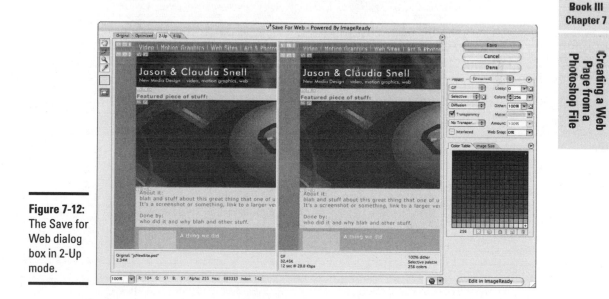

Figure 7-12:
The Save for
Web dialog
box in 2-Up
mode.

You can select each slice individually or select groups of them for optimization.

3. Click the Slice Select tool.

It's located in the left margin of the Save for Web dialog box.

4. Click a slice to select it; shift-click to select multiple slices.

Slices become transparent when they're selected.

5. After you've selected a slice or slices, make your settings for file format and compression amounts.

See the upper-right area of the Save for Web dialog box, as shown in Figure 7-13. JPEGS have presets for low, medium, and high quality. A slider gives you more control. In general, the higher the number, the less the image is compressed, the better it will look, and the larger the file size will be. The file size and approximate download time are displayed at the lower left of the Optimized preview window. You want to adjust the optimization settings until you get the lowest file size while still keeping the best quality in your image. While there are general guidelines to get you started, optimizing properly will take some experimentation because each graphic will have its own unique needs.

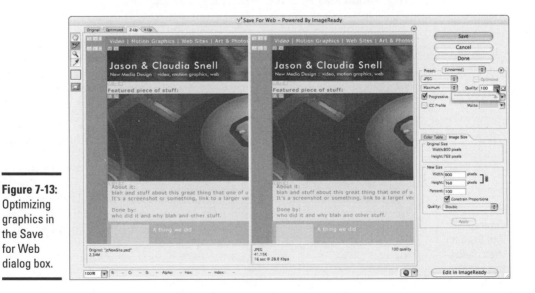

Figure 7-13:
Optimizing graphics in the Save for Web dialog box.

GIFs have different settings; using more colors will generally give better image quality and higher file sizes.

Remember, for all images, the trick to compression is to find the right balance between file size and quality. It can take some playing around, so don't get discouraged. See Book IV, Chapter 1 for more information about which file formats work best with different types of graphics.

6. **If necessary, resize a graphic by using the Image Size tab (in the lower-right of Figure 7-13); enter the new size and click Apply for the changes to take effect.**

   Notice that you don't have to make the same compression settings for each graphic in your document. This is a very useful feature. Your design is very likely to have some areas that will be best as JPEGs and others that need to be GIF. The ability to make different settings also allows you to make different settings for different graphics even if they are going to be the same type. This is handy because some graphics compress better than others. Each one will need special attention. The problem areas to look for are

   • *Around text:* Make sure you don't compress graphics with text (like banners and logos) so much that the text becomes messy looking. If it does get messy, you have gone too far and you need to increase the quality, and consequently the file size, just a bit.

   • *Gradients or other areas with color changes:* An example of this is a person's face, which can get *banding* or *dithering* when it is compressed too much. (To see what this effect looks like, take a photograph that has gradient type color changes and purposely over-compress it. You'll see strange bands of color with blotchy edges start to appear. It won't look good; you'll need to back off the settings a bit.)

7. **After making settings, click Save and navigate to the folder you'd like to save the images in.**

8. **Click Save to save the images and files.**

   Photoshop automatically creates an Images folder and saves your images to it. *Note:* Photoshop doesn't create an Images folder if you're saving out a single image that you didn't slice. The process of using the Save for Web dialog box is the same, except that you make settings for the whole image all at once and the file saved out is the whole document in it's entirety.

Making a Graphic Transparent

The GIF format supports transparency. This is very useful when creating banners or heading text that you'd like to "float" over a background graphic.

1. **Open the Save for Web dialog box by choosing File⇨Save for Web.**

2. **Select GIF as the format you'd like to save your graphic as.**

3. **With the Eyedropper tool, click the color you'd like to make transparent.**

4. **Click the Maps Selected Colors to Transparent button (shown in Figure 7-14) in the Color Table palette.**

   The color becomes transparent in your exported graphic file only; the original is not affected.

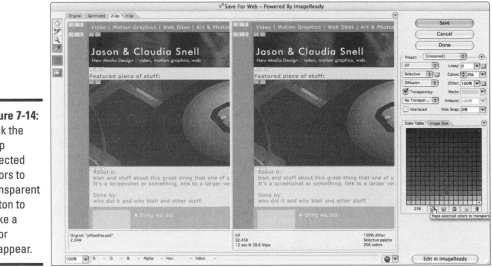

Figure 7-14: Click the Map Selected Colors to Transparent button to make a color disappear.

Make sure the background color is the same as or similar to the color you'd like to float the graphic over. If you have a dark/black background, create your transparent image over that color, and then make it transparent by following the preceding steps. Same goes for light colors. The reason is that when you select a color and make it transparent, it makes just that color go away, but the image actually has a bunch of intermediary colors that are just a little different all around the elements in your graphic. Those won't become transparent. This is a good thing, it keeps the edges of your graphic nice and clean, as shown in the bottom image in Figure 7-15. However, if you have dark intermediary colors but your background is light, you'll get a weird aura or halo all around your graphic, shown in the top image in Figure 7-15.

Figure 7-15:
The halos
disappear
when the
graphic is
placed over
the same
color it was
designed
with.

Chapter 8: Meeting HTML's Powerful Friends

In This Chapter

✔ Discovering Web technologies

✔ Exploring the server side

✔ Inspecting the client side

*W*hen you want to take a Web site to the next level, you add bells and whistles to your designs that make things happen. There are many ways to achieve interactivity on a Web site. Flash is one solution. But we're talking HTML here, and HTML interactivity comes in two flavors: *server side* (interactivity that occurs by code that is interpreted by the server) and *client side* (interactivity that occurs by code that is interpreted in the client's [the person viewing the Web page) browser]. Yes Virginia, that's right; you're actually writing a program to get the interactivity you want. This chapter introduces you to Web technology that is written for both sides of the street.

Web Technologies Defined

All interactive technologies contain code that must be interpreted before the interactivity occurs. What separates the technologies is how the code is deciphered. The software that deciphers the code and causes the interactivity is either a plug-in for the user's browser (client side) or the Web server (server side). When you're deciding what type of code to use, a couple of factors come into play:

✦ If you're deciding to use software that must be interpreted by the user, you need to know if your client's intended audience has the plug-in. If not, will they have the inclination to download the applicable plug-in?

✦ If the technology relies on software that is housed on the server, you'll have to make sure that your client's server has the applicable software available and that it's the proper version of the software for the code you plan to write — or is used in the application (such as a blog) that you're adding to the client's site.

The upcoming sections discuss the objects that are used by many interactive technologies.

Vary your content with variables

Most interactive technologies use variables. A *variable* is quite simply a placeholder for information that can vary. Talk about your logical names. An example of a variable is a form field. When a user enters information, the variable is no longer null (empty). ASP, CGI/PERL, JavaScript, and PHP are a few technologies that use variables. An example of a variable in action is a PHP page transmitting the information from a form into a database. The variable populates the applicable field in the database. Listing 8-1 shows some PHP code with variables.

Listing 8-1:   PHP Code with Variables

```
if ((isset($_POST["MM_insert"])) && ($_POST["MM_insert"] == "RegisterUser")) {
  $insertSQL = sprintf("INSERT INTO users (FirstName, LastName, Address, City,
    `State`, Zip, email, InfoStore, announcements, productsUsed, feedback)
    VALUES (%s, %s, %s, %s, %s, %s, %s, %s, %s, %s, %s)",
                       GetSQLValueString($_POST['FirstName'], "text"),
                       GetSQLValueString($_POST['LastName'], "text"),
                       GetSQLValueString($_POST['Address'], "text"),
                       GetSQLValueString($_POST['City'], "text"),
                       GetSQLValueString($_POST['State'], "text"),
                       GetSQLValueString($_POST['zip'], "int"),
                       GetSQLValueString($_POST['Email'], "text"),
                       GetSQLValueString(isset($_POST['InfoStore']) ? "true" :
"", "defined","'Y'","'N'"),
                       GetSQLValueString(isset($_POST['announcements']) ? "true"
: "", "defined","'Y'","'N'"),
                       GetSQLValueString($_POST['productsUsed'], "text"),
                       GetSQLValueString($_POST['feedback'], "text"));
```

The variables are in single quotations; for example `'FirstName'`. Notice that there's not a space in the variable name. When naming variables, spaces are verboten, as are other symbols, such as punctuation, and so on, as these are used in the actual code.

Variables can hold text, numbers, or Boolean values (`True` or `False`). When you name a variable in your code, you're declaring it. To access the data stored within a variable, you call the variable's name. The data within a variable can be interpreted by a function. When you name a variable, you must

✦ **Give the variable a unique name.** If you give a variable the same name as a variable that has already been declared and is supposed to hold different information, or the same name as a *function* (a sequence of code that performs a task), chaos ensues.

✦ **Give the variable a descriptive name.** For example, when you name a variable `FirstName`, you know exactly what information the variable is destined to hold. For that matter, so does anyone else working with your code.

You declare a variable before it's used in your code. Many types of variables are defined in the head of a document. JavaScript is an example of Web technology that declares variables in the head of an HTML document. (See Listing 8-2.)

Listing 8-2:   Defining Variables

```
function MM_preloadImages() { //v3.0
  var d=document; if(d.images){ if(!d.MM_p) d.MM_p=new Array();
    var i,j=d.MM_p.length,a=MM_preloadImages.arguments; for(i=0; i<a.length; i++)
    if (a[i].indexOf("#")!=0){ d.MM_p[j]=new Image; d.MM_p[j++].src=a[i];}}
}
```

The line of code that begins with `var d=document;` is declaring that variable d is equal to the HTML document. This is part of the JavaScript code that preloads images for a drop-down menu when a user hovers the cursor over a menu link.

A variable also has scope, not to be confused with a popular hygienic product that gives you minty fresh breath or some such nonsense. At any rate, the *scope* of a variable determines where it can be used. A variable can be local or global. You define a new variable by typing **var** followed by the equal sign and then the variable's name. If the variable is declared within a function, as in Listing 8-2, the variable can be used only within that function. However, if the variable is defined outside of a function, it's global in nature and can be used anywhere in the code. When used in a function, a local variable takes precedence over a global variable with the same name. However, to avoid confusion, it's important to give each variable a unique name.

Conditional statements

Another staple frequently used in interactive technologies is the conditional statement. In a nutshell, the *conditional statement* executes code depending on whether one or more conditions are true. If the condition(s) are true, certain lines of code are executed; otherwise, different code is executed. You might think of a conditional statement as the proverbial fork in the road. Listing 8-3 shows the basic structure of a conditional statement.

Listing 8-3:   A Conditional Statement in Its Most Basic Form

```
if (condition)
    {(action);
}else;
    {(else-action);
}
```

A conditional statement almost always begins with the word `if`. If the condition evaluates as true, the next lines of code are executed. If the condition evaluates as false, the script advances to the line of code that begins with `else`, which is followed by the lines of code that execute when the condition evaluates as false. Listing 8-4 is an example of a conditional statement from some PHP code.

Listing 8-4:   A Conditional Statement

```
<?php if ( comments_open() ) : ?>
<h4 id="postcomment"><?php _e('Leave a comment'); ?></h4>

<?php if ( get_option('comment_registration') && !$user_ID ) : ?>
<p>You must be <a href="<?php echo get_option('siteurl'); ?>/wp-
    login.php?redirect_to=<?php the_permalink(); ?>">logged in</a> to post a
    comment.</p>
<?php else : ?>
<form action="<?php echo get_option('siteurl'); ?>/wp-comments-post.php"
    method="post" id="commentform">
```

The code in Listing 8-4 is part of a blog page. If the option for users to leave a comment is open, the next lines of code execute, which enables the user to leave a comment. The second conditional statement queries the blog options to see whether unregistered users can leave comments. If the blog requires registration, the user is told that he must be logged in to leave a comment. The fork in the road, the code that reads `<?php else: ?>`, is interpreted if registration is not required. In this case, a comment form appears on the page, and the user can add a comment about the post.

Here we go loop-de-loop

Another item commonly used in programming is the loop. A *loop* executes lines of code a given number of times. The most commonly used loops are `while` and `for`. A `while` loop executes lines of code while a certain condition is true. A `for` loop specifies how many times the lines of code repeat. Listing 8-5 shows the basic structure of a `for` loop.

Listing 8-5: For This Loop

```
for (initial value; test; increment)
{
    execute this code;
}
```

The loop is set up as follows. The line of code that begins with for shows the initial value, what must occur for the loop to continue, and the amount by which the initial value will increment. As soon as the test evaluates as false, the loop stops and the next bits of code are executed. Listing 8-6 shows a real-world example of a for loop as it would appear in a Web page.

Listing 8-6: Using a Loop

```
$i=0;
while ($i < $num) {
$name=mysql_result($result,$i,"name");
$contact=mysql_result($result,$i,"contact");
$city=mysql_result($result,$i,"city");
echo "<b>Name:</b> $name <br><b>Contact Person:</b>
    $contact<br><b>City:</b> $city</br><hr>";
$i++;
}
```

Let's break down the code in Listing 8-6:

The initial value of the variable i is 0.

The loop continues while i is less than the variable num, which is equal to the number of rows in a database that contains contact information in a mailing list.

The next lines of code retrieve information from a MySQL database and enter the values in a table row.

The line of code that reads i++ increments the value of i by a value of 1, loops the code again, retrieving the next row of information from the database, creating a new row and populating it with the information from the database.

The loop stops when the value of i exceeds the number of rows in the database.

Creating functional functions

You can find lots of ready-made code by surfing the Net. But the fun comes when you create your own code and put it to use in your Web designs. Functions are used in JavaScript, PERL, and C++. When you create a function, you create code that performs a specific task. The function accepts information from the user in the form of an argument. The argument is examined by the function's code, and a result is displayed. Listing 8-7 shows a function in its simplest form.

Listing 8-7: A Really Simple Function

```
function testPassword(argument)
    {
the code;
    }
```

In the example in Listing 8-7, the function's name is `testPassword`. It has one argument. The code determines the end result while evaluating the password. Listing 8-8 shows a real-world example of a function used in JavaScript.

Listing 8-8: A Real-World Function

```
<script language="javascript">
function getPassword () {  Passwords = new Array('x001','xoxo1','de10r');
  var passwordMatches = false;
  var userPassword = prompt ("Enter your password:");
for (i=0; i < Passwords.length; i=i+1)
      {
  if (userPassword == Passwords[i]) passwordMatches = true;
      }
  return passwordMatches;
      }
var theResult = getPassword();
 if(theResult == true) {  alert("Correct")
      }
  else
      {
alert("The password you entered is incorrect");
      }
</script>
```

The name of the function is `getPassword`. The argument defines the passwords as an array and sets the value of the variable `passwordMatches` to false. The next line of code prompts the user to enter his password. A loop evaluates the user-entered password against those in the array. If the password matches, the function alerts the user that the password is correct. Otherwise, the user is notified that the password is incorrect. Code like this is used to password protect a Web site.

Looking on the Server Side

The preceding sections of this chapter (You did read them, didn't you?) are a brief primer in writing code. You write code when using programming languages that are executed on the server side, as well as client side. The following sections give you an introduction to server side programming languages.

ASP/ASP.NET

ASP is an acronym for Active Server Pages, the powerful Microsoft server side language. When a user surfs to a Web site with an ASP page, the Web server determines the content delivered to the user's Web browser. ASP pages are used when content of the page changes frequently. An example of a use for an ASP page is a list that is generated from information in a database. The ASP code on the server side plucks the information from the database and delivers it to the user's browser.

The ASP code is parsed by a DLL (Dynamic Link Library) called `ASP.dll`. Figure 8-1 shows ASP code that is used to retrieve data from a Microsoft Access database.

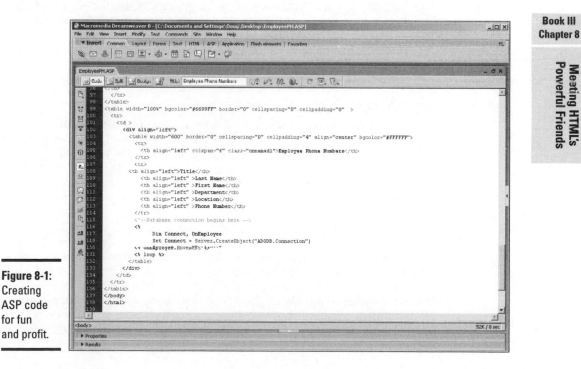

Figure 8-1: Creating ASP code for fun and profit.

To create ASP pages, you must have a Microsoft Web server (the current version is IIS 6.0) on your local system. As of this writing, the URL to find out more information about IIS 6.0 is

`www.microsoft.com/WindowsServer2003/iis/default.mspx`

There is another derivative of ASP pages, ASP.NET. ASP.NET is ASP pages created within Microsoft's .NET Framework. You can think of ASP.NET as ASP on steroids. ASP and ASP.NET feature *session variables,* which are variables that can be accessed by different ASP pages on the site. In essence, a session variable is a variable that is remembered during a user's *session,* which is a visit to the Web site with the ASP.NET pages.

.NET Framework

The .NET Framework is Microsoft's brainchild. Microsoft .NET Framework is an environment for building, deploying, and running Web services and other applications. The .NET Framework consists of three main parts: Common Language Runtime, the Framework classes, and ASP.NET.

The languages available to developers upon installation of the SDK (software development kit) as Managed C++, C#, VB (Visual Basic), and JavaScript. The .NET Framework features multiple language support, offers a vast set of libraries, is open standard friendly, and is supported by HTTP and XML. There is a learning curve, however. If you decide to dip your toe into the vast .NET ocean, you'll have to become familiar with programming in this platform. Currently, .NET is available for Windows only.

JavaScript

JavaScript has been around for some time. Back in the Jurassic period of the Internet, Web pages were static. In other words, what you saw was what you got. Then, someone got the bright idea that it would be "way cool" if visitors could interact with Web pages. Of course, that required some type of language that instructed the pages what to do when visitors interacted with them. Enter JavaScript.

With JavaScript, all sorts of cool things are possible. You can write JavaScript scripts to make a menu drop down when a user hovers his cursor over a menu link, swap images, have form elements interact with each other, and more. JavaScript works with all major browsers.

One of the great things about JavaScript is that you don't need to know a lot about programming. And you don't need a Web server to test your JavaScript code. You can create JavaScript scripts in any HTML editor and test them in your default Web browser.

You can find scripts you can paste into your HTML documents by typing **JavaScript scripts** in your favorite search engine. Using other people's scripts is an excellent way to learn JavaScript. Simply view the source code, and you'll have an idea of how the code achieves the desired result. You can also change the author's code to get a feeling of how JavaScript works. JavaScript uses variables, conditional statements, and functions.

JavaScript is object-oriented programming (OOP). If you've ever dabbled with Flash ActionScript, you've worked with object-oriented programming. JavaScript objects are defined in classes. An image is an object, which is defined by the title of `img`. A class consists of objects that are similar. Objects have properties. For example, the `image` object has the following properties: `name`, `height`, `width`, and `alt`. Objects have methods. For example, the `Form` object has a `submit` method, which is used to submit a form, and a `reset` method, which is used to reset the form. To find out more information on JavaScript, see Book VI, Chapter 1. Figure 8-2 shows a script that is used to validate a user's password.

**Book III
Chapter 8**

**Meeting HTML's
Powerful Friends**

Figure 8-2:
I get by with
a little help
from my
JavaScript.

```
1  <!DOCTYPE html PUBLIC "-//W3C//DTD XHTML 1.0 Transitional//EN" "http://www.w3.org/TR/xhtml1/DTD/xhtml1-transitional.dtd">
2  <html xmlns="http://www.w3.org/1999/xhtml">
3  <head>
4  <meta http-equiv="Content-Type" content="text/html; charset=iso-8859-1" />
5  <title>Untitled Document</title>
6  </head>
7  <script language="javascript">
8  function getPassword () {  Passwords = new Array('x001','xoxo1','del0r');
9      var passwordMatches = false;
10     var enteredPassword = prompt ("Enter your password:");
11 for (i=0; i < Passwords.length; i=i+1)
12 {
13     if (enteredPassword == Passwords[i]) passwordMatches = true;
14 }
15     return passwordMatches;}var theResult = getPassword();
16 if(theResult == true) {  alert("Correct")
17 }
18     else
19     {
20     alert("The password you entered is incorrect");
21     }
22
23 </script>
24
25 <body>
26 </body>
27 </html>
28
```

PHP

PHP is an open source scripting language that you can used in HTML pages. Pages created with PHP code are delivered after being decoded by the server. Pages with PHP code will work only if your Web server has the applicable version of PHP. The version of PHP needed depends on the code you write. Many applications use PHP code. For example, blogs use PHP code to add blog posts to a database and to display them in the blog visitor's browser. If you're working with PHP code, the only way to test the code is to upload the page to a server or to install a Web server with PHP. Pages with PHP code have a file extension of .php.

The beauty of PHP code is that a visitor doesn't need any special plug-in to evaluate the PHP code; it's all done with PHP software on the server. When you create PHP code (shown in Figure 8-3), you will be seeing red. Literally. When you write PHP code in an HTML editor such as Dreamweaver, the code is preceded by <?php, and the text is red in color. (Okay, you can't see the red in this black-and-white book.)

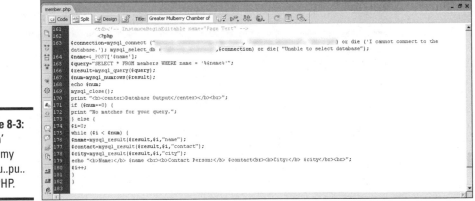

Figure 8-3: Talkin' 'bout my pu..pu..pu.. pu.. PHP.

CGI/PERL

CGI/PERL is another programming language that is executed on the server side. Before you create scripts for a client Web site using this programming language, make sure the Web server supports CGI scripts. UNIX servers generally support CGI scripts.

When your client's needs exceed the capabilities of your bread-and-butter HTML pages — such as creating a chat room or displaying a page counter — you can employ a CGI/PERL script to achieve the desired result. The information is sent from an application on the Web server to the user's browser.

CGI stands for Common Gateway Interface, the protocol that defines the manner in which a Web server interacts with a program. For example, when a Web site visitor fills out a form and presses Enter, the HTML code determines how the form is delivered to the Web server and how it's processed by the PERL script. CGI conventions determine how the script processes the information.

You'll find many Web sites that offer free CGI/PERL scripts. Most of the sites also offer more advanced scripts for a reasonable price.

To show you the power of CGI/PERL scripts, Doug downloaded a script to display the current date on his Web page. The steps were simple and as follows:

1. **Download the nms-textclock script from:** `www.scriptarchive.com/nms-download.cgi?s=nms-textclock&c=zip`.

   The zip file contained a ReadMe page with instructions on how to configure the script as well as the `text-clock.pl` file, which is the PERL script.

2. **Follow the instructions to reconfigure the script and upload it to the applicable folder on your server.**

   I uploaded the file to the cgi-bin on my server. If you're unsure as to what folder the file should be in, contact your Web hosting service. You might also need to change the extension of the file to `.cgi`. Your Web server can provide you with this information as well.

3. **Change the permissions on your server so that the script can be executed. You can use an FTP client to change the Permissions property of the file to 755.**

4. **Add the following to your HTML document where you want the date displayed:**

   ```
   Today is <p align="left">Today is <!--#exec cgi="/
   cgi-bin/textclock.pl"--> </p>
   ```

5. **Save the file with an extension of `.shtml`.**

   This tells the Web browser that the page includes code that will be executed with a server side script.

6. **Upload the page to your server.**

   Figure 8-4 shows my home page with the current date displayed.

Programming for the faint of code

If you've read this chapter from the start, you're probably firmly convinced that there are more programming languages than any mere mortal needs to learn. And yet, there are some developers (pencil-pocket-protected-duct-taped-four-eyed-card-carrying geeks) who know a lot of programming languages. You might be thinking, "I'm a Web designer and I don't need to know all that stuff." And you're right; you don't. You'll find many scripts and applications where someone else has already taken care of the pain of writing and debugging the scripts. And the really cool thing is that many of them are free. You can download them, complete with instructions, and plug them into your pages. Simply type the name of the programming language followed by **scripts** (for example, **CGI/PERL scripts** or **JavaScript scripts**) in your favorite search engine. You'll have pages of results from which to choose. When you find a really useful site, bookmark the page and pillage and plunder to your heart's content.

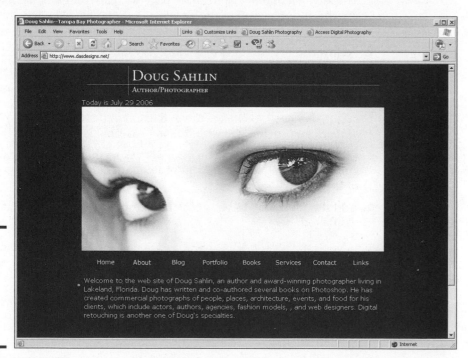

Figure 8-4: Using a CGI/PERL script to display the current date.

Checking Out the Client Side

Server side applications are wonderful, but there's also a good case for applications that execute client side — that is, within the user's browser. The only caveat is that Web site visitors must have the technology (plug-in) to decipher the code installed on their computers. Client side programs come in three flavors: Java, VBScript, and DHTML. The upcoming sections give you the skinny on the client side interactivity you can implement using Java or VBScript.

Java

Java — not to be confused with your morning picker-upper — is an object oriented programming language developed by James Gosling and his colleagues at Sun Microsystems. It's not related to JavaScript. You can implement Java on the client side by writing code that is included in your HTML document. Creating Java code is unfortunately beyond the scope of this book. In addition to checking out *Java For Dummies,* 4th edition, by Barry Burd (Wiley Publishing, ISBN 0-470-08716-1), you can find a number of resources online for writing client side Java code. For example, Java.net has an excellent tutorial at

```
http://today.java.net/pub/a/today/2006/06/27/client-side-
    google-web-toolkit.html
```

Java is chameleon in nature in that it also works server side. The easiest way to implement Java interactivity into your Web designs is through the use of Java applets. When you download a Java applet, the author supplies the software necessary to parse the code. The Java applet is uploaded to your server. You insert the author's code in your HTML document. You can find Java applets by typing **Java applets** in your favorite search engines. The results page will be filled with links to Java applets; many of them are free.

When you download a Java applet, you'll find source code that you add to your HTML document and the actual software for parsing the code. A downloaded Java applet called Mdataclock contained three files in a zip file:

✦ config.html: This included instructions on how to configure the applet.

✦ index.htm: This file contained the code.

✦ Mdataclock.class: This is the code that is parsed by Java at runtime on the user's machine.

The last file must reside in the same folder as the HTML document in which you're inserting the code for the applet. When you upload the site to the server, the .class file that parses the Java applet must be uploaded as well.

Figure 8-5 shows the code as inserted into an HTML document.

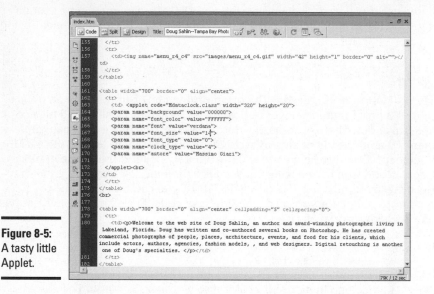

Figure 8-5:
A tasty little
Applet.

VBScript

Guess what folks? VBScript is yet another programming language. VBScript is Microsoft's brainchild. Therefore, it's Windows and Internet Explorer only. VBScript can add functionality to your Web pages. It's relatively easy to learn. But in the end, you'll have to make the decision whether VBScript is something you want to take on.

When you want to create a page with VBScript, you have to include instructions for the browser by using the <script> tag. You can add scripts in the head or body of a document. Listing 8-9 shows a VBScript that will show the date and time on a Web page.

Listing 8-9: Telling Time with VBScript

```
<script type="text/vbscript">
document.write("Today's date is " & date())
document.write("<br />")
document.write("The time is " & time())
</script>
```

In a nutshell, the code uses objects (`date` and `time`) from the VBScript language. The code tells the browser to retrieve the current date and time from the user's computer and display the results (`document.write`) in the user's browser. Figure 8-6 shows the date and time as displayed on a Web page.

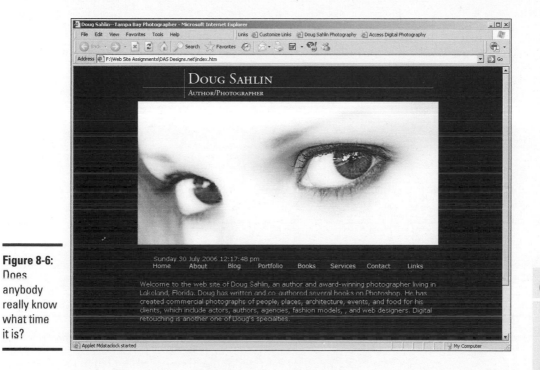

Figure 8-6: Does anybody really know what time it is?

VBScript uses variables, arrays, and conditional statements. You can also use VBScript to jump through hoops by creating functions. A full-blown VBScript tutorial is beyond the scope of this book.

Chapter 9: Web Site Usability and Accessibility

In This Chapter

✔ Avoiding common mistakes that make a site less friendly

✔ Understanding usability

✔ Addressing accessibility concerns

✔ Using Dreamweaver to make your pages more accessible

Designers, developers, and professionals involved in Web site design and implementation work to improve user experience on their sites. Web standards have been developed to help Web professionals create sites that work well for users and producers themselves. If you're in the Web development industry or you're in the midst of developing your own Web site, chances are you have heard the terms *usability, accessibility,* and *standards* and wondered what the buzz is all about.

Ensuring Your Site Is Easy to Use

If you browse the Web regularly, chances are good that you've visited a site that is confusing, difficult to navigate, or hard to use. That experience can be frustrating and often prevents full use of the site. If you've experienced this, you've experienced poor Web site usability. And so have many customers. You might be wondering how these sites are being built. Didn't the designers and developers think of their users? They probably thought they did, but in reality, did not. Web teams often make a couple big mistakes, including

✦ **Assuming users will understand what they're building without asking any of them if they do.** Always make testing a part of your plan up front; that way, you won't be rushed when it's time for testing.

✦ **Viewing negative feedback from users as nitpicking.** Why ask for feedback if you don't plan to improve the site, based on what you find out?

✦ **Not asking themselves, "Who are we building this for?"** If the answer is that they're building a site for themselves, ignoring people who end up visiting the site is okay.

Realistically, all sites are ultimately built for the visitors. You can do your best to build a site that works for them by conducting usability testing. Usability testing can be informal or formal. The approach you take depends on the scope of your project, the size of your budget, and the nature of your audience. You can conduct informal usability testing by sitting down with a person who represents your target audience. As the tester tries to use your site, note any areas that cause problems, ask questions about how easy or hard to use the site is, and give your tester a list of tasks to accomplish (again, noting how easy or difficult any task is to do). More-formal testing might involve e-mailing a link to the site to several individuals, along with a questionnaire that each person fills out and returns to you within a specified timeframe.

After you get some feedback, you'll have a better idea of what your users need your site to do for them. You can start making design choices based on their needs instead of your own. The resulting Web site benefits your users and ultimately helps your site to be successful. Although Book III, Chapter 10 has more detailed information about gathering and implementing feedback, here are some simple rules of the road that every site designer must consider:

✦ **Everything has to work.** Think about the user's point of view: When she clicks a submit button after placing an order, for example, she should see an acknowledgment of receipt of her order, not a presentation about the company. That would be very frustrating, and that user would think twice before trying to use your site again. Figure 9-1 shows an expected `Message Received` screen the user sees after submitting a form.

Figure 9-1:
Make sure you create an acknowledgement page for form submissions.

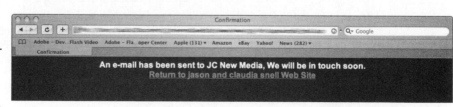

An e-mail has been sent to JC New Media. We will be in touch soon.
Return to jason and claudia snell Web Site

✦ **Pages and graphics should be efficient and easy to navigate.** Users expect instant responses from Web sites, so pages and images must load quickly. Also, the site must be laid out so that users can easily find what they need. If a user has to hunt around your site and read a lot of heavy text, he will leave your site and go to one that helps him get what he wants with less hassle. Your site must have clear navigation. Refrain from using too many buttons and make everything reachable within a couple of clicks. If your site is large, consider a site map to help people get in and get what they want.

✦ **A site needs to be forgiving.** People make mistakes, so plan how to handle user errors cleanly and effectively. Polite error messages with easy-to-understand instructions are important and helpful. Whenever possible, users should have a way to step back and correct errors. Make sure you consider how the experience will work for users and minimize the number of times they have to reenter information if they do make mistakes.

When writing error messages, keep in mind that users don't need to know the technical information about the error. They only need to know how to fix the error — in simple, common language. Remember that your users aren't as familiar with how your system works as you are. Write error messages and instructions accordingly. People appreciate a concise set of bulleted instructions. It's also a good idea to give them correct contact information so they can get hands-on help if they need it. They should be able to call or e-mail your Web site support person. Make sure you put these customers in touch with the person who has the knowledge, training, and experience to help them, not a general-purpose, customer service contact.

✦ **Web sites must look good.** A site should be professional looking and appropriate to the audience and content. After all, visitors to the site are getting an impression about the organization, products, and services it represents. You wouldn't send poorly produced printed materials to your audience. Hold your Web site to the same, professional standard because it's your company's face on the Internet.

Some people believe that content is king. They're only partially right. With so many sites out there boasting good content, you must make a good impression with a good-looking site. You wouldn't send a salesperson to a client meeting wearing pajamas and looking sleep deprived. You shouldn't send your Web site out there looking like that either. Even if the rest of your organization is very professional, users who first encounter your company through a poorly designed site have no way of knowing that. They just see a messy, amateurish site and move along.

Helping Users Access Your Site

Accessibility is closely related to usability but has important differences. Making sites *accessible* involves designing sites that allow people with disabilities to access the content of that site. Many individuals with disabilities (ranging from motor and visual impairments to cognitive and seizure disorders) have special needs when it comes to using Web sites. Some of these individuals depend on assistive technologies, which have special requirements in order to work properly. Other individuals have difficulties with color schemes, blinking content, confusing navigation, or audio-only content. Properly planned and executed Web sites vastly improve the user experience for these individuals.

A site that doesn't plan for accessibility issues can be difficult or impossible for some visitors to use; some types of organizations are required to comply with laws pertaining to Section 508a of the Americans with Disabilities Act. Details about these laws are beyond the scope of this book, but you can find more information at the United States Access Board Web site (www.access-board.gov). The World Wide Web Consortium (W3C), which creates standards for Web development, has created a Web Accessibility Initiative (WAI/WCAG or Web Accessibility Initiative/Web Content Accessibility Guidelines) that helps site developers make their sites accessible. For more information, go to www.w3.org/wai/.

Throughout the rest of this section, we highlight important things to remember when working to improve your site's accessibility and give you pointers on doing so.

Images need alternate content

Alternate content is text that is included within the image tag's alt attribute. This text needs to convey the meaning of the graphic it represents. Web page authors need to include alt attributes for each image on a page, even invisible formatting images (which should actually be avoided in favor of cleaner, easier to maintain CSS for formatting). The alternate text must include the content and/or context of the graphic image. Screen-reading technologies used by visually impaired visitors read the text of the alt attributes, so make sure you write them in a way that makes sense to visitors who can't see the images. It's not helpful to type just **button graphic**. A more helpful tag is Click here to see our specials. (Please note, alt attributes are only one of several coding issues that must be addressed by Web site designers who are trying to make their sites more accessible).

This is the correct way to code alt attributes:

```
<img src="home_but.gif" alt="home page button">
```

```
<img src="mybanner.gif" alt="Claudia Snell, new media
    designer">
<img src="puppies.jpg" alt="image of puppies available for
    adoption">
```

Notice that the alternate content conveys what the graphic is functionally, describes the content of the image, or mirrors the text of the graphic. It's also acceptable to include alt attributes with no content at all, like this:

```
<img src='bullet.gif' alt="">
```

This conveys to a user's screen reader that this is a nonessential image that the user should ignore completely. Without it, some screen readers will read the whole tag to the user. That can create a very frustrating user experience for someone who has to hear each image tag read, especially if there are multiple instances of images with no alternate text.

It's not acceptable to use `alt` attributes as a clever place to hide marketing keywords. This practice was started by marketing and search engine optimization "experts" who didn't understand how Web pages actually work. They discovered that text inside the `alt` attributes is not displayed by the browser as part of the layout but does show up in some browsers when visitors place their cursor over them and they can be "seen" by search engines.

Oddly enough, using `alt` attributes to pack in a bunch of extra keywords can hurt your rankings in a search engine because most search engines are programmed to recognize pages that have an unusually high number of what appear to be keywords or unusual implementations of them. For more information on search engine optimization, look at Book VIII, Chapter 1.

Another reason it is a bad idea to replace useful `alt` attributes with random words is that it will affect not only visually impaired users but also users who have turned off their graphics or are using devices other than browsers — these are all individuals that need `alt` attributes in order to use your Web site.

Use more than one method to convey your information

Colorblind visitors to a site can become confused or miss important information if it is conveyed only through color. While color-coding helps some individuals, you must also convey the information without the color-coding.

Using a set of colors plus icons (as shown in Figure 9-2) can be a way to ensure a good experience for a wider audience. Many people benefit from visual cues, so don't avoid them in favor of designing for those who don't; just make sure you use more than one method to convey your information. Using layout and groupings to signal that information belongs together is also useful. Even a well-planned, color-coding and icon scheme won't save a page that has a poor layout.

If you plan to use color-coding or icons to convey categories, make sure you keep their numbers small. Three or four color-coded categories should work fine; more than that starts to look like a rainbow. Users can start to feel disoriented rather than assisted.

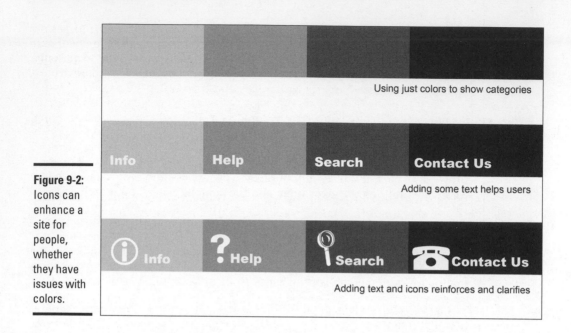

Using just colors to show categories

Adding some text helps users

Adding text and icons reinforces and clarifies

Figure 9-2: Icons can enhance a site for people, whether they have issues with colors.

Pictures are important

Although images without useful `alt` attributes can be confusing for users with visual impairments, pictures assist those who have cognitive disorders. Choose images that support your content. If your pages are about taking care of dogs, include images that illustrate your points or convey the overall message about dog ownership. Don't include images of your last vacation or some other random image "just because it looks pretty." Make sure that the images match the tone or emotion the site is conveying. A site about a serious topic can be confusing if it includes images of laughing children.

Animations are also very popular and can be helpful. If you decide to include animations, be aware that you should avoid creating animations that flicker and flash excessively. Blinking and flickering can cause problems for people who suffer from seizure disorders. Most people don't enjoy these sorts of animations anyway, so avoiding them makes your site more pleasant for everyone.

Orientation tools are helpful

Orientation tools help users navigate the site, as well as tell them where they are, no matter what page they're on. A site map and breadcrumbs are two such tools:

✦ A *site map* (or *site index*) **is a page that lists the links to the pages of your site.** It should mirror the navigation of the site and be presented in an outline style. Users find these to be helpful at some point, especially if the site is large. A site map is particularly helpful to visitors who have cognitive or memory disorders. Users can pinpoint the pages they need very easily with the birds-eye view of the site that the map provides.

✦ *Breadcrumbs* **are a trail of links that show the user the path from the home page to the current page.** Breadcrumbs are typically displayed at the top of the screen and look like this:

```
Home >> About >> Our Products >> Widget
```

Each of the words in the breadcrumb trail should be a link to that page so that a user can backtrack up the trail, if necessary. Just like Hansel and Gretel.

Creating Accessible Web Pages

The good news is that several page-checking utilities are available to help you make accessible pages. Professional Web design software, such as Macromedia Dreamweaver, has many tools, validators, checkers, and resources available to keep you on track.

Using Dreamweaver to insert accessible elements

To use Dreamweaver to help you with properly coding your pages for accessibility, you must have the Accessibility feature turned on. To turn it on, follow these steps:

1. **Open the Preferences dialog box by choosing Dreamweaver⇨ Preferences (on a Mac) or Edit⇨Preferences (on a Windows PC).**

2. **Select Accessibility under Category (as shown in Figure 9-3).**

3. **Enable the check boxes for the elements you want Accessibility help with. It's a good idea to check them all. That way, Dreamweaver will remind you that you need to take special care with these possibly troublesome areas.**

The choices are

- *Form objects*
- *Frames*
- *Media*
- *Images*

4. **Click OK to exit the Preferences dialog box.**

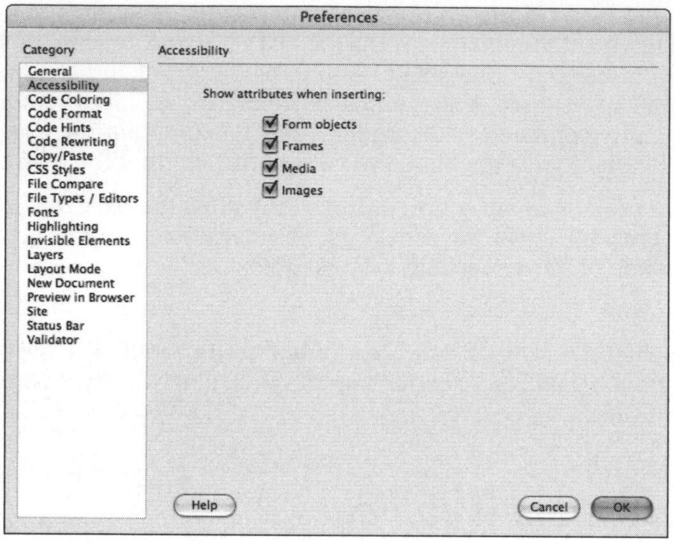

Figure 9-3:
The Dreamweaver Preferences dialog box in Dreamweaver.

To insert an image and `alt` attribute using the Insert menu, follow these steps:

1. **Choose Insert⇨Image.**

The image browse window pops up. Select the image you would like to add.

2. **Click Choose (on a Mac) or OK (on a Windows PC).**

The Image Tag Accessibility Attributes dialog box appears, as shown in Figure 9-4.

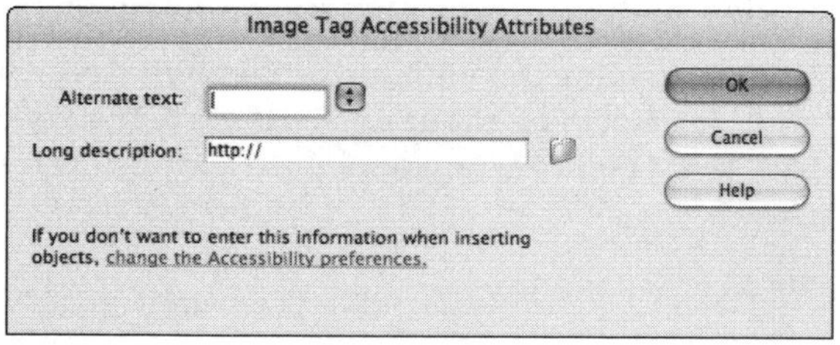

Figure 9-4:
Insert an image and include the alt attributes.

3. Enter the `alt` attribute text and click OK.

The image and proper tag will be inserted into your code.

To insert an image by using the Insert bar, click the Insert Image icon on the Common tab. When the Image Tag Accessibility Attributes dialog box opens, enter the `<alt>` tag text and click OK.

Using Dreamweaver to check your site's accessibility

Dreamweaver has tools to check your code, including code validators and site-testing reports that can check the accessibility of your page or site.

Before you start running reports, you might want to turn on line numbers in your Code view and make sure you're in Split mode in Dreamweaver. To turn on line numbers, choose View➪Code View Options➪Line Numbers. The line numbers appear in the left margin of the Code window, as shown in Figure 9-5.

Figure 9-5:
The line numbers in the Code window help you find your place in the code.

Using Dreamweaver in Split screen mode (as shown in Figure 9-6) enables you to see the code and the design at the same time. Being able to see both code and design helps you make sure you don't code something that looks bad. It also lets you keep an eye on your code to make sure that it doesn't get messy when you use the WYSIWYG tools. To turn on Split screen mode in Dreamweaver, click the Split icon.

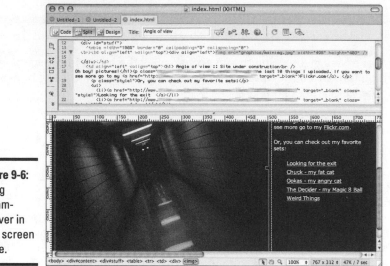

Figure 9-6:
Using
Dream-
weaver in
Split screen
mode.

Running reports

Dreamweaver provides different methods for checking a site's accessibility:

✦ To check the accessibility of the page you're working on, save your document and choose File⇨Check Page⇨Check Accessibility. The Report window opens with the results.

✦ Another way to use the Accessibility report utility is to save your document and choose Site⇨Reports. In the Reports dialog box that appears (as shown in Figure 9-7), select the reports you want to run — for Accessibility testing, enable the Accessibility and the Missing Alt Text check boxes — and click Run. From this dialog box, you can also choose to run the report on just the page you're working on, several selected pages, a whole folder, or the whole site via a drop-down menu at the top.

Click the Run button in the Reports dialog box and the Site Reports window opens with the results.

Fixing mistakes

With the results of your report, you can correct mistakes quickly and easily. The Results window shows code line numbers, the severity of the issue, and some brief information about the issue and where you can research it further. Issues marked with red Xs are things that have completely failed and need to be corrected. Issues with question marks are things that might or might not be an issue and require human judgment to determine whether corrections need to be made. An example of this type of error is `Color is not essential`. The report has no way of knowing if the page is conveying information via color only, so it reminds you to make sure your page makes sense even without the colors. To view the piece of code that's causing an issue, double-click the text of the issue description in the Results window. The code is highlighted for you.

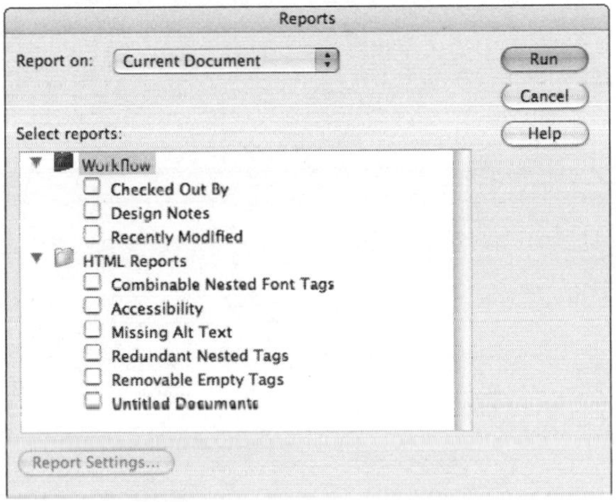

Figure 9-7: Select the reports you'd like to run. You can quickly check several pages at a time with this method.

Reports dialog box:

Report on: Current Document · Run · Cancel · Help

Select reports:

- ▼ Workflow
  - ☐ Checked Out By
  - ☐ Design Notes
  - ☐ Recently Modified
- ▼ HTML Reports
  - ☐ Combinable Nested Font Tags
  - ☐ Accessibility
  - ☐ Missing Alt Text
  - ☐ Redundant Nested Tags
  - ☐ Removable Empty Tags
  - ☐ Untitled Documents

Report Settings...

Chapter 10: Publishing the Web Site

In This Chapter

✔ **Preparing to launch the site**

✔ **Uploading the site**

✔ **What to do after the launch**

Designing Web sites is a creative process that can be lots of fun. But fun doesn't put bread on the table or a Web site on your hard drive, and it isn't going to pay the bills either. After you build it, you've got to upload it before visitors swarm your client's site. But before that blessed event can happen, you've got to make sure you've got your ducks in a row. In other words, make sure it ain't broke, and if it is broke, fix it. There's nothing worse than uploading a site with bugs and ending up with egg all over your face. You guessed it, the yolk's on you. In this chapter, we show you how to exterminate any bugs that might be lurking in your code, how to upload the site to the hosting server, and what to do after the launch.

Look Before You Leap: What to Do before Launch

Your client is all over you like white-on-rice to make the site live, but if you do so before making sure everything is up to snuff, you do yourself and your client a disservice. First and foremost, you damage your reputation, both with the client and potential clients, if you put a site out there that contains code errors, broken links, and so on. In the upcoming sections, we show you a few things you need to consider before uploading the site to the client's server.

Develop a checklist

If you have a checklist you can refer to before you launch the site, you can be sure you won't forget to double-check anything. And you can use the list for all the sites you launch. Write it once; use it countless times. Your list should include the following items:

✦ **Check each and every link.** There's nothing more embarrassing than creating a Web site with links that work on some pages but not on others. You can safeguard against this happening if you create a template that includes the navigation links and then use this for each page you create.

If you're using Dreamweaver to create your pages, choose Site➪ Check Links Sitewide, and Dreamweaver lists any broken links in the Results Panel.

✦ **Does your fancy code work?** If any of the pages in your site are PHP, ASP, or DHTML, make sure each script works as expected.

✦ **Does the site load quickly?** Savvy Web surfers are an impatient lot and won't wait for a site to download. If you've done your homework and optimized all of your images and other interactive content, the site should download in less than 12 seconds.

✦ **Does the site include a call to action?** If your client is selling merchandise or services, Marketing 101 dictates that the site should ask the visitor to do something. At the very least, the site should include some type of special offer that tempts the visitor into clicking the checkout button. Another call to action might be a form that requests contact information for a mailing list or newsletter.

✦ **Is the site easy to navigate?** Make sure that site visitors don't need a PhD to figure out the navigation menu. Try to avoid being cute and designing an avant-garde menu that uses only icons. Some people will get it, but the ones that don't will be visiting the site of your client's competitor. Make sure you have redundant text-only links at the bottom of each page.

✦ **Is the content relevant and easy to understand?** Chances are your client created most of the text for the site and provided images as well. It's your job to put it in a palatable format that visitors can easily digest. Scan each page and make sure the headlines and links provide a message to visitors. This is especially important if the site has a lot of text.

You can break up a lot of content using headlines, bullet points, bold text, white space, hyperlinks, or images. Savvy Internet surfers use these visual clues to quickly find the information they want.

✦ **Read each page.** The information provided by your client should pique visitor curiosity and inform them. The home page should pique the visitor's curiosity and make him want to click through to other pages on the site.

✦ **Make sure that each page has a balance of text and images.** Unless you're doing a portfolio page for a photographer, the images on each page should complement and balance the text. Too much of one or the other presents a confusing message.

✦ **Is the text easy to read?** Make sure the target audience can easily read the text. If your client is a techie, and the visitors aren't, make sure the text doesn't include technical terms. Write the text for the least-common denominator — in other words, the person who knows nothing about your client's product or service. If the content doesn't meet this standard, tell your client she needs to dummy it down before the site goes live. Also, make sure that the text font is easy to read and the font color contrasts well with the background so that visitors can easily read the text.

✦ **Are the paragraphs short?** If not, visitors might shy away from the site as it might look like too much work. If the paragraphs are long, send the text back to your client and ask him to cut out anything that isn't relevant.

✦ **Are the pages consistent?** Each page should have a common look and feel. The navigation menu needs to be consistent on all pages. If it's not, the visitor might think he's clicked out of the site.

✦ **Is the site complete?** In other words, do all or most of the pages have content? It's bad practice to leave a bunch of `Coming Soon` or `Under Construction` messages throughout the site. Missing content frustrates both visitors and your client. If you're under a deadline to launch the site by a certain date and the client hasn't given you all the information, tell her it's in her best interest not to launch the site until all of the pages are complete.

✦ **Make sure every image loads.** If you end up with a place holder with no image, this indicates you might have changed the image file name or inadvertently moved the image to another folder.

✦ **What's above the fold?** The most important (must-see) information on every page should appear above the fold. This is the top portion of a Web page that's visible when the page first loads, without scrolling. This is the most important part of the entire page — use it wisely. At the same time, make sure that no images are cut off by the fold, and that no part of a paragraph is cut off by the fold. When performing this test, make sure to resize your desktop to that of the intended audience.

✦ **How much of the information is below the fold?** If each page of the site has a lot of information that appears below the fold, visitors have to scroll down to access all of the information. If this is the case, consider splitting a lengthy page into two or more pages. Alternatively, have your client edit the content.

✦ **Test all forms and other interactive content.** When you submit a form, make sure the data goes to the intended destination or is added to the applicable database.

✦ **Check the spelling.** Most HTML editors come with a spell checker. There's nothing more unprofessional than having a site with typos or bad grammar. If you're in doubt of the correct spelling of a technical term, ask your client or find the correct spelling at a reputable online dictionary.

✦ **If the site has options to order merchandise, make sure that transactions can be completed.**

Get opinions

A dozen jurors are used in a court of law. You should have at least that many people rendering judgment on your Web site. The people who give their opinions on your design should be totally impartial. In other words, don't use your client's employees or your own when you want feedback on your design.

Do a beta test

If possible, set up a beta test before going live. It's a simple matter to upload your design into a folder on the server and send the URL to your testers. Beta testing is especially useful when you've got a humongous, or a really, really, big, site. A huge site is hard to test fully. In fact, you'll be a candidate for a good hair-coloring product if you tackle the task of testing a huge site by yourself.

In addition to testing the site for usability, beta testers can find any bugs that are lurking in your code. Identifying usability issues and other problems greatly enhances the chances of the site succeeding when it goes public. The test can also determine how real-world users react to the site.

In a typical beta test, you contact a potpourri of users to try out the site for a few weeks. During that time, you get feedback on the site design, usability, any potential problems such as broken links or missing images, and any features that are not clear to the testers. During this time, you monitor the server side to make sure that the data is going to the right places. You also monitor any CGI scripts, such as mail forwarding, to make sure that data is being forwarded to the proper parties. During a beta test, you typically forward all data and e-mails to one address.

Your best candidates for beta testers are actually users of the product or service. Your client might be able to supply some beta testers from his customer base. If you can get a good cross-section of the client's customer base or intended audience, the test is more effective. The information you receive can give you a good idea of site usability and the value of the site from members of your client's intended audience.

Get feedback

Setting up a beta site and enlisted testers is a lot of work. Your beta testers might have a good time checking out the site, but if you don't get feedback, it's an exercise in futility. When you enlist the beta testers, tell them what you're looking for. Any group of individuals has varying degrees of initiative, and beta testers are no exception. Expect some of your testers to give you lots of feedback, others, little or none. Keep tabs on who's saying what, and send e-mails to the people you're not hearing from.

Throughout the course of the beta test, address issues as they come up. If you come across usability issues, tweak your design. Exterminate any bugs. After correcting the issue, contact the person(s) who reported the issue and ask them if your tweak resolved the problem.

E-mail is an excellent way to get feedback, but forms enable the designer to create a set of structured questions. With this type of survey, you can target questions that show how often the tester visits similar sites and how often he uses the product or service. Figure 10-1 shows a mini-survey form for beta testers of a hypothetical photography Web site.

Follow up with beta testers

After the test is over, you've got a lot of data that shows you the high points of the site and issues that need attention. However, you can gain some closure, so to speak, by doing a follow-up survey. Send an e-mail to all test participants and ask them about their overall experience with the test site and, most importantly, whether they liked it and found the content relevant and useful.

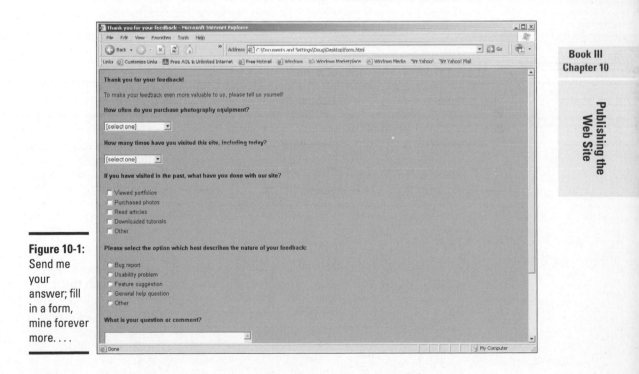

Figure 10-1:
Send me your answer; fill in a form, mine forever more. . . .

In addition to the basic questions, find out how often each participant used the site. You can count on the answers being somewhat inflated (numbers inflated 20 to 30 percent would be the norm), unless you've got a meticulous tester that logged everything concerned with the test. When you're compiling your results, you know that the answers from the power users carry more weight than those of casual users.

Another set of pertinent questions is how the testers like specific features or areas of the site. Find out how often they used specific sections of the site plus how they liked the navigation system and any interactive features on the site. If the site includes forms and features, such as a search engine, make sure you get feedback on those as well.

Another set of questions should address the issues most reported by testers. The answers to these questions can enable you to find out whether your beta test tweaks took care of the issue or not.

Finally, ask your testers to rate the site compared with their experience on similar sites. You can ask users to rate the site on a scale from 1 to 10, or ask them to sum up their experience in a short paragraph. Again, you'll weigh the pertinence of each answer based on how often the tester visited the site.

Tweak your design

The responses from your beta testers enable you to perform last-minute tweaks on the site before it goes live. The issues raised by the beta testers might be related to design, content, or both. If it's design, you have to put your thinking cap on and figure out the best way to overcome the issues. If it's content, your client has to belly up to the table and do some editing. The worst-case scenario would be there are too many issues to resolve given the current design. If this is the case, you'll have to postpone the launch and address the issues, perhaps with a major redesign. If so, you'd be wise to do another beta test before launching.

Going Live

After tweaking the site based on your response from beta testers or from your checklist, you're ready to go live. If you've done your test on the server, it's a simple matter of transferring the files from the beta test folder to the `root` folder of the Web site. If you've done all of your testing on your local machine, you'll need to upload the pages and related files to the server. You can use an application such as Adobe Dreamweaver to upload your content, or use an FTP client. We use a combination of Dreamweaver and an FTP client called CuteFTP to handle all of our file-transfer needs. We cover both applications in the upcoming sections.

Using Dreamweaver to upload content

Dreamweaver features a sophisticated set of commands that enable you to connect to a Web server and upload files to the server (*Put* in Dreamweaverese, as in, *put the files on the server*) or download files from the server (*Get* in Dreamweaverese, as in, *get the files from the server*). To upload pages using Dreamweaver, follow these steps:

1. **Choose Window⇨Files to open the Files panel. (See Figure 10-2.) Alternatively, press F8.**

The Files panel shows the local files associated with the site on which you're working.

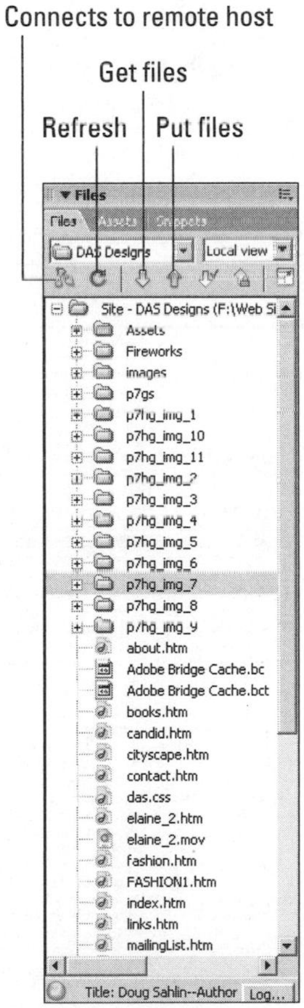

Connects to remote host

Get files

Refresh | Put files

Figure 10-2:
The default
layout of the
Files panel.

2. Click the Connects to Remote Host button.

Dreamweaver connects to the remote server using the credentials you supplied when you set up the site.

3. Click the Expand/Collapse button.

Dreamweaver increases the size of the panel and splits the panel into two panes. The pane on the left shows the files on the remote server, while the pane on the right shows the files on the local machine. (See Figure 10-3.)

4. Select the files you want to upload to the server from the Local Files window.

You don't need to select files associated with the files you're uploading.

5. Click the Put button.

Dreamweaver opens the Dependent Files dialog box. (See Figure 10-4.) This dialog box enables you to upload files associated with the page, such as images and so on.

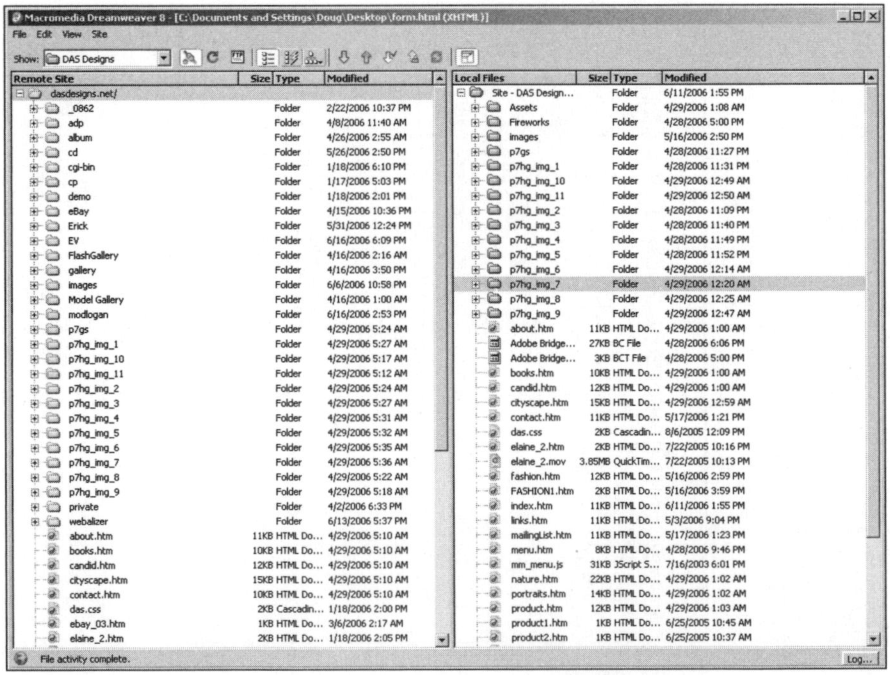

Figure 10-3: Remote on the left, Local on the right. Roger.

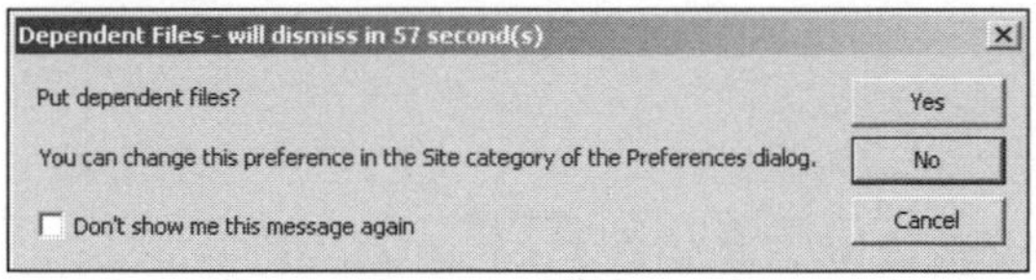

Figure 10-4:
You can
include
associated
files with
the upload,
or not.

Dependent Files - will dismiss in 57 second(s)	✕
Put dependent files?	Yes
You can change this preference in the Site category of the Preferences dialog.	No
☐ Don't show me this message again	Cancel

6. **Click Yes.**

Dreamweaver uploads the selected files, along with all files associated with the selected file.

Alternatively, click No if you know that the files associated with the file you're uploading have not been changed and no new files have been linked to the file.

You can also download files from the remote server by following these steps:

1. **Choose Window⇨Files to open the Files panel. Alternatively, press F8.**

The Files panel shows the local files associated with the site on which you are working.

2. **Click the Connects to Remote Host button.**

Dreamweaver connects to the remote server using the credentials you supplied when you set up the site.

3. **Click the Expand/Collapse button.**

Dreamweaver increases the size of the panel and splits the panel into two panes. The pane on the left shows the files on the remote server, while the pane on the right shows the files on the local machine.

4. **Select the files you want to upload to the server from the Remote Site window.**

You don't need to select files associated with the files you're uploading.

5. **Click the Get button.**

Dreamweaver displays the Dependent Files dialog box.

6. **Click Yes.**

Dreamweaver downloads the selected files into the applicable site's folders on your local machine.

You can also upload a page you're editing by clicking the File Management icon that looks like two arrows (one pointing up and one pointing down) and then clicking Put. Alternatively, you can press Ctrl+Shift+U (Windows) or ⌘+Shift+U (Mac).

Uploading pages with an FTP client

Dreamweaver file management is a wonderful thing. However, if you're working on documents for which you haven't set up a site in Dreamweaver, an FTP client is the ideal solution. An FTP client also comes in handy when you want to download files from a server — for example, when you're doing a site makeover. Quite a few FTP applications are available. We use CuteFTP. It's relatively inexpensive ($39.95, as of this writing), and is flexible enough to upload an entire Web site. To upload files using CuteFTP, follow these steps:

1. **Launch the application.**

The CuteFTP interface is shown in Figure 10-5.

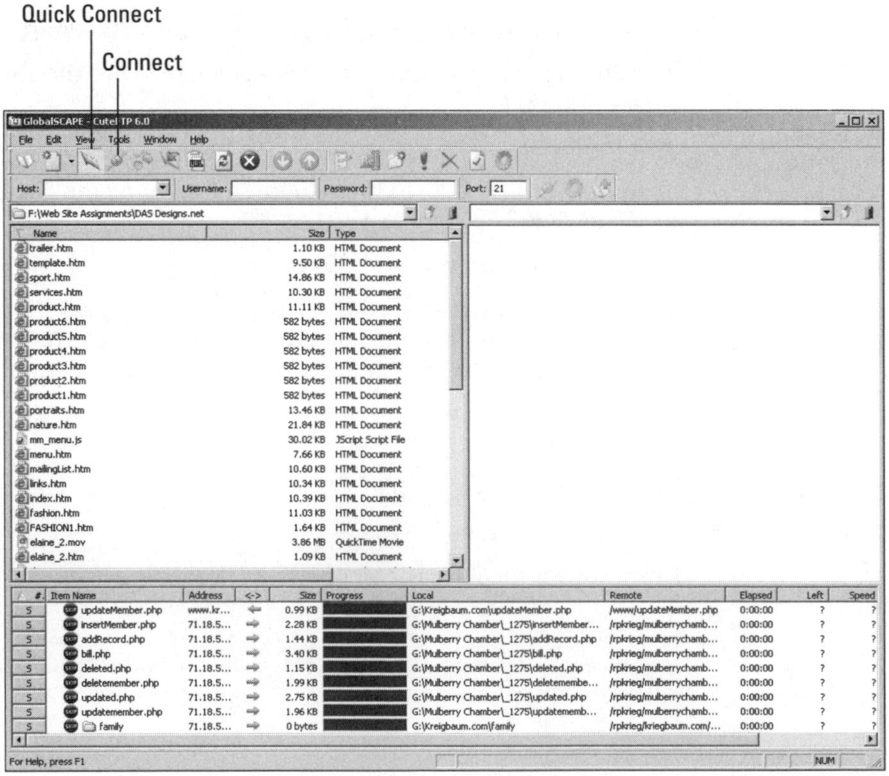

Quick Connect

Connect

Figure 10-5: A cute interface for a cute application.

2. **Navigate to the folder in which you've stored the files you want to upload.**

   The window on the left side of the interface shows the files on your local machine. Click the down arrow to the right of the current folder window to access your system's directory structure.

3. **Click the Quick Connect button.**

   The interface reconfigures to show the Host, Username, and Password text fields.

4. **Enter the host URL, username, and password in the appropriate fields.**

   You don't have to change the default port. Figure 10-6 shows the proper nomenclature for the site URL.

5. **Click the Connect button.**

   CuteFTP connects to the Web site and displays the remote files on the right side of the interface. (See Figure 10-7.)

6. **In the left window, select the files you want to upload.**

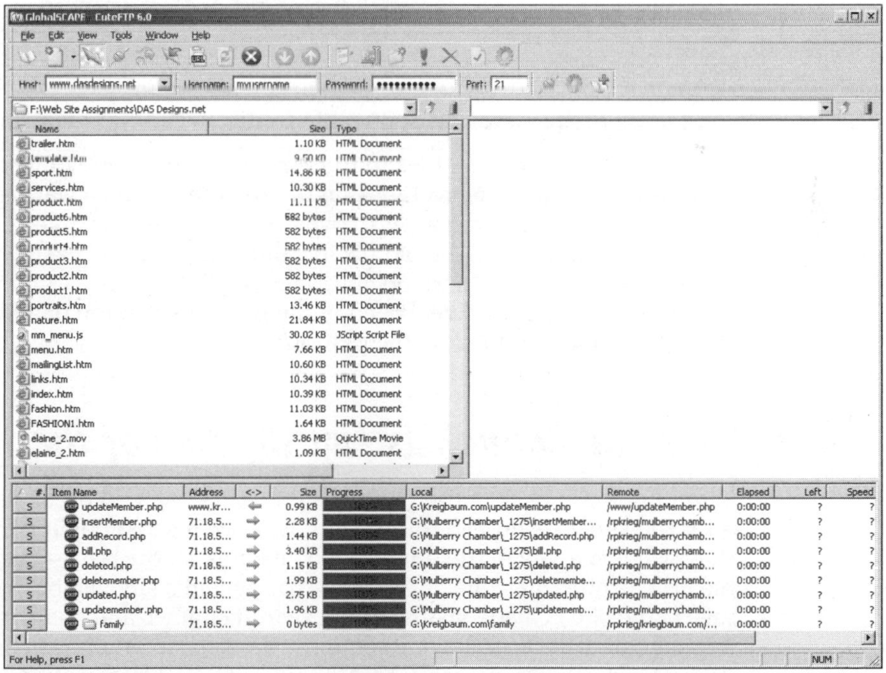

Figure 10-6:
Beam them
up, Scotty.

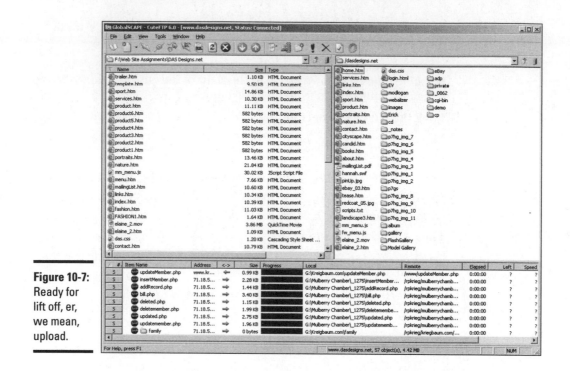

Figure 10-7:
Ready for
lift off, er,
we mean,
upload.

7. Drag the files into the applicable folder in the right window.

CuteFTP uploads the files to the server. If you're uploading edited files with the same name as those on the remote server, a warning dialog box appears asking if you want to overwrite the files. In some cases, you might want to save the old file in a different folder in case you ever need to revert to it. When we need to save old files, we use CuteFTP to set up a folder called Archive. We copy the previous version of a file to this folder before uploading the new one.

What Next? The Launch Is Not the End of the Project

If you think you bask in the glory of a job well done and break out the bubbly after the site goes public, think again. Just because you built it, doesn't mean they will come. Given the number of Web sites on the Net — everyone and his little brother has one, it seems — your client's site will bask in anonymity unless the site is made visible to the search engines and some marketing is implemented. In the following sections, we discuss briefly what needs to be done to make a site succeed. You can find detailed information on making your client's site succeed in Book VIII, Chapter 1.

Submitting the site to search engines

Search engines are technological miracles. Think about it: All you have to do is type in some words regarding what you're looking for, and a few seconds later, you've got hundreds of Web pages to peruse. But search engines are not mind readers. They don't know when you've uploaded your client's squeaky-clean Web site that loads at the speed of sound and is turbocharged with enough interactive bells and whistles to keep visitors entertained for hours. In order to be on a search engine's radar screen, you've got to submit the site.

Submitting the site is like throwing a needle into a haystack. The needle's going to be hard to find unless you do something to make the needle stand out. In order to make your client's site rank high in search engine results pages, you have to optimize the pages for the keywords and key phrases that your client's intended audience is likely to type into the search engine text box to find your client's product or service. You can either optimize the site for yourself or hire a company to optimize the site. Site optimization is a black art that warrants a book of its own.

After you optimize the pages for search engines, you're ready to submit the site to the search engines that your client's intended audience is most likely to use. There are lots of search engines out there. However, you should concern yourself with only the most popular search engines, such as Google and MSN. If, perchance, your client's site caters to a niche market, there might be a search engine dedicated to that market. Your client should be able to tell you whether or not that is the case.

After you've identified which search engines you want to submit to, you can consider several ways of doing that. The topic of search engine optimization and submitting your site to search engines is ever changing, but we cover the current methods of search engine optimization and submission in Book VIII, Chapter 1.

Implementing marketing

Now that you've leapt over the hurdle of search engine submission, you've still got one hurdle to clear: marketing. Very rarely can a bricks-and-mortar business survive on word of mouth. The same is true of Web sites. Granted, the site can get repeat visitors because a friend e-mailed a friend and so on. But in order to achieve your client's lofty goals, marketing has to be implemented.

There are lots of ways to market a Web site. First and foremost, your client should use marketing vehicles he already has in place. For example, the client can add a brief blurb about visiting the Web site in all his print ads. Of course, the URL should be prominently displayed in all ads, and for that matter, on any printed material that leaves the client's place of business.

Traditional marketing techniques work well for a local business in a local market. However, in order for the site to be truly effective, your client might have to resort to online marketing as well. *Pay per click* is a form of marketing where your client budgets how much money he will pay each time a link on a search engine results page is clicked. The client submits a budget, which is the maximum he will pay per month. The frequency with which the link appears is determined by how your client's budget stacks up against those of competitors who are vying for the same keyword or phrase. These are known as *sponsored links*. Web site marketing is a heady topic, which we cover in detail in Book VIII, Chapter 1.

Requesting link exchanges

Like sausages, search engines love links. In fact, your client's site will rank higher in the search engines if more sites link to it. The best way to get sites to link to your client's is to submit a request to the Webmaster of a popular site. Tell the Webmaster that your client's site has content that would be of interest to visitors of his site. Ask the Webmaster to please add your client's URL and a description of the Web site (which you or your client have previously prepared) to the site's link pages. The Webmaster might ask you to supply a link in return.

Another method of marketing is known as *link exchanges*. You can find link exchange services by typing **link exchange** in your favorite search engine. You'll find hundreds of results from which to choose. Typically, a link exchange lets subscribers peruse through their directory and choose the sites they'd like to link to, and vice-versa. The request is submitted to the site Webmaster, who chooses whether to accept the request and ask for a cross-link. Some link exchange services are free. However, as there is no free lunch, a free link exchange service generally comes with strings attached. Before signing up for a free link exchange service, read the fine print and make sure you can live with the service's agreement. You should also make sure that the links propagated by the link exchange are from relevant sites — in other words, sites that relate to your client's business.

Book IV

Web Graphics

The 5th Wave   By Rich Tennant

"See? I created a little felon figure that runs around our Web site hiding behind banner ads. On the last page, our logo puts him in a non lethal choke hold and brings him back to the home page."

Contents at a Glance

Chapter 1: Finding Inspiration

In This Chapter

✔ Finding inspiration

✔ Understanding copyright issues

✔ Getting advice and tools for using colors

✔ Considering font issues

✔ Dealing with image formats: GIF, JPEG, and PNG

When a client hires you to design a Web site, he expects something original and unique. This can be a difficult task. After you pump out a few hundred designs, you have a tendency to rely on old habits and create sites that look similar. And the task is doubly hard because there are really only 27 original ideas. (Everything else is just a subset of the original 27.) To make matters worse, your client wants his original Web site yesterday. So the trick is to be original without spending a whole lot of time doing it. In this chapter, we show you a few ways to feed your creative muse.

Finding Fresh Ideas

Before you search for ideas, it's a good idea to know your client's likes and dislikes. When you initially interview a client, we recommend that you always ask for the URLs of your client's competitors' sites and those of the sites she likes. This can give you an idea of your client's tastes. The client's business and printed material can also give you some ideas. Then, there's the matter of the client's intended audience. If you know the demographics of your client's intended audience, you know their likes and dislikes. If you're dealing with a large company, they probably already have this information. Or perhaps, you and your client can create a persona to define the likes and dislikes of your client's intended audience. For more information on personas, see Book I, Chapter 4.

Another factor you have to consider is the client's industry. Chances are that the sites associated with your client's industry have a common look and feel. It's okay to stretch the envelope, but it's probably not a good idea to venture outside of the envelope. Therefore, your first method of looking for ideas should be entering keywords that relate to your client's business in your favorite search engine. The top-ranking sites might not be the most inspirational, so randomly pick a few sites from the first few pages of results. Bookmark the ones you like. Let your creative muse stir the porridge for a day or two, and then go back to your bookmarks and make notes of what you like.

After you've perused your bookmarked sites, you might still need additional inspiration. If so, find some portals that link to exemplary Web sites. One way to find URLs to inspiring Web sites is to type something like **cool Web sites**, **100 best Web sites**, or **best *type of business* Web sites** in your favorite search engine. You'll come up with a few places to look for inspiration. Here are a few you can try:

+ *Time Magazine's* **50 Coolest Web Sites 2005:**

    www.time.com/time/2005/websites

+ *PC Magazine's* **Top Web Sites 2006:**

    www.pcmag.com/category2/0,1874,7488,00.asp

+ **Web Marketing Association's WebAward, Best Real Estate Web Sites:**

    www.webaward.org/winners_detail.asp?yr=all&award_level=
        best&category=Real%20Estate

+ *Entertainment Weekly Magazine's* **25 Best Music Web Sites:**

    www.ew.com/ew/article/commentary/0,6115,1195793_4_0_,
        00.html

If your search lands you on a site that looks like nothing but advertisements, it probably is. Pick and choose the portals that look like the real deal. Another great source for inspiration is the Adobe Customer Showcase (www.adobe.com/cfusion/showcase/index.cfm). Here, you'll find inspiring designs that were created using Adobe (and the company they acquired: Macromedia) software.

We're not suggesting you blatantly rip off someone else's design but simply that you look at as many Web sites as you can. Incorporate those ideas that you like with your own sense of design. By doing this, you'll take your design skills to the next level and give your client what he wants: a unique Web site.

Respecting the Copyrights of Others

It's one thing to mix and match ideas from other designers with your own. However, blatantly copying someone else's design isn't creative. In fact, the copyright of objects such as photographs and text is owned by the creator. Web sites also fall into this category. Some people might be tempted to steal an image from a Web site, thinking they'll never get caught. When an image or block of text is saved to a hard drive for the first time, the creator retains copyright to the image. Some images might fall under the fair use clause of copyright law. However, when an image is taken (without permission) from one Web site for use on a commercial Web site, this can hardly be considered fair use. If you or your client needs an image that is perfect for your design, consider licensing one from a local photographer or purchasing licensing rights to a photo from a stock agency, such as Comstock or Jupiterimages. And if a Web site owner does give you permission to use his image, make sure you get it in writing. Covering thine own posterior is better than dealing with legal fees and a he said-she said, knock-down, drag-out situation.

If you own Adobe Photoshop CS2, you can search for stock art from within the Adobe Bridge. Open the Adobe Bridge and then choose Edit➪Search Adobe Stock Photos. This command reconfigures the Bridge, which enables you to search for images by entering keywords. Figure 1-1 shows the Adobe Bridge after searching Adobe Stock Photos using the keywords *Statue of Liberty*. You can change the size of the thumbnails to view larger images, download a comp (short for complimentary; a low res version of the image which you can preview at no charge), buy an image online, and so on.

Logos also fall under the copyright laws. You might think it's perfectly okay to take a logo from a manufacturer's Web site and use it in your design because your client is selling the manufacturer's product. However, most manufacturers restrict the use of their logos. To legally use a logo, your client has to accept the manufacturer's terms of use and agree to some kind of licensing. Some manufacturers won't let you alter a logo in any way. For example, you can't get creative in Photoshop with MSNBC's logo and apply it to an image to make it appear as though it was part of a scene or embroidered on an article of clothing.

Figure 1-1: Searching for the perfect, royalty-free image.

If you're designing a lot of sites that do need photos or other elements that you and your client can't supply, consider buying a clip art package of royalty-free images. When you purchase a package like this, you're free to use the image wherever you want.

Protecting Your Own Copyrights

You can't copy or use content created by another Web designer without permission. The same applies to the content you create for your client. You own the copyright to all of the graphic elements you create for the design, such as the interface and buttons, as well as the layout of the page. However, the content you create is often mingled with other content, such as images and text created by the client. Therefore, who owns the copyright to what is kind of a gray area. As the Web designer, you can claim copyright to the content you create for your design by including the following statement on the bottom of each Web page: `Web Design Copyright (c) 2006 `*your name or company name*` All Rights Reserved`. You should copyright your client's original material with the following statement: `Content copyright (c) 2006 `*your client's name*` All Rights Reserved`.

This book is written by Web designers, not legal experts. The information presented in this section should not be construed as advice from legal counsel. In order to fully protect your material and your client's material, you should contact a lawyer whose area of expertise is intellectual property.

Working with Colors (Web Safe versus Not Web Safe)

When you create a Web site, you strive to create an aesthetically pleasing blend of images, text, and graphics such as banners and navigation menus. Your design must be harmonious, a careful blend of what the client supplies you and what you create. If your client supplies you with images for the site, you can often choose a pleasing color palette by sampling colors from the image. If your client has a logo that readily identifies the business, you might be able to create a pleasing color palette by sampling colors from the logo. Limit your design palette to four colors. Figure 1-2 shows a Web site with colors and design elements chosen from the client's logo. It's hard to tell in the black-and-white reproduction of the page, but if you go to `www.acuwest.net`, you can see that the site uses a harmonious selection of blue and green, with a touch of purple as an accent.

Figure 1-2:
Choosing a color palette from a client's logo.

When you design a Web site, the colors must be specified in hexadecimal format, which contains six characters. For example, white is hexadecimal #FFFFFF and black is hexadecimal #000000. The first two characters comprise the red color component of the RGB (red, green, and blue) color model, the third and fourth characters the green component, and the fifth and sixth comprise the blue color component. To designate 256 hues of a color in hexadecimal format, you specify a value from #00 to #FF. Therefore, pure red is #FF0000, pure green is #00FF00, and pure blue is #0000FF.

Common sense tells you that text color is very important. If you create a site with text that is hard to read, you're not doing yourself, or your client, any good. If you take the Santa Claus approach and slap red text on a green background, you've got a recipe for disaster. Traditionally, Web sites have had black text on a white background. Some designers use a shade of gray for text (for example, #333333 or #666666). If you go any lighter than the latter, the text is hard to read.

The Web-safe palette, which has been around since the early days of the Internet, consists of 216 colors that any video card can display, on any monitor, by any platform. The Web-safe color palette is the default color palette of applications such as Adobe Dreamweaver, Adobe Fireworks, and Adobe Flash. The Web-safe palette is shown in Figure 1-3. We know what you're thinking, that figure's black and white; well actually grayscale. If you want to see the Web-safe palette in live, living, and glorious color, create a new Web page in Dreamweaver. Before adding anything to the page, open the Properties inspector, click Page Properties, and then click the Background color swatch. Walla, the Web-safe, 216-color palette appears.

Figure 1-3:
The Web-safe, 216-color palette.

Most modern computers have video cards and monitors capable of displaying millions of colors. Therefore, it isn't imperative that you stick with the Web-safe palette. If you like to err on the side of caution, most Web applications enable you to create a reasonable facsimile of the desired color by picking its closest counterpart from the Web-safe palette.

Many designers are using pure-white text (#FFFFFF) on a black or dark-gray background. If you use this color palette, increase the line height to a percentage of 130 to 150 percent of the text. This increases the space between lines and makes the text easier to read. Figure 1-4 shows a Web page with white text with a line height of 150 percent on a black background.

About Doug Sahlin

Doug Sahlin has been an avid photographer since he was a child. He started his exploration into the world of shadow and light with a box camera capturing images of friends, family, and nature. As a young man, he purchased a 35mm camera and honed his craft, creating award winning photographs of landscapes and seascapes in Florida. In the past 5 years, he has written 15 books on web design, graphic, and image editing applications, co-authored 2 books on Photoshop, and co-authored 1 book on digital video. Many of his books have been best sellers at Amazon.com. While working on his books, Doug has produced commercial photographs of automobile races, fashion models, actors, authors, products, landscapes, architecture and food for his clients. His work has taken him from coast to coast, North to South, and has been seen in print and on the web.

Copyright © 2006 Doug Sahlin All Rights Reserved

Home | About | Blog | Books | Services | Contact | Links
Candid Photography | Cityscape Photography | Nature & Landscape Photography |
Portrait Photography | Product Photography | Sport Photography

Figure 1-4:
Increase the line-height percentage when you use white text on a black background.

Creativity Tools — Color Charts and More

Sometimes, it's hard to visualize what colors will look like when you design a site from scratch. Fortunately, you can easily experiment with different colors in Fireworks or Dreamweaver when you lay out the elements of your design, such as the banner, navigation menu, text, and so on. But when you're under the gun to create a site quickly, it helps to have a bit of inspiration or a tool to help you in your quest. The following list shows some books you can use to inspire your creativity, aid you in choosing colors, and show you some inspiring design ideas:

✦ *Creativity for Graphic Designers: A Real-World Guide to Idea Generation,* **by Mark Oldach (North Light Books):** This book isn't filled with eye candy. Instead, it guides you through processes you can use to come up with ideas. The author also explains the process of creating a good design.

✦ *Artist's Way: A Spiritual Path to Higher Creativity,* **by Julia Cameron (Tarcher):** This book is 14 years old, yet it still contains a wealth of information on being creative. The author leads you through a comprehensive, 12-week course on recovering your creativity from things such as limiting beliefs, self-sabotage, jealousy, and other things that deter your creativity.

✦ *How To Think Like Leonardo da Vinci: Seven Steps to Genius Every Day,* **by Michael Gelb (Dell):** This insightful book lists seven principles found in Leonardo da Vinci's thinking and creative process and shows how to tap into these principles and use them in your own work.

✦ *Color Index: Over 1100 Color Combinations, CMYK and RGB Formulas, For Print and Web Media,* **by Jim Krause (How Design Books):** Keep this handy reference on a bookshelf near your computer. The book is divided into several sections that show color combinations for print and Web. Each color combination shows a graphic using the colors and swatches that list the components needed to create the color using the CMYK and RGB color models. The swatches in the Web design section are designated in hexadecimal format and the RGB color model.

✦ *Color: A Course in Mastering the Art of Mixing Colors,* **by Betty Edwards (Tarcher):** This book delves into color theory. While much of the information is geared towards the artist, you can use the information to create harmonious colors for your Web designs. The author gives you an understanding of primary, secondary, and tertiary colors and shows you how to use the color wheel to understand color values and intensity.

If you're really color challenged, consider purchasing an application such as Color Schemer (www.colorschemer.com). Color Schemer features a color wheel and a section known as Photo Schemer, which enables you to create a color palette using colors from a photo. As of this writing, Color Schemer Studio retails for $49.99.

Font/Type Issues on Web Sites

If you've been designing Web sites for a while, you know that not everyone has the same fonts on their computers as you have on yours. When you design a site, you must take this into consideration. If you design a site with a nonstandard font that's not installed on the client's machine, the page will look fine to you, but won't display as you designed it. There are several fonts that are commonly used for Web sites. These fonts can be used on Web sites that are displayed cross-platform. The fonts are Arial, Times New Roman, Courier New, Courier Mono, Helvetica, and Verdana.

In addition, you can specify serif or sans serif as the font. *Serif* refers to the decoration at the end of strokes that make up letters or characters, such as the diagonal at the end of the angular ascenders of a capital A. When a font is sans serif, there is no decoration at the end of strokes or letters. Figure 1-5 shows a serif and sans serif font.

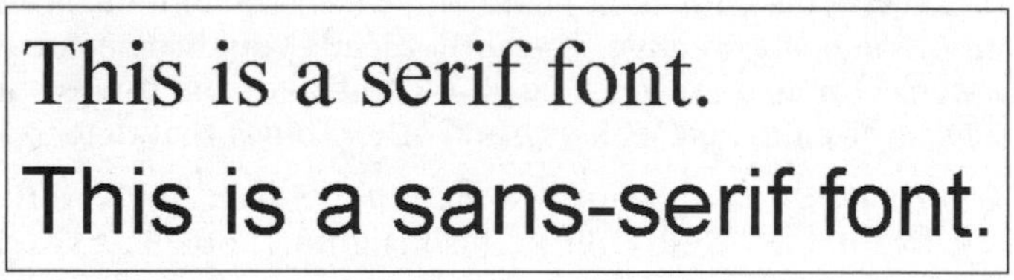

Figure 1-5:
To serif, or not to serif? That is the question.

This is a serif font.
This is a sans-serif font.

When you create Web pages and specify a font, you can specify the default and alternate fonts for a block of text. If the user doesn't have the default font installed on her machine, the HTML page displays one of the alternate fonts. Fortunately, you don't have to hand code the alternate fonts. When you use an application like Dreamweaver, you can choose a set of fonts from a drop-down menu. (See Figure 1-6.)

Figure 1-6:
Vote your choice!

```
Default Font
Arial, Helvetica, sans-serif
Times New Roman, Times, serif
Courier New, Courier, mono
Georgia, Times New Roman, Times, serif
Verdana, Arial, Helvetica, sans-serif
Geneva, Arial, Helvetica, sans-serif
serif
sans-serif
------------------------------------------
Edit Font List...
```

Just when you think it's safe to make an educated choice, there's another issue to contend with: Web browsers. When you use *pixels* (the default unit of measure for text), your text looks fine in the Internet Explorer Web browser. However, if you view the same page in Mozilla Firefox, the text appears smaller. The solution is to use points as the default unit of measure for text. Then your text will display correctly in all browsers.

Use a CSS (cascading style sheet) to specify the parameters for text. This saves you from individually formatting each block of text you add to a Web page. For more information on using CSS to specify text, see Book III, Chapter 3.

Print to Web — Making Your Web Site Work with Existing Materials

What came first, the Web site or the bricks-and-mortar business? In most instances, the bricks-and-mortar business. When this is the case, you need to incorporate as many elements as you can from the client's bricks-and-mortar business on his Web site. The obvious way to do this is to use the client's printed materials as a prototype for your Web design.

When you're thinking about design elements for your client's site, start with the client's logo. That needs to be displayed prominently on every page of the site. If the client has a letterhead with his logo, you can use this as the basis for the site banner. If the client doesn't have a letterhead, use elements from the business card. Figure 1-7 shows a business card for a business coach. Figure 1-8 shows the Web site that was designed using elements from the business card.

Figure 1-7: Using a business card for design elements.

Figure 1-8:
A Web site design using elements from a client's business card.

Understanding Image Formats for Web Design

When you use images on a Web site, you've got two things to consider: the image format and optimization. When you get all of these factors spot on, you've got a crisp-looking image that loads quickly and looks the same in any Web browser. If you get it wrong, you either have an image that loads at the speed of light — but looks horrible — or an image that looks absolutely gorgeous — but takes three forevers to load. In the upcoming sections, I discuss the image formats used in Web designs plus the uses and limitations for each.

Using the GIF image file format

An image saved as a GIF (Graphics Interchange Format) file comprises 256 (8-bit) colors. Images saved with the GIF format can be viewed on all current Web browsers. The GIF (pronounced *giff* or *jiff*) image format is commonly used for images with large areas of solid color, such as logos, or graphic symbols such as buttons. The banner image for the Web page in Figure 1-9 is a GIF image.

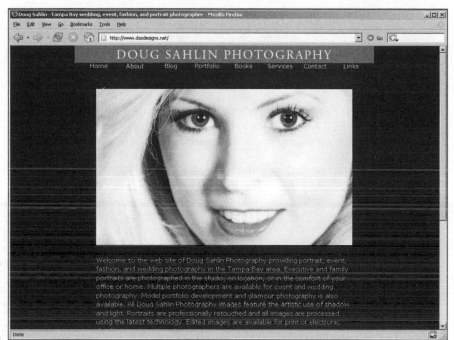

Figure 1-9:
A GIF image
at work as a
banner.

The resulting file size of the image depends on how you optimize the image. When you *optimize* a GIF image, you specify the number of colors with which the image is saved and the color reduction algorithm. The goal is to optimize the image so that it still looks good and loads quickly. Find out more about image optimization in Chapter 4 of this minibook.

GIF images also support transparency. This option is useful when you're displaying text over a background image. When you create the image, use a background color similar to that of the background image for the Web page.

Don't use the GIF format to save photorealistic images with millions of colors. The restrictive color palette degrades the image quality. If you use *dithering* (where colors from the 256 color palette are mixed to create a reasonable facsimile of a color not in the palette), the file size is too large for practical use in a Web page.

**Book IV
Chapter 1**

Finding Inspiration

Using the JPEG image file format

The JPEG (Joint Photographic Experts Group) file format is ideally suited for photorealistic images with millions of colors. The original JPEG (pronounced *JAY-peg*) format also has a derivative known as *JPEG 2000,* which features better image compression that results in smaller file sizes. Unfortunately, JPEG 2000 is not supported by all browsers. The JPEG format does its magic by compressing images. When you compress an image, data is lost, therefore the JPEG format is known as a *lossy* format. Figure 1-10 shows a JPEG image from a photographer's Web portfolio.

The image quality is determined by the amount of compression you apply when saving the image. The ideal compression depends on the amount of detail in the image and the size of the image in the Web page in which you'll insert it. If the image is small without much detail, you can apply higher compression to the image. If the image takes up a large portion of the Web page and contains a lot of detail, you'll have to apply less compression to the image. Otherwise, the detail will be muddy, and the image won't be crisp. Fortunately, most image-editing applications, such as Fireworks and Photoshop, have options that enable you to compare the original image side-by-side to a version of the image with compression applied. The details about image optimization are in Chapter 4 of this minibook.

Figure 1-10: The JPEG format is ideally suited to photographs.

If you have an image with a lot of text, saving the image in the JPEG format will result in jagged edges. This is due to the text anti-aliasing blending the edges of the text with the surrounding image. The best way to overcome this is to use an image-editing application such as Fireworks that enables you to slice an image into sections and then save them in different formats. Save the sliced sections with text in the GIF format and the rest of the image as JPEG files. When you optimize the image, make sure you specify enough colors; otherwise, you'll see jagged edges where the anti-aliasing blends the font to the background.

Using the PNG image file format

The PNG (Portable Network Graphics) format was originally designed to replace the GIF format. For graphics such as buttons and banners, you can save a file using PNG-8 format, which results in an 8-bit file that supports transparency. When you're working with photorealistic images with millions of colors, you can save the files using the PNG-24 format, which saves the file with millions of colors.

The best feature of the PNG (pronounced *ping*) format is that it uses *lossless compression,* similar to the LZW (Lempel-Ziv-Welch) compression used when compressing files saved as TIFFs (Tagged Image File Format). This results in a good-looking graphic with a relatively small file size. The drawback to the PNG format has been differing levels of support by popular Web browsers. Current browsers offer better support for the PNG format, but there are still issues when PNG files saved with transparency are displayed.

Chapter 2: Bringing Your Vision to Life

In This Chapter

✔ Exporting graphics with Fireworks 8

✔ Understanding graphics files

✔ Getting to know that Fireworks interface

✔ Discovering some alternatives: Photoshop, ImageReady, and Corel Painter

You've got a client who needs a Web site. The client has a vision, which might or might not be possible. After you become the voice of reason, you have a workable vision that you can translate into an effective Web site. Now, all you've got to do is start fleshing out the design. But before you can assemble the HTML pages, you've got to take your grand vision and translate it into useable graphics that you can implement in your Web design. In this chapter, we show you the tools you can use to go from concept to completion.

Introducing Fireworks 8

You can use lots of applications to create the graphic elements of your Web design. However, if the elements are exported only as image files, you're going to have to assemble them yourself in your handy-dandy HTML editing application. And that means working with tables and images and spacers, oh my! In other words, the task won't be a whole lot of fun. But some applications can export your graphic design as images and HTML, and you don't have to write the first bit of code. Bingo. That's just the ticket. This section introduces you to Adobe Fireworks, an application you can use to export a graphic design as images and HTML.

Vector and raster images

Fireworks has been around for a long time, but not quite as long as the Internet. Fireworks is an application that enables you to work with vector and raster graphics to create the graphic elements for your Web design. Vector graphics give you the power to edit and resize to your heart's content.

Vector graphics you see are generated using math to determine where the points and paths appear within a graphic. When you resize a vector graphic, mathematical formulas are used to regenerate the graphic. It all adds up. Figure 2-1 shows a vector graphic in Fireworks. Notice the points. Some of the points have what look like handles; these are *curve points*. The handles are tangents. The *tangents* are used to reshape the curve segment between adjoining points.

Raster graphics are also known as *bitmaps*. These rascals are composed of dots of color known as *pixels*. You also have something known as *resolution,* which shows how many pixels per inch (ppi) are used to create an image. Monitor resolution is 72 or 96 pixels per inch. When you create a graphic for print, the ideal resolution is 200 pixels per inch or greater. Now, if you're good at math, you can see the problem when you enlarge a raster graphic. Say, for example, you want to increase the size of an image from 4 inches by 5 inches to 8 inches by 10 inches. You're still working with the same number of pixels per inch; therefore, you're asking the application to double the size of each pixel. The math adds up, but the end result is not very useful, and usually not very pretty. Figure 2-2 shows a small JPEG image. Figure 2-3 shows the same image magnified several times. Notice that you can actually see blocks of pixels.

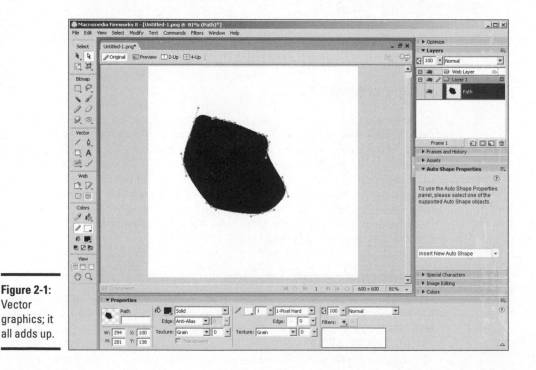

Figure 2-1:
Vector graphics; it all adds up.

Figure 2-2:
Raster
graphics,
mon.

You use a combination of raster and vector graphics to create your Web designs in Fireworks. In fact, in Fireworks you can flesh out the entire Web page, leaving place holders for your HTML text. We use Fireworks to create site banners and navigation menus. The application has powerful tools to optimize graphic images.

Figure 2-3:
Pixels, I've
got pixels.

The PNG file format

Fireworks uses the PNG (Portable Networks Graphics) file format as its native file format. However, it's not the same format as when you export an image from Photoshop using the PNG format. The Fireworks PNG format saves all of the layers and elements used to create the document. The Fireworks file also has a Web layer, which contains information such as the slices and hotspots you've created. Slices and hotspots are used to add interactivity to a document. When you export the document, Fireworks takes all of the pieces you've sliced and diced and houses them in a table. The resulting export is an HTML document and images.

Fireworks interface mini-tour

Fireworks 8 is an incredible application. You can use it to create all of the graphics for your Web designs. You can use the application to create complex interfaces, Web banners, navigation menus, and so on. If your client has more content than will fit comfortably on a navigation menu, you can create drop-down menus that — well — actually drop down. But you get the gist; you can use Fireworks to create some very cool stuff for your Web designs. In the upcoming sections, we show you the Fireworks workspace.

The work area

Fireworks might look like other image-editing applications you have used. However, Fireworks has a few other elements that are specifically related to Web design. For example, in the Layers panel, you find a layer labeled Web Layer. You also find an object called the Button Editor, which — you guessed it — enables you to create buttons. Find out more about buttons in Chapter 3 of this minibook. Figure 2-4 shows a navigation menu being created in Fireworks.

Toolbar   Document window

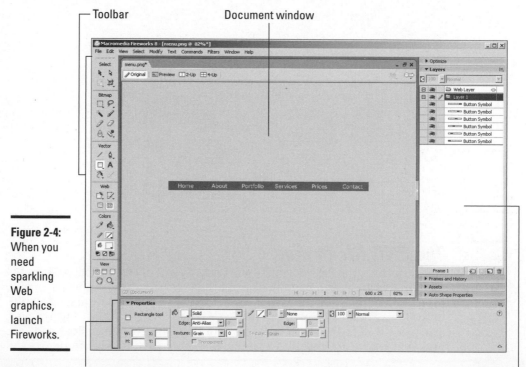

Figure 2-4: When you need sparkling Web graphics, launch Fireworks.

Properties inspector   Panel dock

The Fireworks interface consists of a main window where you assemble the elements of your design, the usual menu bar, a toolbar, and the window in which panels are docked. The Properties inspector has different options depending on the object you've selected. When you're creating text, the Properties inspector is configured as shown in Figure 2-5.

Figure 2-5:
The Properties inspector has several disguises.

The toolbar

Fireworks has a wide array of tools that you use to create and manipulate objects for your Web designs. The toolbar shown in Figure 2-6 houses the following tools:

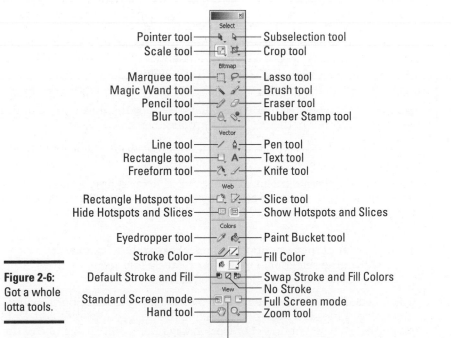

Pointer tool — Subselection tool
Scale tool — Crop tool

Bitmap

Marquee tool — Lasso tool
Magic Wand tool — Brush tool
Pencil tool — Eraser tool
Blur tool — Rubber Stamp tool

Vector

Line tool — Pen tool
Rectangle tool — Text tool
Freeform tool — Knife tool

Web

Rectangle Hotspot tool — Slice tool
Hide Hotspots and Slices — Show Hotspots and Slices

Colors

Eyedropper tool — Paint Bucket tool
Stroke Color — Fill Color
Default Stroke and Fill — Swap Stroke and Fill Colors
No Stroke
Standard Screen mode — Full Screen mode
Hand tool — Zoom tool

Full Screen with Menus mode

Figure 2-6:
Got a whole lotta tools.

✦ **Pointer:** Used to select and move objects.

✦ **Subselection:** Used to select and move objects within a group or points along a path.

✦ **Scale:** Used to resize objects and rotate objects. You can resize objects proportionately by dragging a corner point, change the width by dragging a point in the center of either side, or change the height by dragging a top or bottom center point. When you move your cursor toward a center or corner point and it changes to a curved arrow, you can rotate the object. This is the default tool for this little piece of real estate on the toolbar. There are two other tools that you can access by clicking the down-arrow at the lower-right corner of the Scale tool icon. They are

- *Skew:* Used to slant objects; you know, get them off kilter. You can also use the Skew tool to rotate an object. If you really get miffed at an object, you can tell it, "Skew you and rotate!" And then you can do it.

- *Distort:* Used to change the shape of objects. With this tool, you click and drag individual points to morph an object into something totally different than you started with.

✦ **Crop:** Used to trim the document to a smaller size. Click and drag inside the document to create a cropping rectangle. As you drag the tool, a bounding box appears, showing you the current size of the cropping rectangle. Release the mouse button when the cropping rectangle is the desired size. After creating the cropping rectangle, you see eight small squares that you can use to change the width, height, or width and height of the cropping rectangle. When the rectangle is the desired size, double-click inside the rectangle to crop the document.

✦ **Marquee:** Used to create rectangular selections. Press Shift while dragging the tool to create square selections. Or click the down-arrow in the lower-right corner of the tool icon to round out the corners:

- *Oval Marquee:* Used to create oval selections (or circular selections, if you press the Shift key while using the tool).

✦ **Lasso:** Used to create freeform selections. Click and drag around the area you want to select. Or click the down-arrow in the lower-right corner of the tool icon to access this tool:

- *Polygonal Lasso:* Used to create selections by clicking to define the first point of the selection and then clicking to define the other points of the selection. Fireworks creates a line segment between points. Double-click to close the selection.

You can add to an existing selection by holding down the Shift key and using one of the selection tools to define the area you want to add. Hold down the Alt key (Windows) or Option key (Mac) while using one of the selection tools to remove an area from a selection.

✦ **Magic Wand:** Used to select areas within a document. Click inside an area to select areas of like color. The tool has a Tolerance value from 0 to 255 that you specify in the Properties inspector. A low Tolerance value selects hues that are close to that of the area in which you click. A high Tolerance value selects a wider range of colors.

✦ **Brush:** Used to paint areas of color within the document. You specify the brush parameters such as size, stroke, and edge in the Properties inspector. The Brush tool strokes are divided into categories such as Watercolor and Oil, which enable you to create strokes like those of an artist's brushes. Each stroke has options that enable you to tailor the brush to your liking.

✦ **Pencil:** Used to create freeform lines within a document. You specify the thickness of the stroke within the Properties inspector. You can constrain the tool to a straight line or 45-degree diagonal by holding down the Shift key while creating strokes with the tool.

✦ **Eraser:** Used to erase areas of color within the document. You specify the shape, diameter, edge, and opacity within the Properties inspector.

✦ **Blur:** Used to blur areas. You specify the diameter of the tool, softness of the edge, shape, and intensity within the Properties inspector. This is another spot on the toolbar that is home to many tools. Click the down-arrow in the lower-right corner of the tool icon to access these tools:

  • *Sharpen:* Used to increase the contrast between edges, which makes an object look sharper. You specify the diameter of the tool, softness of the edge, shape, and intensity within the Properties inspector.

  • *Dodge:* Used to lighten areas within the document. You specify the diameter of the tool, softness of the edge, shape, and intensity within the Properties inspector.

  • *Burn:* Used to darken areas within the document. You specify the diameter of the tool, softness of the edge, shape, and intensity within the Properties inspector.

  • *Smudge:* Used to create areas of smudged color within the document. If you've ever dipped your finger into a bucket of paint and rubbed it against a solid object, you have an idea of the effect created with this tool. You specify the diameter of the tool, edge, shape, pressure, smudge color, and intensity within the Properties inspector.

✦ **Rubber Stamp:** Used to clone areas from one part of the document to another. After selecting the tool, press the Alt key (Windows) or Option key (Mac) and click the area from which you want to clone pixels, and then paint in the area to which you want the pixels cloned. This tool comes in handy when you want to retouch images you'll use in a Web design. But the Rubber Stamp tool is just the tip of the iceberg. Click the down-arrow at the lower-right corner of the tool icon to access these tools:

- *Replace Color:* Used to replace areas of solid color in the document with another color. In the Properties inspector, you can choose the color to replace by using the default From option of Swatch and then clicking inside the document to sample a color, or by choosing Image from the From drop-down menu. You then choose the replacement color in the Properties inspector. Click and drag inside the document to replace color. If you choose the Swatch option, the tool replaces the color that matches the swatch. If you choose the Image option, the tool replaces the area of color you first click.

- *Red Eye Removal:* Used to remove red-eye in images. This tool has two parameters, Tolerance and Strength, which you set in the Properties inspector. Click inside the red area of the eye and drag to get the red out.

When multiple tools reside on a toolbar, the last used tool is at the top of the heap. When you click the down-arrow, the other tools appear to fly out of the last used tool, hence the term *fly-out menu.*

✦ **Line:** Used to create vector-based straight lines in the document. After you begin to draw the line, hold down the Shift key to constrain the line horizontally, vertically, or diagonally on a 45-degree angle. The line is constrained in the direction in which you start dragging.

✦ **Pen:** Used to create paths in the document. Click to create a point and then click to create another point. The resulting *path* is comprised of points that are connected by line segments. This tool can be used to create complex shapes. If you click and drag, you create a curve point. Curve points have tangent handles that you can drag to modify the line segment to which the curve point is attached. You can edit paths created with the Pen tool with the Subselection tool. There are other path tools that can be accessed by clicking the down-arrow in the lower-right corner of the tool icon. They are

  - *Vector Path:* Used to create freeform paths that you can edit with the Subselection tool. The tool works similar to the Brush tool, except that when you release the mouse button, Fireworks creates editable points along the path. You set the tool parameters in the Properties inspector. The Precision parameter determines how often Fireworks creates points.

  - *Redraw Path:* Used to modify a path created with the Pen or Vector Path tool. You must first select the path with the Pointer tool, then select the Redraw Path tool, and then click and drag along the path to change its shape.

✦ **Rectangle:** Used to create rectangles. Hold down the Shift key while using this tool to create a square. You set parameters such as stroke shape, stroke diameter, fill, stroke color, and much more in the Properties inspector. But wait, there's more; three more, in fact, that you access when you click the down-arrow at the lower-right corner of the tool icon.

- *Oval:* Used to create ovals — you know, those rotund critters that form the basis for your generic smiley face. Hold down the Shift key while using this tool to create a circle. You set parameters such as stroke shape, stroke diameter, fill, stroke color, and so on in the Properties inspector.

- *Polygon:* Used to created polygons — those multisided wonders that inspired the Pentagon. You set parameters, including the number of sides, in the Properties inspector. Click and drag to create your polygon. The tool also has an option for creating stars, which is a handy option if you're creating a Web site for an actor or rock star.

- *Auto Shape Tools:* These useful critters (Arrow, Beveled Rectangle, Chamfer Rectangle, Connector Line, Doughnut, L-Shape, Pie, Rounded Rectangle, Smart Polygon, Spiral, and Star) are just below the Polygon tool. They work like regular shapes, except you modify them using the Properties inspector and the Auto Shape Properties panel.

✦ **Text:** Used to add words of wisdom to your client's Web site. You use the Text tool to add text to buttons and banners, and other, cool, groovy things you add to your design. And you guessed it — you set the parameters for the Text tool in Ye Olde Properties inspector.

✦ **Freeform:** Used to do yet more cool things with paths. This tool modifies vector paths in a freeform manner. For example, select the tool and drag it across a path you made with the Line tool to transform the path from the straight and narrow to whatever you care to conjure up. And yes, Virginia, Fireworks adds the points to define the reshaped path. If you take a good look at Figure 2-6, you might notice that one of those cute little down-arrows also resides on this tool. Click the arrow to reveal the following:

  - *Reshape Area:* Used to reshape an area previously folded, spindled, and mutilated by the Freeform tool. In the Properties inspector, set the Size and Strength and then drag it across the path to reshape it.

  - *Path Scrubber (Additive):* Used to add points to a path created using a pressure-sensitive tablet. Select the path and then click and drag to redraw the path.

  - *Path Scrubber (Subtractive):* Used to remove points from a path created using a pressure-sensitive tablet. Select the path and then click and drag to remove unwanted portions of the path.

✦ **Knife:** Used to sever (ouch!) a vector object into pieces. Click and drag across the vector object at the point where you want it to split into two pieces. After wielding the knife ("Careful with that axe, Eugene!"), you can use the Pointer tool to move either piece to a different part of the document, or use the Subselection tool to grab one or more points of either piece by the scruff of the neck and modify the shape.

✦ **Rectangle Hotspot:** Used to create *rectangular hotspots,* which are inter-active areas of the document. You can use rectangular hotspots for image rollovers and other delights. We show you more about this tool in Chapter 3 of this minibook. This tool also has close relatives that you can access by clicking the down-arrow in the lower-right corner of the tool icon. They are

  • *Circular Hotspot:* Used to create circular hotspots in the document.

  • *Polygonal Hotspot:* Used to create hotspots for irregularly shaped areas. Click to define the first point of the hotspot and then click to define the other points of the hotspot. Fireworks connects the dots.

✦ **Slice:** Used to divide (hence the name *slice*) a document into pieces. For example, you can create a slice and use it as the basis for a pop-up menu, image rollover, and so on. Each slice becomes an individual image when the document is exported. Click the down-arrow in the lower-right corner of the tool icon to reveal:

  • *Polygonal Slice:* Used to create irregular slices by clicking to define each point of the slice. And if you guessed that Fireworks connects the dots, you would be correct.

✦ **Hide Hotspots and Slices:** Used to hide hotspots and slices (which are designated as light blue and lime green areas) in the document.

✦ **Show Hotspots and Slices:** Used to reveal hidden hotspots and slices.

✦ **Eyedropper:** Used to sample colors from within the document.

✦ **Paint Bucket:** Used to fill an object with the current fill color. You can also set parameters for the tool such as fill color, tolerance, and opacity in the Properties inspector. There's another tool lurking with this tool. Click the down-arrow in the lower-right corner of the tool icon to reveal:

  • *Gradient:* Used to fill an object with a *gradient,* which is a blend of two or more colors. You can choose a preset gradient or mix one of your own in the Properties inspector.

✦ **Stroke Color:** Used to specify the outline color of objects you create with tools such as the Rectangle tool. Click the swatch to open the color-picker and choose a color. Alternatively, you can click the icon to the left of the color swatch and then use the Eyedropper tool to sample a color from within the document.

✦ **Fill Color:** Used to specify the color inside of objects you create with tools such as the Oval tool. Click the swatch to open the color-picker and choose a color. Alternatively, you can click the icon to the left of the color swatch and then use the Eyedropper tool to sample a color from within the document.

✦ **Default Stroke and Fill Colors:** Used to set the color swatches to their default colors: black for the Stroke color and white for the Fill color.

✦ **No Stroke or Fill:** Click the Stroke swatch, and then click this tool to create an object with a fill, but no stroke. Click the Fill swatch, and then click this tool to create an object with a stroke but no fill.

✦ **Swap Stroke and Fill Colors:** Swaps the current Stroke and Fill colors.

✦ **Standard Screen mode:** Used to revert to standard viewing mode, the document, tools, and menu.

✦ **Full Screen with Menus mode:** Maximizes Fireworks to fill the monitor while displaying all elements of the Fireworks workspace.

✦ **Full Screen mode:** Displays the current document, panels, and toolbars but no menus.

✦ **Hand:** Used to pan within the document.

✦ **Zoom:** Used to zoom in on the document. Click inside the document to zoom to the next highest degree of magnification. Click and drag diagonally to zoom to a specific area of the document. Press the Alt key (Windows) or Option key (Mac) to zoom out.

Press the spacebar to momentarily switch to the Hand tool. After panning to the desired area, release the spacebar to revert to the last used tool.

Press Tab to hide the tools and all panels. Press Tab again to display the hidden tools and panels.

Creating Art with Other Tools

Fireworks is considered the workhorse for creating graphics for Web pages. However, you can create some very artistic elements for your Web pages using Photoshop CS2. Photoshop CS2 also ships with a program called ImageReady, which is similar to Fireworks in that you use it to create graphic elements for Web designs. Photoshop has a Save for Web command, which is powered by ImageReady. We show you how to use this command to optimize graphics for the Web in Chapter 4 of this minibook.

Adding Photoshop CS2 to your graphics toolbox

Photoshop CS2 is a powerhouse image-editing application used by professional photographers and artists. The application features an extensive feature set of filters, tools, and commands to perform functions such as color correcting images, removing red-eye, creating images that look like paintings, and so on. Many Web designers use Photoshop to create content such as splash images and banners. The native Photoshop file format, PSD, supports multiple layers, 16-bit color depth, a unique set of blend modes, and much more. Figure 2-7 shows a splash page for a Web site being designed in Photoshop CS2. Notice the Layers palette, which shows the layers that comprise the final image.

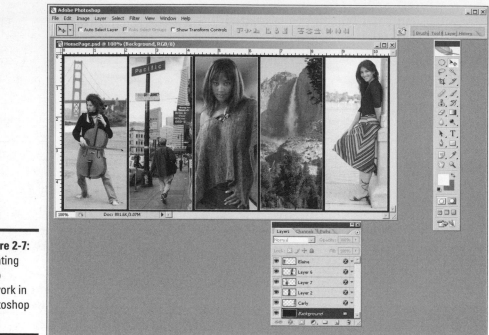

Figure 2-7:
Creating
Web
artwork in
Photoshop
CS2.

The toolset of Photoshop deserves a book of its own. Some of the features appear in Chapters 3 and 4 of this minibook (which covers creating a banner and Web gallery) and in Book III, Chapter 4 (which covers Web and graphics software in general).

Getting graphics ready for the Web with ImageReady

ImageReady is an application that ships with Photoshop CS2. ImageReady features tools that you use to transform artwork you create in Photoshop into Web-ready graphics. ImageReady has a toolset similar to Fireworks. The exception is that ImageReady can decipher everything you do in Photoshop. You can get from Photoshop to ImageReady by using these steps:

1. **Choose File⊏⟩Save for Web.**

The Save for Web dialog box appears. (See Figure 2-8.) Alternatively, you can choose File⊏⟩Edit in ImageReady if you don't want to optimize the image in Photoshop before opening it in ImageReady.

2. **Click the Edit In ImageReady button.**

The image is opened in ImageReady. (See Figure 2-9.)

Figure 2-8:
Launching
ImageReady
from within
Photoshop.

Figure 2-9:
Editing a
design in
ImageReady.

Bringing Your
Vision to Life

The ImageReady interface is similar to Photoshop, but there are a few tools for the Web you should know about. Figure 2-10 shows the ImageReady toolbar.

Slice tool ———————— ——— Slice Select tool
Rectangle Image Map tool ——— ——— Image Map Select tool

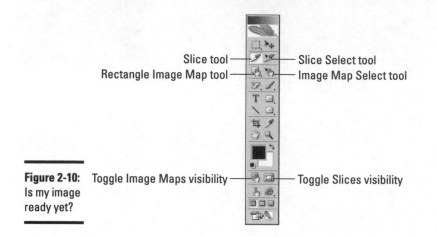

Figure 2-10: Toggle Image Maps visibility ——— ——— Toggle Slices visibility
Is my image
ready yet?

Here are the tools that you use when modifying graphics for the Web:

✦ **Slice:** Used to create interactive areas in the document. A slice can be used to create an image rollover, or it can be used to create as a button. A slice is exported as an image.

✦ **Slice Select:** Used to select slices in the document.

✦ **Rectangular Image Map:** Used to create a rectangular area that will be an interactive hotspot for the image map. When the document is exported as images and HTML, ImageReady creates the code that designates the coordinates (known as *coords* in HTML speak) for an image map. When a user pauses his cursor over an image map hotspot, it becomes a hand with a pointing finger indicating that the hotspot can be clicked and something will happen. The Rectangular Image Map tool has two cousins that are revealed when you click the down-pointing arrow in the lower-right corner of the tool icon. They are

• *Circle Image Map:* Used to create a circular area that will be an interactive hotspot for the image map.

• *Polygon Image Map:* Used to create irregularly shaped hotspots for the image map. You click to define the points of the irregular area. ImageReady connects the dots.

✦ **Image Map Select:** Used to select image map hotspots.

✦ **Toggle Maps Visibility:** Click this tool to show or hide image map hotspots.

✦ **Toggle Slices Visibility:** Click the tool to show or hide slices.

If your image has layers, such as the one in Figure 2-9, you can convert the layers into slices or hotspots by right-clicking (Windows) or Ctrl+clicking (Mac) and then choosing the applicable command from the context menu shown in Figure 2-11.

Figure 2-11: You can create slices from layers.

After you create slices or hotspots, you use the Slice (Window➪Slice) or Image Map (Window➪Image Map) palette to define URLs that will be displayed when the slice or hotspot is clicked. Figure 2-12 shows the Slice palette with a URL and Alt entered.

Figure 2-12: A slice that's good to go — hold the anchovies.

After you set up the interactive areas in the document, choose Save⇨ Optimized As and choose the HTML and Images option. ImageReady exports each slice as an optimized image. The resulting HTML document contains all of the code to reassemble the slices into a table. The document also contains the code for the hyperlinks. Now how good is that?

Creating painterly images in Corel Painter

Many artists use Corel Painter to transform photographs into images that resemble paintings. If you have a client that wants something different, you can supply it with Painter. The current version of Painter is version 9.5. It features a plethora of brushes that make marks that resemble strokes from an artist's brush. There are way too many groups of brushes to mention here, but to give you an idea, Oil, Pastel, and Watercolor are a few groups. You can modify each brush to create a custom brush. Painter also features layers and blend modes that determine how layers interact with each other. You can also use third-party plug-ins with Painter. Figure 2-13 shows an image prior to being cloned and modified in Painter 9.5. Figure 2-14 shows the resulting image.

Figure 2-13:
Creating painterly images from photographs.

Figure 2-14:
The painterly
result of
an image
edited in
Painter 9.5.

Chapter 3: Workhorse Graphics

In This Chapter

✔ Creating buttons

✔ Creating rollover buttons

✔ From concept to completed page

✔ Optimizing your Fireworks design

✔ Exporting your Fireworks design

*W*hen you design a Web site, you've got graphics that you use over and over and over and . . . you get the picture. These graphics become the workhorse graphics for your Web pages. So then, what are workhorse graphics? Well, buttons for one thing. Buttons can range from mundane to passing-for-sane. In other words, you can have a site with buttons ranging from very utilitarian — you know, functional? — to very cool ones that are both functional and artistically gorgeous. Buttons are a part of your design. This chapter shows you how to create buttons and other graphics for your Web design. So roll up your sleeves and get ready for a magical Fireworks tour de force.

Creating Buttons in Fireworks

You've got to have navigation for a Web site. Without navigation, your visitors, looking at the home page, might yawn and say something like, "Is that all there is?" It had better not be if you expect to be a Web designer for any length of time. Clients also have a tendency to frown on one-page Web sites. Therefore, you've got to give visitors a way to navigate from page to page. In the old days before cool applications like Fireworks appeared, navigation menus consisted of underlined text that when clicked, transported the visitor to a related page. Although functional, this method was far from being artistic or compelling. Fortunately, Fireworks makes creating cool buttons child's play. In Fireworks, you can use preset buttons.

Introducing the Button Editor

When you create a button in Fireworks, you use the Button Editor. The Button Editor can create anything from a simple two-state button to a multistate button used for a navigation menu. In case you need a refresher course, a two-state button displays a different graphic when the page first loads (the Up state) and when the user hovers her cursor over the button (the Over state). A two-state button is the default Fireworks button. You can also add a Down and an Over While Down state. Each state has its own tab. Figure 3-1 shows one of the Fireworks preset buttons in the Button Editor.

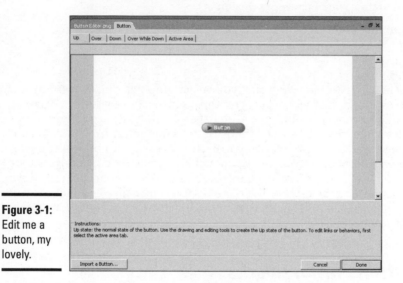

Figure 3-1:
Edit me a button, my lovely.

Creating a simple two-state button

The concept of a two-state button is scary, especially if the states are California and Florida. The left coast meets the right coast. Yikes! But I digress. A two-state button is the default Fireworks button. You create the graphics and text for the Up state, which is what the viewer sees when the page initially loads, and then you modify the same graphics for the Over state, which is what the user sees when hovering his cursor over the button. The different graphics are a dead giveaway that something will happen when the button is clicked. Of course, the site visitor also sees the ubiquitous hand with the pointing finger as he would with a text link, but using different graphics for each button state makes your design much cooler.

Before you can create any button, you've got to figure out what size to make it. When you decide to create a Web site, you do some sort of planning. One method of going from concept to completion is shown in the "Doodle to a Working Page" section of this chapter. Whichever method you use, you know how much area you have delegated for navigation. If you've only got a few links, you can use a horizontal navigation menu. But if you've got lots of links, you need a vertical menu. After you meet with and create a mockup for your client, you know the title for each button. Your button should be slightly larger than the longest title. After you've got all that figured out, you're ready to create a two-state button as follows:

1. **Choose Edit⇨Insert⇨Button.**

The Button Editor appears. (See Figure 3-2.)

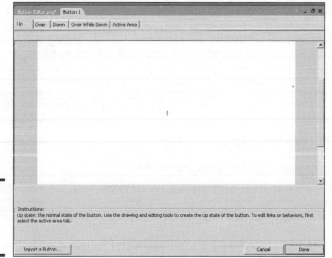

Figure 3-2:
So this is
the Button
Editor!

2. **Choose your drawing tool of choice.**

The logical choice is the Rectangle tool. If you're creating a pill shape button, you can choose the Rectangle tool and then use the Rectangle Roundness parameter to round the corners of the rectangle.

3. **Create a shape with your tool of choice in the Button Editor.**

4. **In the Properties inspector, specify the width and height of your button and any other parameters such as stroke color and fill color.**

Figure 3-3 shows a button under construction.

**Book IV
Chapter 3**

**Workhorse
Graphics**

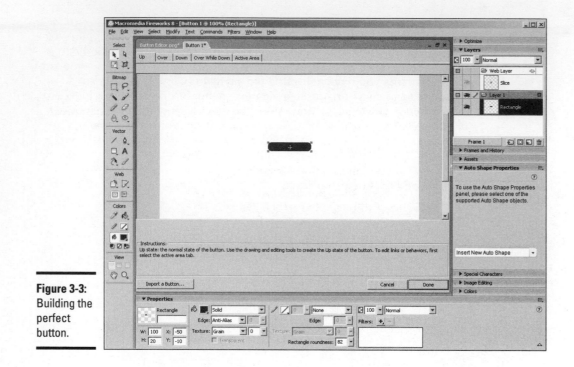

Figure 3-3:
Building the
perfect
button.

5. **Choose Window⇨Align.**

The Align panel opens. (See Figure 3-4.)

6. **Click the To Canvas icon, and then click the middle icons in the Align section.**

This aligns the shape to the center of the Button Editor.

7. **Select the Text tool, and in the Properties inspector, specify the parameters for the button text.**

Verdana and Arial are both good choices for the font face. Choose a color that's harmonious with your design. The font size depends on the size of your button. If you make a small button and try to pack a lot of text on it, the button is hard to read.

Figure 3-4:
Web site
designers
align
objects, not
wheels.

8. **Type the desired text on the button.**

9. **With the text selected, choose Window⇨Align, and then align the button to the center of the canvas.**

   Figure 3-5 shows a button with text on it. The neat thing about Fireworks is you don't have to create a button for each menu item. An upcoming section of this chapter shows you how to flesh out a navigation menu from one button.

10. **Click the Over tab.**

    You've got a blank canvas with which to work.

11. **Click the Copy Up Graphic button.**

    You've got a carbon copy of the shape and text on the Up frame.

12. **Modify or change the graphic you copied from the Up tab.**

    Of course, you could go with a different shape, but that's not practical for a conventional navigation menu button. You modify the button by changing its color and/or the text. For a conventional site, we vote for changing the color of the text. Figure 3-6 shows the button in the Over tab.

13. **Click Done.**

    The button is added to your design.

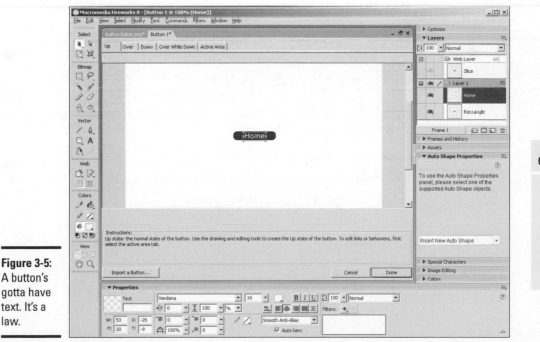

Figure 3-5: A button's gotta have text. It's a law.

Creating buttons with pizzazz

Two-state buttons work great for most Web sites. However, if you want to kick the button up a notch, you can include two more states:

✦ **Down:** The graphic that is displayed on the down stroke of a mouse click.

✦ **Over While Down:** The graphic that is displayed when a user moves his cursor over a button that is part of a nav menu and the page linked to the button is currently being displayed. When you add the Over While Down state to a button, the Include navigation bar's Over While Down state option is automatically selected.

To create a multistate button, follow the instructions for creating a simple two-state button (which was painstakingly detailed in the last section), and then continue with these steps:

1. **Click the Down tab.**

The Down tab of the Button Editor is displayed.

2. **Click the Copy Up Graphic button.**

Fireworks creates a copy of the shape and text in the Over tab.

3. **Modify the graphic and text to suit your or your client's taste.**

4. **Click the Include navigation bar's Over While Down state.**

When you include this option, the Down state of the button displays when the page to which the button is linked loads. This step is used when you're creating a navigation menu.

5. **Click the Over While Down tab.**

This step is optional. You use the Over While Down tab to display a different state when a user hovers his cursor over the button to which the page currently being viewed is linked.

6. **Click the Copy Up Graphic button.**

Fireworks creates a copy of the shape and text in the Down tab.

7. **Modify the graphic and text as desired.**

The completed button is shown in Figure 3-6.

8. **Click Done.**

The button is added to the document.

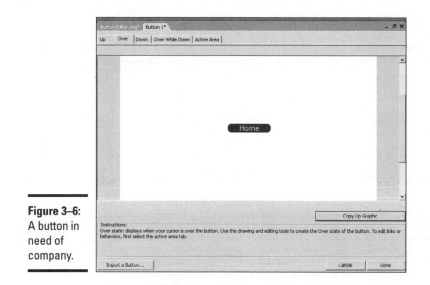

Figure 3-6:
A button in need of company.

Creating a Vertical Navigation Menu

A navigation menu is nothing but a collection of buttons all lined up neatly in a row. You can have a horizontal or vertical navigation menu. You can do all the grunt work in Fireworks and then add the menu to an HTML document you're creating in Fireworks. Talk about your applications that play well with others. To create a vertical navigation menu, follow these steps:

1. **Create a new document in Fireworks.**

The document dimensions are the width and height of the area in which the menu appears in your HTML design.

2. **Create a single button.**

If you fast-forwarded to this section, please rewind to the "Creating Buttons in Fireworks" section of this chapter.

3. **Select the button with the Pointer tool.**

4. **Hold down the Alt key (Windows) or Option key (Macintosh) and drag down.**

This creates an instance of the button. After you start dragging, hold down the Shift key to constrain the motion vertically.

5. **Release the mouse button when the instance is aligned to the bottom of the previous button.**

Objects in Fireworks have a magnetic attraction to each other. The button actually snaps to the bottom of the button above it.

6. **Repeat Steps 4 and 5 to flesh out your menu.**

   At this stage, you've got a column of buttons with the same title. (See Figure 3-7.) Not to worry; you'll give each button its own identity in the following steps.

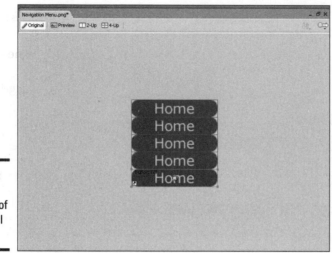

Figure 3-7:
Creating instances of the original button.

7. **Select the first button in your menu, and if the Properties inspector is not already open, choose Window➪Properties.**

   The Properties inspector appears.

8. **Enter the following parameters:**

   URL: The URL to the page that opens when the button is clicked.

   ALT: The alternative text that is displayed in screen readers. ALT text is also used by search engines when indexing a site. Certain browsers, such as Internet Explorer, display ALT text as a tooltip when a user pauses her cursor over the button.

   Target: The target window in which the linked page appears. In most instances, _top is the proper choice. Your options are

   - _blank: Displays the document in a new and unnamed browser window.

   - _parent: Displays the document in the parent window currently displaying the frame.

   - _self: Displays the document in the same window as the one in which the form was submitted.

- _top: Displays the document in the body of the current window. This option ensures the document called by the form action displays in the full browser window, even if the frame was originally displayed in a frame.

Show Down State on Load: Shows the button's Down state when the page to which the button is linked loads.

9. **Select the second button, and if the Properties inspector is not already open, choose Window➪Properties.**

You modify parameters for each button, but you perform one extra step for each button other than those on the home page.

10. **Type the title of the button in the Text field. (See Figure 3-8.)**

This changes the text that is displayed on the face of the button.

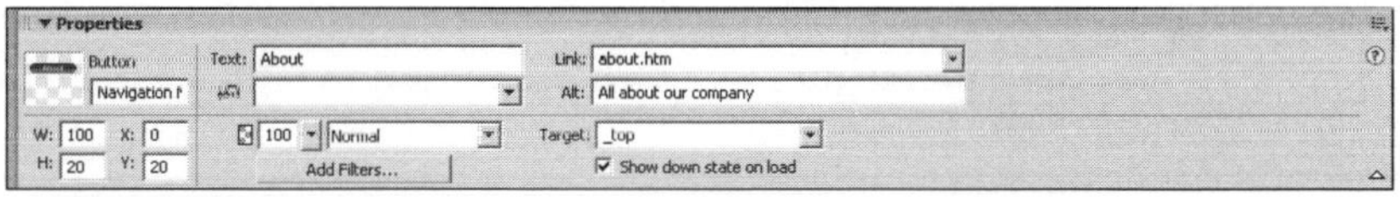

Figure 3-8:
Changing the button face text.

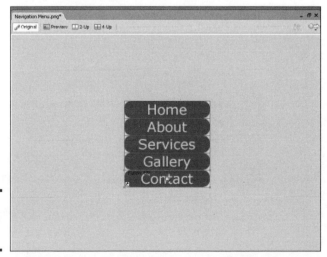

11. **Use the Properties inspector to modify the other parameters of the button.**

12. **Repeat Steps 9 and 11 for the remaining buttons.**

The finished menu is shown in Figure 3-9.

Figure 3-9:
The finished menu.

You can design horizontal navigation menus in the same manner. Create a document that's the height of your button. The width of the document is the button length multiplied by the number of buttons. After you create the first button, use the Alt key (Windows) or Option key (Macintosh) to drag the button right while you hold down the Shift key to create an instance of the button.

Creating a Pop-Up Menu

If you've got a lot of pages to link to and you've only got a limited amount of space, a pop-up menu is the obvious choice. A pop-up menu pops up (hence the name) when a site visitor pauses his cursor over the button that triggers the pop-up menu. That's right, Roy, triggers. You might be thinking doomsday thoughts like JavaScript code, but you'd be only half right. A pop-up menu created in Fireworks uses JavaScript to create its magic. However, Fireworks writes all the code. To create a pop-up menu, follow these steps:

1. **Use the Pointer tool to select the button to which the menu will be attached.**

A white button appears in the middle of the button. This signifies that you can add interactivity to the button. When you create a button, Fireworks creates a slice that conforms to the size of the button. The slice is saved as an image when you export your menu.

2. **Click the white button.**

A menu appears with a list of interactive behaviors you can add to the button. (See Figure 3-10.)

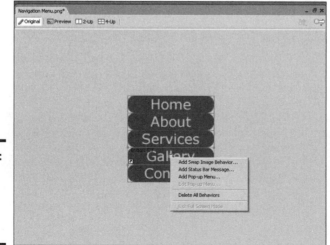

Figure 3-10: Gonna get down, get interactive with the button.

3. **Select Add Pop-Up Menu.**

The Pop-Up Menu Editor appears. (See Figure 3-11.)

4. **Enter the Text, Link, and Target for the item.**

The Text is the button label, the Link is the page to which the button links, and the Target is the window in which the linked page opens. If you're not familiar with targets, check out the "Creating a Vertical Navigation Menu" section of this chapter.

5. **Click the Plus sign (+) to add another item to the menu.**

Fireworks adds blank fields for the button's Text, Link, and Target. Alternatively, you can press Tab to add another item to the menu.

6. **Repeat Step 4 for this button.**

7. **Continue adding the other items to your pop-up menu.**

Figure 3-12 shows a pop-up menu with several items.

To change the order in which items appear on the menu, click an item and then drag it to the desired position.

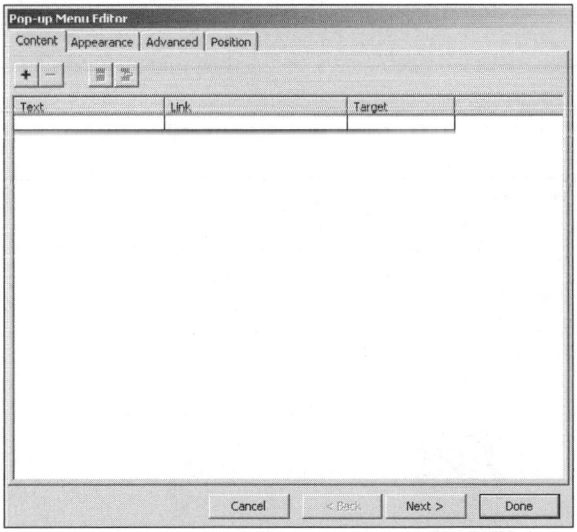

Figure 3-11:
Pop-ups
R us.

To indent menu items, click the Indent Menu button. When you indent menu items, they appear as their own pop-up menu (or submenu if you prefer) when a visitor pauses her cursor over the parent menu item.

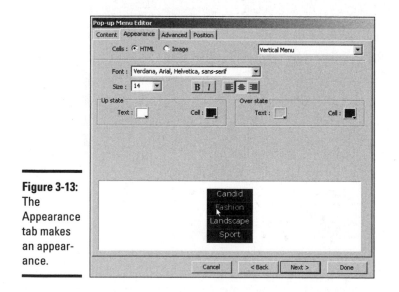

Text	Link	Target
Candid	candid.htm	top
Fashion	fashion.htm	top
Landscape	landscape.htm	top
Sport	sport.htm	top

Cancel   < Back   Next >   Done

Figure 3-12:
Adding
items to the
pop-up
menu.

8. **Click Next.**

The Appearance tab of the Pop-Up Menu Editor displays. (See Figure 3-13.)

Pop-up Menu Editor

Content | Appearance | Advanced | Position

Cells : ⦿ HTML   ○ Image   Vertical Menu ▾

Font : Verdana, Arial, Helvetica, sans-serif ▾

Size : 14 ▾   **B** *I*   ▤ ▥ ▦

Up state
Text : ☐   Cell : ■

Over state
Text : ☐   Cell : ■

Candid
Fashion
Landscape
Sport

Cancel   < Back   Next >   Done

Figure 3-13:
The
Appearance
tab makes
an appear-
ance.

9. **Specify the parameters for the pop-up menu items' appearance:**

- *In the Cells section, choose HTML or Image.* If you choose HTML, Fireworks creates the code for creating the menu items. If you choose Image, Fireworks creates the images for each menu item and saves them when you export the menu.

- *Choose Horizontal Menu or Vertical Menu from the Menu alignment drop-down menu.*

- *Choose a font set from the Font drop-down menu.* These are identical to the font options you have in Dreamweaver. The first font is the default. The Web browser defaults to the next font face if the default font is not installed on the user's computer.

- *Choose the font style and alignment options.* These are the same options you find in your friendly word processing application: Bold, Italic, Underline, left align, center align, or right align.

- *In the Up state section, click the color swatches and choose the color for the cell and text.* As a rule, you choose the same colors as the menu to which the pop-up menu is attached.

- *In the Over state section, click the color swatches and choose the color for the cell and text that appear when visitors pause their cursors over a menu item.*

10. **Click the Next button.**

The Advanced tab of the Pop-Up Menu Editor appears. (See Figure 3-14.)

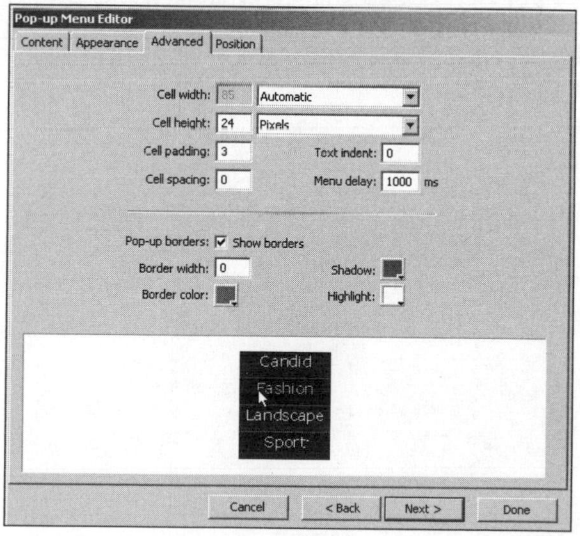

Figure 3-14: And now for the Advanced properties of your pop-up menu.

11. **Accept or modify the following parameters:**

- *Cell Width:* Fireworks determines the width based on the menu item with the longest text. To modify the width, choose Pixels from the drop-down menu. This opens the Cell Width text box into which you can enter a value.

- *Cell Height:* Fireworks chooses a height, which can be modified by entering a different value in the Cell Height field. Alternatively, you can choose *Automatic* from the drop-down menu.

- *Cell Padding:* Accept the default value, or enter a different value. This value determines the area in pixels around the cell text.

- *Text Indent:* Accept the default value (zero) or enter an amount by which to indent the text.

- *Menu Delay:* This is the amount of time for which the menu appears after a visitor pauses his cursor over the button. If no action is taken within that amount of time, the menu disappears. The default delay of 1000ms is 1 second. Enter a different value to increase or decrease menu delay.

- *Pop-up Borders:* The Show Borders check box is selected by default, but the border value is 0, which means that a border is not displayed. Enter a value to display a border, and then click the applicable color swatches for the border: Shadow, Highlight Color, and Border Color.

12. **Click Next.**

The Position tab of the Pop-Up Menu Editor appears. (See Figure 3-15.)

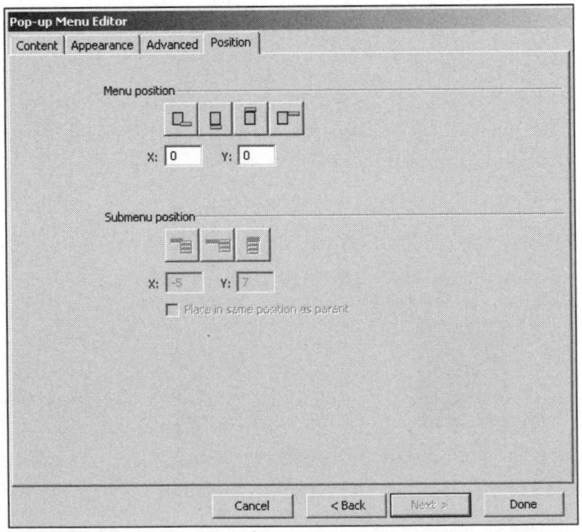

Figure 3-15:
Position is
everything.

13. **Click an icon to align the pop-up in one of the following configurations: to the bottom right of the slice, to the bottom of the slice, to the top of the slice, or to the top-right of the slice.**

After you choose an option, Fireworks inserts values in the X and Y fields. If you want, you can enter different values to further define the positioning of the pop-up menu. If you have indented menu items, the submenu options appear, which enable you to specify the position of submenus.

14. **Click Done.**

The pop-up menu is added to the button.

15. **Press F12 to preview the menu in your default Web browser. (See Figure 3-16.)**

Figure 3-16:
A pop-up menu. Now everyone will want one.

Recycling — Reuse Everything

Creating graphics for your Web designs is time-consuming. When you create something for your own or for a client's site, keep it. Everything you create in Fireworks and save as a PNG file (Fireworks' native file format) is fully editable. For example, if you create a vertical navigation menu in Fireworks, you can change the document size, the size of each button, and the other parameters such as the button text, URL, target window, and so on. If the colors clash with the site where you're going to put them, change the colors. It's a lot easier than creating an item from scratch.

Making a reusable graphic template

Why work harder when you can work smarter? When you create a new Web design, you don't have to reinvent the wheel; just modify it to suit the client. Most designers develop a signature style. If you fall into that category, you can use Fireworks to create templates for the things you use often, such as banners and navigation menus. Fireworks documents are saved with the PNG extension. The resulting document is different from the document you get when you save a file using the PNG format in an application like Photoshop. The Fireworks PNG document is fully editable. Figure 3-17 shows the document for Doug's Web site navigation menu.

Book IV Chapter 3

Workhorse Graphics

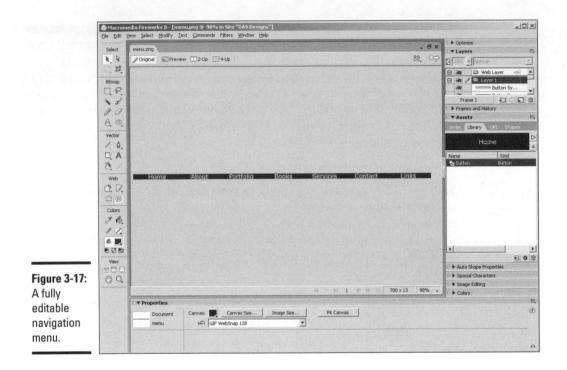

Figure 3-17:
A fully
editable
navigation
menu.

He can easily use this menu on a client's site by doing the following:

✦ **Changing the Canvas size and color in the Properties inspector.**

✦ **Modifying the button color and size by selecting it in the Library, and then double-clicking it to open it in the Button Editor.** If the menu is created using the techniques outlined in the "Creating a Vertical Navigation Menu" section of this chapter, editing the button also changes the color and size of each instance of the button.

✦ **Modifying the text and URL of each button in the Properties inspector.**

Keep a folder of assets that are editable Fireworks and Photoshop files. When you are creating a new site for a client, just pick and choose the assets that you can easily modify to suit the site you're designing.

Organizing a site

When you create a single Web site, you might end up with hundreds of files. Some of them are items supplied by your client that you need to optimize for the Web site. Others are files you create in applications like Fireworks and Photoshop. When you deal with that many files, it's definitely in your best interest to be organized. Consider adopting some version of the system Doug uses to organize site assets:

✦ **Client:** This is the main folder for all files pertaining to the Web site. The folder bears the client's name.

✦ **Client Supplied Assets:** You can lump all assets supplied by the client into this folder. If the assets are of several different types, subdivide the folder keeping all text files in one subfolder, images in another subfolder, multimedia assets such as video in yet another folder, and so on.

✦ **Assets:** Store all the assets you create in this folder. This folder might also be subdivided. For example, you could keep all Fireworks and Photoshop files in a subfolder named Images, and keep Flash and video content in a folder named Multimedia.

✦ **Site:** This folder contains all the files that you'll upload to the site server. In the main folder, keep all the files that will be in the `root` folder on the server. Keep a separate folder for images. If the site needs to be subdivided into different folders on the server, create those folders on your local computer as well.

A Doodle to a Working Page — Concept to Completion

When your client first contacts you, he gives you an idea of the concept behind his Web site. If the first meeting is by phone, jot down as much information as you can and then arrange to meet the client. The meeting can be at his office or your office. Sometimes neither is convenient, and you end up meeting in a coffee shop. Bring your notes from the original phone consultation, a legal pad, and a few writing implements. Bringing a few roller ball pens with different color inks to create sketches helps ensure that you and the client are on the same page. (The strangest client consultation Doug ever held occurred when he was introduced to a potential client in a restaurant. Instead of arranging a meeting for the next day, the client cut right to the chase, and Doug ended up using paper napkins to jot down ideas that he later transferred to a legal pad.)

Mind mapping

You can do mind mapping using an application like Fireworks or using a very large sheet of paper. In a nutshell, the exercise amounts to creating shapes that define the major parts of the Web design. For example, you create a rectangular shape at the top of the document for the banner, another rectangular shape for the menu, and other rectangular shapes for the text and image components of the page. Feel free to experiment with different sizes and locations for the elements that will eventually be incorporated into your design. The next step is to provide the client with a mockup of the Web site, or as some Web designers call it, a comp.

Creating a client mockup

After your mind mapping session, you're ready to create something for your client to approve. It's easy to create several versions of a client mockup in Fireworks. If you used Fireworks to do your mind mapping, use that document as the basis for your client mockup. Flesh out the shapes with actual content. If you've got assets already created, you can incorporate them into the design. Add link titles to the shapes you created for the navigation menu. Then you're ready to create alternative versions of the mockup. To create alternative versions of your mockup in Fireworks, just follow these steps:

1. **Open the Frames palette.**

2. **Select the first frame, and then click the New/Duplicate Frame icon.**

   Fireworks creates a carbon copy of the first frame.

3. **Create a variation of the first frame.**

   This is the second design you present to the client. You can change the manner how the menu is displayed, the placement of objects, choice of colors, and so on.

4. **Create additional frames to create different variations of the design.**

5. **After creating different variations of your design, choose File⇨Export.**

   Fireworks displays the Export dialog box.

6. **Choose the desired file format in which to save the images, and then from the Save As Type drop-down menu, choose Frames to Files.**

7. **Name the document and then click Save.**

   After you Export the frames, you have multiple files with the same file name, appended by the number of the frame. You can now send the individual versions to your client for consideration.

Optimizing Artwork in Fireworks

When you optimize artwork in Fireworks, you choose the file format for export and then specify other parameters. The file format in which you export the document depends on the type of artwork you're creating. When you export the document, you specify other parameters, such as the amount of compression applied to a JPEG file or the number of colors and the palette for a GIF image file.

Optimizing GIF artwork

If your design has large areas of solid color and other elements such as a client logo, the GIF file format is the ideal format in which to optimize your design. Banners and navigation menus are other candidates for the GIF format. To find out more about the GIF format, see Chapter 1 of this mini-book. To optimize an image for export in the GIF format, follow these steps:

1. **Click the 2-Up icon at the top of the document window.**

   Fireworks displays two versions of the image: the original and a copy with the current optimization settings applied. Comparing the original to the optimized version lets you decide the best setting for optimizing the document.

2. **Choose Window⇨Optimize.**

   The Optimize panel is displayed. Figure 3-18 shows the document window in 2-Up display and the Optimize panel. The right side of the window displays the image with the current optimization settings applied. Below the image is the file size, number of colors in the palette, and the estimated time to download the file with an Internet connection speed of 56 Kbps.

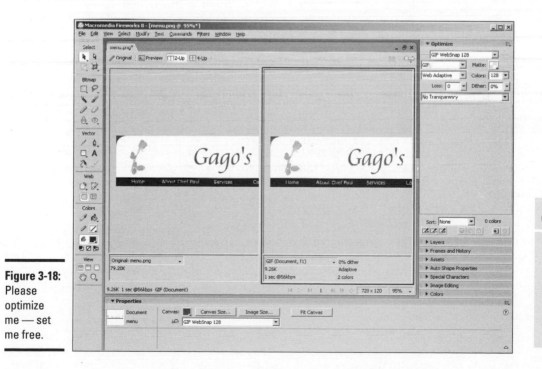

Figure 3-18: Please optimize me — set me free.

3. **Choose a preset from the Saved Settings drop-down menu (in the upper right of Figure 3-18).**

Preview each setting and pay attention to the right pane of the document window. Choose the preset that's the best compromise between image quality and file size. Your choices are

- *GIF Web 216:* Converts all colors to Web-safe colors. The color palette contains up to 216 colors.

- *GIF WebSnap 256:* Converts non–Web-safe colors to their closest Web-safe colors creating a color palette that contains up to a maximum of 256 colors.

- *GIF WebSnap 128:* Converts non–Web-safe colors to their closest Web-safe colors creating a color palette that contains up to 128 colors.

- *GIF Adaptive 256:* This color palette contains only the actual colors used in the document up to a maximum of 256 colors.

4. **Modify the preset to suit your document.**

At this stage, you can experiment with reducing the number of colors in the Indexed palette. You can either enter a value in the Colors text field, or choose a preset from the Colors drop-down menu. If you notice image degradation, you've gone too far. When this occurs, choose the next highest value from the Colors menu.

To export an image with transparency, follow these steps:

1. **Choose Index Transparency from the Transparency drop-down menu.**

2. **Click the Select Transparent Color eyedropper and click inside the document to sample the transparent color.**

Fireworks displays the transparent area as a checkerboard in the right pane of the document pane when displayed in 2-Up mode. (See Figure 3-19.)

Optimizing JPEG artwork

The JPEG format is best suited for artwork that is photorealistic in nature. The JPEG format compresses the file by losing color data; therefore, JPEG is known as a *lossy format*. Your goal is to export the image at the smallest possible file size without noticeable degradation. To optimize a document using the JPEG format, follow these steps:

1. **Click the 2-Up icon at the top of the document window.**

Fireworks displays two versions of the image: the original and a copy with the current optimization settings applied. Comparing the original to the optimized version lets you determine the best setting for optimizing the document.

2. Choose Window⇨Optimize.

The Optimize panel is displayed. When you optimize a document, you can click the 2-Up button to display two versions of the image. The right side of the window displays the image with the current optimization settings applied, while the left side shows the original image. Below the image is the file size, number of colors in the palette, and the estimated time to download the file with an Internet connection speed of 56 Kbps. Make sure you have image magnification set at 100 percent so you see the pixels at their actual size.

3. Choose an option from the Saved Presets drop-down menu.

We recommend starting with the JPEG-High Quality option. The theory is to start with a high quality and apply compression until noticeable degradation occurs.

4. Gradually apply more compression to the image by specifying a lower image quality.

You can enter a value in the Quality text box or drag the Quality slider. When you see noticeable degradation in the image, gradually bump up the image quality until the end result looks good to you.

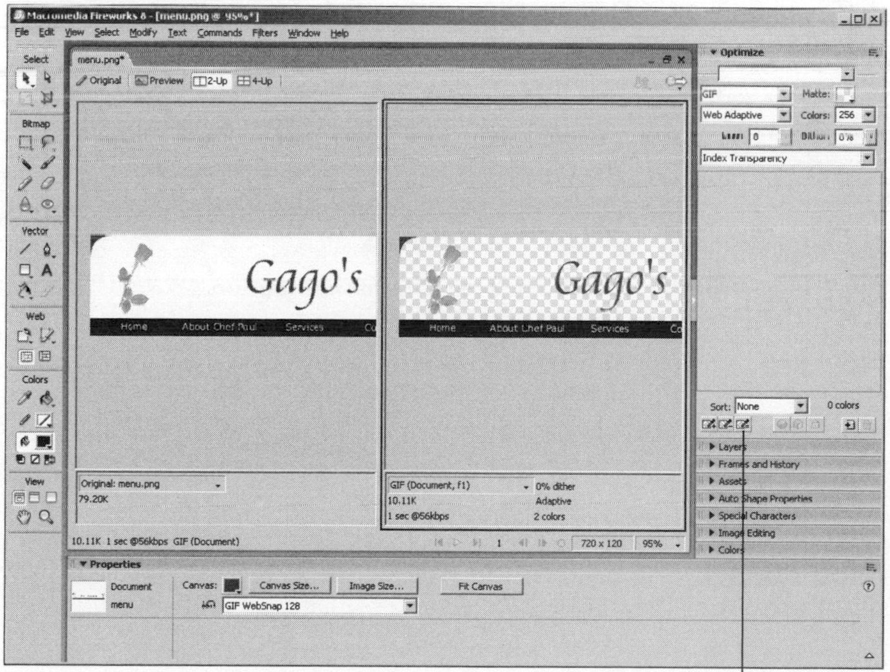

Figure 3-19:
Now you see me; now you don't.

Book IV
Chapter 3

Workhorse
Graphics

Select Transparent Color

If you have to apply heavy levels of compression to get the desired file size, choose an option from the Smoothing drop-down menu to smooth out the jagged edges caused by heavy compression.

Exporting Artwork from Fireworks

After you optimize the image, it's time to export it from Fireworks. Exporting images is fairly straightforward; choose File⇨Export and then specify the folder in which to save the image. When you export a document like a navigation menu with multiple slices, you export the document as images and HTML as follows:

1. **Choose File⇨Export.**

The Export dialog box appears.

2. **Choose HTML and Images from the Export drop-down menu.**

This option exports the document as an HTML file with all the code necessary to reassemble the exported images, create links for navigation menus, and so on.

When exporting a JPEG image, choose Images Only. Normally this is selected by default when you're exporting an image without slices or hotspots.

3. **Choose Export HTML File from the HTML drop-down menu.**

Your alternative is to copy the HTML code to the clipboard.

4. **Click the Export Areas Without Slices check box.**

This exports the areas of your document such as the background that has not been designated as a slice.

5. **Click the Put Images in Subfolder option.**

This helps keep your files neat and tidy. By default, Fireworks creates a folder named Images. You can specify another folder by clicking the Browse button and then navigating to the desired folder.

6. **Click Export.**

Fireworks exports the document as an HTML file and images to the specified folders.

Chapter 4: Creating Compelling Graphics

In This Chapter

✔ **Creating site banners**

✔ **Creating compelling graphics**

✔ **Using Web-friendly photos**

✔ **Incorporating Web photo galleries**

Almost every Web site you see has graphics. Let's face it; a Web site without graphics is text. And how boring is that? To make the sites you design stand out among the plethora of sites on the Web, you've got to incorporate fast-loading, compelling graphics. Graphics come in many flavors. Some of them were covered in the previous chapter. This chapter discusses the graphics that elevate the sites you design above the competition. These include such graphic elements as the banner, splash images, and photo galleries. When you create these elements, you incorporate your own design preferences with the graphic elements from your client's brick-and-mortar business if he has one.

Creating Banner Graphics

Banners are proudly displayed at the top of just about every Web site you visit. The banner often incorporates the client's marketing tools such as the company logo. When you create a banner for a site, you use the company logo and a color scheme that is harmonious with your client's logo. If your client does not have a logo, you use your own sense of design to create the color palette for the site.

Using Photoshop to create a banner

You can create a banner in just about any image-editing application that enables you to create a document from scratch. Photoshop however, gives you the power to augment your creativity with its rich feature-set. Photoshop ships with a set of Adobe Pro fonts that give you the capability to create a very unique banner.

When you design a banner, your first consideration is size. Your client's logo is nestled in the design. Therefore, the banner must be tall enough to display the logo. Fortunately, most professionally designed logos look good in sizes from the sublimely small — the customer's letterhead — to the ridiculously large — the billboard ad. If the client's logo already has text, the logo and a harmonious background color are all you need. If the client logo displays only an artistic arrangement of the client's initials, you have to add text. As a rule, centering banners and site content is preferable.

When you decide on the size for your banner, you must take into account the amount of available monitor real estate for the desktop size of your client's intended audience. A good practice is to optimize Web graphics for the lowest common denominator, which is currently 800 x 600 pixels. In order to keep all your content above the fold, you have to deal with an area of 760 x 420 pixels, which is all you've got left after browser toolbars, menus, scroll bars, and so on. Therefore, the maximum size of any banner you create should be 700 x 80 pixels. This leaves you room for a navigation menu, images, and text.

Figure 4-1 shows a simple banner being designed in Photoshop. The banner is text-only because the business being promoted on the Web site is a start-up and did not have a logo when the initial site was being designed. The banner size is 600 x 80, large enough to elegantly display the company name and tag line using the Adobe Garamond Pro font. The text was further formatted using the Photoshop Character palette, which enables the designer to incorporate font styling such as small caps, faux bold, and faux italic. Faux bold and italic are especially useful if the desired font face does not come with bold or italic styling options. Figure 4-2 shows the banner as displayed on the client Web site.

Figure 4-1: Designing a simple banner in Photoshop.

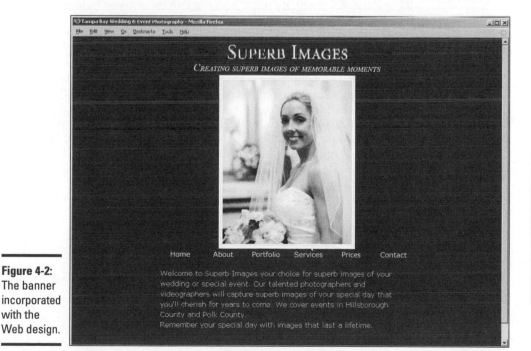

Figure 4-2: The banner incorporated with the Web design.

Including all the important information

The size of your banner is determined by the amount of information your client wants to display. Sometimes your client goes over the top and asks you to include everything but the kitchen sink; for example, the name of the company, address, phone number, Web site URL, and so on. That's simply way too much information, and it's the reason why most Web sites include a Contact Us page. In reality, all a banner needs are the following elements:

✦ **Client Logo:** If your client has a logo, it should be displayed prominently on the banner. Logos aligned to the left side of the banner look good.

✦ **Company Name:** If the client's logo doesn't display the company name, add the company name to the banner. If you're designing a banner for a client who doesn't have a logo, place the company name or Web site name on the banner, centered. When designing a banner for a client with a logo but no company name, display the logo on the left with the company name immediately following. Leave enough space so that the banner does not look cluttered.

✦ **Tag Line:** If the company has a tag line, display it below the company name. If the client has a logo with a company name, the tag line is displayed to the right of the logo, centered vertically. If the company has a logo without a company name, the tag line is centered below the company name. The logo is sized to fill the height of the banner.

Working with an existing logo

When you design a banner, or for that matter a Web site, your client's logo plays an important part in the overall design. If the logo is well designed, you can incorporate elements from the logo into your design. The banner and the Web site should include colors from the client's logo. Figure 4-3 shows a logo being incorporated into a banner design in Photoshop. Figure 4-4 shows the banner incorporated with the Web design. If this book was in color, you'd be able to see that the site colors were pulled directly from the client's logo.

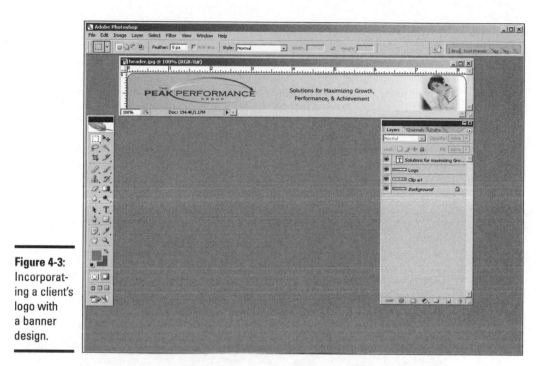

Figure 4-3:
Incorporating a client's logo with a banner design.

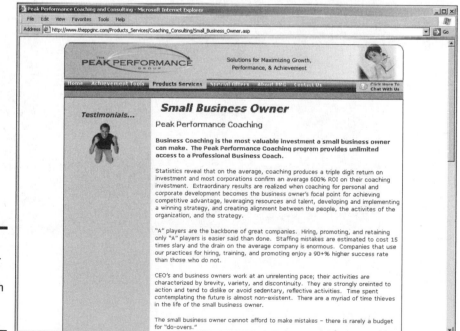

Figure 4-4:
Incorporating the banner with the site design.

Create Promotional Graphics

In today's business climate, a Web site often drives a small business. Therefore, the site often comes before any printed material is created to promote the business. When this is the case, it's logical to use elements from the site design to promote the business. For example, when Doug designed a Web site to promote his photography business, he originally started out with an artistic photo of a very vexing set of eyes. He changed the splash image after doing a ten-minute presentation for a local networking group. He showed a print of an image he had stylized in Photoshop. The image was originally in color, but he converted it to black and white and painted some color from the original image into the subject's lips and eyes. The photo received a lot of oohs and aahs, so Doug now uses it on his home page. (See Figure 4-5.) This photo also appears in Doug's promotional materials. When recipients of the printed material visit the Web site, they immediately see a familiar face.

Figure 4-5: Using Web site elements for promotional items.

Emphasize your point

When Doug decided to create promotional materials to increase his photography business, he knew that the Web site would play an integral part in his marketing plans. When he embarked upon a local marketing campaign, he started with postcards. The front of the postcard features the image from the home page. (See Figure 4-6.)

DOUG SAHLIN PHOTOGRAPHY

Figure 4-6: Incorporating design elements in printed material.

Even though Doug did all the design work for his printed material, he consulted a marketing specialist when deciding what to emphasize on the postcard. She suggested emphasizing a particular service instead of listing all his services. Doug specializes in portrait photography on location. Therefore, he decided to focus on that aspect of the business in the first printed material he created. He laid out the back of the postcard in Adobe Illustrator, using bullet points to bring attention to his portrait photography service. He also added a *call to action* on the back of the card. The marketing guru had told him to give recipients a reason to call. The card has contact information including, of course, the URL to the section of Doug's site where recipients can find examples of his portrait photography. And, of course, his tag line appears below the company name (see Figure 4-7), just as on the Web site.

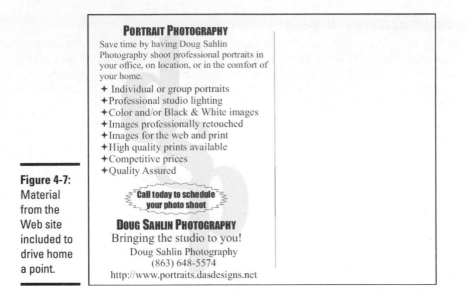

PORTRAIT PHOTOGRAPHY

Save time by having Doug Sahlin Photography shoot professional portraits in your office, on location, or in the comfort of your home.

+ Individual or group portraits
+ Professional studio lighting
+ Color and/or Black & White images
+ Images professionally retouched
+ Images for the web and print
+ High quality prints available
+ Competitive prices
+ Quality Assured

Call today to schedule your photo shoot

DOUG SAHLIN PHOTOGRAPHY

Bringing the studio to you!

Doug Sahlin Photography

(863) 648-5574

http://www.portraits.dasdesigns.net

Figure 4-7: Material from the Web site included to drive home a point.

Complement your style

When you design promotional material to promote a business that is driven by a Web site, the style of the promotional material should be similar to the style of the Web site. The printed material should look as though it was pulled right from the Web design. Fortunately, this is a fairly easy task if you design the graphic elements of your Web site using the Adobe Creative Suite, which as of this writing is Version 2, or CS2. This powerhouse application enables you to use in other applications — such as Adobe InDesign (page layout application) or Adobe Illustrator — the same elements you designed for the Web site in Photoshop.

All applications hinge around the Adobe Bridge, which is available from InDesign, Illustrator, and Photoshop. The Adobe Bridge (see Figure 4-8), enables you to choose items previously saved and open them in their host application. You can then modify the item for the application in which you'll use it. For example, you can resize a photo for use in a poster you're creating in Adobe Illustrator or a brochure you're creating in InDesign. This capability to quickly access assets designed for the Web site in other applications lets you create printed material with the same style as your Web site.

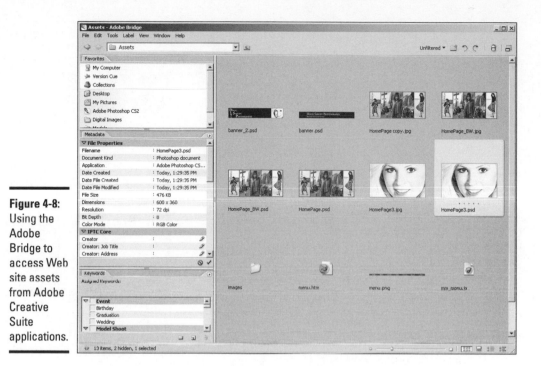

Figure 4-8:
Using the Adobe Bridge to access Web site assets from Adobe Creative Suite applications.

When the time was right to create a brochure, Doug took advantage of the interoperability of Adobe Creative Suite applications. After consulting with his marketing guru, he created the graphic design for the brochure in Adobe InDesign using high-resolution versions of images from the Web site. The brochure emphasized the portrait photography side of the business. The images for the brochure were picked from the portrait section of his Web site. The Adobe Bridge made it easy to see the images ahead of time.

The InDesign Place command (File➪Place) places the image in the design. The Place command is very powerful because it allows you to shrink the original image to fit into a specific portion of your design. If you later decide to increase the size of the image, you can do so with no degradation. When you lay out a brochure using InDesign, you can take advantage of the powerful Text Wrap palette to wrap text around images in the design. (See Figure 4-9.)

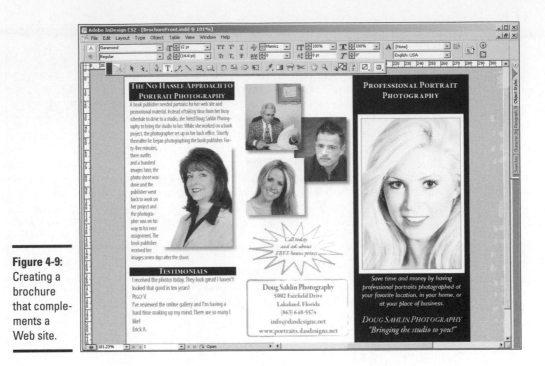

Figure 4-9: Creating a brochure that complements a Web site.

Creating Fast-Loading, Beautiful Photos

Photos are an integral part of any Web site. But the trick is to display photos that look great and load quickly. You can always tell when you're at a site that was not created by a professional designer; the images are either huge and load slowly, or they load quickly but look bad. The next few sections show you how to resize and then optimize your images for the Web.

Resizing your photos for the Web

If you're working with images supplied by your client or images from a clip art disk, chances are that you're dealing with high-resolution images suitable for print. High-resolution images have large file sizes. The combination is totally unsuitable for display on a Web site. Granted, you can control the size at which the image is displayed by entering the desired width and height in the `<img>` tag. But the file size is still the same, and the image will load slowly.

Images for the Web need a resolution of 72 PPI (pixels per inch). Some designers insist on 96 PPI, but this is more than you need. Images with a resolution of 72 PPI are sufficient for all modern computer monitors. Images for print have a resolution of 150 PPI or greater. In addition to resolution, your next concern is image size. The size of the image is determined by where the image will reside. If you're posting the image inline with text, you size the image smaller than you would size an image for a photographer's gallery.

Also consider the desktop size of your audience. Keep in mind that many people are still surfing the net with an 800 x 600 pixel desktop size, which with a maximized browser has an available display area of 760 x 420 pixels. If you resize an image with portrait orientation (an image that is taller than it is wide) to 600 pixels in height, people with an 800 x 600 desktop size will have to scroll to see the entire image. When you resize images for inline display, a good practice is to never exceed 200 pixels in width or height. If the image is being displayed as a splash image on a home page or in an image gallery, we recommend never exceeding an area of 600 x 360 pixels. Granted, this gives the advantage to landscape (wider than tall) images, but the available display area in a Web browser is also wider than it is tall. You can resize images using Fireworks or Photoshop CS2 as shown in the following steps.

To resize images in Fireworks, follow these steps:

1. **Choose Modify⇨Canvas⇨Image Size.**

   The Image Size dialog box (see Figure 4-10) appears.

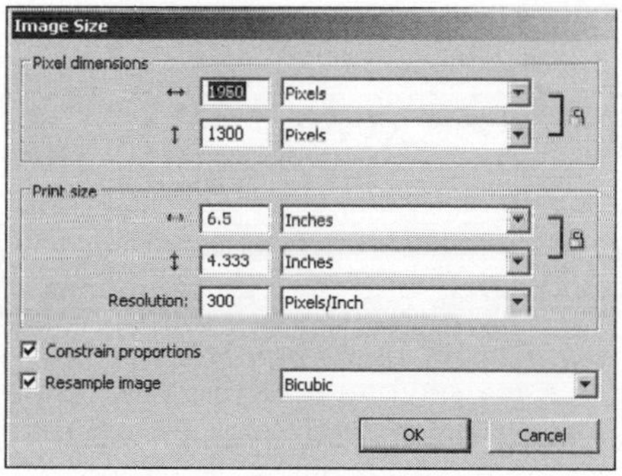

Figure 4-10: Resizing an image in Fireworks.

2. **Enter a value of 72 in the Resolution field.**

   This does not change the Print Size, but it does reduce the Pixel Dimensions of the image.

3. **Enter the desired Width or Height in the Pixel Dimensions section.**

   You can enter either value because the option to constrain proportions is selected by default. It is advised that you never deselect this option because the image will be distorted.

   Downsizing an image is okay, but when you try to upsize a small image, you're asking the image-editing application to increase the size of each pixel in the document. Image degradation is the unhappy result of trying to upsize an image.

4. **Click OK.**

   Fireworks resizes the image to the desired dimensions.

**Book IV
Chapter 4**

**Creating Compelling
Graphics**

Enlarging images with Alien Skin Blow Up

If you have clients that present you with small low-resolution images that need to be enlarged, consider investing in a plug-in called Blow Up that's made by Alien Skin (www.alienskin.com/blowup/index.html). Blow Up works with Photoshop Elements 3 or newer, and Photoshop CS and newer. I've used the plug-in extensively to blow up client photos and my own images. The results are truly amazing. The manufacturer claims you can enlarge a good-quality image four times (1600% area) without jagged edges, halos, or artifacts. The plug-in comes complete with an instruction booklet and can be used with a Macintosh PC G4 processor running MAC OS 10.3.9 or later, or with an Intel Pentium 4 processor running the Windows 2000 or Windows XP operating system. You can download a fully functional demo with a 30-day expiration at www.alienskin.com/downloads/getmail1.asp.

To resize an image in Photoshop, follow these steps:

1. **Choose Image⇨Image Size.**

The Image Size dialog box (see Figure 4-11) appears.

2. **Enter a value of 72 in the Resolution field.**

This does not change the Document Size, but it does reduce the Pixel Dimensions of the image.

3. **Enter the desired Width or Height in the Pixel Dimensions section.**

You can enter either value because the option to constrain proportions is selected by default. It is advised that you never deselect this option because the image will be distorted.

4. **Click OK.**

Photoshop resizes the image.

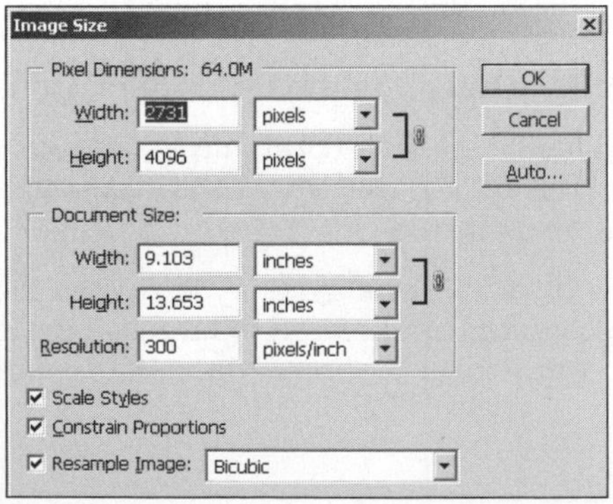

Figure 4-11: Resizing an image in Photoshop.

Using professional optimization techniques

As long as you begin with a high-quality image, you can resize and optimize a photo for the Web in Adobe Photoshop or Fireworks. Optimizing an image in Fireworks is covered in Chapter 3 of this minibook. Photoshop CS2 also has a stout optimization algorithm. You can optimize images in the GIF format or JPEG format.

To optimize GIF images in Photoshop CS2, follow these steps:

1. **Choose File⇨Save for Web.**

The Save for Web dialog box (see Figure 4-12) appears.

2. **Select an option from the Preset drop-down menu.**

Your choices are GIF Dithered, GIF No Dither with a palette of 128, 64, or 32 colors, GIF with a palette of 128 or 64 colors, or GIF Restrictive. Choose the dithered option to have Photoshop mix colors from the palette to simulate colors that are not in the palette. GIF Restrictive pulls colors from the Web-safe, 216-color palette.

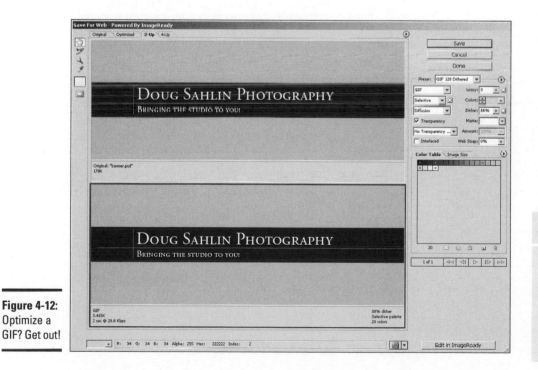

Figure 4-12: Optimize a GIF? Get out!

3. Drag the Lossy slider to reduce file size.

This option discards color data to reduce file size. If you use this option, pay careful attention to the image in the right pane of the Save for Web dialog box. When the image begins to degrade, drag the slider to the left until you no longer see the degradation.

You cannot use the Lossy option if you use the Interlaced option, or with the Noise or Pattern Dither options.

4. Select an option from the Color Reduction Algorithm drop-down menu.

The Color Reduction Algorithm determines the method by which the colors for the image palette are created. Your choices are

- *Perceptual:* Creates a color table by giving priority to colors for which the human eye has greater sensitivity.

- *Selective:* The default option creates a color table similar to that created using the Perceptual algorithm, but it preserves large areas of color in the original image and also Web-safe colors. This algorithm creates a color palette that closely resembles the original image.

- *Adaptive:* Creates a color table using the predominant color spectrum in the image. If you're optimizing an image that is predominantly red and orange, the color table is made up primarily of reds and oranges. Choose this algorithm if the image you are optimizing is made up of similar color hues.

- *Restrictive (Web):* Creates a color palette using colors from the Web-safe, 216-color palette.

- *Custom:* Creates a color palette that you create or modify. If you open a previously saved GIF or PNG(8) file, it will have a custom color palette.

- *Black and White:* Creates a color palette comprised of black and white. Use this algorithm to save images that will be displayed on PDAs that cannot display color.

- *Grayscale:* Creates a color palette comprised of 256 shades of gray from solid black to white. This is similar to how black and white film photos display.

- *MAC OS:* Creates a color palette based on the colors from the Macintosh operating system color palette.

- *Windows:* Creates a color palette based on the colors from the Windows operating system color palette.

5. Modify the number of colors in the palette.

You can modify the number of colors by clicking the spinner buttons or by entering a value in the Colors text field. When you change the number of colors in the palette, you see the results in the color table.

6. **Choose an option from the Dither drop-down menu.**

Dithering creates a facsimile of colors in the image but not in the palette by mixing colors in the palette. Your choices are as follows:

- *Diffusion:* Dithers by creating a random pattern that, in most cases, is less noticeable than Pattern dither. Dithering is diffused across adjacent pixels.

- *Pattern:* Dithers by creating a pattern that looks like halftone squares to simulate image colors not in the color table.

- *Noise:* Dithers by creating a random pattern similar to the Diffusion dither method, but the pattern is not diffused across adjacent pixels. Seams do not show if you use this dithering method.

7. **Transparency is selected by default. Deselect this option if you do not want to optimize the image with areas of transparency.**

Transparency is used when you want areas of the image to be transparent. This option is most often used when you want areas of a tiled background image to show through the image you're optimizing. However, even though transparency is enabled by default, you have to choose the transparent colors by specifying Matte and Transparency colors.

8. **If desired, choose an option from the Transparency menu.**

You have the following options:

- *No Transparency Dither:* Does not apply dithering to partially transparent pixels in the image.

- *Diffusion Transparency Dither:* Dithers by applying a random pattern that, in most cases, is less noticeable than Pattern dither. Dithering is diffused across adjacent pixels. When selecting this option, specify a Dither percentage to control the amount of dithering that is applied to the image.

- *Pattern Transparency Dither:* Dithers by applying a halftone-like square pattern to partially transparent pixels.

- *Noise Transparency Dither:* Dithers by applying a random pattern similar to the Diffusion color-reduction algorithm, but the pattern is not diffused across adjacent pixels. Seams do not show if you use this dithering method.

9. **The Amount option becomes available if you select Diffusion Transparency Dither.**

Drag the slider to specify the percentage of dithering that is applied to the image. Alternatively, you can enter a value in the text field.

10. **Choose the Interlaced option to download the image in stages.**

This option displays a low-resolution version of the image when the page loads. The fully optimized version is revealed when the image loads completely.

11. **Drag the Web Snap slider to specify how close a color must be to the Web-safe palette before it is snapped to a color from the Web-safe palette.**

Choose a higher value to snap more colors to the Web-safe palette. When you choose a higher value, less dithering is applied to the image, thereby reducing the file size.

12. **Click Save.**

Photoshop saves the image in the GIF format using the options specified.

The color table at the bottom of the dialog box shows swatches of the colors that comprise the image color palette. You can modify the palette by adding colors to the palette, snapping colors to the nearest Web-safe color, and defining transparent pixels.

To optimize an image using the JPEG format in Photoshop, follow these steps:

1. **Choose Edit⇨Convert to Profile.**

The Convert to Profile dialog box (see Figure 4-13) appears.

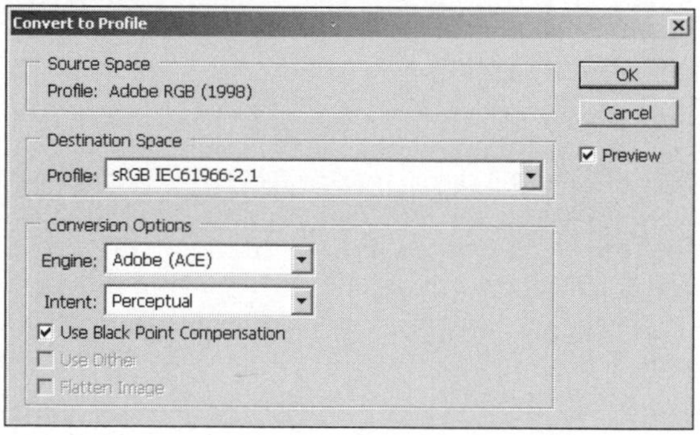

Figure 4-13: Converting the image to a Web-friendly color profile.

2. **Choose sRGB IEC61966-2.1 from the drop-down menu.**

The profile assures that the image displays correctly when optimized for the Web. This is the default profile for many digital cameras. However, if your client gives you an image that has the Adobe 1998 color profile or another print-quality color profile attached, the colors will be *out of gamut* (which means a color cannot be properly displayed on a device) for browser display.

3. **Choose File⇨Save for Web.**

The Save for Web dialog box appears. Figure 4-14 shows the Save for Web dialog box with options for optimizing an image for the JPEG format.

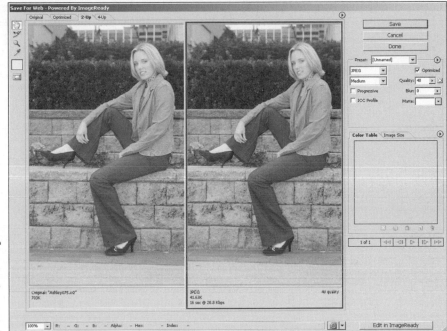

Figure 4-14:
Optimizing
an image for
the JPEG
format.

4. Choose an option from the Preset menu.

Your options are JPEG Low, JPEG Medium, or JPEG High. After choosing
a preset, you can customize the settings to suit your needs.

5. Modify the following parameters if desired:

Quality: Enter a value or click the arrow and drag the slider. Higher
values apply less compression resulting in a better-looking image at the
expense of a larger file size. Lower values apply higher compression
resulting in a smaller file size with poorer image quality. You can tell the
optimal setting for an image by comparing the original in the left pane
of the dialog box to the compressed version in the right. When image
degradation is noticeable, specify a higher value.

Progressive: Downloads the image into the user's browser in multiple
passes. This option enables the visitor to see a low-resolution version
of the image as soon as the page loads. The optimized version appears
when the image finishes loading.

Blur: If you have to apply heavy compression to achieve the desired file
size, enter a value or drag the Blur slider to blur the image and minimize
the appearance of jagged edges.

**Book IV
Chapter 4**

**Creating Compelling
Graphics**

ICC Profile: Includes the current color settings with the file. We recommend against this option unless your default color settings for Photoshop use the sRGB IEC61966-2.1 profile. If this is the case, you can skip Step 2 and use this option to convert the image to the sRGB IEC61966-2.1 color profile.

Matte: Specifies a color to fill pixels that were transparent in the original image. Choose an option from the Matte drop-down menu. Your choices are

- *None:* Choose this option when you do not want to specify a matte color.

- *Eyedropper:* Choose this option, and then click the Matte Color Swatch below the Eyedropper tool on the left side of the interface to choose the fill color from the color picker.

- *White:* Fills transparent pixels with white.

- *Black:* Fills transparent pixels with black.

- *Other:* Enables you to select a matte color from the color picker.

6. **Click Save.**

Photoshop saves the image as an optimized JPEG file.

Creating a Photo Gallery

Many Web sites feature photo galleries. You can create a photo gallery the old-fashioned way by creating thumbnails and optimized full-sized images in an image-editing application like Photoshop or Fireworks. If you do this, you have to house all the thumbnails in an HTML table and create the links to the full-sized versions. If you do it right, the full-sized photos should be in their own HTML document. If that sounds like a lot of work, you're right. If you have Photoshop or Dreamweaver, you can create a photo gallery with a menu command.

Choosing your photos

If you're creating a Web site for a client, your assets should all be neatly assembled in a folder. If you're creating a Web gallery for yourself, your photos should also be in a folder. The easiest way to choose which photos you want to include in a Web gallery is to use an application like the Adobe Bridge or any application that lets you view a folder of photos as thumbnail images. The following steps show you how to choose your photos using Adobe Bridge:

1. **Launch Adobe Bridge.**

   Navigate to the folder that contains the candidates for your Web gallery.

2. **Choose Window⇨Workspace⇨Light Table.**

   The Adobe Bridge displays all images as thumbnails. (See Figure 4-15.)

3. **Examine all the images in the folder.**

4. **When you see an image you want to include in the gallery, press Ctrl+5 (Windows) or ⌘+5 (Mac).**

   This assigns a five-star rating to the photos. Continue assigning five-star ratings to images you want to include in the Web gallery.

5. **Press Ctrl+Alt+5 (Windows) or ⌘+Option+5 (Mac).**

   Adobe Bridge displays only five-star images. (See Figure 4-16.)

6. **Choose File⇨New Folder.**

   Adobe Bridge creates a new folder.

7. **Name the folder Web Gallery.**

8. **Select the images and drag them into the Web Gallery folder.**

Figure 4-15: Separating the wheat from the chaff.

Figure 4-16:
Displaying
the best
images.

Putting the photos in order

After you have the images for your Web gallery neatly sequestered in their
own folder, it's time to arrange them in the order in which you want them to
appear. Adobe Bridge is again the ideal tool of choice for this task. Arranging
images for a photo gallery is as easy as moving slides on a light table, which
is why the following steps show you how to perform this task with the
Adobe Bridge Light Table workspace:

1. **In the Adobe Bridge, open the folder in which you've stored the**
   images for your Web gallery.

2. **Choose Window⇨Workspace⇨Light Table.**

   The Adobe Bridge displays the images you've chosen for your Web
   gallery as thumbnails.

3. **Drag the thumbnails to arrange the images in the desired order.**

   Your images are ready to be converted into a Web gallery. (See
   Figure 4-17.)

Figure 4-17:
Arranging the images in the order in which you want them displayed.

Using Photoshop to create a photo gallery

After you sort your images into a folder, you can quickly create a photo gallery using a Photoshop command. And the cool thing is that you can access that command from within the Adobe Bridge. Here's how:

1. **Select all the images in your Web Gallery folder.**

2. **Choose Tools⇨Photoshop⇨Web Photo Gallery.**

The Web Photo Gallery dialog box appears. (See Figure 4-18.)

3. **Choose a style from your Web photo gallery from the Styles drop-down menu.**

The choice is purely a matter of personal taste. A tiny little display of the style is displayed on the right side of the dialog box. However, the best way to know what style does what is to use six photos and experiment with the different styles until you find one you like.

4. **Enter your client's e-mail address.**

This displays your client's e-mail address below the title of the photo gallery.

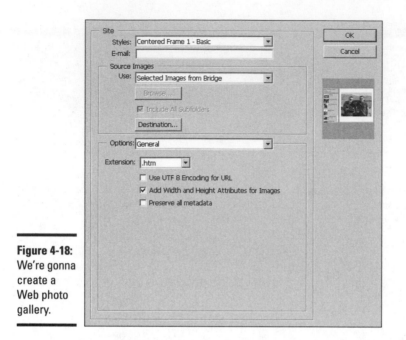

5. Click the Destination button.

The Browse for Folder dialog box appears. Select the folder in which you want to store the gallery and then click OK.

6. Choose Banner from the Options drop-down menu.

The Web Photo Gallery dialog box reconfigures. (See Figure 4-19.)

7. Enter a site name for your Web gallery.

Unless your client has already chosen a name, choose a name that describes what's in the gallery.

8. In the Photographer field, enter the photographer's name if you're creating a Web gallery for a photographer. If your client is not a photographer, you can enter your client's name or business name in this field.

9. From the Options drop-down menu, choose Large Images.

The dialog box reconfigures and displays options to specify the size of the images after the viewer clicks the thumbnail. The options are self-explanatory.

10. From the Options menu, choose Thumbnails.

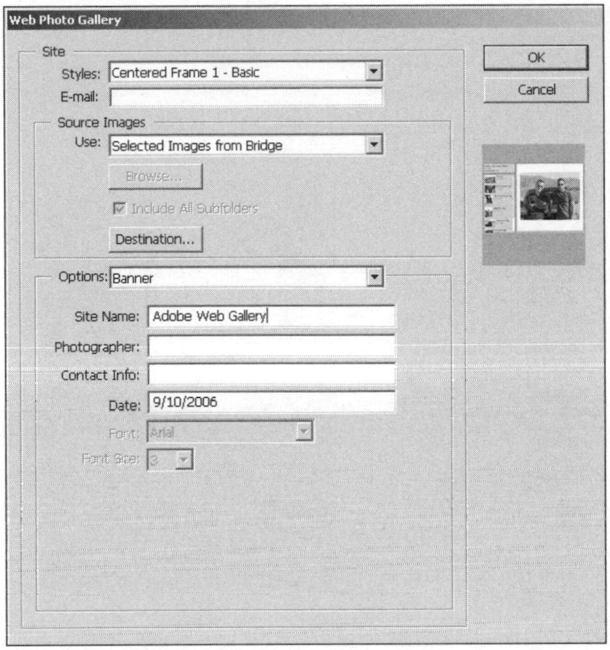

Figure 4-19:
Every good gallery deserves a banner.

The dialog box reconfigures and displays options to specify the size of the thumbnails. The options are self-explanatory.

11. **From the Options menu, choose Security.**

The dialog box reconfigures and displays options that enable you to add a watermark to each image so they can't be stolen from the Web gallery. We recommend that you choose Custom Text from the drop-down menu, and in a word processing application type **(c) 2007, [my client's name]**; then copy it to the clipboard and paste it into the Custom Text dialog box.

12. **Specify the remaining options for security text.**

You might want to lower the opacity of the text to 50 percent. This enables the client to see more of the image. You can also specify that the security text be rotated 45 or 90 degrees in a clockwise or counterclockwise direction.

13. **Click OK.**

Photoshop does its magic — creating HTML pages, thumbnail images, and full-size images that are optimized for Web viewing. Figure 4-20 shows a Web gallery as displayed in the Mozilla Firefox Web browser.

**Book IV
Chapter 4**

Creating Compelling Graphics

Figure 4-20:
A gallery full of lovely landscapes to discover.

Using Dreamweaver to create a photo gallery

If you prefer, you can create a Web gallery in Dreamweaver. When you choose this option, Fireworks creates the thumbnails and full-size images. When you create a Web gallery in Dreamweaver, your only option to resize the images is by using a percentage. We strongly recommend you use Fireworks or Photoshop batch processing to resize the images to the desired size. To create a photo gallery in Dreamweaver, follow these steps:

1. **In Dreamweaver, create a new document.**

2. **Choose Commands⇨Web Photo Gallery.**

The Create Web Photo Album dialog box (see Figure 4-21) appears.

3. **Enter the following information: Photo Album Title, Subheading Info, Other Info.**

This is the information that will be displayed for the title of your album. For the Subheading and Other Info, you might enter your client's name and contact information.

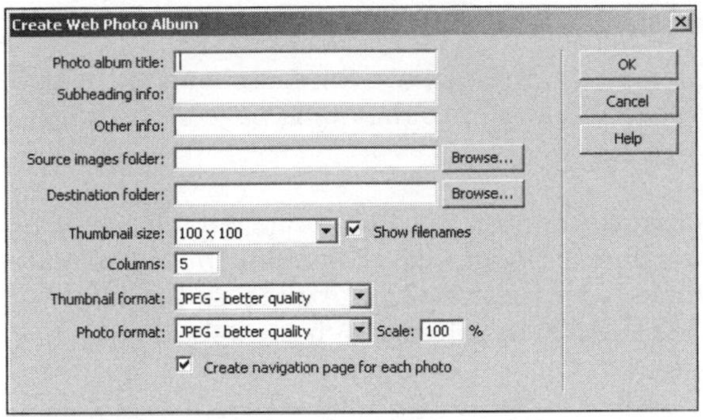

Figure 4-21:
Yet another
way to
create a
Web gallery.

4. **Choose the Source and Destination folders.**

   Click the Browse button to navigate to the folder in which the source images are stored, and then click the Browse button to navigate to the folder where the finished photo gallery will be stored.

5. **Select an option from the Thumbnail Size drop-down menu.**

   This determines the size of the thumbnail that Fireworks creates.

6. **Accept the default option to show filenames.**

   Doug always deselects this option unless the photo gallery is for a photographer whose client will be choosing which images she wants to purchase. The only time you should select this option is when the file name is important, such as when the file name needs to be present in order to identify a photo.

7. **Accept the default value of 5 for Columns, or enter another value.**

   This determines how many columns are created in the HTML page that houses the thumbnails.

8. **Choose options from the Thumbnail Format and Photo Format drop-down menus.**

   These options enable you to choose the image quality and file format. When you're creating a photo gallery, the obvious choice is JPEG. If your client's intended audience accesses the Internet with high-speed connections, choose JPEG-High Quality.

9. **Accept the default Scale value of 100 percent, or enter a different value.**

   The default displays the full-size images at their original sizes. Enter a smaller value to resize the images. Entering a larger percentage is possible, but not advised because image degradation occurs.

**Book IV
Chapter 4**

**Creating Compelling
Graphics**

10. **Accept the default Create Navigation Page for Each Photo.**

This option creates an HTML page for each image with navigation buttons to go forward, back, or to the home page of the image gallery.

11. **Click OK.**

Fireworks launches and creates the optimized full-size images and thumbnails, whereas Dreamweaver handles the task of creating the HTML documents for the image gallery. Figure 4-22 shows the finished gallery as displayed in the Firefox Web browser.

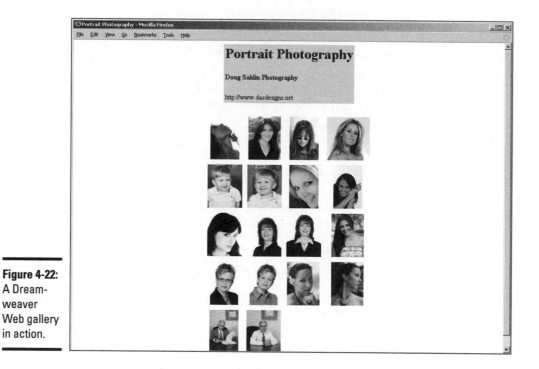

Figure 4-22: A Dream-weaver Web gallery in action.

Book V

Multimedia

The 5th Wave   By Rich Tennant

©RICHTENNANT.COM

Jeez—that's impressive!
Let's see that airbrush
effect again.

Contents at a Glance

Chapter 1: Incorporating Flash Creations

In This Chapter

✔ **Adding Flash interactivity**

✔ **Adding Flash navigation to a Web site**

✔ **Creating Flash animations**

✔ **Creating a Flash presentation**

*I*f you need to kick up a Web design with some multimedia, Flash is an excellent tool to use. With a bit of imagination, you can use this powerful tool to create Web sites that make those of your competition look positively lame. This chapter gives you an introduction to the all-singing, all-dancing Flash 8 workspace. Here you find out how to use it to create flashy navigation in a flash, add animation to your designs, and produce stellar presentations. Let the games begin.

Introducing Flash 8

Flash has been used in the past to create introductions and full-fledged Web sites. However, Flash intros are no longer in vogue, and Flash Web sites are not search-engine friendly. Despite all this, Flash is as strong as ever; Web designers are just using it in different ways.

Designers are able to control the user's experience in a Web site by how they place items on the Flash timeline. They can also control the flow of the Flash movie using ActionScript. Flash navigation menus consist of buttons that can transport the visitor to other parts of the Web site.

Whether you're creating an animation or a menu in Flash, the end result is an SWF file, which is also known as a movie. When constructed properly, Flash movies are relatively small files. Yet a designer can go over the top by adding so many graphics and other bells and whistles that the finished product loads at a snail's pace.

The tempo or pace of a Flash movie is defined by the frame rate. The default frame rate of a Flash movie is 12 fps (frames per second). This is fine for most Flash movies. However, when you're creating a Flash movie with video, you have to specify a higher frame rate. For more information on Flash video and other Web video formats, see Chapter 3 of this minibook.

Touring the interface

The Flash interface may seem daunting to the uninitiated. We certainly had our doubts when we first launched Flash 4. However, the workspace is really quite civil after you work with Flash for a while. To know Flash in all its glory, you need a book on the topic, such as *Building Flash Web Sites For Dummies* by Doug Sahlin (Wiley Publishing, ISBN 0-471-79220-9) or *Macromedia Flash 8 For Dummies* by Ellen Finkelstein and Gurdy Leete (Wiley Publishing, ISBN 0-7645-9691-8). But we bring you up to speed on the various parts of the Flash interface (see Figure 1-1) in the upcoming sections.

Exploring the Toolbox

The left side of the interface is home to the Toolbox, which is shown in Figure 1-2. This part of the interface is home to the tools you use to create objects and text. You can also use them to move and modify objects.

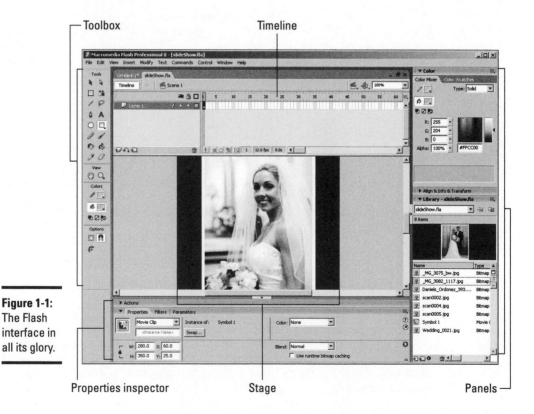

Figure 1-1: The Flash interface in all its glory.

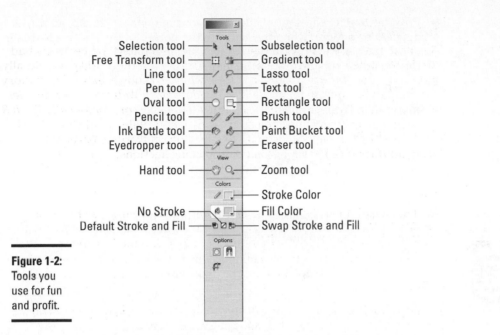

Selection tool —— Subselection tool
Free Transform tool —— Gradient tool
Line tool —— Lasso tool
Pen tool —— Text tool
Oval tool —— Rectangle tool
Pencil tool —— Brush tool
Ink Bottle tool —— Paint Bucket tool
Eyedropper tool —— Eraser tool

Hand tool —— Zoom tool

—— Stroke Color
No Stroke —— Fill Color
Default Stroke and Fill —— Swap Stroke and Fill

Figure 1-2:
Tools you
use for fun
and profit.

The following tools reside in the Toolbox:

✦ **Selection tool:** Selects and moves objects.

✦ **Subselection tool:** Selects points along a path and objects within a group.

✦ **Free Transform tool:** Scales objects; changes the width or height of an object; skews an object; changes an object's center of rotation; rotates an object.

✦ **Gradient Transform tool:** Transforms a gradient that fills an object.

✦ **Line tool:** Creates lines.

✦ **Lasso tool:** Creates a freeform selection.

✦ **Pen tool:** Creates a path.

✦ **Text tool:** Adds text to a document.

✦ **Oval tool:** Creates ovals. Hold down the Shift key while using this tool to create a circle.

✦ **Rectangle tool:** Creates rectangles. Hold down the Shift key while using this tool to create a square. You can add a radius to rectangle corners to create rectangles with round corners by clicking the Set Corner Radius button in the Options area of the Toolbox.

✦ **Polystar tool:** Creates multisided polygons and stars. The Polystar tool appears on a flyout when the arrow in the corner of the Rectangle tool is clicked. When the Polystar tool is selected, it appears on the Toolbox; the Rectangle tool is now on the flyout.

✦ **Pencil tool:** Creates freeform lines in the document.

✦ **Brush tool:** Paints objects within the document.

✦ **Inkbottle tool:** Changes the color of an object's stroke (outline).

✦ **Paint Bucket tool:** Changes an object's fill, which can be a solid color or gradient.

✦ **Eyedropper tool:** Samples a color from an object within the document.

✦ **Eraser tool:** Erases an area or object within the document.

✦ **Hand tool:** Pans within the document.

> While using any tool, press and hold down the spacebar to momentarily activate the Hand tool. Release the spacebar to revert to the previously used tool.

✦ **Zoom tool:** Zooms in on the document. Click to zoom to the next highest level of magnification. Click and drag to zoom to a specific area of the document. Press the Alt key (Windows) or Option key (Mac) and click inside the document to zoom out to the next lowest level of magnification.

✦ **Stroke Color:** Click the swatch to open the Color picker and choose a stroke color. This color will be applied to all tools that create objects with a stroke.

✦ **Fill Color:** Click the swatch to open the Color picker and choose a fill color. This color will be used by all tools that create objects with a fill.

✦ **Default Stroke and Fill:** Click this icon to revert to the default stroke color (black) and fill color (white).

✦ **No Color:** Click the Fill Color swatch, and then click this icon to create an object with no fill, or click the Stroke Color swatch and then click this icon to create an object with no stroke.

✦ **Swap:** Swaps the current stroke and fill colors.

✦ **Options:** This part of the Toolbox changes depending on the tool you have selected.

Someone told me it's all happening on the timeline

The timeline is the tool you use to control the tempo of your Flash movie. The timeline consists of frames. You add keyframes where you want a change to occur. When you create an animation, you add a keyframe and then move the object to a different position.

You create blank keyframes to signify the end of a set of frames. For example, if you're creating a slide show, you add an image to a keyframe where you want the animation to start. The frames downstream from the keyframe duplicate the contents of the keyframe — in this case, the image. The number of frames signifies the length of time for which the image is displayed. We don't show you how to create an animation just yet — that comes later, in the "Creating your first animation" section — but we get you started:

✦ To create a keyframe, click a regular frame and press F6. Alternatively, choose Insert➪Timeline➪Keyframe. A keyframe with objects is signified by a solid dot. (See Figure 1-3.)

✦ To create a blank keyframe, click a regular frame and press F7. Alternatively, choose Insert➪Timeline➪Blank Keyframe. A blank keyframe is signified by a hollow dot. (See Figure 1-3.)

✦ To create a regular frame, press F5. Alternatively, choose Insert➪Timeline➪Frame. Frames duplicate the content of the previous keyframe. The area between keyframes is known as a frame range. The last frame in a frame range is signified by a rectangle. (See Figure 1-3.)

Figure 1-3:
Frames and keyframes and blank keyframes, oh my.

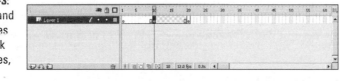

Panels not cast from wood

You use panels to do a lot of your work in Flash. The two panels on the right side of the interface are the Align & Info & Transform panel and the document Library panel. You find other panels on the Window menu. When you use a menu command to open a panel (for example, Window➪Color Mixer), it appears in the workspace as a floating panel. (See Figure 1-4.) Notice that another panel is docked with the Color Mixer panel. The tasks performed by these panels are similar; therefore, the designers of Flash decided to group them together. However, the Flash interface is customizable. If you don't like the layout, you can change it to suit your working preferences.

Figure 1-4:
Panels can
be docked
or floating
in the
workspace.

Many of the panel names are self-explanatory, whereas others require a little clarification. You can use Flash Help (F1) or pick up a copy of the tremendously helpful and infinitely amusing *Macromedia Flash 8 For Dummies* by Ellen Finkelstein and Gurdy Leete (Wiley Publishing, ISBN 0-7645-9691-8).

Inspecting the Properties inspector

Objects have properties. It's a Flash law. When you create an object, such as the lowly and infinitely rotund oval with the Oval tool, you don't have to take what you get. You can change the properties of the oval using the Properties inspector. Figure 1-5 shows the Properties inspector as it is configured when an oval is selected. Notice you can change the width, height, x coordinate, y coordinate, stroke, and fill. Talk about your useful inspectors.

You also use the Properties inspector with other objects. Keyframes also have properties. As mentioned previously, keyframes are used in animation. You can set several parameters for animation by selecting a keyframe and then opening the Properties inspector. (See Figure 1-6.) Notice the options that add sound to a keyframe and give the keyframe a label. A keyframe with a label, isn't that like giving it a name? Yikes!

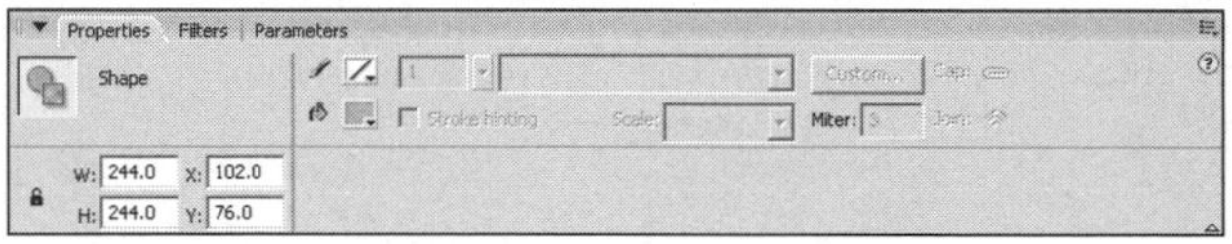

Figure 1-5:
The Properties inspector at work, sans monocle and magnifying glass.

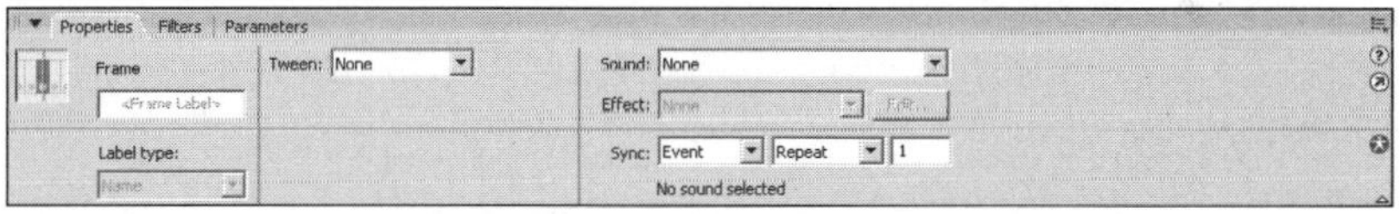

Figure 1-6:
The Properties inspector is also used when creating an animation.

Getting comfortable with Flash

Flash is big, huge, vast. Even if you learn half of the bells and whistles in the application, Flash will never be half vast. But we digress. One chapter just isn't long enough to learn all that Flash has to offer. To do so, you have to get your fingers greasy — get under the hood so-to-speak. However, the next sections show you the fundamentals for creating a new document, an object, and then an animation. Buckle up and enjoy the ride.

Creating a Flash document

When you launch Flash, you get this cute little splash screen that gives you several options. (See Figure 1-7.) One of them is creating a new Flash document. This gives you a document with the default document size, frame rate, background color (refrigerator white, which is boring), and so on. It's a good place to start, but you generally need to modify the document to suit the Web page in which the Flash movie will be embedded.

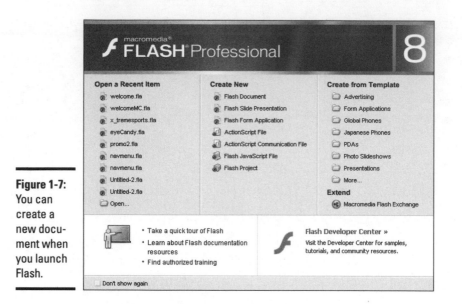

Figure 1-7:
You can create a new document when you launch Flash.

To create a Flash document, follow these steps:

1. **Launch Flash.**

The Flash Start Page appears as shown previously in Figure 1-7.

2. **Click Flash Document.**

Flash creates a new document with the default document size of 550 x 400 pixels, the default frame rate of 12 fps, an appliance-white background color, and the default publishing parameters. You can easily change any or all of these parameters using the Properties inspector.

3. **Open the Properties inspector.**

The default location of the Properties inspector is at the bottom of the interface. You can open the Properties inspector by doing any of the following:

- Click Properties on the title bar of the Properties inspector.
- Choose Window⇨Properties⇨Properties.
- Press Ctrl+F3 (Windows) or ⌘+F3 (Mac).

4. **Click the Size button.**

The Document Properties dialog box (see Figure 1-8) appears.

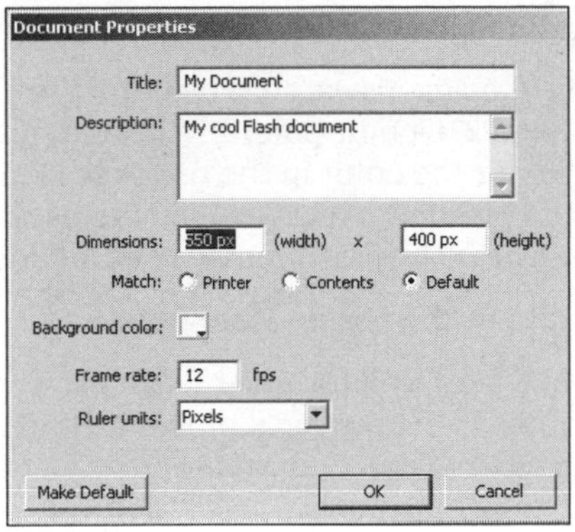

Figure 1-8:
Setting
document
properties.

5. **Type the information in the Title and Description fields.**

This step is optional. It creates meta data, based on RDF (Resource Description Framework) and XMP (Extensible Metadata Platform) standards, that is stored in the Flash movie and is WS3 compliant. Typical information you'd include in the Description is the author, purpose of the document, copyright information, and keywords.

6. **Type values in the Width and Height fields.**

7. **Select an option in the Match section:**

- Choose *Printer* to set the stage size to the maximum printable area, which is determined by the paper size minus margins as specified in the Page Setup dialog box (Windows) or the Print Margins dialog box (Mac).

- Choose *Contents* to set the Stage by putting equal space around the contents on all sides. Before choosing this option, align all elements at the upper-right corner of the Stage.

- Choose *Default* to set the Stage size to that specified in Step 6.

8. **Click the Background Color swatch.**

Flash opens the Swatches palette shown in Figure 1-9.

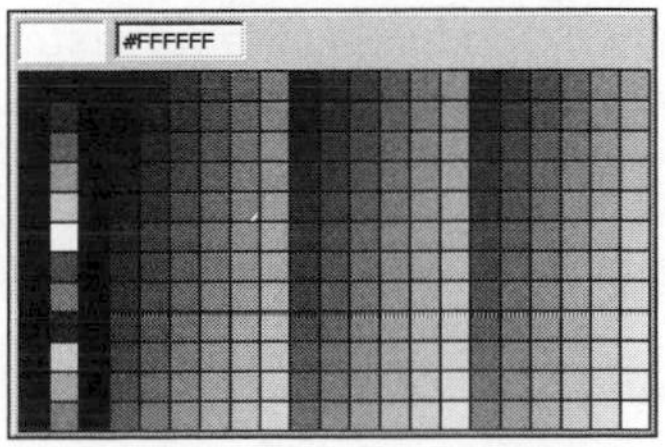

Figure 1-9:
Please, pick
anything but
white.

9. Select the desired background color.

You can choose a color by clicking a swatch. The colors in the default palette are from the Web-safe, 216-color palette. Alternatively, you can enter the hexadecimal value for the color in the text field. This determines the background color of the Flash movie as well as the background color of the HTML document in which the Flash movie is embedded.

10. Type the desired frame rate in the Frame Rate field.

The default frame of 12 fps works well for most Flash movies. However, if you've got a lot of animation or are creating a movie with video, you need a higher frame rate. For video, you need a frame rate of at least 18 fps. If you're streaming video to an audience that has a high-speed cable connection, you can specify 30 fps and deliver beautiful full-motion video.

11. Choose the desired unit of measure from the Ruler Units drop-down menu.

The default unit of measure is Pixels, which works well in most instances. Your alternatives are Inches, Inches (decimal), Points, Millimeters, and Centimeters.

12. Click Default if you want these parameters to be the defaults for future Flash documents you create.

This option applies all parameters except Title and Description, which must be unique, to each Flash document.

13. Click OK.

Flash creates a new document.

Now that you've got a new document, you're ready to create something very cool (or not so cool depending on the needs of your client). The next section points you in the right direction.

Creating an object

After you create a document, you can add objects to the document. Objects can be plain old ho-hum static objects, or they can be symbols. When you create a symbol, you create something that can be used over and over and over again. Just drag the object out of the document Library, and drop it in the desired place on the timeline. When you use a symbol instead of creating a new object, you don't increase the file size of the published movie because Flash re-creates an instance of the symbol using the information stored in the document Library. Symbols come in three flavors: Button, Graphic, and Movie Clip. These steps show you how to create a Graphic symbol:

1. In the Toolbox, set the Stroke and Fill colors.

To set Stroke and Fill colors, you click the applicable swatch to open the Swatches palette. The colors you select are applied to all objects until you change the colors.

2. Select the Oval tool.

3. Click and drag an oval on Stage.

When you release the mouse button, the oval appears on Stage.

Hold down the Shift key to create a circle.

4. If desired, open the Properties inspector and change the parameters for the circle.

In the Properties inspector, you can change the Width, Height, and X and Y coordinates.

5. Use the Selection tool to select the object.

If you created an object with a stroke, you double-click the object to select both the fill and the stroke.

6. Press F8.

The Convert To Symbol dialog box appears.

7. Type a name for the symbol and choose the Graphic option.

Flash gives the symbol a default name. However, it's not very descriptive. It's a good idea to give each symbol a unique name. This makes it easier for you to select the proper object from the Library. This is a distinct advantage when you're creating complex Flash movies with hundreds of symbols.

8. Click the desired Registration Point.

This determines the center of rotation for the symbol. The center point works well in most instances.

9. Click OK.

The symbol is added to the Library.

Creating your first animation

After you add a symbol to the Library, you have the bare bones needed for a Flash animation. In this case, we show you how to make an oval go from Point A to Point B. It's not a way cool animation, but it's a start. To create an animation:

1. Create a Graphic symbol using the Oval tool.

Creating a symbol is easy if you know Flash or if you read the last section. If neither is the case, please rewind and read the previous section.

2. Use the Selection tool to move the symbol to the desired starting point.

To move an object with the Selection tool, click and drag the object to the desired location.

3. **Click a frame on the timeline where you want the animation to end and then press F6.**

Flash creates a keyframe on the desired frame. The number of frames between the beginning and ending keyframes determines the duration of your animation. With the default frame rate of 12 fps, an animation with 12 frames lasts exactly one second.

4. **Move the symbol to the desired end point.**

5. **Right-click any frame between the beginning and ending keyframes and choose Create Motion Tween from the context menu.**

The in-between frames now display an arrow between the beginning and ending keyframes. (See Figure 1-10.) When you create a motion tween animation, Flash interpolates the motion on the in-between frames.

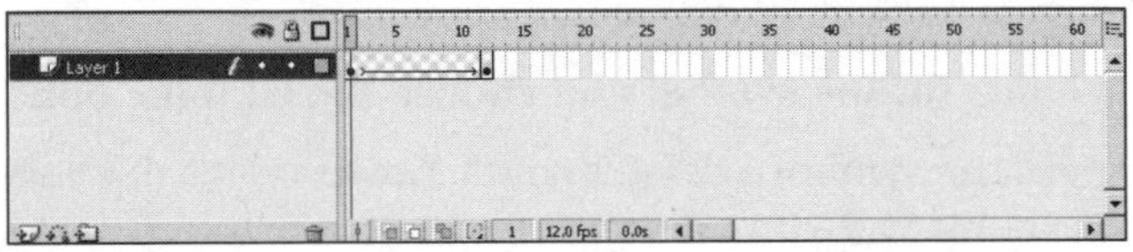

Figure 1-10: Creating a motion tween animation.

6. **Press Ctrl+Enter (Windows) or ⌘+Enter (Mac).**

Flash displays the animation in another window. You're probably thinking that the animation is pretty ho-hum. You're right. So kick it up a notch.

7. **Click a frame in the middle of the beginning and ending keyframes and then press F6.**

You've created another keyframe. The fact that you've already created a motion tween animation means that you can use this keyframe to change the position of the object on this keyframe, which will spice up the animation.

8. **Using the Selection tool, move the object to another position.**

9. **Press Ctrl+Enter (Windows) or ⌘+Enter (Mac).**

Now you're cooking. To give you an idea of what you should be seeing, Figure 1-11 was created using the Onion Skin option, which displays multiple frames at lower opacity.

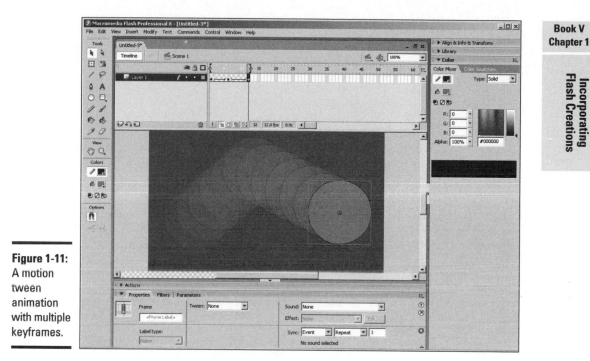

Figure 1-11:
A motion
tween
animation
with multiple
keyframes.

Setting up your workspace

If you're like most designers, you have a set way of doing things. The designers of Flash set up the workspace to suit most Flash users. However, the
Flash workspace can be customized to suit your working preferences. In this
section, we show you a few things you can do to set up the workspace just
the way you like it.

Setting Flash preferences

Everybody's got preferences. Doug prefers blondes, but that's a whole different kettle of fish. You can modify the default Flash Preferences for the way
you work. We don't go through each and every Flash Preference, but we
show you a few that we think are important:

1. **Choose Edit⇨Preferences.**

Alternatively, you can press Ctrl+U (Windows) or ⌘+U (Mac) to open the
Preferences dialog box. By default, the dialog box opens to the General
section. (See Figure 1-12.)

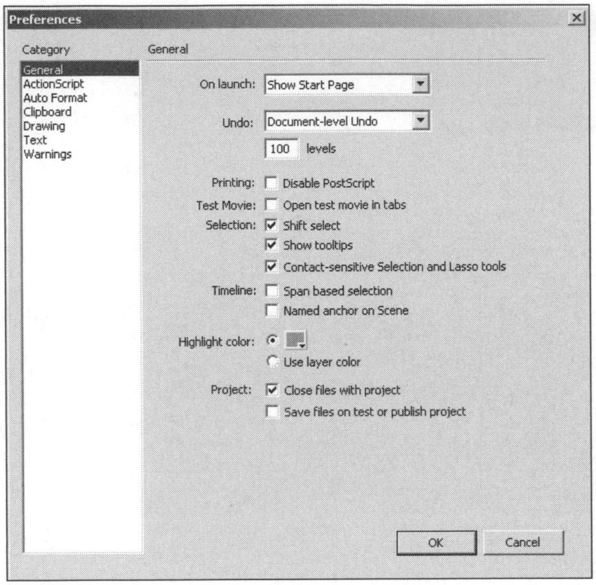

Figure 1-12:
Preferences, and General ones at that.

2. Modify the default preferences to suit your working style.

Most of the preferences are self-explanatory. However, we do recommend that you choose New Document from the On Launch drop-down menu. This option creates a blank document when you launch Flash, enabling you to cut to the chase instead of dealing with the pesky start page. Another option you may consider changing is the number of Undo levels. If you have an older computer or limited memory, lowering the number of Undo levels cuts down on the overhead Flash places on your system.

3. Change the remaining preference categories to suit your working style.

The only other change we recommend you make depends on whether you use ActionScript and have a large desktop size. If both conditions apply, change the font size from 10 to 11 or 12.

4. Click OK to apply the new preferences.

Modifying the workspace

The layout of the Flash workspace suits most designers. You can however, modify the workspace by opening panels and docking them or by placing them in a convenient position. Flash doesn't enable you to save a custom workspace, but the application does remember where you last left things. Here are a few things you can do to customize the workspace:

✦ To float the toolbar, click and drag it to a new location.

✦ To dock a floating toolbar, double-click it.

✦ To float a docked panel, drag it by the upper-left corner and drop it in the desired location. You see icons that look like perforations.

✦ To dock a panel, click the icons that look like perforations and drag the panel into the docking station on the right side of the interface.

✦ To group a panel with another group, click the Option icon in the upper-right corner of the panel and choose the group from the pop-up menu. (See Figure 1-13.)

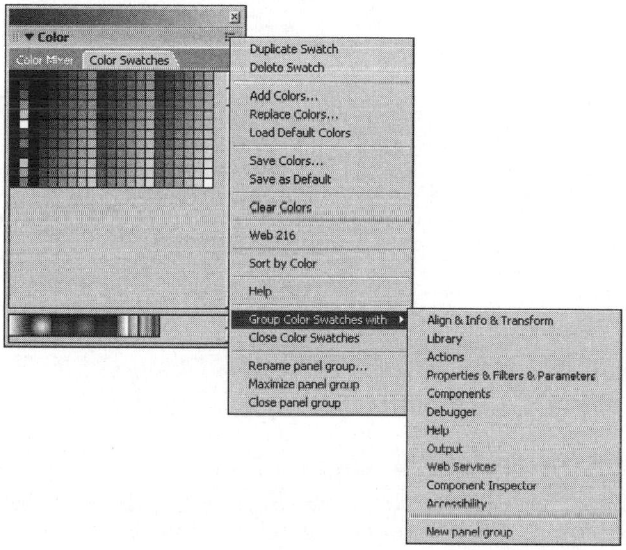

Figure 1-13:
Panels have groups, not groupies.

Building Flashy Navigation

You can do so many things with Flash, and navigation is one of them. You can create cool navigation with HTML, but Flash lets you take it a step further. If you want animated buttons (for instance, a button that makes noise), Flash is your answer. In this section, we show you how to create cool or Flashy navigation, if you will.

Creating the navigation menu document

Before you can create a Flash navigation menu, you create a document to be the base for your menu. Before you create this document, you must know the size of the area in which you plan to place the navigation menu. Typically, this is the width of your site banner and the height you want for your menu. Choose a background color that is harmonious with the Web page in which the menu will be placed. For the purpose of this example, we create a menu that is 600 pixels wide and 25 pixels high with a black background using the default frame rate of 12 fps. (See Figure 1-14.)

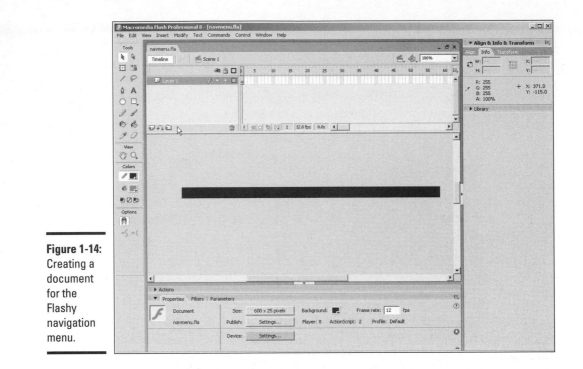

Figure 1-14:
Creating a
document
for the
Flashy
navigation
menu.

Creating buttons in Flash

Navigation menus need buttons. Flash gives you all the tools to create some
really cool buttons. If you've not created Flash buttons before, consider this
your baptism by fire. To create a button for your menu, follow these steps:

1. **Choose Insert⇨New Symbol.**

The Create New Symbol dialog box appears.

2. **Type a name for your symbol and choose the Button behavior.**

You're creating a menu and the obvious place to start a menu is with the
Home button. Therefore, name the button **Home**. (See Figure 1-15.)

3. **Click OK.**

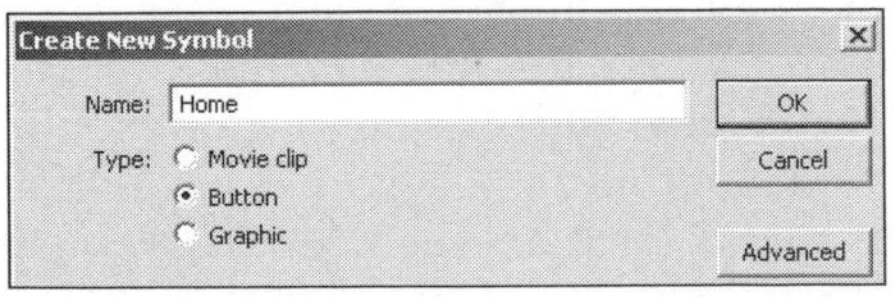

Figure 1-15:
A take me
home kinda
button,
Jenson.

4. **Flash enters symbol-editing mode. (See Figure 1-16.)**

   Notice that you have one layer and four states: Up, Over, Down, and Hit. These states determine what is displayed when the user's cursor is not over the button (Up), when the user passes his cursor over the button (Over), and when the user clicks the button (Down). The final state, Hit, determines the target area of the button. You add the Hit state only if you've got a particularly small button that may be hard to select.

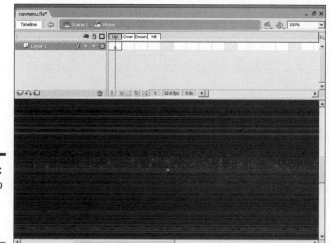

Figure 1-16:
Welcome to symbol-editing mode.

5. **Create the shape for your button.**

   When creating buttons, use the Rectangle tool with a corner radius of 50 pixels to get a generic pill shape. Choosing View➪Rulers enables you to create an object that's the approximate size of the button.

6. **Choose Window➪Properties to open the Properties inspector.**

7. **Type the desired dimensions for your button in the Width and Height fields.**

   To figure out what size to make each button, divide the width of your navigation menu by the number of buttons. In this example, we're creating six buttons for a nav menu that's 600 pixels wide and 25 pixels high. Therefore, each button is 100 pixels wide and 25 pixels high. (See Figure 1-17.)

8. **Select and then Align the button to the center of the Stage.**

   Press Ctrl+K (Windows) or ⌘+K (Mac) to open the Align panel. Click the To Stage icon, and then click the icons that center the button vertically and horizontally.

Insert Layer button

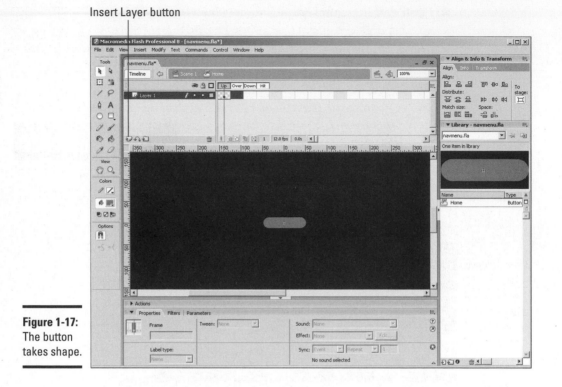

Figure 1-17:
The button
takes shape.

9. Click the Insert Layer button.

Flash creates a new layer. Layers help you organize your work. For the button, I'm creating a separate layer for button text.

10. Double-click the layer title.

This opens a text box into which you can type a new name for the layer. It's not imperative, but it helps you decipher which layer is used for what when you're creating a complex movie or symbol.

11. Enter a name for the label.

Text is as good a name as any. While you're at it, rename the layer on which the button resides. *Button shape* is a good name.

12. Select the Text tool and type the desired name.

In this case, the button is called Home. A full-blown tutorial on the Text tool is beyond the scope of this book. However, if you look at the Properties inspector in Figure 1-18, you see how easy it is to set parameters for the Text tool.

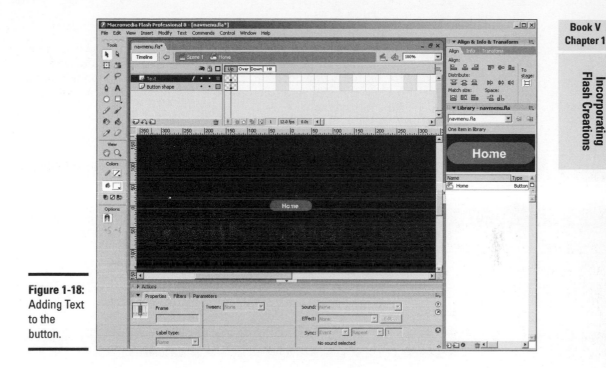

Figure 1-18:
Adding Text
to the
button.

13. **Press F5 in the Down frame on the Text layer.**

This copies the contents of the Up frame to the Over and Down states.

14. **Press F6 to create keyframes for the Over and Down states on the Button shape layer.**

Flash copies the contents of the Up frames to the Over and Down states. The fact that you've created keyframes enables you to change or modify the contents of these frames, or make some other change that will notify users they have indeed found a clickable button. The graphic on the Down state appears when users have successfully clicked the button.

15. **Make changes in the Over and Down states for the Button shape layer.**

For the purpose of this demonstration, we've changed the color of the button to red in the Over frame and orange in the Down frame.

16. **With the Text layer selected, click the Insert Layer icon.**

Flash creates a new layer.

17. **Name the layer** Sound.

18. **Click the Down frame in the Sound layer and press F6.**

Flash creates a keyframe.

19. **Choose File⇨Import⇨Import To Library.**

Select a short sound file. For a button, choose a sound that is less than two seconds in duration. This is the sound that plays when the user clicks the button. If you decide to add sound to a button, choose one that fits the site you're designing. For example, if you're creating a navigation menu for a photographer's Web site, a shutter click is an ideal sound.

20. **With the Down frame of the Sound layer selected, drag the sound from the Library to stage.**

It doesn't matter where you place it. Remember that sounds are heard and not seen. Figure 1-19 shows the completed button. Notice the waveform in the Down frame — Flash's way of notifying you that the sound is in the frame.

21. **Click the Back button that looks like an arrow, and is next to the Scene title above the uppermost layer.**

The button is added to the Library and ready for use.

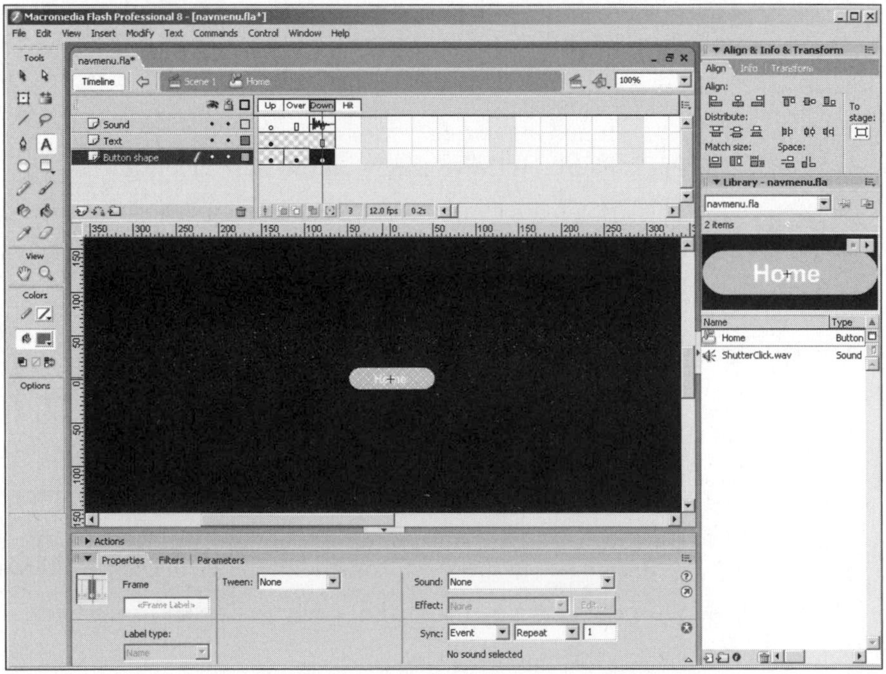

Figure 1-19: A button wired for sound.

Assembling your menu

After you create a button, you can duplicate the button and then change the text to flesh out your menu. If you've done the math right, your button is perfectly sized. When you align the buttons end to end, your menu is assembled. To assemble the menu, follow these steps:

1. **Right-click the Home button in the document Library and choose Duplicate from the context menu.**

   The Duplicate Symbol dialog box appears. (See Figure 1-20.)

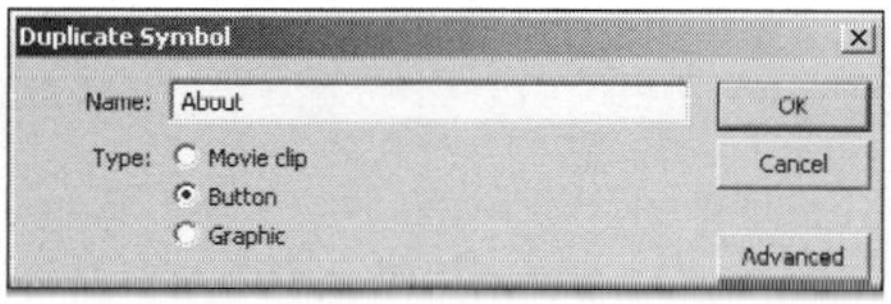

Figure 1-20:
Duplicating
the button.

2. **Name the symbol.**

   The logical choice would be the page to which the button will link.

3. **Click OK.**

   Flash duplicates the button.

4. **Create enough duplicates to flesh out your menu.**

   For the menu we are creating here, you need four more buttons.

5. **Double-click one of the duplicated buttons.**

   Flash enters symbol-editing mode.

6. **Change the button text.**

7. **Repeat for the other buttons in your menu.**

After creating the duplicate, the next step is to arrange the buttons on Stage. To do so, follow these steps:

1. **Select the first button in your menu and drag it on Stage.**

   You don't have to position it exactly. You can use the Align panel to align and distribute the buttons.

2. Drag the remaining buttons onto the Stage.

Position the buttons end to end.

3. Select all the buttons.

You can do this easily with the Selection tool. Simply click and drag around the perimeter of the buttons.

4. Press Ctrl+K (Windows) or ⌘+K (Mac).

The Align panel opens.

5. Click the To Stage icon, and then click the Vertical Centers icon.

Flash aligns the buttons vertically to the stage.

6. Click the To Stage icon, and then click the Distribute Horizontal Center icon.

Flash distributes the buttons evenly to Stage. (See Figure 1-21.)

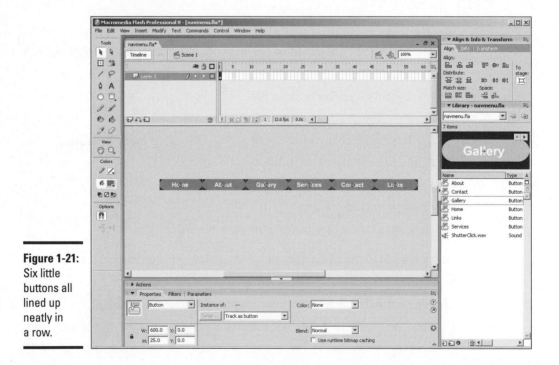

Figure 1-21:
Six little buttons all lined up neatly in a row.

Adding functionality to the buttons

If you test your menu now, the familiar hand icon appears when you pause your cursor over a button, and the button changes color and makes a noise when clicked. However, the button will do zilch, nada. To make the button truly functional, you've got to specify the page to which the button links. To do that, you must venture into the wild and wooly world of ActionScript. To make the buttons truly functional, follow these steps:

1. **Select the first button in your menu.**

2. **Press F9 (or choose Window⇨Actions).**

This opens the Actions panel shown in Figure 1-22. If this is your first introduction to ActionScript, you may think you've opened Pandora's Box. The Actions panel has so many actions, they're divided into what the Flash designers refer to as *books*. When you click a book, you have access to all the actions within that book. But sometimes books open other books.

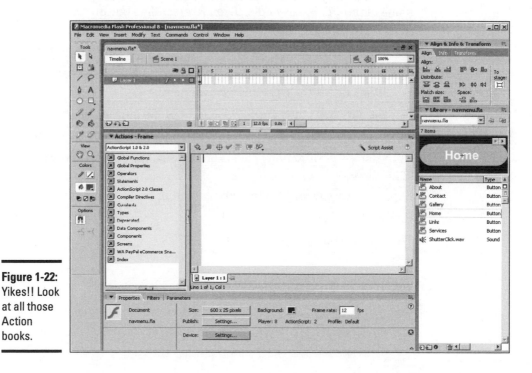

Figure 1-22:
Yikes!! Look at all those Action books.

3. **Click the Script Assist button.**

This button helps novice ActionScript users select the right parameters for each action. If you don't click this button, you've got to write some of the code yourself. Not fun.

4. **Click the Global Functions book, click the Browser/Network book, and then double-click the getURL action.**

Flash adds the action to your script. Just fill in the blanks. Notice that Flash adds a line that begins with: on (release). This is known as an event; in other words, this event that must occur for the action to execute. The default button event, on(release), means the action executes when the user releases the mouse button, just what the doctor ordered for a navigation menu.

5. **In the URL window, type the URL for the Web page that opens when the button is clicked.**

The page you want to open when the button is clicked should be in the same folder as your Flash navigation menu. Therefore, you just type the name of the file. For example, if you're creating a button that links to the home page, the link is index.htm.

6. **Choose one of the following options from the Window drop-down menu:**

- **_self** opens the page in the current frame in the current window.
- **_blank** opens the page in a new window.
- **_parent** opens the page in the parent of the current frame.
- **_top** opens the page in the top-level frame in the current window.

At this stage, your Actions panel should look like the one shown in Figure 1-23.

7. **Repeat Steps 4 through 6 for the remaining buttons in your menu.**

8. **Choose File⇨Save.**

The Save dialog box appears.

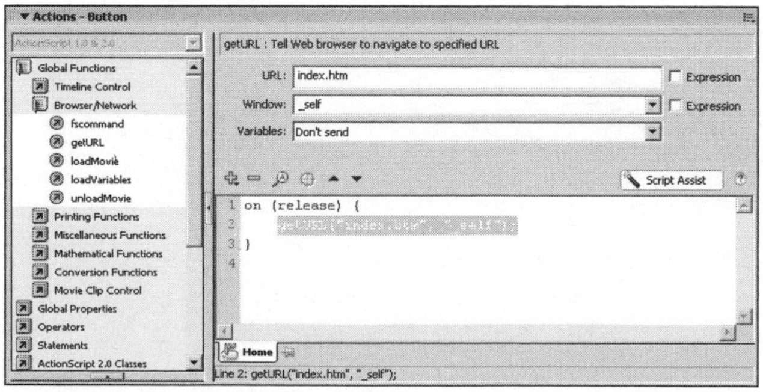

Figure 1-23:
The getURL
action in
action.

9. **Enter a name for the file, specify the location in which you want to save the file, and then click Save.**

   Saving Flash documents in the same folder as the other assets for the Web site is typically a good idea. Flash files are saved with the `.fla` extension. You can modify the `.fla` file at any time by reopening it. All the files you import and objects you create are saved with the file.

Publishing your file and adding it to your page

When you finish your menu in Flash, you publish it as a Flash movie. The default publishing options publish the Flash movie embedded in an HTML document. However, you plan to use the menu in an HTML document with other items. Therefore, you publish the file as follows:

1. **Choose File⇨Publish Settings.**

   The Publish Settings dialog box appears. (See Figure 1-24.) The default settings publish the file as a Flash SWF movie embedded in an HTML document. However, all you need is the Flash movie.

2. **Deselect the HTML option and then click OK.**

3. **Choose File⇨Publish.**

   Flash publishes the file as an SWF movie.

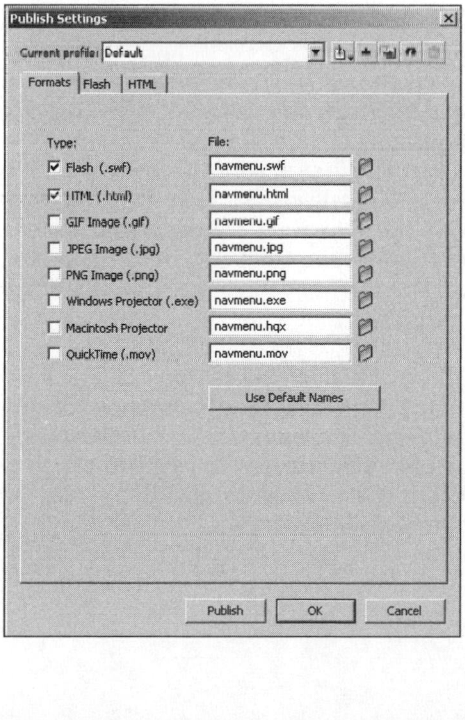

Figure 1-24:
The Publish
Settings
dialog box.

After you publish the navigation menu as an SWF file, you're ready to add it to your Web pages. In Dreamweaver, follow these steps:

1. **Create the document in which you want to add the Flash navigation menu.**

2. **Position your cursor where you want to add the menu.**

3. **Choose Insert⇨Media⇨Flash.**

   The Select File dialog box appears.

4. **Select the SWF file and then click OK.**

   Dreamweaver inserts the Flash movie in your Web page.

5. **Press F12 to test the file in your default browser.**

   Dreamweaver displays the Web page in your default browser.

Flash files have compatibility issues in some Web browsers. Dreamweaver creates a script for browser compatibility and stores it in a folder named Scripts. If your navigation menu does not perform correctly in your default browser, test the page in Internet Explorer. If the menu performs perfectly in Internet Explorer, it will perform correctly in other Web browsers — provided you upload the Scripts folder to the same folder on your Web server where you store uploaded Web pages and the SWF file.

Flash as an Animation Tool

In addition to creating navigation menus with Flash, you can use the application to create impressive animations. Recently Doug needed to create a presentation for his photography business. He wanted something cool and interactive, so he used Flash. The first part of the presentation was an animated intro in which images danced across the screen and stopped to create a collage. Figure 1-25 shows the animation as seen on the stage. Notice the multiple layers. One layer has a sound track, whereas the other layers have motion tween animations. The start of each animation is staggered so that the images fly in at different times.

As you can see, quite a bit was involved in creating the animation. The animation dovetails into the actual presentation. Doug used quite a few high-resolution images to create the animation and presentation. The file size of the published movie is 2MB, clearly too large for the Web, but not too large for a computer or CD presentation. If Doug deletes a few images and optimizes the others for Web viewing, the animation would be a reasonable size for use on the Web.

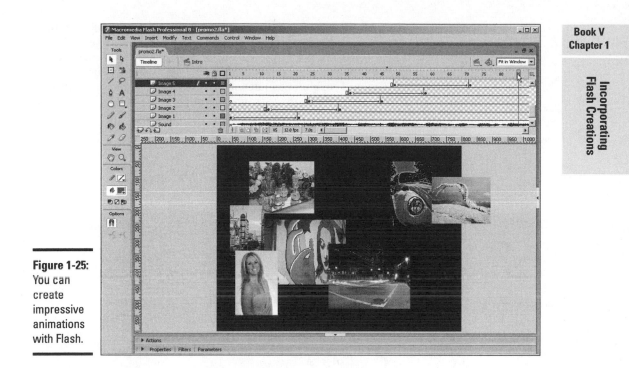

Figure 1-25:
You can
create
impressive
animations
with Flash.

Create a Flash Presentation

When Doug decided to create a presentation for his photography business, he used Flash. He began the presentation with an animation of images (as discussed in the previous section). After the animation played, a menu and a splash screen loaded. The menu contained links that loaded other content into the main Flash movie. A bit of ActionScript wizardry was involved. The menu and splash screen for the presentation are shown in Figure 1-26.

Each button on the menu loads another Flash movie into a target movie clip in the main movie. Working in this manner enables a designer to manage a lot of content using ActionScript. If all the content loads at once, the file size of the movie becomes too large, even for a CD presentation.

Doug wanted to distribute the presentation on business card CDs. He could have published the file as a Flash Projector file, which is a self-contained executable file complete with the Flash Player. However, a Projector file displays Macromedia Flash Player 8 in the title bar, and that's where he wanted to display the business name. The answer was an application known as SWF Studio V3.0. The application converts an SWF file into a self-executing projector file that is customizable. You can add an expiration date to the file after which time it will not play. You can also determine what text is displayed in the title bar. Auto-run is another feature you can add to your presentation. The end result looks like a custom application created solely for his business. You can download a trial version of SWF Studio V3.0 from www.northcode.com.

Figure 1-26: The menu for an interactive Flash presentation.

Exploring the Many Tricks of Flash

No discussion of Flash would be complete without mentioning the power of ActionScript. ActionScript is a scripting language similar to JavaScript. When you sprinkle liberal doses of ActionScript into your Flash movies, you take your designs to the next level. ActionScript comes with a bit of a learning curve. But the good thing about ActionScript is you don't have to master each and every action to get the job done. With a basic knowledge of ActionScript, you can rummage through the Actions panel and learn the actions you need to get the job done. Figure 1-27 shows a design that is powered by ActionScript.

Figure 1-27:
A Flash Web design powered by ActionScript.

The banner across the top of the site moves from side to side. The direction of movement depends on where the user's cursor is. If the cursor is on the right side of the site, the banner moves from left to right. When the user moves his cursor to the other side, the banner reverses direction. The speed at which the banner moves is determined by how far the cursor is from the middle of the design. When the user moves his cursor toward the center of the design, the banner slows to a crawl and then stops. The ActionScript to control the movement of the banner is shown in Figure 1-28. The code relies heavily on a conditional statement. A conditional statement evaluates a condition. If the condition is true, certain lines of code are executed. If the statement is false, other lines of code are executed. In this case, the conditional statement evaluates where the user's mouse is and executes the code that makes the banner move left or right.

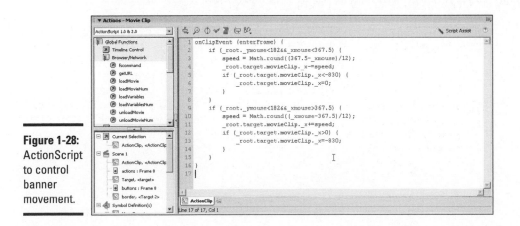

Figure 1-28:
ActionScript to control banner movement.

Chapter 2: Using Sound

In This Chapter

✔ Discovering audio formats for the Web

✔ Working with Flash, QuickTime, RealMedia, and Windows Media audio

✔ Audio tips and tricks

Some people think Web sites are just pretty pictures and text. But that's all changed. You can add sound to a Web site without breaking a sweat. When you add sound to a Web site, the sound streams into the user's browser. The user must have the proper plug-in to hear the audio content. In this chapter, we show you a thing or two about sound. Now Web sites can be seen and heard.

Exploring Audio Formats for the Web

Audio for Web sites is saved in formats that enable the sound to stream into the visitor's browser. Streaming sound is similar to an interlaced picture that loads in stages. With streaming sound, the sound begins as soon as enough of it downloads into the user's browser to play without interruption. The most popular audio formats for the Web are

✦ **AIFF:** The AIFF (Audio Interchange File Format) sound format was once exclusively for Macintosh users but can now be shared cross-platform. This format uses the `.aif` and `.aiff` extensions and is played through the Apple QuickTime Player.

✦ **Flash:** You can import audio into a Flash document, optimize it, and then publish the document as an SWF file. Add the published file to a Web page, and you've got sound, baby.

✦ **QuickTime:** The Apple QuickTime player can play video and audio files. The player recognizes the AIF, AIFF, and MOV sound formats.

✦ **MP3:** The MP3 audio format is a derivative of the MPEG video format. The MP3 sound format combines excellent fidelity with relatively small file sizes.

Copyright issues

The person who created the recording (or the recording company) copyrights songs and recordings. If you use a copyrighted song or recording on a Web site you're designing, you are in violation of the copyright laws. You might be able to obtain a license from the copyright owner. Another option is to obtain royalty-free songs or recordings. You can find these by typing *royalty-free recordings* in your favorite search engine. Some office supply stores sell royalty-free music collections. Or if you're the really adventurous and artistic type, you can create your own background sounds using a program such as Acid Pro (Windows) or Garage Band (Mac). Both applications enable you to create music by mixing and matching royalty-free music loops.

+ **RealMedia:** RealMedia multimedia content has been around for some time. Each version of the player gets more sophisticated. You can save sound files in the RealMedia `.rm` format and embed the RealMedia Player in a Web page to play them.

+ **Windows Media Player:** You can embed Windows Media Player in a Web page and play the WMA and MP3 sound formats.

Adding Flash Audio to a Page

Flash audio is the perfect solution when your client wants background music on a Web page. With Flash audio, you can compress music using the popular MP3 format and choose a data rate that assures good-quality sound and a quick-loading file. The next sections cover how to create Flash audio and add it to a Web page.

Creating Flash audio

Creating Flash audio is not rocket science. But you do need to have a copy of Flash in order to create it. You do, that is, unless you're fortunate enough to have a client who sends you the sound file in the SWF format. To create Flash audio:

1. **Create a new Flash document.**

Accept the default frame rate, choose a color that matches the Web page into which you're adding the sound, and specify a size of 1 pixel x 1 pixel.

2. **Choose File➪Import➪Import to Library.**

   The Import to Library dialog box appears.

3. **Select the sound and then click OK.**

   Flash imports the sound to the document Library.

4. **Select the first keyframe.**

   You've only got one, so it shouldn't be hard to find.

5. **Open the Properties inspector.**

6. **Choose the imported sound from the Sound drop-down menu.**

   The sound file name appears in the Sound text field.

7. **Accept the default Sync options of Event and Repeat, but change the value of the last option to 0 (zero).**

   These settings play the sound once. If you've got a quiet background sound, you might want to change the second option to Loop and then enter the number of times you want the sound to repeat. After you add a sound to a keyframe, your Properties inspector should resemble Figure 2-1.

   A word of caution is in order here. If the song is too loud or doesn't suit all audiences, looping the sound is a surefire way to have part of your intended audience clicking the Back button.

Figure 2-1:
Adding sound to a keyframe — the only keyframe.

8. **Choose Window➪Library.**

   The document Library opens.

9. **Select the sound file and then right-click (Windows) or Control+click (Mac) and choose Properties from the context menu.**

   The Sound Properties dialog box appears.

10. **Choose MP3 from the Compression drop-down menu.**

    The Sound Properties dialog box reconfigures as shown in Figure 2-2.

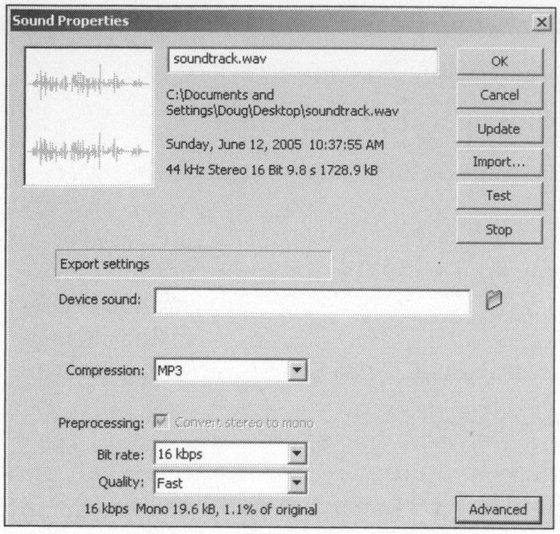

Sound Properties

soundtrack.wav

C:\Documents and
Settings\Doug\Desktop\soundtrack.wav

Sunday, June 12, 2005 10:37:55 AM

44 kHz Stereo 16 Bit 9.8 s 1728.9 kB

OK

Cancel

Update

Import...

Test

Stop

Export settings

Device sound:

Compression: MP3

Preprocessing: ☑ Convert stereo to mono

Bit rate: 16 kbps

Quality: Fast

16 kbps Mono 19.6 kB, 1.1% of original

Advanced

Figure 2-2:
Modifying
the sound
properties.

11. Choose an option from the Bit Rate drop-down menu.

The default option of 16 kbps works well for simple background music
with one or two instruments. However, if you've got more complex
music to entertain your viewers (or your client is a diva, opera star, or
rock musician), you need to specify a higher bit rate to get a better-
quality sound. When you exceed 20 kbps, preprocessing converts stereo
sound to mono. If desired, you can convert the sound to stereo by dese-
lecting the Convert Stereo to Mono check box. A higher bit rate does
increase the file size, so you can't go too far unless you've got a really
short sound clip.

If you import an MP3 sound file, a check box appears in the dialog box
with the option to use the imported MP3 quality. The Bit Rate options
appear if you deselect this option.

12. Choose an option from the Quality drop-down menu.

The default option Fast renders the file quickly. However, you get better-
quality sound if you choose Medium or Best. The latter options take a
while longer to render the sound.

**13. Click Test to preview the sound clip with the current compression
settings.**

If the sound is not to your liking, choose a higher bit rate.

14. After modifying the sound to suit your Web page, click OK.

The new settings are applied to the sound.

15. Publish the document as an SWF file.

Editing sound for fun and profit

If you do a lot of work in Flash with soundtracks or add soundtracks to many of your Web pages, consider investing in a sound editing application. A sound editing application enables you to apply special effects, such as reverb and echo, to a sound to equalize the volume — and to do much more. You can also use a good sound editing application to create voice-overs for a video track, record a podcast, and so on. Another definite bonus is the capability to save the sound in just about any format available today. Sony Sound Forge and Adobe Audition are two of the better sound editing applications. The following illustration shows reverb being added to a sound in Sony Sound Forge 7.0.

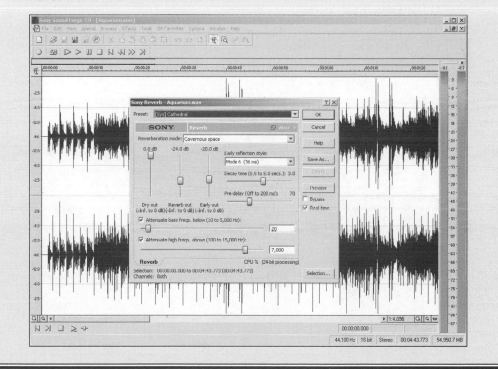

Adding sound to a Web page

After you publish your Flash sound, you're ready to add it to your Web page. Remember, this file is infinitesimally small, as in really, really tiny. No one will see the file, so you can tuck it in just about anywhere. Adding the file above the header section of the document is generally a good idea. Honestly, who's going to notice an extra pixel, especially when it's the same color as the background? These steps show you how to add the sound file:

1. **In Dreamweaver, open the Web page to which you'll add the sound.**

2. **Position your cursor where you want to add the sound.**

You can put the sound anywhere that you've got a blank space — above the header or below the fold.

3. **Choose Insert⇨Media⇨Flash.**

The Select File dialog box appears.

4. **Select the soundtrack SWF file and click OK.**

Dreamweaver adds the soundtrack to the Web page.

5. **Press F12.**

Dreamweaver prompts you to save the file. After you save the file, it opens in your default browser. (See Figure 2-3.) You should hear your soundtrack.

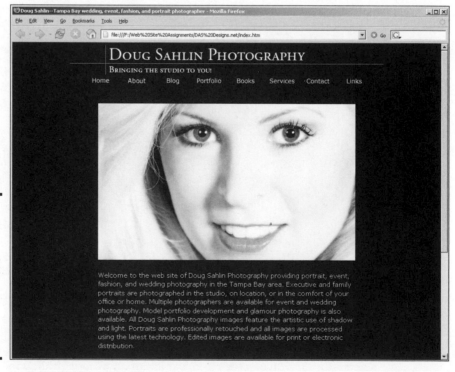

Figure 2-3:
I'm gonna inject your soul with some sweet rock 'n' roll, and shoot you full of rhythm and blues.

Embedding a QuickTime Player in a Page

Another sound format that's quite popular is AIF, which you can play in the Apple QuickTime Player. You can export AIF audio from a good sound editing application. You can also export a sound file as an MOV file from a sound editing application or from Apple QuickTime Pro. However, these files are rather large and not suited for the Web. When you use the AIF form, you embed the applicable controller in the Web page. This enables visitors to play the associated sound file on demand. To embed a QuickTime audio controller in a Web page using the Dreamweaver HTML editor, follow these steps:

1. **Position your cursor at the point in the Web page where you want the video to appear.**

2. **Choose Insert⟹Media⟹ActiveX.**

   Dreamweaver inserts an ActiveX object in the page with the default dimensions of 32 x 32.

3. **Select the ActiveX object in the Document window.**

4. **Open the Properties inspector.**

5. **Enter the following text into the Class ID text box:**

   ```
   clsid:02BF25D5-8C17-4B23-BC80-D3488ABDDC6B
   ```

   This tells the Web browser that the ActiveX content is QuickTime.

6. **In the Properties inspector, specify the following parameters:**

   • Select the Embed check box.

   • Set the width and height in the W and H text boxes. Generally speaking, resizing the object to 320 pixels by 16 pixels is ideal: The default height of the QuickTime controller is 16 pixels, and 320 pixels is wide enough for the visitor to see the progress bar move as the sound plays.

   • Click the Browse folder icon (next to the Src text box) and navigate to and then select the QuickTime AIF sound you want to embed in the page.

   • Enter **http://www.apple.com/qtactivex/qtplugin.cab** in the Base text box.

7. **Click the Parameters button in the Properties inspector.**

   The Parameters dialog box appears.

8. **Add the parameters for the ActiveX object and click OK.**

   Click the plus (+) sign to add a parameter. Each parameter has a value. To run a QuickTime audio file, you need the following parameters and values:

- Parameter 1 = **autoplay**, Value = **false**

- Parameter 2 = **controller**, Value = **true**

- Parameter 3 = **pluginspage**, Value = **http://www.apple.com/quicktime/download/indext.html**

- Parameter 4 = **target**, Value = **myself**

- Parameter 5 = **type**, Value = **video/audio**

- Parameter 6 = **src**, Value = the path and file name of the movie you're embedding in the page.

  At this stage, your Parameters dialog box should resemble Figure 2-4. If desired, you can set the autoplay parameter to `true` to have the sound play as soon as it loads.

9. **Press F12 to preview the page in your default browser.**

  Dreamweaver prompts you to save the document. After you save the document, Dreamweaver launches the page in your default browser. The audio begins playing. Figure 2-5 shows a QuickTime controller in a Web page playing the associated AIF file.

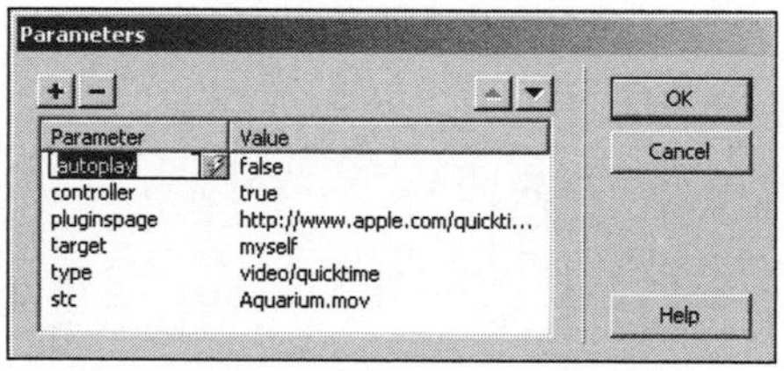

Figure 2-4:
Setting the parameters for a QuickTime sound file.

Adding the RealMedia Player to a Page

The RealMedia RM format is a good format for Web sound. The file sizes are relatively small, and you can embed the RealMedia player in a Web page. This gives visitors the capability to play an RM file. To embed the RealMedia Player in a Web page using the Dreamweaver HTML editor:

1. **Position your cursor at the point in the Web page where you want the video to appear.**

2. **Choose Insert⇨Media⇨ActiveX.**

  Dreamweaver inserts an ActiveX object in the page with the default dimensions of 32 x 32.

3. **Select the ActiveX object in the Document window.**

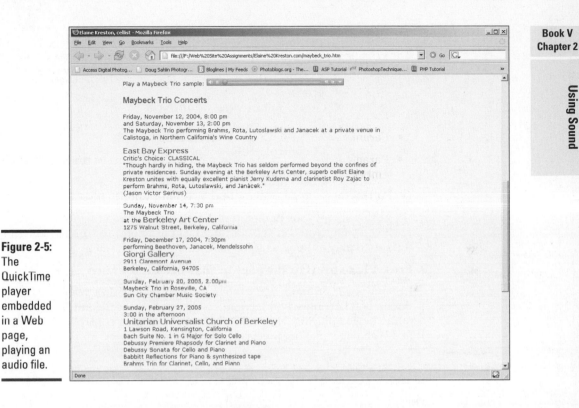

Figure 2-5:
The
QuickTime
player
embedded
in a Web
page,
playing an
audio file.

4. Open the Properties inspector.

5. Enter the following text into the Class ID text box:

```
clsid:CFCDAA03-8BE4-11cf-B84B-0020AFBBCCFA
```

This tells the Web browser that the ActiveX content is RealMedia.

6. In the Properties inspector, specify the following parameters:

- Select the Embed check box.

- Set the width and height in the W and H text boxes. We recommend resizing the object to 320 pixels by 30 pixels because the default height of the RealMedia audio controller is 30 pixels, and 320 pixels is wide enough for the visitor to see the bar move as the sound plays.

- Click the Browse folder icon (next to the Src text box) and navigate to and then select the RealMedia RM sound you want to embed in the page.

- Enter **rvocx** in the ID text box.

7. Click the Parameters button in the Properties inspector.

The Parameters dialog box appears.

8. **Add the parameters for the ActiveX object and click OK.**

Click the plus (+) sign to add a parameter. Each parameter has a value. To run a RealMedia audio file, you need the following parameters and values:

- Parameter 1 = **src**, Value = ***myaudiofile*.rm**

- Parameter 2 = **autostart**, Value = **false**

- Parameter 3 = **controls**, Value = **ControlPanel**

- Parameter 4 = **console**, Value = **audio**

- Parameter 5 = **type**, Value = **audio/x-pn-realaudio-plugin**

    At this stage, your Parameters dialog box should resemble Figure 2-6. If you want, you can set the autostart parameter to true to have the sound play as soon as it loads.

9. **Press F12 to preview the page in your default browser.**

Dreamweaver prompts you to save the document. After you save the document, Dreamweaver launches the page in your default browser. The audio begins playing. Figure 2-7 shows a RealMedia controller embedded in a Web page, playing the associated RM file.

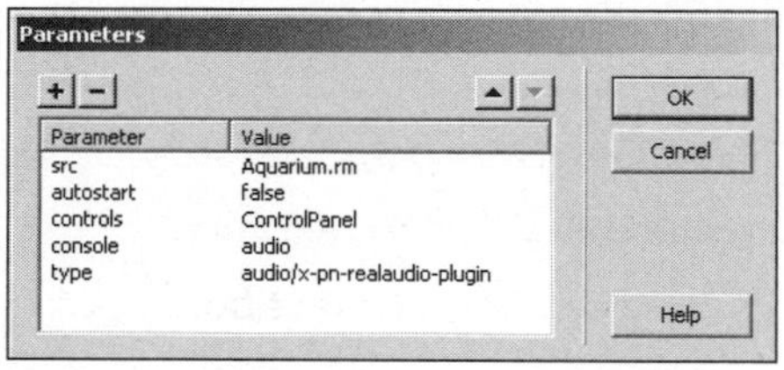

Figure 2-6: Setting the parameters for a RealMedia sound file.

Adding the Windows Media Player to a Web Page

The Windows Media Player is a versatile application. It can play video files as well as audio files. You can embed the Windows Media Player in a Web page and play WMA (Windows Media Audio) and MP3 sound files. To embed the Windows Media Player configured for audio in a Web page using the Dreamweaver HTML editor, follow these steps:

1. **Position your cursor at the point in the Web page where you want the video to appear.**

2. **Choose Insert⇨Media⇨ActiveX.**

Dreamweaver inserts an ActiveX object in the page with the default dimensions of 32 x 32.

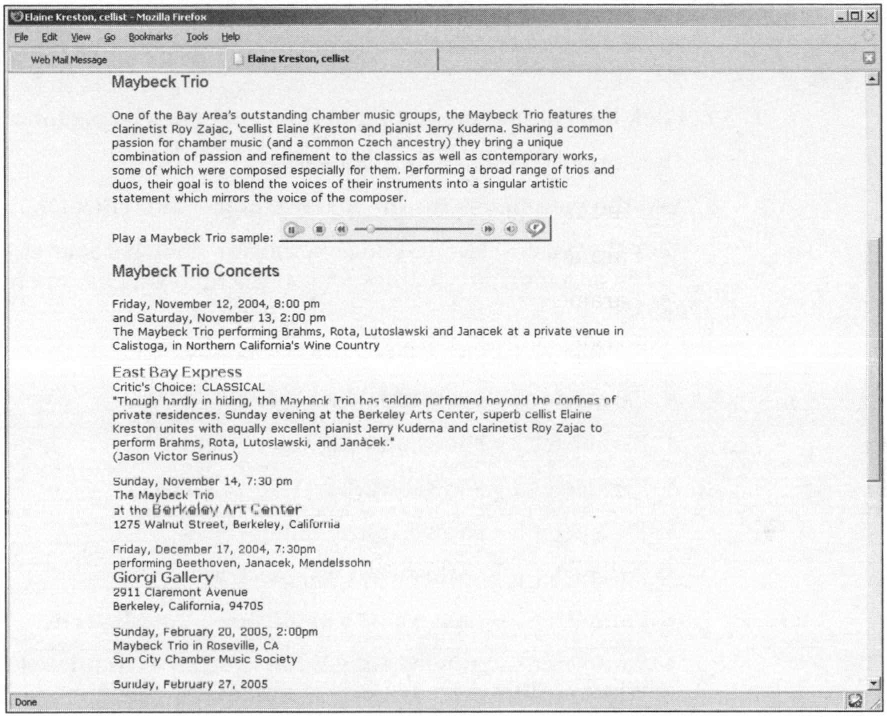

Figure 2-7:
A
RealMedia
audio
console
embedded
in a Web
page.

3. **Select the ActiveX object in the Document window.**

4. **Open the Properties inspector.**

5. **Enter the following text into the Class ID text box:**

   ```
   clsid: 22d6f312-b0f6-11d0-94ab-0080c74c7e95
   ```

   This tells the Web browser that the ActiveX content is Windows Media
   Video or Audio.

6. **In the Properties inspector, specify the following parameters:**

   - Select the Embed check box.

   - Set the width and height in the W and H text boxes. Set the height to
     42 (the height of the Windows Media Audio controller) and the width
     to 320.

   - Click the Browse folder icon (next to the Src text box) and navigate
     to and then select the Windows Media Video WMV movie you want
     to embed in the page.

   - Enter **mediaplayer2** in the ID text box.

The Windows Media Player can also play MP3 audio files. You can link an MP3 file to the Windows Media Player by browsing for the desired MP3 file.

7. Click the Parameters button in the Properties inspector.

The Parameters dialog box appears.

8. Add the parameters for the ActiveX object and click OK.

Click the plus (+) sign to add a parameter. Each parameter has a value. To run a QuickTime video, you need the following parameters and values:

- Parameter 1 = **src**, Value = the file name of your movie
- Parameter 2 = **autostart**, Value = **false**
- Parameter 3 = **showcontrols**, Value = **true**
- Parameter 4 = **showstatusbar**, Value = **false**
- Parameter 5 = **showdisplay**, Value = **false**
- Parameter 6 = **autorewind**, Value = **true**
- Parameter 7 = **type**, Value = **application/x-mplayer-w**
- Parameter 8 = **pluginspage**, Value = **http://www.microsoft.com/ Windows/Downloads/Contents/MediaPlayer/**

At this stage, your Parameters dialog box should resemble Figure 2-8. If you want, you can set the autostart parameter to true, which means the audio plays as soon as it loads. The site visitor can use the controller to pause or stop the file.

Figure 2-8:
Parameters
for an
embedded
Windows
Media
Audio
controller.

9. Press F12 to preview the page in your default browser.

Dreamweaver prompts you to save the document. After you save the document, Dreamweaver launches the page in your default browser. The audio file begins playing. Figure 2-9 shows the Windows Media Player configured for audio in a Web page, playing the associated sound file.

Figure 2-9: A Windows Media Audio controller embedded in a Web page.

If you attempt to test an embedded Windows Media Player in the Mozilla Firefox browser on your local machine, it won't play. It will, however, play when you upload the HTML page and associated files to your server.

Delivering Your Message

When you add audio to a Web site, you're entertaining site visitors or informing them. When you entertain visitors, it can be in the form of music or perhaps comedy. When you inform people, it's generally in the form of the spoken word with, perhaps, some background music. In either event, your goal is to deliver a professional audio track that's clear and easy to understand. Here are a few things to consider when preparing audio for a Web site:

✦ **If your client is recording audio for a Web site, make sure he uses a professional microphone and an application such as Sony Sound Forge or Adobe Audition to record the track.** Making a professional recording from a Web cam isn't possible. You should also make sure your client positions the microphone in such a manner that the sounds of his breath are not recorded. The microphone also needs to be far enough away from his mouth to ensure the plosive sounds from the letters such as P and S are not recorded.

✦ If the sound of your client's voice isn't pleasing or if she speaks with a heavy accent, tactfully suggest she hire a professional to record the narration.

✦ When compressing soundtracks for the Web, strive for the smallest possible file size, while still maintaining a clean, crisp sound.

✦ Don't compress music soundtracks to 8-bit depth. The recording will sound scratchy in soft passages.

✦ Make sure the soundtrack isn't over-modulated. The loudest parts of over-modulated soundtracks are distorted. If your client is recording the track, tell him to make sure the levels don't go into the red area.

✦ Don't use recordings from other Web sites unless you can secure a license to use the recording in your Web design.

✦ Don't use digital versions of copyrighted recordings unless you can secure a license to use the recording in your Web design.

✦ Don't use an application such as Musicmatch or iTunes to create a digital version of a commercial recording for use on your Web site. This is a clear violation of the copyright laws.

Chapter 3: Using Web Video

In This Chapter

✔ **Understanding Web video formats**

✔ **Incorporating streaming video on a Web page**

✔ **Working with Flash, QuickTime, and Windows Media video**

✔ **Encoding video**

*I*f sound is cool, well then, motion and sound must be cooler, right? Well of course it is; that's why you see so much video on the Web these days. Web video can be anything from something as simple as your talking head introducing visitors to a Web site to full motion video of sporting events such as auto races. Video for the Web streams into the viewer's browser. Before the advent of streaming video, Web pages with video weren't feasible. After all, who in their right mind would wait for a 15 or 20MB file to download? Not too many people. But with streaming video, large file sizes are possible due to the fact that the video starts playing as soon as enough data downloads for the movie to begin playing. This chapter gives you the skinny on what you need to know to add a lean, mean, streaming video machine to your Web designs.

Exploring Web Video Formats

There aren't quite as many video files as Carter has little liver pills, but close. During the infancy of video for the Web, video was segregated to platforms. Macintosh users had Apple QuickTime and Windows users had Windows Media Video. After a while, both platforms could play both formats. Then, along came RealMedia, and finally, the designers of Flash invented their own video codec (a file format that compresses the video when it's rendered and decompresses the video when it's played). Here are the popular video formats for the Web:

✦ **Apple QuickTime:** One of the granddaddies of video for the Web, QuickTime has been around since 1992. The Apple QuickTime player is required to view QuickTime video. The most popular QuickTime video format for the Web is MOV, which, you guessed it, is derived from *movie*.

✦ **RealMedia:** RealMedia is the brainchild of RealNetworks. RealMedia incorporates RealVideo and RealAudio. RealMedia streaming files for the Web can contain RealAudio and RealVideo streams, and several other formats, including SMIL (Synchronized Multimedia Integration Language). The RealPlayer is required to view RealMedia content. Really! Yes, there are a whole lot of *reals* in the previous sentences, but not a single *reel,* as in *movie.*

✦ **Windows Media Video:** Microsoft's answer to the Web video wars is Windows Media Video, the WMV (Windows Media Video) format. This format has improved steadily over the years and can be viewed cross platform. The Windows Media Player acts as a plug-in when Web pages with WMV video are displayed.

✦ **Flash Video:** Those wild and crazy guys (and probably gals) at Macromedia jumped on the video bandwagon with their showpiece application Flash. Before Macromedia invented their own video codec, Apple Quick-Time MOV video files could be incorporated into a Flash Web design — in fact, they still can be. But Macromedia wanted their own format and must've taken lessons from that Portuguese chef when they kicked it up a notch and invented the Flash Video codec known as FLV (Flash Video). Flash video can be played by Flash Players 6, 7, 8, and 9. Google uses Flash video quite extensively on its video site (www.video.google.com), which, as of this writing, is in beta but likely won't be for long.

Working with Digital Video

Video is very much a part of the Web. Therefore, to be successful as a Web designer, you need to know about Web video and how to incorporate it on your page. As mentioned previously in this chapter — which was toiled over late in the evening and with great precision, even though the deadline was looming perilously close, and which, hopefully, you read and enjoy — there are lots of video formats for the Web. Like images, video files start out as something completely different than what you end up putting on a Web page. If you're lucky, you have a client who knows all about video and gives you perfectly encoded video all ready to plop onto your Web pages. Right! And we have a bridge in Brooklyn, New York, we'll let you have for a song.

The reality of the matter is, you're likely to get a video cassette from your client and instructions on which bits he wants for the Web site. When that happens, you'll have to encode the video yourself or hire a professional videographer to do it for you.

Capturing video

If your client hands you a cassette tape, you have to get the contents of it into your computer (*capture* it) before you can encode it. To capture video, you need either a video capture card or an application such as Adobe

Premiere or Sony Vegas. Well, for that matter, Windows Movie Maker and Apple iMovie can also capture video. Most applications capture video in a proprietary, digital video (DV) format. We say *proprietary* because even though the file format name is the same, different applications seem to use slightly different algorithms to capture video as DV files. If you've dabbled with digital video, you're familiar with these terms. However, if you need a full-course serving that shows you how to capture and process digital video, trot on down to your local bookstore and pick up a copy of *Digital Video For Dummies,* 4th edition, by Keith Underdahl (Wiley Publishing, ISBN 0-471-78278-5).

But the application's not all you need. You need a connection between the digital video camera or digital video deck and the computer. Most digital cameras and digital video decks use FireWire (IEEE 1394) or USB connections. On the computer side, either a FireWire card or a video capture card is required. Capturing video is a fairly boring process. There's no way you can speed it up. If your client gives you a cassette with 20 minutes worth of video, it takes 20 minutes to capture it. But that does give you an excuse to catch up on something more important, like creating a shag rug with recycled hairballs. Figure 3-1 shows video being captured by Sony Video Capture 6.0, which is part of the Sony Vegas 6.0 video editing application.

Figure 3-1:
Video doesn't stand still, but it's easy to capture.

Encoding video

When you *encode video,* you employ a video codec. A *video codec* compresses the video to the desired data rate, which also determines the file size. When the encoded video is played, the codec decompresses the video. When you encode video, you specify the frame size and data rate. The data

Editing digital video

We know what you're thinking: This is a book about Web design. However, it never hurts to master multiple skills, especially where digital video is concerned. Many video editing applications are sheer torture to work with. We won't name names, but some video timelines show only the beginning and end of a clip, which makes it pretty difficult to know what to leave in and what to leave out. Other video editing applications show intermediate frames, and if you zoom in close enough, every frame on the timeline. This makes it easy to slice and dice a video to perfection.

If you've worked with Flash, you're familiar with timelines. Video editing application timelines are no different. You navigate to a specific spot in the timeline to perform a task such as splitting a video, inserting a video clip, adding a video transition, and so on. If you use a video editing application with an intuitive interface, creating a video production can be extremely rewarding.

The following illustration shows a video being edited in Sony Vegas 6.0. If you're interested in getting your feet wet in video editing, try editing some video in Windows Movie Maker II or Apple iMovie.

rate is specified in kbps (kilobytes per second). Where Web video is concerned, data rate is directly related to bandwidth. If you try to cram a video with a data rate of 512 kbps through a modem with a connection speed of 56 kbps . . . well, you can see it just won't happen.

So how do you know what data rate to use? And why do you need to worry about data rate when you've already got your hands full with CSS and other HTML delights? Well, you really don't *need* to know a lot — that is, if you have a good application to encode your video. A good video encoding application, also known as a *compression application,* shows you which options to use for a specific destination. If you're preparing video for a client whose intended audience will be viewing the video with a broadband connection, you can choose the proper preset to suit the need.

Sorenson Squeeze is an excellent compression suite that enables the user to compress a file in the following Web video formats: Flash Movie (SWF), Flash Video (FLV), QuickTime (MOV), Windows Media Player (WMV), and Real-Media (RM). In addition, you can compress audio in the popular MP3 format and encode video for DVD. The current version of Sorenson Squeeze is 4.3. Although the application lists for $419, you'll recoup that in a heartbeat if you work with a lot of video. You can process a video into single or multiple formats. If your client needs three different versions of a video in the MOV format for dialup connections, DSL connections, and cable connections, you simply open the source video, select the presets, and click the Squeeze It button. Within a few minutes (or hours, if you're processing a long video into several different formats), you'll have perfectly compressed video ready to embed in your Web page. Another added bonus is the ability to batch process a folder of videos. Figure 3-2 shows a video being encoded using the Sorenson Squeeze 4.3 Compression Suite.

Creating and Encoding Flash Video

If you read the early parts of this chapter and start reading this section with tears in your eyes, swearing you'll never do video — take a deep breath. Flash has its own video encoder. Yup, it's part of Flash 8 Professional. The upcoming sections show you how to encode digital video into the FLV format within Flash. Now that you've caught your breath, read on.

If you have a client who wants to add video to his Web site, you can do so easily with Flash. Full motion video in Flash is a beautiful thing. You tailor the video for your client and the type of equipment used by the client's audience. You can also add a controller to the video, which enables visitors to control playback of the video.

Figure 3-2:
Isn't compression like a diet or something?

When you need to quickly add a video to a Flash movie, you can do so by encoding the video within Flash. When you encode a video in Flash, you can choose whether the video will work with the Flash 7 Player or Flash 8 Player, and you can choose the data rate. These handy steps show you how to encode a video in Flash:

1. **Create a new document that is the same size as the video you'll be incorporating on your Web page.**

   Make sure you match the frame rate of the main movie.

2. **Choose Import⊏>Import Video.**

   The Import Video dialog box (see Figure 3-3) appears.

3. **Click Browse.**

   The Open dialog box appears.

4. **Select the video you want to import and then click Open.**

   The path to the video and file name appear in the File Path field.

5. **Click Next.**

   The Deployment section of the Import Video dialog box appears. (See Figure 3-4.)

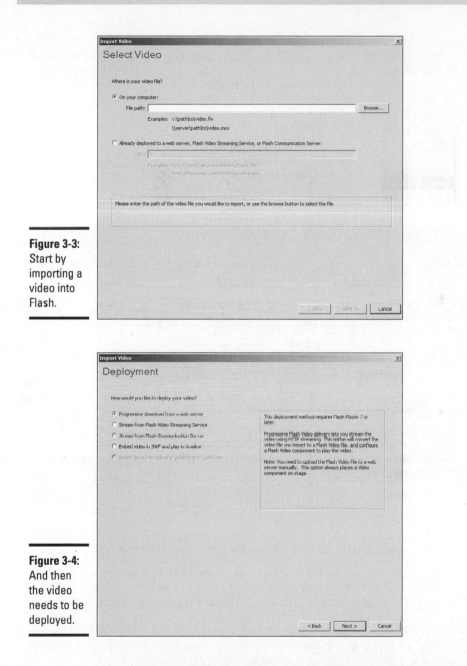

Figure 3-3:
Start by
importing a
video into
Flash.

Figure 3-4:
And then
the video
needs to be
deployed.

6. **Accept the default Progressive Download from a Web Server option,
unless you have a client who owns several Ferraris and is rich enough
to afford Flash Video Streaming Service or Flash Communication
Server.**

7. **Click Next.**

The Encoding section of the Import Video dialog box appears. (See Figure 3-5.) In this section of the dialog box, you can preview the video by dragging the Preview Scrubber. You can trim the video by dragging the In Point slider to the point where you want the video to begin and by dragging the Out Point slider to the point where you want the video to end. This doesn't affect the original clip, only the FLV file that's created during the encoding process.

In Point slider   Out Point slider

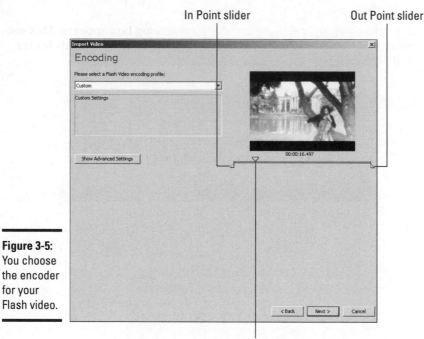

Figure 3-5:
You choose the encoder for your Flash video.

Preview Scrubber

8. Choose an option from the Encoding drop-down menu.

Your choices are Modem, Low, Medium, or High Quality for the Flash 7 or Flash 8 Player. If your audience will access the Internet with a dialup modem, choose Low; with a DSL connection, choose Medium, or with a fast cable connection, choose High. If you're certain your intended audience has the Flash 8 Player, choose Flash 8 Player. The encoding for the Flash 8 Player is the latest and greatest. If high quality with fast streaming is your main concern, choose one of the Flash 8 options.

If you're familiar with encoding digital video, click the Show Advanced Settings button and tweak the settings to suit the Web page in which the video will appear. When you modify the settings, Custom appears in the encoding window instead of one of the defaults.

If you choose one of the Flash 8 options, you can hedge your bets by warning your audience that they need the Flash 8 Player to view the video and provide the link where they can download the application.

9. Drag the In Point slider to determine which frame of the source video is the starting point of your Flash video.

10. Drag the Out Point slider to determine which frame of the source video is the ending frame of your Flash video.

11. Click Next.

The Skinning section of the Import Video dialog box appears. This section enables you to choose a skin (the interface) and controls for the video. (See Figure 3-6.)

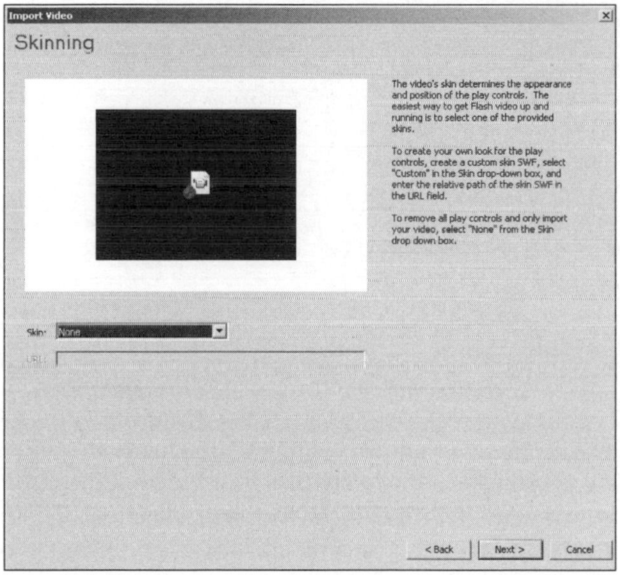

Figure 3-6:
A video without sheepskin.

12. Choose a skin from the Skin drop-down menu.

Unless you're going to use the video as part of a Flash Web site, choose None. All you need is the encoded Flash video. You can add a skin when you add the video to your Web page in Dreamweaver.

The minimum width of the skin is listed after you choose it. If the minimum width is larger than the width of your video, choose a skin that doesn't have as many controls.

13. Click Next.

The Finish Video Import dialog box shown in Figure 3-7 appears. This lists all of the options specified in other sections of the Import Video dialog box.

14. **Click Finish to encode the video.**

Alternatively, you can click the Back button to navigate to a section and make a change. After you click Finish, the Flash Video Encoding Progress dialog box appears, as shown in Figure 3-8. This useful rascal tells you how long it's going to take to encode your video. If the remaining time is longer than a minute, relax and tune in and tune out.

After the video is encoded, an FLV file appears in the folder in which you saved the FLA file. An FLV playback component appears in the document Library. However, if you're going to use the video on a Web page, all you need is the FLV file.

15. **Choose Control⇨Test Movie to preview your video.**

Figure 3-9 shows a preview of a Flash video without controller.

16. **Save the document.**

This step is optional, as all you really need is the FLV file.

Figure 3-8:
But I want it
yesterday.

Figure 3-9:
Previewing
the encoded
video.

When you encode video from within Flash, the video encoder creates an
FLV (Flash Video) file with the same name as the source file with the `.flv`
extension. You need to upload this file to your Web server along with your
Web page.

Adding Flash Video to a Web Page

It's easy to add Flash video to a Web page in Dreamweaver. As an added
bonus in Dreamweaver, you can add controls to the video that enable Web
site visitors to start and stop the video as they please. This is much better
than having the video loop endlessly while the visitors are trying to pay
attention to the other content on the page. To add Flash video to a Web page:

1. **Position your cursor at the point in the Web page where you want to
   insert the video.**

2. **Choose Insert⇨Media⇨Flash Video.**

   The Insert Flash Video dialog box appears. (See Figure 3-10.)

Encoding video with the Flash 8 Video Encoder

If you're encoding multiple videos, use the Flash 8 Video Encoder that ships with Flash 8 Professional. This gem gives you the capability of encoding multiple video files. The settings options are identical to those you find when you import video into Flash and use the progressive download method of deployment.

After you apply settings to a file, you can duplicate the file and modify the settings. This option is useful if you need to deploy different versions of the video for visitors that access the Web with dialup modems, DSL modems, or cable modems. You can add as many videos as you want to the queue. The application encodes one video at a time. The following illustration shows the Flash 8 Video Encoder with two video files that will be encoded with three settings. The application will encode a total of six videos.

Here's a good tip: When encoding multiple videos, set up the application prior to finishing work for the day. Then before you leave, just click the Start Queue button. The encoded files will be ready to use in a Web page when you start work the next day.

3. **Accept the default Progressive Download Video option for Video Type.**

   The other option is Streaming Video, which requires a special server.

4. **Click the Browse button next to the URL field.**

   Navigate to the FLV file you want to add to the Web page. If you've been neat and tidy, the file should be in the Web site folder. If you haven't been neat and tidy, Dreamweaver lets you know by displaying a dialog box, which offers you the option of copying the file to the Web site folder. Take it.

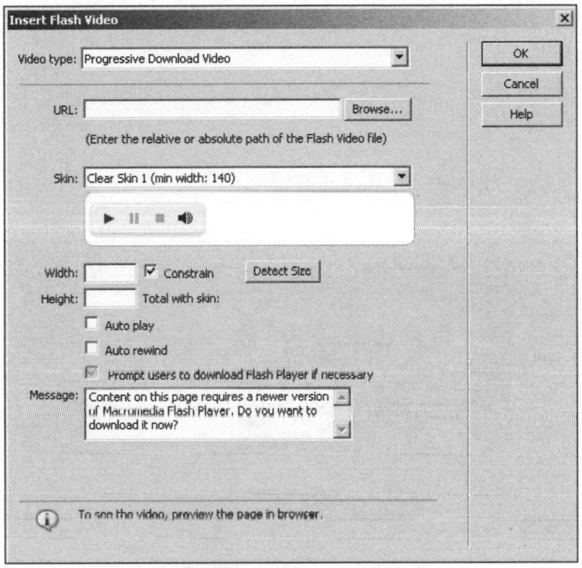

Figure 3-10:
Inserting
Flash video
in a Web
page.

5. **Choose a skin from the Skin drop-down menu.**

   There are several options that give Web site visitors different options, such as playing the video or playing and pausing the video as well as adjusting the sound volume. Each skin lists the minimum width required to display all of the controls. Your video width must be equal to or larger than the width of the skin you choose.

6. **Enter values in the Width and Height fields.**

   These are the dimensions of the video you're adding to the page. Alternatively, you can click Detect Size and Dreamweaver fills in the blanks.

7. **Choose additional options as needed.**

   You can have the video autostart when fully downloaded and rewind when finished. If you choose both options, the video will loop endlessly until the user clicks the Stop button on the skin.

8. **Click OK.**

   Dreamweaver adds the video to the page.

9. **Press F12 to preview the page in your default browser.**

Dreamweaver prompts you to save the document. After you save the document, Dreamweaver launches the page in your default browser. The video controller becomes partially transparent after the video begins playing. (See Figure 3-11.)

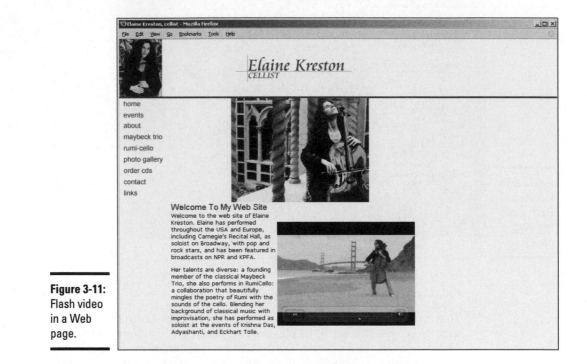

Figure 3-11: Flash video in a Web page.

Adding QuickTime Player to a Page

QuickTime video is another popular choice for Web video. Unfortunately, Dreamweaver has no menu choices to add QuickTime video to a page. You can, however, add ActiveX content to a page, which is what QuickTime video is. You specify the parameters to get the file to play correctly within the page. To embed a QuickTime player that plays an associated MOV file in a Web page, open a Web page in Dreamweaver and follow these instructions:

1. **Position your cursor at the point in the Web page where you want the video to appear.**

2. **Choose Insert⇨Media⇨ActiveX.**

Dreamweaver inserts an ActiveX object in the page with the default dimensions of 32 x 32 pixels.

3. **Select the ActiveX object in the Document window.**

4. **Open the Properties inspector.**

5. **Enter the following text into the Class ID text box:**

```
clsid:02BF25D5-8C17-4B23-BC80-D3488ABDDC6B
```

This tells the Web browser that the ActiveX content is QuickTime.

6. **In the Properties inspector, specify the following parameters:**

- Select the Embed check box.

- Set the width and height in the W and H text boxes. Add 16 to the height if you're including a controller.

- Click the Browse folder icon (next to the Src text box) and navigate to and then select the QuickTime MOV movie you want to embed in the page.

- Enter **http://www.apple.com/qtactivex/qtplugin.cab** in the Base text box.

7. **Click the Parameters button in the Properties inspector.**

The Parameters dialog box appears.

8. **Add the parameters for the ActiveX object and click OK.**

Click the plus (+) sign to add a parameter. After you click the plus sign, a text box appears in which you type the parameter. Each parameter has a value that you type in the next text field. To run a QuickTime video, you need the following parameters and values:

- Parameter 1 = **autoplay**, Value = **true**

- Parameter 2 = **controller**, Value = **true**

- Parameter 3 = **pluginspage**, Value= **http://www.apple.com/quicktime/download/indext.html**

- Parameter 4 = **target**, Value= **self**

- Parameter 5 = **type**, Value = **video/quicktime**

- Parameter 6 = **src**, Value = the path and file name of the movie you're embedding in the page

At this stage, your Parameters dialog box should resemble Figure 3-12. If desired, you can set the autoplay parameter to false, in which case the video won't play until the visitor clicks the Play button on the controller. You can also set the value for controller to false, in which case a controller isn't displayed. Logic dictates it's not advisable to set both of these parameters to false, as your visitor will only see the first frame of the movie and have no way to play it.

Figure 3-12:
Setting the parameters for a QuickTime video.

9. **Press F12 to preview the page in your default browser.**

Dreamweaver prompts you to save the document. After you save the document, Dreamweaver launches the page in your default browser. The video begins playing. Figure 3-13 shows a QuickTime Player in a Web page playing the associated video file.

Figure 3-13:
A QuickTime video embedded in a Web page.

If you embed a lot of video in Web pages, switch to Code view and select the code that embeds the ActiveX object into the Web page. Open the Snippets palette and click the New Snippets button at the bottom of the palette. You can now insert the snippet into other pages. After inserting the snippet, change the parameters that specify the source video in the Properties inspector.

Adding Windows Media Player to a Page

Choices are a good thing. When it comes to Web video, you've got quite a few. Yet another option you have to satisfy your client's need to have full motion video on her Web site is Windows Media Video. You can embed the Windows Media Player in a Web page that gives visitors the controls they need to play the associated video file. To embed the Windows Media Player in a Web page, open the Web page in Dreamweaver and follow these steps:

1. **Position your cursor at the point in the Web page where you want the video to appear.**

2. **Choose Insert⇔Media⇔ActiveX.**

   Dreamweaver inserts an ActiveX object in the page with the default dimensions of 32 x 32 pixels.

3. **Select the ActiveX object in the Document window.**

4. **Open the Properties inspector.**

5. **Enter the following text into the Class ID text box:**

   ```
   clsid: 22d6f312-b0f6-11d0-94ab-0080c74c7e95
   ```

   This tells the Web browser that the ActiveX content is in Windows Media Video.

6. **In the Properties inspector, specify the following parameters:**

   • Select the Embed check box.

   • Set the width and height in the W and H text boxes. Add 50 to the height if you're including a controller.

   • Click the Browse folder icon (next to the Src text box) and navigate to and then select the Windows Media Video WMV movie you want to embed in the page.

   • Enter **mediaplayer1** in the ID text box.

7. **Click the Parameters button in the Properties inspector.**

   The Parameters dialog box appears.

8. **Add the parameters for the ActiveX object and click OK.**

   Click the plus (+) sign to add a parameter. Each parameter has a value. To run a QuickTime video, you need the following parameters and values:

   • Parameter 1 = **src**, Value = the file name of your movie

   • Parameter 2 = **autostart**, Value = **false**

   • Parameter 3 = **showcontrols**, Value = **true**

- Parameter 4 = **showstatusbar**, Value = **false**
- Parameter 5= **showdisplay**, Value= **false**
- Parameter 6 = **autorewind**, Value= **true**
- Parameter 7 = **type**, Value = **application/x-mplayer-w**
- Parameter 8 = **pluginspage**, Value = **http://www.microsoft.com/ Windows/Downloads/Contents/MediaPlayer/**

At this stage, the Parameters dialog box should resemble Figure 3-14. If desired, you can set the autostart parameter to true, in which case the video plays as soon as it loads. You can also set the value for showcontrols to false, in which case a controller isn't displayed. Logic dictates it's not advisable to set both of these parameters to false, as your visitor will see only the first frame of the movie and have no way to play it.

Figure 3-14: Parameters for an embedded Windows Media Video.

Parameter	Value
src	Elaine768K_Stream.wmv
autostart	false
showcontrols	true
showstatusbar	false
showdisplay	false
autorewind	true
type	application/x-mplayer-w
pluginspage	http://www.microsoft.com/Wi...

9. **Press F12 to preview the page in your default browser.**

Dreamweaver prompts you to save the document. After you save the document, Dreamweaver launches the page in your default browser. The video begins playing. Figure 3-15 shows a Windows Media Video in a Web page complete with controller.

If you attempt to test an embedded Windows Media Player and associated video file in the Mozilla Firefox browser on your local machine, it won't play. It will, however, play when you upload the HTML page and associated files to your server.

Avoiding DV Pitfalls

Nobody likes to wind up with egg on his face. For most, the additional cholesterol is unwelcome — not to mention the mess. But we digress. Egg on your face where Web video is concerned is a file that doesn't play, or doesn't play properly. Here are some handy tips and tricks to help you keep your client's Web video squeaky clean:

Figure 3-15:
A Windows
Media Video
embedded
in a Web
page.

✦ **Don't copy video from other Web sites and use them on yours.** This violates copyright laws.

✦ **Don't use a video from one of your client's suppliers before reading the licensing rights to the video.** After you read the rights, make sure your client agrees to them. Being named as a second party in a copyright infringement suit isn't a good thing.

✦ **If your client is recording a video for his Web site, which you or someone else will later compress and encode for the Web, make sure he uses a good-quality camcorder and not some el cheapo Web cam.** Garbage in, garbage out.

✦ **Make sure your client's intended audience has the necessary plug-ins to view the video.** When in doubt, list the required plug-in and link to the Web site from which visitors can download it.

✦ **Apply the right level of compression for your intended audience.** If your client's intended audience accesses the Internet with dialup modems, don't embed a video with a 756 kbps data rate.

✦ **If your client's intended audience accesses the Internet at different connection speeds, create links to videos with different compression rates.** Have one file with a data rate of 40 kbps for dialup access, one file with a data rate of 400 kbps for DSL access, and another file with a data rate of 756 kbps for cable access.

✦ **Don't embed more than one video per Web page.** If your client wants multiple videos to be accessible from a page, use a video editing application to export one frame of the video as an image. Do this for each video the client wants to be accessible from the page. On the Web page, each photo serves as a link to the full video.

Chapter 4: Slideshow Pro

In This Chapter

✔ **Introducing Slideshow Pro**

✔ **Creating a slide show**

✔ **Adding effects and links**

✔ **Editing a slide show**

The first chapter of this minibook covers using Flash to add interactivity to your Web pages. Some people love Flash. Others would rather have a tooth pulled than learn how to use a new application. If you fall in the latter group and still want to add cool interactivity to your Web pages, you can easily do so from within Dreamweaver by using an extension known as Slideshow Pro. Slideshow Pro enables you to easily add Flash slide shows to your designs — slide shows with special effects such as motion and frame overlays. In this chapter, we show you some of the cool things you can do with Slideshow Pro.

About Slideshow Pro

Active Slideshow Pro is a Macromedia Dreamweaver extension created by the folks at DMXzone. The extension makes it possible for you to add compelling multimedia slide shows to your Web pages. Adding a slide show is as simple as invoking a menu command, navigating to a folder of images you want to include in the slide show, and then choosing the options you want in your slide show. The options you can include are lengthy. You can choose an overlay for your slide show, which, incidentally, is a Flash SWF file. You can add motion to your slide shows, cool transitions, dazzling text effects, and more.

If you want a truly custom slide show, you can add your slides one at a time, add a text overlay, control motion for the slide and text independently, add a custom fade between slides, and more. You can also add a music soundtrack to your slide show, complete with a Mute button if site visitors don't like your choice of music. The options allow you to create a one-of-a-kind slide show guaranteed to dazzle site visitors. As of this writing, Active Slideshow Pro sells for $149. For more information, visit www.dmxzone. com/ShowDetail.asp?NewsId=11360.

The Ken Burns effect

Ken Burns is a documentary filmmaker. He intersperses his documentaries with original prints and photographs. In his documentaries, Ken Burns often gives life to still photographs by slowly zooming in on subjects of interest and panning from one subject in the image to another. For example, in a photograph of a baseball team, he might slowly pan across the faces of the players and come to a rest on the player whom the narrator is discussing. Ken Burns didn't originate this technique, but he is so associated with it that it is now known as the *Ken Burns effect*.

The effect is also used when transitioning from one clip to another. For example, to segue from one person in the documentary to another, he might open a clip with a close-up of one person in a photo and then zoom out to make another person in the photo visible. Burns used this technique extensively when creating documentaries about subjects who lived when video cameras weren't available or in wide use. The zooming and panning across photographs creates the feeling of motion and keeps the viewer visually entertained.

Active Slideshow Pro gives you the capability to pan across a photo and zoom in, thereby replicating the Ken Burns effect. This technique has become a staple of documentaries, slide shows, presentations, and even computer screen savers.

Installing the Extension

You purchase the Active Slideshow Pro extension from DMXzone.com. It's available as a download. After you download the extension to your hard drive, follow these steps to install the extension:

1. **Double-click the extension.**

Slideshow Pro is an MXP file, like all Adobe extensions for products originally created by Macromedia. Extension Manager launches and installs the extension. After the Extension Manager launches, a dialog box appears with a disclaimer from Macromedia. This is included because any developer can create extensions, and Macromedia doesn't claim responsibility for them. However, you can install extensions from a reputable source like DMXzone safely.

2. **Click Accept to agree to the disclaimer**

Macromedia begins installing the extension. After the extension is installed, the Macromedia Extension Manager dialog box displays information about the extension. (See Figure 4-1.)

3. **Restart Dreamweaver to complete the installation.**

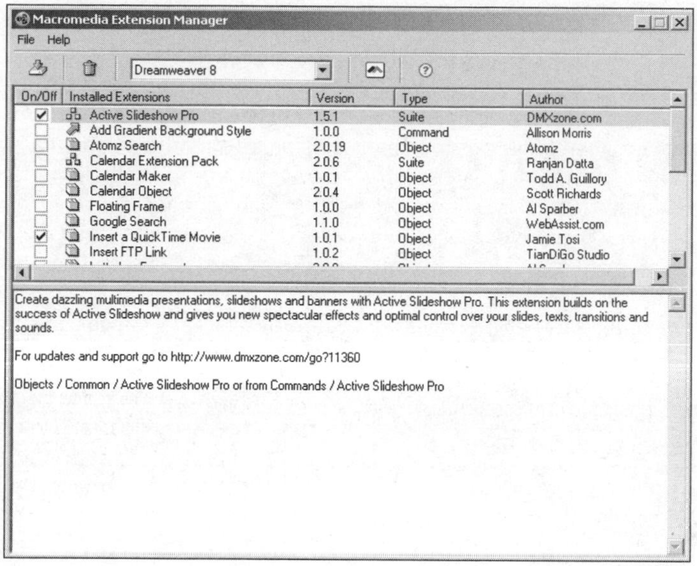

Figure 4-1:
Installing
the
extension.

Creating a Slide Show

After installing the extension, you're ready to rock and roll and create your first slide show. You access Active Slideshow Pro from within Dreamweaver. The resulting Flash file is linked to your HTML document. You can use a slide show anywhere, but a slide show is particularly effective on the home page of a Web site. It's a classy way to show people what your client does. If your client is a photographer, it's a really classy way to showcase his best pieces to his potential customers.

Launching Slideshow Pro

To create a slide show, you begin with an HTML document. You can create the slide show anywhere in the document. However, a slide show is a thing of beauty, and a thing of beauty is a joy forever. Therefore, it makes sense to give your slide show a place of prominence on the page. To start your slide show:

1. **Create an HTML document.**

Start with a template from the site that includes the navigation menu, site banner, and all the other associated accoutrements. (See Figure 4-2.)

2. **Choose Commands⇨Active Slideshow Pro.**

The Active Slideshow Pro dialog box appears. (See Figure 4-3.)

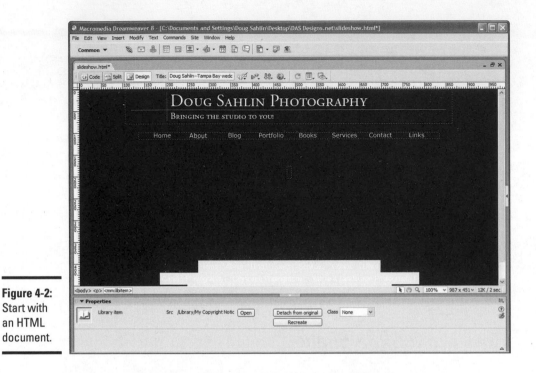

Figure 4-2:
Start with
an HTML
document.

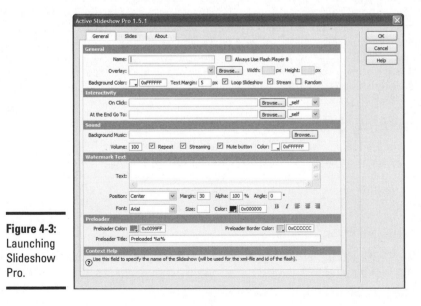

Figure 4-3:
Launching
Slideshow
Pro.

3. **Enter a name for the slide show.**

4. **Click the Always Use Flash Player 8 check box if desired.**

This option determines whether the slide show works in only the Flash 8 Player. If you choose this option, make sure you inform site visitors that the Flash 8 Player is required and provide a link they can use to download the player.

5. **If you wish, choose an overlay from the Overlay drop-down menu.**

Overlays are SWF files that play over the slide show. They run the gamut from fancy frames to moving objects and frames. If you choose an overlay, the application fills in the Width and Height fields.

6. **Click the Background Color swatch to choose the background color for the slide show.**

If you specify a border, choose a color that complements the background color of the HTML page; otherwise, choose the same color as the document.

7. **Accept the default Text Margin value of 5 pixels or enter another value.**

This option determines how far text is indented. If you choose an overlay, make sure you specify a large enough value so that the text isn't partially eclipsed by the overlay.

8. **Select the Loop Slideshow check box if desired.**

If you choose this option, the slide show starts again at the beginning after it finishes.

9. **Select the Stream check box if you wish.**

This option begins playing the slide show and music while data is still streaming into the user's browser.

10. **Select the Random check box if you wish.**

This option plays the slides in a random manner.

11. **If desired, enter a URL in the On Click field.**

If you enter a URL, site visitors can launch the Web page by clicking the slide show. The option is available only if you deselect the Loop Slideshow option. You can also specify a file within the Web site, such as an image that is the same size as the slide show.

12. **If desired, enter a URL in the At the End Go To field.**

This option is available if you deselect the Loop Slideshow option. It loads the Web page when the slide show is finished. You can also specify a file within the Web site, such as an image that is the same size as the slide show. The file or Web page does, however, load in the same window if you choose _self. When you're creating a slide show for a Web page, we don't recommend using this option because it takes the viewer away from the client's Web site.

13. Click the Background music Browse button.

This enables you to browse to an MP3 file to use as background music for your slide show.

14. Accept the default Volume value of 100 or enter another value.

The default option plays the soundtrack at 100 percent of its volume. Enter a lower value to play the soundtrack at a lower volume.

15. Specify the other options for your soundtrack as follows:

- *Repeat:* The default option repeats the soundtrack, as long as the slide show is playing.

- *Streaming:* Begins playing the soundtrack while the data is still streaming into the user's browser.

- *Mute Button:* Determines whether a mute button is displayed with the slide show. If you accept this default option, users can click the button to mute the sound.

- *Color:* Enables you to choose the color for the Mute button from the Color picker. The default color is white.

16. If you want to display watermark text on the slides, specify the following options in the Watermark Text section:

- *Text:* Type the text you want to display over each slide.

- *Position:* Choose an option from the drop-down menu to determine how the text is positioned over each slide. The options are self-explanatory.

- *Margin:* Determines how much the text is indented. Specify a larger value if you're using an overlay with your slide show.

- *Alpha:* The default option of 100 displays the text at full opacity. Specify a lower value if you want the text to be partially transparent and let some of the underlying slide show through.

- *Angle:* Enter a value to tilt the watermark text.

- *Font:* Choose an option from the drop-down menu.

- *Size:* Accept the default value of 30 pixels or enter a different value.

- *Color:* Click the Color swatch and choose the text color from the Color picker. Choose a color that you can see over the images.

- *Style:* Choose one or more options to style the text. Your choices are Bold and/or Italic.

- *Align:* Choose an option to align the text. Your options are Left, Center, or Right.

17. **Specify the following options in the Preloader section:**

- *Preloader Color:* Click the Preloader Color swatch and choose the preloader color from the Color picker.

- *Preloader Border Color:* Click the Preloader Border Color swatch and choose the color of the preloader border from the Color picker.

- *Preloader Title:* Accept the default preloader title or select the text and type the title you want. Loading is a good option.

Adding slides to your show

A slide show with no slides is like popcorn with no pop, which, incidentally, is corn. But you're not creating a corny slide show, so the next logical step after you get past the General tab of the Active Slideshow Pro dialog box is to add some slides as follows:

1. **Specify the general options for your slide show as specified in the previous section.**

If you didn't read the previous section, please do. Doug spent a good amount of time writing it in his favorite Wi-Fi café. Besides, this section makes more sense if you do read the previous section.

2. **Click the Slides tab.**

The Active Slideshow Pro dialog box reconfigures to show the options for adding slides. (See Figure 4-4.)

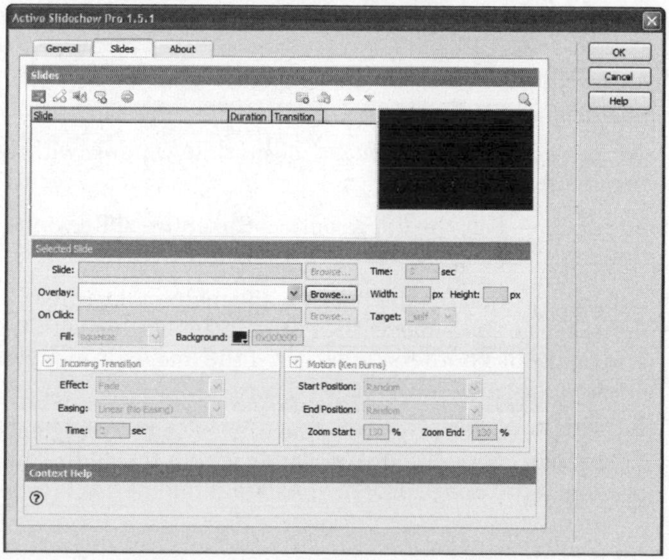

Figure 4-4:
Adding a
slide.

3. Click the Add Slide button.

A folder icon appears in the Slides Window.

4. In the Selected Slide section, do the following:

- *Click the Browse button to the right of the Slide field.*

  This opens the Select File dialog box.

- *Navigate to and select the slide you want to start your show. Then click OK.*

The first slide is the first impression site visitors will get of your client's handiwork. Hit them with your best shot.

- *Accept the default time of 3 (seconds) or enter a different value.*

  This determines the number of seconds for which the slide is displayed after the transition from the previous slide ends.

- *Choose an option from the Overlay drop-down menu.*

  If you choose an overlay for an individual slide, it overrides (for this slide only) the overlay you chose from the General section. I advise you to choose one overlay style and stick with it. The slides are the stars of the show, not the overlays.

- *Enter a file name or URL in the On Click field.*

  This option enables the visitor to click the slide and load a Web page or file. You can manually enter the URL or file name or click the Browse button and navigate to the desired file. This supersedes what you specified for this option in the General tab.

- *Choose a Fill option.*

  This determines how the slide is displayed if you don't choose an Incoming Transition option. Your choices are

  Center — Centers the image in the slide window without resizing the image.

  Stretch — Fills the image across the entire slide window. This option can change the image proportions.

  Squeeze — Resizes the image while maintaining the original proportions. This option makes the entire image visible within the slide. The image has borders, however, if the image proportions are different from those of the slide.

  Trim — Resizes the image while preserving the original proportions. This makes the entire image visible within the slide. The image has borders if the image proportions are different from those of the slide.

- *Choose a Background Color.*

    Click the Background Color swatch to determine the slide background color. This overrides the background color you might have chosen in the general section.

5. **Click the Incoming Transition check box.**

    This option is selected by default. If you accept the option, choose the effect you want for the slide transition from the Effect drop-down menu:

    - *Fade:* This option gradually increases the opacity of the incoming slide until it's fully visible at the end of the transition period.

    - *Slide In:* The incoming slide transitions in from the direction specified in the option you choose and overlaps the previous slide. For example, if you choose Slide In Right, the incoming image transitions in from the right.

    - *Push:* The incoming slide pushes the previous slide out of the frame, transitioning in from the direction specified in the option you choose. For example, if you choose Push Left, the incoming slide transitions in from the left and pushes the previous slide to the right.

6. **Choose an option from the Easing drop-down menu.**

    Easing allows you to add special effects to the transition, such as acceleration or elastic movement. The best way to understand what each choice does is to experiment and remember which effects you like best.

7. **Accept the default Time value of 2 (seconds) or enter a different value.**

    This option determines how long it takes the incoming slide to complete its transition.

8. **Click the Motion check box.**

    This option is selected by default and enables you to create a slide show with the Ken Burns effect. If you accept this option, specify the following options:

    - *Start:* Choose an option from the Start drop-down menu. You can choose Random, which moves the slide into the frame from a random direction. This emulates the original Ken Burns effect. Alternatively, you can choose one of the Slide From options, which slides the image in from a specified direction.

    - *Finish:* Choose an option from the Finish drop-down menu. You can choose random, which places the slide in a random position at the end of its duration. Alternatively, choose one of the Slide To options, which slide the image to a position specified in the option you choose.

9. **Accept the default Zoom Start value of 130 percent or enter a different value.**

   This determines how large the image is when it appears in the slide window. If you specify 100, the image fills 100 percent of the frame; larger values magnify the image by the value entered.

10. **Accept the default Zoom End value of 130 percent or enter a different value.**

    This determines how large the image is at the end of its duration. Specify a lower value than the Zoom Start value to zoom in and a higher value than the Zoom Start value to Zoom out.

11. **Click the Interactive Preview button, which looks like a Play button, at the lower-right corner of the slide preview.**

    If the slide preview is to your liking, you can add slides to the show. Alternatively, you can modify any parameter to improve your show before adding slides to the show.

You can add a folder of files to a slide show by clicking the Folder button and then selecting the desired folder of images. After adding a folder of slides, click each slide in the Slides window to set Incoming Transition, Motion, and other parameters.

12. **After adding slides to your show, you can modify the order in which they appear by selecting a slide and then clicking the Up or Down arrow.**

If you decide that a slide doesn't belong in the show, select it and then click the Delete button that looks like a minus (–) sign.

Adding text and sound to a slide

You can display text on a slide and also have a sound play when a slide appears. The sound is in addition to any background music you select in the General tab. Logic dictates that you shouldn't display watermark text and text on an individual slide. In fact, we rarely use text in slide shows. Let the images do the talking. Adding tasteful background music is, however, a nice touch. To add text and sound to a slide:

1. **Select the slide to which you want to add text.**

2. **Click the Add Text icon, which looks like a pencil.**

   The Slides tab reconfigures to show options for adding text. (See Figure 4-5.)

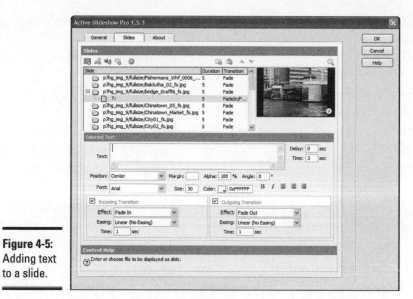

Figure 4-5:
Adding text
to a slide.

3. **Accept the default Delay value of 0 (seconds).**

The default value displays the text as soon as the image fully transitions into the slide window. If you specify a value larger than 0 (zero), the text doesn't appear until the duration expires.

4. **Accept the default Time value of 3 (seconds) or enter a different value.**

This option determines the length of time for which the text is displayed over the image.

5. **Enter the desired text in the Text field.**

6. **Specify parameters for the text. Your options are as follows:**

- *Position:* Choose an option from the drop-down menu to determine how the text is positioned over each slide. The options are self-explanatory.

- *Margin:* Determines how much the text is indented. Specify a larger value if you're using an overlay with your slide show; otherwise, the overlay might hide some of the text.

- *Alpha:* The default option of 100 displays the text at full opacity. Specify a lower value if you want the text to be partially transparent and let some of the underlying slide show through.

- *Angle:* Enter a value to tilt the watermark text.

- *Font:* Choose an option from the drop-down menu.

- *Size:* Accept the default value of 30 pixels or enter a different value.

- *Color:* Click the Color swatch and choose the text color from the Color picker. Choose a color that you can see over the images.

- *Style:* Choose one or more options to style the text. Your choices are Bold and/or Italic.

- *Align:* Choose an option to align the text. Your options are Left, Center, or Right.

7. Click the Incoming Transition check box.

This option is selected by default. This option adds a transition effect to the text as the image appears. If you accept this option, choose an option from the Effect drop-down menu. Your choices are

- *Fade In:* The text gradually fades in from transparent to full opacity.

- *Zoom In:* The text zooms into view.

- *Blur In:* The text is blurry when it first appears and is clear when the transition period ends.

- *Time:* Accept the default transition time of 1 second or enter a different value.

8. Click the Outgoing Transition check box.

This option is selected by default. If you accept this option, choose an option from the Effect drop-down menu. Your choices are

- *Fade Out:* The text gradually fades out from full opacity to transparent.

- *Zoom Out:* The text zooms out of view.

- *Blur Out:* The text is clear when it is displayed and is blurred during the transition out.

- *Time:* Accept the default transition time of 1 second or enter a different value.

9. Click the icon that looks like a speaker to have a sound play when the slide is displayed.

This reconfigures the dialog box for sound options.

10. Click the Browse button and navigate to and select the sound.

Select a sound with a duration of a second or two. If you specify a sound with a longer duration, it continues playing while the next slide loads. A perfect example of that is a shutter click for a photographer's slide show.

11. Accept the default Volume value of 100 or enter a different value.

The default value plays the sound at 100 percent volume. Enter a lower value to lower the volume of the sound.

12. **Accept the default delay of 0 (seconds) or enter a different value.**

This option determines whether the sound is delayed and, if so, by what amount of time.

13. **Accept the default Repeat value of 1 or enter another value.**

The default value repeats the sound once. For a slide with a display time of 3 to 5 seconds, the default is the ticket. Besides, too much noise is going to detract from the beauty of the images.

14. **Click OK to add the slide show to your Web page.**

Active Slideshow Pro does its work quickly and adds a Flash file to your Web page.

15. **Press F12.**

Dreamweaver prompts you to save the file. After saving the file, it's displayed in your default browser. (See Figure 4-6.)

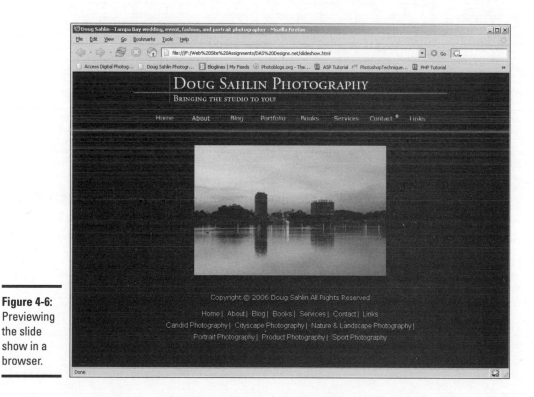

Figure 4-6:
Previewing
the slide
show in a
browser.

Editing a slide show

After you create a slide show and preview it, you might find that you need to tweak it. You can make minor tweaks in Dreamweaver and, if need be, edit the show in the Active Slideshow Pro extension. To edit a slide show:

1. **Select the slide show.**

It's the big rectangle with the capital F for Flash.

2. **Choose Window⇨Properties.**

The Properties inspector opens. From within the Properties inspector (see Figure 4-7), you can edit many of the same parameters found in the General tab of the Active Slideshow Pro dialog box.

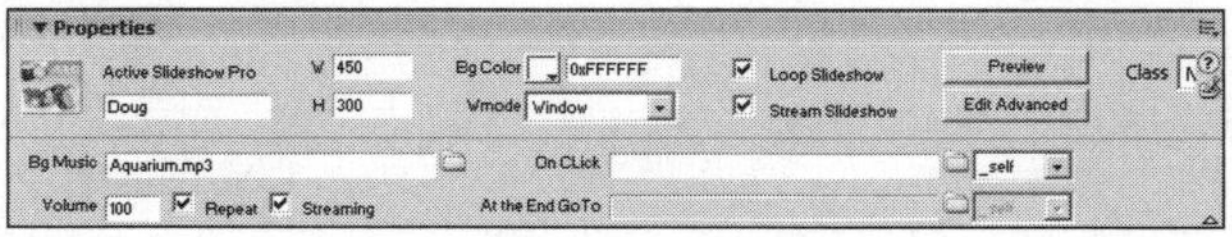

Figure 4-7:
Editing slide show properties in the Properties inspector.

3. **Click Preview.**

The slide show previews from within Dreamweaver.

4. **Click Edit Advanced.**

The slide show appears in the Active Slideshow Pro dialog box.

5. **Make your edits and click OK.**

Book VI

Audience Interaction

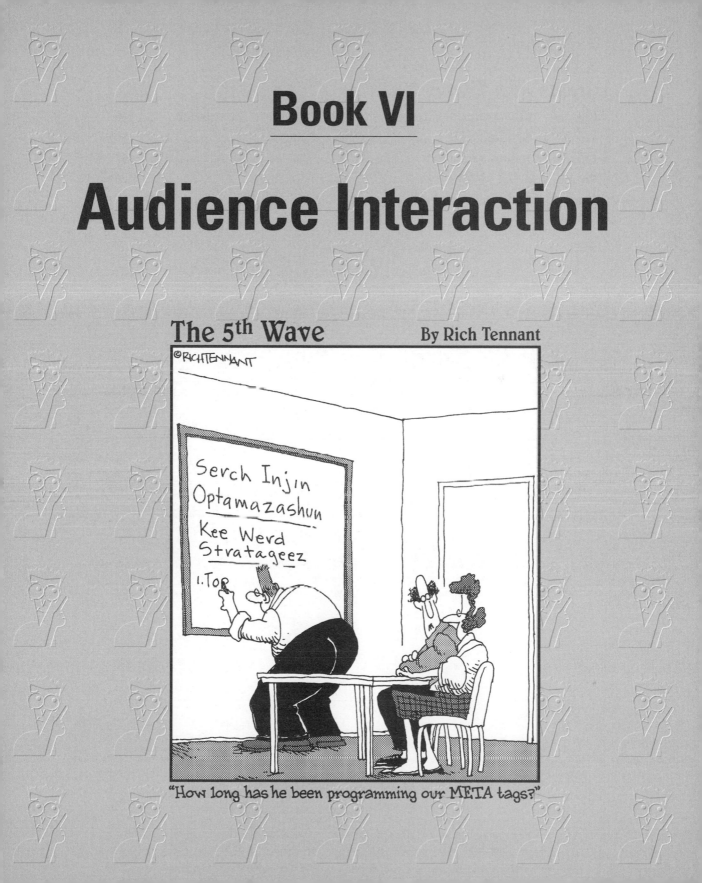

The 5th Wave   By Rich Tennant

Serch Injin
Optamazashun

Kee Werd
Stratageez

1. Top

"How long has he been programming our META tags?"

Contents at a Glance

Chapter 1: Adding Basic Interactivity with HTML Forms and JavaScript

In This Chapter

✔ Engaging Web site visitors with interactive content

✔ Considering coding

✔ Creating HTML forms

✔ Adding buttons and boxes to Web forms

✔ Working with password fields, hidden fields, and text areas

✔ Giving Web site visitors multiple choices

✔ Using JavaScript event handlers

✔ Thinking about server side technology

Interactivity is a wonderful thing. It can make a Web site dance and sing. But as Web designers, we are devout cowards when the need arises to write code. However, you can create many forms of interactivity without writing the first word of code. The Web form is a perfect example, which is comprised of items like text fields, check boxes, radio buttons, submit buttons, and so on. You can create one in an application like Dreamweaver by selecting the proper menu commands. In this chapter, we show you how to create forms and master JavaScript event handlers.

Understanding Interactivity

An interactive Web site is one that does more than appear on your monitor — it has bells and whistles that the user can interact with. Any Web site that requires input from a visitor and delivers different content based on user input can be considered interactive. Interactivity can be as simple as greeting a visitor based on the name she inputs in a Web form, or as complex as delivering information from a database. You can add a lot of interactivity to your designs by adding a bit of JavaScript code to a page, by creating a DHTML page, or by using VBScript (Visual Basic Script). The most-complex types of interactivity take place on the server side and involve adding code to a page that is interpreted by server software. ASP, PHP, and CGI/PERL are examples of programming languages that are interpreted on the server side. Now, just because we've mentioned a lot of scary acronyms that are related to code, don't think this chapter will have a lot of geek-speak. We mention code only where we need to. In most instances, you won't have to write any code, and when you do, we explain it in terms that you're sure to understand. Now that you have an idea of what interactivity is, let's get interactive.

Getting Ready to Code

Yes, at times you do need to manually write code for the pages you design. But that means learning a language like JavaScript, VBScript, or one of the other Script Sisters. That's, like, a lot of work. But in most cases, you don't have to learn an entire programming language, just like you don't have to know the entire English language to communicate.

Working with code is kind of like working for the government on a need-to-know basis. You learn only the code you need to know to get the job done. In many instances, a good HMTL editor like Dreamweaver can create the difficult code for you. All you need to know is which menu command to select. Fireworks, Dreamweaver's partner in interactivity, can also create code for you. For example, in Fireworks, you can create a functional navigation menu with a drop-down menu thrown in for grins and giggles. You exercise your creativity in graphic design when creating the menu. You can then export the menu as images and HTML. Figure 1-1 shows a menu as created in Fireworks. After exporting the file as HTML and images, the images are all neatly stored in a folder, and the code that most designers couldn't even think of creating is stored in an HTML file. To get the menu into one of your designs, you use the Fireworks HTML command in Dreamweaver to plop the menu (which is neatly sliced and diced inside a table) in your document, as well as all of the code needed to make the menu work. Figure 1-2 shows just some of the code created by Fireworks. In all, Fireworks generated 105 lines of code for the menu. Can you imagine writing all of that by hand? No wonder hardcore Web developers have carpal tunnel syndrome and an addiction to Naproxen.

But what happens when the dynamic duo of Dreamweaver and Fireworks can't create the effect you're after? You can find lots of code on the Internet. All you need to do is type the desired programming language and examples into your favorite search engine. You'll have lots of results from which to choose. Granted, you'll have to change some of the code to suit your design. But it's a lot easier than thumbing through a manual on the programming language that's heavy enough to be a doorstop. Another alternative is to grab someone else's code — provided it's not on a page generated by server side technology. If you see a way-cool effect on a Web site that you want to mimic on your Web site, you can view the code by choosing the proper View Source command from your Web browser. You must remember, there are only about 27 original ideas. Everything else is a mutation, permutation, or combination of the original ideas.

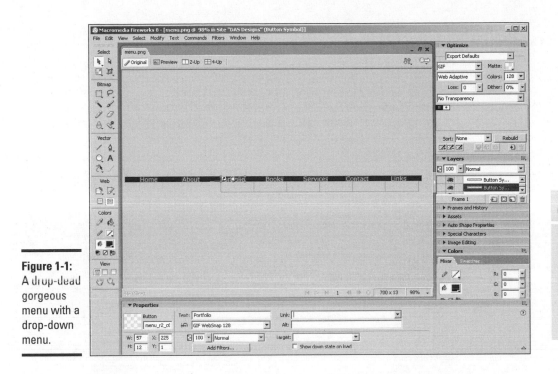

Figure 1-1:
A drop-dead
gorgeous
menu with a
drop-down
menu.

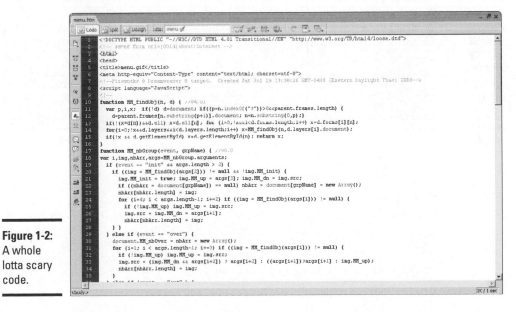

Figure 1-2:
A whole
lotta scary
code.

Building an HTML Form

One of the most basic and useful forms of interactivity is the lowly Web form. You see them on just about every Web site. *Forms* are used to gather information for mailing lists, add entries to blogs, subscribe to RSS (Real Simple Syndication) feeds, and more. Figure 1-3 shows a form used by a catering service. In the following sections, we show you how to create a Plain Jane form that gets 'er done.

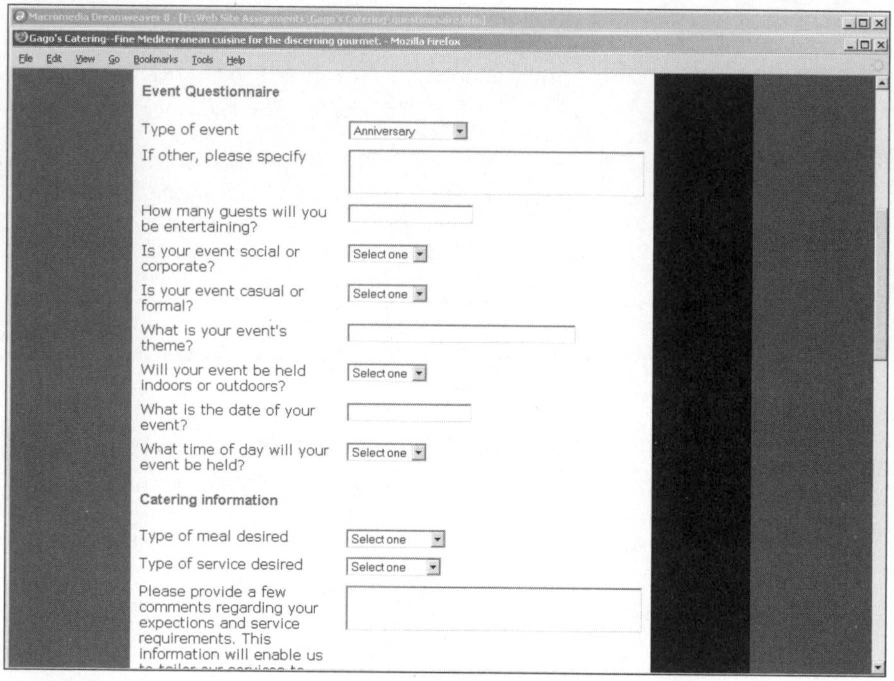

Figure 1-3: An HTML form in all its glory.

Form tags: <form> </form>

Everything has a beginning. In the case of a form, the <form> tag designates where the form starts in a document. And a form's got to end somewhere; it's a law. The </form> tag neatly bookends the form. If you're a geek, you type the beginning and ending <form> tags, and for that matter, all the code in between. But if you're a smart Web designer, you let your HTML editor do the heavy work for you. If you use Dreamweaver, you're in luck. Dreamweaver has a Forms toolbar and a menu devoted to creating form elements.

Your HTML editor takes care of another task for you: It lets you specify the action that occurs when the form is submitted and the method used. The action can be another Web page or it can be a script on the server, such as a mail-forwarding script. If the form is appending information on a Web page, GET is the method. If the form is being used to send information to a user, or posts information to a database, the method used is POST.

Text fields: <input type="text">

You can add all manner of elements to a form. One of the most useful form elements enables visitors to add text. When you add a text field to a form, you give the field a unique name. When the information is submitted, the name of the field is used in the ensuing code. For example, the information in the text field can be inserted into a variable, which has the same name as a field in a database. The name of the text field is what the programmer uses when creating the code to make the leap from text field to variable to database.

When you create a text field, you specify the width of the text field. You also determine whether the text is a single line, multiple lines, or password text. Another option is to limit the number of characters the end user can type into the field. If you don't limit the number of characters for a text field, you end up having a character (the smart-aleck type that likes to wreak havoc) enter 50 pounds of gibberish in your svelte, 25-character field.

Submit buttons: <input type="submit">

The </form> tag might be the end of your form in HTML, but it isn't the end of the form as far as the user is concerned. The last interactivity (you might remember that this is a chapter on interactivity) the user sees is a button that enables him to submit the form, a button that might be accompanied by its faithful companion, Reset. The Submit button executes the action specified by the beginning <form> tag. When you add a button to a form, you also have the option to change the default text, change the style of the dull and drab default text with a style from your style sheet, or choose Submit Form, Reset Form, or None as the action. You choose None as the action if you want the button to function as something else — for instance, a hyperlink that loads another Web page. Reset does just as you would expect, it clears all of the fields in the form in case the user changes her mind and wants to start from scratch.

Creating a simple form in Dreamweaver

The previous sections of this chapter cover the basic elements of a form. If you fast-forwarded to this section to create a form, you should probably at least skim the previous sections. It can make the process of creating a form a little easier. Now, you could *hard code* — developer-speak for typing the code by hand — the form. But that's a lot of work, and if you don't know all of the parameters, your form will be as useless as clothes in a nudist colony. The easy way to create a form is to choose menu commands from your HTML editor. This section shows you how to create a form in Dreamweaver 8, which comes with a handy-dandy Forms toolbar. (See Figure 1-4.)

**Book VI
Chapter 1**

**Adding Basic
Interactivity**

Figure 1-4:
The all-
singing, all-
dancing
Forms
toolbar.

You can create a form within a new Dreamweaver document or add the form to an existing document. Follow these steps to create a simple form with a text box (or *text field,* as Dreamweaver calls it) and a Submit button to submit user information using a Web site's mail redirect script:

1. **Launch Dreamweaver and open an existing document into which you want to insert a form, or open a new document.**

2. **Position your cursor where you want the form to begin.**

3. **Choose Insert➪Form➪Form.**

   Dreamweaver designates the form area with a dotted, red line.

4. **In the Properties inspector, enter the action that will take place when users submit the form.**

   The action can be another Web page with a script or a script at a Web server. In the case of this form, the action executes a mail-forwarding script on a Web server.

   Book III, Chapter 5 has more detailed information on using the Properties inspector.

5. **In the Action field of the Properties inspector, specify the method by which the form data will be submitted.**

   You have three options:

   • *Default:* Uses the browser's default method of submitting form data — which is usually GET.

   • *GET:* Appends the information to a URL.

   • *POST:* Sends the data as a body of data.

6. **Choose the target from the Target drop-down menu (if applicable).**

   This option is applicable only if the action calls another Web page that will be displayed in the browser. The target is the window in which the page will be displayed. By default, the page will open in the same window. Your choices are

- *_blank:* Displays the document in a new and unnamed browser window.

- *_parent:* Displays the document in the parent window currently displaying the form.

- *_self:* Displays the document in the same window as the one in which the form is submitted.

- *_top:* Displays the document in the body of the current window. This option ensures the document called by the form action displays in the full browser window, even if the form was originally displayed in a frame.

7. **If applicable, specify the MIME encoding type of the data from the Enctype drop-down menu.**

    The default encoding type of Application/x-www-form is generally used with the POST method. If you're creating a file-upload field, choose the Multipart/form-www encoding type.

8. **Insert the desired form object. For the purpose of this demonstration, choose Insert⇨Form⇨Text Field to begin creating a text field.**

    A *text field* is the same thing as a *text box* — it's a place for users to type information.

    The Input Tag Accessibility Attributes dialog box appears. (See Figure 1-5.) This information is designed to aid disabled people who visit the Web site.

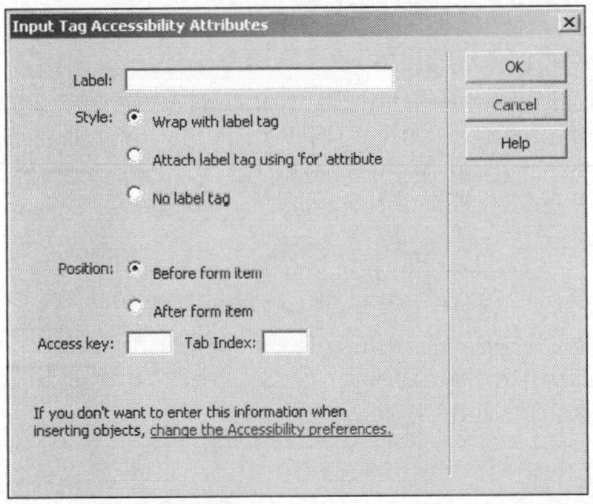

**Book VI
Chapter 1**

**Adding Basic
Interactivity**

Figure 1-5: Enter the attributes, please.

9. **Enter the desired information in the Input Tag Accessibility Attributes dialog box.**

    If your client's site will not have disabled visitors, the dialog box still has one useful attribute, Label.

10. **Type the desired label for the text field you're creating in the Label text box and click OK.**

This is the label that visitors see to the left of the text field you're creating — the name of the text field. So if, for instance, you're creating a text field that asks for an account number, your label would probably be something like, `Account Number`.

11. **In the workspace, select the text input field you just created and fill in the parameters in the Properties inspector. (See Figure 1-6.)**

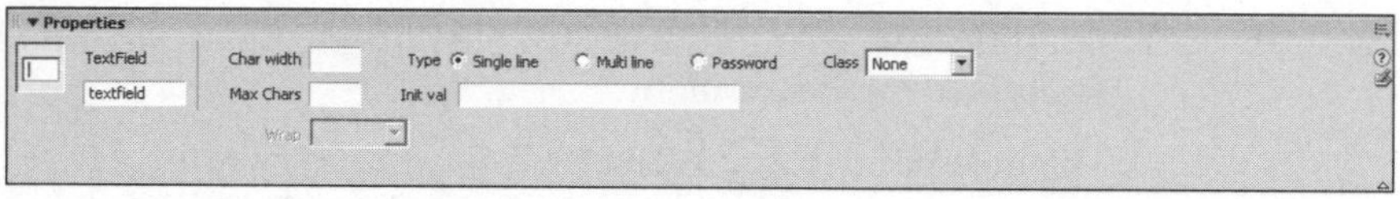

Figure 1-6:
Every form
element has
properties.

12. **In the Properties inspector, type a name in the name text box.**

The default name for a form object is its actual name, which is appended by a number if there is more than one in a document. In this case, we're renaming a text field, which has a default name of TextField. Each form element must have a unique name. Names cannot contain spaces. Choose a logical name that reflects the type of information users will enter in the field. For example, if the text field requires the user to enter his first name, a logical name for the text field is `firstName` or `first_name`.

13. **Enter the other parameters for the text field you're creating.**

- *Type:* Sets the type of text field that will be displayed on the Web page. Choose Single Line to display the text field as a single line in the document, or choose Multi Line to display a text box in which users can type more than one line of text. Or, you can choose Password, which displays each character as an asterisk or filled-in circle to preserve the anonymity of the user's password.

- *Char Width:* Sets the maximum number of characters that can be displayed in the field. This number can be less than Max Chars, which specifies the maximum number of characters that can be entered in the field. The default value is 20.

- *Max Chars:* Specifies the maximum number of characters that can be entered in the field. You can use this parameter to limit the number of characters for a zip code field to five. In some browsers, an alert sounds if a user enters more than the Max Chars value.

- *Num Lines:* Becomes available if you specify Multi Line as the Type. This value determines the height of the text box, in lines.

- *Wrap:* Becomes available if you specify Multi Line as the Type. Choose Off or Default to prevent the text from wrapping to the next line. Virtual wraps the text to a new line when the user enters enough text to exceed the width of the text field — but doesn't wrap the text when the data is sent. Physical wraps the text to a new line when the user enters enough text to exceed the width of the text field *and* wraps the text when the data is submitted.

- *Init Val:* Displays an initial value in the text field when the form loads. This parameter is useful for displaying instructions to the user. The user then selects the text and types the desired information into the field.

- *Class:* Lets you stylize the text entered in the text field using a style from the document or an attached CSS.

14. Add other form fields as needed.

If you've got a complex form with multiple fields, create a table and then add each element to the desired cell. This creates a good looking form that is easy to use.

15. For the purpose of this demonstration, choose Insert⇨Form⇨Button to begin creating a button.

The Input Tag Accessibility Attributes dialog box, which you use in Step 9 of this list, appears.

16. Enter the desired information in the Input Tag Accessibility Attributes dialog box and click OK.

Dreamweaver adds the button to the document.

17. In the Properties inspector, click the Submit Form radio button to select an Action.

While you're in the Properties inspector, you can modify other attributes of the button. (See Figure 1-7.) For example, you can change the text displayed on the button by entering new text in the Value field. You can also apply a style to the button by choosing an option from the Class drop-down menu. The items on the Class menu are from styles defined within the document or within an attached style sheet.

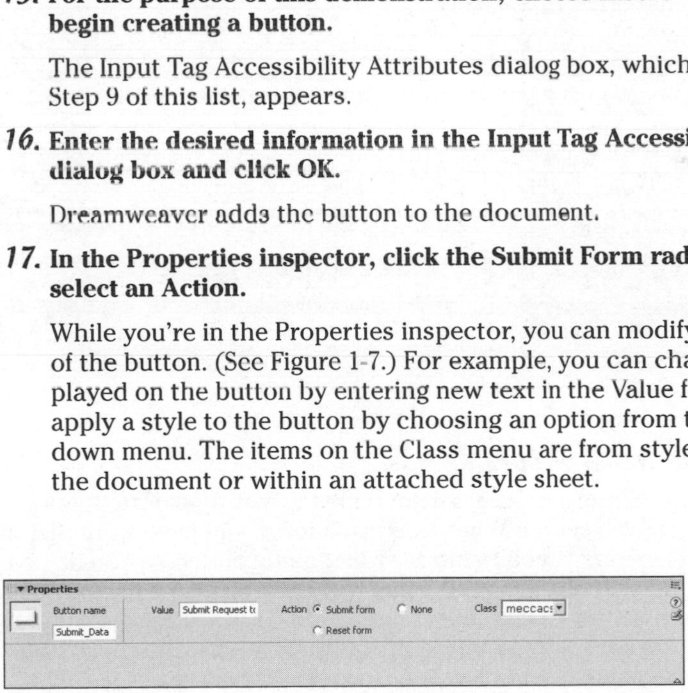

**Book VI
Chapter 1**

**Adding Basic
Interactivity**

Figure 1-7:
Setting
properties
for a Submit
button.

18. **Accept the default name for the button (Submit), or in the Properties inspector, enter a different name.**

Select the default name in the Value field, and type the desired name.

19. **Repeat Step 16, only this time use the Properties inspector to define a Reset button. In the Action area, click the Reset Form radio button.**

Figure 1-8 shows a form with several text fields and a Submit button, as displayed in the Firefox Web browser.

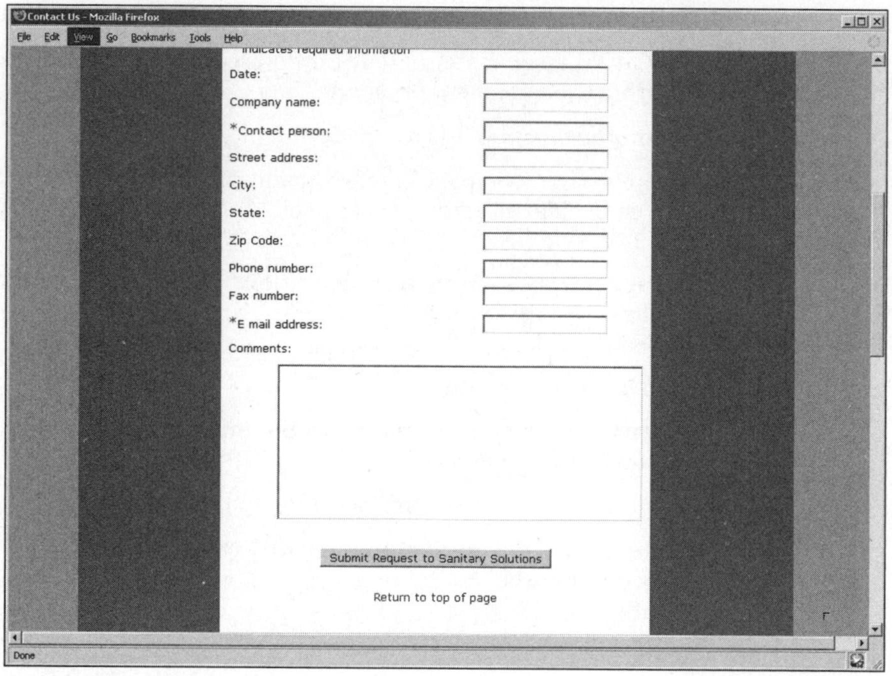

Figure 1-8: Previewing the completed form.

Testing the form

After creating a form, it's a good idea to test it prior to uploading it to your client's Web server. When you test a form, you make sure that all of the fields and elements in your form are functioning perfectly. You do so by entering data in each text field and using the other elements in your form, such as radio buttons, check boxes, and list boxes. Click the Submit button to make sure the data is transmitted properly. Depending on the action, this might require being online or using a local testing server.

Adding Elements to Your Form

It would be difficult to get the job done if the only form elements available were the text field and button. Fortunately, that's not the case. You can flesh out a form by adding check boxes, radio buttons, and list boxes. And then there are form elements that are so shy, they stay in hiding.

Password fields

If you're creating a form that requires a user to submit confidential information, such as a password to a Web site, you can preserve the anonymity of the information by creating a text field in the form and assigning Password to the Type parameter (in the Properties inspector) of the Text Field form object. Listing 1-1 shows the code for a password text field.

Book VI
Chapter 1

Adding Basic
Interactivity

Listing 1-1: A Password Text Field

```
<input name="Password" type="password" id="Password"
    size="20" maxlength="20" />
```

Creating a password field is identical to creating a text field, except you choose Password as the field type. If you're creating a password field in Dreamweaver, choose Insert➪Form➪TextField and then choose the Password option in the Type section of the Properties inspector. (See Figure 1-9.) When information is entered in the password field, it appears as asterisks or filled-in circles on the computer monitor.

If you're creating a form that requires a user to submit confidential information, such as a password to a Web site, you want to preserve the anonymity of the information. If you specify a field in your form as a password field, you can prompt users' Web browsers to replace each character they type with an asterisk or filled-in circle.

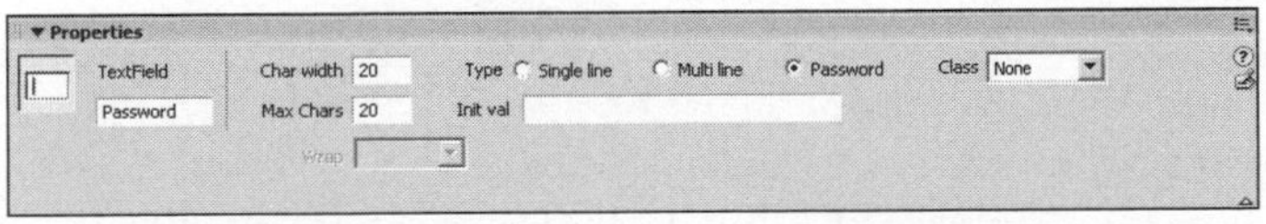

Figure 1-9:
Choosing the Password option for a text field.

Hidden fields

Hidden fields are very useful form elements. They contain information that is pertinent to the form, such as the form method, but they don't need to be seen by the person filling in the form — hence the name. When you add a hidden field to a form, you add pertinent information to the form. A hidden field has a name that indicates the purpose of the hidden field. Listing 1-2 shows the first few lines of code for a form used on a caterer's Web site.

Listing 1-2: A Form with Hidden Fields

```
<form method="post"
    action="http://www.myhypotheticalcateringsite.com/cgi-
    bin/webform.cgi">
<input type="hidden" name="recipient" value="paul@
    myhypotheticalcateringsite.com">
<input type="hidden" name="redirect" value="http://
    myhypotheticalcateringsite.com/thankYou.htm">
<input type="hidden" name="subject" value="Catering
    Questionnaire">
```

The form is used in conjunction with a mail-forwarding script on the site's Web server. Typically, scripts reside in the site's cgi-bin folder. The script calls for the recipient's e-mail address. This is stored in the first hidden field. The script also redirects the visitor to another page after submitting the form. This information is stored in the second hidden field. The third hidden field contains the subject that appears in the e-mail that is sent to the recipient.

If you use an application like Dreamweaver, you don't have to write all the code. In Dreamweaver, choose Insert⇨Form⇨Hidden Field and the Tag Editor - Input dialog box, shown in Figure 1-10, appears. All you need to do is fill in the blanks, and Dreamweaver writes the code for you.

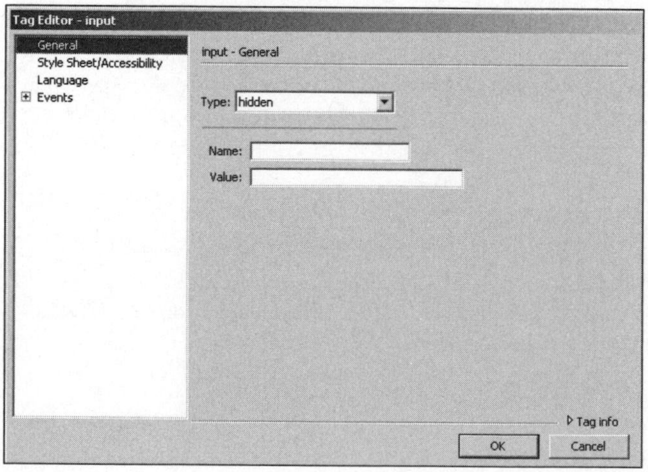

Figure 1-10: Adding a hidden field to a document.

Textarea form objects

Extra, extra, tell us all about it in a big-ol' text box. If your client wants a space in a form for his visitors to leave copious amounts of information, a text box, also known as a *text area,* is the ideal solution. You can specify the width of the text box and the number of lines in the text box, which in essence, sets the width and height of the text box. You can create a text box that is 80 characters wide and 15 lines tall by adding the code in Listing 1-3 to your form.

Listing 1-3: Code to Add a Text Area to a Form

```
<textarea name="textarea" cols="80" rows="15"
    wrap="physical"></textarea>
```

If you use Dreamweaver to create your Web pages, the solution is much simpler than writing out the code yourself. Choose Insert⟿Form⟿Textarea. After you add the field to the document, specify the following parameters in the Properties inspector:

✦ **Char Width:** Sets the maximum number of characters that can be displayed in the field. This number can be less than Max Chars, which specifies the maximum number of characters that can be entered in the field. The default value is 20.

✦ **Wrap:** Becomes available if you specify Multi Line as the Type. Choose Off or Default to prevent the text from wrapping to the next line. Virtual wraps the text to a new line when the user enters enough text to exceed the width of the text field — but doesn't wrap the text when the data is sent. Physical wraps the text to a new line when the user enters enough text to exceed the width of the text field *and* wraps the text when the data is submitted.

✦ **Init Val:** Displays an initial value in the field when the form loads. This parameter is useful for displaying instructions to the user. The user then selects the text and types the desired information into the field.

✦ **Class:** Lets you stylize the text entered in the text field using a style from the document or an attached CSS.

A text box has a scroll bar that enables the user to scroll up or down if the entered text exceeds the text area. Figure 1-11 shows a text field in a form with the scroll bars on full alert.

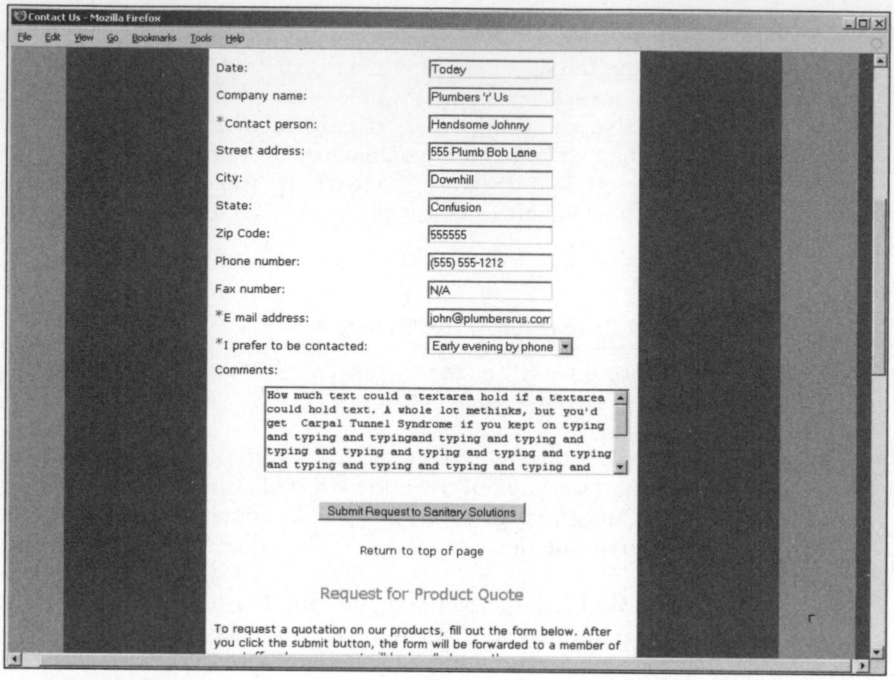

Figure 1-11:
Fill the Comments text box to overflow and a scroll bar appears.

Multiple choice types (check box and radio)

As a rule, people like it when you give them the opportunity to make a choice. Visitors to Web sites like choices, too; that's why some Web genius invented the navigation menu. But we're straying from the topic at hand, which is forms. When you want Web visitors to make a choice, they can easily do so by clicking a check box or radio button. The value for the form element is transmitted with the form data.

Check boxes: <input type="checkbox">

When you add a check box to a form, you give the visitor an option of making a choice by clicking the check box. This is an efficient way of laying out a form when you require multiple responses to a question. You add the question to the form, and then list the answers, with a check box next to each answer. The value for the check box tells the form recipient what the visitor's answer or choice is. Listing 1-4 shows the code needed to add several check boxes to a form with a multiple choice question.

Listing 1-4: Check Off, Check On!

```
<tr>
        <td colspan="7" valign="top"><div align="left">Will you require any
of the following services? Check all that apply? </div></td>
```

```
                    </tr>
                    <tr>
                      <td colspan="7" valign="top"><div align="left">
                        <table width="100%" border="0" cellspacing="0"
cellpadding="5">
                          <tr>
                            <td width="35%">Bar/Liquor</td>
                            <td width="6%"><input name="bar/Liquor"
type="checkbox" id="bar/Liquor" value="Bar_Liquor"></td>
                            <td width="49%">Expresso/Cappuccino bar </td>
                            <td width="10%"><input name="Serving_Equipment"
type="checkbox" id="Serving_Equipment" value="Expresso_Cappuccino"></td>
                          </tr>
```

If you use Dreamweaver to create your HTML forms, you add a check box to a document by choosing Insert⇨Form⇨Checkbox. After you add the element to the form, you set the parameters in the Properties inspector. Check boxes have the following parameter choices:

✦ **Checkbox Name:** By default, Dreamweaver assigns the name checkbox, followed by a number if you add more than one to a form. Unless I'm working on a drop-dead simple form with less than four check boxes, I rename the check box to something more descriptive. Each check box must have a unique name and cannot contain spaces or special characters.

✦ **Checked Value:** This is the value that will be transmitted when the form is sent. In other words, the answer to your question or the choice, depending on the type of form you're designing.

✦ **Initial State:** Determines whether the check box is selected when the form loads in the user's browser.

✦ **Dynamic:** Lets the server dynamically determine the initial state of the check box. For example, you can use a check box to visually display information stored in a database record. When the page loads, the server plucks the information from the database and fills in the check box if applicable. This option is only applicable if your document was created using one of the options from the Dynamic Page category.

✦ **Class:** Lets you apply a class from a CSS style sheet to the check box.

Radio buttons: <input type="radio">

Radio buttons are another option when you want users to make only one choice — for example, when you want the site visitor to choose which method should be used to reply to his query. You'd set up a group of radio buttons with the input name of Response. The values would be: Email, Phone, Fax, and so on. The user would be limited to one choice from the group as they all have the same input name. A radio button looks like a round dimple in the document that gets filled with black (or another color if you play with CSS styles) when the user clicks the radio button, instead of a square that gets filled with a check. But the button doesn't tune into anything. Where they came up with the name *radio button* is beyond me. Listing 1-5 shows the code for inserting a radio button in a form.

Listing 1-5: You Can Tune a Radio, but You Can't Tune a Radio Button

```
<input name="CreditCard" type="radio" value="Master Card" />
```

If you use Dreamweaver to create your HTML forms, you add a radio button to a document by choosing Insert⇨Form⇨Radio Button. After you add the element to the form, you set the parameters in the Properties inspector. Radio buttons have the following parameter choices:

✦ **Radio Button:** By default, Dreamweaver assigns the name `radiobutton`, followed by a number if you've got more than one in your form. Unless I'm working on a drop-dead simple form, I rename the radio button to something more descriptive. When you want to restrict a visitor to only one choice from a group, all buttons will have the same name and the Checked Value will be different.

✦ **Checked Value:** This is the value that will be transmitted when the form is sent. In other words, the visitor's choice.

✦ **Initial State:** Determines whether the radio button is selected or not when the form loads in the user's browser.

✦ **Dynamic:** Lets the server dynamically determine the initial state of the radio button. For example, you can use a radio button to visually display information stored in a database record. When the page loads, the server plucks the information from the database and fills in the radio button, if applicable. This option is applicable only if your document was created using one of the options from the Dynamic Page category.

✦ **Class:** Lets you apply a class from a CSS style sheet to the radio button.

Radio groups

If you want to limit visitors to one choice, you insert a group of radio buttons. The buttons all have the same input name, but have different values. Therefore a user can select only one radio button per group to be submitted with the form. Listing 1-6 shows the code for a group of radio buttons, neatly housed in a table. Notice the name of each button is the same.

Listing 1-6: No Multiple Choice For You!

```
<table width="200">
   <tr>
      <td><label>
<input type="radio" name="CreditCard" value="Visa" />
Visa</label></td>
   </tr>
   <tr>
      <td><label>
         <input type="radio" name="CreditCard" value="Master
   Card" />
         Master Card</label></td>
   </tr>
   <tr>
      <td><label>
         <input type="radio" name="CreditCard"
   value="American Express" />
         American Express</label></td>
   </tr>
   <tr>
      <td><label>
         <input type="radio" name="CreditCard"
   value="Discover" />
         Discover</label></td>
   </tr>
</table>
```

If you use Dreamweaver to create your HTML forms, you can easily insert a radio group as follows:

1. **Open an existing document in Dreamweaver and position your cursor where you want the radio group to appear.**

2. **Choose Insert⇨Form⇨Radio Group.**

The Radio Group dialog box appears. (See Figure 1-12.)

Figure 1-12:
Look, it's a
radio group.

3. **Change the default Name of the radio group.**

   It's always a good idea to give an object a name that makes sense. But there is one rule: no spaces and no special characters in the name.

4. **Rename each Label and Value.**

   The Label is what users will see, whereas the Value is what will be transmitted with the data. If, for example, the group is a list of credit cards, you'd name one Label and Value `Visa`, another Label and Value `Mastercard`. You have two buttons in the group, by default.

5. **Click the plus sign (+) button to add additional buttons to the group.**

6. **Rename the Label and Value of the new buttons.**

   At this stage, you probably want the buttons to appear in alphabetical order.

7. **To change the order in which the buttons appear, click the button label and then click the ↑ or ↓ to rearrange the list.**

8. **Determine how the buttons will be displayed and click the applicable Lay Out Using radio button to lay out the buttons with line breaks or in a table.**

9. **Click OK.**

   Look Ma, I created a radio group without writing any code!

Drop-down lists

Drop-down lists are cool. They take up one little slot on your Web page, but click the little down arrow and a list of choices appears. You can use drop-down lists anywhere in a form where you need to give the visitor lots of choices but don't want to waste a lot of real estate doing it.

When you create a drop-down list, you can enable the user to select multiple items. Listing 1-7 shows the code needed to create a drop-down list. Notice the lines of code that start with `<option value=`. These are the choices on the drop-down list.

Listing 1-7: Code for a Drop-Dead Gorgeous Drop-Down List

```
<select name="select" size="1">
<option value="Select one please.">Select one
    please.</option>
<option value="By  phone">Mid-morning by phone</option>
<option value="Mid-afternoon by phone">Mid-afternoon
                        by phone</option>
<option value="Early evening by phone">Early evening
                        by phone</option>
```

```
<option value="By fax">By fax</option>
<option value="By E-mail">By E-mail</option>
<option value="By mail">By mail</option>
</select>
```

You can write out your own code, but if you've read this chapter from the start, you know there's a better way to build this mousetrap in Dreamweaver. Here's how you do it:

1. **Open an existing document in Dreamweaver and position your cursor where you want the drop-down list to appear.**

2. **Choose Insert⇨Form⇨List/Menu.**

A drop-down list is born.

3. **In the Properties inspector, click the List Values button.**

The List Values dialog box appears. Your cursor is hovering in the Label position, signifying that the dialog box is ready for you to do your thing.

4. **Type the name for the first Label.**

This is what visitors will see in your drop-down list. You have the option of displaying an initial value. This is a great way for you to tell visitors what you want them to do.

5. **Press the Tab key and type a name for the Value.**

6. **Click the plus sign (+) button to add another option to the list.**

Yep, you guessed it. You've got to type another value for the Label and Value. Figure 1-13 shows a drop-down list under construction.

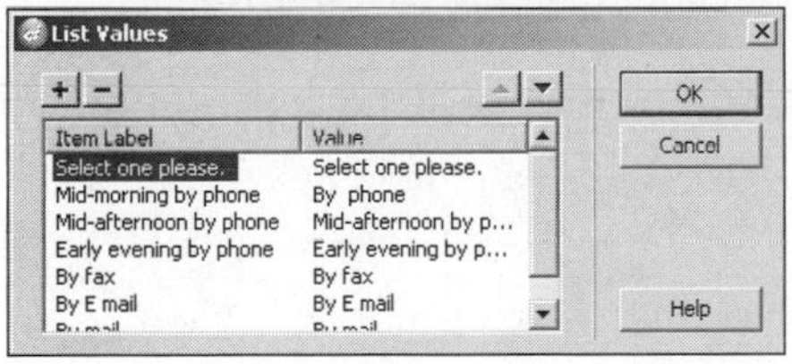

Figure 1-13:
This List
Values
dialog box is
filled with
choices.

7. **Click the Item Label of a button and then click the ↑ or ↓ to rearrange the order in which buttons appear in the list.**

8. **Click OK.**

Dreamweaver inserts the drop-down list in your form.

9. **In the Properties inspector, choose the rest of your options. (See Figure 1-14.)**

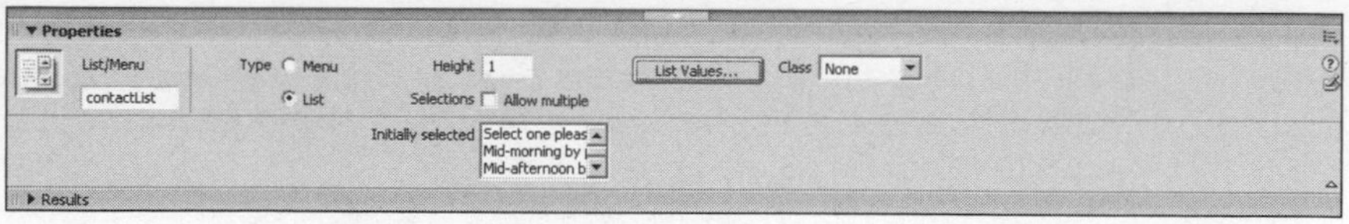

Figure 1-14:
Choosing options for the drop-down list.

- Enter a name for the list in the text field in the upper-left corner of the Properties inspector. Dreamweaver gives the list a default name, such as `select`. It's considered good practice to give the object a name that reflects what it does in the document. The name can't contain spaces or special characters.

- Click the option you'd like displayed when the list loads from the Initially Selected window. If you don't choose an option, the drop-down list window is blank.

- Click the Allow Multiple check box if you want viewers to be able to select multiple items from the list. To select multiple items, viewers must hold down Ctrl (Windows) or ⌘ (Macintosh) while clicking.

- In the Type area, click the List radio button to have the form object function as a drop-down list, or click Menu to have the form object function as a jump menu. Of course, if you choose Menu, your values have to be URLs to the pages you want to open when users click the labels. If you choose Menu, the option to allow multiple selections is grayed out, which is logical because even the best multitasker can't navigate to more than one page at a time.

You can add other elements to a form by choosing Form➪Insert and choosing an option from the submenu, including the following:

✦ **Image Field:** Enables you to insert an image in a form.

✦ **File Field:** Inserts a Browse button and field in a form. (You see this type of field on a form that wants you to attach a file saved on your hard drive.)

✦ **Fieldset:** Add a border around data.

✦ **Label:** Enables you to insert label tags in your form. When you add this option, the split workspace appears. In the Code section of the workspace, you enter the name for the label between the tags.

Event handlers and JavaScript

When you add JavaScript to the body of a document, you need to specify when the code is executed. For example, you've probably visited more than one Web site where one of those annoying pop-ups appeared before all of the page content loaded. The designer was responsible for that piece of magic by using the onload event handler. An *event handler* tells the Web browser when to execute *(handle)* the code. But there's more than just knowing which event handler to use when creating a script. You've got to know which browser your client's intended audience is using. That's right — the browser wars come into play because different browsers have different event handlers. When you work in Dreamweaver and use Behaviors, you can choose the browser used by the intended audience from the Show Events For drop-down menu. Listing 1-8 shows code to open a Web page in another browser window. The code refers to a JavaScript function "MM_openBrWindow" that is in the head of the document. The onload event handler instructs the browser to execute the function when the page loads.

Listing 1-8: You Will Open a New Window onLoad

```
<body
    onLoad="MM_openBrWindow('http://www.dasdesigns.net/blog','
    ','scrollbars=yes,width=640,height=480')">
```

The onLoad event handler has other purposes. For example, the event handler is used to load all images used in the page as soon as the page loads. This makes it possible for images that appear when a user pauses his cursor over an image to appear immediately because they've already been loaded into the host computer's memory. Here is a list, with descriptions, of a few more event handlers:

✦ onBlur Code executes when a text field loses focus. A text field *gains focus* when a user clicks inside the text box, and it *loses focus* when the user clicks outside of the text box. A common use for this event handler is to display a message if a user clicks inside a text box and then outside the text box without entering data.

✦ onClick Code executes when a user clicks the left mouse button on an object. For example, you can write code to redirect a user to a Thank You page when the users clicks a form's Submit button.

✦ onDblClick Code executes when a user double-clicks the left mouse button on an object.

✦ onError Code executes when a JavaScript error occurs. Developers often use this event handler with code that displays an error dialog box or suppresses all JavaScript errors in the document.

✦ onFocus Code executes when a text field *gains focus* (when a user clicks inside the text box). Code with this event handler can be used to display a dialog box with instructions on what information to enter into a form when the first text field in the form gains focus.

✦ onKeyDown   Code executes when a user presses a key.

✦ onKeyPress   Code executes when a user presses and holds a key.

✦ onKeyUp   Code executes when a user presses and then releases a key.

✦ onMouseDown   Code executes on the down stroke of a left mouse button click.

✦ onMouseMove   Code executes whenever the user moves his mouse.

✦ onMouseOut   Code executes when a user moves his mouse over and then out of a specified object on the page. In other words, the object gained and then lost focus.

✦ onMouseOver   Code executes when a user pauses his cursor over active text or an object.

✦ OnMouseUp   Code executes when the user releases the left mouse button.

✦ onUnload   Code executes when a user leaves a page. If you've ever seen a window pop up when you navigate to another Web page, you've been a victim of a script with an onUnload event handler. These are almost as annoying as pop-up windows that occur when a page loads.

Making dynamic pages with server side technology

Every single section in this chapter — with the exception of this one — concerns code that is interpreted by the client, who is the visitor to the wonderful page you created for your wonderful client. But some Web technology requires server side technology to decipher your code. We describe two prime examples of pages that require server side technology to decipher in the list that follows.

✦ **ASP (Active Server Pages):** ASP is Microsoft's server side technology for generating Web page content on the fly. When you create a Web page with ASP code, you can simplify the process by using built-in objects. ASP has six built-in objects:

- *Application*

- *ASPError*

- *Request*

- *Response*

- *Server*

- *Session*

ASP pages are generated on-the-fly, using software on the server. The page delivers information based on how the user interacts with the page. ASP code is often used to deliver information from a database. For example, you can design a Web page to display contact information from a database of members. The page visitor can then search for members in a certain zip code, and the ASP code causes the page to display members in that zip code.

The default script language for ASP is VBScript. ASP is designed to run on a Windows server. However, other servers might have software that will interpret ASP pages. When in doubt, check with your Web hosting service.

To create ASP pages, you should read a book devoted to the subject. Chapter 2 of this minibook, however, introduces you to the kiddy side of the ASP pool.

✦ **PHP (PHP HyperText Processor):** PHP is an alternative for ASP pages. Most Web hosting services have the software to interpret PHP code. Blog applications rely heavily on PHP code. PHP runs on different platforms and is compatible with most Web servers. PHP supports many databases. In fact, most blog applications use a combination of PHP with a MySQL database. PHP syntax is similar to PERL and C programming languages.

Dipping your toe into the shallow end of the PHP pool requires only that you read Chapter 3 of this minibook.

Chapter 2: An Introduction to ASP

In This Chapter

✓ **What is ASP?**

✓ **Running ASP on your computer**

✓ **Installing the IIS**

✓ **Introducing ASP scripting**

✓ **Rotating images and ad banners**

The thought of writing code sends a shiver down the spine of many Web designers, including yours truly. However, at times you have to buck up and actually dive into the deep end of the pool to satisfy a client. *ASP* (Active Server Pages) is code that is parsed by the server, therefore it's known as *server-side technology*. ASP pages can change on-the-fly to suit the need of the site visitor. One prime example of ASP pages is plucking information from a database and then serving it up to the client (the Web site visitor). The client submits the request to the server, which can be in the form of a query. The server responds to the query, writes the page, and sends it back to the client. With a fast server, the transaction is seamless. While this miniscule chapter is by no means a substitute for the heady subject of creating ASP pages, it shows you enough to know whether you want to venture further or put a clove of garlic on a piece of string and wave it in front of any client that says, "Oh by the way, do you do ASP?"

Understanding ASP

ASP is the brainchild of Microsoft, the same people who brought you Windows Me. Okay, Windows Me was a bust, but ASP isn't. ASP can do a lot of things that HTML could never even dream of. If you're going to create ASP pages for a client, you must run them on a Windows server. You can create ASP pages in Dreamweaver or any good HTML editing application.

An ASP page shares many attributes with an HTML page. The page consists of tags, text, and images. But where ASP pages differ is when interactivity is needed. In order to obtain the interactivity, you add scripts to the page. You can write scripts using the VBScript or JavaScript language. ASP pages have the `.asp` extension. When a visitor accesses an ASP page, the server hands off the page to IIS (Internet Information Services), an application that reads each line of the ASP page and returns the results as an HTML page to the visitor's browser. Using ASP pages has several advantages, including that you can

✦ Dynamically change or add to the content of a Web page.

✦ Respond to visitor queries or data submitted from HTML forms.

✦ Access any data or databases and return the results to the visitor's browser.

✦ Customize a Web page to make it personal for individual users.

✦ Quickly learn ASP script, which executes faster than CGI and Perl.

✦ Gain security because visitors can't view your ASP source code from the browser.

✦ Have your ASP files viewable in any browser because they're returned as plain HTML.

✦ Cut down on network traffic with clever ASP programming.

Creating ASP pages is made easier due to seven, built-in IIS objects. The objects are grouped based on the functions they perform. The IIS objects used within ASP pages are

✦ **ASPError:** Objects that give detailed information when an error occurs.

✦ **ObjectContext:** Objects that are used to control ASP transactions, which are managed by the Microsoft Transaction Server (MTS).

✦ **Request:** Objects that get information from the user.

✦ **Response:** Objects that send information to the user.

✦ **Server:** Objects that control the Internet Information Server.

✦ **Session:** Objects that store information about, and change settings based on information gathered during, the user's current Web-server session.

✦ **Application:** Objects that share application-level information and control settings for the lifetime of the application.

You might be familiar with objects if you've ever delved into an Object Oriented Programming language such as ActionScript. Each object can perform a set of functions, and each object has methods and properties. For example, the `Response` object has a method known as `Write` that displays information for the user.

Creating ASP Pages and Testing Them on Your Local System

It might seem like a case of the blatantly obvious, but ASP pages have the .asp extension. You can write ASP pages in a word processing application like Windows Notepad. However, most designers prefer the safety net of an HTML editing application like Dreamweaver. In Dreamweaver, you don't have to write all of the code, and the application can help you in some instances. You can write the pages with Dreamweaver, but you'll need another application (such as ISS) installed on your system to test the pages.

Working with IIS

ASP pages need IIS (Internet Information Server) to process ASP pages and return them as HTML pages. In order to test ASP documents on your local machine, you need to install IIS, which functions as a Web server. IIS is included with Windows XP Professional, and you can install it as follows:

1. **Insert the Windows XP Professional CD into your CD-ROM drive.**

2. **Choose Start⇨Settings⇨Control Panel.**

3. **In the Control Panel window, click Add/Remove Programs.**

4. **In the Add/Remove window, click Add/Remove Windows Components.**

The Windows Components Wizard appears. (See Figure 2-1.)

5. **Click the Internet Information Services (IIS) check box and then click Next.**

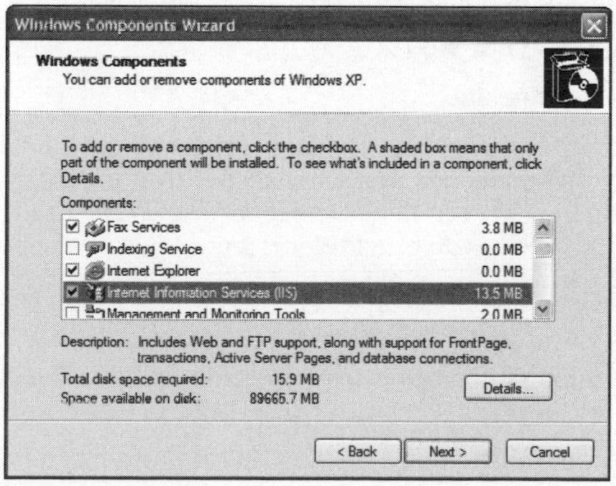

Figure 2-1:
Installing
the IIS.

Windows installs the IIS on your system. This process takes a few minutes, but Windows entertains you with a progress bar while the application is installed. When the installation is complete, Windows displays a message telling you that the component has successfully installed.

6. **Click Finish.**

IIS is installed on your system.

Setting up the Web site

After successfully installing IIS on your computer, you're ready to start creating ASP pages. But you can't create the pages in just any folder on your computer. You've got to set them up in a special folder, which is the equivalent of a Web server. To set up your Web site:

1. **Navigate to C:\Inetpub\wwwroot.**

2. **Right-click and choose New⇨Folder from the shortcut menu.**

Windows creates a new folder.

3. **Name the folder.**

Defining the site in Dreamweaver

After you create the folder, you're almost ready to start creating pages in Dreamweaver. But as mentioned previously, ASP pages don't work without a local server. Before you can create a little ASP magic in Dreamweaver, you've got to tell the application where the local server is. You do that when you define the site as follows:

1. **Choose Site⇨New Site.**

The Site Definition dialog box appears.

2. **Enter the name of your site.**

3. **Enter the URL of the site.**

So you might be thinking, "The site is on my local machine; how do I enter a URL?" The answer is that when a site is on a local machine, the machine is the host server, hence the name *localhost*. The URL for a site named mysite in the wwwroot folder is http://localhost/mysite/. (See Figure 2-2.)

4. **Click Next.**

The Site Definition dialog box refreshes, and you have the option to specify a testing server.

5. **Select the Yes, I Want to Use a Server Technology radio button.**

The Site Definition dialog box does its chameleon thing and adopts a new guise.

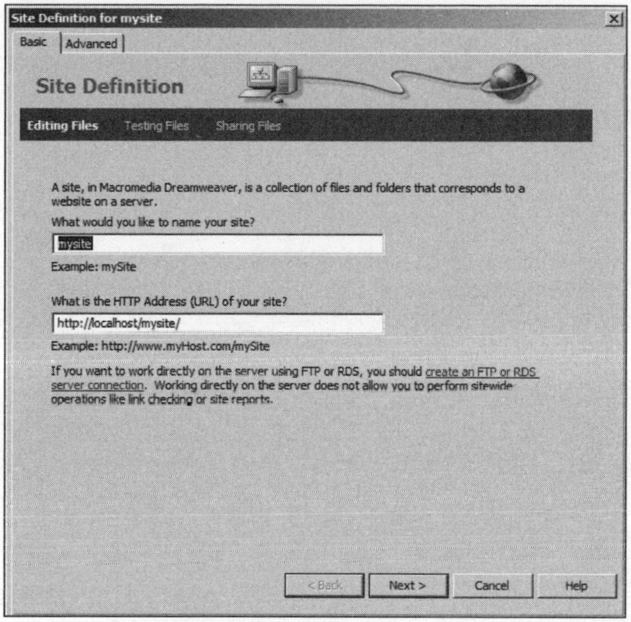

Figure 2-2:
But my sites
are always
well
defined.

6. **Choose an option from the server technology drop-down menu.**

Choose the applicable ASP server technology. (See Figure 2-3.) The upcoming examples will be VBScript. If your code will be VBScript, your choice would be ASP VBScript.

7. **Click Next.**

The Site Definition dialog box dons another disguise; this time you get the option of choosing how you will test your files. (See Figure 2-4.)

8. **Accept the default option to test on your local machine. Verify that the folder where you store your files is correct.**

9. **Click Next.**

The dialog box reconfigures, giving you the option to specify the `root` URL of your site. This should already be filled in. (See Figure 2-5.)

10. **Click the Test URL button.**

Dreamweaver runs a test to ensure that the application can test ASP files on the specified folder. If the test is successful, Dreamweaver displays a dialog box informing you that the test is successful.

11. **Click OK to close the Macromedia Dreamweaver dialog box and then click Next.**

The dialog box reconfigures and gives you the option of copying the files to another machine when you're finished editing.

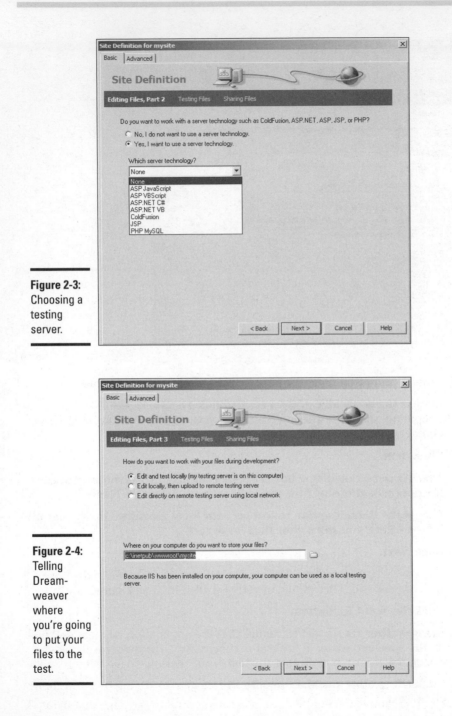

Figure 2-3: Choosing a testing server.

Figure 2-4: Telling Dream-weaver where you're going to put your files to the test.

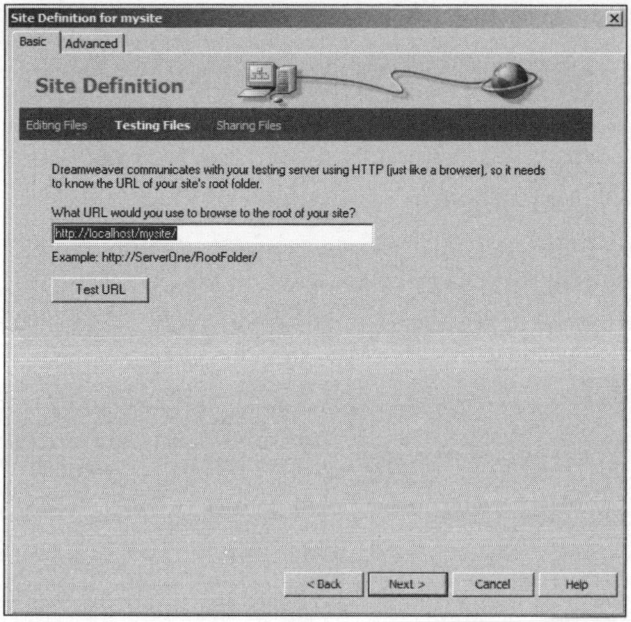

Figure 2-5:
Specifying
the root URL
of your site.

12. **Accept the default option of No and then click Next.**

The Site Definition dialog box reconfigures and shows a summary of the setup. If anything is incorrect, click the Back button to navigate to the page that contains the parameters you need to change.

13. **Click Done.**

The dialog box closes and you're ready to venture into the wild and wonderful world of ASP.

If you ever test an ASP page and you don't get the results you're expecting, make sure IIS is running. You can check this by opening the Administrative Tools section of the Windows Control panel. Open the Services section and double-click the World Wide Web Publishing icon. If the Status reads Stopped, click the Start button to enable IIS.

Creating ASP Pages in Dreamweaver

After you install IIS, set up a Web folder, and define the site in Dreamweaver, you're ready to begin creating pages. An ASP page looks a lot like HTML; it has images, text, HTML tags, and so on. Where the ASP magic comes into play is when you use ASP objects and create scripts in the page that define how the page looks after IIS reads the code. Sometimes, you've got only a few lines of script; other times, you've got a lot. If half of your page is script, you could say the page is half-ASP. At any rate, it's time to create an ASP page in Dreamweaver.

1. **Choose File⇨New.**

   The New Document dialog box appears.

2. **Choose Dynamic Page from the Category column and ASP VBScript from the Dynamic Page column.**

   These are the options you need when creating ASP pages with the VBScript language.

3. **Click Create.**

   Dreamweaver creates a new document that is ready to receive your VBScript.

4. **Click the Code button.**

   Dreamweaver switches to Code view.

5. **Position your cursor after the `<body>` tag and press Enter.**

   Dreamweaver creates a new line.

6. **Enter the following code:**

   ```
   <%
   Response.Write("Hello World")
   %>
   ```

7. **Press F12.**

   Dreamweaver prompts you to save the document. After you save the document, Dreamweaver displays the page in your default browser. You should see the words `Hello World`.

Although it doesn't look very impressive, you've changed the Web page based on the instructions you included between the `<%` and `%>` tags. The code uses the `Write` method of the `Response` object to display the information between the opening and closing parentheses. The information is enclosed with quotation marks, which designates that it is a text string. In fact, you might have noticed Dreamweaver displays a tooltip that says `Write(string)` after you type the opening parentheses.

You can also format text by adding HTML tags. Change the code in Step 6 to the following:

```
<%
Response.Write("<h2>Hello World</h2>")
%>
```

Figure 2-6 shows the text with the <h2> tags applied.

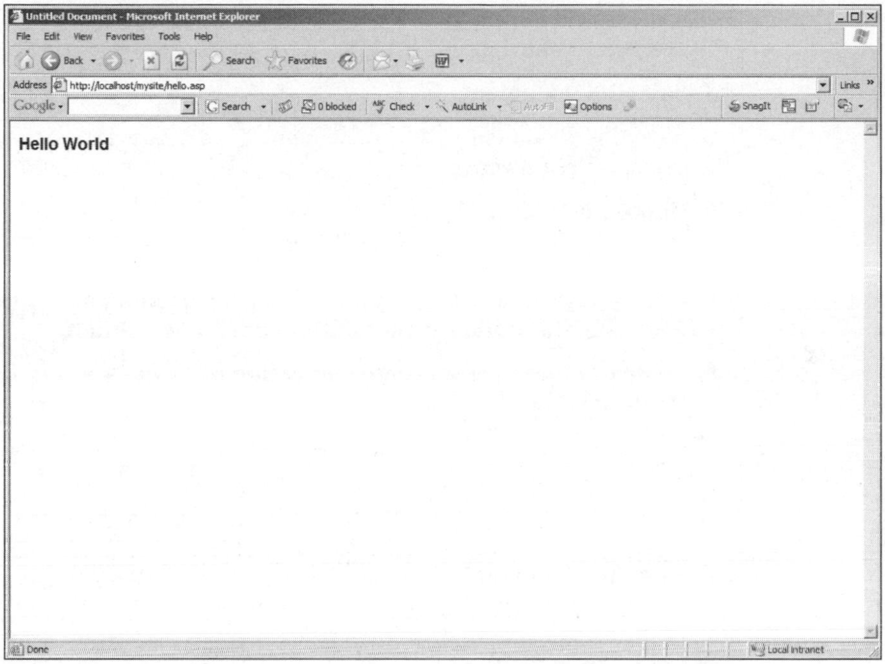

Figure 2-6:
Format text
with HTML
tags.

Using variables

Variables store information. It's kind of like giving a Web browser a brain. When you incorporate variables on your ASP pages, you can store and dispense information. Also, you can use variables to store information entered in forms and display them on an ASP page. The steps that follow show you how to create a form that collects user information and then displays it on another page. To explore the power of variables, launch Dreamweaver and then do this:

1. **Create a new HTML document.**

That's right, the form you use to collect the information is an HTML document.

2. **Switch to Code view, create a new line after the <body> tag, and enter the following:**

```
<form method="GET" action="welcome.asp">
First Name: <input type="text" name="fname" />
<br />
Last Name: <input type="text" name="lname" />
<br /><br />
<input type="submit" value="Submit" />
</form>
```

The code you enter creates a simple form that collects the visitor's first and last name. The form action opens another document, `"welcome.asp"`, when the site visitor clicks the Submit button. The `form` method, `get`, makes the information available to other documents. The variables are `fname` and `lname`.

3. **Save the document.**

   Save the document with the file name `form.htm`. Leave the document open in Dreamweaver.

4. **Choose File⇨New.**

   Dreamweaver displays the New Document dialog box.

5. **Choose Dynamic Page from the Category section, and then choose the ASP VBScript option from the Dynamic Page column.**

6. **Switch to Code view, create a new line after the `<body>` tag, and enter the following:**

   ```
   Welcome
   <%
   Response.Write(Request.QueryString("fname"))
   Response.Write(" " & Request.QueryString("lname"))
   %>
   ```

7. **Save the document.**

   Save the document as `welcome.asp`.

8. **Click the form.htm tab.**

   Each open document in Dreamweaver has its own tab.

9. **Press F12.**

   Dreamweaver opens the document in your default browser. If you entered your code correctly, your browser should show the form shown in Figure 2-7.

10. **Fill in the form and click Submit.**

    The form action calls the ASP page, which uses the variables from the form to greet the visitor. (See Figure 2-8.)

Before moving on, you need to know a bit more about the code used in the ASP page. The code is using the `write` method of the `Response` object to greet the visitor. The code is using the `QueryString` property of the `Request` object to pluck the information from the variables `fname` and `lname`. But there's yet another method to interact with a form, and that's using the `POST` method. When you use the `POST` method, the information from the form isn't displayed in the address window of the user's browser.

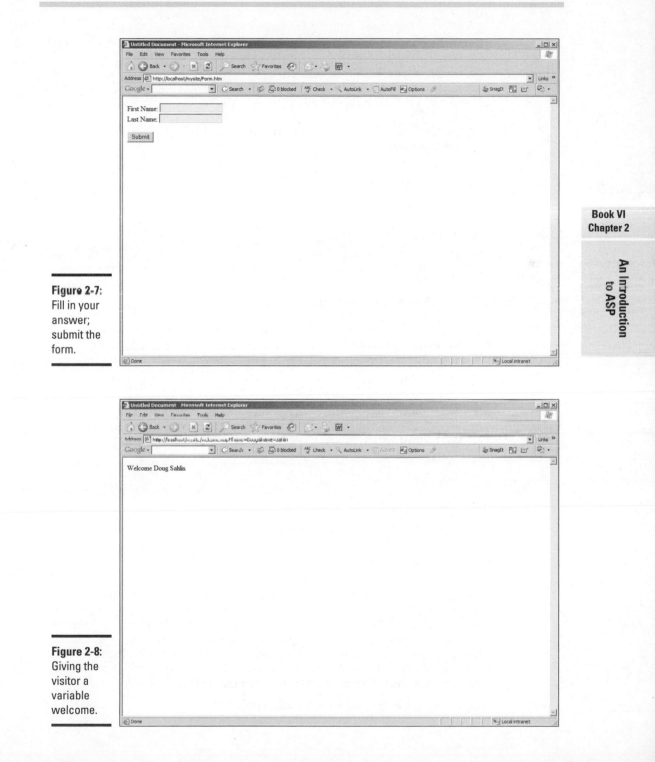

Figure 2-7:
Fill in your
answer;
submit the
form.

Figure 2-8:
Giving the
visitor a
variable
welcome.

To interact with form elements using the POST method, follow these steps:

1. Create a new HTML document.

That's right, the form you use to collect the information is an HTML document.

2. Switch to Code view, create a new line after the <body> tag, and enter the following:

```
<form method="POST" action="welcomePost.asp">
First Name: <input type="text" name="fname" />
<br />
Last Name: <input type="text" name="lname" />
<br /><br />
<input type="submit" value="Submit" />
</form>
```

The code you enter creates a simple form that collects the visitor's first and last name. The form action opens another document, "welcomePost. asp". The form method, get, makes the information available to other documents. The variables are fname and lname.

3. Save the document.

Save the document with the file name formPost.htm. Leave the document open in Dreamweaver.

4. Choose File⇨New.

Dreamweaver displays the New Document dialog box.

5. Switch to Code view, create a new line after the <body> tag, and enter the following:

```
<%
dim fname
fname=Request.Form("fname")
dim lname
lname=request.fForm("lname")
%>
Response.Write("Hello" & " " & fname & " " & lname & "!<br >" & "How are
    you?")
        %>
```

6. Save the document.

Save the document as welcomePost.asp.

7. Click the form.htm tab.

Each open document in Dreamweaver has its own tab.

8. Press F12.

Dreamweaver opens the document in your default browser.

9. Fill in the form and click Submit.

The form action calls the ASP page, which uses the variables from the form to greet the visitor. (See Figure 2-9.)

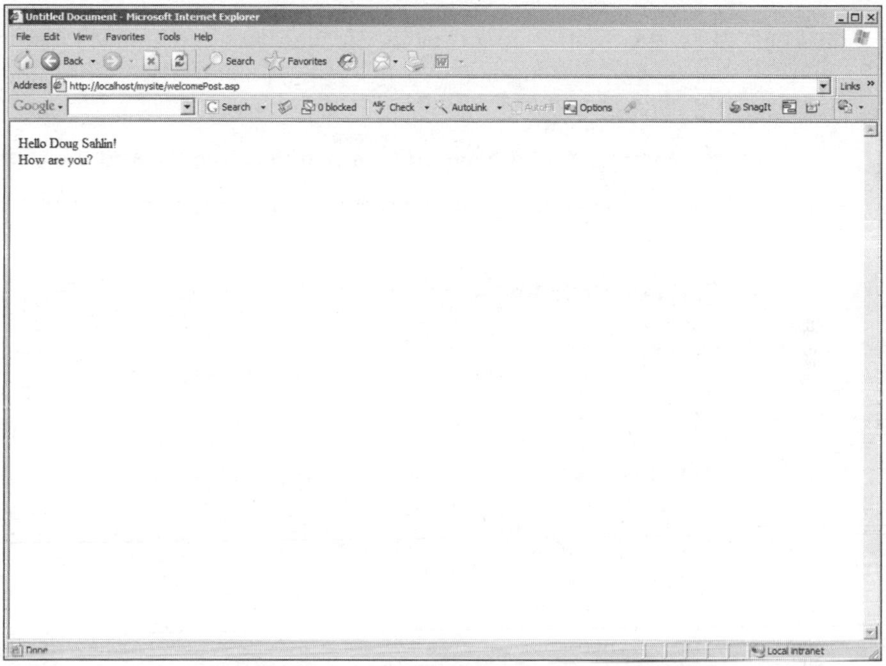

Figure 2-9:
Giving the
visitor a
hearty hello.

Differences between this scenario and the previous scenario include these:

✦ **The method in which the data is transmitted: post.** With the post method, the information is not displayed in the address window of the user's browser.

✦ **The manner in which the data is transmitted to the ASP page.** The code dim fname declares a new variable. The next line of code sets the value of the variable equal to the data "fname" that was posted from the form. The form collection of the Request object is used to get the information.

✦ **The manner in which the information is written.** Instead of creating several lines of code using the Write method of the response object, it's compiled on one line of code. The variables and *text strings* (the text surrounded by quotation marks) are *concatenated* (string speak for combined to form a single phrase). The HTML tag <br />, which is used to create a line break, is also in quotes. Notice that there are two spaces surrounded by quotation marks. If these were not in the script, the greeting, first name, and last name would run together.

Introducing VBScript functions

VBScript has some built-in functions that enable you to perform certain tasks. The functions are divided into groups such as Math Functions, Format Functions, String Functions, and so on. To demonstrate the power of functions, this section covers using the date/time functions to display the date and time on the server's machine. To add the date and time to an ASP page, complete the following steps:

1. **Open an ASP document to which you want to add the date and time.**

Position your cursor where you want to display the date and time.

2. **Switch to Code view.**

3. **Enter the following code:**

```
<%

Response.Write("Today is" & " " & (Date()) & "<br />" & "The Server's
     local time is" & " " &(Time ()))

%>
```

4. **Press F12.**

Dreamweaver prompts you to save the page. After you save the page, it is displayed in your default browser. Figure 2-10 shows the date and time added to an ASP page.

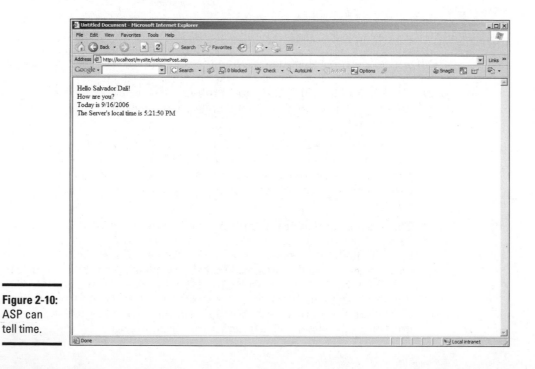

Figure 2-10:
ASP can
tell time.

When you use the VBScript `Date` function on an ASP page, it gets the date from the server's computer, not the user's computer. However, this is still useful information, especially if your client has a Web site in a different time zone than that of the visitors. You can incorporate the date and time in the greeting; for example: `The date and time in London, England is . . . .`

You also have formatting options when you add the `Date` function to a script. The default formatting displays the short version of the date showing the month, day, and year in this format: mm/dd/yyyy. Table 2-1 shows the formatting you can use for the `Date` function.

Table 2-1		Formatting the Date and Time
Constant	*Value*	*Description*
vbGeneralDate	0	Display a date in format: mm/dd/yy. If the date parameter is Now(), it also returns the time, after the date.
vbLongDate	1	Display a date using the long date format: weekday, month day, year.
vbShortDate	2	Display a date using the short date format, like the default (mm/dd/yy).
vbLongTime	3	Display a time using the time format: hh:mm:ss PM/AM.
vbShortTime	4	Display a time using the 24-hour format: hh:mm.

By adding either a constant that you're previously defined and given a value or the value, you can format the date and time. For example, change the code used in the previous example to:

```
<%
Response.Write("Today is" & " " & (FormatDateTime (Date(),1)) & "<br />"
    & "The Server's local time is" & " " &(Time ()))
%>
```

Figure 2-11 shows the result. The day of the week and month are spelled out.

Discovering Cool ASP Tricks

If you've read this chapter from the start, you know that you can do a lot of things with ASP. The previous sections show you how to do some useful things with ASP; now it's time to take it to the next level. The upcoming sections show you how to add some cool features to your designs using ASP.

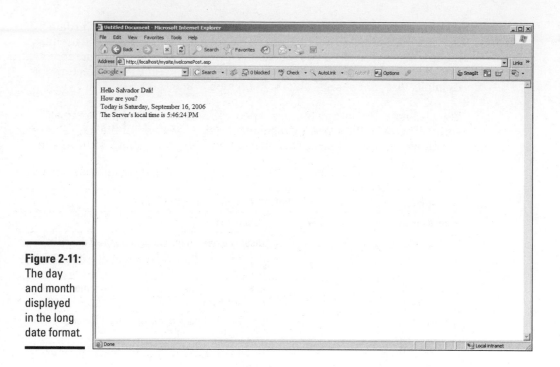

Figure 2-11:
The day
and month
displayed
in the long
date format.

Displaying a random image

If you have a client, say a photographer, who wants to display a different image each time a page loads, read on. VBScript can generate random numbers. ASP pages are generated when the browser loads the page. Combine the two and you can easily display a different image every time the page loads. To create a page that displays a random image each time the page loads, complete the following steps:

1. **Rename the images you want to display randomly, adding a sequence of number suffixes, starting with 1.**

   We recommend using the Adobe Bridge to rename the photos to `IMG_` followed by a number. You end up with a folder of images named `IMG_1.jpg`, `IMG_2.jpg`, and so on.

2. **Open the ASP document in which you want to display a random image each time the page loads.**

3. **Position your cursor where you want the image to appear.**

   To constrain the position of the image, put the VB code in a table row.

4. Enter the following code:

```
<%
RANDOMIZE
Dim RndNum
RndNum = Int(30 * Rnd) +1
%>
<img src="images/IMG_<% =RndNum %>.jpg">
```

That's not a lot of code, but what it achieves is powerful:

- The first line of code, `<%`, tells IIS that this is a script.

- The first statement, `RANDOMIZE`, generates the `Rnd` function's capability to create a random number.

- The third line of code declares a variable called `RndNum`, which is my shortcut for random number.

- The fourth line of code sets the value of the variable. `Int` is a function that generates an *integer,* which you might remember is a whole number.

- The computation in the parentheses takes the number of images, which in my case is `30`, and multiplies that by the `Rnd` function. This generates an integer between `0` and `29`; therefore, a value of `1` is added, so the range is `1` to `30`.

- The fifth line of code, `%>`, ends the VBScript.

- The `<img>` tag has the VBScript code `<% =RndNum %>`, which appends `IMG_` with the randomly generated number. If your client has a fairly large number of images, say ten or more, chances are his visitors will see a different image each time they visit the site.

5. Press F12.

Dreamweaver prompts you to save the document. After you save the document, the page launches in your default browser. Click the Refresh button a few times, and you'll see the script do its magic. (See Figure 2-12.)

Create a rotating ad banner

If you've got a client that wants to generate extra revenue, you can create ASP code to generate an ad banner every time a page is visited. The ad banner, when clicked, of course, redirects the visitor to another site. To add a rotating ad banner to a page, you take advantage of the ASP `AdRotator` component. To add a rotating ad banner to a Web page, complete these steps:

1. Open the ASP document to which you want to add the ad banner.

2. Add a table where you want the ad banner to appear.

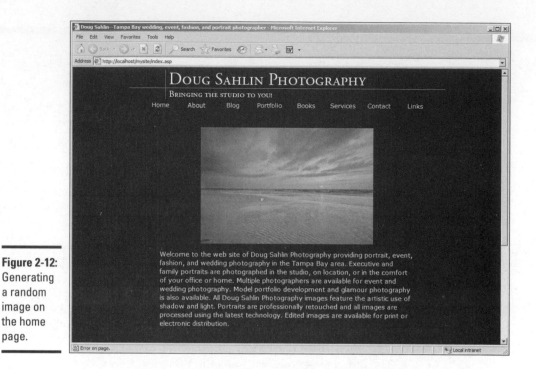

Figure 2-12:
Generating
a random
image on
the home
page.

We recommend putting the ad banner at the top of the document. If you're adding the ad banner to an existing ASP page, position your cursor at the top of the document and then choose Insert➪Table. The table should be 1 row and 1 column.

3. **Position your cursor inside the table and then switch to Code view.**

4. **Enter the following code:**

```
<%
set adrotator=Server.CreateObject("MSWC.AdRotator")
adrotator.Border="1"
Response.Write(adrotator.GetAdvertisement("ads.txt"))
%>
```

The first line of code tells IIS to compile a script. The second line of code creates the `AdRotator` object. The third line of code puts a 1-pixel border around the ad. The fourth line of code uses the `Write` method of the `Response` object to read an advertisement from a text file. The fifth line of code ends the script.

5. **Create a new document in Notepad (Windows) or TextEdit (Mac).**

This is the text file that contains the path to the images, the URL, and the frequency with which the ad should be displayed.

6. **Enter the information for your ads. The following is a sample:**

```
REDIRECT banners.asp
*
banners/adp.gif
http://www.accessdigitalphotography.com/
Visit Access Digital Photography
50
banners/si.gif
http://www.superbimages.net
Visit Superb Images
30
banners/pp.gif
http://www.theppginc.com
Peak Performance Group--Business Coach
20
```

The first line in the document specifies the document that contains the code to redirect the visitor to the ad site URL. The asterisk tells IIS that the ads follow. There are three ads in this document, and they'll be rotated by the AdRotator component. Here's a rundown of what each line in the ads designates:

- **Path:** The first line of each ad is the path to the image file. In this case, all of the image files are in a folder called Banners.

- **URL:** The second line of each ad is the URL to which the visitor will be redirected.

- **ALT text:** The third line of each ad is the ALT text that will be generated for the image.

- **Frequency:** The fourth line of each ad is the frequency in which it will appear. The first ad will appear 50 percent of the time, the second ad 30 percent, and the third ad 20 percent.

7. **Save the document as ads.txt.**

Save the document in the root folder of your Web site.

8. **In Dreamweaver, create a new ASP document.**

Choose the ASP VBScript option from the Dynamic page column of the New Document dialog box.

9. **Switch to Code view.**

10. **Create a new line after the <body> tag and enter the following code:**

```
<%
    url=Request.QueryString("url")
    If url<>"" then Response.Redirect(url)
%>
```

In a nutshell, the script reads the URL associated with the image from the `ads.txt` document and redirects the visitor to the page.

11. Save the document as `banners.asp`.

You also need to save this file in the `root` folder of your Web site.

12. In Dreamweaver, click the tab for the document in which you inserted the `AdRotator` component.

13. Press F12.

Dreamweaver prompts you to save the document. After you save the document, Dreamweaver opens it in your default browser and displays a banner ad. (See Figure 2-13.) Refresh the browser a few times to see the ads rotate.

14. Click an ad.

The `banners.asp` page is summoned, the script runs, and the visitor is redirected to the URL associated with the ad. (See Figure 2-14.)

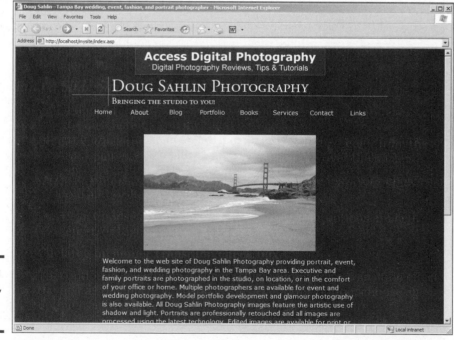

Figure 2-13:
Banner ads, love 'em or ignore 'em.

Figure 2-14:
The
`adbanner`
`.asp` page
redirects
the visitor
to the URL
associated
with the ad.

Chapter 3: Introduction to PHP

In This Chapter

✔ **Understanding PHP**

✔ **Discovering PHP server side requirements and PHP syntax**

✔ **Adding variables to the code**

✔ **Creating conditional statements**

✔ **Getting loopy: While and For**

*I*f your client needs an interactive Web site, PHP is yet another language you can use. Like ASP (the subject of the previous chapter), PHP scripts within PHP pages are interpreted by the server. PHP supports databases. In fact, many bulletin board and blog applications are created with PHP code. These applications use a MySQL database to store bulletin board and blog data. You can also create your own PHP pages using an HTML editing application like Dreamweaver. So if you need interactive pages that update when they're visited, read on, for the pages that follow introduce you to PHP.

What Is PHP?

PHP originally stood for Personal Home Page. Now, the acronym means PHP HyperText Processor. PHP pages contain HTML tags and PHP scripts to create a page that can change depending on user interactivity. The PHP page, when visited, is converted into HTML by the server. You can't view the original PHP code by viewing the source code from the browser. All you see if you do this is the HTML code generated by the server after parsing the PHP code. PHP pages can have all the other goodies that HTML pages have, such as text, hyperlinks, and so on. Many applications, such as interactive calendars, blogs, and bulletin boards, are powered by PHP. Unlike ASP, PHP is *cross-platform,* which means it can be used on servers running Unix, Windows, Macintosh, and other operating systems.

Fulfilling PHP Server Side Requirements

If you're creating PHP pages for a client's Web site, you'll have to choose a server that supports PHP. Originally, PHP required an Apache server. However, many Linux servers can also parse PHP code. In the same regard, you should choose a server that supports MySQL databases. Your client might not need a database in the beginning. However, as his site grows, he might decide to add a blog or create a mailing list from user e-mail addresses he's collected. When this occurs, having a server with MySQL database capabilities is a definite plus. You'll also need to make sure that the server has the version of PHP and MySQL to support the application you intend to use or the pages you intend to create. As of this writing, the current version of PHP is 5.1.6, and the current version of MySQL is 5.0. Check with your Web server's technical staff to see which version they currently have installed on their system.

You can download an Apache server, PHP, and MySQL for installation on your local machine. However, if you already have an IIS server installed, these items will be in conflict. Doug creates his PHP documents on his local machine and uploads them to the server for testing.

Creating PHP Pages

When you create PHP code, you must create the code with the correct syntax. Otherwise the code won't execute properly when parsed by the server. If you've created ActionScript code from scratch, you're familiar with the need for proper syntax. All PHP code begins with `<?php` and ends with `?>`. A semicolon (`;`) is required at the end of each line of code. In the following steps, I show you how to create a PHP page with a simple script:

1. **In Dreamweaver, choose File⇨New.**

   The New Document dialog box appears.

2. **Choose Dynamic Page from the Category column and choose PHP from the Dynamic Page column.**

3. **Click Create.**

   Dreamweaver creates a new PHP page.

4. **Switch to Code view.**

   Your cursor is positioned after the `<body>` tag.

5. **Press Enter (Windows) or Return (Mac) to create a new line.**

6. **Enter the following code:**

```
<?php
   echo "Hello World";
?>
```

The echo command tells PHP to display the text between the quotation marks. Dreamweaver displays the beginning and ending PHP tags (<?php and ?>) as red, boldfaced text. If desired, you can use print in lieu of echo.

7. **Save the document and upload it to your server.**

8. **When you view the page in a Web browser, you see the text Hello World. (See Figure 3-1.)**

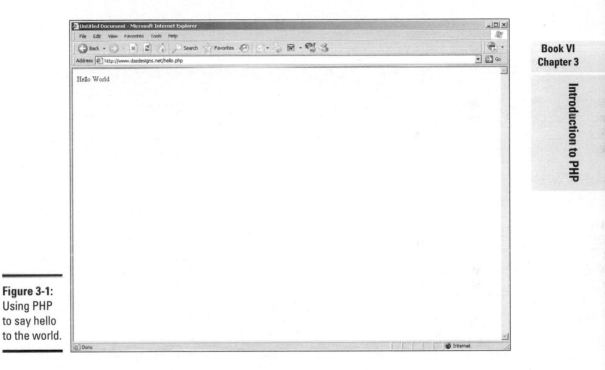

Figure 3-1:
Using PHP to say hello to the world.

Declaring and Using Variables

Variables are a very important part of any code language. *Variables* are code objects that are used to store and dispense information. For example, you can have a variable with no content, which is known as a *null variable,* that is filled with the content a user enters into a form. You use variables when sending information to a database or retrieving information from a database. Variables in PHP are preceded by a dollar sign ($). Listing 3-1 shows a simple script that contains variables.

Listing 3-1: Using Variables

```php
<?php
    $fname="Doug";
    $lname="Sahlin";
    print "Hello $fname $lname";
?>
```

If this was added to a PHP page, the resulting page that would be delivered to the user's Web browser would display as shown in Figure 3-2.

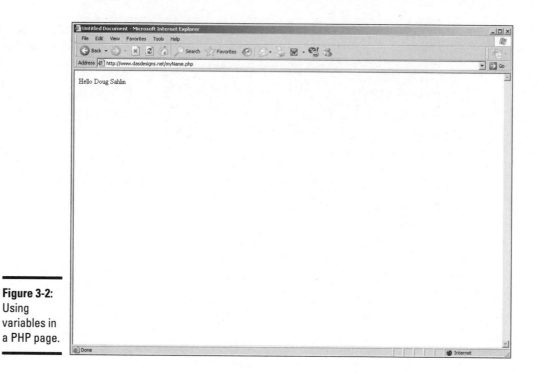

Figure 3-2:
Using variables in a PHP page.

But variables are much more powerful than that. As mentioned previously, you can use them to transfer data from a form to a database, or from a form to a page. Listing 3-2 shows a simple form that asks the user for her first and last name.

Listing 3-2: Retrieving Data from a Form

```html
<form id="form1" name="form1" method="post" action="welcome.php">
    <table border="0" cellspacing="0" cellpadding="0">
    <tr>
```

```
<td>First name </td>
<td><input type="text" name="fname" /></td>
</tr>
<tr>
<td>Last Name </td>
<td><input type="text" name="lname" /></td>
</tr>
</table>
<p>
<input type="submit" name="Submit" value="Submit" />
</p>
</form>
```

The form has two fields named fname and lname. The form method is post, which means the data is transferred transparently and isn't visible in the visitor's browser. When the visitor clicks the Submit button, the form action calls a page named welcome.php. The PHP code for the welcome.php page is shown in Listing 3-3.

Listing 3-3: PHP Code That Retrieves Variables from a Form

```php
<?php
        $fname=$_POST['fname'];
        $lname=$_POST['lname'];
        print "Welcome $fname $lname";
        ?>
```

The first line of code signifies that the script is PHP. The second line of code defines a variable called fname and sets it equal to the value of the fname form field using the POST method. The third line of code defines a variable called lname and sets it equal to the value of the lname form field using the POST method. The fourth line of code prints the result with the text Welcome. The fifth line of code ends the script. Figure 3-3 shows the result when the script is parsed by the server.

Working with Conditional Statements

Conditional statements are like a fork in the road. When you create a dynamic Web site with PHP, you want your Web page to be as smart as possible, with code that can make decisions based on the information visitors input, the type of browser they're using, and so on. With a conditional statement, you can achieve this. If the condition is true, one thing happens; if not, another thing happens. For example, a conditional statement can verify a user's e-mail address by seeing whether it has a valid format (*somebody@ somewhere.com*). If the user didn't enter a valid e-mail address, the code you created asks the techno-phobic user to enter a valid e-mail address.

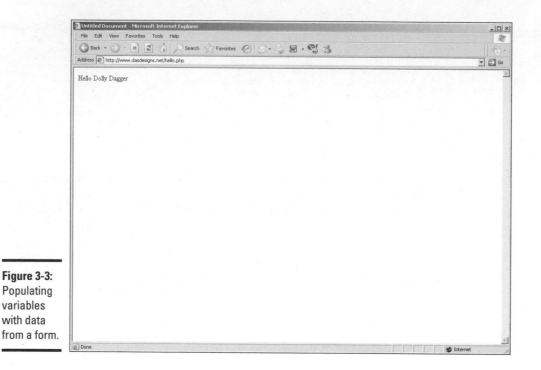

Figure 3-3:
Populating
variables
with data
from a form.

Putting conditional statements into action

The easiest conditional statement is to verify whether a condition is true. To do this, you use the `if` statement. The syntax for the statement is shown in Listing 3-4.

Listing 3-4: Proper Syntax for an if Statement

```
if (condition is true) {
        do this
}
more code
```

If the condition verifies as true, the code within the curly brackets is executed; otherwise, the next line of code is executed. For example, say you have a form on your Web site that asks for the visitor's first and last name. You can use the `if` statement to validate the form. Listing 3-5 shows the HTML code for the form.

Listing 3-5: A User Information Form

```
<form id="form1" name="form1" method="post" action="validate.php">
        <table border="0" cellspacing="0" cellpadding="0">
        <tr>
```

```
<td>First name </td>
<td><input type="text" name="fname" /></td>
</tr>
<tr>
<td>Last Name </td>
<td><input type="text" name="lname" /></td>
</tr>
</table>
<p>
<input type="submit" name="Submit" value="Submit" />
</p>
</form>
```

The form is pretty straightforward, asking for the user's information. As soon as the user clicks the Submit button, the validate.php page loads. This page contains the code shown in Listing 3-6, which tests to see if the user has entered her first and last name.

Listing 3-6: Validating the Form

```php
<?php
    $fname=$_POST['fname'];
    $lname=$_POST['lname'];
    if ($fname=="" Or $lname==""){
    print '<meta HTTP-EQUIV="refresh" content=0;url="form.htm">';
    }
?>
```

The variable $name is set equal to the information entered in the form field fname, and the variable $lname is set equal to the information entered in the lname form field. The information is retrieved using the POST method. The conditional statement uses the logical operator "Or". The comparison operator (==) is used to see if either variable contains no information — quotation marks with nothing between them indicate that the variable is null. If either variable contains no information, the next line of code refreshes the browser to the form. However, if there is information in both fields, you need additional code; otherwise, the user is stuck on the validate.php page. Enter the else statement. Listing 3-7 shows the code with the addition of an else statement.

Listing 3-7: Creating a Fork in the Road

```php
<?php
    $fname=$_POST['fname'];
    $lname=$_POST['lname'];
    if ($fname=="" Or $lname==""){
    print '<meta HTTP-EQUIV="refresh" content=0;url="form.htm">';
    } else {
    print '<meta HTTP-EQUIV="refresh" content=0;url="index.php">';
    }
?>
```

The addition of the `else` statement creates another course of action when both variables do contain data. There is a third statement that can be added to evaluate a condition: `elseif`. This statement enables you to add an alternative outcome if the `elseif` statement evaluates to be true. You can add as many `elseif` statements to cover any possible scenario. Listing 3-8 shows an example of an `elseif` statement added to evaluate another possible outcome.

Listing 3-8: Using an elseif Statement

```php
<?php
    $password=$_POST['password'];
    $fname=$_POST['fname'];
    $lname=$_POST['lname'];
    if ($password=="" Or $fname=="" Or $lname==""){
    print '<meta HTTP-EQUIV="refresh" content=0;url="form.htm">';
    } elseif ($password!= "letmein") {
    print '<meta HTTP-EQUIV="refresh" content=0;url="http://www.google.com">';
    } else {
    print "Welcome $fname $lname ";
    }
?>
```

This scenario evaluates a login form for a Web site. The code creates three variables, retrieving the first name, last name, and the password submitted by the user. The `if` statement checks to be sure the user entered data in each form field. The `elseif` statement evaluates to see if the password does not equal `letmein`. If the `elseif` statement evaluates as true, the visitor is redirected to Google. The final scenario is what happens when the previous statements evaluate as false and welcome the visitor to the Web site.

Using comparison operators

Comparison operators test for equality, inequality, or whether a value is greater than or less than another value. You use comparison operators in conditional statements to compare elements, such as whether a variable contains certain information. Comparison operators are often confused with assignment operators. For example, when you create a variable, you use the assignment operator =. When you create a conditional statement and want to verify if the content of a variable is equal to a specific value, you use the comparison operator ==. Table 3-1 shows the comparison operators you can use when creating conditional statements.

Table 3-1		Comparison Operators	
Operator	*Example*	*Operator Name*	*Result*
==	$a==$b	Equal	True if the value of $a equals the value of $b
!=	$a!=B	Not equal	True if the value of $a does not equal the value of $b

Using logical operators

You use logical operators when you want to evaluate multiple conditions. When you evaluate multiple conditions, you can specify whether a statement is true if all conditions are met, or if only one condition is met. Table 3-2 shows the Logical Operators you can use when creating conditional statements.

Table 3-2	Logical Operators	
Operator	*Example*	*Result*
And	`$a=="Jack" And $b=="Jill"`	True if both sides of the statement evaluate as true.
Or	`$a=="Jack" Or $b=="Jill"`	True if either side of the statement evaluates as true.
Xor	`$a=="Jack" Xor $b=="Jill"`	True if either side of the statement evaluates as true, but false if both sides of the statement evaluate as true.

Repeating Lines of Code Using Loops

Loops are very handy when you need to repeat certain lines of code for a specified number of times. You can loop through a database while searching for certain data. A loop continues as long as a given condition is true. There are different types of loops you can add to your PHP code. We show you how to get loopy in the upcoming sections.

Using the while loop

A `while` loop is a loop in its simplest form. The loop executes while a given condition is true. As soon as the condition is false, the next lines of code are executed. Listing 3-9 shows an example of a `while` loop.

Listing 3-9: Using a while Loop

```php
<?php
    $MyNum = 1;
    while ($MyNum <= 10)
    {
    print ("$MyNum");
    $MyNum++;
    }
?>
```

The code in Listing 3-9 will print the numbers 1 through 10. The loop continues as long as the value of the $MyNum (a variable) is less than or equal to

10. The line of code that reads `$MyNum++;` increases the value of `$MyNum` by a value of `1` every time the loop executes.

Using the for loop

The `for` loop executes code for a given set of iterations. The value by which the loop increments can vary. For example, you can use a `for` loop to search every record in a database, or every other record in a database. Listing 3-10 shows a `for` loop.

Listing 3-10: The for Loop

```php
<?php
        for ($MyNum = 1; $MyNum <= 10; $MyNum+=2) {
            print $MyNum;
        }
?>
```

This loop also executes as long as the value of `$MyNum` is less than or equal to `10`. The `for` loop has three statements that are separated by semicolons. The first statement in the loop sets the value of `$MyNum` to `1`; the second statement tells the PHP compiler to execute the loop as long as the value of `$MyNum` is less than or equal to `10`; and the third statement specifies that the loop increment the value of `$MyNum` by a value of `2`. The code will print the following: `13579`.

Generating a Random Image

The previous sections give you a look at PHP code. If you've read through it, you might now be interested in seeing a real-world application using PHP code. You can find plenty of applications on the Web. For that matter, you can even find examples of code on the Web. This chapter is but a brief introduction showing you some of the building blocks of PHP code. If your interest is piqued, consider picking up a copy of *PHP 5 For Dummies,* by Janet Valade (Wiley Publishing, ISBN 0-7645-4166-8). And now, on to the real-world example of PHP in action.

When people visit a Web site, they like to see new and different things. One way to ensure that they do is to generate a random image on the home page. If you have ten or more images that are generated randomly, the visitor is likely to see a different image every time he visits the site. To generate a random image on a home page, follow these steps:

1. **Rename the images and add a number suffix starting with 1.**

We recommend using the Adobe Bridge to rename the images to `IMG_` followed by a number. You end up with a folder of images named `IMG_1.jpg`, `IMG_2.jpg`, and so on.

2. **Open the PHP document in which you want to display a random image each time the page loads.**

3. **Position your cursor where you want the image to appear.**

   To constrain the position of the image, put the PHP code in a table row.

4. **Enter the following code:**

   ```
   <?php
   $image = rand(1,30);
   print '<img src="images/IMG_'.$image.'.jpg">';
       ?>
   ```

   You get a lot of bang for your buck with just a few lines of code. The first line tells the server it is parsing PHP code. The second line of code creates a variable named `$image` and sets it equal to a random number between 1 and 30 (the number of images renumbered to display randomly). The third line of code uses an HTML image tag to add the random image to the page. The `$image` variable is used to append the number to the `image` file name.

5. **Upload the file to your server and preview it in your Web browser.**

   The script causes an image to be displayed randomly. (See Figure 3-4.) Refresh the browser a few times to test the script.

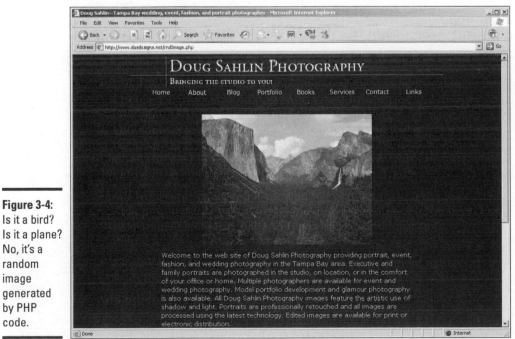

Figure 3-4:
Is it a bird?
Is it a plane?
No, it's a
random
image
generated
by PHP
code.

Chapter 4: MySQL and PHP

In This Chapter

✔ Building a mailing list form

✔ Creating a MySQL database

✔ Transferring data to the database

✔ Reading data from the database

MySQL and PHP are almost like a marriage made in heaven. PHP likes to send stuff to MySQL, and MySQL accepts it with open arms, er, fields. Like Batman and Robin, MySQL and PHP are a dynamic duo. So dynamic in fact, that quite a few applications out there use the combination to good effect. Blog, bulletin board, and calendar applications are good examples of the dynamic duo at work. You can write a PHP script in a PHP Web page that sends information to and plucks data from a MySQL database. MySQL databases keep the information safely locked away until its good buddy PHP comes calling.

In case you rushed right to this chapter expecting to find out everything you need to know about MySQL and PHP, well, you almost came to the right place. To learn everything about integrating MySQL databases with PHP pages would require a good book. However, in this chapter, on these very pages written with tender loving care, with blisters on your authors' fingers, we show you how to use PHP and MySQL to create a mailing list.

You can choose from a lot of applications for managing mailing lists. The applications enable you to easily manage a mailing list, send information to people who have opted in to the mailing list, and so on. However, if you have a client who doesn't need all the bells and whistles, why give them to him? If your client's only need is to store a limited number of names and e-mail addresses in a database and occasionally retrieve the information, you can easily accomplish this by creating a form for your client's Web site visitors, a MySQL database on your client's Web server, and then the PHP code to send and retrieve information from the database.

Creating a Mailing List Form

The first step in the process of creating a mailing list is setting up a mailing list form. In case you haven't read the chapter on creating forms, this step list leads you through the process. It's easy. Really. To create a mailing list form:

1. **In your favorite HTML editor (ours is Dreamweaver) open the document into which you want to insert a mailing list form.**

    Some designers have the audacity to create a pop-up window on the home page, asking the visitor to sign up for a mailing list. Really, how can you tell if you want to sign up for a mailing list when you haven't even seen the site yet? We'll leave the absolute location to you and your client and jump off the soapbox now.

2. **Position your cursor where you want to insert the form.**

3. **Choose Insert⇨Form⇨Form.**

    Dreamweaver inserts the first building block for a form.

4. **Choose Window⇨Properties.**

    The Properties inspector opens.

5. **In the Action field, enter** addrecord.php.

    This is the document you'll create to add the information to the database. The action tells the Web browser to launch the page when the visitor clicks the Submit button.

6. **Position your cursor within the form (the red border) and then choose Insert⇨Table.**

    The Table dialog box appears. Using a table for a form enables you to keep text and form fields segregated. For a simple e-mail collection, you need three rows and two columns.

7. **Enter 3 in the Rows field and 2 in the Columns field. Set the other parameters to suit the page in which you're inserting the form.**

8. **Click OK.**

    Dreamweaver creates a table.

9. **Enter the desired text in the first column.**

Name and **E-Mail** makes a lot of sense to us.

10. **Position your cursor in the second column in the first row and then choose Form⇨TextField.**

Dreamweaver inserts a text field in the table cell.

11. **Choose Window⇨Properties.**

The Properties inspector appears.

12. **Label the TextField Name.**

The default name of the first text field in a document is Text. Highlight the default name and type the desired name in its place. In this case, type **Name**. (See Figure 4-1.)

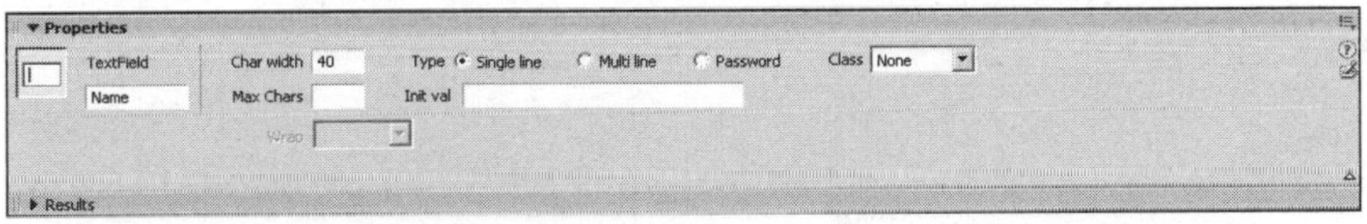

Figure 4-1:
Setting the parameters for the text field.

13. **Enter a value of 40 in the Char Width and Max Chars fields.**

These values size the text field and limit the maximum number of characters users can input to 40. If your client has visitors with long names, you might want to increase these values.

14. **Position your cursor in the second column of the second row and repeat Steps 10 to 13.**

This time, name the TextField **E-Mail**.

15. **Position your cursor in the first column of the third row.**

16. **Choose Insert⇨Form⇨Button.**

Dreamweaver inserts a button in your form. If desired, you can change the button text in the Properties inspector. Your finished form should resemble Figure 4-2.

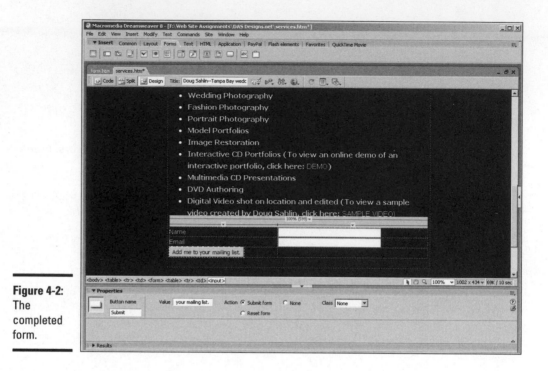

Figure 4-2:
The
completed
form.

Creating the Database

After you know what fields you want in your database, you're ready to create
it. Now, we could show you a whole lot of complex code that creates a new
database, but why work harder when you can work smarter? Most Web hosting services that have MySQLAdmin installed also have a little gem called
PHPMyAdmin, which enables you to create databases from within the service's control panel. Here's how to do it:

1. **Log in to your Web server.**

If you're not sure how to do this, check with your hosting service's technical support.

2. **Create a new MySQL database.**

Your Web hosting service probably has something like a MySQLAdmin
icon. Click the icon and create a new database. You'll submit a username
and password. Jot these down, as you'll need them to connect to the
database. Also, make sure that you choose the DBA User option, which
means *database administrator.* If you're unsure, check with your Web
hosting service's technical support.

3. **After you create the database, launch PHPMyAdmin.**

There should be an icon for this on your server's control panel. If you're not sure of how to launch PHPMyAdmin, check with your Web hosting service's technical support.

4. **Select the database you just created.**

5. **Click Operations.**

The Operations section of the PHPMyAdmin dialog box appears. (See Figure 4-3.)

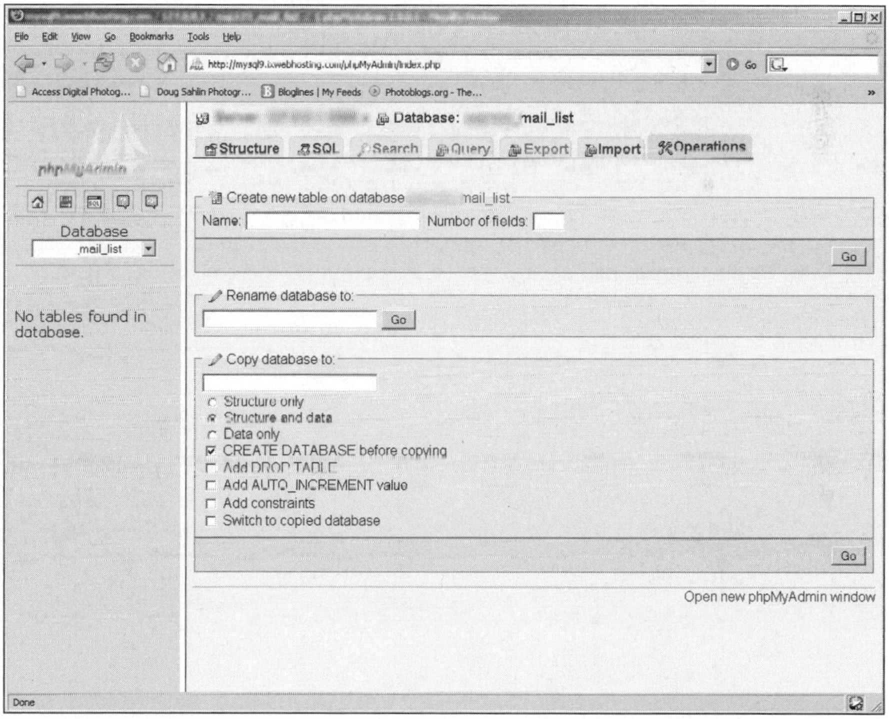

**Book VI
Chapter 4**

MySQL and PHP

Figure 4-3:
Configuring
the
database.

6. **Enter a name in the Name text box (underneath Create New Table on Database).**

You can have multiple tables in a database. However, for a simple database like this, you need only one table. Give the database a name that reflects its purpose. Don't create a name that has spaces.

7. **Enter a value in the Number of Fields text box.**

For this database, we need **3** fields.

8. **Click the Go button.**

The dialog box refreshes, and you're faced with the task of naming your fields. (See Figure 4-4.)

9. **Enter the names and characteristics for your fields.**

Name the first Field **ID**, choose INT from the Type drop-down menu, enter **5** in the Length/Values field, choose Auto_Increment from the Extra drop-down menu, and then click the Primary radio button. Name the second Field **Name**, accept the default VARCHAR (*variable characters,* which means the field will accept text and numbers, which are read as text data and can't be used for arithmetic operations) option for Type, and then enter **40** in the Length/Values field. Name the third Field **E-Mail**, accept the default VARCHAR option for Type, and then enter **40** in the Length/Values field.

The second and third Field names are the same names as those in the form you created. The Value you enter is the same Value you specified for Max Chars when you created the form. The first Field generates a number every time a record is added to the database. This number is used to locate information in the database. The ID is incremented by a value of 1 every time a record is added to the database.

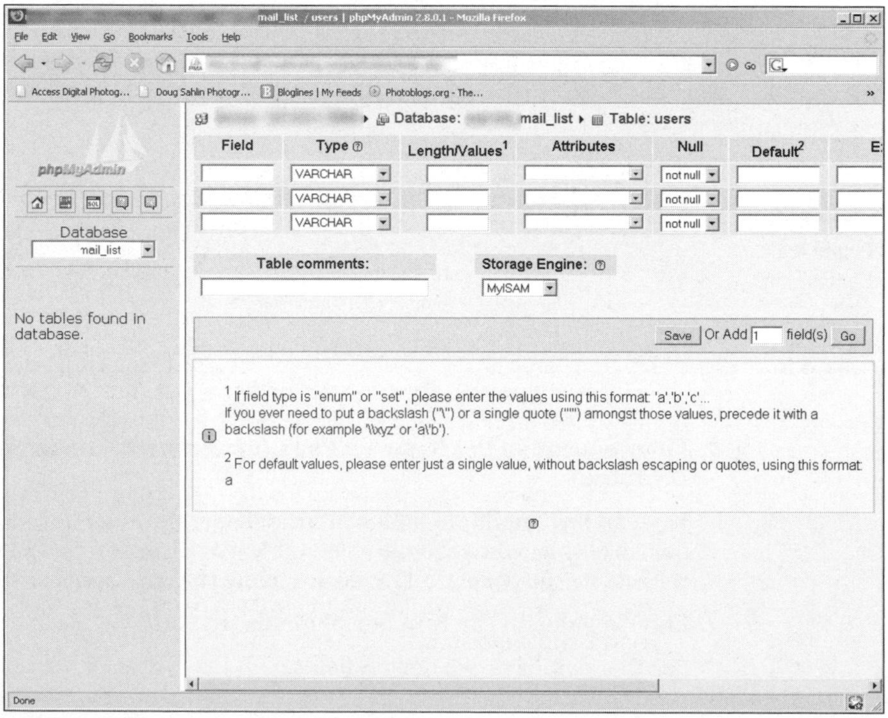

Figure 4-4: Setting the field characteristics.

10. **Click Save.**

PHPMyAdmin creates the table and fields. Next, you create the PHP code that transfers the information from the form to the database.

Creating the PHP Code

When you've got the form and the database ready to go, it's time to create the PHP code that will populate the database with e-mail addresses. What you do is create variables for each form field and then create a connection to the database. Your code also puts the information in the database. Just follow these steps:

1. **Create a new document in Dreamweaver.**

Choose Dynamic Page from the category column and choose PHP from the Dynamic Page category.

2. **Switch to Code view.**

3. **Create a new line after the <body> tag and enter the following code:**

```
<?php
  $Name=$_POST['Name'];
  $EMail=$_POST['EMail'];
  $connection=mysql_connect ("localhost", "myusername", "mypassword") or
    die ('I cannot connect to the database.');
  mysql_select_db ("mydatabase",$connection) or die( "Unable to select
    database");
  $query = "INSERT INTO `mytable` (`ID`, `Name`, `EMail`) VALUES
    ('','$Name','$EMail')";
  mysql_query($query);
  mysql_close();
?>
```

You'll have to change the code to suit your Web server and the database information, but the first three lines of code will remain unchanged. Here's what's happening in this code:

- The first line signifies that PHP code follows.

- The next lines of code create two variables, $Name and $EMail, which are set equal to the names of the fields from the form you created where users enter their names and e-mail addresses.

- The line of code that begins with $connection creates a variable with the information needed to connect to the database. Most Web hosting services use localhost as the location for the database; however, with some Web servers, you're required to enter a URL. Check with your Web hosting service's technical support staff for more information.

- The line of code that begins with `mysql_select_db` selects the database using the information from the `$connection` variable. You'll have to replace *mydatabase* with the name of your database.

- The line that begins with `$query` creates a variable with the instructions that insert the data into the database. You'll have to replace *mytable* with the name of the table into which you're inserting the form data. You might recognize the information (`` `ID` ``, `` `Name` ``, `` `EMail` ``). These are the fields in your database into which the information is being inserted. The information being inserted is specified by the word `VALUES`. The values being inserted are (`''`, `'$Name'`, `'$EMail'`). The single quotes are a place holder for the ID field in the database. When the information is inserted in the database, MySQL assigns a number to the record. The ID field is the primary field in the database and is set to *auto increment,* which means that sequential numbers are assigned to the records entered: 1, 2, 3, 4, and so on.

- The line of code that begins with `mysql_query` tells MySQL that a query operation is being requested. The query performed gets instructions from the variable `$query`.

- The line `mysql_close();` closes the connection to the database. And if you've read Chapter 3 of this minibook, you know that `?>` ends the PHP code.

4. **Save the document.**

   Save the document as `addrecord.php`, the same file name specified in the action of the form you created.

When you upload the HTML page with the form and the ASP file to your server, site visitors can enter their names and e-mail addresses into the form. When they click the Submit — or whatever clever name you've given the button — button, their information is added to the database.

You need to add additional code to the head of the `addrecord.php` document. Otherwise, the site visitor will click the Submit button and get stuck on the `addrecord.php` page . The code you need to add is

```
<meta http-equiv="REFRESH" content="0; URL=http://www.mywebsite/thanks.htm">
```

After adding this code to the `addrecord.php` page, you need to create a new page called `thanks.htm`. The browser refreshes with this page after the code executes. The Thank You page contains site navigation and a message to site visitors thanking them for adding their information to the database.

Retrieving Information from a Database

Okay, after you have a database that accepts information from a Web page, how do you access it? You can choose from a lot of different commands to search a database. You can set up a form where the user enters the information he's searching for and then create the code that searches a particular field of the database and returns information that is identical to or similar to the user's request. This is known as a *query*. To show you everything you can do with a database requires several chapters. To show you everything you can do with PHP and a MySQL database requires an entire book. Neither option is available, and our project editor was chomping at the bit for this chapter. To learn everything you ever wanted to know about MySQL and PHP, consider *PHP and MySQL For Dummies,* 2nd edition, by Janet Valade (ISBN 0-7645-5589-8) or *PHP & MySQL Everyday Apps For Dummies,* by Janet Valade (ISBN 0-7645-7587-2). (Both are published by Wiley.)

Now that the disclaimer's out of the way, we want to show you how to retrieve the data from the simple mailing list we show you how to create in the previous section.

If you didn't read the previous section, do so now.

To retrieve the data from the mailing list database, follow these steps:

1. **Create a new document in Dreamweaver.**

Choose Dynamic Page from the category column, and choose PHP from the Dynamic Page category.

2. **Switch to Code view.**

3. **Create a new line after the `<body>` tag and enter the following code:**

```
<table>
<tr>
<th width="120"  align="Left">
Name</th>
<th width="120"  align="Left">
E-Mail</th>
</tr>
</table>
<table>
<?php
$connection=mysql_connect ("localhost", "myusername", "mypassword") or
    die ('I cannot connect to the database.');
mysql_select_db ("mail_list",$connection) or die( "Unable to select
    database");
$query="SELECT * FROM users ORDER by name";
$result=mysql_query($query);
$num=mysql_numrows($result);
mysql_close();
$i=0;
```

```
while ($i < $num) {
$name=mysql_result($result,$i,"Name");
$email=mysql_result($result,$i,"EMail");
?>
<tr>
<td width="120" align="left" ><? print $name ?>
<td>
<td width="120" align="left" ><? print $email ?>
 </td>
</tr>
<?php
$i++;
 }
 ?>
</table>
```

4. **Save the file and upload it to your server.**

When you load the `.php` file in a browser, it plucks all of the data from the database. Figure 4-5 shows a hypothetical mailing list displayed using the code in the previous steps.

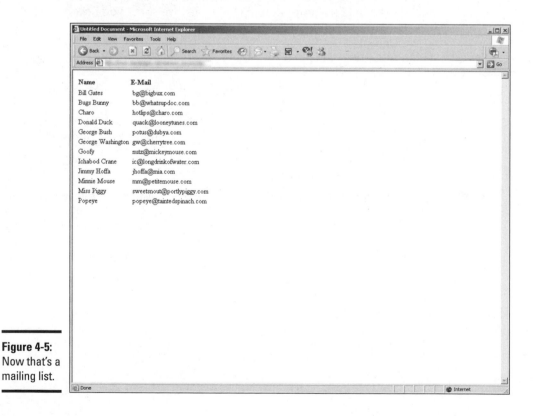

Figure 4-5:
Now that's a mailing list.

You're probably thinking, Yikes, that's a lot of code! We don't leave you in a lurch, though. Read on to find out what the code means.

Listing 4-1 shows the code for the table that displays the titles for the information that will be retrieved. The titles use the <th> tag (table header) which boldfaces the text. The headers are sized and the text is aligned to the left.

Listing 4-1: The Table Titles

```
<table>
<tr>
<th width="120"  align="Left">
Name</th>
<th width="120"  align="Left">
E-Mail</th>
</tr>
</table>
```

In Listing 4-2, the first line of code creates a new table and the second line begins the PHP script.

Listing 4-2: Connecting to the Database

```
<table>
<?php
$connection=mysql_connect ("localhost", "myusername", "mypassword") or die ('I
    cannot connect to the database.');
mysql_select_db ("mail list",$connection) or die( "Unable to select database");
$query="SELECT * FROM users ORDER by name";
$result=mysql_query($query);
$num=mysql_numrows($result);
mysql_close();
```

The new table stores the results of your query, which in this case is all of the names and e-mail addresses in the database. The second line of code creates a variable that contains all of the information needed to connect to the database. The line of code that begins with mysql_select_db creates a connection to the database, which in this case is named mail_list. The $query variable in the fourth line of code is set equal to the query that will be performed to select the information from the users table of the database. The results will be ordered by name. The $result variable in the fifth line of code is set equal to the mysql_query command, which queries the database using the information in the $query variable. The $num variable in the sixth line of code is set equal to the number of rows of data returned from the query. The final line of code closes the database.

Listing 4-3 shows the final lines of code. It's not as bad as it looks.

Listing 4-3: Using a while Loop to Extract the Data

```
$i=0;
while ($i < $num) {
$name=mysql_result($result,$i,"Name");
$email=mysql_result($result,$i,"EMail");
?>
<tr>
<td width="120" align="left" ><? print $name ?>
<td>
<td width="120" align="left" ><? print $email ?>
 </td>
</tr>
<?php
$i++;
 }
 ?>
</table>
```

The $i variable is set to 0 (zero), which, incidentally, is the ID number of the first record row returned from the database. The while loop will run as long as the value of $i is less than the variable $num. The next variable in our lineup is $name, which is set equal to the result of the first query. The variable $i, which is initially set to 0 (zero), is the first record that matches the search criteria and returns the data from the Name field of the database. The $email variable is similar but returns the result from the E-Mail field of the first record that matches the criteria. Now that we've got our variables in a row, let's put some data in the table rows.

The next line ends the PHP code and is immediately followed by a table row, which has two cells. The first cell contains the contents of the $name variable, which contains the data from the Name field of the first record that matches our results. Notice the manner in which the PHP code is entered: <? print $name ?>. This is a shortcut when you need to insert PHP in an HTML tag. The <? tag signifies the start of PHP code and the ?> tag ends it. The next table cell contains the contents of the $email variable, which contains the data from the E-Mail field of the first record that matches the query results. And now we have more PHP code. Basically, the code $i++ is increasing the value of the variable $i by a value of 1. The ++ shortcut is code to increase a value by 1. The closing curly bracket (}) signifies the end of the instructions included in the while loop. The loop continues until all of the records are displayed.

Chapter 5: Additional Site Interactivity

In This Chapter

✔ Considering adding a blog

✔ Letting users speak: message boards and wikis

✔ Setting up automatic notifications: RSS feeds

✔ Keeping in touch with e-mail

*I*t seems as though interactivity is the buzzword when it comes to Web sites. If you design sites that aren't interactive, you're not a happening designer. And it's a well-known fact that happening designers get most of the work. If you've read previous chapters of this minibook, you have an idea of the type of interactivity you can create when you design pages for your clients. But wait; there's more! In fact, a whole lot more. This chapter shows you other forms of interactivity you can add to your pages. In fact, it shows you a whole lot of interactivity in this chapter.

Engaging Visitors with an Online Journal (Blog)

Blogs have become the hottest thing since sliced bread. It seems as though everyone and his little sister has a blog these days. Some of them are vanity blogs, while others contain useful information or points of view. Figure 5-1 shows a blog that contains useful information about digital photography. The creators are two best-selling authors of books on digital photography and Photoshop. The blog is interactive in that readers can leave comments on blog posts.

Savvy business people also use blogs. Because the information in a blog is updated frequently, Web sites with blogs are ranked highly by search engines. If a commercial blog site is optimized for search engines, it attracts traffic that might include potential clients.

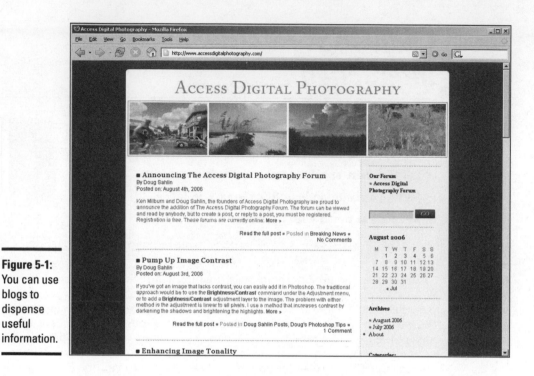

Figure 5-1:
You can use blogs to dispense useful information.

You can download two popular blog applications for free. One is b2evolution. You can find information about b2evolution and download the application at `http://b2evolution.net`. WordPress is another popular blog application. You can find information about WordPress and download the application at `http://wordpress.org`. You can customize both applications to suit a Web site. Figure 5-2 is Doug's personal blog that complements his photography business. Notice the navigation menu, which is a carbon copy of the menu on Doug's main site. He customized the blog template to include the menu, which enables blog visitors to return to any page on his main site.

The aforementioned blog applications use PHP and a MySQL database. Both applications enable users to post and manage blogs using a browser-based interface. Before you add one of the aforementioned blog applications to your site, or to your client's site, make sure that your server has the proper version of PHP and MySQL at your disposal. For more information on blogs, see Book IX, Chapter 2.

**Book VI
Chapter 5**

Additional Site Interactivity

Figure 5-2:
You can
easily
customize
blogs.

Initiating Online Conversations: Forums and Message Boards

If your client has a product or service that includes a user base that likes to exchange information about topics related to the product or service, an online forum or bulletin board is an ideal addition to the main Web site. Forums give users a chance to interact with each other. Someone on your client's staff moderates the bulletin board. The moderator can add his two cents to a forum thread. Forums can create customer loyalty. Forums also turn visitors into potential customers.

A *forum* or *bulletin board* is an application that enables visitors to post information. The information in a bulletin board changes; therefore, the page needs to be generated on the fly when someone visits the site. Most bulletin board and forum applications use ASP or PHP code to generate the page and pluck the required information from a database. The application writes new forum posts to the database, which also contains subscriber information and so on. One forum application that you can download for free is phpBB. The application uses PHP code combined with a MySQL database. For more information about phpBB and to download the application, visit www.phpbb.com.

The forum application enables the administrator to determine whether guests can make a post or if only registered members can post messages in the forum. The administrator can subdivide a forum site into forums that pertain to related topics. The forum site administrator manages the forums. The administrator also grants rights to visitors of the forum site, which determines who can view posts, write posts, moderate forums, and so on.

When someone posts a new topic on a bulletin board, other visitors (or registrants, depending on the permissions allowed by the forum administrator) can respond to the post. The topic and replies are known as a *thread*. The information in the forums is stored in a database on the server. Ken Milburn, a photographer and author, and Doug recently used phpBB to create a forum for digital photography. Figure 5-3 shows the home page of the forum.

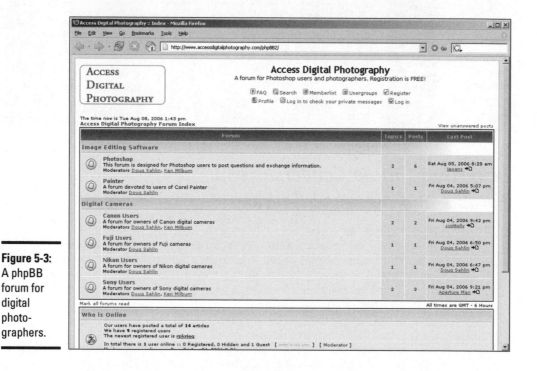

Figure 5-3: A phpBB forum for digital photographers.

The forum site in Figure 5-3 is divided into several interest areas, including forum areas devoted to Photoshop, Painter, and specific brands of digital cameras. Site visitors can view other visitors' comments in a topic area by clicking the appropriate link on the home page. Each topic area lists the most recent posts. (See Figure 5-4.) A forum page generated with the phpBB application shows a visitor what rights she has in a list at the bottom of the page.

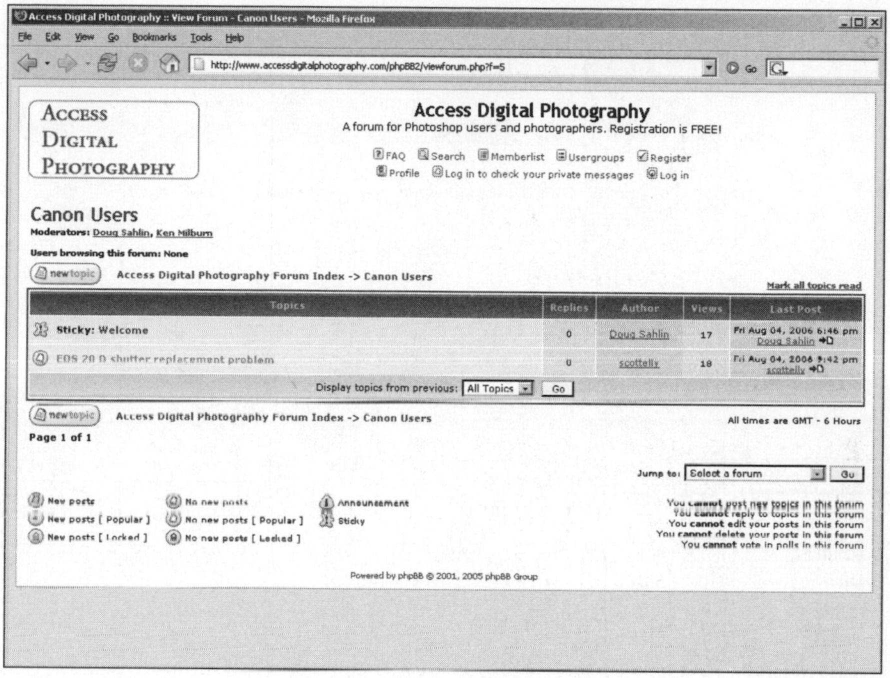

Figure 5-4:
A topic area
in a phpBB
forum.

Another nice feature of a forum using the phpBB application is the ease of administration. After logging in, an administrator can manage every aspect of the forum using the Administration panel. From within the panel, the administrator can assign rights to user ranks, create new user ranks, delete users, manage and create forums, and so on. Figure 5-5 shows the Forum Administration section of the Administration panel.

Establishing an Online Community: Wiki

A *wiki* (pronounced just like it looks, *WICK-ee*) is an online community of users that can share documents and spreadsheets, create Web pages, and more. The name *wiki* comes from *wiki wiki,* which means *quick* in Hawaiian. The software that runs a wiki enables members of the community to use a common interface to create content for the community. *Wiki* is server software that enables users to create and edit Web page content using any Web browser. Wiki software enables visitors to insert hyperlinks and uses a simple text syntax to create new pages and cross-links between internal pages. Users can modify the organization of wiki content as well as edit the documents. To check out a very busy and active wiki community, visit www. wikipedia.org/. Figure 5-6 shows a page from a wiki site where visitors can edit the page.

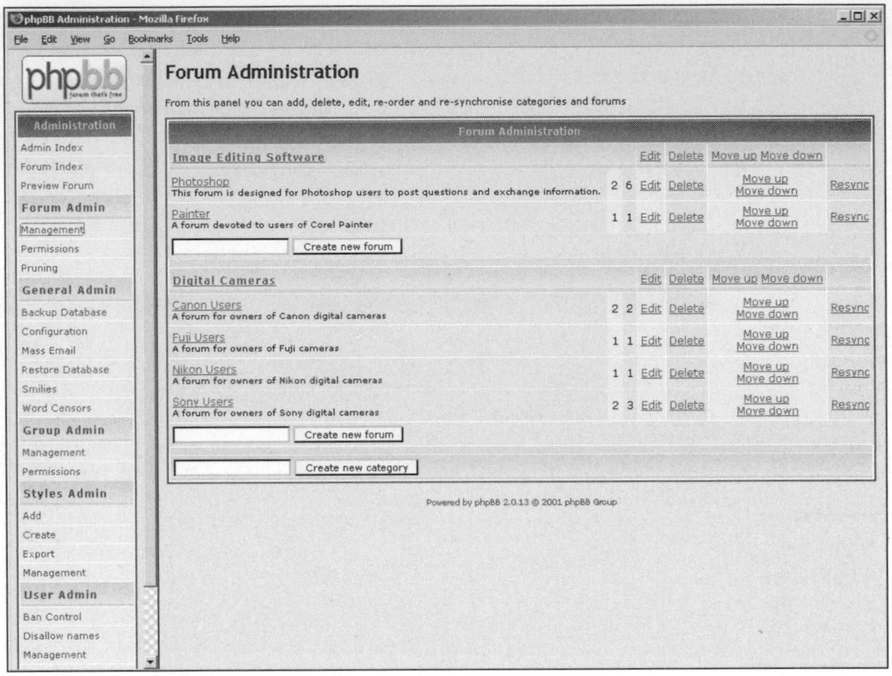

Figure 5-5: Admin-istering a phpBB forum.

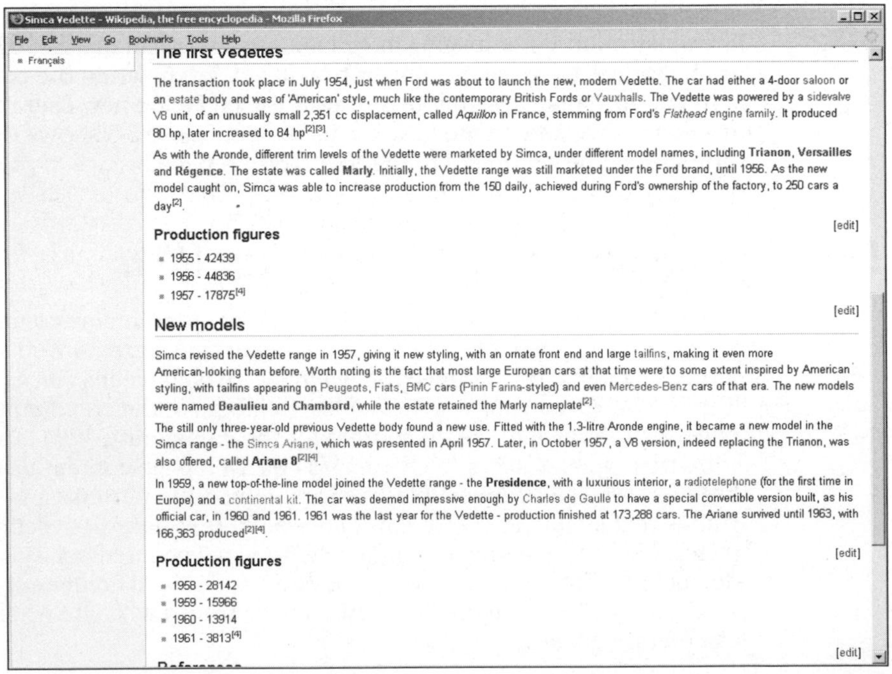

Figure 5-6: Edit me. Go ahead and make my day.

The very nature of a wiki means that literally anyone who can access the wiki can edit pages within the wiki site. Some wiki communities require users to register before they can edit pages. Others require an authentication code, while others let the user freely edit the page — but they record the user's IP. You might wonder if pages could be wiped out. The answer is yes. However, most communities are fairly civil and pages are rarely wiped clean. Figure 5-7 shows a wiki page that's ready for editing. You can find wiki software by typing those very words in your favorite search engine. A tutorial on using Wiki software is beyond the scope of this book.

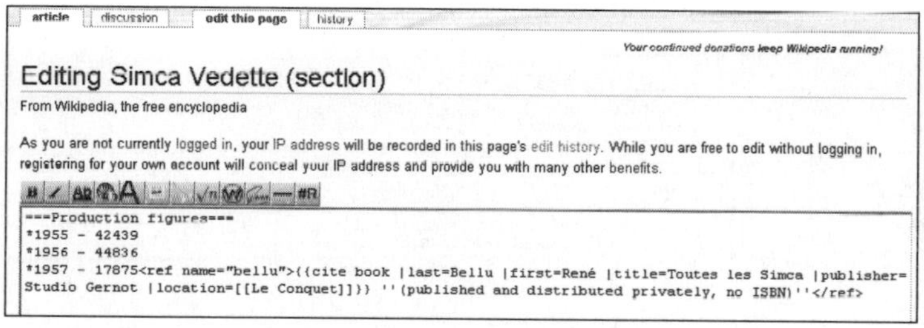

Figure 5-7:
Now let's
see, if we
boldface
this and
italicize
that . . .
yada, yada,
yada.

Feeding Them Your Content: RSS

If you set up a blog or a wiki for a client, you can create an RSS (Real Simple Syndication) feed to notify subscribers when new information is posted. Subscribers can use an online RSS feed service or download an RSS feed reader to keep track of desired RSS feeds. Either method notifies a subscriber when you update the RSS feed. RSS delivers information to RSS feed readers through an XML document, which is known as an *RSS feed, Webfeed, RSS stream,* or *RSS channel.* The RSS feed notifies users when newly released content is added. The type of notification differs depending on the vehicle reading the stream. Figure 5-8 shows the free RSS reader being used to track several RSS feeds.

The RSS reader shown in Figure 5-8 enables the user to peruse the newest headlines — or all headlines. If a user finds a headline that piques his interest, he can click the Read More link to read the article in the reader (as shown in Figure 5-9) or click the Open in Browser link to read the article in his default Web browser from the Web site hosting the RSS feed. The Open in Browser option enables visitors to peruse more of the host site after reading the article.

Figure 5-8:
Feed me,
baby.

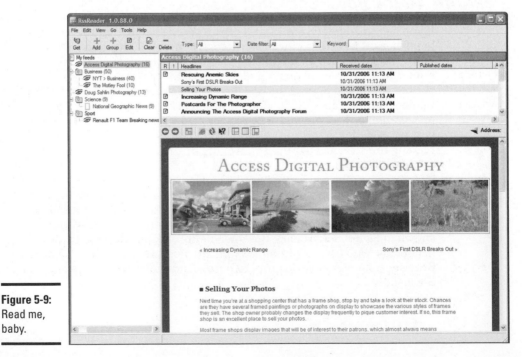

Figure 5-9:
Read me,
baby.

Using an online feed reader

Many people prefer to use online RSS feed reading services instead of down-loading and installing an RSS feed reader. An *online RSS feed reading service* enables you to track feeds through something you're already familiar with, a Web browser. There are many online services. We've personally explored two online RSS feed reading services: Bloglines (www.bloglines.com) and Pluck (www.pluck.com). If you haven't explored the wonderful world of RSS feeds, you can subscribe to either service for free. Figure 5-10 shows an RSS feed as it appears in Bloglines. Clicking the name of the blog transports the user directly to the blog site in a new browser window. Clicking the title of the post displays the entire post in a new browser window from the URL of the post.

**Book VI
Chapter 5**

**Additional Site
Interactivity**

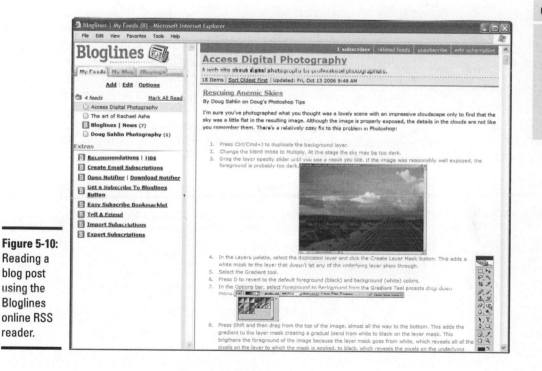

Figure 5-10:
Reading a
blog post
using the
Bloglines
online RSS
reader.

Creating an RSS feed

To broadcast an RSS feed, you create an XML (eXtensible Markup Language) document. Even if you're not familiar with XML language, you can create an RSS feed in no time flat using a word processing application such as Notepad. The document needs the following tags:

✦ `<rss>` Encompasses the entire feed. It tells feed readers what version of RSS the feed is.

✦ `<channel>` Houses all of the information about the feed. You can have more than one channel in a feed.

✦ `<title>` Displays the title of the blog.

✦ `<link>` Contains the URL of the blog.

✦ `<description>` Explains the purpose of the blog and the type of information in the blog posts.

✦ `<language>` Chooses the language in which the blog is written.

✦ `<item>` Displays the information for each blog post included in the feed. Each item needs the following tags:

  • `<title>` Shows the title of the blog post.

  • `<link>` Adds the URL for the blog post.

  • `<description>` Provides a description of the blog post. For this tag, I cut and paste the first few sentences from the blog post.

That's pretty much it in a nutshell. You can add other bells and whistles to the post, such as the time it was created, and so on. Listing 5-1 shows a simple RSS feed for a single blog post.

Listing 5-1: A Really Simple XML Document for an RSS Feed

```
<!DOCTYPE rss PUBLIC "-//Netscape Communications//DTD RSS
    0.91//EN" "http://my.netscape.com/publish/formats/rss-
    0.91.dtd">
<rss version="0.91">
    <channel>

<title>Doug Sahlin Photography</title>
    <link>http://www.dasdesigns.net/blog</link>
    <description>A digital photography and Photoshop blog
    with news, tips, and tutorials.</description>
    <language>en-us</language>
<item>
<title>Rescuing Anemic Skies</title>
    <link>http://www.dasdesigns.net/blog/?p=21</link>
    <description>I'm sure you've photographed what you thought
    was a lovely scene with an impressive cloudscape only
    to find that the sky was a little flat in the resulting
    image. Although the image is properly exposed, the details
    in the clouds are not like you remember them. There's a
    relatively easy fix to this problem in
    Photoshop:</description>
</item>
</channel>
</rss>
```

To add an item to an RSS feed, open a browser and navigate to the URL for the blog post you're adding. Then, it's a simple matter of cutting and pasting the title, link, and description for the new item. For the description, you can use the first few sentences from the blog post. The first lines of a blog post should be interesting enough to pique a visitor's curiosity and make her want to read the rest of the post. Each post is a new item with a title, link, and description as shown in Listing 5-2.

Listing 5-2: An RSS Feed with Multiple Posts

```
<?xml version="1.0" encoding="UTF-8"?>
<!DOCTYPE rss PUBLIC "-//Netscape Communications//DTD RSS
    0.91//EN" "http://my.netscape.com/publish/formats/rss-
    0.91.dtd">
<rss version-"0.91">
    <channel>
<title>Doug Sahlin Photography</title>
    <link>http://www.dasdesigns.net/blog</link>
    <description>A digital photography and Photoshop blog
with news, tips, and tutorials.</description>
    <language>en-us</language>
<item>
<title>Rescuing Anemic Skies</title>
    <link>http://www.dasdesigns.net/blog/?p=21</link>
    <description>I'm sure you've photographed what you thought
    was a lovely scene with an impressive cloudscape only to
    find that the sky was a little flat in the resulting
    image. Although the image is properly exposed, the details
    in the clouds are not like you remember them. There's a
    relatively easy fix to this problem in
    Photoshop:</description>
</item>
<item>
<title>Selling Your Photos</title>
    <link>http://www.dasdesigns.nct/blog/?p=20</link>
    <description>Next time you're at a shopping center that has a
    frame shop, stop by and take a look at their stock. Chances
    are they have several framed paintings or photographs on
    display to showcase the varioius styles of frames they sell.
    The shop owner probably changes the display frequently to
    pique customer interest. If so, this frame shop is an
    excellent place to sell your photos.</description>
</item>
    </channel>
    </rss>
```

Book VI
Chapter 5

Additional Site Inte-activity

You can use Listing 5-1 as a template for your own RSS feed. As long as you create a carbon copy of the first three tags, you can fill in the blanks. In fact, to show you how nice we are, we'll leave you a template (see Listing 5-3) from which to work.

Listing 5-3: An RSS Feed Template

```
<?xml version="1.0" encoding="UTF-8"?>
<!DOCTYPE rss PUBLIC "-//Netscape Communications//DTD RSS
    0.91//EN" "http://my.netscape.com/publish/formats/rss-
    0.91.dtd">
<rss version="0.91">
<channel>
<title></title>
<link></link>
<description></description>
<language></language>
<item>
      <title></title>
      <link></link>
      <description></description>
</item>
</channel>
</rss>
```

After you create your feed, save it as an XML document. We call this one `feed.xml`. Upload the document to the `root` directory of your blog. You're now ready to start feeding the masses, so to speak.

There is another way of creating an RSS feed, for those who don't like manually typing the code shown in the previous examples. There's a free application called RssPublisher. You can download it from `www.rsspublisher.com`. The application (see Figure 5-11) consists of three tabs: Feed, Headlines, and Publish. On the Feed tab, you enter the information about your feed. On the Headlines tab, you enter the title, description, and link to each post you want to feed to the public. The Publish tab enables you to publish the feed directly to the Web site hosting the blog, to your local machine, or both.

Validating your feed

You validate parking tickets, so why not validate your RSS feed? If all RSS readers can't read your RSS feed, it's not useful. You can validate your RSS feed for free by following these steps:

1. **Log on to the Internet and navigate to `www.feedvalidator.org`. (See Figure 5-12.)**

2. **Enter the URL to your RSS feed.**

   Enter the URL plus the document name; for example: `http://www.mywebsite/feed.xml`.

3. **Wait.**

   The feed validator checks your feed and tells you the status of your feed. Figure 5-13 shows the results when a feed is valid.

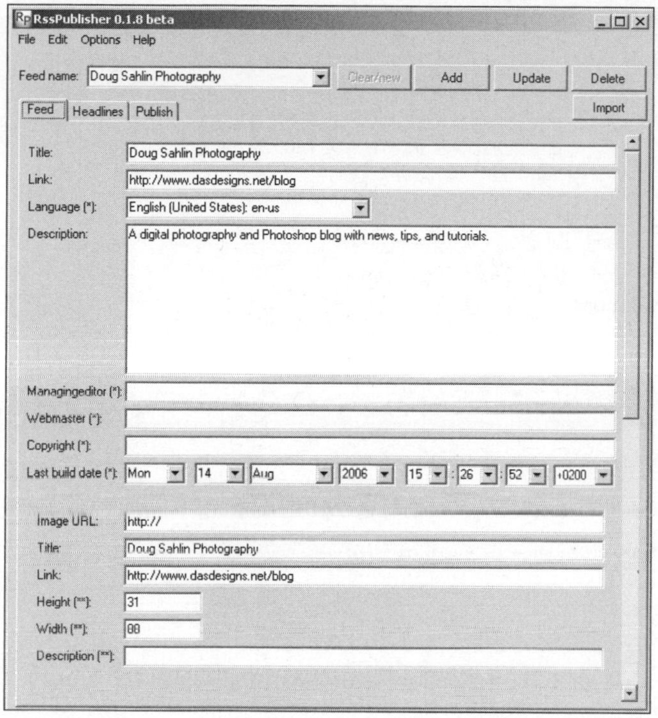

Figure 5-11: Using RssPublisher to create a feed for those in need.

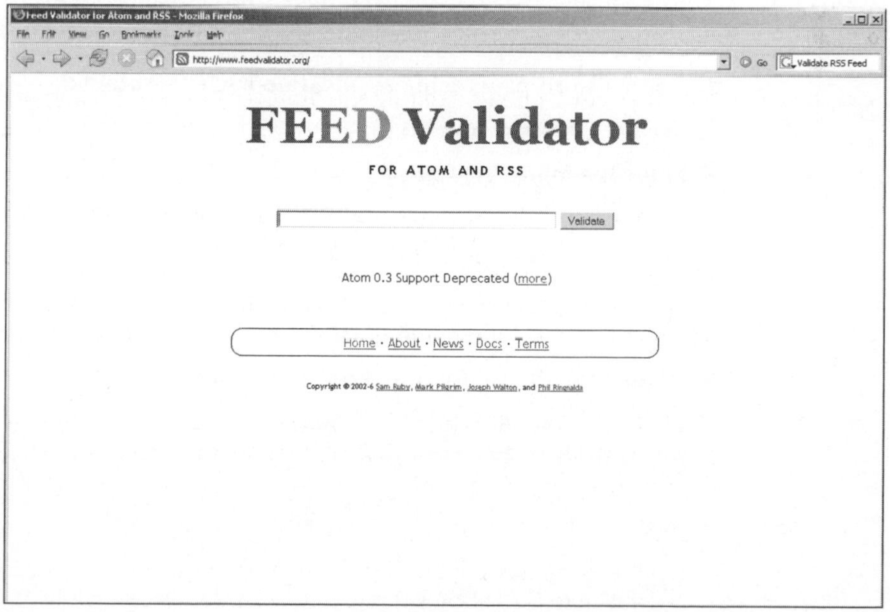

**Book VI
Chapter 5**

**Additional Site
Interactivity**

Figure 5-12: Please validate me; set me free.

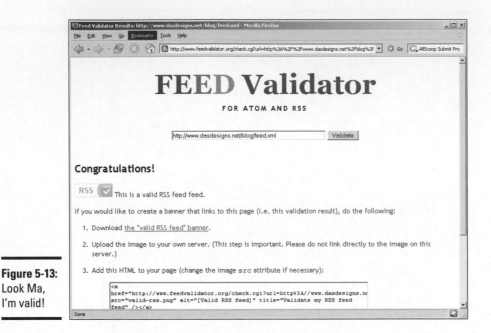

Figure 5-13:
Look Ma,
I'm valid!

If your feed isn't valid, the feed validator highlights the troublesome lines of code and lets you know what steps to take to correct the problem. You need to save an RSS feed with UTF-8 encoding. However, some Web servers read the file as having ANSI encoding. If this occurs, the error will show up when you validate the feed. To correct this problem, follow these steps:

1. **Open a word processing application such as Notepad.**

2. **Create a new document.**

3. **Enter the following text:**

```
AddType 'application/xml; charset=UTF-8' xml
```

4. **Save the file as .htaccess.**

Your word processing application might save the file with an extension. If this is the case, rename the file prior to uploading it.

5. **Upload the file to the blog `root` directory.**

When you validate the blog now, the `.htaccess` document ensures that the XML file is delivered with UTF-8 encoding.

Getting your feed going

Now that you've got an RSS feed, it's time to announce the fact to the world. Of course, you want to let current visitors to the blog know that it's syndicated with an RSS feed. You can do this by adding the code in Listing 5-4 to the applicable place in your blog page. This code uses three RSS feed reading services: Yahoo!, Bloglines, and Rojo. In addition, you may want to consider adding text that shows the URL to your feed. For example, you could add a line of text that reads: To add our blog to your RSS feed reader, enter the following URL: www.*mysite.com*/blog/feed.xml in the applicable field in your feed reader.

Listing 5-4: Code to Subscribe to a Blog

```
<h2>Subscribe to my blog!</h2>
<form name="subscribe">
<p>Subscribe to this blog via RSS feeds.
</p> <select name="feeds">
<option value="http://add.my.yahoo.com/rss?url=<?php
    bloginfo('url'); ?>/feed.rss">My Yahoo!</option>
<option value="http://bloglines.com/sub/<?php
    bloginfo('url'); ?>/">Bloglines</option>
<option value="http://rojo.com/add-subscription?resource=
    <?php bloginfo('url'); ?>/">Rojo</option>
</select><br /><p></p>
<input type="button"
    onclick="location=document.subscribe.feeds.options
    [document.subscribe.feeds.selectedIndex].value;"
    value="Subscribe">
  </form>
```

Finding the place in your page code where you add the code in Listing 5-4 will take a bit of searching when you're using a blog application. After all, you didn't write the code. You should be able to figure it out by determining where you want to place the form in the blog page, by viewing it online, and then examining the code in your HTML editor with a fine-toothed comb. When you successfully add the code to a blog, you'll see a window with a down-arrow that opens a drop-down menu with your subscription choices. (See Figure 5-14.)

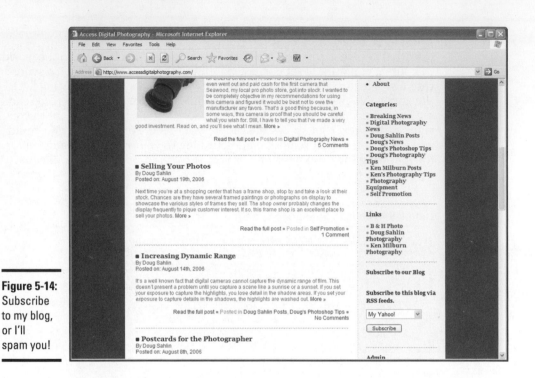

Figure 5-14: Subscribe to my blog, or I'll spam you!

You can publicize a blog by submitting it to online blog readers, such as www.bloglines.com or www.pluck.com. Another alternative is to use an application that submits your blog feed to multiple sources. One such application is Submit Pro by Allscoop. This works like the software you can purchase to submit Web sites to search engines. And the wonderful thing is that it's free. We've submitted two blog feeds to numerous sites with the software and have noticed an increase in the amount of traffic that comes to each blog. The application is self-explanatory. You launch the application and then add the RSS feeds you want to submit. (See Figure 5-15.) You then select the sites to which you'd like to submit the feed. (See Figure 5-16.) When you click the Next button (the right-pointing arrow), the application submits the blog to the sites you selected while you sit back and enjoy a fresh cup of your favorite beverage. You can download Submit Pro from www.allscoop.com/tools/rss-submit.

Branding through E-Mail

Anyone who is serious about doing business online should have an e-mail address associated with the Web site. Sure you can conduct business by sending an e-mail with one of the free online services, but who wants to do business with `friendlyfred@hotmail.com`? In addition to the credibility factor, the free services limit the number of messages you can receive. The better solution is to set up one or more e-mail addresses using your Web server's control panel. E-mail addresses are also a wonderful way to make a Web presence seem like a huge company. The following list shows examples of addresses you can set up for a fictitious Web site called `widgetsrus.biz`:

✦ `john@widgetsrus.biz`

✦ `sales@widgetsrus.biz`

✦ `info@widgetsrus.biz`

✦ `service@widgetsrus.biz`

Figure 5-15:
Select the feeds you want to submit.

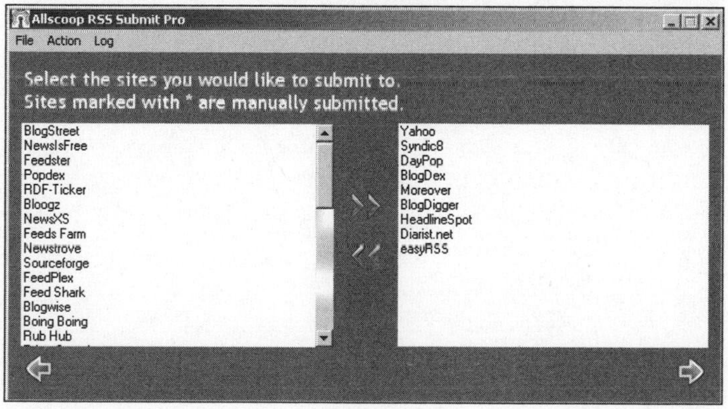

Figure 5-16:
Select the site to which you want to submit the feeds.

If your client uses an application like Microsoft Outlook to manage mail, he can easily set up accounts to receive and send messages from each e-mail address. The recipient will never be the wiser. When the business grows, your client can add additional e-mail addresses for other employees and transfer the other addresses he's currently managing to the applicable employee.

Keeping Them Up to Date: Newsletters

If your client's site changes frequently — and it should — he'll want to get the word out when new material is posted on the site. One of the easiest ways to do this is telling people who have visited the site that new information is posted. You're probably thinking that there's no way your client is going to e-mail each and every person who has stopped by his site. And you'd be right; this is way too much work. The easy way to keep visitors abreast of new information is to send them newsletters on a regular basis. When you design the site, you create a form that enables visitors to subscribe or opt in to the newsletter list. The visitor's information is stored in a database. You could create your client's monthly newsletter, but there's an easier way: an application that enables your client to create a newsletter from a template you've designed and send that newsletter to subscribers. The application should also give your client the option of managing the mailing list. Such applications exist. If you don't have access to one, type **e-mail list manager** in your favorite search engine. Better yet, mosey on over to Book IX, Chapter 3, which shows you a list management application in action and some newsletter examples.

Book VII

E-Commerce

The 5th Wave   By Rich Tennant

"Our customer survey indicates 30% of our customers think our service is inconsistent, 40% would like a change in procedures, and 50% think it would be real cute if we all wore matching colored vests."

Contents at a Glance

Chapter 1: An E-Commerce Primer

*Y*our client is an entrepreneur with a product or service for sale and wants to take the business to the next level. Or perhaps you're creating a Web site for a bricks-and-mortar business that wants to kick the business up a notch. Your solution for either client is quite simple: Design an interactive e-commerce site for your client. When done correctly, an e-commerce site makes it possible for your client to conduct business worldwide, 24 hours a day, 7 days a week. That's right — a store that never closes.

Of course, any venture has its pitfalls. Your goal as a Web designer is to create an attractive, interactive site that your client's customers can easily navigate. In addition to the usual bells and whistles you'll include on an interactive site, you also need to provide a manner in which Web site visitors can order and pay for their wares and a method for your client to collect her money. In this chapter, you'll learn basic e-commerce concepts such as setting up the site, working with credit card authorization packages, and obtaining a secure server.

Nailing Down E-Commerce Concepts

If you build it, they will come. Not! The world of e-commerce enables a merchant to branch out and present her service or product to a worldwide audience. However, if the merchant does not address certain issues, the site won't succeed. It often falls on the shoulders of a savvy Web site designer — that would be you, reader — to advise your client. The following sections show you what to consider when creating an e-commerce site.

Establishing an online identity

Every Web site has a domain name — it's a law. A *domain name* is like a phone number. It is unique. When entered in the Address field of a Web browser, preceded by www, it leads the flock to the proper Web site. The domain name for an e-commerce site should serve two functions: It describes the business to potential customers, and it is used to navigate to the merchant's online catalog. Your client might already own a domain name. However, if the name was not carefully chosen, you should recommend to your client that a more appropriate name be registered. After all, you can register a domain name rather inexpensively these days.

So what's in a name? Everything. The domain name should be easy to remember, short, and tell something about the business. The name should also be unique. For example, people associate the Amazon.com domain with the largest online seller of books — and other assorted sundries — in the world. A domain name of Isellbooks.com, tells the visitor about the business, but it is not unique, nor is it short.

If your client already has an established bricks-and-mortar business, you should use that name as the domain name — or a clever derivative thereof. For example, if your clients are attorneys and their domain name is carnettsmithLaw.com, consider changing it to Cslaw.com. Many firms personalize a domain name by using the word "my" as part of the domain name. For example: mycslaw.com.

Researching domain names

A domain name is like a phone number. When a Web surfer enters the domain name into the Address field of his browser window, the browser refreshes to the Web site's home page. That's right; domain names are unique. There are zillions of Web sites out there, and each one has a unique name. When you or your client is trying to come up with a unique domain name for the e-commerce site you'll design, you can quickly cut to the chase and figure out whether a domain name has already been reserved by following these steps:

1. **Log on to the Internet and navigate to www.betterwhois.com.**

   You can research a domain name at most *registrars* (the companies that take your money in exchange for registering a domain name). However, this Web site searches all domain registrars to see if the name has been reserved.

2. **Enter the desired domain name in the Search field as shown in Figure 1-1.**

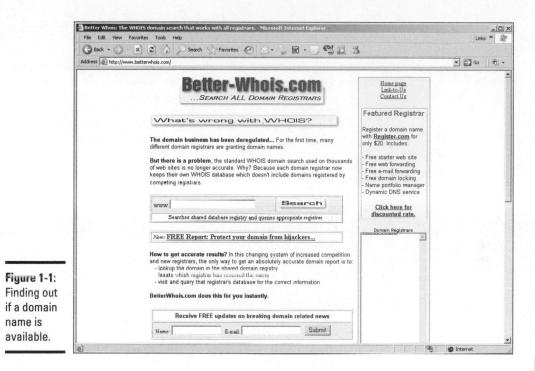

Figure 1-1:
Finding out
if a domain
name is
available.

**Book VII
Chapter 1**

**An E-Commerce
Primer**

3. **Click Search.**

You are prompted to enter the security code shown on your monitor.

4. **Enter the security code and click Continue.**

The domain registrar databases are searched. If the domain name is reserved, a message to that affect appears on the results page. If the domain is reserved, you can get further information about the domain by clicking one of the links shown in Figure 1-2. If the domain name is available, the Web page refreshes with a message to that affect, and you have the opportunity to register the domain name.

If the desired domain name is not available, see if the same name is available with one of the other domain name suffixes. Most businesses like to register their domain as a top-level (.com) domain. However, the .net, .biz, and .info suffixes are also acceptable for e-commerce sites.

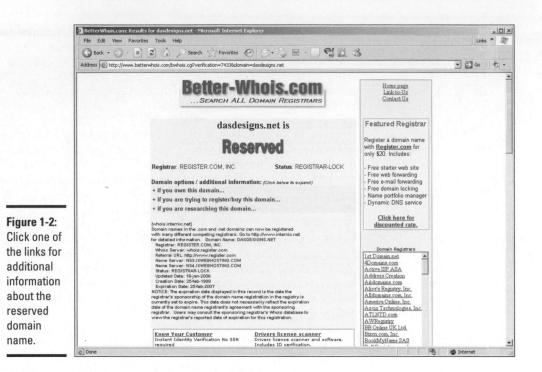

Figure 1-2:
Click one of the links for additional information about the reserved domain name.

Purchasing domain names

After you find that a desired domain name is available, you can reserve the domain by purchasing it. Domain registrars are not regulated. There are many from which to choose. You can reserve a domain name for as little as $6.95 per year. However, make sure you research the domain registrar before reserving the name with them. Many of the low-price registrars come with strings attached, or they try to sell you Web hosting along with the domain name. And the Web hosting provided by the domain registrar might not be applicable for e-commerce.

Many Web hosting services include domain registration as part of their hosting fee. Of course, your client is responsible for renewing the domain name after the registration expires. It is also possible to get a better deal if you register the domain for more than one year. Like everything else on the Internet, the price of registering domains is in a constant state of flux. If you do a bit of research before registering your client's desired domain name, you'll find the best package currently available. If you type **domain registrars** into your favorite search engine, you'll have enough results to keep you busy for a few hours.

If you're able to get your desired domain name with the .com suffix, consider purchasing .net, .biz, .info, and .org suffixes for your domain name as well. It's also good practice to register misspellings of the chosen domain name. This enables your client to prevent competitors from registering other suffixes with your client's domain name and similar spellings to ride on the coattails of your client's successful site.

Just because a domain name has been registered doesn't mean it's being used. Many domain name brokers buy names on speculation. Additionally, unused domain names can be purchased. You might be able to purchase your desired but currently registered domain name from a company such as BuyDomains.com or Afternic.com.

Choosing an e-commerce-friendly server

Web hosting services are a dime a dozen these days, or so it seems. Choosing the right server can mean the difference between a successful e-commerce site and one that fades into oblivion after a few hundred visitors. Web hosting services offer a variety of features. The following sections offer some sage advice for choosing a Web hosting service for your e-commerce site.

To share or not to share

Most Web hosting companies offer shared and dedicated hosting. The option you choose depends on your client's budget and how much traffic you anticipate will be generated for the e-commerce site you're designing. Of course, when it comes to traffic, your client will want the moon, Alice.

If your client is just dipping his toe into the e-commerce tidal pool, a shared server suffices nicely. When a site is hosted by a *shared server,* this means that the site information is stored on a host with several other Web sites. Shared servers are more economical than dedicated servers. The only potential drawback with a shared server is that if your client's site (or one of the other sites on the server) starts getting a lot of traffic, visitors might not be able to access the site quickly during busy times, or — worst-case scenario — visitors might not be able to access the site 100 percent of the time.

If your client has an established, bricks-and-mortar business that is doing well and you have a stout plan for marketing the site — you do have a marketing plan, don't you? — consider paying the extra to get a dedicated server. When you host a site on a dedicated server, the server is dedicated to your client's site. That's right, your client's site is the only one on the server, which means visitors get faster access, even when the Internet is busy, and they get access 100 percent of the time.

If your client's initial needs warrant only a shared server, make sure that the Web hosting company can upgrade the client to a dedicated server without penalty when the need arises.

Getting the best deal

When searching for a service to host an e-commerce site, the best price is not necessarily the best deal. And in some instances, the best price is an absolute disaster. As the Web designer, you need to be in control and tell your client which server you're going to use. But what features do you need? That, like the proverbial well, is a deep subject. However, here are a few items to consider when shopping for the quintessential, e-commerce, Web hosting service:

✦ **Does the Web hosting company provide shared servers or dedicated servers?** If the company is providing a shared server, visitors may experience problems connecting to the Web site during peak traffic periods.

✦ **How much hard disk space does the Web hosting service provide?** This usually differs depending on the plan you choose. If the site you're designing is relatively small, you can get by with 300–500 megabytes (MB) of hard disk space. If the site you're designing has copious amounts of multimedia elements such as full-motion video or Flash movies, subdomains, and other bells and whistles, you might need up to 9 gigabytes (GB) of space. Choose the amount of space that best serves your client's current needs. But make sure the hosting service is flexible, and your client can upgrade to a different plan that provides more disk space when the need arises.

✦ **What percentage of up time does the Web hosting service guarantee?** E-commerce sites need to be available 24/7. In an ideal world, there would never be power outages or problems with Internet hub connections. However, these interruptions in service are a fact of life, and the best Web hosting services have redundancy built into their system to guard against down time. Choose a Web server that can guarantee you near 100 percent availability.

✦ **How many e-mail accounts does the Web hosting service provide?** Most Web hosting services provide 50 e-mail accounts with a hosting package. Having an e-mail account linked to a Web site adds an air of authenticity to the site. Most consumers would rather send a query to, let's say, an e-mail address like `info@widgetzrus.com` than to `fred@aol.com`. With 50 e-mail addresses that have your domain name, you can use generic e-mail addresses like: `info@`*mysite.com*, `sales@`*mysite.com*, and if needed, personal e-mail addresses like `fred@`*mysite.com*.

✦ **Does the Web hosting service provide a user-friendly method of managing the Web site?** Most Web hosting services provide a control panel that clients use to manage the Web site, add e-mail addresses, manage databases, control FTP access to the site, and so on. If you're going to manage the account for the client, make sure you understand how to use the control panel. If your client is going to manage the site, make sure the control panel is extremely user friendly.

✦ **Does the Web hosting service provide support? If so, is the support by phone or online?** You'll also need to know if support is available 24/7 in case of an emergency.

✦ **Can you set up a database for the Web site?** This feature is especially important if your client requires a Web site that receives data from clients for future use. You'll also want to know what type of database the hosting service supports.

✦ **Does the Web hosting package support pages with PHP code?** If so, make sure the version of PHP offered by the Web hosting service matches the version you'll be using for your code.

✦ **Does the Web hosting service provide statistics?** If so, how much information is provided? You or your client needs to know how many visits the site is getting each day, where the traffic is coming from, what keywords are being used to find your site from search engines, what the most popular entrance and exit pages are, and so on. This information is imperative when you and the client fine-tune the content of the site.

✦ **Can you host more than one domain with the hosting package?** This information is important if the client is setting up more than one e-commerce site. Many Web hosting services enable you to host up to ten domains with one hosting package at a reasonable cost.

✦ **Does the hosting service enable you to create subdomains?** This feature is useful if the client wants to set up different Web sites for different aspects of the company's services. For example, you could design pages for the client's customer service and store them in a subdomain that you might name `customerservice.mye-commercesite.com`.

As a Web designer, you can host your own Web site with a Web hosting package that permits more than one domain. You can then host your client Web sites using your Web hosting service and bill the client for hosting service, enabling you to add additional profit to your bottom line. Many Web hosting services also have reseller packages. You can purchase Web hosting for additional domains at a reduced price. You then mark up the hosting service and bill your client.

Planning a user-friendly site

Before you begin designing the site, it's time to sit down with your client and find out what his goals are for the site. If the client wants to use the site to dispense information and collect sales leads, you'll need to create an online catalog, as well as a database that records the names and e-mail addresses submitted by interested parties. You can collect this information using an online form.

If the site is being used to sell products and your client wants visitors to be able to purchase products online, you'll have to get additional information in order to create a successful site. Here are a few important items that must be included when designing an e-commerce Web site:

✦ **An About Us section:** This section gives your client credibility. Here you'll include information about your client and the reasons visitors should purchase your client's products or services.

✦ **A comprehensive description of your client's products or services:** This section of the site should include the features of your client's offering and information on how each feature benefits the client's potential customer. If your client is selling a product or interactive service, this section should also explain the function of each feature and its benefit to the customer.

✦ **A section that features testimonials and/or success stories from your client's existing customer base:** This section builds tremendous credibility for your client's product or service.

✦ **FAQs:** An FAQ (frequently asked question) section anticipates and answers questions or concerns potential customers might have.

When you design the site, make it easy for potential customers to gather all the information they need to make an informed buying decision. Add as many graphic elements as you need to add sizzle to the steak. Images are a must when it comes to selling a product. You should include an image with each product description. If your client's catalog is extensive, you'll be displaying many items on each page, which equates to a small image size. If your customer's products bear close scrutiny, make sure to include links to different views of the product as well as links to larger versions of the image.

If appropriate, you can also include multimedia elements in your Web design. Video clips are great ways to explain complicated details about a product or service. And you can spice up an e-commerce site with the liberal use of Flash movies. For that matter, Flash is also an excellent vehicle for incorporating full-motion video on a Web site.

Don't overload a page with multimedia elements, especially if part of your client's intended audience accesses the Internet with dialup modems. If your client insists on multimedia elements or you feel multimedia elements are essential for the site, consider creating two versions of the site: one for high bandwidth and one for low bandwidth. Make sure that the multimedia for the low bandwidth version of the site is smaller in size with higher levels of compression to ensure that it loads in a reasonable amount of time.

Clean navigation is essential. If you design a site with a cluttered navigation menu with multiple choices, visitors can be confused and have a hard time figuring out what to click to get the information they need. If your client has more products or information, you can divide the site into sections. Each section is like a minisite with pertinent information to a specific part of your client's business.

Brainstorming the site

When you and your client brainstorm to create the ultimate e-commerce site, your goal is to arrive at a common vision: a marriage of your creative talent and your client's vision. During your meeting of the minds, you should strive to take the upper hand. Unless your client is familiar with Web sites and e-commerce, some of her ideas might be over the top, or simply undoable. Designing an e-commerce site is covered in detail in Chapter 2 of this minibook. When initially planning the site, take the following factors into consideration:

✦ **Research e-commerce sites of businesses similar to your clients.** In fact, ask your client for the URLs of his fiercest competitors. Most business Web sites have a common look and feel. It's generally not a good idea to design a site that's considerably different than your client's competitors'. Researching your client's competitors' sites gives you an idea of what are considered standard design staples for that type of business.

✦ **Display your client's company name and logo prominently on each page.** The easiest way to do this is to create a banner and display it at the top of each page, as shown in Figure 1-3.

✦ **Create a separate page for contact information.** On this page, include the client's physical address, phone number(s), fax number(s), and e-mail addresses.

✦ **Create a What's New section to showcase your client's newest products and other pertinent news.** This is also a great place to announce special promotions. This section should be updated frequently to encourage customers to visit the site often.

✦ **In addition to the main navigation menu for the site, add a text-only menu at the bottom of each page.** This information can improve the site's ranking in search engines. It also gives customers a convenient way to navigate when they scroll to the bottom of a page.

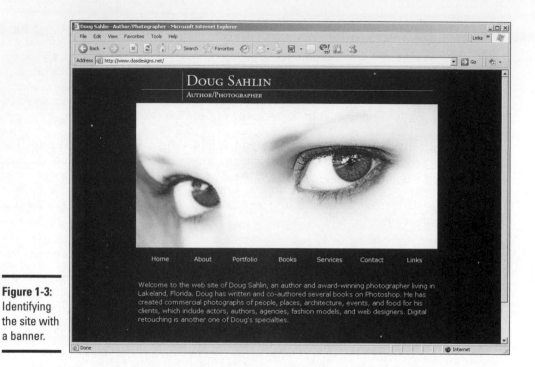

Figure 1-3:
Identifying
the site with
a banner.

✦ **Add a privacy statement that clearly describes your client's policy for protecting customers' personal information.**

✦ **Keep your navigation simple.** Customers should not have to click more than six times to go from the site's home page to checkout.

✦ **Don't use any trick navigation.** The navigation menu you design should be simple and not distract the customer's attention from the reason for the site: the product or service your client is selling.

✦ **Use meaningful link names.** If your client suggests using obtuse, yet creative, link names, it's your job to become the voice of reason and suggest readily identifiable link names. That is, of course, unless your customer is selling an avant-garde product or service whose target audience consists of eclectic people with a creative bent.

When creating an e-commerce Web site, set up an info@myclientsbiz. com e-mail address. This can be a catchall e-mail for customer queries. Most Web hosting services provide more than enough e-mail addresses with each hosting package. Contact the service hosting your client's Web site for more information on setting up new e-mail accounts.

Adding Basic E-Commerce with PayPal

If your client is on a budget, or isn't sure if the product or service he or she is promoting will take off, PayPal is a viable alternative to hosting with a secure server and purchasing a credit card authorization package. In fact, many successful e-commerce sites use PayPal to complete transactions. PayPal is the brainchild of the folks who created eBay. Initially, PayPal was used to complete eBay auctions. The buyer could set up a free, personal PayPal account to pay the seller. Online shoppers with a personal PayPal account can pay for purchases using a debit card, credit card, or by transferring funds from the bank account associated with the PayPal account.

Online merchants can use PayPal to accept payments using either a Premier or Business account. Merchants can sign up for either account for free. The fees for transactions up to $3,000 per month is 2.9 percent plus $0.30 per transaction. The beauty of a PayPal account is that the merchant incurs no setup fees, no monthly maintenance fees, and no fraud-protection fees. A merchant can transfer money from his PayPal account to his bank account at any time. There is no charge for a wire transfer, which takes three to four days, depending on the bank account routing.

When you use PayPal to accept payments, you can create a custom payment page. When you create a custom payment page, it looks like the payment is being conducted with your own secure server. To create a custom page in PayPal, follow these steps:

1. **Log on to your PayPal Premier or Business account and navigate to the Profile page.**

   The Profile section of PayPal's Web site is where you specify your account information, financial information, and seller preferences.

2. **From the Seller Preferences menu, choose Custom Payment Pages.**

   The Custom Payment Page Styles section of the site appears. The default payment style is PayPal, unless you've previously created a custom payment page. In this case, all payment page options are displayed, as shown in Figure 1-4, and a custom style is selected.

3. **To create a new custom payment page, click Add.**

   The Edit Custom Page Style page appears, as shown in Figure 1-5.

4. **Enter a name for the custom page style.**

   This name is added to the list of custom styles associated with your profile.

5. **Enter the URL for the custom banner that will be displayed at the top of your custom payment page in the Header Image URL field.**

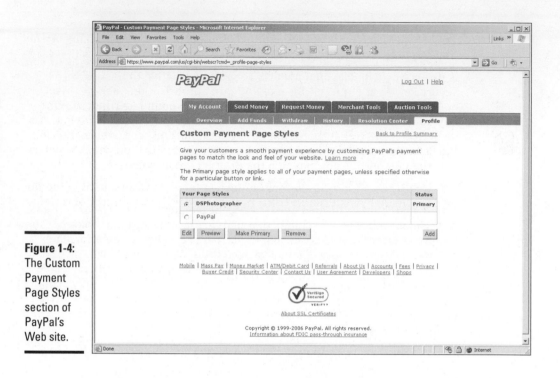

Figure 1-4:
The Custom
Payment
Page Styles
section of
PayPal's
Web site.

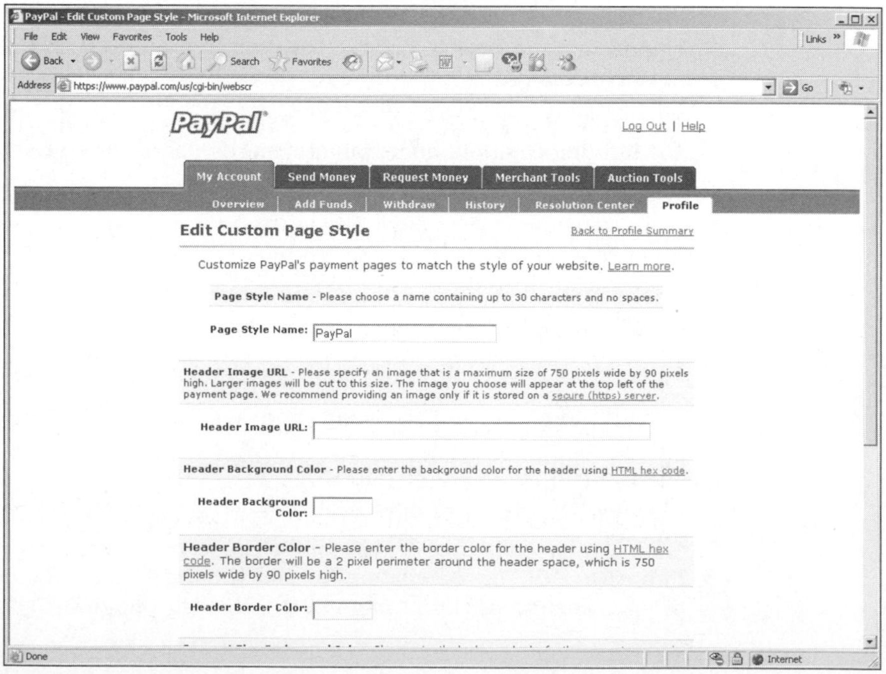

Figure 1-5:
Creating a
custom
payment
style.

The ideal size for the banner is 750-pixels wide by 90-pixels high. Ideally, the banner should contain your client's logo or the name of the e-commerce site. You can easily create an image in Fireworks that loads quickly. Unless the banner contains photorealistic images, export the image in the GIF format.

You should store the image for a custom payment page on a secure server. If it isn't, a warning is displayed in the customer's Web browser notifying him that the payment page contains insecure items. The URL for a secure server begins with `https//` instead of `http://`, which is used for Web pages in which the data is not encrypted.

6. **If you're not using a custom banner, enter the hexadecimal value for the header background color in the Header Background Color field.**

    Choose a background color that matches the background color of the e-commerce page from which the payments will be made. (For more information on hexadecimal values, see Book II, Chapter 4.)

7. **Enter the hexadecimal value for the header border in the Header Border Color field.**

    This places a 2-pixel border with the specified color around the payment page header.

8. **Enter the hexadecimal value for the background color in the Payment Flow Background Color field.**

    This changes the background color of the page from white to the color specified. Note that certain colors such as red and fluorescent green are not permitted as these colors clash with the payment page warning messages, making them hard to read. And of course, you should not choose a dark color as the text will be illegible as well.

9. **Click Save to save the custom style and return to the Custom Payment Page Styles page.**

    Alternatively, you can click Preview to preview the custom style. If the style is not to your liking, change the parameters until the custom style matches the look and feel of the e-commerce site from which the payments are being made.

10. **Click the radio button for the style you just created.**

    This makes the selected style the style that is displayed when payments are made from the e-commerce site.

11. **Click the Make Primary button.**

    The style you created is now the default style for any PayPal transactions. Figure 1-6 shows a custom PayPal payment page.

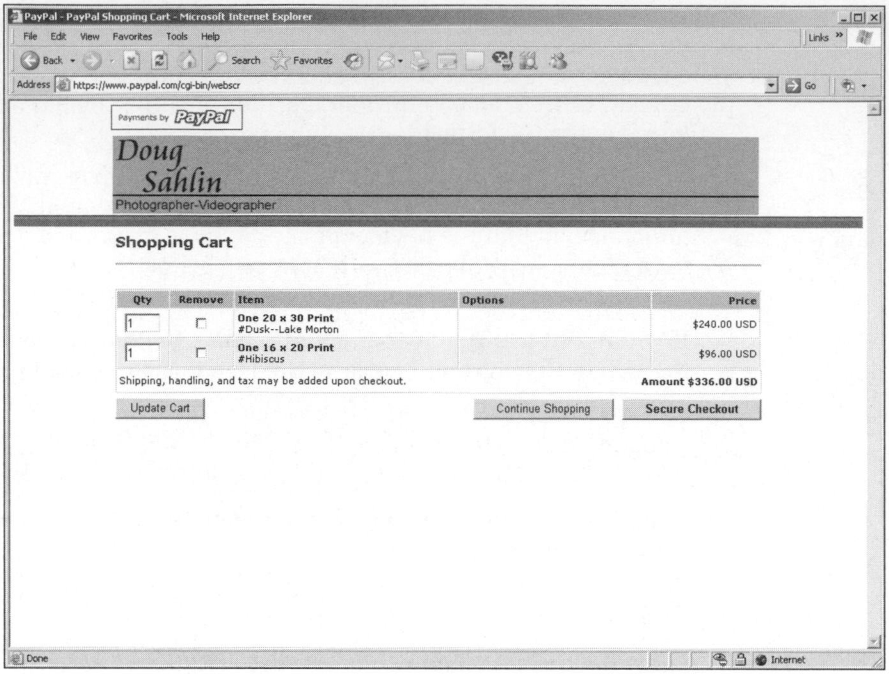

Figure 1-6: A custom PayPal payment page makes it appear as though the payment is being made through the site's secure server, and not PayPal.

Integrating with Credit Card Authorization Packages

The traditional way to handle transactions from a Web site is using a credit card authorization package. When you integrate a site with a credit card package, the payments from the site are handled by a number of banking institutions and processes. The service charges a setup fee and a monthly maintenance fee. The maintenance fee is based on the number of transactions handled per month. A thorough review of each of the many authorization packages available is beyond the scope of this book. However, you can find some information by logging onto the Internet and pointing your Web browser to `http://www.dummies.com/WileyCDA/DummiesArticle/id-142.html`.

Credit card authorization packages enable you to run your online business with minimum overhead. In a traditional bricks-and-mortar store, you have to hire salespeople to show customers the product, take orders, and accept payments. With a properly designed e-commerce site and credit card authorization package, these tasks are handled automatically. If the e-commerce site you're designing sells a service, you can schedule regular payments through the credit card authorization package.

Online payments are quite involved, flowing through a complex network of financial institutions and processes. The complexity is exacerbated when you accept payment from foreign countries. Fortunately, technology has simplified this process, and the proper credit card authorization package provides the gateway for this process. When a customer makes an online payment, the process occurs in the background, and the payment process occurs fairly quickly.

Solving the online payment maze

When a customer makes a payment, the payment must go from the issuing bank (the institution that funds the customer's credit card) to your client's bank. The process appears seamless when a payment is made online, but there are many supporting players in what seems like a one-act play. The following list introduces the various actors in this one-act play that happens when the Checkout button is clicked:

✦ **Acquiring bank:** The acquiring bank provides Internet merchants with an Internet merchant account. An online merchant must have an Internet merchant account to enable credit card authorization and payment processing. Your client's bank can probably serve as an acquiring bank.

✦ **Authorization:** This part of the process is when the credit card submitted by the customer is validated and checked to ensure there is a sufficient credit balance to cover the purchase. At the same time, the information submitted by the customer is verified to ensure it matches the credit card company's records.

✦ **Customer issuing bank:** Banks such as SunTrust or Citibank that provide a credit card or other payment instrument to the customer are considered customer issuing banks. During the transaction, the customer issuing bank verifies that the payment information submitted by the merchant is valid and that the customer has sufficient funds or credit balance to cover the purchase.

✦ **Internet merchant account:** An account set up with an acquiring bank that enables a merchant to accept credit card payments over the Internet. Applying for a merchant account is similar to applying for a commercial loan. Typically, the acquiring bank charges a monthly maintenance fee based on the number of transactions posted to the merchant's account. A setup fee applies as well.

✦ **Payment processing service:** This is a service that provides the gateway for the customers, merchants, and financial institutions to process authorizations and payments. The service is usually provided by a third party such as Authorize.Net or VeriSign.

✦ **Processor:** The processor is a large, online data center that processes credit card payments and settles funds to merchants. The processor is linked to the merchant's e-commerce site on behalf of the acquiring bank via the payment processing service.

✦ **Settlement:** The process by which transactions with authorization codes are sent to the processor for payment to the merchant is called a *settlement.* Think of this as electronic bookkeeping that causes funds from authorized transactions to be routed for deposit into the merchant's account at the acquiring bank.

Fees for credit card authorization packages vary depending on the institution you choose and the number of bells and whistles included with the chosen credit card authorization package. As of this writing, a basic credit card authorization package that allows the merchant to conduct up to 500 transactions per month has a setup fee of $179 and a monthly maintenance fee of $19.95. If the merchant exceeds 500 transactions, an additional fee of $0.10 per transaction is charged to the merchant's account.

Internet fraud: An e-commerce merchant's worst nightmare

Not unlike things that go bump in the night, Internet fraud can rear its ugly head when you least expect it. Online merchants are responsible for fraudulent credit card transactions conducted through their sites. In addition to incurring heavy penalties and fees incurred by the credit card association, there is the matter of product costs and shipping fees incurred by your client. Fortunately, you can protect the site against credit card fraud, even with a start-up online business that has limited transactions.

The first and most obvious step in safeguarding against fraud is to choose a payment solution that is secure and reliable. Choose a payment package that includes standard processing and anti-fraud features such as Card Security Code (CSC) and Address Verification Service (AVS). In addition, the payment solution should have options that enable your client to upgrade to the new buyer verification systems such as MasterCard SecureCode and Verified by Visa. Your payment solution might have additional options to safeguard against fraud. Ask your representative for details.

SSL — What Is It?

The world is full of acronyms these days, and the wonderful world of e-commerce is no exception. But remember, if it weren't for acronyms, you'd have to type or write a whole lot of words. The acronym of concern for any e-commerce site is SSL, which stands for *Secure Sockets Layer.* See, we told you it was a lot of words.

In a nutshell, when a site has SSL, that means that the transaction is encrypted and cannot be deciphered by a third party. All pages that are secure are listed as `https`, followed by the rest of the Web address. Users can transmit any amount of information from a secure site and know that a third party cannot decipher the information. Sending credit card information via a secure site is safer than whipping out your credit card in a local store where prying eyes — and for that matter, the salesperson — can see the information. When you purchase goods or services from a secure site, the data is *encrypted* when it is submitted. When the recipient — that would be the bean counter for your client's e-commerce site — receives the data, it is *decrypted*. The bean counter adds the money to your client's P&L statement, and the goods are shipped to your client's customer.

Using a secure server

When you conduct your e-commerce using a secure server, the SSL certificate is linked to the site from which the transactions are being conducted. The SSL certificate is in your client's name and the domain name of the e-commerce site.

Hosting an e-commerce site through a secure server is an expensive proposition. To host an e-commerce site on a secure server using an SSL certificate with 128-bit encryption costs several hundred dollars per year — and as much as a thousand dollars and up per year depending on the services included with the package. However, the less-expensive alternative of using PayPal's secure server is always an option. You might pay a bit more per transaction, but the cost of a secure server isn't added to your overhead. The other alternative is sharing an SSL certificate, if your Web hosting service provides this option.

Sharing an SSL certificate

Many Web hosting services allow their customers to share an SSL certificate. This service is included with your hosting, and therefore can be considered free. When you share an SSL certificate, you do so through a third-level domain alias, for example: www.*yourdomain*.c2.*yourWebhostingserver*. com. When you share an SSL certificate, you must use the domain alias in the code you use to create the buttons for your site's shopping cart. Alternatively, you can purchase a shopping cart package, which you can integrate into the site.

The problem with sharing an SSL certificate is that Internet Explorer issues a warning saying the domain name on the certificate does not match the domain name of the site from which the transaction is being conducted. Even so, the data is still encrypted, and the transaction is secure. This may cause a customer to back out of a transition.

E-commerce Do's and Don'ts

When you create an e-commerce site, your goal is to sell your merchandise — or your client's merchandise. In keeping with these goals, there are certain things you should consider and certain things you should avoid (such as designing an e-commerce site that looks like a board game). The following lists of do's and don'ts can keep you on the straight and narrow:

✦ **Do make the site user-friendly.** Make sure your site navigation is easy to decipher. If your visitors need a manual to figure out how to use your site, it's not a good thing.

✦ **Do include a privacy statement.** If you request the visitor's contact information, make sure to include a link to your privacy statement that is readily visible on any page that requests sensitive information.

✦ **Make sure the site has the look and feel of other e-commerce sites in your client's industry.** Customers shy away from something that looks different from what they've come to expect. After all, no department stores look like the hip boutiques in Haight-Ashbury.

✦ **Avoid using buzzwords and hype in the product descriptions.** These raise a red flag with many buyers.

✦ **Don't write the content.** Your client knows more about his business and product than you could ever hope to. After all, you wouldn't have your client write the content for your Web site, would you?

✦ **Spice up the pages.** Many Web sites have too much text on the page, while others rely solely on graphics. A good design has a nice mix of text and graphics.

✦ **Use Flash content judiciously.** If you need to add some razzle-dazzle, Flash can provide it for you, but don't make your site exclusively Flash. Search engines tend to avoid Flash content like the plague. However, you can safely add a small Flash animation to an otherwise HTML page.

✦ **Keep it fresh.** Make sure your client understands that an e-commerce site needs to be updated frequently in order to ensure return visitors. Either negotiate a fee for periodic revisions up front, or design the site in such a manner that your client can update it with Contribute. If you choose the latter, be sure to add extra for Contribute tutoring and the inevitable calls for advice. For more information on Contribute, see Book VIII, Chapter 2, or purchase a copy of *Macromedia Contribute For Dummies,* by Janine Warner and Frank Vera (Wiley Publishing, ISBN 0-7645-3751-2).

Pumping it up with eBay

eBay is without a doubt the largest online merchant in the world. Thousands of people use eBay to auction off their unwanted techno-toys, digital cameras, musical instruments, and so on. One man's trash is another's treasure. A NASCAR driver used eBay to auction off a helmet he had thrown at a competitor's car after being forced off the track. The proceeds went to charity. In fact, a section of eBay is devoted to selling cars that sell anywhere from a few hundred dollars to several hundred-thousand dollars.

Savvy owners of e-commerce Web sites duplicate their efforts on eBay by setting up an eBay store. The fees for selling and setting up an eBay store are reasonable. Many bricks-and-mortar businesses that also have Web sites set up eBay stores. To drive traffic to their eBay stores, they auction off popular, fast-selling items. The eBay store features items other than those being offered for auction. Once the vendor starts racking up sales on eBay, they can add the buyers to their e-mail list and send them news about specials from their e-commerce Web site. The figure shows an eBay store run by the owners of a successful bricks-and-mortar business, who also run a successful e-commerce Web site. There's profit in redundancy.

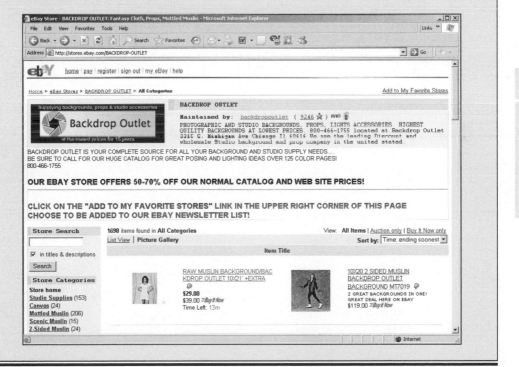

✦ **Don't clutter the home page.** Some e-commerce sites look like the front page of the daily news and are way too busy to be useful. The home page of the e-commerce site should be like the cover of a book: inviting and a reason for the visitor to click a few links to see what your client has to offer.

✦ **Give visitors a reason to return.** Set up the site with a news section, or create a small section of the home page devoted to new products or information. Make sure this content is updated at least twice a month.

✦ **Don't create content that disappoints the visitors.** If your client insists on a section that promises response, such as a section that accepts customer comments, make sure your client is aware that he must live up to the promise and provide feedback.

Chapter 2: Building an E-Commerce Site

In This Chapter

✔ Coping with technology

✔ Dealing with the law and privacy

✔ Using Web hosting and payment system tools

✔ Getting the word out

✔ Protecting your site

All the good intentions in the world won't get the job done, especially when you're creating an e-commerce Web site. In order for an e-commerce site to be successful, it's got to be usable. If potential customers can't navigate the site without a manual thick enough to be a doorstop, they'll never come back. In addition to being usable, the site needs technology in order to perform tasks such as capturing the e-mail addresses of customers for a mailing list, taking orders online, and so on. And of course, any time you're doing business, there are legal considerations. Doing business online has its own grab-bag of legal issues — and you thought you were just designing another pretty site on the Net. In this chapter, we show you the technological and legal considerations involved with an e-commerce site as well as how to build some of the elements for your e-commerce site.

Technological Considerations

Technology is everywhere in some shape or form. When it comes to creating an e-commerce site, consider several technological issues. Some of the technological issues concerning e-commerce, such as secure servers and credit card authorization are covered in Chapter 1 of this minibook. However, additional technological issues are involved with building the site.

The technology you use depends on the needs of your client. Perhaps your client requires a form that collects information from customers. You could use a CGI mail-forwarding script to transmit the data from customer to e-commerce client via e-mail. However, a technologically advanced method for doing this is to create PHP code that transmits the information to a database.

If you're like many Web designers, the thought of creating code causes you to break out in a cold sweat. If this is the case, you need to form an alliance with a Web developer who is as happy as a clam in salt water when writing complex code. Like most human beings, Web developers come in varying forms of initiative, skill, and honesty. Make sure you're working with a developer who will stay the course and not turn tail at the first sign of a bug in his code. You'll also have to pad your price to the client to include the Web developer's fee.

After you take care of the technological issues on the design side, you might think it is safe to jump off the deep end and begin designing the site. Nay, nay, Nanette. Did you ever hear of *server side?* The technology you use to create your Web site must be present on the server side. You must address these considerations when you choose a hosting service for the e-commerce site. Most standard Web hosting packages include the latest version of PHP and the ability to create one or more MySQL databases. These are generally handled with a Linux-based server. However, if your site requires ColdFusion, ASP, MS SQL databases, or MS Access databases, you'll need to opt for a Win NT server, which is generally more expensive.

Usability: Thinking Like a Customer

The customer is always the customer. But then again, without the customer, the snazzy e-commerce site you're designing for your client would be absolutely worthless. The trick here is to get yourself and your client into a customer frame-of-mind. How many Web sites have you and your client gone to and clicked out of almost immediately? Probably quite a few. When you and your client are brainstorming, bring up the topic of Web sites you absolutely refuse to visit again. Then jot down the reasons you'd never return to them. Now that you know what you don't like, consider the following usability issues:

✦ **Can I easily find my way around the site?**

✦ **How many clicks does it take to go from the home page to checkout?**

✦ **Can I easily get back to where I've been?**

✦ **Is the navigation menu consistent on all pages?**

✦ **Do all pages on the site have a consistent look and feel?**

✦ **When I get to the bottom of the page, can I easily navigate to another page?** If the answer to this question is no, create text links at the bottom of the page that contain all of the links in your navigation menu. The text links also help your rating with search engines.

✦ **Does each page have a descriptive title?** You wouldn't open a book in a bookstore if it didn't have a descriptive title on the cover, would you? Titles are also used by search engines to rank Web sites.

You can easily add a title to a Web page by changing the page properties in an application such as Dreamweaver.

✦ **Does each page have a link to the site's home page?** Many designers add a hyperlink to an image such as the company's logo and place it in the upper-left corner of the page. This is considered good practice, but Web neophytes might not be hip to this trick. Always include a navigation menu link that clearly indicates that clicking it returns the customer to the site's home page.

✦ **Does the site have alternative navigation?** If you're designing a large site with hundreds of pages, create a text-based site map. Include a link to the site map on each page. As an added bonus, with a site map, search engine robots have easy access to all of the site's pages.

✦ **Does the site have a search field?** Adding a search field makes it easy for customers to find the information they're after. You can find inexpensive — or perhaps even, free — search utilities by typing **Web site search utility** in your favorite search engine. Weed through the results to find the best solution for the site you're designing.

✦ **Is the most important content of each page clearly visible?** Think like a newspaper editor and put the most important content of each page at the top of that page. You can further draw attention to pertinent content through the use of a header style, which functions just like a newspaper's headline.

You can customize heading styles with a CSS (Cascading Style Sheet). See Book III, Chapter 3 for more about CSS.

✦ **Can a page be summed up in a glance?** Customers should be able to quickly scan each page and get an idea of the content contained within. You can use header styles, bold text (which can be created as a style using a cascading style sheet), bullet lists, or graphics to emphasize the important content on each page.

✦ **Is text included in an image?** Text in an image is not visible if customers have disabled images in their browser, or for visually challenged customers accessing the site with a screen reader. If text is needed to describe the contents of an image, create the text when designing the page in your HTML editor.

✦ **Does each `<image>` tag specify alt text?** When you add alt text to an `<image>` tag, the tags show up as tooltips in many browsers. An added benefit is increased visibility to search engines.

✦ **Does the site enable visitors to provide feedback?** If not, consider adding feedback forms in applicable sections of your site — pages such as Contact Us or Feedback. You might also consider creating a Feedback Forum where customers can post feedback and read feedback from other customers. The type of feedback you're looking for includes whether visitors enjoyed the site, would visit a similar site, understood the site content, were easily able to navigate the site, and so on.

✦ **Can your client's target audience easily understand the site content?** If your client provides content for the site and uses technical jargon and hard-to-understand terms, become the voice of reason and tell your client to "dummy it down." Pun intended.

Legal Considerations — Call a Lawyer

When you create an e-commerce site for a client, the client is liable for the content of the site. Of course, your name is also linked to the site. Therefore, you have two concerns in that regard: your reputation and your client's reputation. One of the most important things to consider is copyright law. Don't use anything on an e-commerce site — or for that matter, any Web site — for which you or your client don't own the copyright or for which you or your client have not purchased a license. This includes photos, videos, and music. In the long run, the only way to be positively sure is to run everything past your client's legal counsel.

Other legal concerns involve the privacy of Web site customers. Every commercial Web site that collects information from customers should have a privacy statement. Then there's the issue of cookies — the software kind, not the ones that cause love handles. Speaking of edible — well almost edible — objects that have become part of Internet lingo, there's spam. Cookies and spam, which won't be found on any menus other than at the Internet Café, are covered in upcoming sections.

Cookies that don't crumble

Cookies are small text files that are automatically downloaded to Web site visitors' computers. Cookies are used to track Web site visitors' habits, such as what sites they visit, how they found the site that issued the cookie, what pages they navigate to, and so on. They're a useful tool that shows e-commerce marketing gurus which sections of their sites are the most popular, which need updating, where Web site traffic is coming from, and so on. Cookies are also used to save passwords, site preferences, and so on. Any Web site that uses cookies must notify visitors in some shape or form that this software is being downloaded to the user's computer. Failure to do so is an invasion of the visitor's privacy.

Spam, spam, spam, spam!

Marketing a Web site is a whole different kettle of fish. One tried-and-true method of marketing used by most e-commerce sites is a mailing list. With the use of a mailing list, e-commerce marketers can inform customers of new products and special offers. You can send this information in the form of a classy HTML newsletter, such as the one shown in Figure 2-1. However, commercial e-mail messages can be sent to only people who *opt-in.* (In other words, the customer requests the information.) Previously, marketers could send the messages to anyone as long as the recipients had a means of *opting-out* (making the messages stop coming). If an unsolicited e-mail message is sent and that message presents a commercial advertisement, an offer to purchase a product or service, or a link to an offer to purchase a product or service, it is considered *spam*.

Figure 2-1:
HTML
newsletters
requested
by the
customer
are not
spam.

The CAN-SPAM (Controlling the Assault of Non-Solicited Pornography and Marketing) Act of 2003 is an attempt to control spam. Many e-commerce marketers mistakenly think that because they have purchased a list with hundreds or thousands of e-mail addresses of likely prospects, they can barrage their inboxes with all manner of advertisements and such, which contain deceiving subject lines or false headers. Sending messages of this type to multiple recipients (100 e-mails in a 24-hour period, 1,000 e-mails in a 30-day period, or 10,000 e-mails in a one-year period) is a felony. The CAN-SPAM act also regulates what merchants need to do when sending messages to recipients who have elected to receive commercial e-mails from the merchant.

The message header must clearly indicate that the message is a solicitation. There must be a valid e-mail address in the message header, and there must be a means by which the recipient can unsubscribe from the list.

Creating HTML newsletters and advertisements can be a lucrative business for Web designers. If you decide to do this type of work for your client, you'll need to create an unsubscribe link in the messages. It's also a good idea to include a link to the merchant's privacy notice, plus a link to the merchant's legal notice if he has one.

Creating an E-Commerce Site

After you brainstorm with the client to get his grand vision and consider usability and technology, you're ready to begin designing the site. Setting up an e-commerce site isn't rocket science, but keep in mind that some design elements are critical and unique to e-commerce sites. For example, commercial Web sites need e-mail addresses that are associated with the domain. An e-mail address with an actual domain name other than a generic ISP service such as AOL lends credibility to the e-commerce business. And of course, there's the matter of how to pay for the goods. In the upcoming sections, we show you how to add these components to your e-commerce design and more.

Setting up the e-mail addresses

Most visitors to e-commerce sites don't feel comfortable sending an e-mail to an address like fredswidgets@aol.com. It just doesn't seem very professional to have an e-mail address that's not associated with the domain from which the goods are being sold. In most instances, you set up the e-mail addresses through the Web hosting service's control panel. Each Web hosting service is different, but the following shows an example of how this works.

1. **Log in to your Web hosting service control panel.**

This is a secure part of the server's site. You'll need a username and password to access the control panel. This information is generally included with the e-mail confirmation after you set up a hosting account. Figure 2-2 shows an example of a control panel.

2. **Click the e-mail link.**

This section of the control panel enables you to add and edit e-mail addresses associated with the domain. An example of the e-mail section of a control panel is shown in Figure 2-3.

3. **Click the link to add a new e-mail address.**

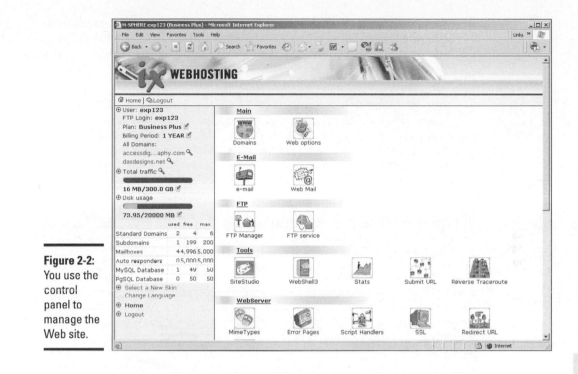

Figure 2-2:
You use the control panel to manage the Web site.

Figure 2-3:
Most hosting services enable you to configure e-mail addresses.

The control panel refreshes and shows the options available for setting up new e-mail accounts. You have several options from which to choose. Your best option is to set up a mailbox. Doing so means that you or your client has to configure her e-mail client to accept messages from the new mailbox.

Your other option is to forward mail from the domain to an existing e-mail address. The problem with this option occurs when your client needs to respond to a customer. That's right, the response is from the existing e-mail address, not the new e-mail address with the client's domain name. A response from `Jillswidgets@aol.com`? Not very professional.

4. Choose the desired option.

The control panel refreshes and contains the necessary dialog box to set up an e-mail address and password. Figure 2-4 shows the typical dialog box for setting up a new e-mail address.

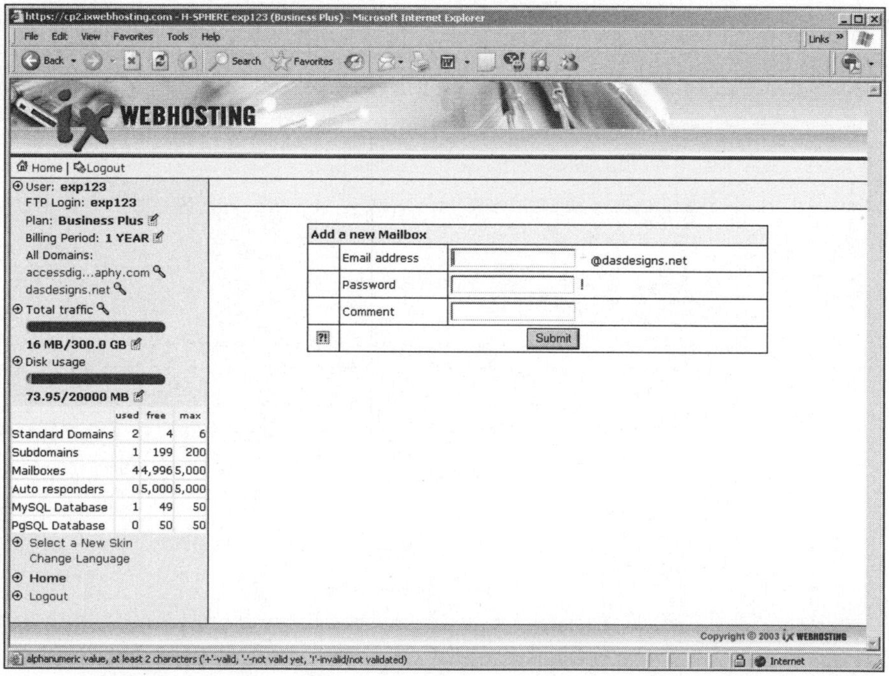

Figure 2-4: Creating a new mailbox.

5. Set up other mailboxes as needed.

Most Web hosting services enable you to set up a plethora (more than 2, less than 51) of mailboxes. This enables the savvy designer and client to make the company behind the Web site seem larger than it actually is.

You can set up multiple mailboxes such as: info@*mywebsite*.com, sales@*mywebsite*.com, service@*mywebsite*.com, and so on. The customer never needs to know that only one person is responding to the messages.

Selling items with a PayPal account

If your client prefers to dip a toe in the e-commerce waters, she can save considerable money by accepting payments with a PayPal account. As mentioned in Chapter 1 of this minibook, the rates are reasonable. All you need is a bank account and an e-mail address to set up a PayPal account. Once the account is set up, you can accept payments online. Adding PayPal Add to Cart buttons to any Web page you create in Dreamweaver is a breeze, thanks to a free plug-in from WebAssist (www.webassist.com). To add PayPal Add to Cart buttons to a Web Page, do the following:

1. **Navigate to www.webassist.com/professional/products/ ProductDetails.asp?PID=18.**

   As of this writing, this is the URL from which you download the free PayPal eCommerce Toolkit for Dreamweaver.

2. **Download and install the plug-in.**

   The plug-in, PayPal410.mxp, is a Macromedia extension. By default, it is downloaded to your desktop. Double-click the extension to install it.

3. **Launch Dreamweaver and create the page from which the customer will check out.**

   You have a lot of flexibility here. Many Web designers create a page where several products are displayed along with a description. The Add to Cart button appears below the product description. Figure 2-5 shows a photographer's Web site from which images can be purchased. The portfolio consists of thumbnails that, when clicked, reveal a larger image in a separate window. Figure 2-6 shows a basic HTML page with the image. Now it's time to insert the Add to Cart buttons.

4. **Choose Insert⇨PayPal⇨Add to Cart Button.**

   The first dialog box of the Insert PayPal Add to Cart Button Wizard appears.

5. **Enter the e-mail address of the PayPal account to which the sale will be credited. (See Figure 2-7.)**

6. **Click Next.**

   The second dialog box of the Insert PayPal Add to Cart Button Wizard appears.

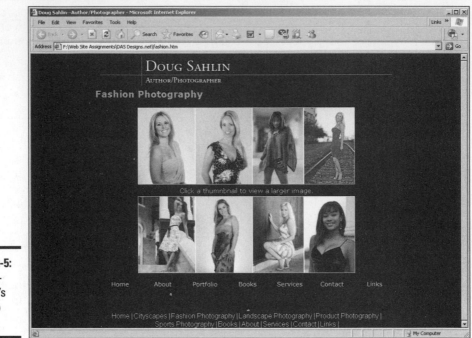

Figure 2-5:
A photographer's portfolio page.

Figure 2-6:
An image that needs an Add to Cart button.

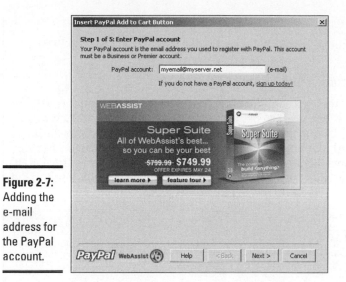

Figure 2-7:
Adding the
e-mail
address for
the PayPal
account.

7. **Choose the desired button style from the dialog box shown in Figure 2-8.**

   You can choose one of the preset styles, or choose a custom button. If you choose the latter option, the Button Image URL field becomes active. In this field, enter the URL where the button image is stored.

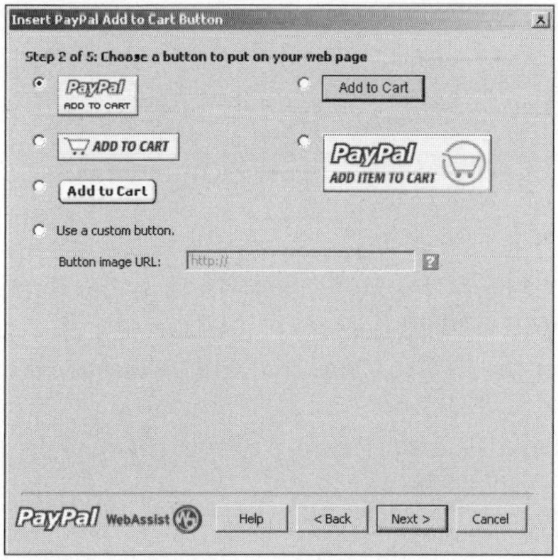

**Book VII
Chapter 2**

**Building an
E-Commerce Site**

Figure 2-8:
Choosing a
button style.

8. **Click Next**

   The third dialog box of the Insert PayPal Add to Cart Button Wizard appears.

9. **Enter the product information.**

   The product information you enter indicates which product to ship to the customer. You need to use a unique product name for each item. Select Yes or No for the options to request a shipping address from the customer and to include a comments field at checkout time. After the customer pays for the purchase, this information is sent to the e-mail address entered in Step 5. Figure 2-9 shows the dialog box for Step 3 of 5 of the Insert PayPal Add to Cart Button Wizard.

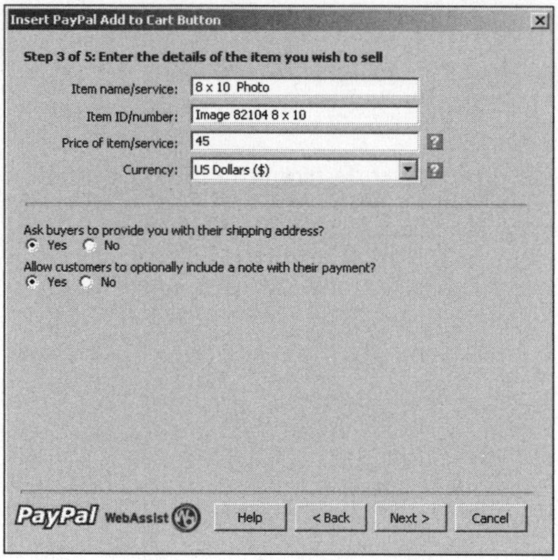

Figure 2-9:
Entering product information.

10. **Click Next.**

    The fourth dialog box of the Insert PayPal Add to Cart Button Wizard appears, as shown in Figure 2-10.

11. **If desired, enter the URL to a logo that will be displayed on a custom checkout page.**

    You can also create a custom PayPal payment page online, as outlined in Chapter 1 of this minibook.

12. **Click Next.**

    The last dialog box of the Insert PayPal Add to Cart Button Wizard appears, as shown in Figure 2-11.

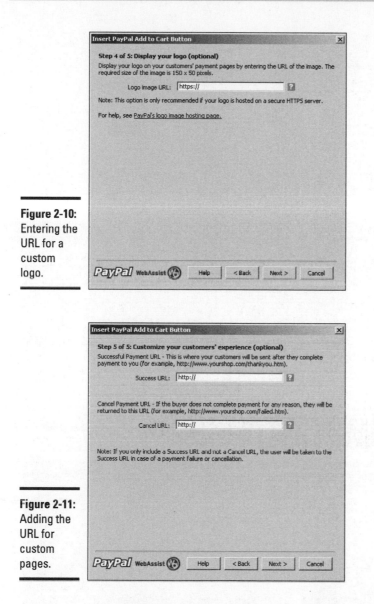

Figure 2-10:
Entering the
URL for a
custom
logo.

Figure 2-11:
Adding the
URL for
custom
pages.

13. [Optional] **Enter the URLs to custom pages that will appear after buyers complete the purchase, or when the customer completes a purchase or cancels a purchase.**

14. **Click Next.**

The Review dialog box of the Insert PayPal Add to Cart Button Wizard appears, as shown in Figure 2-12.

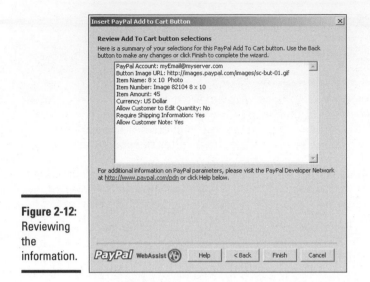

Figure 2-12:
Reviewing
the
information.

15. **If the information is correct, click Finish to add the button to the page. Alternatively, click the Back button to return to a step that you need to modify.**

    Figure 2-13 shows the completed page with the PayPal button added.

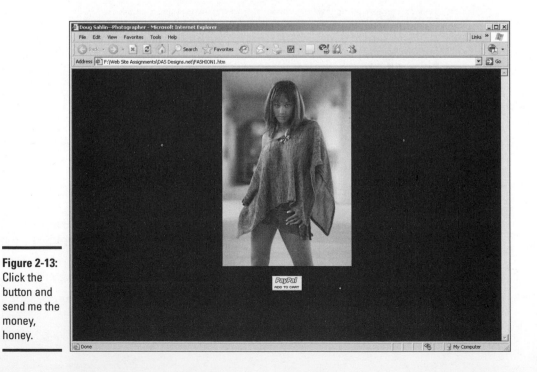

Figure 2-13:
Click the
button and
send me the
money,
honey.

Using a Shopping Cart

If the site you're designing will be hosted at a secure server, integrate the items for sale with a credit card authorization package, as discussed in Chapter 1 of this minibook. However, if you attempt to integrate the items for sale with the authorization package *without* a little help from a friend, you're a card-carrying geek — also known as a Web developer. This means writing code baby. The thought of writing code sends shivers down most Web designers' spines, but you have an alternative. Enter the shopping cart.

You can find shopping cart applications online. In fact, the service hosting the site might include a shopping cart application. Figure 2-14 shows an example of the type of features you can get with a Web hosting shopping cart application. Figure 2-15 shows an online shopping cart created using a Web hosting service shopping cart application.

Another solution is to purchase an e-commerce shopping cart template that integrates with Web design software such as Dreamweaver or FrontPage. A full-featured shopping cart template gives you complete control with features such as the ability to calculate shipping, integration with a product search page, the ability to add unlimited product features such as size and color, the ability to integrate with popular credit card authorization packages, and much more.

Figure 2-14: Choosing a shopping cart application.

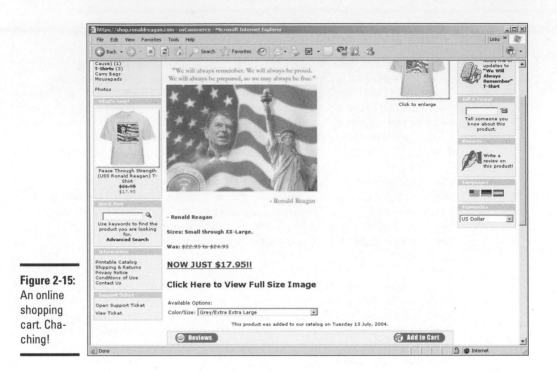

Figure 2-15:
An online shopping cart. Cha-ching!

You can find a plethora of shopping cart templates by going to your favorite search engine and typing the name of your Web design software followed by **shopping cart template**. When you review the results, look for a template that has all the features you need. Many templates let you design a store from scratch using a generic template that you can integrate with your existing design. These templates include the PHP or ASP code you'll need to create a functional shopping cart that you can integrate with a credit card authorization package. Figure 2-16 shows an e-commerce store that was created using a shopping cart template.

Creating a mailing list form

If your client wants to keep customers updated about new products, changes to the Web site, and so on, the easiest way to accomplish this is to have customers opt-in to a mailing list. You can easily do this by creating a form such as the one in Figure 2-17.

For more information on creating forms, see Book VI, Chapter 1.

Figure 2-16:
We're only
in it for the
money.

Figure 2-17:
Send me
your
answer, fill
in a form. . . .

The form itself if pretty straightforward. What makes the form tick is the form action. When the customer clicks the Submit button, a PHP page is summoned. The form action for the HTML form (see Listing 2-1) summons a PHP page that sends the form results to the database. We show you the code for the PHP page in the next section of this chapter.

Listing 2-1: Summoning the PHP Page

```
<tr>
    <td colspan="2"><form action="addRecord.php"
    method="post">
      <p>Doug is  maintaining a mailing list to notify
    visitors when new content is added to the site. <br />
    To be added to our mailing list, fill in the form.</p>
      <p>PRIVACY NOTICE: Your E mail address will not be
    forwarded to third parties. It will only be used to notify
    you
    when new material is posted on our site. </p>
      <table width="564" border="0" cellspacing="0"
    cellpadding="5">
        <tr>
          <td width="168"><p>Your Name:</p></td>
          <td width="376"><input name="Name" type="text"
    size="60" /></td>
        </tr>
        <tr>
          <td><p>Your E Mail:</p></td>
          <td><input name="E_Mail" type="text"  /></td>
        </tr>
      </table>
      <p> </p>
      <table width="451" border="0" cellspacing="0"
    cellpadding="5">
        <tr>
          <td width="56"><div align="center">
            <input type="submit" name="Submit"
    value="Submit" />
</div></td>


    </form></td>
    </tr>
</table>
```

Forwarding the information to a database

Most Web hosting services make it possible for you to quickly set up a database through their control panel. When you set up a database, you define the fields that store the information. Figure 2-18 shows a database as set up through a hosting service's control panel. Listing 2-2 shows the PHP code needed to connect to the database.

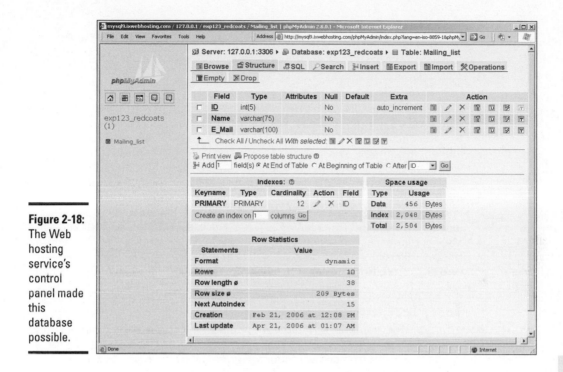

Figure 2-18:
The Web
hosting
service's
control
panel made
this
database
possible.

Listing 2-2: Forwarding the Information to a Database

```
<!DOCTYPE HTML PUBLIC "-//W3C//DTD HTML 4.01
    Transitional//EN" "http://www.w3.org/TR/html4/loose.dtd">
<html>
<head>
<meta http-equiv="Content-Type" content="text/html;
    charset=iso-8859-1">
<meta http-equiv-"REFRESH" content="0;
    URL=http://www.mywebsite/thanks.htm">
<title>Successfully Added Record</title>
</head>
<body>
<?php
$name=$_POST['Name'];
$E_Mail=$_POST['E_Mail'];
$connection=mysql_connect ("mywebhostingservice.com",
    "myusername", "mypassword) or die ('I cannot connect to
    the database.');
mysql_select_db ("mydatabase",$connection) or die( "Unable to
    select database");
 $query = "INSERT INTO `Mailing_list` (`ID`, `Name`,
    `E_Mail`)  VALUES ('','$Name','$E_Mail')";
```

```
mysql_query($query);
mysql_close();
?>
</body>
</html>
```

A full dissertation in PHP code is beyond the scope of this book. We do, however, explain how the code makes it possible to connect to the database and transfer the data. The objects with the dollar sign ($) before them are variables. The variable $name is set as equal to $_POST['Name']. In other words, the code is posting the name entered by the customer. The variable $E_Mail is set equal to the e-mail address entered by the customer on the mailing list form. The line of code that begins with $connection makes the connection to the database. The line of code that begins with $query inserts the data into the mailing list. For more information on PHP and MySQL databases, check out *PHP and MySQL For Dummies,* 2nd Edition (ISBN 0-7645-5589-8) or *PHP & MySQL Everyday Apps For Dummies* (ISBN 0-7645-7587-2), both by Janet Valade (published by Wiley).

Test, test, and then test again

After your e-commerce site is created, test the site to make sure everything works. Yes, we know, this is just common sense. But an e-commerce site does have items that are not found on garden-variety Web sites. The following list shows the obvious — and not so obvious — things for which you need to test:

✦ **Make sure all the links work.**

✦ **Time the pages as they download.** If any page doesn't download in less than 12 seconds, optimize the graphics until it does. Alternatively, delete graphics you don't need. If possible, strive for pages that download in 8 seconds or less.

✦ **Test the pages using the type of connection the majority of your client's intended audience will be using.**

✦ **If the site uses forms that submit information to a database, test the form to make sure the data makes the trip to the database.**

✦ **Test the site on real users.** While the site is still under development, invite employees of your client and friends to test the beta version of the site. Create a customer survey form to get feedback from your beta testers and incorporate this feedback in future iterations of your design.

After securing a server for the e-commerce site, create a generic home page to let people who find the site before it goes public know what they can expect. Create a separate folder — Test is a logical name — on the server to store the site while you're creating it. After you've finished testing the site, transfer the pages and associated folders to the root directory for the site.

Selling Online

After you've test the e-commerce site, your client is ready to dive into the deep end of the pool and begin selling his wares. Selling online is like selling from a bricks-and-mortar operation. Your client can stock the best-looking shop in town with the finest goods, but if he doesn't promote it, the business will fail. Security is another concern. Web sites are vulnerable to hackers, scams, and so on. And then there's the matter of the customer, who is the very reason the e-commerce site exists. Getting sales is one thing, but getting customers to come back again is a different story. Not getting customers to return is another reason businesses fail.

If you build it they won't care

So you've set up a fancy e-commerce site with all the bells and whistles that the law allows. And you think that just because the site's the coolest thing since sliced bread, it will be overcome with visitors who place large orders. Well, dream on because it won't happen. No one will care about your Web site — until you give them a reason to care. And they won't have a reason to care if they can't find you. The only way you'll attract traffic to your Web site is to get the word out. Many Web site owners spend copious amounts of money employing online marketing and search engine optimization companies. (These methods of promotion are covered in Chapter 3 of this minibook.) However, here are a couple of things a Web site owner can do to get the word out:

✦ **Send out a press release.** Many local newspapers will let you post a free press release. Lots of online companies specialize in press releases as well. Type **press release** in your favorite search engine, and you'll come up with Web sites specializing in press releases as well as information on how to write a press release.

✦ **Add your URL to your business cards, letterheads, and other written literature.** Include the URL in your e-mail signature.

✦ **Have the site featured in online and traditional business directories.** Let your fingers do the walking and type **online business directories** in your favorite search engine. You'll end up with more than enough results.

✦ **Submit the site to search engines.** Many Web hosting services enable you to submit a site through their control panel. If not, navigate to your favorite search engines and look for a link that says, Submit a URL, or something similar. Follow the prompts to submit the site.

✦ **Create cross-links with other sites.** Links help a site's rank with search engines. Encourage your client to write the Webmaster of other popular Web sites asking for permission to link to their site and vice versa. This one-hand-washes-the-other form of linking draws visitors from your site to theirs and vice versa.

✦ **Market the site's merchandise through other Web sites.** A network of affiliates that sell similar items or services can expand the sales of any e-commerce site. The affiliate creates links to merchandise on your client's site. The affiliate gets a commission for each sale.

✦ **Provide free information.** If your client's site targets a certain niche market, such as photographers, free tutorials give potential customers a reason to return. In order for this technique to work, the information must be of value to the target group and updated frequently. Tell your client to visit forums associated with the niche market and answer user questions. In the signature of the message, include the URL to the e-commerce site along with a description of the free information available.

✦ **If your client has promotional funds, consider using a pay per click option offered by some search engines.** The search engine company charges a fee for each click to your client's site with a particular phrase of keywords. For example, if your client is a wedding photographer in Houston, the obvious keyword phrase to choose for a pay per click would be *Houston Wedding Photographer*.

✦ **Use search engine ads.** Many Web sites offer ads on the right side of the results page. The ads that appear in the results page are relevant to the keywords entered by the search engine visitor.

✦ **Advertise the site in print media such as trade publications associated with the product being sold from the e-commerce site.**

Security concerns

The Internet can be a nasty place. Web site owners have to contend with hackers, online theft, fraud, and viruses, to name a few. Any owner of an e-commerce site must be prepared for problems. In addition to these security issues, you must consider security for e-commerce transactions as discussed in the previous chapter of this minibook. Here are a few things that you can do to bolster the security of any e-commerce site:

✦ **Add a copyright notice to the bottom of each page.**

✦ **If your client is a photographer or is selling fine art online, make sure each image bears either the copyright symbol and the name of the creator or a watermark.** Furthermore, you can incorporate JavaScript on the page, which prevents visitors from right-clicking an image and downloading it to their computer.

✦ **To prevent high-resolution images from being downloaded, use JavaScript to implement an image swap when users mouse over the image.** The replacement image can either be a warning that the image is protected by copyright laws, or it can be a low-resolution version of the same image that the visitor would not want to download.

✦ **Copy all of your client's Web site files to CD or DVD.** In the event that the server's equipment crashes or a hacker destroys the site, you can quickly get your client up and running again by uploading the files to the server.

✦ **Advise your client to protect business computers by firewall and antivirus software.** This prevents hackers from accessing your client's business records or sending virus-laden e-mails to your client.

✦ **Advise the client to install some sort of anti-spam software on the business computers.** Spammers are relentless, and your client's e-mail addresses are up for grabs once the site is live.

✦ **Make sure the Web hosting service has adequate protection.** Hackers often know how to access hosting service control panels. A successful attack on an e-commerce site through a control panel can be devastating. For example, the hacker can clean out your client's database.

✦ **Advise your client to change his password frequently and to choose one that cannot be easily guessed by competitors or hackers.** This is very important because many hosting services use a combination of the client's e-mail address as the username and a client-generated password to gain access to the control panel. The best password is alphanumeric and at least eight characters in length.

✦ **To ensure security for all transactions on an e-commerce site, choose a secure server that offers 128-bit SSL encryption.**

Following through on every sale

Businesses that succeed rely on repeat customers to keep the ball rolling. It's expensive to entice new customers to use a product or service. Happy customers who use a product repeatedly and refer friends and business associates are the hallmark of a successful business. The easiest way to get customers to use a product again and again is to treat them like royalty before and after the sale. Here are some tips for following through on a sale:

✦ **Send each customer a thank you letter via e-mail.** The letter also serves as a confirmation of the order.

✦ **Send each customer a copy of the invoice via e-mail.** This is yet another confirmation of the order, and it shows customers that their business is valued.

✦ **Send each customer a message letting her know when her order will be shipped.** This is another opportunity for the e-commerce company to get its name in front of the customer.

✦ **Send each customer a tracking number when the order has been shipped.** Keeping customers informed is good business.

✦ **Invite each customer to participate in a survey a few days after the order has been received.** Asking customers to participate in a survey makes them feel more important. A discount on future orders can be used as an incentive to ensure that a high percentage of customers participate in the survey.

Chapter 3: Maintaining An E-Commerce Site

In This Chapter

✔ Coping with client-side and server-side technology issues

✔ Working with customers

✔ Optimizing and marketing the site

✔ Upgrading your hosting service

After your client's squeaky-clean e-commerce site is uploaded to the server, your job is done. Well, . . . maybe. If your client is techno-phobic, he'll rely on you for advice when the going gets rough. And like anything else technical, the going will get rough. Believe me.

In many instances, your job as a Web designer ends when you hand off the shiny new site to your client. Your client, however, might not be the most technologically savvy person on the planet. Therefore, you'll have to serve another role after the site has been uploaded to the Web hosting service, that of advisor. In this chapter, we show you what to recommend to your client when the going gets rough.

When Technology Breaks Down

The best-laid plans go to waste, and the best-engineered technology can and will break down at the most inconvenient time. Technology comes in two forms: client side and server side. The code on your HTML pages marries client-side technology with server-side technology. Your role as Web-design guru means that you end up doing some handholding with your client when technology breaks down. The following sections deal with both client-side technology problems and server-side technology problems.

When client-side technology runs amuck

An example of client-side technology is code within your HTML pages that is executed with client-side technology such as the Web site viewer's browser and associated plug-ins. If you've done your homework, you should know what scripting works with the technology used by your client's target audience. Therefore, the only potential problem with client-side technology rests firmly on your shoulders. If the code doesn't work, you end up looking like a jerk. The best medicine against code errors is to test, test, and then test again. After you're sure your code is up to snuff, you can add the following safeguards to ensure that your client's target audience sees exactly what you intend it to see:

✦ If your Web design is optimized for a specific browser, make sure to leave a note to that effect on the home page of the Web site. You can also include code that identifies the browser with which the user is accessing the site and redirect the user to the appropriate page that is optimized for that specific browser.

✦ If you're using technology that is dependent on DSL or cable modem connections, make sure you include an alternate page for users that still connect with dialup modems.

✦ If your Web design is optimized for a certain-size desktop, make sure this information is clearly noted on the home page of the Web site.

✦ If your design needs plug-ins, such as the latest version of the Flash player or the Adobe Reader, make sure to include a link to the site from which the browser plug-in can be downloaded.

✦ Another potential JavaScript problem can occur when you rely on JavaScript drop-down menus or links. Most search engine spiders cannot follow a JavaScript link. If you use JavaScript links, create a text navigation menu at the bottom of each page for search engines to pick up on.

✦ If you include mailto: links in your design, make sure your client's target audience uses e-mail applications that support this method of launching a client e-mail application and opening a blank message. Knowledge of your client's target audience can enable you to ascertain whether this might be a problem.

✦ Include a section where visitors can comment on site usability. This section can provide any red flags to usability problems related to client-side technology. Negative feedback can tell you what you need to know to revise your code so that such problems don't occur in the future.

✦ Entirely out of your control are the limitations of the user's processor and memory. In this regard, design your site to be compatible with the lowest common denominator of current computer technology.

Server-side technology, or code sleight of hand

You enhance the usability of your client's site by adding items such as blogs, forums, databases, and so on. This technology relies on the server to interpret the code in your pages to return a desired result. For example, PHP code is commonly used for blogs and user forums. Before you create any page that relies on server-side technology, you must be sure that the service that hosts your design supports the technology. Again, the best defense against server-side technology issues is to test your code thoroughly before the site goes public.

Another server-side technology issue is the availability of the hosting service. If your client's site is not accessible 100 percent of the time, you might need to consider changing your client's hosting service. Web server outages can be another problem. If your client's Web hosting service is hit by a natural disaster such as a tornado or hurricane, your client's site is definitely down for the count. However, if your client's hosting service is out for any other reason, consider getting another server. Most Web hosting servers have generators that kick in whenever the local power company has a failure.

If your client's customers complain that the site takes too long to download and you've designed the site as lean and mean as possible, the server's connection might be the problem. A good Web hosting service has *OC3 lines,* which enable a data transfer of 155 megabits per second, or *DS3 lines,* which enable a transfer rate of 45 megabits per second. Most Web hosting services have several incoming lines that are a combination of OC3 and DS3 lines.

Handling Customers

Customers are the lifeblood of any business, and Web design is no different. Whether you're creating a Web site for a small, mom-and-pop operation or a Fortune 500 company, you have to deal with client issues on a repeated basis. The key to working with any client is communication. Even though you might be an accomplished vocal communicator, the type of communication called for here is the written variety. Your client has to deal with customers as well. While the following can't be considered a primer in working with customers, we do offer some sound advice in that regard.

Getting it in writing

If you're an experienced Web designer, you'll start the project after your initial consultation with the client. Your portfolio does your talking, and the client hires you based on your experience and what you say during the consultation. If you don't have too many Web sites notched on your totem pole, you'll have to first sell yourself and your skills to the client and then create a mockup for the client to peruse. Then you're hired by the client to design a Web site and look after it in sickness and in health, 'til death do you part. Oops, wrong vow. At any rate, whether you're an experienced pro or an accomplished designer earning your stripes, you need a contract to cover your posterior — and for that matter, your client's.

When you write a contract, make sure you list in detail everything you're going to do for the client. You should list every phase of your work, such as optimizing photos, scanning images, publishing the Web site, optimizing the site for search engines, uploading the site to the server, submitting the site to search engines, and so on. If you list every phase of the project, your client sees the added value in the services you're providing. The added value justifies the cost of your services and often helps you get a job when bidding against a competitor who is not as meticulous as you when it comes to contractual issues.

You should also include details such as whether you're including hosting with your design fee — and if so, for how long. Another detail you need to address is whether you'll revise the site as time goes on. Major revisions are time consuming, and minor revisions are annoyances when you have other work to do. And of course, your client wants any revision done immediately, if not sooner. We strongly advise you to address revisions in another contract. If you take our sage advice, your revision contract should be as detailed and ironclad as your original Web-design contract.

Schedule revisions at the same time every month. This enables you to schedule the workload when it's convenient for you. Your revision contract should include a clause that says that your client is responsible for getting all materials such as revised text and images to you in a timely manner. If the client drops the ball, you're not responsible for a tardy release of an update.

You also need to address contingencies such as the client being late in delivering material that is imperative to your design. After all, if the client is going to hold your feet to the fire on the final delivery date, you need to hold your client's feet to the fire as far as the delivery of needed material. You should also cover legal issues, such as the venue in which any disagreements that require the services of an attorney will be resolved.

Your contract should also include a payment schedule. Typically, you're paid a percentage when the client signs the contract and receive additional payments when you've achieved certain milestones — such as completing 50 percent of the design, completing 100 percent of the site and making it available for client review, and launching the site to the public. Make sure you include a clause that covers you in the event that the client doesn't deliver the material you need to complete the site. There will be times when you've completed the design, and all you're waiting for is the client's text to fill in the blanks. Your contract should include a clause to the effect that the applicable milestone payment is due even if your client doesn't deliver the text in a timely manner.

You also need to cover the client who waffles — ahem, you know, changes her mind. Time is money, and in case the client significantly changes the design from what she originally signed for, you need to include a clause that covers this eventuality. Bill changes at your hourly rate. You do have an hourly rate, don't you? Another factor you need to cover is additional material you need to create that is not covered in the contract, such as additional sections of the site or additional images the client supplies that you must optimize for the design. In our contracts, we add a clause that if the total scope of the site exceeds what is listed in the contract, the client will be notified so that we can negotiate an agreeable fee for the additional work. Most Web designers do extra work on an hourly basis.

Create a boilerplate contract that lists all the things you usually include with your Web design. This is a tremendous timesaver. While your prospective client is still thunderstruck with your presentation, you can open your boilerplate contract, add any needed clauses, and quickly send it to him. Strike while the iron is hot and don't give your prospective client a chance to shop your services with another designer.

To make sure you have dotted all the I's and crossed the T's, you should have an attorney review your boilerplate contract.

Documenting everything

Never do business on a handshake. It always comes back to haunt you. Make sure your client signs and dates your original contract. If you need to make minor changes to the contract, cross out the original text and then write in the revision. Both you and the client need to initial the revision. If the client requests significant changes in the contract, rewrite it — or tell the client to take a hike.

Make sure all additional client requests — with the exception of really small details — are handled with a change order. Now, we know what you're thinking: That's a lot of paperwork. But the change order doesn't need to be anything elaborate; a quick note to the client on your letterhead will suffice. Leave an area for the client to accept and date the change order. Include a SASE (self-addressed, stamped envelope) with the change order and don't do any additional work until you receive the signed change order.

You should also document the client's feedback. When you create new content and upload it to the server, send the client an e-mail requesting that she review the changes and comment on them by return e-mail. Print out the e-mail with your client's comments and put it in the client's folder.

Handling e-commerce customers

No Web designer in his right mind should take on the task of handling e-commerce customers. After all, taking care of your own clients is a full-time

Book VII
Chapter 3

Maintaining an
E-Commerce Site

job. However, if you're dealing with a client who did fall off the turnip truck yesterday, she might not have a clue as to how to handle customers. Just because your client's online shop is selling the neatest new gadget since the wheel doesn't mean she'll be able to handle the going when the going gets tough. You can provide value-added services that separate you from your competition if you can give your customer advice on how to deal with her customers.

First and foremost, your client should keep copies of all electronic communication with customers and keep fastidious records. She should meticulously document every sale. Unless your client's product can be downloaded electronically, he will have to deal with shipping. If your client is inexperienced, advise him to develop a relationship with a shipper. This makes it easier to deal with goods damaged in shipment. If your client has a good, working relationship with the shipper, it's easier to resolve damaged goods claims. Whenever we ship something, we err on the side of overkill and package the item so it will survive a 6-foot fall.

Search Engine Optimization (SEO) and Marketing

If you build it, they will not come. And that's the truth. There are more sites on the Web than Carter has little liver pills — in other words, way too many for people to care about the masterpiece you just designed for your client. If your client's site is to succeed, you've got to give customers a reason to care, Bunky. Hopefully, your design and your client's content is enough to keep them there, but first you need to grab that herd of horses by the scruff of the neck and drag them to water. You can achieve part of the task by optimizing the site for search engines. This brings some of the horses to the pond. But to search out the thoroughbreds for their sip of Perrier, you'll have to resort to more esoteric marketing techniques. Search engine optimization, like the proverbial well, is deep. We show you how to optimize your site and present some marketing techniques in the upcoming sections. These are really just the tip of the iceberg. For a heaping plateful of Web site optimization techniques, pick up a copy of *Search Engine Optimization For Dummies,* 2nd Edition, by Peter Kent (Wiley Publishing, ISBN 0-471-97998-8).

Optimizing the site for search engines

If you know how to properly optimize a Web site for search engines, you can make a lot of money — in fact, maybe enough money to give up your day job as a Web designer. Many visits to commercial Web sites occur as the result of users typing pertinent keywords in a search engine. Your job as a Web designer is to have your client's site show up at or near the top of the first page of results from a keyword search. We know, that's easier said than done. Scores of words have been written on optimizing a site for search engines — enough to fill several books. The following are a few tips you can use to optimize your client's site:

✦ Brainstorm with your client and come up with a list of keywords or phrases that you think users enter into search engines to find sites similar to your client's. Test the keywords and phrases in the major search engines such as Google and Yahoo! to test your theory. Discard the phrases or keywords that don't bring up sites similar to your client's. If a keyword or phrase brings up the Web site of your client's fiercest competitor, put that keyword at the top of the list.

✦ Jot down the titles of your client's competitors' Web sites and those of similar businesses that are in the top 10 percent of a search result using keywords or phrases that customers use to find sites similar to your client's. Use a variation of these titles for your client's Web site.

✦ Create a keyword-rich title for each page of the Web site. You can modify the title by changing page properties. Create a unique title with keywords that are likely to be used to find your client's site. A site's title is displayed in the search engine's results page. Some designers think that a series of keywords or phrases will get the job done. But just because the site's title vaults a site near the top of the first page of search results, it won't necessarily drive traffic to the site. In addition to being keyword rich, the title must make sense and give users a reason to click through to the site.

✦ Make sure that the URLs entice visitors to click through to the site. For example, if a search for *telephoto lenses* returned these results:

```
www.photosuppliesrus.com/products123.asp

www.photosuppliesrus.com/telephotolenses.asp
```

Which site would you visit?

✦ Mirror the keywords from your title tag in the alt text of each image on the home page.

✦ Mirror the keywords from your title page in the text on the home page. The redundancy of keywords gives the site a higher ranking with search engines.

✦ If your design uses JavaScript for menu navigation links, create a text menu at the bottom of the page. Search engine spiders have a difficult time following JavaScript links but can easily follow the redundant text links you place at the bottom of the page.

✦ If possible, include keywords anytime you use a heading style on the home page.

✦ Add content to the meta tags in the head section of each page's HTML. The `<meta name>` tag enables you to add a keyword-rich description of the e-commerce site. Limit the description to 250 characters, including spaces, as this seems to be the limit that search engine spiders recognize. The `<meta keywords>` tag enables you to add keywords and key phrases that pertain to sites such as the one you're creating. You can include up to 255 keywords/key phrases. Enter a comma to separate keywords and key phrases. Remember to mirror the key phrases you include in the `<title>` tag. Search engines like redundancy — to a limit. It is considered good practice to not repeat a keyword more than five times in the `<meta keywords>` tag.

When creating keywords for the site, include common misspellings of words in your key phrases. Remember to include the town(s) or regions in which your client does business. You might also want to consider adding all lowercase and all uppercase variations of what you and your client feel are the most popular key phrases, as many people type with all caps or all lowercase.

✦ Create links to other Web sites and have them link to yours. Many search engines increase a site's rank due to its popularity. These search engines include the number of links to your site in that criterion.

Don't resort to trickery to try to vault your client's site to the top of the heap. In the past, Web designers repeated keywords and key phrases relentlessly beneath the regular site content. In order to make these invisible to the user, they used the same color as the background, or a color that was one decimal different. Visitors couldn't see the words, but search engine spiders could. Search engines are wise to this trickery and drop a site from their index when they discover a designer's chicanery. Other spamming techniques include adding keywords that are not related to the site, creating multiple instances of the home page with a different URL and title, or using multiple instances of the same tag.

Finding sites to link to the e-commerce site

Reciprocal links are great, but you should also have a plethora of sites that link to your client's because of the content on your client's site. Oh yes, your spiffy design is also a good reason for them to link to your client's site. We know what you're thinking: That's not an easy task. But it is if you follow these simple steps:

1. **Navigate to** www.google.com.

Google is currently one of the most popular search engines.

2. **Enter a keyword that relates to your client's business.**

Your search will reveal the most relevant Web sites that pertain to your client's business. As you peruse the results, look for bona fide Web sites, not directories of sites. Your goal is to find Web sites of your client's competitors or similar businesses.

3. **Type** Link: **followed by the domain name of a Web site from the results of Step 2.**

   For example, to find out which Web sites are linked to Yahoo!, type **Link: yahoo.com**.

   This command, followed by the domain name, returns the URLs of sites that are linked to the domain.

4. **Click Search.**

   Google returns a list of Web sites that are linked to the domain you entered in Step 3.

5. **Make a list of the domains that you'd like to link to your client's Web site.**

   The easiest way to accomplish this is to open a new document in your favorite word processing application, and then in your Web browser, select the URL that you want to link to your client's site. Press Ctrl+C to copy the URL, and then with your cursor in the word processing application, press Ctrl+V to paste the URL into the document. Alternatively, if you have the full version of Adobe Acrobat, you can use the Web Capture feature to capture the entire page as a PDF document.

6. **Contact the Webmaster of the domains that you'd like to link to your client's site.**

   Compose a simple e-mail to the Webmaster explaining that your client's site has information that would be beneficial to the visitors or the Webmaster's site. The Webmasters will ignore you, disagree, agree, or ask you to provide a reciprocal link. If the Webmaster doesn't agree to link to your site, thank him and try to find out why he refused. This information might help you fine-tune the site.

**Book VII
Chapter 3**

**Maintaining an
E-Commerce Site**

You can perform a similar search at Yahoo.com to find out which sites are linked to your client's competitors. Type **Link:** followed by the domain name in Yahoo!'s search engine to find out which sites are linked to your client's competitors.

If your client uses a particular product to perform his service, ask the Webmaster of the manufacturer's Web site to link to your client's. For example, if your client is a musician and exclusively uses Gibson guitars, ask the Webmaster of www.gibson.com to link to your client's site.

Danger, Will Robinson! These do not compute

Certain elements of Web design are frowned upon for commercial sites because search engines have problems with them. If possible, you should avoid these elements like the plague, but if your client insists on using elements such as framesets and Flash, take a look at the following sections, which discuss the problems and workarounds.

Optimizing sites with frames

If your client wants to get framed, you'll need a private investigator or a good attorney to untangle the mess. But we digress. Web site search engines do a notoriously bad job of indexing frames sites — so bad that you should insist your client shy away from frames. The problem is that when you submit the site, you're submitting the page with the code that designates how large each frame is, how many frames there are, and so on. In other words, there's no real content, such as text, images, alt text, and other items, that search engine spiders can sink their teeth into and properly index the site. If, however, frames are the only logical solution for the e-commerce site you've been hired to design, there is a workaround.

Add the `<no frames>` tag to the frameset page. This tag was originally used for browsers that didn't support frames. Most modern browsers do support frames. However, the content you add within the `<no frames>` tag helps get your client's site listed. Listing 3-1 shows HTML code for a frames page with the `<no frames>` tag.

Listing 3-1: Optimizing a Site with Frames

```
<html>
    <head>
    <title>Example Framed Site</title>
    </head>
    <frameset cols="150,*">
    <frame name="contents" target="main">
    <frame name="main">
    <noframes>
<body>
    Optimized page content for search engine optimization goes
        here.
</body>
    </noframes>
    </frameset>
    </html>
```

Within the `<body>` tags, place your optimized content for the search engines. You can copy and paste content from the page that shows up in the main frame when the site first loads. You can include all content from a page including HTML within these tags. Use the optimization tips discussed earlier in this chapter. Be sure you include content in the `<title>` tag and the meta tags.

Jumpin' Jack Flash is not such a gas

A Flash movie is a thing of beauty — what with dancing images, flying letters, and whatnot. Many designers like to use Flash for an intro or splash page. They look cool, but search engines think they've hit a major fog bank 'cause they can't see links, text, and all the other stuff they use to index a site. In spite of this, you can do a few things to increase the visibility of a Flash intro or splash page:

✦ Use the `<title>` and meta tags to add information that contains keywords relevant to the site you're designing.

✦ Add text that will appear below the fold (the area below the browser status bar that viewers will have to scroll to). The text you add should be meaningful, as some people might be curious and scroll down to see what is there.

✦ Add a text navigation menu below the fold. Search engine spiders can't see what links are in a Flash movie, but they can read the text links and use them to spider the other pages in the site.

Using search engine software

You can use other methods of optimizing your site and then submitting it to search engines. Some software applications can analyze your Web design in regards to popular search engines. The actual options depend on the application. Some applications make suggestions on what you can do to optimize the site; some generate keywords, while others provide means for submitting your site to the most popular search engines. WebPosition 4 is considered the granddaddy of optimization applications. You can download a trial version by visiting its Web site: `www.web-position-gold-pro-software.com`. You can find other optimization packages by typing **"search engine optimization software"** in your favorite Web browser. You can also find reviews of optimization software to determine which package best suits your needs. Some applications enable you to track a given number of optimized sites. As of this writing, the standard edition of Web Position 4 enables you to optimize and track five domains, whereas the pro version of the application features unlimited domain support.

Marketing the site to the world

You can use many different methods to market an e-commerce site. The client usually does this after the site goes live. However, your client will probably count on you for suggestions, or you might decide to include marketing as part of your design contract. In either event, you need to know something about marketing an e-commerce site — or you have to employ the services of a professional Web site marketing company. As with any organization, Web site marketing companies come in all flavors. Your best defense against a snake-oil salesman masquerading as a professional Web site marketing company is to do some research or take advantage of some of the services you can purchase through search engines.

Using a pay per click promotion

Many search engines offer the option of a paid ad that shows up in a results page when users enter a certain keyword or key phrase. Like anything else, he who swings the biggest club gets the game. With most search engines, you specify how much you'll pay for each click on an ad that appears when users enter a specified keyword while at the same time specifying your maximum budget per month. The placement of your ad is determined on how much you bid per click versus your total budget. In other words, if your bid on a keyword and budget is higher than another advertiser's, your add will appear before hers. If your bid is high, but your budget is low, your ad will appear lower in the list. To get a concise idea of how this works, we suggest you visit Google's AdWords Help Center at `https://adwords.google.com/support/?hl=en_US`.

When you take out an AdWord, you create the content for your ad. The resulting ad appears in a prominent position in the search engine's result pages for the particular keyword(s) you purchase. Figure 3-1 shows the results page for the key phrase, *Tampa Photographer*. The paid ads are on the right side of the page.

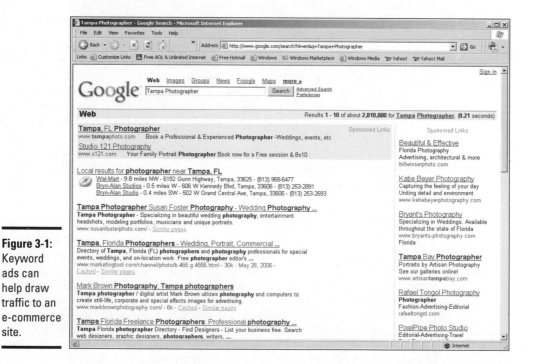

Figure 3-1:
Keyword ads can help draw traffic to an e-commerce site.

When you decide to include paid keyword ads in your online marketing campaign, you have four steps to complete before that paid keyword ad is in place:

1. **Determine which keywords are relevant to your client's business.**

If your client markets many products, he'll quickly go bankrupt paying for ads for each product he sells. If your client sells multiple products, the key is to break the phrases related to your client's offerings' genres. For example, if your client sells three brands of acoustic and electric guitars, a logical choice would be *acoustic guitars* and *electric guitars.* Your client pays for two key phrases instead of six.

2. **Find the most popular keywords and key phrases that relate to the particular genre.**

You can employ an online marketing company to do this work. If your client is on a budget, he can use one of the online tools, such as Overture's Keyword Selector Tool, which you can find at `http://inventory.overture.com/d/searchinventory/suggestion`. Simply enter the word for which you'd like to find keywords, and the site comes up with a page of results. Figure 3-2 shows the results for the key phrase, *Tampa Photographer.* The results page shows the most key phrases used in conjunction with searches for a photographer in Tampa, Florida. Note that the key phrase, *photographer tampa,* was used the most times when searching for a photographer doing business in Tampa. The most popular keyword or key phrase is also the most expensive. Review the list and find a keyword or key phrase that is most relevant to your client's business and will result in customers perusing his Web site. To take the Tampa photographer scenario a step further, the fourth keyword on the keyword suggestions page, *tampa bay photographer,* might be the ideal choice.

You can also use the keyword suggestion page to find keywords and key phrases you can use in the `<title>`, `<meta description>`, and `<meta keywords>` tags.

3. **Write the ad that will display in the results page with your client's chosen keyword or key phrase.**

Create compelling ad copy that will make people want to click through to your client's site. You should also include the URL to the Web site in your ad. Even if users don't click through, they might remember the URL to the site and visit it in the future. But the most compelling ad copy in the world is wasted if the landing page to which the ad is linked is not relevant. For example, if your ad copy is about wedding photography, the wise choice would be to link to the page about wedding photography on your client's site, and not the home page.

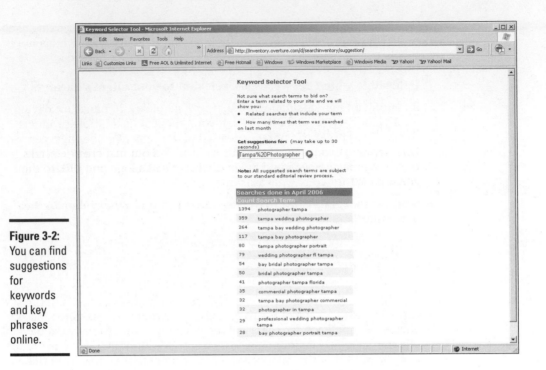

Figure 3-2:
You can find suggestions for keywords and key phrases online.

4. **Fine-tune the ad.**

    Google and Yahoo! enable you to target an ad by language or location. For example, you can target an ad to appear in one or more of the following: countries, territories, regions, and/or cities. Furthermore, you can specify that the ad be available to only a specific language audience. Targeting enables you to get more bang for your buck.

The only way you'll know for sure if the pay per click campaign is working is to monitor the site statistics. Google and Yahoo! supply statistics with their campaigns. Over time, a thorough review of statistics enables the e-commerce site owner to edit the key phrases and, if necessary, choose new ones. In addition, you can monitor the statistics log supplied by your Web hosting service to see if a campaign is effective.

Other marketing techniques

If your client has a startup company, her budget might not be able to afford a pay per click campaign. Never fear; there are other ways to get visitors to her site. The following are a few techniques you and your client can employ:

✦ **Use link exchanges.** As mentioned previously, you can popularize a Web site by exchanging links with other sites. The easiest way to accomplish this is to solicit links from e-commerce Web sites that offer similar services but aren't in competition with your client's services. The link to your client's site appears on the other site's link page. In return, your client posts a reciprocal link to the other Web site on his links page. Many Webmasters are familiar with this valuable marketing tool and might have hundreds of links on their site.

One way you can make your client's site stand out in a crowded links page is to create a small graphic with the client's logo and URL to the site. Export the graphic as a GIF file.

✦ **Use banner exchanges.** You can publicize your client's site by participating in a banner exchange. Your client's banner is displayed on other sites that subscribe to the service. When clicked, the banner drives visitors to your client's site. Many banner exchange programs are free. When you sign up for a banner exchange program, make sure to read the fine print. Sometimes you have to prominently display the banner exchange company's logo on your client's site in exchange for the free service.

✦ **Offer free content.** If your client is an acknowledged expert in her field, advise her to offer free content, such as articles, to established sites that might be frequented by visitors who would be interested in your client's product or service. In exchange for the content, the site provides a link to your client's site.

Figuring Out When to Upgrade

When you initially consult with a client, your first concern is what type of Web site you'll design to best suit your client's need. The second concern is what features your client needs from the Web hosting service. When you first consult with the client, you can get a pretty good idea of what he needs from a Web hosting service. However, if you, or your client, monitor the site statistics, you'll know when it's time to upgrade. Other hints can come from visitor feedback. This vital information tells whether the site is immediately accessible or downloads slowly.

As the site evolves, your client might need additional features that are not included in the hosting package. When you initially choose a company to host your client's site, make sure it is flexible and will let you change hosting packages when needed. Another useful option is a money-back guarantee if the hosting service doesn't live up to its promises. Additionally, some hosting services will let you cancel the service, without penalty and for any reason, with a 30-day notice. The Web hosting business is very competitive. You can pick and choose to get the service that best suits your needs and your client's.

Upgrading to a more robust Web hosting package

When you initially design your client's site, you might be under budgetary constraints, which means you'll choose a hosting package that can take care of the client's immediate needs and nothing more. However, when the site gets off the ground, and your client's bank account can no longer be balanced with an abacus, your client might need another tax deduction or four. One way you can accomplish this is by upgrading to a better Web-hosting package. Of course, your client has to justify any additional expense to her accountant. Here are a few reasons why she should consider upgrading her Web hosting package:

✦ **Your client needs to host more domains.**

If your client expands into different ventures that need their own unique domain names, you'll have another project to create. In addition, your client will need the ability to host more domains.

✦ **Your client needs more space for the Web site.** E-commerce sites are often used to sell a multitude of products. When more products are sold, more Web pages are needed, more images are needed, multimedia applications such as video are added, and so on. This takes up space on the server's system. A Web hosting service offers a limited amount of disk space. When your client is close to using her allotted space, it's time to upgrade to a package that offers more.

✦ **Your client needs features such as FTP access for customers, one or more databases, CGI forms, SSI, and so on.** Entry-level hosting packages generally don't offer these features. When your client needs one or more of these features, it's time to upgrade to a different hosting package.

✦ **Your client needs content that is updated on the server side.** Most entry-level Web hosting packages don't support server-side technology such as ASP or ColdFusion. Additionally, if your client needs a robust database using MS SQL or MS Access, you'll need to upgrade to a Web hosting package that supports these applications.

✦ **Your client needs additional subdomains.** A *subdomain* is like a different Web site, but it has the same domain name. For example, if your client wants to separate his customer service from the main Web site, the subdomain would be something like `service.mydomain.com`. When your client has used his allocation of subdomains, it's time to upgrade to a more robust Web hosting package.

✦ **Your client needs more e-mail addresses.**

Most Web hosting services give you a finite number of e-mail addresses. If your client's needs exceed this number, you'll have to purchase additional e-mail addresses or opt for a more robust Web hosting package.

✦ **Your client exceeds his monthly data transfer allotment.** If you design a site with bells and whistles such as video and audio clips, visitors are downloading more data when compared to a site with just text and graphics. When the site gets popular, the sheer number of visitors tax the data transfer allotment. Rather than paying a premium when your client exceeds his monthly data transfer, he should upgrade to a hosting package that features a higher data transfer allocation.

Each site has different requirements, and each Web hosting company is different. You should always endeavor to get the best package, based on your client's needs. When you shop for hosting space for your client, make sure you're dealing with a hosting service that is flexible and will let you upgrade your client's service at any time. The best advice we can offer in this regard is to find a reliable hosting service for your personal Web site that treats you right and has a great track record. Based on your personal and hopefully acceptable experience with the Web hosting service, you'll know you can use the company for your clients as well.

Upgrading to another server

If you've done your homework, the server you choose for your client's e-commerce site will perform flawlessly. As the old saying goes: "If it ain't broke, don't fix it." However, not all servers are created equal. And sometimes, servers sign up more users than they can comfortably accommodate. When this happens, visitors experience longer download times due to server traffic, or they might not be able to connect to the site at all. If your client's site experiences any usability issues that can be attributed to the server, you'll either need to work out the issues with the server or upgrade to another hosting service.

Sometimes server issues can be attributed to the type of server on which your client's site is hosted. If your client's site is hosted on a shared server and visitors report usability issues such as long download times, it's time to upgrade to a dedicated server. A dedicated server costs more money. However, if the site has the traffic to justify a dedicated server and the traffic is purchasing goods or services, the additional cost is well spent.

Book VIII

Site Management

The 5th Wave   By Rich Tennant

"Hey-here's a company that develops short memorable domain names for new businesses. It's listed at www.CompanyThatDevelopsShort-MemorableDomainNamesForNewBusinesses.com."

Contents at a Glance

Chapter 1: Helping a Site Succeed

A successful Web site is an ever-changing work in progress. You use your skills as a Web designer to bring your client's business to life on the Web. You take the seed of your client's idea, plant it, and nurture it to fruition. However, the fruit will fall from the vine and rot unless you or your client does something to bring it to the public eye. The first step in making the site successful is optimizing the site for search engines. This step can help your client's site rank higher in the search engines. That, however, might not be enough, especially if the Web site is promoting a popular product or service. If this is the case, your client has to resort to marketing the site online. In addition to marketing the site online, your client can use conventional methods to popularize the site. After visitors are coming to your client's site in droves, there must be a reason for them to return. That's right — you or your client needs to update it on a regular basis. After all, you wouldn't buy the same magazine month after month if the content never changed. In this chapter, we show you how to implement SEO (search engine optimization), online marketing, and other techniques to help the site succeed.

Planning and Incorporating Search Engine Optimization (SEO)

After you decide what type of content the site will have, you begin building the site in your favorite HTML editor. However, if you don't include one other important step, your client's site will be the virtual equivalent of a store that relies on word of mouth to get its customers. If your client's site is to succeed, it has to be found by the masses. And the way the masses get most of their information is by using search engines such as Google. Be forewarned that search engine optimization has become a fairly exact science. And like any science, there's a bit of magic involved as well. A full-course, soup-to-nuts serving of search engine optimization tips is beyond the scope of this book. However, in the upcoming sections, we show you a few pointers on optimizing your client's site for the search engines.

Seeing why SEO is essential

If you're a relatively inexperienced Web designer, you might wonder why all the hubbub about search engine optimization. Quite simply, the Web is a competitive place. Literally thousands of sites sell similar product lines, promote similar services, and have similar causes — all of them competing for Joe Public's visit, which will hopefully end with a visit to the checkout. And they all want to be at the top of the first page of a search engine's results. If one of your client's goals is to achieve a high ranking in the search engines, it is imperative that the site be optimized, either by you or by a company that specializes in search engine optimization and marketing.

Understanding the mechanisms: Meta tags, keywords, descriptions, and alt text

Search engine optimization might seem like smoke and mirrors to the uninitiated. But in reality, it's a matter of tweaking what's at your disposal. Search engine robots index a site based on the information they find in certain tags. It's your job as a Web designer, or the job of the search engine optimization company, to put the right information in these tags, which will propel your client's site to the top of the results page when certain keywords are entered in the search engine's text field. The keywords or key phrases relate to businesses or organizations similar to your client's. You judiciously place these keywords in meta tags and alt tags. Meta tags are found in the head of the document, while alt text is an alternate description for an image.

SEO defined

A search engine might seem like it's a fairly simple beast. You enter a keyword — or several keywords (also known as a *key phrases*) — and magically, results pages appear that list sites that are supposed to be related to the words you typed in the search engine text box. The results are listed by relevancy, whoever he is. But seriously, the sites on the pages are ranked in accordance to how closely the keywords entered by the user relate to the site. But how is the ranking determined? How does one site magically pop to the top of the first results page, while others are lost in relative anonymity on the eighth or ninth results page? The answer lies in the skill of the Web designer or the company hired to optimize the site for search engines. Optimizing a site for search engines involves adding the right words to the HTML tags that the search engine robots analyze when adding the site to the search engine index. The most skilled SEO wizards know exactly what will improve a site's ranking with the most popular search engines. They don't resort to trickery such as typing a bunch of keywords the same color as the background, which is known as *spamming the search engines*. Most search engines are aware of the old tricks. Therefore, a Web designer who knows how to optimize sites for search engines will always be in demand.

What's in a name?

Meta tags appear in the head of the document. With the exception of the `<title>` tag, visitors don't see the tags in the head of the document. Search engine robots can, however, read the information in meta tags and the title tag. Listing 1-1 shows the `<title>` tag and meta tags from a hypothetical coin-collecting company.

Listing 1-1: The Title and Meta Tags

```
<html>
    <head>
    <title>Coin Collectors Paradise--A 1-Stop resource for
    coin collectors.</title>
    <meta name="description" content="Coin Collector's
    Paradise is a buyer and seller of rare American and
    foreign coins. Coin collector books and research material
    are also available.">
    <meta name="keywords" content="coins, coin dealers, coin
    collectors, American coins, foreign coins, buy coins, sell
    coins, appraise rare coins, gold coins, rare coins, paper
    money, un-circulated coins, proofs">
    </head>
```

The `<title>` tag is prominently displayed in the Web visitor's browser. This information tells Web site visitors what they can expect to find on the site. The `<title>` tag is also displayed in most search engine results pages. Notice that the word *coin* is repeated twice in the title of our fictional coin collector's Web site.

The first meta tag in the hypothetical HTML document is `description`. The description should also make sense as it is also displayed in a search engine's results page. A keyword-rich description will help your site rank higher in a search engine index. A logical description that tells visitors what they can expect to find at your client's site is more likely to result in a click-through to the site. You can have up to 250 words in your description. However, many search engine robots record only the first 30 words or so. The `description` tag for our hypothetical Web site is short, sweet, and to the point with only 23 words, yet the keyword `coin` is repeated three times, and the key phrase `coin collector` is repeated twice. If you don't add the `description` meta tag to a page, search engine results pages display the first few lines of text in lieu of a site description.

The final meta tag in the document is `keywords`. You can include up to 255 keywords and key phrases. Keywords and key phrases are separated by commas. Listing 1-1 has a total of 13 keywords and key phrases in the fictional `keywords` tag. Most search engine robots use the first 25 key phrases as part of their indexes, so there's no need to go overboard with this tag. Note that the word `coin` is used repeatedly in most of the key phrases. The only thing I'd add would be the state, county, and town in which the client's bricks-and-mortar business is located. If the business was associated with a region, such as Tampa Bay, Florida, I'd include that as well. For example: `Tampa Bay coin dealer`.

Initially, all search engines supported the `keywords` tag. However, currently, this isn't so. The major search engines still support this tag. If you have to scrimp anywhere in your search engine optimization, this is one tag you can ignore.

Increasing site visibility with alt text

In addition to using meta tags, you can also increase the visibility of your client's site by adding alt text to each `<img>` tag in a page. In a nutshell, alt text is text that you add to images. Adding alt text does several things. In some Web browsers, it shows up as a tooltip when a user positions her cursor over the image. If someone is accessing the site using a text-only browser, the tag shows up in a box that is the same dimensions as the image. For the visually impaired viewing the page with a screen reader, the tag is displayed in lieu of the image. When search engine robots index the site, they use the information in the alt tags for indexing the site. When you add alt text to the `<img>` tags on your site, include the keywords and key phrases used in the title, description, and keywords meta tags. The alt text should also be a logical sentence. If you jam an alt tag full of keywords and key phrases, it might cause the search engine robots to disregard the information. Worse yet, the gibberish can distract site visitors when the tooltip appears.

Improving site searchability

After you optimize a site for search engines, you might think you're ready to upload the site and submit it to search engines. But you can do other things to make your client's site easier for potential visitors to find.

Clean up your code

Before you submit your site to the search engines, your code must be impeccable. Most Web designers use HTML editors to create their pages, which creates fairly bulletproof code. However, if you've manually modified any of the code, you run the risk of sending mixed signals to the search engine robots. Here are a few things to review:

✦ **If you have any JavaScript-based menus, create a text equivalent at the bottom of the page.** Search engine robots cannot follow JavaScript links to index the rest of the site.

✦ **If any of the code is created using a word processing application, check the code for redundant tags.** Dreamweaver has a Clean Up Word HTML command, which removes markup specific to the Microsoft Word application. It also cleans up font tags and a plethora of other tags created by the application.

✦ **Avoid adding custom styles to each document.** Add styles to the head of a document. Use a CSS (Cascading Style Sheet), which will create cleaner code for the search engine robots to follow. For more information on CSS, see Book III, Chapter 3.

✦ **Use a unique `<title>` tag for every page on your site and make sure the title is relevant to the content of each page.** This enables the search engine robots to accurately index each page of your site. For example, if one page shows a map and directions of how to get to your client's site, the page title might read: `Directions to your client's bricks-and-mortar store`.

✦ **Add an alt tag for every image on the page.** Make sure the tag text matches the content of the page and mirrors the keywords and key phrases used in the title and meta tags.

✦ **Validate your code.** Most HTML editors have a command to validate or clean up the code. For example, Dreamweaver has a Clean Up HTML command. This command removes empty and redundant tags, plus it has an option to combine nested tags when possible. You can also validate your markup in Dreamweaver by choosing File➪Check Page➪Validate Markup.

Create a title, alt tags, descriptions, and keywords

Prior to the site being submitted to the search engines, you need to add the elements that will propel your client's Web site to the top of the desired results page. You do so by creating a unique title for each page, alt tags for each image, a description for each page, and keywords. This is especially important if your client's site promotes multiple products or multiple services. When this is the case, you optimize the pages for each product or service as if they were individual Web sites. Therefore, the title, alt tags, descriptions, and keywords for these pages will be tailored for the product or service your client is promoting. The following steps show you how to optimize a page in Dreamweaver:

1. **Open the document you want to optimize.**

2. **Open the Properties inspector.**

When you initially open a document and have not selected any elements, the Page Properties button in the Properties inspector is available.

3. **Click the Page Properties button.**

The Page Properties dialog box appears.

4. **Click the Title/Encoding category.**

The Page Properties dialog box refreshes to show the current title and encoding.

5. **Type the desired title in the Title text box. (See Figure 1-1.)**

The title you choose for the page is the result of your tireless research to determine the optimum keywords to optimize the page for search engines. Redundancy intended.

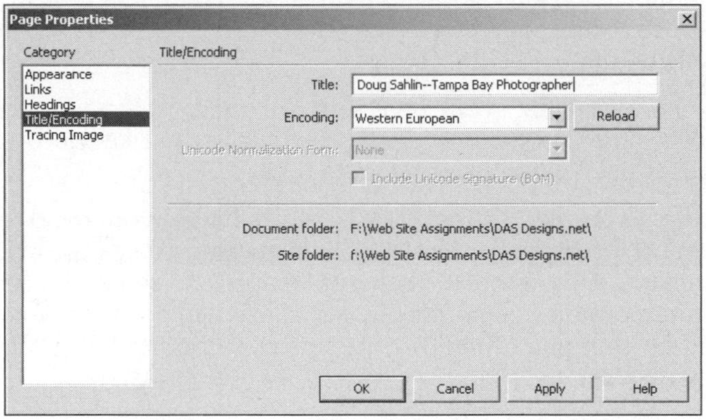

Figure 1-1:
Adding a
title to the
document.

6. **Choose Insert⇨HTML⇨Head Tags⇨Description.**

The Description dialog box appears.

7. **Type the desired description in the text box. (See Figure 1-2.)**

The description you type depends on the product or service your client performs. If your client performs multiple services or sells multiple products, each page needs to have a different description.

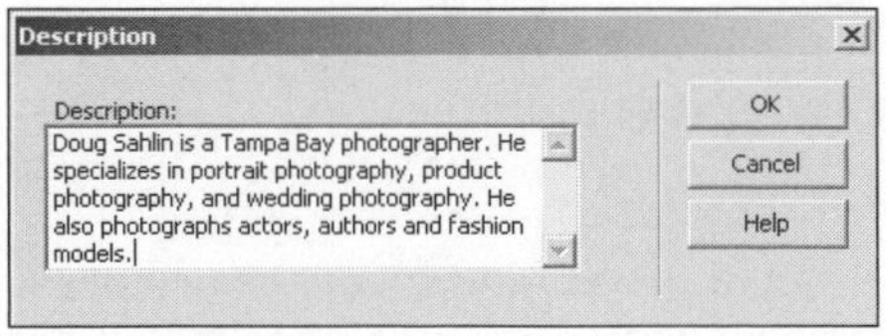

Figure 1-2:
Adding a
description
to the Web
page.

8. **Click OK.**

   The description meta tag is added to the head of the document you're optimizing for search engines.

9. **Choose Insert⇨HTML⇨Head Tags⇨Keywords.**

   The Keywords dialog box appears.

10. **Type the desired keywords.**

    The keywords and key phrases you enter are the result of your research of other Web sites selling products or services similar to your client's. Keywords or key phrases are separated by commas. (See Figure 1-3.)

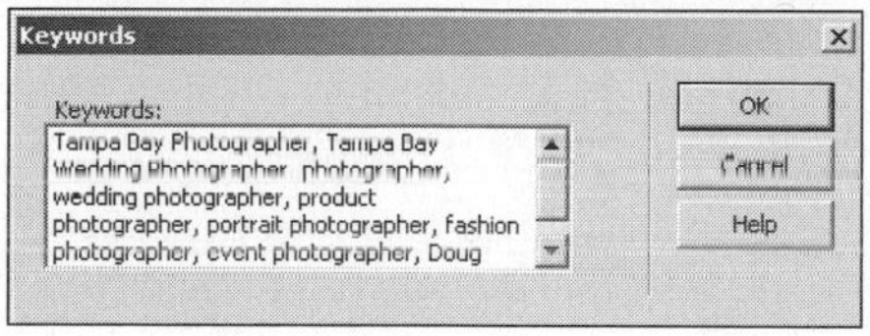

Figure 1-3:
Adding keywords to the document.

11. **Click OK.**

    The keywords are added to the head of the document you're optimizing.

12. **Select the image to which you want to add the alt tag.**

13. **Open the Properties inspector.**

    The Properties inspector enables you to change many parameters of the image, including the alt tag.

14. **Type the desired text in the Alt text field, as shown in Figure 1-4.**

    The alt tag is added to the document when you save it. Figure 1-5 shows the code of the document that was optimized in the preceding steps.

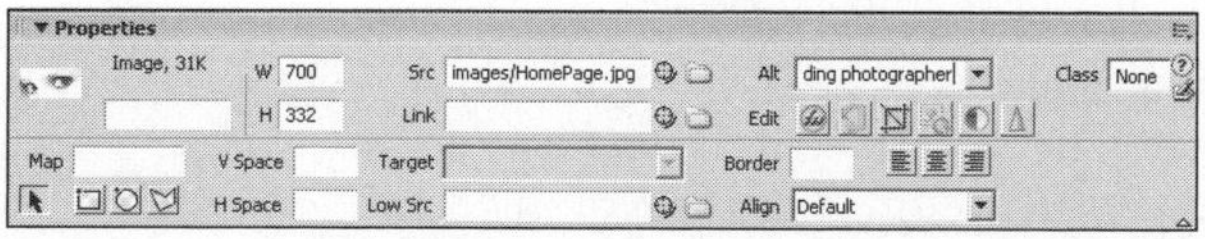

Figure 1-4:
Adding a descriptive alt tag to an image.

```
1  <!DOCTYPE HTML PUBLIC "-//W3C//DTD HTML 4.01 Transitional//EN"
2  "http://www.w3.org/TR/html4/loose.dtd">
3  <html>
4  <head>
5  <meta http-equiv="Content-Type" content="text/html; charset=iso-8859-1">
6  <title>Doug Sahlin--Tampa Bay Photographer</title>
7  <meta name="description" content="Doug Sahlin is a Tampa Bay photographer. He specializes in portrait photography, product photography,
8  <meta name="keywords" content="Tampa Bay Photographer, Tampa Bay Wedding Photographer. photographer, wedding photographer, product photo
9  <style type="text/css">
10 <!--
11 body {
12     background-color: #000000;
13     margin-left: 0px;
14     margin-top: 0px;
15     margin-right: 0px;
16     margin-bottom: 0px;
17 }
18 -->
19 </style>
20 <link href="das.css" rel="stylesheet" type="text/css">
21 <script language="JavaScript">
22 <!--
23 function mmLoadMenus() {
24     if (window.mm_menu_0428213624_0) return;
```

Figure 1-5:
The code
of the
optimized
Web page.

Hiring the Right Professional Help

If you're not a guru when it comes to search engine optimization, you or
your client has to hire someone to take care of this task. If not, your client's
site will be all but invisible to people using search engines to find Web sites
of similar products or services. After all, if a site isn't optimized, it ends up
on the fifth or sixth results page of a search — or higher if the product or
service is extremely popular. For example, a Google search for *same day
shipping* yields 97,000,000 results. FedEx doesn't rank number one because
of their expertise in shipping the product on the same day; a team of SEO
experts was employed to get this result.

Many companies claim to optimize Web sites for search engines. Most SEO
companies use a combination of proprietary software and consultation with
the client to optimize a site. The company suggests changes that the client
needs to make to ensure that the site ranks near the top of the major search
engines. Of course, your client's major competitors are also working to have
their sites rank near the top of the major search engines. If you think SEO is
a one-time shot, you're sadly mistaken. The site will need to be optimized
on an ongoing basis. If you or your client thinks you can get off cheaply by
hiring a company that claims they can do it in one shot, think again.

As mentioned previously, lots of companies claim to be SEO experts. When
choosing a company, here are a few questions to ask:

✦ How long has the company been doing SEO?

✦ Is SEO their main business, or just a service offered?

✦ Does the company have a proven track record of getting results for their
clients?

✦ Can they provide testimonials and references from satisfied clients?

✦ Can the company clearly demonstrate a logical process by which they optimize the site for maximum visibility in the search engines?

✦ Does the company offer ongoing optimization as part of their contract?

✦ Will the company submit the site to the major search engines?

✦ How often will they resubmit the site?

✦ How many members does the company have on its staff?

When you're searching for a search engine optimization company, you should also find out the company's code of ethics — in other words, what steps they take to optimize the site. If it seems as though they'll employ some non-ethical tactics to optimize the site, look elsewhere. Search engines quickly catch when any form of chicanery is used to vault a site to the top of the search engines. In fact, you can examine the code of one of the SEO company's clients and see for yourself whether anything is rotten in Denmark.

Deciding between SEO and paid advertising

In addition to, or in lieu of, search engine optimization, you can use keyword advertising, which shows your client's paid ad on results pages. The ad is listed in the Sponsored Links section of the results page for the keyword or key phrase your client pays for. The frequency and the page on which the ad appears is determined by the amount your client agrees to pay per click and the total amount the client has budgeted for pay per click advertising with the search engine company. If your client allocates a large enough budget for pay per click advertising, his site will appear in the sponsored links section on the first or second results page. Therefore, search engine optimization is redundant and an unnecessary expense.

However, certain keywords and key phrases, such as *wedding photographer,* are in high demand. Therefore, the only way to ensure that your client's pay per click ad appears in a desirable position on the first or second results page is to allocate a large budget for pay per click advertising. When faced with a large pay per click advertising budget, your client will have to determine whether it is more economical to employ a top-notch SEO company or sign up for the pay per click advertising campaign.

Submitting your site to search engines

After your client's site is optimized for search engines, it's time to submit the site to search engines. Some of them are highly specialized and might not be relevant to your client's type of business. There are so many search engines out there that you could go nuts trying to submit the site to multiple Web sites. Therefore, you should submit the site to the most popular search engines. Of course, what is popular now might be passé in two or three years. The following is a list of popular search engines and the URLs to the pages where you submit your site:

✦ **Google:** It's currently considered the most popular search engine for the masses. You can submit a site to Google at:

> www.google.com/addurl/?continue=/addurl

✦ **MSN Search:** This is another popular search engine affiliated with MSN.com. You can submit your site to MSN Search at this URL:

> http://search.msn.com/docs/submit.aspx

✦ **AltaVista:** AltaVista has been around for a while. It's a popular search engine that offers alternative services such as Yellow Pages, a directory, a shopping and travel section, a people-finder section, and much more. You can submit a site to AltaVista, which is powered by Yahoo! Search Technology. In order to submit a site, you must be a registered Yahoo! user. After you register as a Yahoo! user (it's free), you can submit a site at the following URL:

> http://submit.search.yahoo.com/free/request

✦ **Yahoo!:** You can submit a site for inclusion in Yahoo!'s search engine at the same URL for which you submit a site to AltaVista. However, in order to guarantee that your site appears in Yahoo!'s search engine, you'll have to pay to submit the site, and then pay per click. You can find out more at this URL:

> http://searchmarketing.yahoo.com/srchsb/sse.php?mkt=us

Many of the sites in the previous list have specialized directories to which you can submit a site. However, a complete tutorial on submitting your site to search engines is beyond the scope of this book.

Don't resubmit your client's site to a search engine unless you have made significant changes to the site or have re-optimized pages using a different title or description, or you have changed the keywords. If you continually submit a site with no changes, this is considered spamming the search engine and can negatively affect the site's rank within the search engine.

You can find services that enable you to submit your site to multiple search engines for no fee by typing *free search engine submission* in your favorite search engine. However, many of these sites will try to sell you on using their paid services or will add you to some sort of mailing list. If you decide to use one of these services to submit your client's Web site, read the fine print. Remember, there are no free lunches.

Your Web hosting service might offer submission to search engines as part of their package. Contact your Web hosting service's customer support for more information. If your Web hosting service offers this feature, you'll probably submit the site using their control panel, as shown in Figure 1-6.

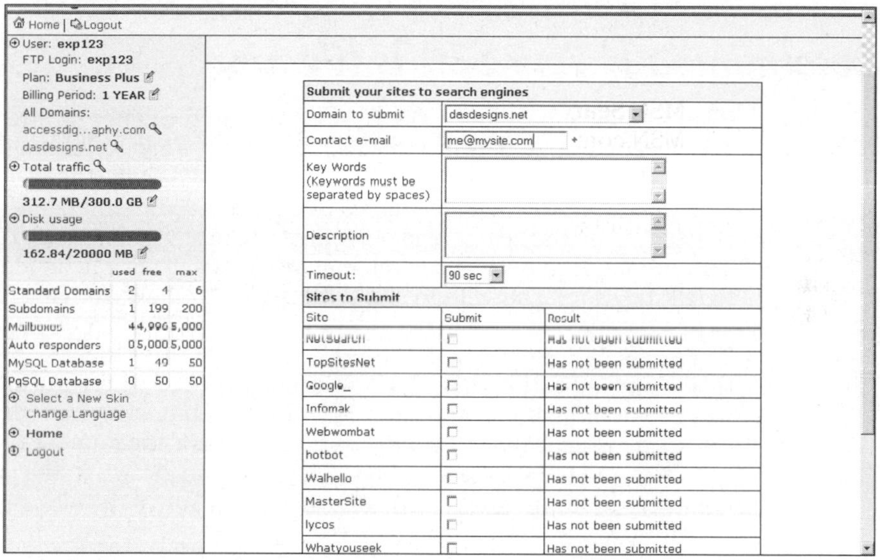

Figure 1-6: Many Web hosting services offer search engine submission with Web hosting packages.

Using a service to submit your site

If you contract an SEO company to optimize the site, chances are they will also submit it for you. If you've optimized the site yourself and don't want to go through the hassle of submitting the site to multiple search engines, you can employ a service to submit the site for you. Like all services, site submission services come in multiple flavors and varying degrees of initiative. The price charged by the company depends on the number of search engines to which it submits the site, how often it resubmits the site, and other services included in the package such as sponsored links and so on. Most services use proprietary software to submit the site. A good search engine submission company will also know the ins and outs of each search engine and whether the search engine has specialized directories for products and services to which they can submit your client's site.

You can find a plethora of search engine submission companies by typing *search engine submission service* in your favorite search engine. Just because a submission service's site is listed at the top of a results page doesn't mean it's a good service. (Can you say, "sponsored links"?) Like any other service, make sure the company is legitimate and their employees didn't fall off the turnip truck yesterday. A reputable service has testimonials from satisfied customers. Be a savvy buyer. Don't take the service's word for it. See if the sites listed in the testimonials are still active. If so, see if you can contact the person who wrote the testimonial and ask him for his opinion — off the record, so to speak.

Determining If Your SEO Is Working

Even though you submit a site to several search engines or hire a site-submission firm to perform this task, it takes a while to determine what effect search engine optimization is having for your client's Web site. First and foremost, search engines don't index a submitted site overnight. Depending on the search engine, it might take several weeks to get indexed. The submit page on each search engine usually gives you an idea of how long it takes for a submitted site to be added to the search engine's index.

If your client is getting more orders or inquiries after the site is submitted, this is one indication that SEO is working. However, there are more scientific ways to determine the impact of SEO. Most Web hosting services provide a means by which you and your client can monitor the number of visits to your site and the means by which the traffic was drawn to the site. The following sections provide useful information on Web site stats, plus what to do with the information you receive.

Reading your Web stats

Web site statistics are a wonderful thing. With most Web hosting services, stats are accessed through the Web service's control panel. In addition to being a wonderful thing, they are artistic and colorful, what with all the bar charts and pie graphs. To read site stats, log on to the site's control panel, click the applicable icon, and . . . *walla!* Instant stats! Many stat packages show a graphical representation of site traffic. (See Figure 1-7.) In addition, you'll see other information, such as the number of hits, files, pages, and visits. With most services, you click the desired month to get more details. (See Figure 1-8.) We know what you're thinking: What does all this stuff mean? Fear not, intrepid designer! Please fast-forward to the next section for nontechnical definitions of Web stat terms.

Defining Web stat terms

After you crack open the statistics for a site, you have to decipher what they mean. But unless you're a trained professional, the stats might seem like gibberish. The following list is designed to demystify Web stat terms.

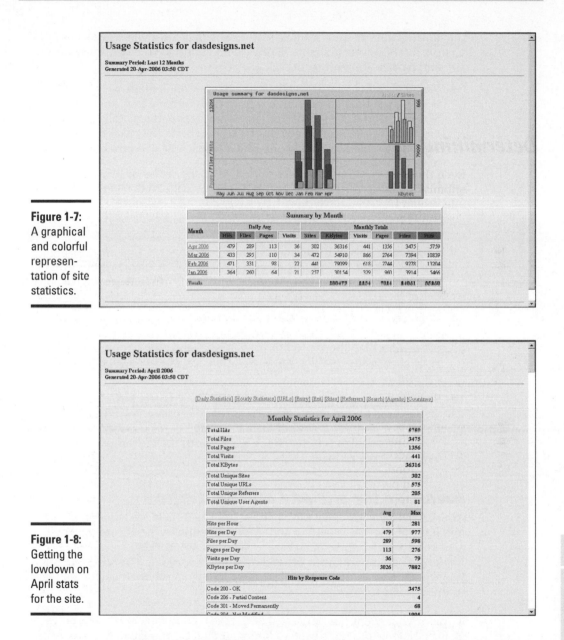

Figure 1-7: A graphical and colorful representation of site statistics.

Figure 1-8: Getting the lowdown on April stats for the site.

✦ **Hits:** A hit occurs any time the Web server delivers a file. Hits can be misleading, as several files might need to be downloaded for an individual page. For example, in addition to the HTML document for a Web page, images, a cascading style sheet, Flash movies, and so on must be downloaded as well. A single visit to any page on a site results in multiple hits. Copious amounts of hits do not justify breaking out the bubbly and patting yourself on the back.

✦ **Visits:** A visit is logged whenever a unique visit is made to the site. This is by far the best barometer you have to determine how successful your SEO efforts are. A word of caution: Some stats services tally a visit whenever a new page is accessed on the site. If this is the case, the stats service provides a listing for Unique Visits, which tells you how many visitors have accessed the site.

✦ **Entry pages:** This statistic gives the URL for the page on which the visitor first landed. If your client sells many products and services, this information shows you which optimized pages are doing the best job of driving visitors to the site.

✦ **Exit pages:** This statistic shows you which page visitors are viewing prior to exiting the site. While everybody's got to leave sometime, if one page shows up more than others, it could indicate that the page isn't being received well by visitors.

✦ **Referrers:** A *referrer* is a Web page that contains a link to one of the pages in your client's site. Referrals might come from search engines or other sites that choose to link to you. Knowing how people are finding your client's site enables you to fine-tune the methods used to market the site.

✦ **Search strings:** This stat shows which keywords and key phrases the visitor used to find your client's site. If keywords or key phrases that have been used for a pay per click campaign don't show up, you know that the campaign is not yielding results with the currently chosen keywords and key phrases.

Adjusting the site and driving traffic

After analyzing your client's Web site stats, you'll have a good idea of how much traffic the site is getting and from where the traffic is coming. You'll also know which online marketing techniques are working, how well SEO is working, and how well your other marketing is working. The site stats tell you which areas of the site need revision and what other steps you can take to drive traffic to the site.

If you or your client has employed SEO, take a good look at the search strings that visitors have used to find your site. Do they match the keywords and key phrases you've peppered heavily in the title, description, and keywords? If so, your efforts are working. If the search strings are obscure text in any of the head tags or actual text in the body of the page, you'll have to revise the tags to reflect the keywords and key phrases that people have used to find the site — which of course, will help drive more traffic to the site.

If you use pay per click marketing to drive traffic to the site, search strings are once again useful. If the search strings match the pay per click words you've budgeted with various search engines, the campaign is doing its job. If not, you'll have to adjust the pay per click campaign, budgeting the keywords and key phrases that show up most frequently in search strings. You can also use referrers to determine the effectiveness of a pay per click campaign. If the referrers are those that your client has employed a pay per click campaign with, your client's money is well spent. If not, advise your client to suspend the pay per click campaign or lower the budget.

Entry pages are another useful statistic to study when a site sells multiple products or multiple services, especially when you've used marketing or SEO to draw attention to the site. The most popular entry pages tell you how effective your SEO efforts are. If certain pages are not being visited and these are popular products or services, you'll have to optimize these pages again. If you've used a pay per click campaign on the pages that aren't getting their fair share of visits, you'll have to adjust the budget or budget different keywords or key phrases.

Stats on exit pages can tell you if the content is effective. The pages that visitors exit most frequently might need to be tweaked if the pages are products or services that are vital to the client's business. In a perfect world, the most frequently used exit page would be the checkout of your client's secure server.

Using Reciprocal Links to Boost the Site's Visibility

Search engines pay special attention to the number of sites that link to your client's site. If all other parameters are equal and one site has more external sites linking to it, the site with more links ranks higher on a results page. In other words: "He who dies with the most links wins." Therefore, it's in your client's best interest to have as many sites as possible linking to his. If your client's site has interesting content and a compelling design — You did give your client a compelling design, didn't you? — it's relatively easy to get other sites to link to his site. Ask. That's right, send e-mails to Webmasters of sites that you'd like to link to your client's, telling them you like their site, would like to link to it, and would appreciate it if they'd do the same for your client's site. Keep at it until you've got a slew of sites linked to your client's and then monitor the stats to see which sites are referring visitors to your client's. At the same time, monitor where your client's site appears in search engine results pages. It won't happen overnight, but in a few months, your client's site will rank higher, thanks to the power of reciprocal links.

**Book VIII
Chapter 1**

**Helping a
Site Succeed**

TIP

Navigate to www.yahoo.com or www.google.com and type **Link:** *PopularWebsite*, replacing the phrase *PopularWebsite* with the domain of a popular Web site that sells the same product or service as your client's. The domain should be in the following format: *PopularWebsite. com* — for example, Wiley.com. You'll get a list of sites that link to the popular Web site. Send an e-mail to the Webmasters of these sites, requesting that they link to your client's site.

Promoting a Site with Traditional Marketing

Web designers should provide their clients with owner's manuals. Just think about the grief it would eliminate, not to mention the phone calls. In addition to telling clients that they won't get results immediately, the owner's manuals would tell clients the obvious things they can do to promote their sites. When you write your Web site owner's manual, be sure to include the following advice for your clients:

✦ Add the URL of your Web site to your business card and the business cards of your employees.

✦ Add the URL of your Web site to every piece of stationery for your company, especially note pads and letterheads.

✦ Add the URL of your Web site to every brochure and catalog you print.

✦ Add the URL of your Web site to every magazine and newspaper ad you purchase.

✦ Add the URL of your Web site to every television ad you purchase.

✦ Have a sign maker add the URL of your Web site to every company vehicle and every sign. You'd be surprised how many people jot down the URL of a Web site when they see it.

✦ Add the URL to any other type of vehicles used to promote the business, such as billboards and ads on park benches.

Keeping Them Coming Back

After you and your client have done your best to launch an informative Web site, you'll have to think about the future. If you don't, the site can quickly lose popularity, and your client's business can dwindle. The best way to keep visitors returning to a site is to keep the content fresh. In this regard, you'll have to think ahead and plan for future content. In the upcoming sections, we give you a few tips to ensure a steady stream of visitors to your client's site.

Ongoing content development

A successful Web site should have new information at least once every two weeks. That's not really as difficult as it seems. If your client is an expert in his field, he can post articles or tutorials on the Web site. The articles should be compelling enough to ensure that visitors will look forward to bi-weekly installments. The articles can include hyperlinks to the product or service the client is featuring in the article. For example, if the Web site's purpose is to sell art supplies, an article could show visitors how to mix colors. I'm sure you've seen Web sites with a headline that gives a short introduction to an article with a Read More link at the bottom of the blurb. Savvy Web surfers know that this content is usually updated on a regular basis. If your client is not a writer, perhaps someone on his staff can write the articles. In lieu of that, perhaps the client's vendors can create content. In lieu of that, there are Web sites that offer free material for reprint, in exchange for an ad.

As of this writing, you can find an index of free Web content at www. freesticky.com/stickyWeb.

The best way to plan for ongoing content is to know the clientele that are likely to visit the site. Knowledge of your client's intended audience is the key to planning new development. Advise your client to find interesting new stories that relate to her product or service. Include links to these articles on the client's Home or What's New page. If the client has a blog (a Web log, which we discuss in further detail in Book VI, Chapter 5), this is an excellent place to mention interesting news articles or product developments.

Another way to keep customers returning is to post success stories on the Home or What's New page. This takes a bit of planning on your client's part. If the client has an established bricks-and-mortar business, advise her to solicit customers for testimonials or success stories. For example, if your client is promoting a weight-loss service, before-and-after pictures are great testimonials. Advise your client to obtain a release from her customer before posting the pictures and success story. Contact your lawyer for more information on what information a model release should include. If your client is a savvy marketer, she can exchange goods or services in exchange for a good article or success story.

The key to successful content development is to do it like clockwork. It will take between four and seven visits before visitors realize that the site is updated frequently. When planning new content, your client should be on the prowl, visiting industry-specific Web sites in search of new material. Your client can set up alliances with Web sites that sell similar products or services to her intended audience. Your client can find articles on these Web sites that interest her customers, and she probably has content that is of interest to other Web sites. This information can be exchanged between sites with a short ad and hyperlink to the marketing partner's Web site.

**Book VIII
Chapter 1**

**Helping a
Site Succeed**

Tell visitors that site content is updated on a regular basis and ask them to bookmark the page.

Another way to develop content for the site is to recycle. As long as the information is timely, there's no reason your client can't post an article again in another three or four months. If your client uses this tactic, make sure he keeps track of when the articles are posted and mixes it up. In other words, advise him not to repost the articles in the same order they were originally posted. Your client can also do a bit of creative cutting and pasting to create a new article from information that has already been posted on the site.

Creating content to keep them coming back

In addition to creating articles and tutorials, you can employ other devices to ensure that visitors want to return. This type of content is the fun and informative stuff. The following are a few time-honored techniques that can be used to have visitors flocking to the site on a regular basis:

✦ **Add short-term specials to the home page.** The specials can be on new products or services. Make sure the special is really a value and not just an attempt to get rid of old inventory. If the visitor perceives the short-term special as a value, he's likely to purchase the product or service. Or even if he doesn't make the purchase, the seed is planted and the visitor is likely to return when the special expires to see what is offered next.

✦ **Provide tutorials.** If your client has a service that includes instructional material, consider giving away a short tutorial in PDF format. When you give something away, make sure you ask for something in return: the visitor's e-mail address so you can inform her of the next, free tutorial.

✦ **Give away free stuff.** If your client's business has promotional material, such as t-shirts or baseball caps, give the materials away to every twenty-fifth visitor who registers contact information on the Web site.

✦ **Create a What's New page and update it frequently.**

✦ **Create an online newsletter.** Have visitors register their e-mail addresses, and notify them when the newsletter is updated.

✦ **Hold a contest related to your client's products or services.** The grand prize can be a product or a discount. The visitor submits his contact information when registering for the contest.

✦ **Create fun, interactive pages.** The pages can be quizzes related to your client's products or services. You can create content like this in Flash, which is covered in Book V, Chapter 1.

Chapter 2: Maintaining a Web Site

In This Chapter

✔ Updating Web pages

✔ Using Adobe Contribute

✔ Managing the site with Dreamweaver

✔ Tricks and tips for maintaining Web sites

You've worked hard to create a compelling Web site for your client. But in order for the site to succeed, someone needs to update the content. Updating or maintaining a Web site is usually not included in a designer's contract, as the amount of work varies depending on whether the client needs a major overhaul on a section of the site or the update is simply a matter of making some changes on an existing page. If your client has contracted you to maintain the site, you can do so by using an HTML editor such as Adobe Dreamweaver. Or perhaps, your client is relying on you to do the major maintenance and his staff will be responsible for the "grunt" work. If this is the case, people who have little or no experience in Web design will edit your pages. We cover both scenarios in this chapter, including some tips and tricks to make the job easier.

Updating Pages without Destroying Them

Clients change their minds when you least expect it. It's one of Murphy's Laws — number 327, most likely. So what are you to do when your client comes to you with a bunch of updates and then decides — after you've created them — that he doesn't like them and wants to revert to the old ones? Well, if you've modified the pages, you're up the proverbial creek without a paddle. Whenever a client presents us with the first set of revisions, we do the following in Dreamweaver:

1. **Choose Window⇨Files.**

This opens the Files panel for the Web site on which you're currently working.

2. **Click the Expand to Show Local and Remote Sites button.**

3. **Click the Connects to Remote Host button.**

Dreamweaver connects to the remote host and displays all files and folders on the remote host. (See Figure 2-1.)

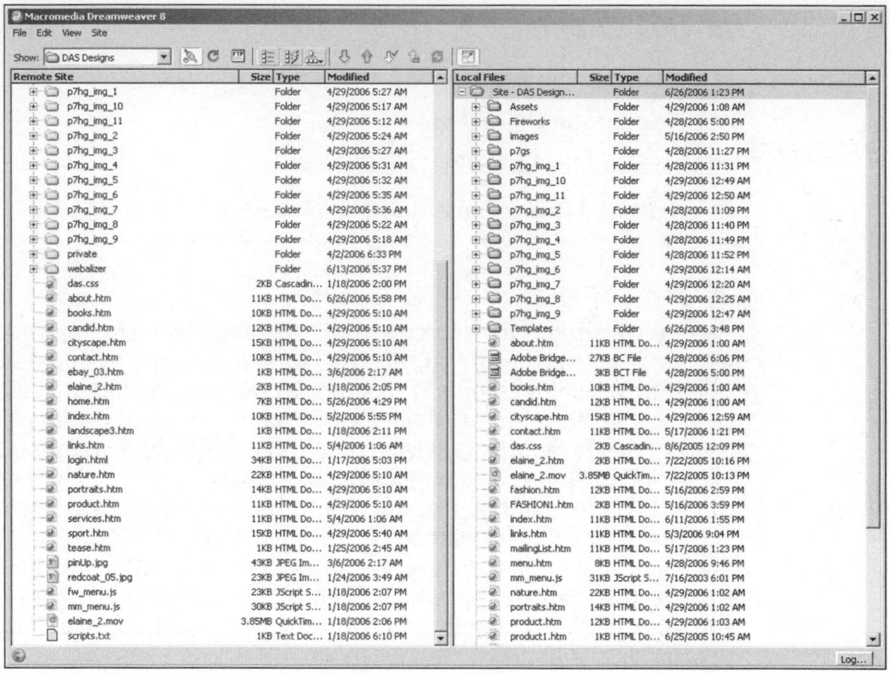

Figure 2-1:
You can manage files on your local machine and the remote host.

4. **Right-click (Windows) or control-click (Mac) the remote host `root` directory and choose Create New Folder from the menu.**

   Dreamweaver creates an unnamed folder.

5. **Change the name of the folder to Archive.**

   This is where you'll store the original HTML files for the Web site.

6. **Select all of the original HTML files for the site, including any CSS (Cascading Style Sheets) files and JS (JavaScript) files.**

7. **Choose Edit⇨Copy.**

   Dreamweaver copies the files to the clipboard.

8. **Select the Archive folder.**

9. **Choose Edit⇨Paste.**

   Dreamweaver pastes the original HTML files into the Archive folder.

Now that you have the original files archived, you can modify the Web site. To revert to the old page, delete the revised file and then drag the page from the Archive folder, which will replace the deleted revision. When you do the next update, create a subfolder of the Archive folder, and name it Revision_1. You'll store the files from the previous revision in there. Archiving the latest three revisions should be sufficient unless you've got a client with a photographic memory. In case of server problems, consider keeping a copy of the archive on your local machine or on a CD.

Sharing the Work with Contribute

If your client's personnel will be responsible for some of the updates, chances are they won't know how to use a sophisticated application like Dreamweaver. But they will be familiar with office applications such as Microsoft Word. The goal of the people who created Adobe Contribute was to create an application that anyone familiar with office applications could use to update a Web site. The application can be used to browse to a Web page. (See Figure 2-2.) If the user has a connection to the Web page, she can edit the page with the click of a button. That's right, the page can be edited on your computer, just like you were editing a Word document. When you're satisfied with the changes, click Publish and the edited page is uploaded to your server. One of the other cool features about Contribute is that the application enables the user to roll back to a previous version of the page, which is a blessing if one of your client's staff really messes up a page while editing it.

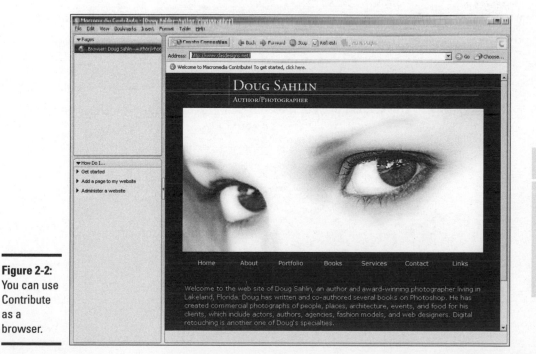

Figure 2-2:
You can use
Contribute
as a
browser.

Creating a connection

Before you can edit a Web site with Contribute, you must make a connection to it. This is similar to defining a site in Dreamweaver, but different enough to warrant some instruction. To create a connection to a Web site with Contribute, follow these steps:

1. **Use Contribute to navigate to the home page of the site to which you want to make a connection.**

2. **Click the Create Connection button.**

The first page of the Connection Wizard appears. (See Figure 2-3.)

Figure 2-3:
The Connection Wizard makes a cameo appearance.

3. **Click Next.**

The second page of the Connection Wizard appears. (See Figure 2-4.)

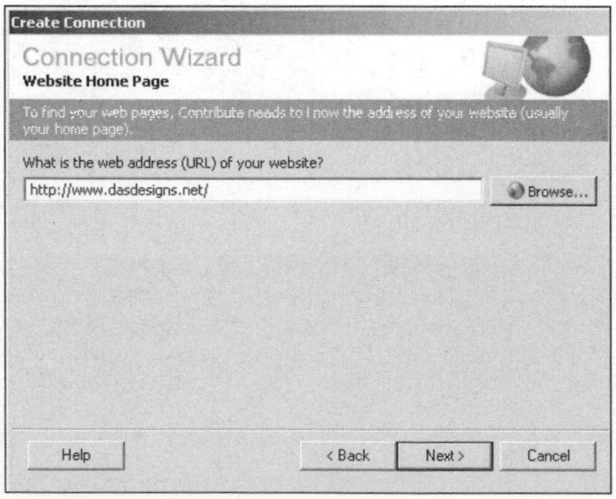

Figure 2-4:
Get ready to be connected.

By default, this page shows the URL to which you have navigated. If this is not the home page, enter the URL to the home page in the text field. Alternatively, you can click the Browse button and browse to the site's home page.

4. **Click Next.**

   The third page of the Connection Wizard appears.

5. **Choose the method by which you'll connect to the Web site from the drop-down menu. (See Figure 2-5.)**

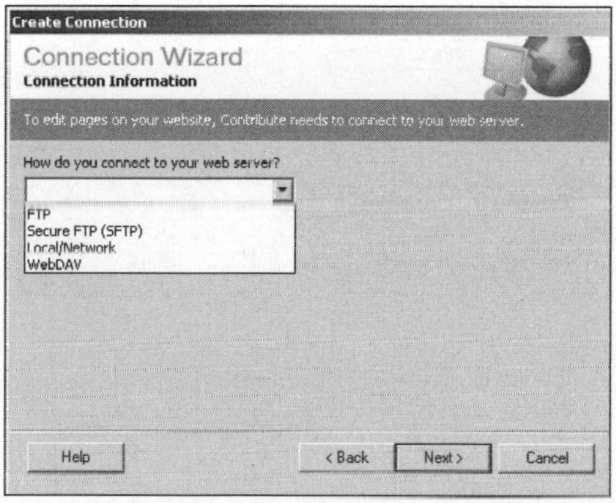

Figure 2-5: There's a method to this connection madness.

If the site is a remote host, your choice is FTP. If you're configuring Contribute for an intranet, the choice is Local/Network.

After you make a choice, the Connection Wizard reconfigures.

6. **Enter your credentials.**

   Figure 2-6 shows the Connection Wizard as configured for an FTP connection with FTP server, username, and password entered.

7. **Click Next.**

   Contribute tests the connection. (See Figure 2-7.) After verifying the connection, the Connection Wizard reconfigures.

8. **Enter the root folder in which the Web site files are stored. (See Figure 2-8.)**

   Alternatively, you can click the Choose button to display folders on the remote server.

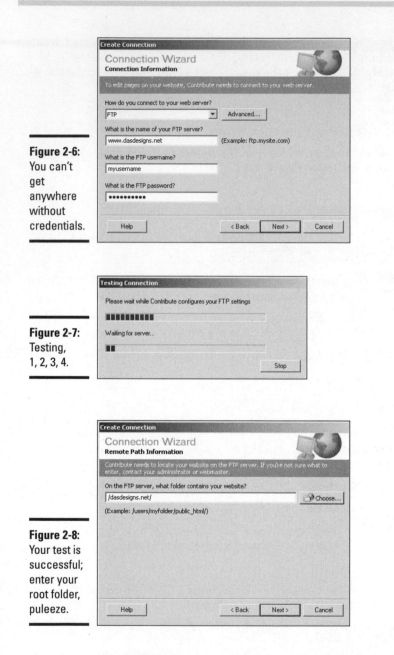

Figure 2-6:
You can't get anywhere without credentials.

Figure 2-7:
Testing, 1, 2, 3, 4.

Figure 2-8:
Your test is successful; enter your root folder, puleeze.

9. **Click Next.**

Contribute tests upload speed and performs other diagnostic tests on the remote server. After performing the tests, the Connection Wizard reconfigures, as shown in Figure 2-9. On this page, you enter your user information, which is how Contribute identifies users that can edit the Web site. The information Contribute needs is your name and e-mail address.

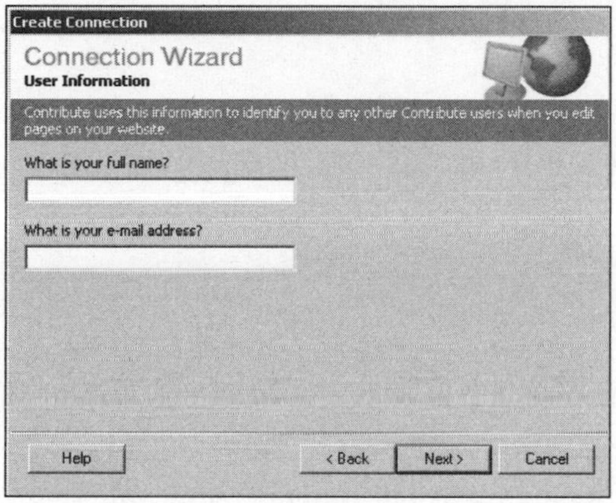

Figure 2-9:
Who are
you? Who,
who are
you?

10. Enter your user information and click Next.

The Create Connection Wizard reconfigures to show the Summary page, which summarizes the information you've submitted in the previous steps. If the information is accurate, go to the next step. If not, click the Back button as needed to navigate to the page that contains the information that you need to change.

11. Click Done.

The connection information is stored on the remote server. The Create Connection button becomes the Edit Page button.

Congratulations, you've now made a connection to your client's Web site, which can now be edited with Contribute. Your next step is to administer the site and determine whether you'll accept the role of administering the site from this point on, or transfer this role to one of your client's lackeys, err, personnel.

Administering the Web site

After making a connection to a Web site, you *administer* the site. In essence, what that means is that you set permissions for the people that will edit the site. When you set permissions, you can limit the type of editing each team member can do, as well as set limits on the size of images and so on. To administer a Web site to which you've made a connection, do the following:

1. **Choose Edit⟶Administer Websites and then choose a Web site to which you've made a connection.**

All sites to which you've been the first to connect to show up on a sub-menu of the Administer Website menu. After you choose, a dialog box appears asking you what type of editing you'll want for the site and if you'll accept the role of administrator. (See Figure 2-10.)

2. **Choose an editing option by clicking the applicable radio button.**

We strongly advise you to choose the Standard Word Processing option, as it's the easiest for most office personnel to learn.

3. **Click Yes to become administrator of the site.**

Alternatively, you can choose No and bestow the honor on someone else.

After you make a choice, the Administer Website dialog box appears, as shown in Figure 2-11. The Users and Roles section of the dialog appears by default. This shows all users who have a connection to the Web site and the roles they play. If you select a user role and click the Edit Role Settings button, you can set permissions for this type of user. The options are largely self explanatory. You can limit the sizes of images that are added to pages, the type of editing allowed, the type of code Contribute writes when a user from the role group edits a page, and so on. You can also create new roles or remove roles from this section of the Administer Website dialog box.

4. **Click Administration.**

The dialog box reconfigures, as shown in Figure 2-12.

5. **Click Set Administrator Password.**

The Change Administrator Password dialog box appears, as shown in Figure 2-13.

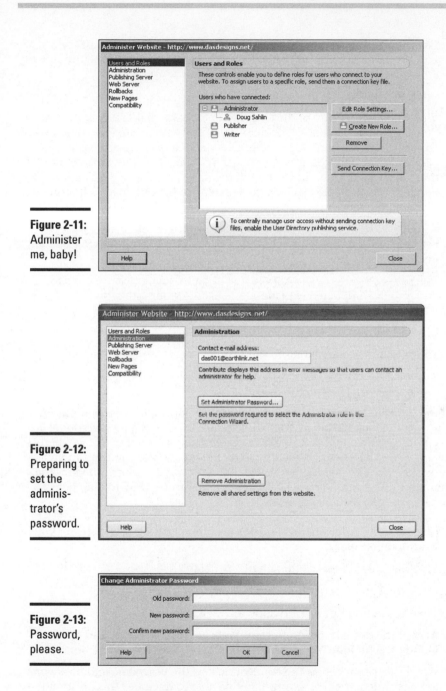

Figure 2-11:
Administer
me, baby!

Figure 2-12:
Preparing to
set the
adminis-
trator's
password.

Figure 2-13:
Password,
please.

6. **Enter a password and then confirm the password.**

7. **Click OK.**

The Change Administrator Password dialog box closes. The password you entered has to be entered any time a user tries to choose the role of administrator when making a connection to the Web site.

8. **Click Rollbacks.**

The Rollbacks section of the Administer Website dialog box appears. This section of the dialog box allows you to enable rollbacks. When you enable rollbacks, Contribute makes a copy of a page as soon as a user clicks the Edit Page button. A user can roll back to a previous version of the page, which is a handy option if the page gets messed up eight ways to Sunday or the boss decides he doesn't like the employee's handiwork. The default number of rollbacks is 3. Enter a higher number if you think the client will need it.

9. **Set options in other sections of the Administer Website dialog box as needed.**

The other sections of the Administer Website dialog box are easy to understand. A detailed explanation of each section is beyond the scope of this book.

10. **Click Close.**

Your settings are uploaded to the server.

Sending a connection key

If your client's personnel are techno-phobic, they probably know nothing about FTP credentials and all that stuff. In fact, if your client's personnel are really young, they might think FTP are the initials of a rapper. But we digress. When you're using Contribute with nontechnical people, you send them a connection key. The connection key is their gateway to Contribute nirvana, or something like that. A *connection key* is a no-brainer way to connect to a Web site. To send a connection key:

1. **Choose Edit⇨Administer Websites and then choose the Web site you want to administer.**

The Users and Roles section opens by default.

2. **Click the Send Connection Key button.**

The Connection Key Wizard appears. (See Figure 2-14.)

3. **Accept the default option to send your current settings, and then enable the Include My FTP Username and Password check box.**

When the user receives the connection key, the username and password are encrypted; the recipient will not be able to decipher this information.

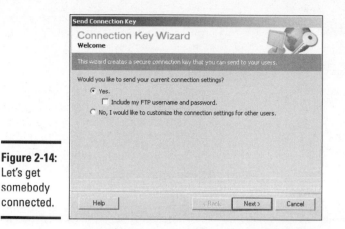

Figure 2-14:
Let's get
somebody
connected.

4. **The Role Information page of the Connection Key Wizard appears. (See Figure 2-15.)**

If the person you're sending the connection key to will only be editing pages, choose Writer, or if the person will also be creating new pages, choose Publisher. Alternatively, you can choose another person to become an administrator. This option is handy if you and your client will jointly administer the site.

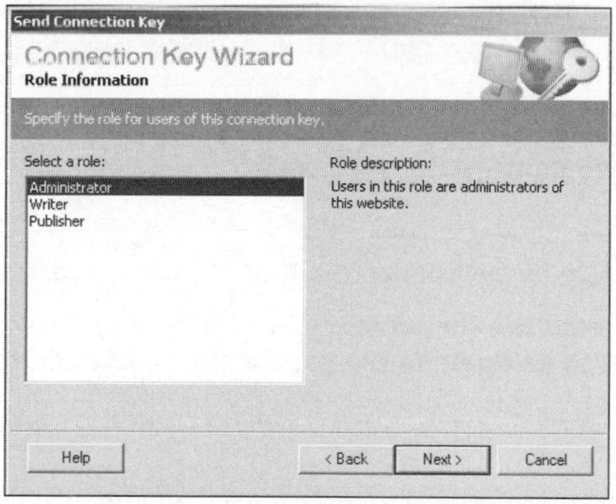

Figure 2-15:
Time for a
little role
playing.

5. **Choose a role and then click Next.**

The Connection Key Information page of the Connection Key Wizard appears. (See Figure 2-16.)

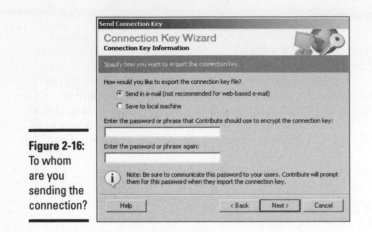

Figure 2-16:
To whom
are you
sending the
connection?

6. **Choose the manner in which you're going to send the connection key.**

   You can send a connection key via e-mail, choose to save the connection key to your local machine for distribution via floppy disk, or upload it to a secure folder on a local server. The wizard recommends that you don't send the key via Web-based e-mail, which is an excellent suggestion as it isn't secure. If you're dealing with a local client, save the key to your local machine, transfer it to a floppy disk (remember those?) or Flash drive, and then deliver it to the client when you're showing her personnel how to use Contribute. If your client is distant, send the floppy disk via the most convenient method. Send the password under separate cover.

7. **Enter the password that the recipient will need to unlock the connection key and then confirm the password.**

8. **Click Next.**

   The Summary page of the Connection Key Wizard appears.

9. **Review the information for accuracy. If something is incorrect, click the Back button to navigate to the page where you need to change the information.**

10. **Click Done.**

   If you've specified saving the key to the local machine, you'll be prompted for a location in which to save the key. If you've already got a floppy disk loaded, save the key to your floppy drive. If you've specified sending the key via e-mail, your default e-mail application opens. Fill in the blanks and let the e-mail fly, Guy.

Editing Web pages

Now that you've got your client's Web editing team up and running with Contribute, they can begin editing pages. Editing pages in Contribute is as simple as navigating to the site and then to the page that needs to be edited. The following steps show you some of the basic editing tasks you can perform with Contribute. A full tutorial on all the features of Contribute is beyond the scope of this book. If you need to know more information about Contribute, refer to the online help. The online help can also show you how to create new pages with Contribute. To edit a page in Contribute, follow these steps:

1. **Launch Contribute.**

   When you launch Contribute, the application connects to Web sites to which you've made a connection. The sites are listed on the Contribute start page. (See Figure 2-17.)

2. **Click the site you want to edit.**

   Contribute navigates to the site's home page. Alternatively, you can enter the URL to the page you want to edit after Contribute loads.

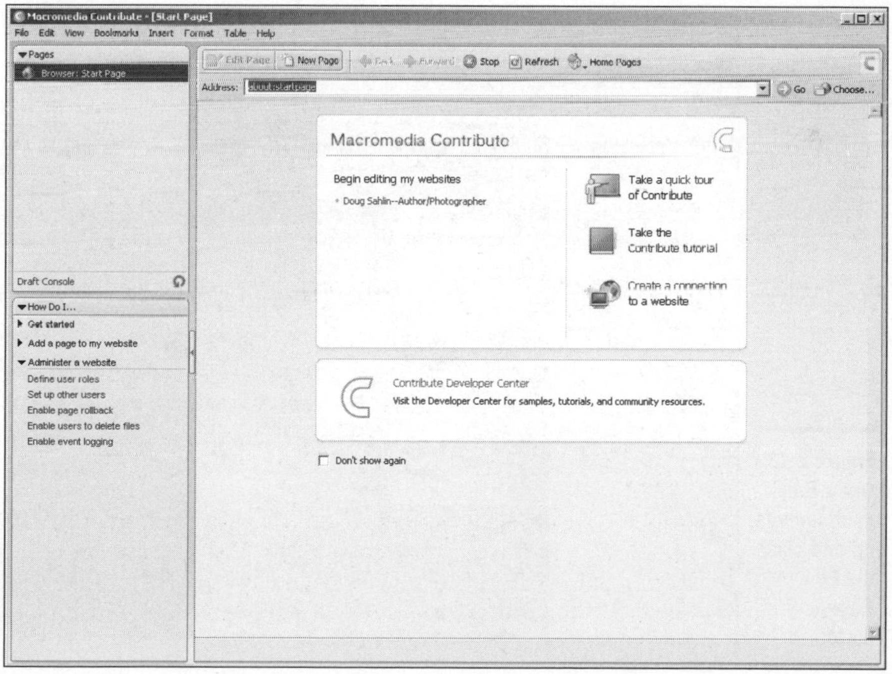

Figure 2-17: You've got connections.

3. **Use the site navigation menu to navigate to the page you want to edit.**

   After navigating to a page on a site to which you've made a connection, the Edit Page button appears. (See Figure 2-18.)

4. **Click the Edit Page button.**

   Contribute creates a draft of the page. (See Figure 2-19.) At this stage, you can edit any part of the page that isn't locked. If you've set up the site using templates, the parts of the pages such as the navigation menu should be locked to prevent users from tampering with your hard work. While in draft mode, you can change text, do minimal image editing, change image properties, and so on. Notice the toolbars at the top of the page. You can use the buttons on them to insert images, create links, and insert tables. Notice the tools for formatting text. They look quite similar to what you find in most word processing applications.

   If a page needs extensive editing, click the Save For Later button. When you do this, Contribute saves the draft to your local machine. You can edit any draft by clicking the desired page in the Pages panel. After editing the page offline, click the Publish button to upload the edited page to the server.

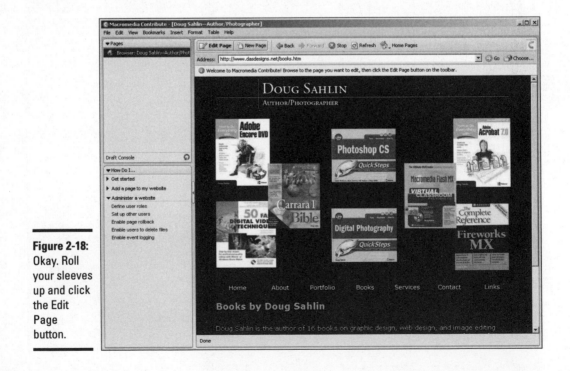

Figure 2-18: Okay. Roll your sleeves up and click the Edit Page button.

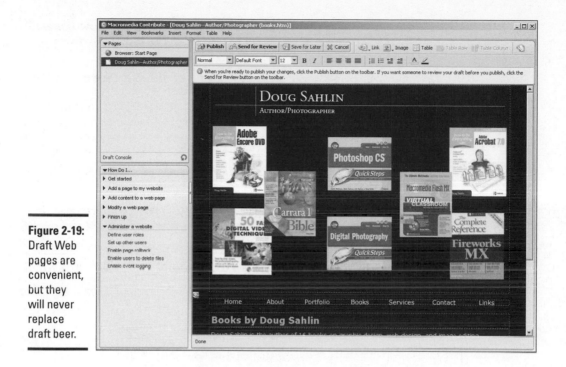

Figure 2-19:
Draft Web pages are convenient, but they will never replace draft beer.

5. **After editing the page, click the Publish button.**

   Contribute publishes the edited page to the server. If you've enabled rollbacks, Contribute has saved the previous version of the page in case you're not satisfied with your edits and want to revert (*rollback,* in Contributese) to a previous version of the page. The default number of rollbacks is 3.

Managing a Site with Dreamweaver

If you and your staff have been contracted to manage your client's site, the obvious application for editing is the application with which the pages were created. Dreamweaver is a robust application that enables the savvy Web designer to create a way-cool Web site and edit it as well. The following sections show you how to edit your pages in Dreamweaver.

Editing new pages

The beauty of editing pages in a full-featured HTML editor like Dreamweaver is that you can edit the pages as well as the underlying code. When you edit pages in Dreamweaver, you can work in one of three modes: Design, Code, or the chameleon Split mode, which enables you to view the page and code at the same time. Now, how cool is that? To edit pages in Dreamweaver:

1. **In the Files panel, select Local View from the View drop-down menu and then select the site you want to edit from the Site drop-down menu.**

Dreamweaver displays the files associated with the site. (See Figure 2-20.)

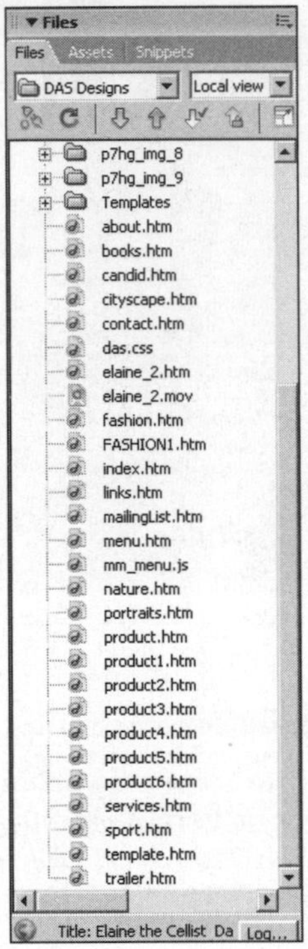

Figure 2-20: The Files panel is your friend.

2. **Double-click the page you want to edit.**

Dreamweaver opens the page in Design mode. (See Figure 2-21.) Editing pages in Dreamweaver is pretty straightforward. The Properties inspector is your friend in Dreamweaver. You use it to change links, CSS styles, images, and so on.

3. **Edit the page as needed.**

If you need to modify the code, click the Code button to display the page in Code view. (See Figure 2-22.) If you need to view both the code and page at the same time, click the Split button to display the page in Split view. When working in Split view, you can select items in the Display pane, and the underlying code is displayed in the Code pane. (See Figure 2-23.)

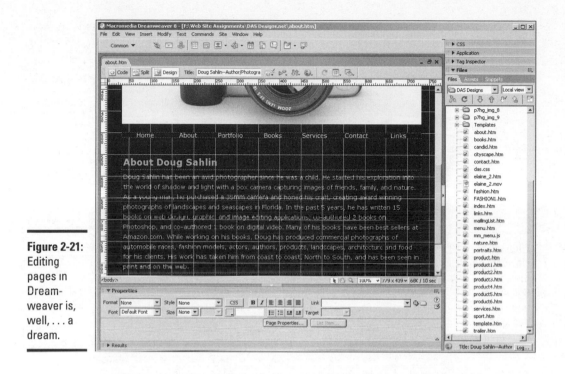

Figure 2-21:
Editing pages in Dream-weaver is, well, . . . a dream.

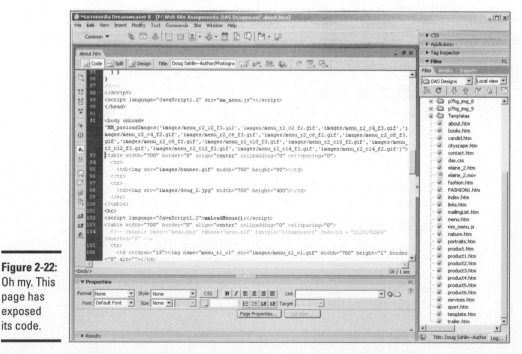

Figure 2-22:
Oh my. This page has exposed its code.

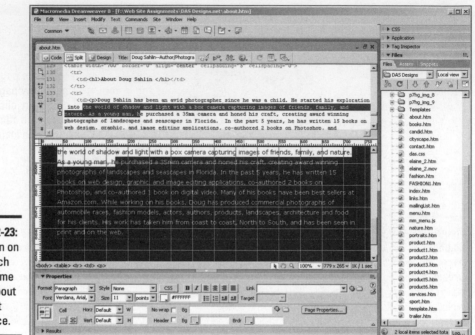

Figure 2-23:
Lie down on
the couch
and tell me
more about
this split
existence.

4. **After editing the page, click the Put button, which looks like an up-pointing arrow.**

Dreamweaver uploads the edited page to the server.

Archiving pages

You work hard to create compelling Web sites for your clients. If you follow our sage advice in the "Updating Pages without Destroying Them" section of this chapter, you archive pages on the server. But what happens if the server has a major malfunction (known as a *hissy fit* to your nontechnical client) and all of your client's files are erased? Most Web servers have some kind of redundancy, which enables them to restore your client's files. But in the case of a natural disaster, the computers on which the backup files are kept might be toast. You probably have the latest version of your client's pages on your local machine. However, hard drive failure isn't out of the question. To prevent problems, we always archive a Web site to CD after we publish it. If you have sophisticated CD-burning software, you can set up a multisession disc and update the disc whenever you change a page. In either worst-case scenario (a server meltdown or a local machine hard drive meltdown), you've still got everything you need to restore your client's Web site on a CD. Oh yeah, CDs are prone to failure as well. Make a copy of the CD and store it in a safe place. It's always better to be safe than sorry.

Templates in Dreamweaver can save your sanity

If your client changes her mind frequently, you might find yourself frequently creating new pages for her Web site. When this occurs, you turn on the meter and start charging your client your going rate for revisions. But why re-invent the wheel? We mean, after all, the new pages will have common elements such as the site banner, the footer, the navigation menu, and so on. Rather than creating these items from scratch every time you create a new page, you can save yourself a lot of time by creating

templates when you create the site. If you create a template for every possible page that you'll need to create, making a new page is a snap. Choose File⇨New and then click the Templates tab. Choose the desired template and go to town. You'll save yourself a lot of time by working with templates, as you don't need to re-create the common items that are used in the site. But there's no need to pass the savings on to the client. For more information on creating templates, refer to Book III, Chapter 6.

Tips for Managing Tasks

Many of your tasks as a Web designer are repetitive. At times, you have to enter the same bit of code and at other times you use items that are the same, but different. When you perform repetitive tasks on a regular basis, Snippets are a Web designer's best friend. And for items like a site copyright notice that changes once a year, you can't beat a Library item. Another way you can streamline your workload is with Assets. Assets are items, such as Flash movies and images, that you use when designing a site. Assets have their own panel and are neatly organized in folders by content type, ready to use in an existing page or a new page. The upcoming sections show you how to streamline your work when creating or editing pages.

Simplifying repetitive tasks with Snippets

Did you ever wish you could do away with the boring tasks in your everyday life? We mean, wouldn't it be wonderful to step in front of a mirror, push a button, and get your face washed, followed by a close shave and a quick trim? Well, modern grooming technology hasn't gotten that far, but Web design has. If you find yourself doing repetitive tasks in Dreamweaver, such as inserting the same image or the same bits of code in a page multiple times, you'll love Snippets. With Snippets, you can save code that you'll be using frequently in the Snippets panel. You can then use the Snippet in any Web page you create.

Creating Snippets

One task that many e-commerce Web designers do over and over is insert
Buy Now links and the associated code into Web pages. Many of our clients
use PayPal in their sites. The following steps show how to record PayPal
code as a Snippet.

1. **Open the page that contains the code you want to save as a Snippet.**

You can record any combination of code, even code to insert images,
create hyperlinks, and so on. Just make sure that any assets such as
images will be present on the site in which the Snippet code will be used
and that the relative path is the same.

2. **Click the Code button.**

When you create a Snippet, you select the code associated with the task
you want to convert to a Snippet. You can create a Snippet in Designer
mode, but when you're recording several lines of code, it's hard to
ensure you've selected everything in Designer mode. If, however, you're
recording a single object such as text with a hyperlink, you can accomplish this in Designer mode.

3. **Select the desired code.**

4. **Choose Window⇨Snippets.**

The Snippets panel opens. The Snippets panel consists of several preset
Snippets that ship with Dreamweaver. You can also create folders for
your own Snippets. We store our Snippets in a folder, oddly enough,
named My Snippets. (See Figure 2-24.)

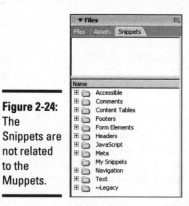

Figure 2-24:
The
Snippets are
not related
to the
Muppets.

5. **Select the folder in which you want to store the Snippet.**

6. **Select the code you want to convert to a Snippet.**

7. **Click the New Snippet icon.**

The Snippet dialog box appears.

8. **Name the Snippet (see Figure 2-25) and then click OK.**

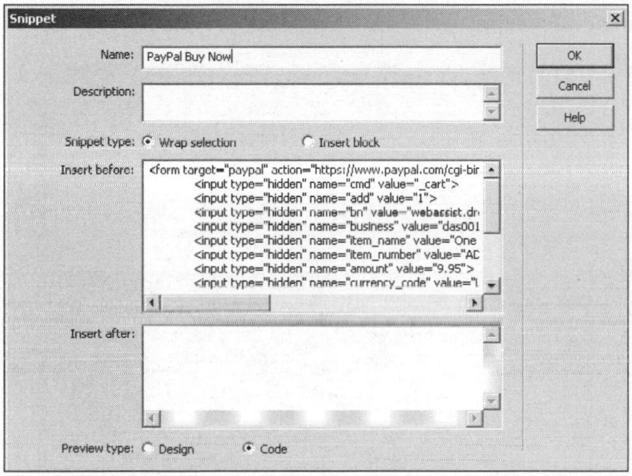

Figure 2-25:
We hereby
christen
thee: Joe
Snippet.

The Snippet is added to the desired folder.

Using Snippets

After you amass a panel full of spicy Snippets, you can liberally sprinkle them on the new pages you create or the pages you edit. And you do so with the simple click of a button. To use a Snippet in a Web page, do this:

1. **Create a new page or open an existing page where you want to add a Snippet.**

2. **Choose Window⇨Snippets.**

The Snippets panel opens.

3. **Navigate to the folder that contains the Snippet you want to use.**

4. **Drag the desired Snippet onto the page.**

You can do this in any mode. If you decide to add a Snippet while working in Code mode, make sure you position your cursor in the proper place. Otherwise, you run the risk of messing up the page. Of course, you can always undo inserting the Snippet.

Figure 2-26 shows a page in Split mode where the PayPal Buy Now Snippet was added to a page. The only thing that you'll need to change is the PayPal item number. But that's a small price to pay for not having to enter all that code.

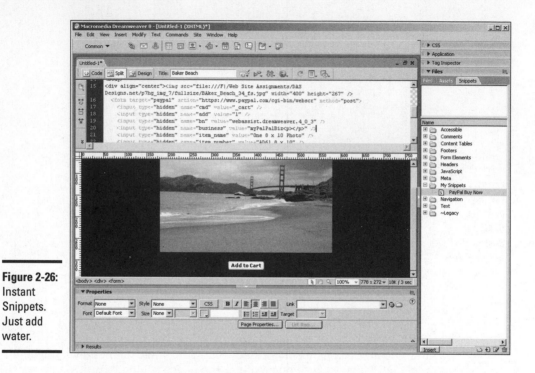

Figure 2-26: Instant Snippets. Just add water.

The Snippets panel is a powerful feature that can save you lots of time. In addition to recording your own Snippets, you'll find several, useful, preset Snippets neatly tucked away in folders. If you don't like JavaScript because of all the code work, check out the JavaScript folder in the Snippets panel. When you start using some of these gems, your clients will think you're a genius. Don't let on that you had a little help from a friend.

To edit a Snippet, select it and then click the Edit Snippet button at the bottom of the Snippets panel. This opens the Snippet dialog box. Edit the code as needed and then click OK to save the edited Snippet.

Taking advantage of your assets

Everything's got assets, including the Web pages you design. Whenever you define a site and begin creating pages, the images, colors, Flash movies, hyperlinks, and so on are saved in the Assets panel. Whenever you want to use an asset on a new page, all you need to do is grab it by the scruff of the neck and drop it on the page. What could be simpler? And if you really, really like an asset and think you'll use it on other pages for the site you're creating, you can save it as a favorite. To use assets, follow these instructions:

1. **Choose Window⇨Assets.**

The Assets panel opens. The panel has several icons on the left side, which, when clicked, display all the assets in the categories. When you click an item such as an image, the image is displayed in the window at the top of the Assets panel. (See Figure 2-27.)

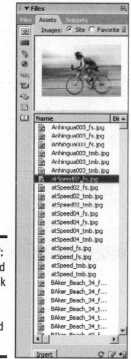

Figure 2-27: Hot, roasted assets; click an icon to get your hot, roasted assets.

2. **Select the desired asset and drag it onto the page.**

To use an asset on any Web site, select the asset and then click the Add To Favorites icon. To access the favorites for a Web site, click the Favorites icon to reveal the site favorites for that category.

Using the Dreamweaver Library

The Dreamweaver Library is a wonderful thing. Anything you add to the Library can be used on any page you create within the site. The really cool thing about Library items is that when you edit them, you have the option of updating the pages that already contain the Library item, which is a perfect solution if you've got an item such as a copyright or anything else that's date sensitive and needs to be updated in multiple pages.

Creating Library items

Consider creating a Library item anytime you have an object that will be used in multiple Web pages. The beauty of a Library item is the fact that you can use it on any Web page in any Web site. To create a Library item:

1. Open the Web page that contains the item you want to convert into a Library item.

We include a copyright notice on most of the Web sites we create. When we finish creating the home page, we add the copyright notice to the bottom of the page and then convert it to a Library item.

2. Choose Window⇨Assets and then click the Library icon.

The Assets panel opens to the Library section. (See Figure 2-28.)

Figure 2-28: The Dreamweaver Library has no librarian.

3. Select the item you want to convert to a Library item.

When you select an item, such as a menu with links — or in this case, a copyright notice with HTML tags — it helps to view the page in Split mode. This ensures that you select the object and the tags that format the object. In the case of the copyright notice, we also want to include the tags that center the text and format it as paragraph text. (See Figure 2-29.)

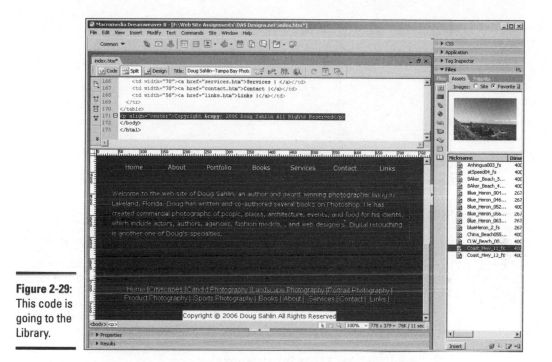

4. **Drag the item from the Web page into the Library when working in Design view.**

Alternatively, you can click the New Library Item icon. The item appears in the Library as Untitled.

If you add an item to the Library that is formatted with a CSS (Cascading Style Sheet), a warning dialog box appears telling you the item might not look the same on other pages because the CSS formatting information is not copied with the item. In the case of text, the formatting defaults to the HTML formatting for the text object.

5. **Enter a name for the item.**

We use a descriptive name that is easy to decipher when using the item in another Web page. For example, if you're managing multiple Web sites and each one has a copyright notice, precede the copyright notice with the client's name. Figure 2-30 shows my copyright notice as it appears in the Library.

Using Library items

If you set up your Library items when you create the first page of a site, you can easily add it to other pages in the site. To add a Library item to a Web page you're editing:

Figure 2-30:
A copyright notice in the Dreamweaver Library.

1. **Position your cursor where you want the Library item to appear.**

If the page includes a lot of formatting tags or code that is specific to items on the page, view the page in Split mode to ensure that the Library item is placed in the correct position.

2. **Choose Window⇨Assets and then click the Library icon.**

The Assets panel opens to the Library.

3. **Drag the Library item into the page.**

The Library item is added to the page. Text items appear as a white rectangle in Display mode (see Figure 2-31) but display perfectly in a browser.

Editing Library items

You can edit a Library item at any time. When you edit a Library item, any pages that use the Library item can be automatically updated, which is a tremendous timesaver. To edit a Library item:

1. **Choose Window⇨Assets and then click the Library icon.**

The Library section of the Assets panel appears.

2. **Select the item you want to edit.**

3. **Click the Edit icon.**

The Library item appears in the main window of the Dreamweaver workspace. (See Figure 2-32.)

4. **Edit the file.**

5. **Choose File⇨Save.**

The Update Library Items dialog box appears. (See Figure 2-33.)

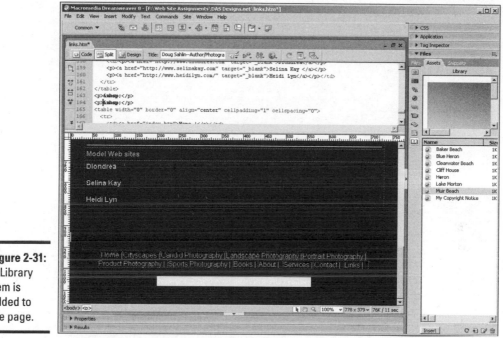

Figure 2-31:
A Library
item is
added to
the page.

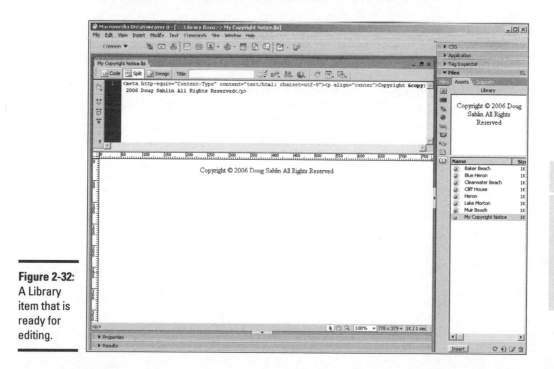

Figure 2-32:
A Library
item that is
ready for
editing.

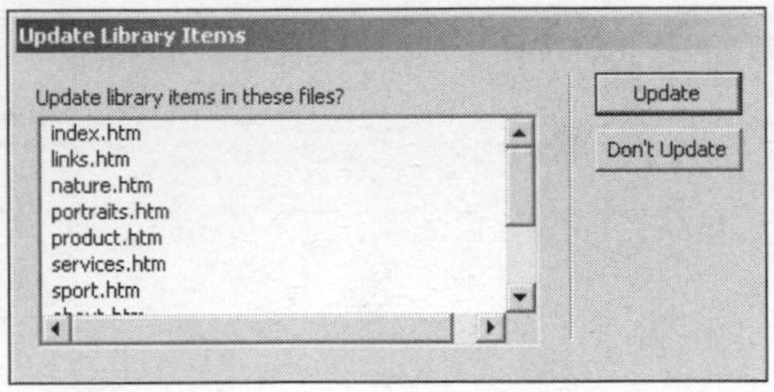

Figure 2-33:
Whoopee!
I'm gonna
update
some
pages.

Update Library Items

Update library items in these files?

index.htm
links.htm
nature.htm
portraits.htm
product.htm
services.htm
sport.htm

Update

Don't Update

6. Click Update.

All pages that contain the Library item are updated. Alternatively, click Don't Update if you don't want to update the pages.

Chapter 3: Expanding a Site

In This Chapter

✔ **Deciding between expanding and adding on**

✔ **Starting again from scratch**

✔ **Doing a redesign**

✔ **Publicizing the relaunched site**

*L*ike a toddler using a bike with training wheels, there comes a time when your client needs to make the next step, knock off the training wheels, and ride with the big boys. When this blessed event occurs, you've got some decisions to make: whether to update the existing design or start from scratch and redesign. Many factors are involved in your decision. After you make that decision, you have to design the site in such a manner that the revision or redesign doesn't interrupt your client's current site. So then, if you're in an expansion frame of mind, this chapter shows you the factors to consider when expanding the site. Doug takes the lead in this chapter, showing you the steps he took to update his own site.

Use It or Lose It: Should You Add On or Redesign?

You've designed a wonderful Web site for a client; you uploaded the design and went on your merry way, designing sites for other clients. Several months later, the client comes back to you and — guess what? You've got another gig. He wants you to do more work on the site. The Web site is very important to your client, and he wants you to add information about his new products and services. You meet with the client, and he lays out the grand vision for the site expansion. Now, you're faced with an important decision. Do you add on to the existing site or redesign it from scratch?

Adding on to an existing site

When it's time to expand a Web site, you can always add on to the site. When you add on to a Web site, you keep the look and feel of the current Web site, and the expansion is almost seamless. Your client's visitors are coming to a place they know and are familiar with the features. But your client has given you some cool new stuff that he wants included on the site. Consider the following when making the decision whether or not to add on to an existing site:

✦ If the site is less than a year old and doesn't look outdated when compared to the competition, adding on to the site is a viable option.

If the site is a few years old and sports features such as a Flash intro or beveled buttons, remove them. Like beehive hairdos, these features have gone the way of the dodo.

✦ If you can do the expansion without a massive renovation to the existing navigation menus, update the site.

✦ If your client only wants you to add additional features such as a forum or blog (Web log), you can easily accomplish this using the existing site framework.

✦ If the current site has been received well by the client's customers and the expansion can be accomplished using the existing site framework, update the site.

✦ If you can expand the current site without incurring usability issues or otherwise confusing visitors, update the existing design.

Redesigning the site from scratch

When you redesign a site from scratch, it's almost the same as designing a new Web site. The obvious advantage is that you've already worked with the client, so you know her foibles and follies. Figure 3-1 shows my personal Web site prior to redesign. My goal for the redesign was to create a Web site that focused on my skills as a photographer. Web design is still a major part of my business. However, I now work in conjunction with other designers. Therefore, I can change the focus of my personal Web site to photography. The redesigned Web site is shown in Figure 3-2.

Consider the following when deciding if a site needs to be redesigned:

✦ If the site is more than a year old and appears outdated, redesign the site from scratch.

✦ If the site isn't up to snuff with Web sites of your client's competitors, it's time to do a redesign from the ground up.

✦ If the site no longer accurately reflects your client's main focus, a total redesign is needed.

✦ If an expansion will cause usability issues such as cluttered menus, hard-to-follow navigation, and confusing content, redesign the site.

✦ If you've already made substantial changes and added new features prior to the client's expansion request, redesigning the site from scratch will enable you to use the latest technology and create a state-of-the-art redesign for your client.

Figure 3-1:
Bend me,
shape me,
any way you
want to.

Figure 3-2:
The URL is
the same
but the
content
has been
changed to
protect the
innocent.

✦ If the current Web site can't easily accommodate your client's future expansion plans, redesign the site.

✦ If your client's intended audience is accessing the Internet with faster connections, redesign the site and incorporate items such as streaming video, Flash movies, and other interactive features in the new site.

Your client might expect a price break because you previously did work for her. If a price break or discount comes up in the course of discussion, you have to put your foot down and tell the client that a redesign from scratch involves just as much work as a new site design. In fact, if it's been more than a year since the initial site design, your price should be higher.

Headache-Free Expansion

When you expand a site, everything must go off without a hitch. Whether you revise the existing site or redesign the site, the finished product must be error free. This is even more important when you're expanding an existing site, as visitors are used to surfing the current site, which, if you've done your homework and tested the original design, is error free. You did test the original site, didn't you?

If the site is a total redesign, you must consider other things before jumping in with both feet and cranking out new Web pages. In the upcoming sections, we give you some food for thought when it comes to redesigning a site. We also show you how to make sure the site expansion goes off without a hitch.

Things to consider when redesigning

When you redesign a site that's been out there for a while, you do so because the client has new material to show site visitors and because the existing site is getting a bit long in the tooth. When you redesign a site, you need to put the same effort into the redesign as you did when you created the original site for the client. You need to see what's out there. In other words, do your research and view sites of businesses or organizations that are similar to your client's. Just because the first site you designed for the client was state of the art doesn't mean a redesign that is simply a rehash of the original design will draw "oohs" and "aaahs" from people who visit the new site. While you're doing your research, you should also check out the current sites of your client's competition. If your client is in a dog-eat-dog business, chances are the sites of his competitors have been significantly changed since you viewed them while designing the original site. For that matter, your client's top competitors might have changed since you did the original design. Check with your client to see who are currently his top competitors.

A logical workflow for a site redesign includes the phases we describe in the following sections.

Consultation

Meet with your client to get the scope and breadth of the client's expansion. Get as much information as you can from the client. This meeting is very similar to your initial consultation with the client, except that you know her better now and can talk frankly with the client based on your previous experience.

+ **Find out everything about the client's current needs.** What are her goals for the revised site? Also, ask her to think about future expansion.

+ **Discuss the previous site.** What pages and sections work and which don't? Your client is bound to have feedback from site visitors. The site stats can tell you which pages are hits and which aren't.

+ **Address the client's intended audience.** Is the intended audience the same as when you did the original site, or is the audience different or expanded based on the new information that will be incorporated in the redesign?

+ **Address your client's competitors.** Is she competing against different businesses, or does the list of the client's competitors expand along with the Web site expansion?

+ **Determine your client's timetable for going live with the redesign.** You'll have to incorporate her timetable with the other phases of the project and your current workload. If the timetable isn't reasonable, become the voice of reason and tell the client what the timetable will be based on the scope and breadth of the redesign.

Review

Review the client's existing site in conjunction with the desired expansion. During this review, you're looking for answers to these questions:

+ **What does the client's current site say to the intended audience?**

    When reviewing the information, make note of which information is concurrent with your client's new goals, and which is not.

+ **Will the intended audience change based on the new information you'll incorporate with the client's current site?**

    If the audience will change, you'll have to consider which content from the old site will be appropriate for the new site and whether you'll have to change material based on the demographics of the new audience.

+ **Can you incorporate the current graphics into the redesign?**

    You might need to change the navigation menu or site banner based on your client's new goals.

✦ **In the new design, can you improve navigation and the organization of information?**

If the client's audience complained about any items on the old site, now is the perfect time to change them.

✦ **Which pages are the most popular and which pages have the fewest hits?** If the pages that have the fewest hits contain important information, you have to tweak these pages during the redesign.

✦ **Which pages have been bookmarked by site visitors?** You have to incorporate a version of bookmarked pages in the new design, and these pages must have the same URL.

You want to include some familiar items in order to provide some continuity to people who visited the original version of the site. Two of the most common items in a design are the banner and the footer. If possible, include both in the redesign so your client's Web site visitors won't think they've landed on the wrong Web site.

Analysis

Analyze the information you learned while reviewing the site and incorporate that with the content that the client wants incorporated with the redesign. Determine if the information can be incorporated with that presented on the client's current Web site or if you'll have to create new pages for the material.

Analyze the client's intended audience. Has it changed since your first design for the client? Has the technology used by your client's intended audience changed since your first design? Has Web technology changed since your first design? The answers to these questions shape your redesign. You also need to know what bandwidth your client's audience is using to access the Internet, their average desktop size, and so on.

A redesign is more than simply rehashing material from the old site. While you do want to keep some continuity, analyze the material that the client is presenting to you for the redesign. Unless you're forgetful or have more business than you know what to do with, you're bound to remember the content of the old site. If not, analyze the content of the current site thoroughly before analyzing the new content proposed by the client. After analyzing the new content, come up with a plan to marry the old with the new.

Planning

This stage of the redesign is similar to creating a mockup for client review. Incorporate all of the information you've learned to create a user-friendly navigation system that combines the old and new. After you've jumped this hurdle, consider how you'll organize the information on each page. The information you learned while consulting with the client, reviewing the client's existing pages, and analyzing the other important factors in the redesign shows you which information is the most relevant in the redesign. This information must be easily accessible by your client's intended audience.

You have to address other issues in your redesign, such as the following:

✦ **Does the current site's server have enough features to implement your redesign?** For example, if your redesign incorporates a database, does the server have provisions for creating a database? Alternatively, can you upgrade the features on the server side to incorporate the new features in your redesign?

✦ **What software will you need?** For example, if the client asks you to include a site-wide search engine, you need to find the applicable software and include the cost plus markup of the software in your revision.

✦ **How much of the old can you wed with the new?** Consistency is important to Web site visitors. Therefore, you should keep some of the old images and, if at all possible, the site banner. When you plan the redesign, you must keep the client's intended audience in the forefront of your mind. Your redesign incorporates the client's goals with the intended audience's expectations. In the viewer's eyes, the redesigned site should have value-added services.

Archive the original Web site. You might be able to incorporate some of the material in the original design in future revisions of the redesigned site.

✦ **What technology is your client's intended audience using?** Do they have the necessary browser and plug-ins to access the technology you plan on using in the redesign? If not, use a different technology or add links to sites where site visitors can download the plug-ins needed to view the redesigned site. In the long run, your best bet is to plan the redesign around the lowest common denominator; in other words, go with the oldest technology used by your client's intended audience.

Alternatively, you can create two versions of the site: one for the techies who have the latest software plus fast Internet access, and another version for the lowest common denominator. Use a gateway page with links to direct visitors to the site that matches their technology.

✦ **Have you incorporated future expansion in the redesign?** Make sure your navigation menus are laid out in such a manner that you can easily incorporate future additions to the Web site. Use templates to simplify the construction of each page. Templates will also be indispensable when incorporating future expansion into the redesigned site.

Book VIII Chapter 3

Expanding a Site

Include search engine optimization (SEO) in your redesign. If you don't, the client's expanded site will be virtually invisible in search engine results pages. See Book VIII, Chapter 1 for more about SEO.

Implementation

At this stage of the process, you start with a clean slate in your HTML editor and incorporate your planning to create the actual pages. This is no different than creating a new Web site. You design a home page that's a brief overview of your client's business, service, or organization that is compelling enough to draw visitors to the site. Then you must lay out the ensuing pages in a logical manner with the most important information at the top of the page. The main pages in any section of the site should be short, simple, and to the point. Pages that are deeper in a section can have more text.

Testing

Finally, test the site to ensure a smooth transition from the old to the new. If the site is small, you can test most of it on your local machine, or if the site uses ASP, ColdFusion, or PHP, you can test the pages using a testing server on your local machine. At the risk of being blatantly obvious, check everything: navigation menus, links, interactive content, and so on. Another option you can choose is doing an online beta test, as outlined in Book III, Chapter 10. After testing the site, evaluate your findings and tidy up any loose ends or faulty code. Then you're ready to go live.

Trauma-free site expansion

Whether you're expanding existing pages or redesigning the site from scratch, your task is a lot easier if you follow certain steps during the project. Most of this is common sense, but even the best designer might forget a step or take things for granted because he's worked with the client before. Well, the long and the short of it is, don't take anything for granted. Otherwise, one of Murphy's Laws will come into play when you least expect it. At any rate, here are a few things to consider when expanding a Web site:

✦ **Write a proposal for the expansion project.** After you and the client come to terms with the scope and breadth of the project, prepare a proposal and get the client to sign the proposal before you begin work.

✦ **Present a mockup to the client for approval.** Just because you've worked with the client before doesn't mean you know her like the back of your hand. You might be in for a nasty surprise if you assume that she'll fall in love with your expansion sight unseen.

✦ **Use existing pages as the basis for the site expansion.** When you begin the site expansion, download the old pages from the Web hosting service. Worst-case scenario, you'll have to create a new navigation menu to incorporate new sections of the site. You can create a new menu in Fireworks and insert it in the proper place in your HTML pages.

✦ **Archive the original Web site so you can refer to the old content if you need to.**

✦ **Maintain links and the page's listing in a search engine index.** When revising a page that is currently on the site, begin with the document you downloaded from the Web hosting service. Change the page as needed and save it using the same name. This keeps all of your links intact and preserves the page's listing in a search engine index.

✦ **Keep your client abreast of the project.** If you're uploading your work as you do it, tell the client when the revised work is posted and get the client to sign off on the work. If you're working on a total redesign, upload the content to a different folder at the Web hosting service and ask your client to review and comment on the work you've done so far.

✦ **Test, test, test, and then test again.** Make sure everything on the pages you're creating or revising works perfectly. That includes links and any code you're using. A site expansion should be handled with the same kid gloves as a new design.

   In fact, if you've got the luxury of time and the scope of the expansion is massive, consider doing a full-blown beta test, as outlined in Book III, Chapter 10. In lieu of a beta test, use your friends, employees, or the client's employees to test the revised site.

✦ **Upload pages *only after* securing the client's approval.** Never upload pages to the root directory of the Web hosting service until the client agrees that the work is to her liking and you've tested the pages to ensure against any problems. Your best bet is to upload the new pages to a different folder on the server and send the URL to the client and anyone else who is testing the pages.

✦ **Set up a testing server.** If you're creating ColdFusion, PHP, or ASP pages, set up a testing server on your local machine, which enables you to test the pages as you create them.

✦ **Work smarter, not harder.** Use the features of your HTML editor to modify the previous work you've done for the client as part of the site expansion. If you're using Dreamweaver, read the upcoming sidebar, "Making Dreamweaver work for you," to find out how you can whip through a site expansion without breaking a sweat.

**Book VIII
Chapter 3**

Expanding a Site

Making Dreamweaver work for you

You've already created a lot of material for the site you're about to expand. Whether you're revising the old site or redesigning it, there's no sense in reinventing the wheel. The Assets panel is chock-full of items you used on the old site: images, Flash movies, URLs, and so on. To use them in the revision or redesign, simply open the Assets panel and drag the asset into the new or revised page. Snippets can also be a great timesaver, especially if the site uses a lot of code. If you've added items to the Library, such as footers, copyright notices, and so on,

you can use these in the site expansion as well. And last, but not least, consider recycling templates you used when creating the site. If it's a total redesign, you might be able to get by with revising templates. To revise a template, open the document as a .dwt file. You can then edit locked regions of the template and make other necessary changes to suit the revision. As an added bonus, when you save the template, you have the option of updating all pages that were designed with the template.

After Launching the Expanded Site

You might think the work is done after you've uploaded the revised or redesigned site to the server. Nay, nay, Nanette; your work, or your client's work, has just begun. You've posted something new and hopefully exciting for the world to peruse. But like anything else, nobody will know what you've done unless you tell them about it. That's right — you've got it, so flaunt it. The following is a list of things you or your client should do to publicize a revised or redesigned site:

✦ **Send a press release to the local media.** The press release should include the reason the client changed the Web site along with information about the client and the client's business or organization. Don't forget to include the URL to the site in the press release.

✦ **Notify members of your client's mailing list that the site has new content.**

✦ **Send a newsletter to existing clients telling them about the expanded Web site.**

✦ **Request link exchanges.** If your client's expanded Web site contains information that is pertinent to Web sites not currently linked to the site, request a link exchange.

✦ **Include an invitation to visit the expanded Web site in all of the client's printed media, including advertisements.**

✦ **Re-register the site with the search engines.**

✦ **Use other online marketing techniques, such as pay-per-click ads, to draw visitors to the expanded site.**

After you launch the redesigned or revised site, pay careful attention to the site statistics to determine the overall success of the expanded site. Notice which pages are getting the most visits and from which pages visitors are exiting the site. If viewers are exiting the site from pages that contain important new content, you'll have to revise the pages. The information learned from the site statistics will drive future changes, revisions, and redesigns.

Convince your client to add an online survey with your redesign or revision. The survey should ask visitors what they like and dislike about the redesigned site. If the survey is long, consider including a special offer as a reward for submitting the completed survey. The information garnered from the survey can help you and the client gauge the overall success of the site.

Book IX

Case Studies

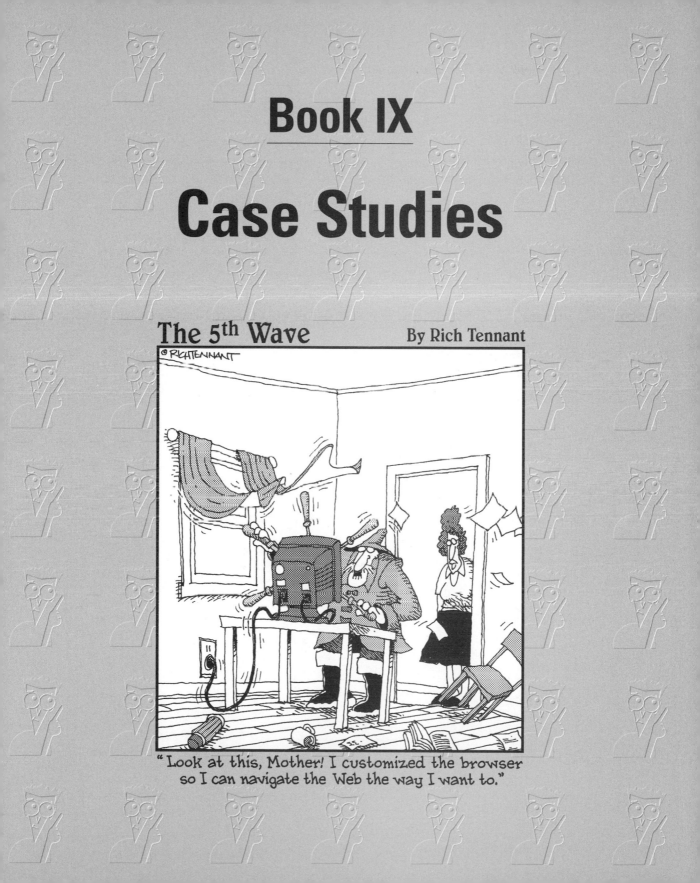

The 5th Wave   By Rich Tennant

"Look at this, Mother! I customized the browser
so I can navigate the Web the way I want to."

Contents at a Glance

Chapter 1: Personal Web Sites

In This Chapter

✔ **Self-promotion on the Web**

✔ **Getting your message out there**

✔ **Defining the site**

✔ **Creating the pages**

The Web is accessible to anyone. If you're an artist, author, or musician, a Web site is a wonderful way to promote your skills. Whether you're published or not, a Web site is a way to show your work to the masses. Many personal Web sites, however, are poor reflections of what the artists have to offer. In this chapter, Doug takes the lead and shows you the prototype he's creating — the makeover of a musician's Web site.

Tailoring the Site to Your Client

When you design a site for a creative person, the site needs to reflect your skill as a designer as well as your client's personality and personal taste. Some creative types have a tendency to go over the top. You might end up having to be the voice of reason if you encounter a client like this.

When I first began the task of redesigning a Web site for a busy cello player, my first step was to find out more about her needs and what type of Web designs she liked. She sent me the URLs of a few sites she likes, and we discussed her needs, likes, and dislikes. She wanted

+ A site that's easy to update and maintain.

+ A site with tasteful colors and graphics.

+ A photo gallery she can easily update.

+ A page with video and audio clips.

+ A discography page with links to sites where people can purchase her work.

+ A page with a schedule of upcoming performances.

Creating the Home Page

The home page is the window to every site. Therefore, it should load quickly and be inviting and compelling enough to entice the visitor to click a few links. Before coming to grips with the design for my cello-playing client's site, I created the navigation menu for the site. I used Fireworks to create a vertical navigation menu with rollover buttons. (See Figure 1-1.) I created the banner in Fireworks as well. I exported the menu as HTML and images and the banner as images. I optimized the buttons and banner as GIF files.

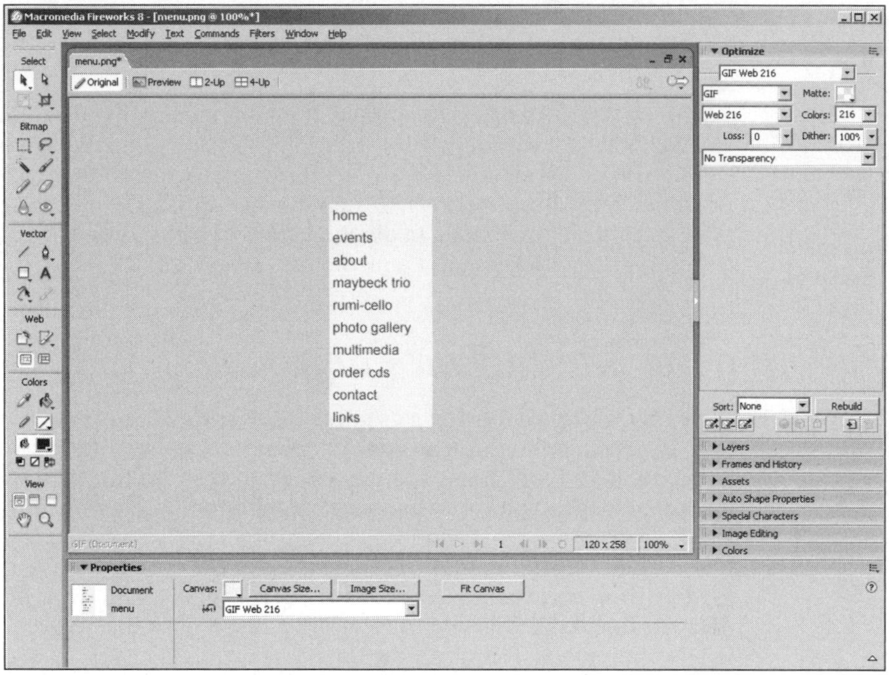

Figure 1-1:
Creating the navigation menu.

Her original site had a lovely picture of her playing her cello beside some ornate columns. I loved the shot and decided to use Active Slideshow Pro (which is covered in Book V, Chapter 4) on it. I started with random motion and then used the Slide To Center option. (See Figure 1-2.) In essence, it's a one-slide slide show, but the effect draws the viewer into the site.

To finish off the home page, I decided to add a bit of sound. I didn't want to increase the amount of time it took the page to download, so I used a five-second clip from a Bach Cello Concerto. I created the sound file for the home page in Flash and added it to the HTML document. (See Book V, Chapter 2 for more about incorporating sound on a Web site.)

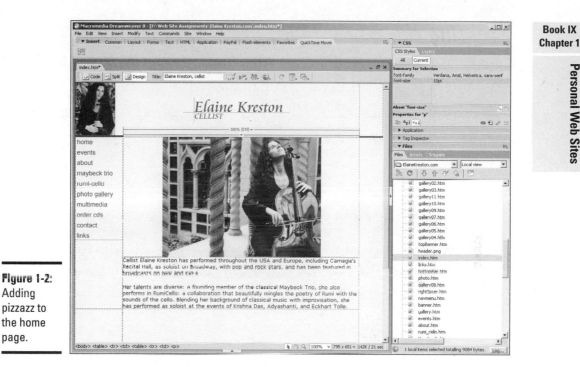

Figure 1-2:
Adding
pizzazz to
the home
page.

Creating Other Pages

To meet my client's goals (see the earlier section, "Tailoring the Site to Your Client"), I had a slew of pages to add after creating the home page, which I discuss in the preceding section. This section covers those other pages.

The photo gallery

One of the site owner's requests was that the site be easy to edit. That left me with a few concerns regarding the photo gallery. I could have used the Image Gallery Magic plug-in in Dreamweaver to create a stunning gallery, but that would have required that a Web designer make the updates. I ended up creating a gallery in Flash. The gallery was published as an SWF file and added to the Web page. When the gallery loads, the first image in the gallery is displayed. The gallery (shown in Figure 1-3) comes with buttons that load the previous or next image. The images are numbered sequentially. When the cellist wants to change images, she can keep the same file names (img1.jpg, img2.jpg, and so on). She just resizes the images to fit the gallery and uploads them to the Images folder on her server. Based on our initial conversation, I knew she had the software and knowledge to perform this task.

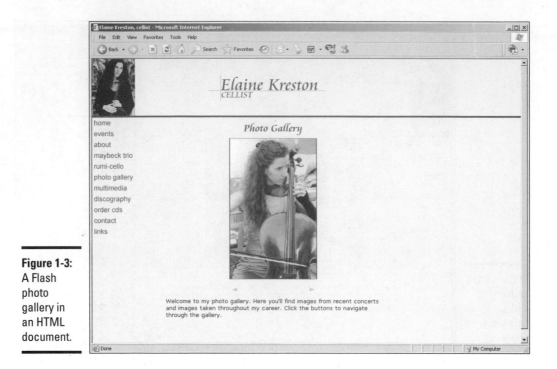

Figure 1-3:
A Flash photo gallery in an HTML document.

The discography page

The cellist for whom I'm creating the site is quite prolific. She has an album of her own and has played on several others. In addition, she's created original soundtracks for two yoga DVDs. The volume of work had to be presented in a logical manner that she could easily edit. The albums were resized into thumbnails in Fireworks. Each thumbnail is housed in a table. Each thumbnail is a hyperlink to the Web site where visitors can purchase the work. (See Figure 1-4.) In addition, the site has a page to order CDs.

When you're creating a Web site, you can never take a visitor for granted. The visitor might not think of going to the Order CDs page, but when he sees the pointing hand appear when passing his cursor over one of the images, he'll be tempted to click it just to see what happens. It could result in a sale.

The events page

In addition to teaching music and recording, the cellist frequently performs. Therefore, she needed an events page, such as the one shown in Figure 1-5, to keep visitors informed. I created a table with two columns and multiple rows. The left column contains the date and time of the event, whereas the right column contains information about the event. An events page like this is easy for a site owner to edit.

Figure 1-4:
The
discography
page.

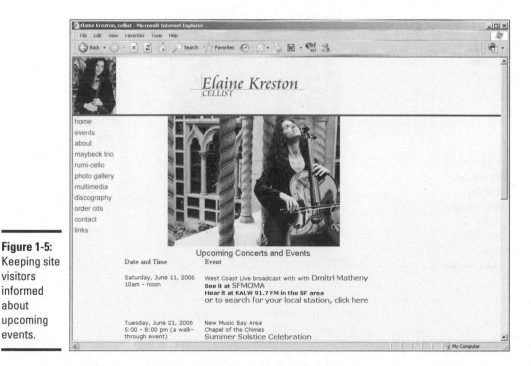

Figure 1-5:
Keeping site
visitors
informed
about
upcoming
events.

The multimedia gallery

With the advent of high-speed cable modems, adding video and audio to a Web page is feasible. When you create a Web site for a musician, a page with multimedia clips (as shown in Figure 1-6) is the ideal way to showcase her talent. I recorded video of the cellist while I was attending a writing conference in San Francisco. I recorded her in several picturesque areas of San Francisco. The last clip was recorded on Baker Beach with the Golden Gate Bridge in the background. I edited the video and replaced the audio captured by the video camera with the cellist's studio recording of Bach's "Suite No. 1 for Cello" — the same piece she played while I shot the video. I edited the video and rendered it as a QuickTime MOV video file. The QuickTime Player was embedded in the page and linked to the video. In addition, I added several audio clips to the page. Book V covers incorporating multimedia elements in your Web design.

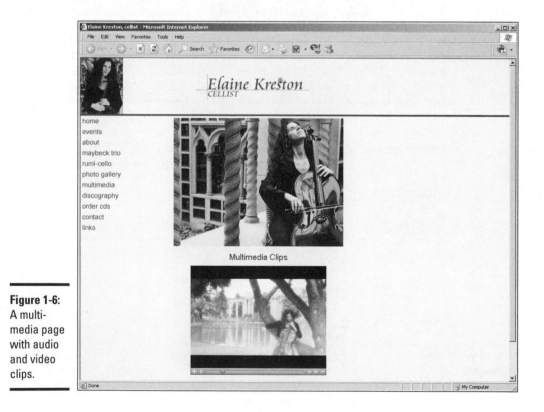

Figure 1-6:
A multimedia page with audio and video clips.

Editing a Personal Web Site

When you create a personal Web site, you take the same care as you do with any Web site. However, most people who can afford to hire a designer to create a personal site want to edit the site themselves. Therefore, you need to put some safeguards in place so the site owner doesn't turn your handiwork into something that looks like an experiment from a 4th grade student gone amuck. Make sure you create the page with a template. Create editable regions in which the site owner can update material. The areas that can cause the most problems are menus nested within a table. Most menu buttons are rollovers. If the client accidentally deletes a button, the results can be disastrous. This area should be locked. You should also lock the header and footer.

If your client tells you she wants to edit the site, include the cost of a copy of the Contribute application with your design fee. Just about anyone can master Contribute, including the aforementioned 4th grader. But don't just drop a copy of Contribute in your client's lap and wish her good luck. Sit down with your client and show her how to connect to a site and edit a page. You should also show her how and when to use tables, insert images, create links, and so on. If you take some time to show your client the right way to edit a site with Contribute, it can save you from having to deal with a phone call from a panicked client who messed up your design so badly that even you won't recognize it.

Chapter 2: Blog Site

In This Chapter

- ✔ Knowing how blogs work
- ✔ Adopting the b2evolution blog application
- ✔ Running multiple blogs with WordPress
- ✔ Using a blog hosting service
- ✔ Incorporating a blog with an existing site

A *blog,* for those of you who have been couch potatoes instead of Net potatoes, is short for *weblog.* A blog is like an online diary. You post your thoughts, photos, or information of interest to your viewing audience and collect comments from people who read your blog. Kids use blogs, and so do politicians. Blogs come in many different varieties. There's the *vanity blog,* which is a blog that's put up by someone who absolutely thinks it's the coolest thing since wireless pointing devices but fills the blog with vacuous text, and there's the *serious blog,* which is put up by someone who has important information to convey to his Web site visitors. In this chapter, we explore two pieces of blog software and explore a blog that was added to a Web site.

Examining Blog Software and Services

If you type **blog software** into your favorite search engine, you get pages of results to explore. Many of the most popular blogs are free.

Before actually showing you some blogs, we tell you a bit about how they work. When you add a blog to your Web site, you're adding PHP pages to your Web site. The pages enable you to display your blog online and accept comments from visitors to your blog. You post entries to your blog from the administration pages. From the administration pages, you can also delete pesky comments or comments you feel aren't suitable for your blog. When you post an entry to your blog or a user posts a comment, the information is stored in a MySQL database on the server. When someone visits a blog site, the PHP page plucks the information from the database and displays it.

b2evolution

The b2evolution blog software is completely free. It's a blogger's dream, with a full-featured administration section that enables the user to post blogs and manage comments posted by users. The b2evolution blog is multilingual, multi-user, and supports multiple blogs. You can download different blog skins (user interfaces) to change the way the blog looks to visitors. If you're conversant with PHP code and CSS (cascading style sheets), you can modify the blog to match the look and feel of other Web pages on the site. In the following sections, we show you some of the features of a b2evolution blog.

Introducing the b2evolution application

The b2evolution blog is powered by PHP and a MySQL database. As of this writing, the current version of b2evolution is b2evolution 0.9.2, which is also known as Sparkle. You can download b2evolution at `http://b2evolution.net`. Follow the links to the Download section.

In order to run b2evolution, your Web server needs PHP 4.1 or above and MySQL 3.23 or above. The designers of the application claim that it works best with an Apache server. Everything on the blog is done online through a Web browser. b2evolution has been tested with the following browsers: Firefox 1.0+, Internet Explorer 6.0, and Konqueror 3.5+. Display issues are experienced with the following browsers: Safari, Mozilla Firefox 1.2, and Netscape 4.0.

The b2evolution application has an impressive manual, which you can view at their Web site. You can see the full manual at `http://manual.b2evolution.net/Main_Page`. The manual covers every conceivable question about the application, including how to change the look of the blog, how to create blog entries, how to manage multiple blogs, and so on. The downloaded application comes with installation instructions that link to the b2evolution Web site and complete manual.

Installing b2evolution

If your Web server has the required features (listed in the preceding section) to run b2evolution, you're ready to install b2evolution on your server. You can find detailed instructions with the application. The following steps are condensed, but they give you an idea of how simple it is to install the application on your server.

1. **Download and unzip the b2evolution application.**

   All of the necessary files you need to run the application are downloaded into a folder named Blogs.

2. **Create a new MySQL database on your server.**

   You can easily create a MySQL database through your Web hosting service's control panel or a server application called phpMyAdmin. When you create the database, you're prompted for a name, username, and password. You don't have to configure the database, as the b2evolution application handles that task for you.

3. **Upload the Blogs folder to your server using an FTP (File Transfer Protocol) application such as CuteFTP.**

   When you unzipped b2evolution, all of the files required to run the application appeared in the Blogs folder.

4. **Change permissions on several pertinent files.**

   Using your FTP application, you change the permission of files that configure the blog, enable uploading of image files when creating blog entries, and so on. Detailed instructions on which files need permission changes are revealed in the complete instructions.

5. **Install the application.**

   To install b2evolution on the server, you access the Install folder, which, on a typical installation, can be found at www.*mywebsite*.*com*/blogs/install/. After you access this folder, the install dialog boxes appear. Follow the prompts to enter your MySQL database name, username, and password.

6. **After entering your database information, choose New Application and follow the prompts.**

   The installation software writes the config files and populates the database. During the installation, you receive a username and password, which you'll use to log in to the blog. If desired, after logging in to the blog for the first time, you can change the default password.

7. **After you install b2evolution on your server, click the log in link.**

   This takes you to the blog's log in page, where you're prompted for your username and password. But before you can actually post to the blog, you have to change a few files.

8. **After the installation, you need to change a few permissions on the server and make some changes to the `config.php` file.**

   Most FTP applications give you the option to change permissions. The blog installation instructions tell you what changes to make. After making these changes, you're ready to go blogging.

Posting a blog entry in b2evolution

After you install and set up a b2evolution blog, you or your client can begin posting entries to the blog. When you post entries to a b2evolution blog, you do so through the Back Office, which you access by logging in as administrator. Several tabs in the Back Office enable you to perform myriad blogging tasks. The Back Office is well documented in the online manual. It's also fairly intuitive — almost as easy as writing an e-mail. If your client is familiar with working in a Web browser, you'll have him up and blogging in no time flat.

When you create a blog post, you enter the information on the Write tab of the Back Office. You use the various buttons to add hyperlinks, images, and so on. (See Figure 2-1.)

After writing a blog entry, you can preview it (see Figure 2-2) before clicking the Upload button. After you upload the post, visitors to the blog can read it and add comments.

Managing a b2evolution blog

You manage a b2evolution blog through what is known as the Back Office. In the Back Office, you configure your blog and add other users to the blog. If you're maintaining the blog for your client, you're the administrator and you set up other users on the Users tab. (See Figure 2-3.)

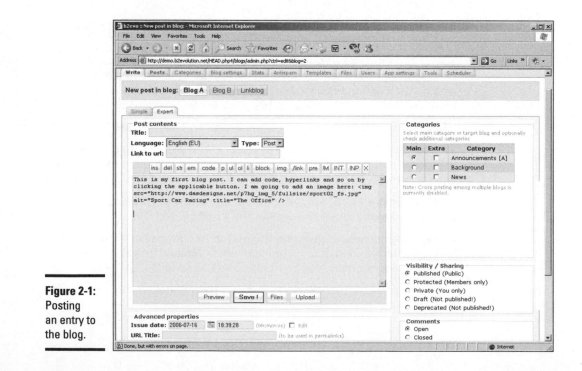

Figure 2-1:
Posting an entry to the blog.

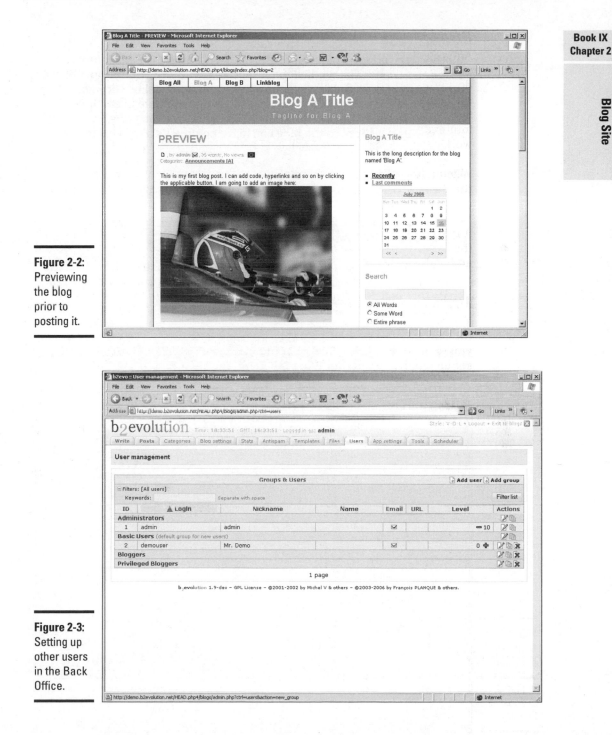

Figure 2-2:
Previewing the blog prior to posting it.

Figure 2-3:
Setting up other users in the Back Office.

WordPress

Another very popular blog application is WordPress. Like b2evolution, WordPress is free. The application is feature rich. After you set up a blog on a server, you (or your client) can manage everything online through a Web browser. WordPress supports multiple blogs and multiple users. If desired, you can have users create profiles with WordPress. Depending on the template you use, visitors to the blog can leave comments about each post.

About WordPress

WordPress also uses a combination of PHP code and a MySQL database to display and maintain the blog. As of this writing, the current version of WordPress is WordPress 2.03. You can download WordPress at `http://wordpress.org/download`.

After you have the blog up and running, you can manage posts as well as user comments. You can edit previous posts, delete posts, and delete comments that you deem inappropriate for the blog. You do this on the Posts tab of the Back Office. (See Figure 2-4.)

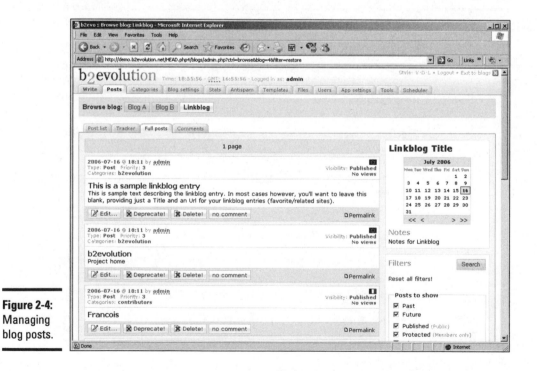

Figure 2-4: Managing blog posts.

To run WordPress, your Web server needs PHP 4.2 or above and MySQL 3.23.23 or above. The designers of the application claim it works best with an Apache or LiteSpeed server.

WordPress comes with installation instructions. While the application doesn't have a full-fledged manual, you can find impressive documentation on the application at `http://codex.wordpress.org/Main_Page`. The WordPress Web site also features an impressive support section (`http://wordpress.org/support`) that covers many installation issues as well as how to modify templates.

Installing WordPress

If your server has the necessary features (listed in the preceding section) to run WordPress, you're ready to install the application. Installation instructions are included with the application. To give you an idea of how easy it is to install the application, here is a condensed version of the installation process.

1. **Download the application and unzip the files.**

The files needed to run the application are downloaded into a folder called WordPress.

2. **Create a new MySQL database on your server.**

You can easily create a MySQL database through your Web hosting service's control panel or a server application called phpMyAdmin. When you create the database, you're prompted for a name, username, and password.

3. **Open `wp-config-sample.php` in a word processing application.**

4. **Change the database information.**

Modify the file by changing the default name of the database, username, and password.

5. **Save the file as `wp-config.php`.**

6. **Upload the files to a folder on your server.**

Create a folder on your server. The logical name for that file is Blog. Upload the files to this folder.

7. **Install the application on your server.**

To install the application, navigate to the `install.php` file on your server. The default location is www.*mywebsite.com*/blog/wp-admin/`install.php`.

8. Follow the prompts to install the application.

The installation dialog box prompts you for a name for your blog and your e-mail address. After you supply that information, WordPress automatically fills in the table for your database. The application generates a username and password.

9. Write down your username and password.

You need these to log in to your blog, administer it, and post entries. If you're not crazy about the username or password, you can change it when you administer the blog.

10. Log in to your blog.

You'll find a `wp-login.php` link at the bottom of the installation dialog box. Click the link to begin blogging.

Modifying a WordPress blog

After you install a WordPress blog, you can modify the blog to suit the Web site to which it is linked. You can do so by modifying an existing theme (skin) or uploading a new theme to your server. The downloaded version of WordPress has two themes. However, WordPress is a popular application and lots of developers have created themes for the application. To modify the look and feel of your WordPress blog with a theme, follow these steps:

1. Open your Web browser and navigate to `http://themes. WordPress.net`.

The WordPress ThemeViewer appears. (See Figure 2-5.)

2. Navigate to a theme you like.

As of this writing, there are 42 pages of themes. You can speed up your search by displaying themes that have color schemes similar to the site to which they'll be linked. You can sort by color by enabling one or more check boxes.

3. Click the Test Run link to preview the theme in your browser.

The test site appears in a new browser window. (See Figure 2-6.)

4. When you find a theme you'd like to use, click the Download link and then follow the prompts to download the file to your desktop.

5. Unzip the file.

6. If desired, modify the theme in your HTML editing application.

You'll find tutorials on modifying themes at this URL: `http://codex. wordpress.org/Blog_Design_and_Layout#Themes_and_ Templates`.

Figure 2-5:
Selecting
a new
theme for a
WordPress
blog.

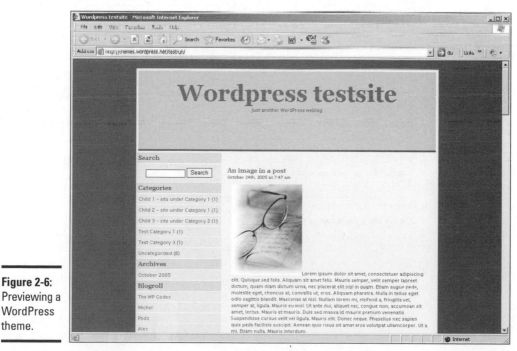

Figure 2-6:
Previewing a
WordPress
theme.

7. **Upload the Themes folder to the following directory on your server** `www.mywebsite.com/blog/wp-content/themes`.

   After uploading a Themes folder to this directory, you can change the look of your blog.

8. **Log in to your blog.**

   When you log in as administrator, the Dashboard section of your blog appears, which is where you administer the blog, write new posts, add new users, and so on. (See Figure 2-7.)

9. **Click the Presentation tab.**

   Your Web browser refreshes and displays the themes you have uploaded to your server. (See Figure 2-8.)

10. **Select the desired theme.**

    The previously used theme is replaced.

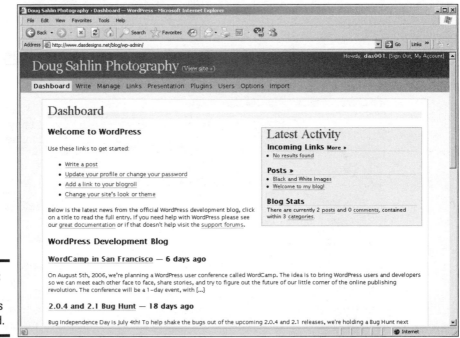

Figure 2-7: The WordPress Dashboard.

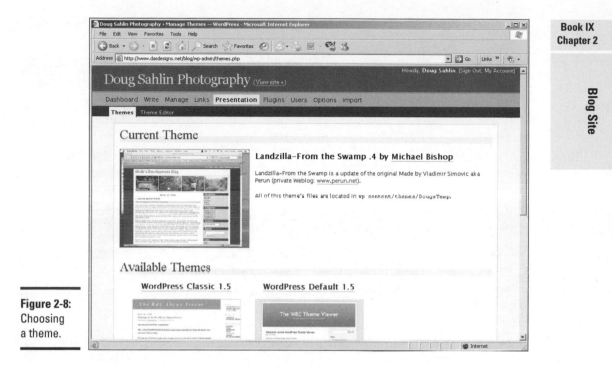

Figure 2-8:
Choosing
a theme.

Posting a WordPress blog entry

Blogs are all about getting the word out. WordPress makes it easy for you to post entries to your blog. You can add images and hyperlinks when posting a message to your blog. To add an entry to your blog:

1. Log in to your WordPress blog.

When you log in as administrator, WordPress displays the Dashboard, which enables you to administer your blog.

2. Click the Write tab.

Your Web browser refreshes to the Write page of your blog.

3. Enter the desired information.

When you post an entry to your blog, you can format the text and add images to the post. You can also add hyperlinks by clicking the Link icon. This opens a dialog box that enables you to enter the URL and determine whether the Web page opens in the same browser window or a new one. Figure 2-9 shows a post being written. Figure 2-10 shows the post as it appears on the blog.

Figure 2-9:
Writing
a post.

If you or your client posts information on several different topics, you can create a category for each topic. This makes it easier to manage your blog.

Managing a WordPress blog

If you're setting up a blog that has multiple authors and multiple categories, you can easily manage the blog through the WordPress Dashboard. You can also edit or delete posts. To edit posts in a WordPress blog, follow these steps:

1. Log in to your WordPress blog.

When you log in as administrator, WordPress displays the Dashboard, which enables you to administer your blog. If you have other people creating content for the blog, users with editor status can also edit blog entries.

2. Click the Manage tab.

Your browser refreshes to show all entries posted to the blog. (See Figure 2-11.)

Figure 2-10:
The entry,
as it
appears on
the blog.

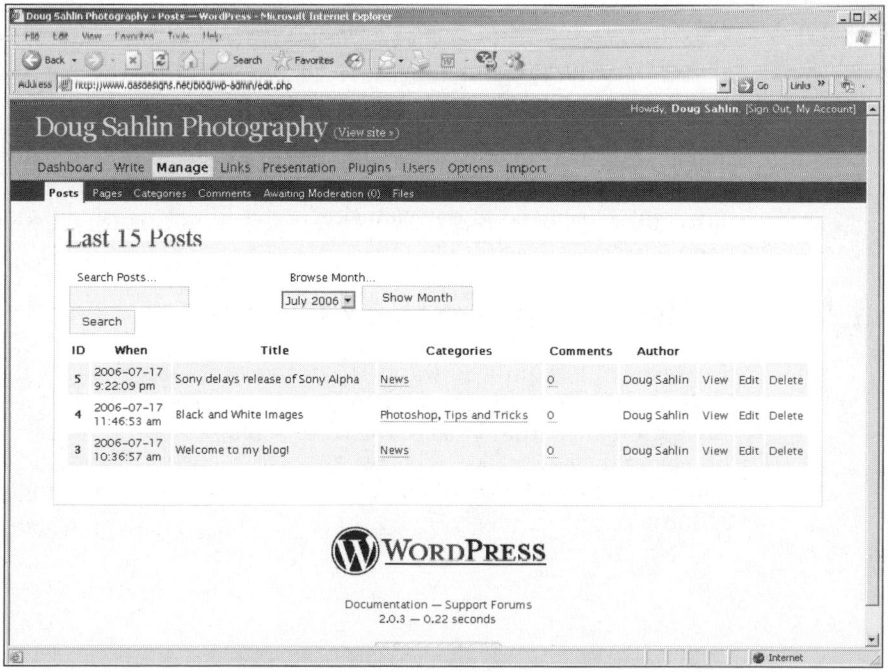

Figure 2-11:
Managing
posts.

3. **Click the Edit link for the post you want to edit.**

   WordPress opens the entry on the Write tab.

4. **Edit the message and then click the Save button.**

   WordPress publishes the edited post.

You can also add categories to the blog, modify comments, and more on the Manage tab. You can add links to the blog through the Links tab, plus add and manage users through the Users tab.

Exploring other options: Blogger.com

If your client doesn't have PHP capability on his Web server and still wants to go blogging, many online sources can host a blog. The online blog is linked to the blogger's site. Google acquired Blogger.com in 2003. Google has made improvements to the service, and it now features the capability to upload images with blog posts. You don't have to download any software; you do everything online. Blogger.com users can choose from a variety of templates.

Of course, like anything else that is free, strings are attached. The free blog is supported by ads that appear on the user's blog. If you want no strings attached, you've got to pay for it and post your blogs at BlogSpot.com.

Hosting a blog with Blogger.com is a three-step process. You create an account, name your blog, and then choose a template. After choosing a template, you or your client can begin posting words of wisdom — or a reasonable facsimile thereof.

Blogger.com was the perfect solution for a busy author/attorney/business coach who wanted to have her voice heard. Figure 2-12 shows the author's blog, which is linked to her Web site.

Adding a Blog to an Existing Web Site

If you've got a client who wants to get the word out, a blog is the ideal way to do it. Adding a blog to an existing site is as easy as adding a button to a navigation menu that links to the blog. A blog can do wonders for an existing site. Search engines like blogs because the material is updated frequently. All things being equal, a search engine ranks a site with a blog higher than one without.

Figure 2-12:
A free blog
linked to an
author's
Web site.

When you add a blog to a site, you've got to match the look and feel of the other pages on the site. Many Web designers shy away from creating blog templates, as there is quite a bit of PHP code involved, not to mention style sheets. Fortunately, literally hundreds of blog templates are available for the most popular blog software. If you start out with a blog that is similar to the look and feel of your client's Web site, you can get it to match perfectly by tweaking the PHP code, the CSS associated with the template, or both.

A blog was the ideal situation for a Web site another photographer and myself were starting. I didn't have time to create a full-blown Web site, so to get the site up and running, I used the WordPress blog. Figure 2-13 shows the finished blog with several posts.

Figure 2-13:
A blog added that matches the look and feel of an existing Web site.

Chapter 3: Online Newsletter

In This Chapter

✔ **Creating mailing lists**

✔ **Adding people to a mailing list**

✔ **Maintaining a newsletter mailing list**

✔ **Making a useful newsletter**

After you create, optimize, and submit a Web site to the search engines, it's the client's job to make sure that people return on a regular basis. One way to get people to return is to update the site content frequently. But how will the client's customers and Web site visitors know when the content is updated? Well, your client could be real subtle, use the blunt hammer approach, and send an e-mail to all visitors asking them to "Look at my new content!" Well, begging usually doesn't get you very far, at least not in the business world. To get people to visit the Web site again, you've got to pique their interest. A great way to do this is to present them with useful information or special promotions that entice them to visit the site again. One of the best ways to do this is to send newsletters via e-mail. The newsletter contains information that is useful to the recipient and links to pertinent areas of new content on the Web site. For example, in the case of a merchant's Web site, the links would be to sales items.

Building a Mailing List

You build the most beautiful newsletter in the world for your client. Your client scratches his head and asks, "What's next?" You politely answer, "Send it to your mailing list." Your client goes to marketing and asks if they have a mailing list. Marketing says they'll buy one. WRONG! Can you say, "spam"? These days, if you send out a newsletter without the recipient's permission, it's highly unlikely that recipients read it. If the recipient of your client's newsletter hasn't requested (also known in geek-speak as *opted in*) to the newsletter, chances are it will be caught by the recipient's spam filter. The only logical solution is to build a mailing list of people who want to receive the newsletter.

The old-fashioned way of creating a mailing list is to store e-mail addresses in a folder using an application such as Outlook. When it's time to send the newsletter, the client has to create an HTML e-mail and then plop the e-mail addresses of the subscribers into the BCC (blind carbon copy) field and let the message rip. (When you send a message as a BCC, you assure the anonymity of the subscribers.) Of course, if the mailer forgets to put the subscribers' e-mail addresses in the BCC field, he'll have a lot of angry people to respond to. And then there's the drudgery of maintaining the list by manually adding and deleting e-mail addresses. If you think this sounds like a lot of work, you're right.

The modern way to create a mailing list is by storing the information in a database on the site's server. Web designers and developers have no problem extracting the information from the database and compiling a mailing list. But your client's not a Web designer and is probably not a card-carrying geek either. Therefore, you've got to make it easy for him to get the information out of the database. The best way to do this is to purchase an e-mail management application and include it in the cost of creating the Web site — plus markup, of course. One such application is called Email List Manager 2.5. As of this writing, a single server license for the application is $99 and is available at www.adminprotools.com. The Enterprise version of the application sells for $249. You can use the Enterprise version on multiple domains as well as multiple servers in a local Enterprise network. Email List Manager 2.5 works with a ColdFusion server. The application features the following:

✦ **Subscriber and e-mail address storage:** Email List Manager 2.5 stores an unlimited amount of subscribers, including e-mail addresses and contact information. You can import a CSV (comma-separated values) list of subscribers or paste a block of text into the application's import window. The application also features a custom HTML tag, which enables a designer to add the necessary code to have a subscriber added or removed from a subscription list.

✦ **HTML e-mail and newsletter tool:** The application features a built-in HTML editor that enables users to create an HTML e-mail campaign for distribution to a subscription list. The application also enables the user to create and store an alternate text version of the newsletter, which is sent out as a multipart message. The application also has the capability of using variables in an HTML message, which enables the user to personalize the message with information, such as the subscriber's name, from the database. In addition, the application also makes it easy to use any stored e-mail newsletter as a template for a new campaign. Newsletters can be previewed before distribution. But for the ultimate litmus test, the user can use the Send Message to 1 Recipient option and send the e-mail to himself or another user before sending it to the entire list.

✦ **Subscriber management tool:** E-Mail List Manager 2.5 makes it easy to automatically purge the list of bad or delinquent e-mail addresses. The application also retrieves and processes all *bounced messages* (messages that return an error message to the sender, most likely because the e-mail addresses are incorrect or the inboxes are unavailable). Bounced messages are logged, and you can view the log at any time. Another feature enables a user to determine if a message bounced because the user exceeded his message allotment. Another feature enables users to search subscribers who have bounced messages and remove those subscribers from the list. The application is flexible, enabling users to change the parameters for list management at any time.

✦ **Personalization feature:** This feature enables users to personalize newsletters and messages with variables. The current build of the application enables the use of the following variables: first name, last name, e-mail address, subscription list name, and the current date, as well as custom variables. All of this information (except for the date) is derived from the fields of the database.

✦ **Attachments manager:** The application helps you easily manage one or more attachments per message.

✦ **Tracking feature:** The application enables users to track how many subscribers clicked a link within an HTML newsletter. This feature helps users to fine-tune their content for future newsletters.

In short, the application makes it easy for anyone to create and maintain mailing lists, create effective HTML newsletters, and monitor newsletter campaigns.

Making It Easy to Add People

The easiest way to add subscribers to a mailing list is to include some type of link on the Web site you're creating. The link connects to a form that makes it easy for users to subscribe to the mailing list. The data collected is added to the database. When you create a link for subscribers, it should stand out on the page. (See Figure 3-1.)

The magic needs to happen after the user clicks the link. As a Web designer, it's your job to create a form that populates the database with the subscriber's information. The code behind the form varies, depending on the type of database you create. Figure 3-2 shows the form used to populate the database for the mailing list for the acupuncturist's Web page shown in Figure 3-1. Notice that the form has fields for the users to add contact information other than their e-mail addresses. And notice that subscribers can use a radio button to unsubscribe from the mailing list. For more information on creating forms, see Book VI, Chapter 1.

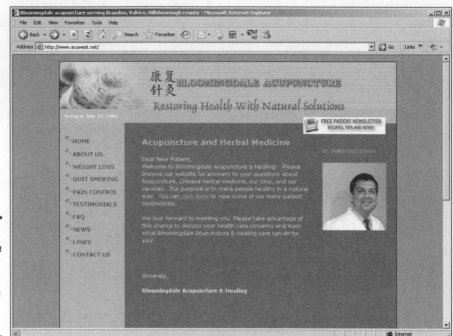

Figure 3-1:
A noticeable link entices site visitors to subscribe to a mailing list.

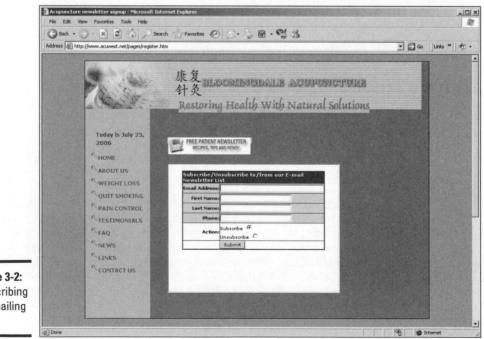

Figure 3-2:
Subscribing to a mailing list.

Managing the Mailing List

After the mailing list is up and running, you or your client have to manage it. When you manage a mailing list, you can add or delete members. Applications like Email List Manager 2.5 make it easy to manage a subscriber list and messages sent to subscribers through the use of a browser-based interface. (See Figure 3-3.) This is much easier than manually managing a mailing list through a server's control panel. As an added benefit, it's easy to teach your client how to manage the list.

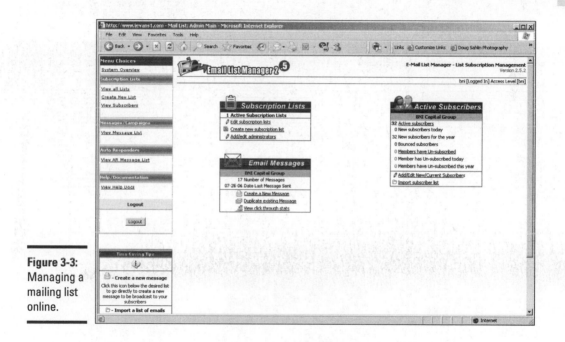

Figure 3-3:
Managing a mailing list online.

From within the interface, you can add new users, delete existing users, and update records, as shown in Figure 3-4.

Give Subscribers Something Useful

When sending a newsletter to subscribers, be sure that it contains useful information. Otherwise, your subscriber list will dwindle quicker than stock in fast-food restaurants after a mad cow disease report. The best way to pique a newsletter reader's interest is to include a special sale or a useful article. For example, a newsletter sent to subscribers of an online art supply store includes an art tip in every newsletter. They also have a newsletter that features their art products. (See Figure 3-5.) Notice that the top of the newsletter features an offer to pique the reader's interest. It also has a link to the online version of the newsletter.

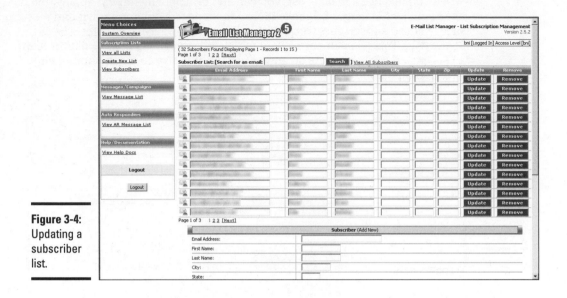

Figure 3-4:
Updating a subscriber list.

Figure 3-5:
An e-mail newsletter designed to get the reader's attention.

Email List Manager 2.5 enables you to create HTML newsletters. The built-in HTML editor gives you the option of starting from scratch or editing an existing newsletter. (See Figure 3-6.) The HTML editor is fairly easy to use. With a bit of tutoring (for which you'll charge cold cash), you'll have your client creating her own HTML newsletters in no time. Notice the icons at the top of the editor. Many of them are similar to those you find in word processing applications.

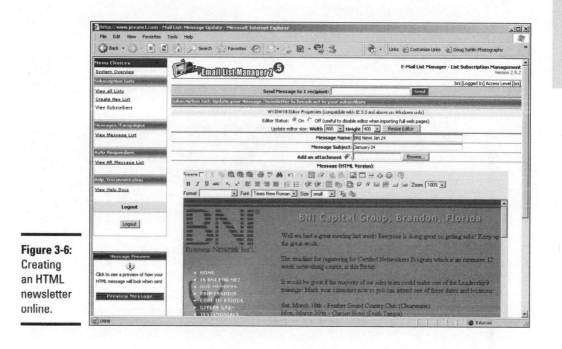

Figure 3-6:
Creating
an HTML
newsletter
online.

Case Study: Newsletter for an Acupuncture Clinic

A doctor of traditional medicine, also certified as a doctor of oriental medicine, opened an acupuncture clinic. To generate business, the doctor contacted a local Web designer, who created a Web site for him. The Web site was optimized and submitted to the search engines. After the search engines indexed the site, it began attracting quite a bit of traffic. The doctor asked the Web designer what else could be done to pique visitor curiosity and have them return to the site on a regular basis. She suggested a newsletter. Email List Manager 2.5 was used to set up a subscriber list, and a link was added to the Web site home page. The link opened a form that visitors used to subscribe to the list. Once the list had a considerable number of subscribers, the Web designer showed the doctor's office manager how to use Email List Manager 2.5 to send newsletters and maintain the mailing list. The Web designer created a newsletter that had a similar look and feel to the clinic's Web site. The newsletter also used the same navigation menu as the Web site. (See Figure 3-7.) The links were fully functional, enabling newsletter recipients to visit the site after reading the newsletter. Several hundred people are currently subscribed to the list, thanks to the useful information supplied in each newsletter.

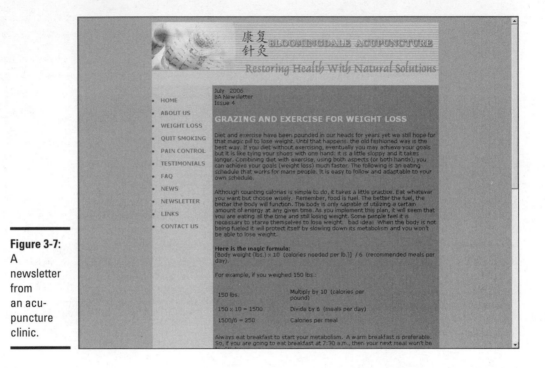

Figure 3-7:
A newsletter from an acu- puncture clinic.

Chapter 4: Photographer/ Portfolio Site

In This Chapter

✓ Knowing what you want

✓ Creating a navigation menu and thumbnail page

✓ Doing preliminary work in Fireworks

✓ Creating the portfolio

*E*very client has special needs, and photographers are no exception. The old saying that a picture is worth a thousand words has never been truer than when a photographer chooses to use a Web site for promotion. Photographers need to include information about themselves and their services, but by far, the most important part of a photographer's Web site is the portfolio section. We can share some first-hand insight into this topic because when Doug is not building Web sites and writing books, he's also a professional photographer. In this chapter, Doug takes the lead and dissects a photographer's Web site — his own, in fact.

Defining Goals for the Site

If a Web site doesn't have a reason for existence, it's just another domain name taking up space on a server. When I decided to turn the photography skills that I'd spent most of my life learning into a source of income, I realized I needed to have a Web presence. I already had a domain name and Web site. However, the Web site focused on my skills as an author, graphic artist, and Web designer. When I decided to add photography as an income source, I realized that including the information about my other skills would be counterproductive. When I decided to transform my site into a photographer's portfolio, I was doing the majority of my Web design work with a team who already had a Web site. Therefore, I could easily convert the domain to a photographer's Web site without skipping a beat. The following is a list of goals I wanted to accomplish with the Web site, including creating

✦ A clean, uncluttered design to showcase my photography.

✦ A simple, easy-to-understand navigation system.

✦ Fast-loading pages.

✦ Portfolio pages of thumbnail images that, when clicked, revealed full-size images.

✦ Multiple portfolio pages of similar images.

✦ A page to feature the books I've written.

✦ An About page to give viewers information about me and my achievements as related to photography.

✦ A Contact page.

✦ A Links page.

Designing the Site

After I defined the goals for the site, I was ready to design the site. I reviewed many photographer sites and bookmarked those that matched my design goals. Then, it was just a matter of relying on my creativity to come up with a Web site that's immediately identifiable as a photographer's Web site — but with my own spin.

Creating the navigation menu in Fireworks

I knew how many buttons I would need for the navigation menu. I wanted a horizontal navigation menu, but the number of buttons exceeded the available space for a clean, horizontal layout. Therefore, I decided to use the Fireworks pop-up menu feature for the subpages in the portfolio section of the site. When I designed the menu in Fireworks, I added the URL in the Link text field in the Properties inspector. The basic menu is shown in Figure 4-1.

After laying out the main menu, it was time to add the pop-up menu. My first step was to define the links in the Content tab of the Pop-Up Menu Editor. (See Figure 4-2.) Thanks to the flexibility of Fireworks, I was also able to define the URL for each link.

After defining the content of the pop-up menu, I specified the parameters in the Appearance, Advanced, and Position tabs of the Pop-Up Menu Editor. I decided to use HTML to generate the pop-up links. Figure 4-3 shows the finished menu as previewed in Internet Explorer.

I exported the finished menu from Fireworks as HTML and images. This option creates HTML code for the menu, which neatly houses the buttons in a table. The menu, complete with HTML, can be inserted into another HTML document.

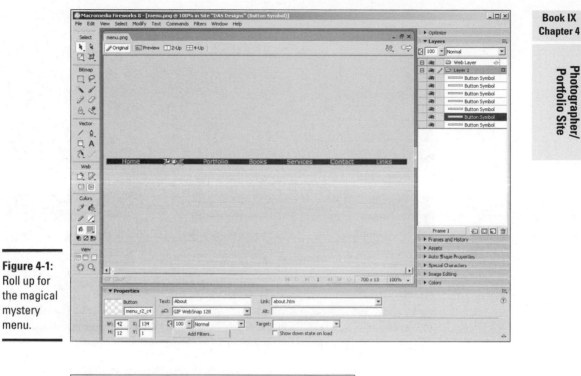

Figure 4-1:
Roll up for
the magical
mystery
menu.

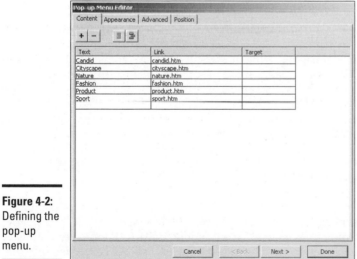

Figure 4-2:
Defining the
pop-up
menu.

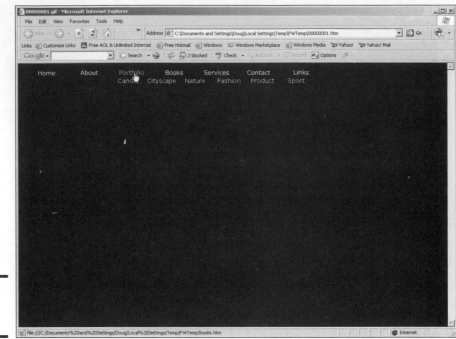

Figure 4-3:
Pop goes
the menu.

Optimizing images in Fireworks

I'm a photographer who uses Photoshop extensively for image editing, touchup, and so on. Fireworks 8 is a remarkably versatile application in the hands of an adept designer. While it doesn't have the image-editing features of Photoshop, Fireworks makes it easy for a Web designer to optimize a folder of images for display in a photographer's portfolio. Prior to optimizing images for a Web portfolio, I use the Adobe Bridge to rename images and add other meta data, such as copyright information, keywords, and so on. If you're a photographer and want to know more about workflow in Adobe Photoshop CS2, including the Adobe Bridge, pick up a copy of *Photoshop CS2 for Digital Photographers Only,* by Ken Milburn and Doug Sahlin (Wiley Publishing, ISBN 0-471-74689-4).

I create uncompressed copies of the original images in the Web site Images folder and rename them to reflect the portfolio in which they'll appear. For example, if I'm renaming images for a portfolio called Fashion, I end up with a folder of images named Fashion1, Fashion2, and so on. I then use the Fireworks Batch Process command to optimize the images in JPEG format and resize them for the Web. (See Figure 4-4.) For a photographer's portfolio, image quality is an important factor. As a rule, I use a quality value of 60 as the minimum. The size to which you optimize the image depends on the desktop size used by your intended audience. After optimizing the images, you can delete the copies of the originals.

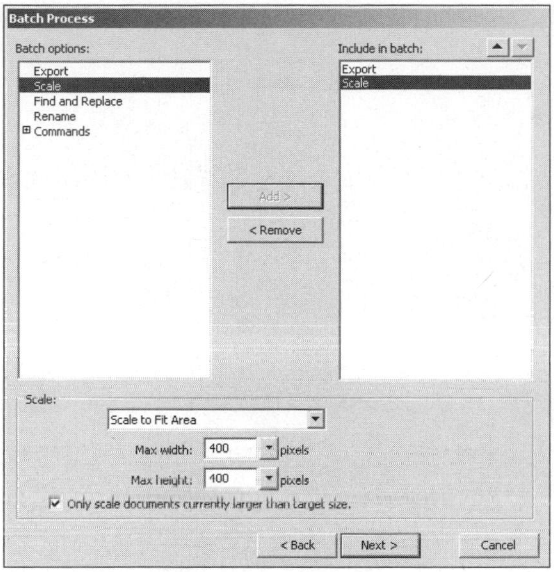

Figure 4-4:
Optimize me,
Fireworks.

Creating thumbnails in Fireworks

One of the goals of my site was to have fast-loading pages. Therefore, I decided to display thumbnails of the images, which, when clicked, would reveal full-size images in another browser window. You can easily resize a folder of images using the Fireworks Batch Process command. When I process thumbnails in Fireworks, I use the Scale and Rename options. I add a suffix th to the file name so as not to overwrite the original image. (See Figure 4-5.) Adding th to the file name tells me the images are thumbnails, which makes it a breeze to insert them (rather than the full-size images) into the gallery page. For more information on using Fireworks to optimize images, refer to *Macromedia Studio 8 All-in-One Desk Reference For Dummies*, by Damon Dean and Andy Cowitt (Wiley Publishing, ISBN 0-7645-9690-X).

Creating the other assets

I used Photoshop to create the site banner and the original image on the home page. I used the Text tool to create the banner text. I used the Adobe Garamond font. I used the Character palette to format the text with the small caps option. (See Figure 4-6.)

The original image for the home page was a collage of five images. I cropped each original image to make it a vertical panel and then copied the cropped image into the document I used to create the image for the home page. Photoshop automatically created a new layer for each image that was copied into the document. I then used Layer Styles to add a 1-pixel white border around each panel. (See Figure 4-7.)

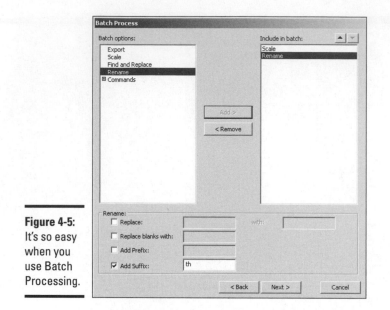

Figure 4-5:
It's so easy
when you
use Batch
Processing.

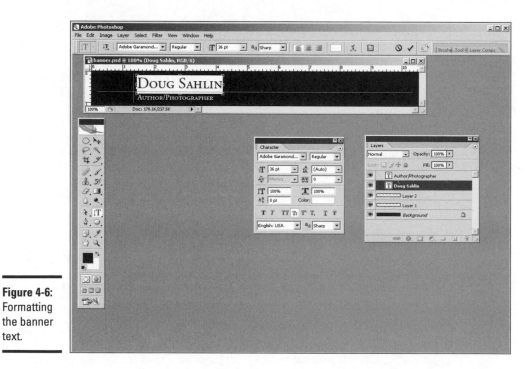

Figure 4-6:
Formatting
the banner
text.

Figure 4-7:
Creating the image for the home page.

After creating the banner and home page image, I used the Export For Web command. The banner was exported as a GIF image, and the home page image was exported as a JPEG file. (See Figure 4-8.)

Putting it together in Dreamweaver

After creating the assets in Fireworks and Photoshop, it was time to put it all together in Dreamweaver. I began by defining the site. With that task out of the way, I was ready to create a template that I could use on all pages. I created a table into which I put the banner and home page image. I then chose Insert⇨Image Objects⇨Fireworks HTML to insert the pop-up menu. I followed up by creating an editable region in which I could add text. To finish the template, I added a text menu at the bottom of the template (see Figure 4-9) because search engines can't read the links in the Fireworks pop-up menu, which is generated by JavaScript. I saved the document as a template. For more information on using Dreamweaver to create a site, refer to *Macromedia Studio 8 All-in-One Desk Reference For Dummies,* by Damon Dean and Andy Cowitt (Wiley Publishing, ISBN 0-7645-9690-X).

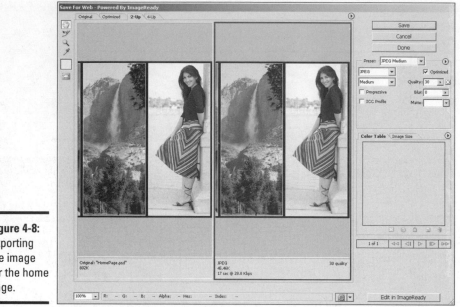

Figure 4-8:
Exporting
the image
for the home
page.

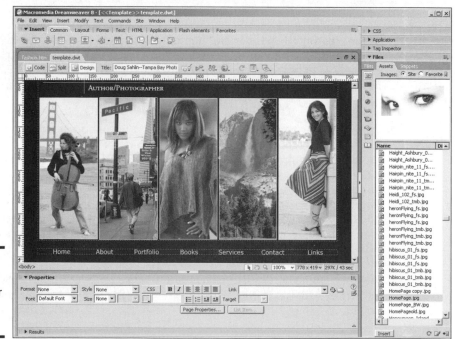

Figure 4-9:
Creating a
template for
the Web
site.

I used the template to create most of the content for the site. Because I used a template, I didn't have to re-create the navigation menu and other content common to the site. I also created a Cascading Style Sheet to modify the default styles to suit the site and create new styles. Figure 4-10 shows the site's home page.

Figure 4-10:
Creating pages from a template.

Creating the portfolio pages

To create the portfolio pages, I modified the template. When I modified the template, I deleted the image that was used on all other pages, which was an editable region, and replaced it with a title — in this case, Fashion Photography. I then created a table to house the thumbnails. Each cell in the table was created as an editable region, with the exception of the explanatory text in the second row. The modified template was saved with a different name. I used the template to create the portfolio pages. (See Figure 4-11.)

Each thumbnail is a link to a page that contains a larger version of the image. The Open Browser behavior is used to open the link in another browser window. The behavior also enables you to specify the size of the new browser window, which, in this case, is just slightly larger than the image. Figure 4-12 shows the portfolio page as it appears in the Internet Explorer browser. Note the larger version of the image that appears when the visitor clicks the applicable button.

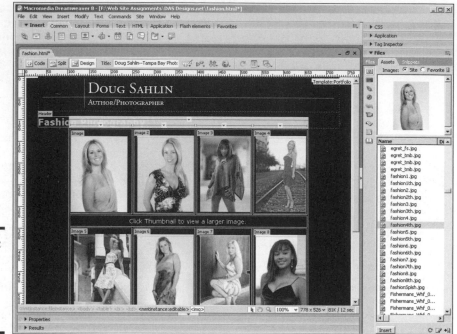

Figure 4-11:
Creating a
portfolio
page from
the
template.

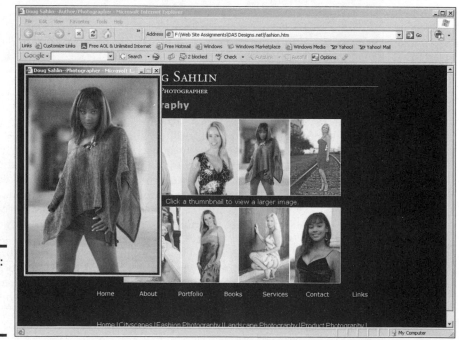

Figure 4-12:
The
completed
portfolio
page.

Showing off without snootiness

I was pleased with the original portfolio galleries of my Web site. I also received positive comments from site visitors. However, I saw an image gallery plug-in that just blew my socks off. As soon as I saw a gallery created with the plug-in, I just knew I had to use it to create the portfolio pages for my Web site. The name of the plug-in is Image Gallery Magic. You can find it at the Project VII Web site:

www.projectseven.com/products/galleries/hgmagic/index.htm

TIP

As of this writing, the plug-in retails for $95 and is compatible with Windows and Macintosh versions of Dreamweaver 8. If you're doing a Web site for a photographer or, for that matter, any other client who wants to display a large number of images with a touch of class, add the cost of this plug-in to your proposal. Your client will be pleased with the end result, and you can use the plug-in for other clients.

Image Gallery Magic enables you to create new pages using one of six gallery presets. Alternatively, you can add an Image Gallery Magic gallery to an existing page, which is what I did on my site. (See Figure 4-13.) The application dovetails nicely with Fireworks, which handles the creation of the thumbnails and full-size images. The application enables you to scale the images to fit within a desired size, specify the caption under each photo, and so on.

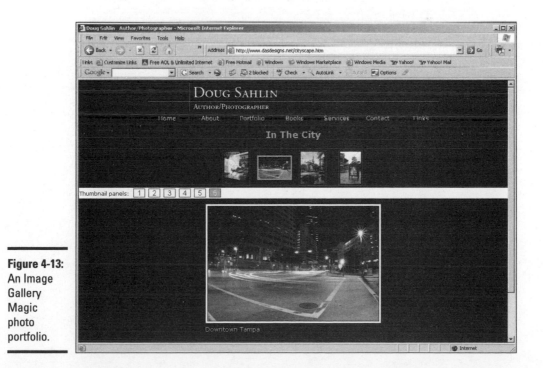

Figure 4-13:
An Image Gallery Magic photo portfolio.

Index

• *U* •

• *V* •

Notes